Bourgeois Radicals

Bourgeois Radicals explores the NAACP's key role in the liberation of Africans and Asians across the globe even as it fought Jim Crow on the home front during the long civil rights movement. In the eyes of the NAACP's leaders, the way to create a stable international system, stave off communism in Africa and Asia, and prevent capitalist exploitation was to embed human rights, with its economic and cultural protections, in the transformation of colonies into nations. Indeed, the NAACP aided in the liberation struggles of multiple African and Asian countries within the limited ideological space of the Second Red Scare. However, its vision of a "third way" to democracy and nationhood for the hundreds of millions in Asia and Africa was only partially realized because of a toxic combination of the Cold War, Jim Crow, and die-hard imperialism. *Bourgeois Radicals* examines the toll that internationalism took on the organization and illuminates the linkages between the struggle for human rights and the fight for colonial independence.

Carol Anderson is an associate professor of African American studies and history at Emory University.

Bourgeois Radicals

The NAACP and the Struggle for Colonial Liberation, 1941–1960

CAROL ANDERSON

Emory University

CAMBRIDGE
UNIVERSITY PRESS

CAMBRIDGE
UNIVERSITY PRESS

32 Avenue of the Americas, New York NY 10013-2473, USA

Cambridge University Press is part of the University of Cambridge.

It furthers the University's mission by disseminating knowledge in the pursuit of education, learning and research at the highest international levels of excellence.

www.cambridge.org
Information on this title: www.cambridge.org/9780521763783

© Carol Anderson 2015

First published 2015

A catalogue record for this publication is available from the British Library

Library of Congress Cataloguing in Publication data
Anderson, Carol (Carol Elaine), author.
Bourgeois radicals : the NAACP and the struggle for colonial liberation, 1941–1960 / Carol Anderson, Emory University.
pages cm
Includes bibliographical references and index.
ISBN 978-0-521-76378-3 (hardback) – ISBN 978-0-521-15573-1 (pbk.)
1. National Association for the Advancement of Colored People – History – 20th century. 2. Anti-imperialist movements – United States – History – 20th century. 3. African Americans – Political activity. I. Title.
E185.5.N276A53 2015
323.1196'073 – dc23 2014020153

ISBN 978-0-521-76378-3 Hardback
ISBN 978-0-521-15573-1 Paperback

To Aaron and Drew
my heart, my soul, my rock

Contents

List of Figures   *page* viii

Acknowledgments   xi

    Introduction: De-Centering Du Bois   1

1   Rising Wind   10

2   "The White Man's Burden Has Not Been Very Heavy":
The NAACP's Anticolonial Struggle against South Africa,
1946–1951   69

3   "An Even Larger Issue Than 'Containing Communism'":
The NAACP and the Italian Colonies   133

4   So Weak, So Seventeenth Century: Indonesia and the
Domestic Jurisdiction of Dutch Colonialism   204

5   Regime Change   268

    Conclusion: Beyond the Single Story   330

Bibliography   337

Index   363

Figures

1.1. Pan-Africanist strategist George Padmore   *page* 12
1.2. Walter White testifying before Congress   43
1.3. Roy Wilkins   44
1.4. W. E. B. Du Bois   52
2.1. Shantytown near Johannesburg, South Africa   85
2.2. Herero Chief Hosea Kutako   89
2.3. South African Prime Minister Daniel Malan   105
2.4. The Reverend G. Michael Scott lobbying at the UN   112
2.5. NAACP board member Channing Tobias   127
3.1. Paul Robeson at the Soviet embassy   162
3.2. Roy Wilkins meeting with Somali Youth League leaders
      Abdullahi Issa and Ali Noor   185
3.3. Italian Foreign Minister Carlo Sforza   188
3.4. Ralph Bunche with the NAACP's Roy Wilkins and Henry
      Lee Moon   198
3.5. Italian military rolling ashore at Mogadishu to begin
      trusteeship   201
4.1. Colonel Blimp cartoon   210
4.2. Sign of Indonesian defiance and independence during
      Surabaya Campaign   212
4.3. Walter White with children in Dutch New Guinea during
      the Second World War   229
4.4. U.S. Ambassador Philip Jessup   246
4.5. Dutch Ambassador to the United States Eelco Van
      Kleffens   258
5.1. Kenyan mother carrying child and all her worldly
      possessions   274

5.2. Jomo Kenyatta and Mau Mau leader Field Marshal
       Mwariama   314
5.3. Standing beneath portrait of recently deceased Walter
       White, Roy Wilkins, who was named executive secretary
       of the NAACP by Arthur Spingarn   319
5.4. Ghana President Kwame Nkrumah in Harlem   321
5.5. Meeting of the presidents – Kwame Nkrumah and Dwight
       Eisenhower   326

Acknowledgments

This has been a journey. And although the scholarly pursuit appears to be a solo flight, it is anything but. I must thank Franklin Knight, always. Dianne Stewart, forever. David Levering Lewis, for everything. Eric Arnesen, for believing. Robert Collins, for always having my back.

I also thank Jim Meriwether, for clarity. Jake Adam York, for having the brilliance to keep it real. You will be sorely and truly missed. Emilye Crosby, no one does S.O.S. like you. That is an incredible cape you are wearing. Odd Arne Westad, for insight. Leroy Davis, for perspective. Brett Gadsden, for listening and reasoning. George White, for reading and reading and reading some more. David Chappell, for vision. Dorothy Brown, for peace and laughter. Susan Whitlock, for a brilliant eye.

The opportunity to test-drive some of these chapters was priceless. Thank you Clifton Crais and Gyan Pandey for fabulous feedback from the Post-Colonial Seminar at Emory University. The Human Rights Reading Group at the University of Connecticut – aka the A-Team (Emma Gilligan, Glenn Mitoma, Luis Van Isschot, Kathyrn Libal, Henry Krisch, and especially Fiona Vernal for being willing to read not just the first but also the second draft!) – was such an amazing experience. The insight, perspective, and rigor you brought to the work are appreciated. I have been blessed, as well, to be in two sane, supportive departments throughout this journey: History at the University of Missouri and African American Studies at Emory. Thank you.

The ability to research deeply would have been impossible without generous grants and fellowships from the Eisenhower Foundation, the Research Board of the University of Missouri System, the Research Council of the University of Missouri, the Charles Warren Center at

Harvard University, the Gilder Lehrman Institute of American History, the Franklin and Eleanor Roosevelt Institute, the Human Rights Institute at the University of Connecticut, the College of Arts and Science and the Laney Graduate School at Emory University, and the Center for Faculty Development and Excellence at Emory.

The archivists and librarians deserve special praise. The legendary Liz Safly may be gone now but she will never be forgotten. Her colleagues at the Truman Presidential Library, Dennis Bilger, Randy Sowell, and Dave Scott, were phenomenal. Lucy McCann at Rhodes House and the Bodleian at the University of Oxford went above and beyond. Thank you. Additional thanks go to Shugona Campbell, Brenda Square, and Lori Carr at Amistad, Tulane University; Joellen El Bashir at the Moorland-Spingarn Research Center, Howard University; Chalsea Milner and Dwight Strandberg at the Eisenhower Presidential Library; Dagmar Getz at the YMCA Archives, University of Minnesota; Chris Burns, Ingrid Bower, Sylvia J. Bugbee, Prudence Doherty, and Peggy Powell at the Special Collections at the University of Vermont; Kathy Nusco at the Massachusetts Historical Society; Sarah Hutcheon at the Radcliffe Institute for Advanced Study, Harvard University; Tamar Dougherty at the Lehman Suite, Columbia University; Delores Fisher and Erin Grant of Interlibrary Loan at the University of Missouri; and the indomitable Elizabeth McBride at the Government Documents and African Studies, Emory University.

At the heart of this journey is my family, Aaron and Drew. You two have been warriors and troupers. Thank you for bearing with me through it all. And to my brothers, Earl, David, and Wendell, there are no words that can ably capture the strength and the confidence that you give me. Thank you.

Finally, to my editors at Cambridge University Press – first Lewis Bateman, then Eric Crahan, and then Deborah Gershenowitz – who were so supportive, thank you.

Introduction

De-Centering Du Bois

I'm for truth, no matter who tells it. I'm for justice, no matter who it's for ... or against.

– Malcolm X[1]

Nearly a decade ago, while beginning the archival research for this book, I happened to run into historian Gerald Horne at the Library of Congress. We chatted a bit and then he asked me what I was working on. I said, "The NAACP's anticolonialism." He smiled and half jokingly replied, "Well, that's going to be a short book!"

Horne would have been right, if the archival record confirmed the orthodoxy that has reigned for more than forty years. The standard, accepted saga is straightforward. The National Association for the Advancement of Colored People's (NAACP) anticolonialism began and ended with co-founder W. E. B. Du Bois, whose second stint at the Association was only four brief, tumultuous years, 1944–1948. In that short space of time he brought an enormous wealth of insight, experience, and intuitive brilliance to the subjects of colonialism, economic exploitation, and Africa.[2] His intellectual and anticolonial light was so bright – blinding almost – that it has appeared to many scholars that when he left the NAACP, he took the fire and the sun with him. All that remained of the Association

[1] Malcolm X and Alex Haley, *The Autobiography of Malcolm X* (New York: Ballantine Books, 1964), 421.
[2] W. E. B. Du Bois, *Color and Democracy: Colonies and Peace*, introduction by Herbert Aptheker (New York: Harcourt Brace, 1945; reprint, Millwood, NY: Kraus-Thomson Organization Limited, 1975); Du Bois, *The World and Africa: An Inquiry into the Part Which Africa Has Played in World History* (New York: International Publishers, 1946).

I

was a darkened, desiccated husk. The NAACP was just a shell of what it used to be and certainly a mere shadow of what it could have been. The ouster of Du Bois, these scholars contend, not only hobbled and destabilized the Association's anticolonialism but also had a disastrous effect on the struggles for liberation in the United States.

That powerful, haunting story has been reaffirmed in book after book, article after article. The problem is that it cannot withstand archival scrutiny.

I liken this conundrum to the troubles of physicists and astronomers using the Ptolemaic, earth-centered model of the universe. The only way that tha planetary system could hang together was through continual mathematical gymnastics: recalibrations, ellipses, equants, and epicycles to account for astral movements that simply made no sense otherwise. Ptolemy's geocentric system, for example, could not explain lunar orbits around Jupiter. Only when scientists placed the sun, not the earth, at the center and posited gravity's elliptical orbit did the model begin to correlate fully with the evidence. Further, this change led to subsequent breakthroughs that moved knowledge well beyond the solar system and into the galaxies. In the end, de-centering the earth did not trivialize the importance of the planet; it just made it possible to see that there was more to explore.[3]

Similarly, this book had to de-center Du Bois to make sense of a phenomenon that by all accounts was not supposed to be there. Just as the telescopes trained on the moons orbiting Jupiter called into serious question Ptolemy's geocentric model, rigorous research in the records of the NAACP undermined the assertions of scholars that the Cold War, anticommunism, and, finally, Du Bois's 1948 ouster had silenced the NAACP. For here was this organization, working in the late 1940s and throughout the 1950s within an array of transnational alliances based in Cape Town, Mogadishu, Jakarta, and London, as well as with allies and covert supporters in the White House, State Department, and United Nations (UN), wading into liberation campaigns against the South Africans, the British, the Italians, the Dutch, and the French. How was this even possible given the Ptolemaic construction of black liberals' dormant Cold War anticolonialism?[4]

---

[3] James M. Lattis, *Between Copernicus and Galileo: Christoph Clavius and the Collapse of Ptolemaic Cosmology* (Chicago: University of Chicago Press, 1994).

[4] Erik McDuffie, "Black and Red: Black Liberation, the Cold War, and the Horne Thesis," *Journal of African American History*, 96, no. 2 (Spring 2011), 236–247; Gerald Horne, *Black and Red: W.E.B. Du Bois and the Afro-American Response to the Cold War,*

Penny Von Eschen, Gerald Horne, James Roark, and others have all described how the lure of civil rights bait, the toxin of anticommunism, and the pressures of the Cold War led the NAACP to abandon those struggling to be free from colonial oppression. Although Horne invokes the image of Faust selling his soul to Mephistopheles, the better metaphor might be Judas Iscariot accepting a few pieces of civil rights concessions in exchange for betraying global liberation struggles.[5] Scholar Robert L. Harris Jr., quoting Du Bois, notes that the NAACP "traded 'breaks in the American color line for acquiescence in American and West European control of the world's colored peoples.'"[6] Historian Francis Njubi Nesbitt explains, "Truman's concessions to civil rights groups and his strong-arm tactics against the left convinced moderate groups, such as the NAACP ... that 'full American nationalism apparently promised greater immediate rewards than racial internationalism.'" The Association, in Nesbitt's estimation, decided that it was "safer to conform to the new order" than to fight for "Du Bois's leftist and anti-imperialist politics."[7]

Indeed, Gerald Horne writes that the NAACP's growing anticommunism led to "the purge of W.E.B. Du Bois ... and ultimately the retreat of the association from its deeply engaged and left-leaning posture on the global stage."[8] Murali Balaji notes that the firing occurred because Du Bois had attached "himself to radical causes that promised immediate liberation for colonized and exploited people," whereas the Association's policies "only confirmed his long-held suspicions that the NAACP's

---

1944–1963 (Albany: SUNY Press, 1986); Horne, *Mau Mau in Harlem? The U.S. and the Liberation of Kenya* (New York: Palgrave MacMillan, 2009); Horne, *Race Woman: The Lives of Shirley Graham Du Bois* (New York: New York University Press, 2000); Horne, *Communist Front? The Civil Rights Congress, 1946–1956* (London: Associated University Presses, 1988); Horne, *The End of Empires: African Americans and India* (Philadelphia: Temple University Press, 2008); Kenneth Janken, "From Colonial Liberation to Cold War Liberalism: Walter White, the NAACP, and Foreign Affairs, 1941–1955," *Ethnic and Racial Studies*, 21, no. 6 (November 1998), 1091; Kate Baldwin, *Beyond the Color Line and the Iron Curtain: Reading Encounters between Black and Red, 1922–1963* (Durham, NC: Duke University Press, 2002), 19.

[5] Horne, *Black and Red*, 56, 57; Penny Von Eschen, *Race Against Empire: Black Americans and Anticolonialism, 1937–1957* (Ithaca, NY: Cornell University Press, 1997), 116, 143, 144; James Roark, "American Black Leaders: The Response to Colonialism and the Cold War, 1945–1953," *African Historical Studies*, 4 (1971), 265–266.

[6] Du Bois quoted in Robert L. Harris Jr., "Ralph Bunche and Afro-American Participation in Decolonization," in *The African American Voice in U.S. Foreign Policy since World War II*, ed. Michael L. Krenn (New York: Garland, 1999), 177.

[7] Frances Njubi Nesbitt, *Race for Sanctions: African Americans against Apartheid, 1946–1994* (Bloomington: Indiana University Press, 2004), 10.

[8] Horne, *The End of Empires*, 180.

activism would only go so far."[9] Similarly, James Roark insists that, "[j]ust as Du Bois' hiring during the [Second World] war had symbolized the new international commitments of the association, his firing gave notice of a return to domestic concerns."[10]

The invisible but all-powerful force shaping this narrative's trajectory is Du Bois's assertion that the Association was just a "bourgeois set-up afraid to do anything that is not respectable" and that the organization had jumped on President Harry Truman's "bandwagon" and shackled the NAACP to the "reactionary, war-mongering, colonial imperialism of the present administration."[11] Du Bois looms so large in the assessment of the Association's anticolonialism that scholars have adopted his framework seemingly without interrogation. They have not, for example, seriously asked about the biases inherent in a critique from an octogenarian who was essentially thrown out of the organization he helped found. They have not stripped away his anger to analyze the essence of his criticism. Instead, historians have jumped down the same semantic rabbit hole that Du Bois did, one that equates anticommunism with support of colonial regimes.

The syllogism is simple and, in the end, historically misleading. The logic chain's first premise is that the U.S. government was staunchly anticommunist. The second, based on the first, is that the Americans were determined to keep the Soviet Union away from any territory it did not already control. The third contends that to contain the USSR, the United States decided to prop up and prolong the rule of European colonizers throughout the globe. Once scholars have established the imperialistic outcomes of an anticommunist foreign policy, the NAACP's own anti-Marxist bent invariably leads to the conclusion that the Association was in league with the United States to do whatever it took to keep the USSR out of Africa and Asia, even if that meant aligning with Europeans at the expense of colonized peoples' freedom.

---

[9] Murali Balaji, *The Professor and the Pupil: The Politics and Friendship of W.E.B. Du Bois and Paul Robeson* (New York: Nation Books, 2007), 246.

[10] Roark, "American Black Leaders," 265.

[11] W.E.B. Du Bois to George Padmore, April 7, 1949, *Papers of W.E.B. Du Bois* (Sanford, NC: Microfilming Corporation of America, 1980), Reel 64, microfilm, (hereafter *Du Bois*); W.E.B. Du Bois to Walter White, November 14, 1946, Box A241, File "William E.B. Du Bois–General, 1946," *Papers of the National Association for the Advancement of Colored People*, Library of Congress, Washington, DC (hereafter *Papers of the NAACP*); Du Bois to the Secretary (White) and Board of Directors of the N.A.A.C.P., memo, September 7, 1948, Box A241, File "W.E.B. Du Bois – General (Jan–Sept 1948)," *Papers of the NAACP*.

Horne emphasizes, for example, that "[t]he Association's move ... from militant anti-imperialism to virulent anticommunism, ... was a tortuous path." The NAACP's "board liberally populated with fat cats and ideological biases" received "a defined attitude and certain civil rights concessions at home in exchange for steely eyed anticommunism abroad."[12] Von Eschen writes that "in accepting the legitimacy of the United States as the leader of the free world," the NAACP had severed "the argument that linked the struggle of black Americans against Jim Crow with that of Africans against colonialism."[13] With the onset of the Cold War, Von Eschen continues, the NAACP developed "a new exclusive focus on domestic discrimination and silence on foreign policy issues."[14] Roark similarly explains that the pervasive anticommunism that enveloped the Association and others in the African American political center meant that "most American black leaders had abandoned the cause of the world's colored peoples."[15]

Meanwhile, the virulence of the anticommunist witch hunts in the United States, coupled with the historical sexiness of heroes who challenged the era's reign of fear, has led scholars to render the anticolonial trail of the Association and its allies so small that it was almost invisible, while disproportionately magnifying the footprints of the Left. A preponderance of the scholarship has, indeed, focused on leftists, such as Paul Robeson and Du Bois, who were hammered hard by the Second Red Scare. These men, and many more like them, embodied a commitment to anticolonialism as well as a deep affinity for communism as a panacea for the world's ills. Their unshakable faith in the power of communism (and especially the Soviet Union) to destroy imperial rule and end the subjugation of hundreds of millions of people of color led historians to conflate communism and anticolonialism and treat these two separate phenomena as synonymous. In other words, scholars have made the mistake of believing that communism was the sine qua non of anticolonialism.

In the end, therefore, the semantic rabbit hole that made the NAACP a standard bearer for imperialism and the Soviet Union synonymous with anticolonialism greased the way into a Wonderland where the Association disappeared, like the Cheshire Cat, from the histories of colonial liberation struggles. Roark makes clear that while the NAACP crumpled beneath the

---

[12] Horne, *Black and Red*, 56, 57.
[13] Von Eschen, *Race Against Empire*, 117.
[14] Ibid., 143, 144, 116.
[15] Roark, "American Black Leaders," 265–266.

weight of Cold War pressures, a "handful of black leaders, mostly on the left, refused to make the switch in 1947 ... these black leaders redoubled their attack on Western capitalism and racism."[16] Based on the power of that narrative, which has been repeated so often that it has become truth, subsequent works have focused on the nexus between black radicals and colonial liberation movements and, in the process, silenced the important work of anticommunist, anticolonial groups. Nesbitt, for example, simply dismisses the NAACP and other "moderate groups" and then asserts that African Americans' drive against global racial oppression could only have "emerged in radical black politics of the 1940s."[17]

If that is the case, then how do scholars explain the NAACP disrupting a brokered deal in 1949 to carve up North Africa and the Horn of Africa among U.S. allies? How can historians account for the actions of an Association board member who, in 1951, sowed so much anticolonial discontent in the Fourth Committee of the UN that the British were convinced that it was a seminal moment that would make continued colonial rule infinitely more difficult? Jupiter's moons are crying out for an explanation. In fact, historians Brenda Gayle Plummer, Jason Parker, and James Meriwether as well as political scientist Alvin B. Tillery Jr. have begun to provide great insight into the contributions of black liberals to a series of liberation strategies.[18] It is time now to train the telescope on how the NAACP was able to operate, sometimes quite effectively, in a political environment that had toppled other anticolonial activists.

If we de-center Du Bois, the organizing methods the Association used to discredit the legal and normative pillars that propped up the "white man's burden" come into view. The NAACP, working – often through the UN – in partnership with a range of liberal organizations and indigenous freedom fighters, took direct aim at the tenets of national sovereignty, domestic jurisdiction, white supremacy, unsubstantiated claims of uplift,

---

[16] Ibid.

[17] Nesbitt, *Race for Sanctions*, viii; also see Thomas Dyja, *Walter White: The Dilemma of Black Identity in America* (Chicago, IL: Ivan R. Dee, 2008), 177.

[18] Jason Parker, "'Made-in-America Revolutions'?: The 'Black University' and the American Role in the Decolonization of the Black Atlantic," *Journal of American History*, 96, no. 3 (December 2009), 727–750; James H. Meriwether, "'Worth a Lot of Negro Votes': Black Voters, Africa, and the 1960 Presidential Campaign," *Journal of American History*, 95, no. 3 (December 2008): 737–763; Brenda Gayle Plummer, *In Search of Power: African Americans in the Era of Decolonization, 1956–1974* (New York: Cambridge University Press, 2012); Alvin B. Tillery Jr., *Between Homeland and Motherland: Africa, U.S. Foreign Policy, and Black Leadership in America* (Ithaca, NY: Cornell University Press, 2011), 72–98.

and geostrategic necessity to help render colonialism anachronistic and unacceptable.

De-centering Du Bois also allows for greater insight into how the goal of human rights diverged from that of colonial independence although they were coterminous and, initially, intertwined. The Association posited a "third way" of postcolonial nation building, one that sought to curb the potential excesses of private capital accumulation and avoid Soviet–style institutions while infusing human rights into the process of modernization. The NAACP argued that the ravages of capitalism without the benefits of democracy and human rights would be so exploitive that people of color would be unable to find any sense of justice and hope in their societies, moderate nationalist influences would be discredited, political extremism would take root, and the end result would be more violence, more deprivation, and more human rights violations.[19] This framework emerged from a series of meetings with Africans and Asians in the early 1940s. During the Second World War, indigenous leaders, such as Nigerian Nnamdi Azikiwe and President-General of the African National Congress (ANC) A. B. Xuma, envisioned a decolonized world predicated on political independence *and* human rights. Within a few short years, however, those interwoven fibers of national viability frayed in the course of UN battles, concerns about development aid, and the Cold War. As a result, colonial independence was, in many ways, "fast-tracked," while human rights were left at the UN's starting gate.

De-centering Du Bois underlines self-determination, not communism or the Soviet Union, as the gravitational force pulling hundreds of millions of people into struggles against better financed, better equipped colonizers. The core, guiding principle was a people's right to choose their own government. That dogma allowed the NAACP's anticolonialism to have a sense of clarity not mired by ideological haze. For example, as long as "the wishes of the inhabitants" were denied, the Association refused to back Ethiopia's bid to absorb Eritrea, derided

---

[19] Walter White to Chester Williams, October 25, 1948, Box 181–8, Folder 3, *Papers of Rayford Logan*, Moorland-Spingarn Research Center, Howard University, Washington, DC (hereafter *Logan-MSRC*); Walter White to Arthur [Spingarn], n.d., ca. February 1950, Box 6, File "Spingarn, Arthur B.," *Walter Francis White and Poppy Cannon White Correspondence*, Beinecke Rare Book and Manuscript Library, Yale University, New Haven, CT (hereafter *White Papers*). See Barbara F. Walter, "Does Conflict Beget Conflict? Explaining Recurring Civil War," *Journal of Peace Research*, 41, no. 3 (2004), 371–388.

the Soviets' imperialistic power play in North Africa, and mounted a full-throttle campaign against an American-backed plan to dole out Libya, Somalia, and Eritrea to U.S. allies. De-centering Du Bois provides insight into the ways the NAACP adapted its strategies when its access to the White House was closed off after Dwight D. Eisenhower came to power. During Truman's presidency, the Association leadership had managed to obtain various appointments to the U.S. delegations to the UN. The NAACP's foreign policy consultants also attended State Department briefings and gained access to decision makers to wield some influence.[20] The Eisenhower years, however, were very different. The NAACP, especially because of its high-profile work on destroying legal racial segregation in the United States, was persona non grata at the White House. Although the propaganda nightmare that was Jim Crow forced the Eisenhower administration to search for African Americans to appoint to UN delegations, it soon became clear that no matter how strong, viable, capable, or even Republican a candidate might be, if he was "an NAACP man," he was not getting through the vetting process.[21] The Association leaders were, therefore, instrumental in the shaping of another organization that could focus on decolonization, the American Committee on Africa (ACOA).

In short, de-centering Du Bois opens up a universe of African Americans' anticolonial efforts that have heretofore been ignored or written off as "ritualistic" anomalies.[22] It renders visible the all-

---

[20] See, for example, the discussion to invite Haitian President Paul Magloire for a visit to the United States, Dean Acheson to the President [Harry S. Truman], January 17, 1952, Box 42, File "State Department Correspondence, 1951–52 [5 of 6]," *Papers of Harry S Truman: White House Confidential File: Confidential File*, Harry S Truman Presidential Library, Independence, MO (hereafter *HST:WHCF:CF*); Walter White to Dean Acheson, January 31, 1952, Box A617, File "State Department: General, 1952–54," *Papers of the NAACP*.

[21] R[obert] E. H[ampton], Memorandum for the Record, January 13, 1958, Box 4, File "Be-Bl," *Papers of John Foster Dulles, 1951–59*, Personnel Series, Special Liaison Staff Sub-series, Dwight D. Eisenhower Presidential Library, Abilene, KS (hereafter *Dulless:PS:SLSS*); Robert E. Hampton, Memorandum for the Record, January 10, 1958, Box 4, File "Be-Bl," *Dulles:PS:SLSS*; David S. Smith to Mr. Hanes, memo, June 29, 1954, *Papers of John Foster Dulles, 1951–59*, Personnel Series, Chiefs of Mission Sub-series, Box 3, File "Subject File (Strictly Confidential) Negro Problem," Dwight D. Eisenhower Presidential Library, Abilene, KS (hereafter *Dulles:PS:CMS*); Telephone Conversation Re: UN Delegation, July 20, 1953, *Papers of John Foster Dulles, 1951–59*, Telephone Calls Series, Box 1, File "Telephone Memos (Except to and from White House) July–Oct. 31, 1953 (5)," Dwight D. Eisenhower Presidential Library, Abilene, KS hereafter *Dulles:TCS*).

[22] Roark, "American Black Leaders," 263.

important constellation of alliances and strategies used to dismantle colonial empires. It opens up lines of inquiry about human rights and decolonization that have not been explored in this context.[23] And it reveals how that activism was motivated by a force more powerful than communism: freedom.

---

[23] Roland Burke, *Decolonization and the Evolution of International Human Rights* (Philadelphia: University of Pennsylvania Press, 2010); Samuel Moyn, "Imperialism, Self-Determination, and the Rise of Human Rights," in *The Human Rights Revolution: An International History* (in Reinterpreting American History), eds. Akira Iriye, Petra Goedde, and William I. Hitchcock, series ed. Wm. Roger Louis (New York: Oxford University Press, 2012), 159–178.

I

Rising Wind

It won't hurt you guys to struggle for the things you love to talk about.
After a while you'll get a revolutionary conscience.
                                                    – George Streator[1]

By 1919, thick, dark smoke billowed out of Europe's crumbling empires.
The flames of self-determination, sparked by the Wilsonian principles of
the First World War, licked the outskirts of Europe itself, then spread to
Africa, Asia, the Middle East, and the Caribbean. The colonial powers
tried to douse it, harness it, defuse it, but the ember of independence still
burned. All of the maneuvering at Versailles had not quelled the fervor.[2]

In fact, the horse trading at the peace talks, the bartering of peoples
back and forth, and the refusal of the great powers to acknowledge racial
equality as a bedrock principle of international law and peace added a
powerful accelerant to the quest for freedom.[3] As African leader Lamine
Senghor remarked in 1927 at the conference of the League Against
Imperialism, "We have assembled to defend ourselves against these injus-
tices": that "the imperialists very democratically reserve the right to sell
an entire Negro people to another imperialist," that "you are forced to
work ten hours a day in the ... African sun, and can only earn 2 francs,"
that confessions for so-called crimes are extracted through methods

[1] George Streator to Henry Moon, n.d., Box 5, File "Streator, George & Olive," *Papers of Henry and Mollie Moon*, Schomburg Center for Research in Black Culture, New York (hereafter *Moon Papers*).
[2] Erez Manela, *The Wilsonian Moment: Self-Determination and the International Origins of Anticolonial Nationalism* (New York: Oxford University Press, 2009).
[3] Paul Gordon Lauren, *The Evolution of International Human Rights: Visions Seen*, 2nd ed. (Philadelphia: University of Pennsylvania Press, 2003), 119–126.

"worthy of the darkest Middle Ages," and that when the "Negroes of the Antilles ... demand too many rights," the French press advocates that these twentieth-century slaves be sold "to the Americans; then one would at least make a profit out of it." "Beware!" Senghor warned. Although blacks had been in a long slumber, they "will not fall asleep again."[4]

In 1930, Walter White, secretary of the National Association for the Advancement of Colored People, sensed the same restlessness and anger. Blacks throughout the globe, he remarked, were simmering with "resentment" and becoming increasingly "militant." He pointed to the "situation in South Africa and in other parts of the Continent, in the United States and in the world," which, "so far as color is concerned, is so very serious and threatens to become so much more" if racism, discrimination, and colonialism continued to be the modus operandi of governments.[5]

The wounded European powers, however, believed that they could put out the fire of independence and salvage their disintegrating empires. They imprisoned, they shot, they gassed; they did whatever it took to subdue those who demanded political and economic freedom. But campaigns of terror and repression could not reinforce the bonds of colonialism; the mere hint of self-determination was just too powerful.

With the onset of the Second World War, the colonies' ties to the metropole, already frayed and singed by Versailles's liberatory zeitgeist, began to snap. In 1942, the Office of Strategic Services (OSS), the forerunner of the Central Intelligence Agency (CIA), conducted an initial assessment of the impact of nationalism on "the Allied war effort." From the U.S. government's standpoint, the news was not good. It was obvious that "disrespect for British rulers" was not only intense but also extensive. The OSS discerned a "vigorous and growing nationalist feeling among important elements in the native population of British West Africa." In addition to being "young, fearless, intelligent, and shrewd," the leadership of these colonial liberation movements was also "fanatically nationalistic and racialistic (i.e., pan-African, pan-blackman), bitterly anti-imperialist and anti-British." A worried OSS concluded that "widespread resentment smolders beneath the surface."[6]

---

4 Lamine Senghor, "The Negro's Fight for Freedom," in *Ideologies of Liberation in Black Africa, 1856–1970: Documents on Modern African Political Thought from Colonial Times to the Present*, ed. J. Ayo Langley (London: Rex Collings, 1979), 255–260.
5 Walter White to Thomas Jesse Jones, January 16, 1930, Box 31, File "11," *Phelps-Stokes Collection*, Schomburg Center for Research in Black Culture, New York, (hereafter *Phelps-Stokes Collection*).
6 "Preliminary Statement of Nationalism Among British West African Natives," *OSS/ State Department Intelligence and Research Reports, Part XIII, Africa: 1941–1961*

FIGURE 1.1. Pan-Africanist strategist George Padmore (in hat).
Source: Photo by Philippe Le Tellier/Paris Match via Getty Images. Courtesy of
Getty Images, Editorial Image #166561904.

That assessment, however, was only partially correct. By now, the
resentment was no longer smoldering; it was out in the open and burned
with an intensity for all to see. Trinidadian and Pan-Africanist George
Padmore, one of the chief strategist for colonial liberation in Ghana
and a journalist for the NAACP's magazine *Crisis*, had already defined
his mission as "getting rid of the damn white blood suckers from the
W[est] I[ndies]."[7] He longed for the day when he could launch a "'Holy
War' against the perfidious whites and drive them out of Africa"[8] (see
Figure 1.1). That sentiment was shared by Kwame Nkrumah, the future
prime minister of Ghana, who in 1942 exclaimed, "I was so revolted by
the ruthless colonial exploitation and political oppression of the people

   (Washington, DC: University Publications of America, 1980), Reel 2, microfilm (hereafter
   OSS/Africa).
[7] George [Padmore] to Cyril [Ollivierre], April 18, 1941, File, "George Padmore," *George
   Padmore Letters*, Schomburg Center for Research in Black Culture, New York (hereafter
   Padmore); George [Padmore] to Cyril [Ollivierre], March 30, 1938, *Padmore*; George
   [Padmore] to Cyril [Ollivierre], September 26, 1932, *Padmore*.
[8] George [Padmore] to Cyril [Ollivierre], July 28, 1934, *Padmore*.

of Africa that I knew no peace."[9] Nkrumah later seethed that "Africa's exploiters ... strode across our land with incredible inhumanity, without mercy, without shame, and without honor."[10] For him, colonialism had to be "liquidated" so that Africa could be free.[11]

Japan's onslaught in Asia hastened that possibility as the British, French, and Dutch suffered spectacular, high-profile defeats or, even worse, the humiliation of bow-down, groveling "capitulation."[12] Unable to defend their prized colonial possessions in the Pacific, Europe called on the peoples in those areas to resist the invaders from Tokyo. But the response throughout the empires was defiant. In Indonesia, for example, "by the time Japanese troops landed in Java, a frantic atmosphere of welcome had overwhelmed the island." Independence, which the Dutch had blocked with every maneuver, now seemed within reach, especially with Japan's help.[13] Even when it became clear, within a few weeks, that Emperor Hirohito's forces were no liberators – that, in fact, the "last thing the Japanese military wanted was the fostering of Indonesian nationalist aspirations" – for many Indonesians that Japanese occupation still "symbolized the breakdown of detested colonial rule and the collapse of a racialized system of alien norms and values which had been forced upon them."[14]

Not surprisingly, then, after witnessing the supposedly invincible British and Dutch scramble across oceans searching for cover from Japan's

---

[9] Quoted in Carol Anderson, "The Cold War and the Atlantic World," in *The Atlantic World: 1450–2000*, eds. Toyin Falola and Kevin D. Roberts (Bloomington: Indiana University Press, 2008) 294.

[10] Quoted in Christopher Andrew and Vasili Mitrokhin, *The World Was Going Our Way: The KGB and the Battle for the Third World* (New York: Basic Books, 2005), 426.

[11] Kwame Nkrumah to Walter White, June 9, 1953, BoxA4, File "Africa: General, 1952–53," *Papers of the NAACP.*

[12] See, for example, "The Netherlands East Indies," *Netherlands News Digest*, 1, no. 1 (March 15, 1942), 13–16; Christopher Bayly and Tim Harper, *Forgotten Armies: The Fall of British Asia, 1941–1945* (London: Allen Lane, 2004); Christopher Thorne, *Allies of a Kind: The United States, Britain, and the War against Japan, 1941–1945* (New York: Oxford University Press, 1978), 4; John E. Dreifort, "Japan's Advance into Indochina, 1940: The French Response," *Journal of Southeast Asian Studies*, 13, no. 2 (September 1982), 292; Tran My-Van, "Japan through Vietnamese Eyes, 1905–1945," *Journal of Southeast Asian Studies*, 30, no. 1 (March 1999), 135–146.

[13] Elly Touwen-Bouwsma, "The Indonesian Nationalists and the Japanese 'Liberation' of Indonesia: Visions and Reactions," *Journal of Southeast Asian Studies*, 27, no. 1 (March 1996), 8.

[14] László Sluimers, "The Japanese Military and Indonesian Independence," *Journal of Southeast Asian Studies*, 27, no. 1, (March 1996), 27; Marc Frey, "Visions of the Future: The United States and Colonialism in Southeast Asia, 1940–1945," *American Studies*, 48, no. 3, (2003), 365–366.

military might, the Malaysians and Indonesians were "unwilling to kick the conquerors out merely to welcome the white man back again."[15] One State Department analysis emphasized that "it is not clear to Asia ... that the Asiatics have anything to gain from this war – to millions the choice is merely one between Japanese imperialism and Western imperialism." The department's report concluded that the only way to defeat the Axis would be for the Western powers to "face the fact that the survival of the very democracy which they are fighting to defend demands the *spread* of democracy and the spread of democracy means the end of imperialism."[16]

That was just too bitter a pill for the British to swallow. Prime Minister Winston Churchill was more than willing to meet in August 1941 with President Franklin Roosevelt to craft a series of majestic-sounding war aims, known as the Atlantic Charter, which enshrined and expanded on the Four Freedoms and tied the United States closer to Britain.[17] However, Churchill was not willing to "expose ... our whole Empire to great embarrassment." He stated emphatically, "I have several times ... informed the President that I did not accept *universal* application of the Atlantic Charter."[18] The prime minister's staunch resistance centered on the realization that if the colonies had the right to free speech, freedom of religion, freedom from want, and freedom from fear, the mechanisms that

---

[15] *Newsweek*, March 23, 1942, cited in Earl Brown and George R. Leighton, "Negroes and the War," May 1942, File "Public Affairs Committee, The Negro and the War, 1942 [50]," *Papers of the YMCA: Channing Tobias*, YMCA Kautz Family Archives, University of Minnesota, Minneapolis (hereafter *Tobias Papers*); F. Tillman Durdin, "Tokyo Tanks Roll in Malay Jungle," *New York Times*, December 13, 1941; "British Fall Back on Malay Coasts: Japanese Are Just 65 Miles from Singapore," *New York Times*, January 20, 1942; Sluimers, "The Japanese Military and Indonesian Independence," 26.

[16] U.S. State Department, "Summary of Opinion and Ideas on International Post-War Problems," No. 3, August 12, 1942, Box 24, File "U.S. Senate: Political Studies – Postwar + Foreign Affairs, Oct. 1942–June 1943," *Papers of Warren Austin*, Bailey-Howe Library, Special Collections, University of Vermont, Burlington (hereafter *Austin Papers*). Emphasis in original.

[17] The Four Freedoms were first articulated by President Roosevelt in a speech to Congress, January 6, 1941: "We look forward to a world founded upon four essential human freedoms. The first is freedom of speech and expression – everywhere in the world. The second is freedom of every person to worship God in his own way – everywhere in the world. The third is freedom from want ... everywhere in the world. The fourth is freedom from fear ... anywhere in the world." http://www.archives.gov/exhibits/powers_of_persuasion/four_freedoms/four_freedoms.html. Accessed June 19, 2012.

[18] Prime Minister to Deputy Prime Minister and Foreign Secretary, September 15, 1943, DO 35/1897, British National Archives, Kew, United Kingdom. Emphasis added.

Britain used to maintain control of its far-flung empire would be wholly discredited.[19]

In Kenya, for example, the most arable land had already been ripped from the indigenous Kikuyu and doled out to a handful of European settlers, creating a death spiral of overcrowding, landlessness, and poverty among the Africans.[20] George Padmore, in *How Britain Rules Africa*, explained that "apart from low wages, long hours, bad food when supplied, and floggings for minor offences," the colonial government had crafted a legal system in which the "administration of justice between Black and White in East Africa [was] a farce." Africans were whipped to death for petty theft, whereas white settlers were exonerated or sentenced to only a few months in a hospital for committing murder.[21]

In Malaysia, tin miners were "paid from twenty-five to thirty-seven cents a day" for "nine hours of back-breaking labor."[22] The rubber plantations were equally brutal sites of exploitation. By design, imported Chinese indentured servants earned so little that they could never pay off the debt for their transportation to Malaysia. Finally in 1937, the plantations were rocked with a series of strikes as the workers demanded a mere "$1.00 a day, an increase of around thirty-five to forty cents" more than their present earnings. Within the span of two weeks, the rebellion spread, as nearly 24,000 workers crippled the production on forty-four plantations. The colonial administration fired back with violence, imprisonment, and intimidation to force the indentured and barely paid to return to servitude in the fields.[23]

---

[19] For the issue of freedom of religion, see Chinua Achebe, *Things Fall Apart* (New York: Fawcett Crest, 1959); Rosiland Shaw, "The Invention of 'African Traditional Religion,'" *Religion*, 20 (1990); Jean Comaroff and John Comaroff, *Of Revelation and Revolution: Christianity, Colonialism, and Consciousness in South Africa*, 2 vols. (Chicago: University of Chicago Press, 1991, 1997); Kevin Boyle and Juliet Sheen, eds., *Freedom of Religion and Belief: A World Report* (London and New York: Routledge, 1997), 148–149.

[20] David Anderson, *The Histories of the Hanged: The Dirty War in Kenya and the End of Empire* (New York: W. W. Norton, 2005), 10, 31, 188–189.

[21] George Padmore, *How Britain Rules Africa* (London: Wishart Books, 1936; New York: Negro Universities Press, 1969), 122–123 (page citations are to the reprint edition).

[22] "Address of Walter White … at Shrine Auditorium, Los Angeles, California," July 19, 1942, *Papers of the National Association for the Advancement of Colored People: 1909–1950*, Part 1, (Washington, DC: University Publications of America, 1981), Reel 11, microfilm (hereafter *NAACP*).

[23] John A. Tully, *The Devil's Milk: A Social History of Rubber* (New York: Monthly Review Press, 2011), 270–272; W. G. Huff, "Entitlements, Destitution, and Emigration in the 1930s Singapore Great Depression," *Economic History Review*, 54, no. 2 (May 2001), 290–323.

Similarly, in Trinidad "the island's largest oil company paid its shareholders a 35% dividend in the same year that it lowered workers wages by roughly the same figure."[24] Not only were wages intolerably low, with some employees making only seven cents an hour, but also the conditions were dangerous and workers were treated with disdain as the managers contemptuously sputtered that "these black dogs only bark – they cannot bite."[25] By 1937, the firebrand trade unionist Tubal Uriah "Buzz" Butler exclaimed: "The hour has come to show our might and power and to get things for ourselves. Our brutal taskmasters have ... challenged us to prove our right to life and happiness!"[26] The ensuing revolt convulsed the island. The British rolled in with warships and troops, banished any colonial official who even whispered that seven cents an hour was a bit low, and imprisoned Butler – twice. In the aftermath, fourteen died, fifty-nine were injured, and hundreds were arrested.[27]

In short, the hard, cold realities of what it took to control a people who refused to accept their subjugation made clear that the Four Freedoms and colonialism were irreconcilable. And for exactly that reason, the language and principles of the Atlantic Charter caught the attention of nongovernmental organizations around the world.

A month after the Atlantic Charter was issued, the Phelps-Stokes Fund, a New York-based foundation that was endowed to create a "new deal' for the people of Africa," formed the Committee on Africa and Peace Aims to determine how "to help protect the interests of the Natives of Africa in connection with the Peace Treaty which will follow the present war."[28] Almost immediately, the Committee, which included NAACP board member Channing Tobias and several other prominent African

[24] Jason C. Parker, *Brother's Keeper: The United States, Race, and Empire in the British Caribbean, 1937–1962* (New York: Oxford University Press, 2008), 21.
[25] The Oilfields Workers' Trade Union, "OWTU History: 1937–1947," http://www.owtu.org/content/owtu-history. Accessed October 29, 2012.
[26] Parker, *Brother's Keeper*, 21.
[27] Paul Buhle, *Tim Hector: A Caribbean Radical's Story* (Jackson: University Press of Mississippi, 2006), 55–57.
[28] James Waldo Fawcett, "Fund of Two Sisters Premises 'New Deal' for African Peoples," n.d., Box 62, File "Pictures, Press Clippings, 1924(?)-1939," *Papers of Ralph Bunche*, Schomburg Center for Research in Black Culture, New York (hereafter *Bunche Papers*); Minutes of Preliminary Meeting of Committee on Africa and Peace Aims, September 8, 1941, attachment to Anson Phelps Stokes to Walter White, September 30, 1941, Box A3, File "Africa: General, 1941–43," *Papers of the NAACP*.

Americans, believed that the Atlantic Charter "should be considered the heart" of the recommendations.[29]

To ensure that it was on the right track, the Committee deliberately sought the advice and expertise of Africans who had experienced colonialism firsthand. At the February 21, 1942, meeting, representatives from the Gold Coast (present-day Ghana), Nigeria, and Sierra Leone reaffirmed that they were "especially interested" that the Atlantic Charter "would be applied to Africa." In addition to a range of opportunities and rights, they sought the creation of "additional facilities for higher and technical studies for Native students either at home or abroad, and greater assurance that when so trained they could secure governmental posts." They emphasized that if the Atlantic Charter "could be applied in the way indicated it would be of inestimable value to the future development of the African people."[30]

Anson Phelps Stokes, chairman of the foundation, was himself a bit more reticent. Bewitched by the "remarkable achievements" of Britain's stewardship "in certain parts of Africa," he had envisioned a gradualist, benevolent, metropole-led path to self-government. However, as he explained to a disgruntled British official, the sizable number of African Americans on the Committee and the fact that "some of them may have been rather radical in the past" led, instead, to a strident critique of colonialism as racist, exploitative, and antithetical to human rights.[31] Stokes grudgingly had to admit that African Americans' construction of colonialism as anything but some beneficent "civilizing" force led the Committee to embrace the Africans' framework.

Over several months, the Committee explored the "significance of the Atlantic Charter" with particular "emphasis on the fact that [it] requires the abandonment not only of territorial aggrandizement but of commercial aggrandizement at the expense of the native people; the need of changing the psychological attitude of European powers toward the people of Africa; the importance of economic improvement as a basis for social welfare development; ... the larger and more effective participation of African peoples in the Government; ... the provision by Government

---

[29] Minutes of the Meeting of the Executive Committee of the Committee on Africa and Peace Aims, February 7, 1942, Box A3, File "Africa: General, 1941–43," *Papers of the NAACP.*

[30] Minutes of the Meeting of the Executive Committee of the Committee on Africa and Peace Aims, February 21, 1942, ibid.

[31] Anson Phelps Stokes to Harold Butler, July 17, 1942, Box 37, File "1," *Phelps-Stokes Collection.*

of more scholarships for home or foreign advanced study ...; greater emphasis on education in all its stages"; and the elimination of racism and the resulting pernicious policy of "stratifying [individuals] from birth into classes with widely different privileges." In addition, the Committee considered that "the land ... be the property of the permanent residents of Africa" and be distributed to "meet the present and future needs of the African people."[32]

As these ideas circulated and solidified, they gained momentum. In August 1943, determined not to be "left in the lurch in the post-war days to come," the West African Press Delegation, led by Nnamdi "Zik" Azikiwe, who would become Nigeria's first president, issued a bold and brilliantly conceived document – "The Atlantic Charter and British West Africa," which laid out a human rights agenda for the "post-war reconstruction of the colonies and protectorates" of Ghana, Nigeria, Gambia, and Sierra Leone. The initial premise was that "capitalism and imperialism have stultified the normal growth of these territories," and now, given all that Africans had contributed to Britain's defense, this was the time for the colonies "to evolve into full-fledged democratic States." That transformation would require – in addition to free speech, freedom of the press, and religious tolerance – the right to education, health care, and housing and the reorganization of the penal system "on corrective rather than punitive lines, more in accord with the principles of indigenous African society"; economic programs in agriculture, including land redistribution, in which "the welfare of the peasant farmer shall be paramount" rather than that of "private enterprise"; "nationalisation or public ownership and control of the mines"; and employment laws that improved working conditions and raised wages while eliminating forced labor "with a view to raising the ... standard of living." Azikiwe conceded that the horrific effects of British colonialism had made immediate independence simply impossible. Nationhood would have to be phased in, but with a definite timetable and hundreds of readily available scholarships to prepare a governing and civil service class to take on the "Africanisation ... [of] all aspects of the political and administrative life of the Colonies and Protectorates of British West Africa."[33]

---

[32] Minutes of the Meeting of the Executive Committee of the Committee on Africa and Peace Aims, February 21, 1942, Box A3, File "Africa: General, 1941–43," *Papers of the NAACP*; Minutes of the Meeting of the Committee on Africa and Peace Aims, May 23, 1942, ibid.

[33] West African Press Delegation to Great Britain, "The Atlantic Charter and British West Africa: Memorandum on Post-War Reconstruction of the Colonies and Protectorates of

In South Africa, however, there was real concern that the Atlantic Charter's "grandiose language," although a wonderful comfort for those who already had their rights, was laced with a dangerous blend of intoxicating hope and crushing disappointment for the oppressed. For "the Black races that inhabit South Africa, this charter can mean something great and epochal if given a close and conscientious interpretation" – or, as Davidson Don Tengo Javabu, the first black professor hired by the University of Ft. Hare, observed, "[I]t may amount to nothing more than empty words." If the Atlantic Charter did not grant Africans "under the terms of the Third Article 'the right of all peoples to choose the form of government under which they will live,'" if it applied only to "people who governed themselves before the present war," and if the document's "fifth point 'improved labour standards'" did not include "land rights, betterment of agriculture, industry, health services and training of Africans," Javabu concluded, "then the charter is an empty shell so far as Africans are concerned."[34]

Still, as both the "completed document from West Africa" by Azikiwe and the one from the Phelps-Stokes Fund made their way to A. B. Xuma, president-general of the African National Congress, it was clear that there was a determination to give that "grandiose language" real meaning, especially for those living under colonial and oppressive conditions.[35] The ANC, therefore, convened a series of meetings throughout 1943 to craft "The Atlantic Charter from the African's Point of View."[36] "The time is no longer such that our needs and aspirations can be dictated by any other than the Africans themselves," one man declared.[37] The preliminary draft, *African Charter*, did not equivocate. The "Native is the foundation on which the country's whole economic structure is built.

British West Africa," August 1943, Box A3, File "Africa: General, 1941–43," *Papers of the NAACP*. For the role of more than one million African troops in the war effort and the effects on decolonization, see Martin Plaut, "The Africans Who Fought in WWII," *BBC*, November 9, 2009, http://news.bbc.co.uk/2/hi/africa/8344170.stm. Accessed November 23, 2012; Rita Headrick, "African Soldiers in World War II," *Armed Forces & Society*, 4, no. 3 (Spring 1978), 501–526.

[34] D. D. T. Jabavu to A. B. Xuma, June 26, 1943, Reel 3, *Papers of A.B. Xuma*, Thomas Dodd Research Archive, University of Connecticut, Storrs (hereafter *Xuma*).

[35] A. B. Xuma to Sir/Madam, November 22, 1943, ibid.; Anson Phelps-Stokes to A. B. Xuma, December 2, 1943, ibid.

[36] A. B. Xuma to Paramount Chieftaness Matsaba, April 15, 1943, ibid.; A. B. Xuma to Secretary African Trade Unions, June 2, 1943, ibid; A. B. Xuma to Paramount Chief Bathoenall, April 15, 1943, ibid; Moses Kotane to A. B. Xuma, April 9, 1943, ibid.; African National Congress Calls the People!, November 20, 1943, ibid.

[37] Sol Sidzumo to A. B. Xuma, May 4, 1943, ibid.

The recognition of this undoubted fact carries with it both the moral and the logical obligation to recognise ... as belonging to the African, those fundamental human rights which are upheld in the Atlantic Charter."[38] The point, Xuma asserted, was to "convey ... our undisputed claim to full citizenship." The ANC's expanded document, *Africans' Claims in South Africa*, laid out why there had to be a "plan for our freedom." Currently, "Africans have no freedom of movement, no freedom of choice of employment, no right of choice of residence and no right ... to purchase land or fixed property." This systematic oppression was cloaked "under the guise of segregation" in which Africans were "subjected to serious educational, political and economic disabilities and discriminations." As a result, the ANC asserted that it wanted the Allies "and the people of South Africa to know the full aspirations of the African peoples so that their point of view will also be presented at the Peace Conference." That meant, in no uncertain terms, that "the Atlantic Charter must apply to the whole British Empire, the United States of America and to all the nations of the world and their subject peoples," including especially "the Union of South Africa which, although representing itself abroad as a democracy," had "the same characteristics as Fascism" – namely, "the ruthless trampling underfoot of all human rights."[39]

The response to the Atlantic Charter in India was less hopeful. For Indian nationalists, nothing emanating from Whitehall, including the Atlantic Charter, suggested that Britain was ready to relinquish its colonial grip. Churchill had, after all, explicitly clarified to members of Parliament that at "the Atlantic meeting, we had in mind, primarily, the restoration of the sovereignty, ... of the States and nations of Europe now under the Nazi yoke." The British Empire, he insisted, was a completely different matter; one in which the Four Freedoms were just not applicable.[40] Both the *Star of India* and the *Hindu Times* were, therefore, highly "suspicious of the underhand game" played by the prime minister. Although eloquent and seductive, the Atlantic Charter simply rang hollow. "India cannot be expected to accept those principles," the newspapers asserted, until

[38] African National Congress, *African Charter*, June 7, 1943, ibid.
[39] African National Congress, *Africans' Claims in South Africa*, December 16, 1943, ibid.; Pan African Congress: Declarations and Resolutions, October 21, 1945, Reel 4, *Xuma*; A. B. Xuma to Secretariat Pan African Congress, October 16, 1945, Reel 4, *Xuma*.
[40] House of Commons Debate, September 9, 1941, Vol. 374, cc67–156, http://hansard. millbanksystems.com/commons/1941/sep/09/war-situation#S5CV0374P0_19410909_HOC_292. Accessed September 23, 2012. Also see Wm. Roger Louis, *Imperialism at Bay: The United States and the Decolonization of the British Empire, 1941–1945* (New York: Oxford University Press, 1978), 130.

independence from British imperial rule was also included.[41] Gandhi similarly dismissed the altruistic high ground staked out by the Atlantic Charter: "The Allies have no moral claim for which they are fighting, so long as they are carrying this double sin on their shoulders – the sin of India's subjection and the subjection of Negroes and other African races."[42]

Over the course of the war, the NAACP, too, raised its voice to insist that the human rights battle against the Axis could not be solely about European liberation. The Association's board of directors was appalled that a possible result of millions killed and billions spent was "freedom for white people ... on the one hand and continued exploitation of colored peoples on the other." The "exploitation of India, China, Abyssinia and other African areas, the West Indies, or of any other part of the world" had to end – or the Third World War was not far off.[43]

Channing Tobias warned that "there will be trouble down the road if the victorious nations, following this war, insist upon holding unbroken the ring of white dominance that now encircles the darker peoples of the earth." He particularly singled out the "great Winston Churchill," who was "confessedly an imperialist of the most pronounced Victorian rootage." Tobias asserted: "[A] world based on ... empire and imperial behavior is now impossible. It cannot exist. We must make clear our determination for real democracy for all peoples."[44]

Walter White also did not equivocate: "[T]he day of the white man's imperialistic rule is over."[45] In a letter to Churchill, which Anglophile Anson Phelps Stokes found highly objectionable, White slammed the prime minister for using "stirring language [to] denounce ... the racial theories on which Hitler has built a sinister philosophy and a diabolic

---

[41] Developments in India: Immediate Freedom of India Demanded by Indian Press, September 17, 1941, *Daily Report: Shortwave Broadcasts*, Foreign Broadcasts Information System database (hereafter *FBIS*).

[42] Preston Grover, "Gandhi Plans Early Move Against British in India," *Christian Science Monitor*, June 16, 1942.

[43] Resolution by Board of Directors on Control of Reoccupied Territories, September 11, 1944, Box A639, File "United Nations: UNCIO, General, 1945, March-May 10," *Papers of the NAACP*.

[44] Channing H. Tobias, "World Implications of Race," in the *Challenge of Race* (New York: Foreign Missions Conference of North America, 1944), File "Biographical Material Re: Bernays Award, 1944, [2A]," *Tobias Papers*.

[45] "Pacific Charter for the 400,000,000," *Philadelphia Record*, May 9, 1942, attached to Walter White to Sumner Welles, May 9, 1942, Box 86, File "White, Walter, 1942," *Papers of Sumner Welles*, Franklin D. Roosevelt Presidential Library, Hyde Park, NY (hereafter *Welles Papers*).

war machine" while stubbornly refusing to acknowledge that that same racism was the foundation that had "been devised and developed to justify the cruel exploitation of black, brown and yellow people" and to "exploit the vast wealth of Africa, the West Indies, of India, of the Far East and other portions of the world whose resources were originally owned by the non-white races." White warned Churchill that "unless such theories are abandoned, other and more destructive wars will follow as inevitably as the night does the day."[46]

Not surprisingly, at a number of NAACP annual conferences during the war, the issue of independence for colonial peoples in India, Malaysia, Burma, and throughout Africa echoed around the assembly halls.[47] During the Association's 1942 annual convention, R. Lal Singh, editor of *India News*, implored NAACP members "to go on record here as demanding the rights of the colonial peoples to national government so that we can mobilize to fight Fascism." He asserted that African Americans' "struggle is linked with the struggle of Indian people." Singh concluded, "The burden is heavy," but "at the end ... is an abundance of justice and security."[48] A few months later, in October 1942, the *Pittsburgh Courier* found that 87.8 percent of African Americans surveyed believed that "India should contend for her rights and her liberty now."[49]

However, as principled as the NAACP's stance on colonialism, racism, and imperialism may have been, and as hopeful as a united front seemed, the sense of shared oppression, the Association noted, was not

[46] Walter White to Winston Churchill, press release, September 26, 1941, Box 31, File "11," *Phelps-Stokes Collection*. For Anson Phelps Stokes's objections, see Anson Phelps Stokes to Walter White, October 22, 1941, Box 31, File "11," *Phelps-Stokes Collection*; Walter White to Anson Phelps Stokes, October 28, 1941, Box 31, File "11," *Phelps-Stokes Collection*; Anson Phelps Stokes to Lord Halifax, October 29, 1941, Box 31, File "11," *Phelps-Stokes Collection*; Anson Phelps Stokes to Walter White, November 3, 1941, Box A3, File "Africa: General, 1941–43," *Papers of the NAACP*.

[47] "Address of Walter White, ... at Shrine Auditorium," July 19, 1942, Reel 11, *NAACP*; Walter White, "Keynote Address of Emergency Conference on the Status of the Negro in the War for Freedom," June 3, 1943, Box A130, File "Board of Directors: William Hastie, 1943–45," *Papers of the NAACP*; Resolutions Submitted by NAACP Branches for Consideration of the Resolutions Committee of the Wartime Conference, July 12–16, 1944, n.d., Reel 11, *NAACP*.

[48] "Remarks by R. Lal Singh, Editor of *India News*, before the Thirty-third Annual Conference of the National Association for the Advancement of Colored People – Los Angeles, CA," July 17, 1942, Reel 11, *NAACP*.

[49] C. L. R. James, *Fighting Racism in World War II* (London: Pathfinder, 1980), 201. Also see Quinton Dixie and Peter Eisenstadt, *Visions of a Better World: Howard Thurman's Pilgrimage to India and the Origins of African American Nonviolence*, foreword by Walter Earl Fluker (Boston: Beacon Press, 2011).

universal among its constituents. Many African Americans feared that once Asians and Africans gained their independence, any sense of kinship with African Americans would evaporate. Sometimes this fear masked itself by amplifying the "American" component of African American – no matter how horribly compromised that identity was. The *Atlanta Daily World*, located in a city that had seen one of the worst mass acts of violence against African Americans in the twentieth-century, expressed some "sympathy" for India's quest for independence but made clear that the two freedom struggles were not analogous. "In the first place," the editorial asserted, "the American Negro is neither vassal nor subject but an American citizen, entitled to ... every right and privilege of any other American citizen." Second, Gandhi's insistence that Britain had no right, regardless of how loathsome the Nazis were, to declare war in India's name, and his strategies of nonviolence and civil disobedience during the war were highly inappropriate because they were unpatriotic. Therefore, "[w]hile extending the fullest sympathy and support to the people of India," the editorial concluded, "as Negro American citizens, ours must first and always be based upon the complete fullness of our effort in support of the nation's war effort, and for victory over the Axis Powers."[50]

At other times, the fear that led some to question the very concept of shared struggle reflected an uneasy sense that blacks were not really hallowed American citizens, at all, but rather the quintessential global pariah.[51] In 1942, Howard University history professor Rayford Logan

[50] "Sympathy and Support for India," *Atlanta Daily World*, August 30, 1942. For the Atlanta Race Riot of 1906, see David Fort Godshalk, *Veiled Visions: The 1906 Atlanta Race Riot and the Reshaping of American Race Relations* (Chapel Hill: University of North Carolina Press, 2005); Allison Dorsey, *To Build Our Lives Together: Community Formation in Black Atlanta, 1875–1906* (Athens: University of Georgia Press, 2004).

[51] Richard Durham, "Gary Strikers Like Their Equality White," *Chicago Defender*, October 6, 1945; Venice T. Spraggs, "8 Nations Ban Negroes," *Chicago Defender*, June 16, 1945; Robert E. Washington, "Brown Racism and the Formation of a World System of Racial Stratification," *International Journal of Politics, Culture, and Society*, 4, no. 2 (Winter, 1990), 209–227; Kofi Apraku, *Outside Looking In: An African Perspective on American Pluralistic Society* (Westport, CT: Praeger, 1996); Jorge Duany, "Reconstructing Racial Identity: Ethnicity, Color, and Class among Dominicans in the United States and Puerto Rico," *Latin American Perspectives*, 25, no. 3 (May 1998), 147–172; Ruel Rogers, "Black Like Who?: Afro-Caribbean Immigrants, African Americans, and the Politics of Group Identity," in *Islands in the City: West Indian Migration to New York*, ed. Nancy Foner (Berkeley: University of California Press, 2001), 163–192; Mary C. Waters, "Ethnic and Racial Identities of Second-generation Black Immigrants in New York City," *International Migration Review*, 28, no. 4 (Winter 1994), 795–820; Mary C. Waters, *Black Identities: West Indian Immigrant Dreams and American Realities* (Cambridge, MA: Harvard University Press, 1999); Kevin A. Yelvington, "A Life In and Out of Anthropology: An Interview with Jack Sargent Harris," *Critique of Anthropology*, 28, no. 4 (2008), 451.

observed that the world's racism just seemed to roll downhill onto African Americans. "Not only do whites exploit darker peoples but Japanese exploit Koreans and Chinese, Serbs exploit Croatians, and minority groups fleeing persecution in Europe come over here and persecute us." Logan was, therefore, taken aback that an Indian scholar, S. Chandrasekhar, whom he met at a conference, "was quite congenial," and "unlike many Indians, he made no effort to run away from me." The Howard University professor was even more surprised by this after he learned that Chandrasekhar had previously been warned by an "Indian who had lived in the United States for twenty years ... not to be too friendly with Negroes."[52] There was, as one immigrant explained, "'a strong prejudice' among Indians against 'associating with the negroes in America.'" This disdain emanated from not only a "feeling of race superiority" but also a keen awareness that "the negroes [sic] are socially ostracised by the Americans themselves."[53] And that simple construction exposed the subtext that "negroes" were not "Americans." Nor were U.S. blacks easily welcomed into the larger community of color. As one Indian fumed, "Too much has been written by the Negro papers, magazines and fourth rate writers like Du Bois, about the darker races, but who in the hell wants to join the caravan with the black ones."[54] Secretary of State Cordell Hull reinforced that point when he emphasized to President Roosevelt that while Walter White and the NAACP seemed to believe that there was some kind of people of color kinship, in reality, there were "well-recognized racial prejudices on the part of Indian leaders themselves" against African Americans.[55]

Without question, as historian Nico Slate notes, this "shared struggle for freedom" was fraught with complications. Indians and African Americans wrestled with malleable definitions of freedom, the differences between Jim Crow and British imperialism, and the caste system and its implications for the language of equality. Nonetheless, Slate observes, given the brutality, violence, and discrimination they faced in their respective lands, "while the nature of freedom was debated, most Indians and African Americans knew–this was not it."[56] The common experience of

[52] Rayford Logan, diary entry, July 18, 1942, Box 3, File "Diaries, 1942," *Papers of Rayford Logan*, Washington, DC: Library of Congress (hereafter *Logan Papers*).

[53] Nico Slate, *Colored Cosmopolitanism: The Shared Struggle for Freedom in the United States and India* (Cambridge, MA: Harvard University Press, 2012), 27.

[54] Ibid., 88.

[55] Cordell Hull to Franklin Roosevelt, May 22, 1942, Box 86, File "White, Walter, 1942," *Welles Papers*.

[56] Slate, *Colored Cosmopolitanism*, 1–35, quotes on cover and on p. 4.

dealing with omnipresent subjugation and forced inequality was powerful enough to bridge very divergent circumstances and to cast the struggle for freedom as mutually reinforcing, even symbiotic. In other words, despite the divisions among a conflicted mass of human beings, there was also a constant: they did not enjoy anything akin to the vaunted Four Freedoms. And this extended well beyond Indians to include other colonized peoples.

The sense of "shared struggle" would lead to eventual alliances between the NAACP and the Somalis, Libyans, Indonesians, and Hereros. To be sure, each of these anticolonial struggles came with its own history, obstacles, and strategies. Yet, the goal was the same. Walter White keenly observed that "[a] wind *is* rising – a wind of determination by the have-nots of the world to share the benefits of freedom and prosperity which the haves of the earth have tried to keep exclusively for themselves."[57] One State Department official would come to explain that the colonized "have been engaged in a revolution in which they have been trying to throw off the poverty and oppression of past centuries. They have been striving for independence, better education, more widespread ownership of land and control over their own identity."[58]

Thus, in 1942, Roy Wilkins, the assistant secretary of the NAACP, remarked that African Americans were "just a segment of a people's revolution."[59] But make no mistake, it was a revolution – and one in which the Association had a critical role to play. Wilkins invoked the Mt. Rushmore of black liberation as he declared that in this epic struggle to upend white supremacy, the Association stood on the shoulders of the "Sojourner Truths, the Denmark Veseys, the Nat Turners, ... [and] Frederick Douglass." Given their powerful legacies, Wilkins exhorted, the NAACP "cannot sell out. We cannot step to one side. We cannot and will not remain silent. The fight goes on and on, until we win."[60]

[57] Walter White, *A Rising Wind* (Garden City, NY: Doubleday, 1945), 155. Emphasis in original.
[58] Address by the Honorable Dean Acheson, "Secretary of State Before the Commonwealth Club of California, San Francisco ... March 15 ...," Press Release No. 246, March 13, 1950, Box 30, File "United Nations: Dean Acheson – Corres., Addresses & Press Releases, Jan.–Dec. 1950," *Austin Papers.*
[59] Fragment that begins "fellow citizens.... Let no one underrate ..." July 14, 1942, *NAACP,* Reel 11.
[60] "Fight for Rights to Continue during War, NAACP Delegates Told: Keynote Address at Los Angeles Repudiates 'Wait-until-after-the-War' Philosophy and Pledges Double Effort for Victory at Home and Abroad," July 17, 1942, Reel 11, *NAACP.*

Any attempt to harness this transnational, transracial, seething discontent would be faced with a juggernaut of resistance. No matter how wounded, bloodied, and wearied the British, Dutch, and French may have been by the war, they were determined to maintain their colonial rule and forestall independence. To be sure, the imperial powers' resolve still had the cracked, yellowed veneer of benevolence. An OSS report explained that the "fundamental premise underlying all colonial policies has been that native populations are too backward culturally and insufficiently experienced politically to shoulder the responsibilities of self-government – as conceived by Westerners."[61] Bestial images of the primitive only seemed to reaffirm that assessment. The American consul in Lagos, for example, reported on widespread "cannibalism" in Nigeria, which, he was sure, could only be "attributed ... to the depravity, ignorance, and superstition of some of the wild people of the 'bush.'"[62] Francis B. Sayre, high commissioner of the Philippines, asserted that "premature independence for primitive, uneducated peoples can do them more harm than good."[63] "Do not be deceived," he warned. "[T]he most profound issues and struggles will come after independence, not before."[64] Similarly, Henry Villard, assistant secretary of state for Near East Affairs, noted that while the Four Freedoms opened the "question of political advancement for the natives of Africa, ... that does not mean we intend to ... listen seriously to the extremists who advocate the instant liberation of" colonial peoples "from external control." Africa has a "relatively primitive native population," Villard remarked, and there would be inevitable "chaos and confusion ... from casting adrift on the uncertain political seas great masses of inexperienced people."[65] The British also extolled the necessity of colonialism because "many parts of the Colonial Empire are still so little removed from their primitive state that it must be a

[61] "Indigenous African Political Systems: An Appraisal of Native Attitudes," June 13, 1944, Research and Analysis No. 1878, Reel 3, *OSS/Africa*.

[62] Andrew G. Lynch to Secretary of State, March 27, 1945, Reel 2, *Confidential U.S. State Department Central Files, British Africa, 1945–1949, Internal Affairs* (Bethesda, MD: University Publications of America, 1991) (hereafter *Confidential British Africa*).

[63] Francis B. Sayre, "The Problem of Underdeveloped Areas in Asia and Africa," *Proceedings of the American Academy of Arts and Sciences*, 81, no. 6 (April 9, 1952), 292, Box 13, File "United Nations: Printed Matter," *Papers of Francis B. Sayre*, Library of Congress, Washington, DC (hereafter *Sayre Papers*).

[64] "Sayre's Warning," *Manila Bulletin*, April 3, 1940, Box 10, File "8," *Papers of John Nevin Sayre*, Peace Collection, Swarthmore College, Swarthmore, PA (hereafter *JNSayre Papers*).

[65] "Address by Mr. Henry S. Villard ... at the Chautauqua Institute," August 19, 1943, Box 33, File "20," *Phelps-Stokes Collection*.

matter of many generations before they are ready for anything like full self-government."[66]

However, just beneath the veneer of beneficence and concern lurked the real needs of the West: "great power" status, raw materials, and geo-strategic bases. The Dutch, who were laboring under a brutal Nazi occu-pation, desperately needed to piece back together what they viewed as their national honor and rightful place at the table of great powers; the rapid collapse of their armed forces in Indonesia and Europe had left both seriously in doubt.[67] Despite its rhetoric of aiding Indonesia to throw off the "armed robber-state of the Far East ... to prepare for the relief and rehabilitation of the Indies," Holland knew that what was truly at stake was not Indonesia's revitalization but its own rebuilding.[68] The Nazis had stripped the nation of much of its industrial plant, confiscated foodstuffs, and decimated the harbors. The Dutch estimated that it would require roughly 18 billion guilders, approximately $696 billion in 2011 dollars, just to get back to prewar levels.[69] Indonesia was rich in resources – oil, tin, kapok – that could provide the capital needed to finance a massive reconstruction effort in the Netherlands. As historian Robert McMahon noted, "most [in the Netherlands] believed that Indonesia was indispens-able to the Dutch economy and would continue to be indispensable in the postwar period, especially in view of the desperate needs of their war-ravaged homeland."[70]

Britain had also absorbed a devastating economic blow as it liquidated many of its assets, including hundreds of millions in gold reserves, and threw "financial caution" to the wind "to obtain vital supplies from North America" to weather the Nazi onslaught.[71] The colonies, however, were

[66] Notes of a Meeting held at No. 11 Downing Street, May 3, 1943, DO 35/1897.
[67] Sluimers, "The Japanese Military and Indonesian Independence," 19–20; Gerhard Hirschfeld, *Nazi Rule and Dutch Collaboration: The Netherlands under German Occupation, 1940–1945* (Oxford, New York, and Hamburg: Berg, 1988); Louis de Jong, *The Netherlands and Nazi Germany*, foreword by Simon Schama (Cambridge, MA: Harvard University Press, 1990).
[68] *Netherlands News Digest*, 3, no. 8 (July 1, 1944), 277; "The Netherlands East Indies: A New Government for the East Indies," *Netherlands News Digest*, 3, no. 1 (March 15, 1944), 24, 25.
[69] Nehemiah Robinson, "Problems of European Reconstruction," *Quarterly Journal of Economics*, 60, no. 1 (November 1945), 5–6, 7, 11; Alan Bullock, *Hitler, A Study in Tyranny*, rev. ed., (New York: Harper & Row, 1964), 695–696; Measuring Worth, http://www.measuringworth.com/uscompare/relativevalue.php. Accessed December 9, 2012.
[70] Robert McMahon, *Colonialism and Cold War: The United States and the Struggle for Indonesian Independence, 1945–49* (Ithaca, NY: Cornell University Press, 1981), 93.
[71] A. J. B., "American Aid to Britain," *Bulletin of International News*, 18, no. 6 (March 22, 1941), 319–324; Thorne, *Allies of a Kind*, 110.

clearly not on the auction block; British identity was too inextricably linked to an empire on which the sun never set. Already rankled that the Americans were buying up England's assets at fire sale prices, the British response was "stiff" and "distinctly chilly" when several State Department officials suggested that it would be imprudent for the colonized to come out of this war "neglected in the general settlement."[72] The very idea of "independence," Foreign Secretary Anthony Eden stressed, "would not be acceptable." Even the tenet of "'self-government' ... would be quite unacceptable."[73] Similarly, the British Dominion high commissioners found an American proposal for postwar alterations in the colonial system "most unsatisfactory." "Particularly objectionable," they declared, was the "unfortunate emphasis on independence" and the "impracticable suggestion for a timetable," which would have set a definite date for nationhood and the transfer of sovereignty.[74] Winston Churchill was even less restrained: he "hit the roof" when asked to contemplate a world where even a handful of colonies were not under imperial rule. As one State Department official noted, "the mere mention of the phrase 'territorial trusteeship' almost gave [Churchill] an attack of apoplexy. He said that he would never consent to such a thing and he went on muttering 'never, never, never' for several minutes."[75] As the prime minister saw it, Britain had everything to lose and absolutely nothing to gain by this "vague American aspiration" for the eventual liquidation of colonial empires, which, he noted most acidly, "cost them nothing to make."[76]

While that response might have been expected from Churchill's Tory Party, the Labour Party also equated British greatness with empire.[77]

---

[72] Isaiah Bowman to John Winant, April 28, 1944, Box 1, File "Bowman, Isaiah, 1944," *Papers of Benjamin Gerig*, Library of Congress, Washington, DC (hereafter *Gerig Papers*).

[73] Anthony Eden to Viscount Halifax, May 26, 1943, DO 35/1897.

[74] Extract from Note of Meeting with Dominion High Commissioners held at 4.0 p.m. on Monday, 10th May, 1943, May 18, 1943, DO 35/1897.

[75] Alger Hiss to Benjamin Gerig, February 14, 1945, Box 4, File "State Department Colonial Policy: Memoranda and Correspondence," *Gerig Papers*.

[76] Winston Churchill to Deputy Prime Minister and Foreign Secretary, September 15, 1943, DO 35/1897.

[77] See Ritchie Ovendale, "The South African Policy of the British Labour Government, 1947–51," *International Affairs*, 59, no. 1 (Winter, 1982–1983), 43; Paul Kelemen, "The British Labor Party and the Economics of Decolonization: The Debate over Kenya," *Journal of Colonialism and Colonial History*, 8, no. 3 (Winter 2007): 1–33; Mary Davis, "Labour, Race, and Empire: The Trades Union Congress and Colonial Policy, 1945–51," in *The British Labour Movement and Imperialism*, eds. Billy Frank, Craig Horner and David Stewart (New Castle upon Tyne: Cambridge Scholars Publishing, 2010), 89–106;

Proposal after proposal for increasing international accountability over the colonies, or expanding the League of Nations' Mandate system, which, after the First World War, had placed a few colonies on the long road to independence, indicated how "resistant the British may be."⁷⁸ Sounding eerily similar to Foreign Secretary Eden, Labour Party M. P. Arthur Creech-Jones denounced international accountability as "definitely unacceptable." His solution was to dissolve the mandates, treat these colonies as spoils of war, and absorb them into existing imperial systems. The growth of empires, he insisted, "would really be to the advantage of the mandated territories and their development." Creech-Jones anticipated that there might be some backlash, but that would simply be the result of a misinformed public "thinking in terms of the out-worn concepts of the old imperialism and the old type of colonial administration."⁷⁹

Even the creation of a Division of Dependent Areas Affairs in the State Department annoyed British officials, who were certain that their American "ally" was openly scheming to supplant the United Kingdom in every nook and cranny of the globe. Creech-Jones and another member of Parliament asked, with no hint of subtlety, whether the new division would be appropriately focused on the U.S. colonies of Puerto Rico, Hawaii, and the Philippines and, of course, "concern itself with the problems of the 'fifteen million dependent peoples in the United States proper' by which they meant … the American Negro."⁸⁰

France, too, desperately hoped to hold onto its colonies. Like Britain, the French strongly suspected that "American imperialism," under the guise of aid and support, planned to "swallow up" France's colonial empire.⁸¹ The source of this fear, U.S. diplomats reported, was that the rapid collapse of French forces in 1940 was so devastating and the Nazi occupation so humiliating that France had all of the weaknesses, paranoia, and

---

Billy Frank, "Labour's 'New Imperialist Attitude': State-Sponsored Colonial Development in Africa, 1940–51," in *The British Labour Movement and Imperialism,* 107–130.
⁷⁸ Benjamin Gerig to Leo Pasvolsky, January 10, 1945, Box 4, File "State Department Colonial Policy: Memoranda and Correspondence," *Gerig Papers.*
⁷⁹ Ralph Bunche to Benjamin Gerig, January 7, 1945, ibid.
⁸⁰ Ralph Bunche to Benjamin Gerig, January 7, 1945, ibid.
⁸¹ Jefferson Caffery to Secretary of State, March 21, 1945, 711.51/3-2145, Reel 3, *Confidential U.S. State Department Central Files, France, 1945–1949, Foreign Affairs* (Bethesda, MD: University Publications of America, 1986) (hereafter *Confidential France Foreign Affairs*); Kim Munholland, "The Trials of the Free French in New Caledonia, 1940–1942," *French Historical Studies,* 14, no. 4 (Autumn 1986), 561; Martin Thomas, "Deferring to Vichy in the Western Hemisphere: The St. Pierre and Miquelon Affair of 1941," *International History Review,* 19, no. 4 (November 1997), 809–835.

pretensions associated with faded-great-power syndrome.[82] Moreover, the French had been here before. Their defeat by Prussia in the nineteenth century meant that "the conquest of Africa took on the character of a national compensation through which the country could regain its rank in the European concert.... As a result, the defense of Africa – the largest part of the French Empire – became closely associated with the defense of France itself."[83]

During the Second World War, however, the British and the Americans did the overwhelming majority of the fighting in North Africa against the Germans and the French collaborationists, Vichy France.[84] For the first few years of the war, the Free French forces, led by Charles De Gaulle, "were held down by a firmly pro–Petain [Vichy] administration."[85] In fact, the primary saga of the Free French is one of little substantive, effective action, demands for recognition disproportionate to its contribution to the war, and repeated violations of the Geneva Convention in the treatment of German and Italian prisoners of war who had been captured by British and American forces and turned over to the French for safekeeping.[86] Even the invasion of Normandy, which eventually ousted the Germans from France, was handled by American, Canadian, and British troops.

The Free French also bungled what could have been the triumphant liberation of one of France's colonies, Lebanon. The situation was so

[82] Philippe Burrin, *Living with Defeat: France under the German Occupation, 1940–1944*, trans. Janet Lloyd (London: Arnold, 1996); Julian Jackson, *France: The Dark Years, 1940–1944* (New York: Oxford University Press 2001); Eric T. Jennings, *Vichy in the Tropics: Pétain's National Revolution in Madagascar, Guadeloupe, and Indochina, 1940–1944* (Stanford, CA: Stanford University Press 2001); France: Policy and Information Statement, September 15, 1946, 711.51/9–1546, Reel 3, *Confidential France Foreign Affairs.*

[83] Pierre Lellouche and Dominique Moisi, "French Policy in Africa: A Lonely Battle against Destabilization," *International Security*, 1.3, no. 4 (Spring, 1979), 110.

[84] Ronald Lewin, *Rommel as Military Commander* (New York: Ballantine Books, 1968), 80–235; Rick Atkinson, *An Army at Dawn: The War in North Africa, 1942–1943* (New York: Henry Holt and Company, 2002), 82–84, 86–89, 115–118, 137, 141–148, 159.

[85] C. M. C., "French North Africa since June 1940: Main Political Developments," *Bulletin of International News*, 19, no. 25 (Dec. 12, 1942), 1127.

[86] Edward L. Bimberg, *Tricolor over the Sahara: The Desert Battles of the Free French, 1940–1942* (Westport, CT: Greenwood Press, 2002); Munholland, "The Trials of the Free French in New Caledonia, 1940–1942," 562; Anthony Clayton, *The Wars of French Decolonization* Modern Wars in Perspective, ed., B. W. Collins and H. M. Scott(London and New York: Longman, 1994), 19–20; Bob Moore, "Unruly Allies: British Problems with the French Treatment of Axis Prisoners of War, 1943–1945," *War in History*, 7, no. 2 (2000), 180–198.

mismanaged that, according to the *Chicago Defender*, it put De Gaulle's forces "on trial in the eyes of the world, which [were] looking to see if these men [had] learned anything from their harrowing experiences from the Nazis."[87] The answer appeared to be "no." In 1941, the Free French had made a clear promise of independence to Lebanon but then clumsily followed up two years later by intimating that nationhood would only occur if the Lebanese leadership granted France "land, air, and sea bases as essential" for "communications with [French] territories in the Far East and Africa." Lebanon swatted away those pretensions and proudly declared its independence. Instead of accepting this fait accompli and finding a way to gracefully put their imprimatur on it, French authorities arrested and imprisoned the president and seven other leading politicians. The Lebanese responded so furiously that not even bullets could quell the rebellion. Within a few days, with the Levant in the throes of what could easily escalate into a revolution, the Free French retreated, licked their wounds, and released the leaders. Almost immediately, Lebanon re-declared and reasserted its independence.[88]

That is to say, the French who "won" the war actually had very few victories and were, in many ways, barely a "junior ally."[89] One State Department analysis, therefore, concluded that the "humiliation" of the Nazi occupation and limited French contributions to the war effort had "rendered them exceptionally sensitive to questions involving their sovereignty and their national prestige."[90] Not surprisingly, then, France was sure its ills could be cured with another strong dose of pure, uncut empire.[91] As scholar Anthony Clayton noted, "it was argued that if France was to remain a world power she had to retain the Empire in order to resist subordination to *les anglo-saxons*, whatever the rest of the world might think."[92] Indeed, Gaston Monnerville, a leading politician, observed, "Without her empire, France would today be nothing more than a liberated country. Thanks to her Empire France is a victorious

[87] John Robert Badger, "World View," *Chicago Defender*, February 19, 1944.
[88] W. G. E., "France, Syria, and the Lebanon," *The World Today*, 2, no. 3 (March 1946), 116.
[89] Moore, "Unruly Allies," 180.
[90] France: Policy and Information Statement, September 15, 1946, 711.51/9–1546, Reel 3, *Confidential France Foreign Affairs*.
[91] Jean Chretien (pseudonym for French Colonial Administrator), "The French Colonial Ideal," *Free World*, January 1946, 23–26, Box 79, File "United Nations – Trusteeship Council," *Papers of Vernon McKay*, Melville Herskovits Africana Library, Northwestern University, Evanston, IL (hereafter *McKay Papers*).
[92] Clayton, *The Wars of French Decolonization*, 3.

country."[93] The French, therefore, made it clear that "there can be no question of giving up French rights over her colonial territories 'where the work achieved by our colonizers justifies our presence.'"[94]

Even South Africa wanted a special key to the colonial club. Since 1919 it had held South West Africa as a League of Nations mandate, but it now was angling to strengthen its grip on that international territory, while also trying to stitch together a network of white settler communities in Kenya, the Rhodesias, Eastern Congo, Uganda, and Tanganyika to "end the isolation of South Africa's white population and secure the future of European civilization on the African continent." South African officials worried aloud about "how long they can sit on the lid" as the "economic strength and political consciousness" of the indigenous people and Indians who had settled there grew. The problem was that, whereas the government in Pretoria depicted South Africa as "a warm and friendly land … [with] a rich tradition of freedom – freedom of thought, freedom of speech and freedom of worship," the OSS accurately described a nation where the "Natives are excluded from any effective voice in the government, of a country in which they are the overwhelming majority; their educational opportunities are meager; their movements are restricted by pass laws; outside of their crowded, unproductive reserves they are forbidden to engage in any but the most unskilled types of labor and are remunerated on a scale which does not ensure them the bare necessities of existence."[95] Prime Minister Jan Christian Smuts, therefore, fretted that the more "liberal" colonial policies practiced by the Portuguese in Angola, Belgians in the Congo, and British in Kenya and Tanganyika would undermine Pretoria's ability "to confine her Bantu to unskilled labor" and the "Zulu, the proudest fighting race in southern Africa" to "labor battalions because the Union dares not arm its natives." Smuts's proposed solution was a Pan-African Conference of the colonial powers to develop a more "rigid" European strategy to corral the indigenous populations so that South Africa would not be buried "by an avalanche of color in a generation or two."[96] In addition, the prime minister

---

[93] Ibid., fn 2, p. 3.
[94] Official and Unofficial Opinion of the Mandatory Countries as to the Future of the African Mandates, April 10, 1945, Reel 3, *OSS/Africa*.
[95] Union of South Africa, "South Africa on Service: A Pictorial Record of the Union of South Africa's Work on the Home Front, 1939–1943," 1944, File "World War, 1939–1945 – South Africa," *Vertical File*, Franklin D. Roosevelt Presidential Library, Hyde Park, NY; The Pan-African Movement, December 15, 1943, Reel 10, *OSS/Africa*.
[96] The Pan-African Movement, December 15, 1943, Reel 10, *OSS/Africa*.

sought U.S. assent to annex South West Africa, although it was legally international territory. As far as he was concerned, particularly with the rising tide of black consciousness and anticolonialism, the League's mandate system had "outlived its time."[97]

All of these colonial (or would-be) powers knew that to achieve their ends, they needed the United States to put the might of American political and economic power behind their imperial projects. The executive branch, however, had its own evolving and often contradictory plans. In mid-1942, John Foster Dulles had just returned from London and shared with the Roosevelt administration his assessment of the situation. He noted that the Atlantic Charter was not "taken as seriously in England as here," the British government "resent[ed] the American condemnation of so-called 'imperialism,'" and he had to douse Whitehall's hopes about U.S. support in restoring the British Empire because, as he explained, the "opposition in the United States [would] be formidable" if the public believed the American government was "collaborat[ing] in imperialism and exploitation."[98] Also at stake was the perception of the United States in Asia. Thus, Secretary of State Hull had nixed a joint Anglo-American film project concerning "military operations in the Southeast Asia theatre." He was adamant that the United States could not be seen as supporting, advocating, or fighting for the British Empire. We must, he insisted, "avoid ... confusion in the minds of the peoples of the area with regard to American and British policies." There could be no intimation that U.S. troops "in the Far East ... were waging a war of imperialism."[99] The Joint Chiefs of Staff (JCS) also raised concerns about the appearance of American power propping up the Empire. "British interests and objectives in that area [Asia], are ... both military *and* political, while those of the United States are concerned with the defeat of Japan." After coming to the realization that Churchill's aims were about not just ousting Hirohito's army but also reinstalling British imperial rule, the JCS, with the concurrence of the State Department and the Office of War Information, demanded that an Anglo-American committee on

[97] Official and Unofficial Opinion in the Mandatory Countries as to the Future of the African Mandates, April 10, 1945, Reel 3, *OSS/Africa*.

[98] Draft of Proposed Confidential Report of John Foster Dulles to the Commission to Study the Bases of a Just and Durable Peace, July 30, 1942, Box 20, File "Dulles, John Foster," *Papers of Henry A. Wallace as Vice-President*, Franklin D. Roosevelt Presidential Library, Hyde Park, NY.

[99] Cordell Hull to Henry L. Stimson, October 9, 1944, Reel 5, *Confidential U.S. State Department Central Files, Southeast Asia, 1944–1958* (Bethesda, MD: University Publications of America, 1989) (hereafter *Confidential Southeast Asia*).

propaganda be "abolished" immediately.[100] Throughout Asia, one State Department report noted with concern, "there has been constant repetition of the theme that the oppression of colored peoples was due to 'Anglo-American imperialism.'" Given that the brutality of the Japanese did "not mean the acceptance by Asiatic peoples of a restored Western imperialism" – indeed, all "available evidence indicates that the peoples of" Asia "have become much more nationalistic during the course of the war" – the "colonial problem will not be solved by the restoration of European rulers who will continue to bear the white man's burden." Therefore, "it is imperative that the subject peoples should have some idea of the extent to which *this* country," the United States of America, was "bringing pressure to bear for their liberation." Of course, the report concluded, U.S. liberation efforts "must take place under the watchful eye of European colonial administration."[101] Nonetheless, the State Department advised, the United States not only had to distance itself from "imperialistic policies" but also had to recognize that "the change in attitude of all people towards white imperialism [was] reaching revolutionary proportions."[102]

However, the United States could not maintain that distance and stay fully engaged with its allies. In November 1942, FDR had offered a vision of a world comprised of no colonies, just independent nations free from religious and racial discrimination. For the president, the "steps to complete statehood" included "a period of preparation, through the dissemination of education and the recognition of the fulfillment of physical and social and economic needs," as well as a trusteeship "period of training for ultimate independent sovereignty."[103]

A year later, in 1943, however, deeper into the war, postwar planning, and the possibility of an Allied victory and its implications for U.S. national security, the president indicated that it would be "drastic"

---

[100] Draft of Proposed Letter to the President, January 29, 1944, Reel 2, *Confidential Southeast Asia*. Emphasis added.

[101] Need for an Intensive Short-Term Information Program in SEA, n.d., Reel 5, *Confidential U.S. Southeast Asia*. Emphasis added.

[102] Proposal for an International Trusteeship System (Memorandum Prepared by Mr. Moffat), May 27, 1944, PWC-248, Reel 4, *State Department Documents of the Post-War Programs Committee, 1944* (Washington, DC: National Archives and Records Service, 1979) (hereafter *State Post-War Committee*).

[103] "Significant Comments and Suggestions Emerging from Discussion in the United States: … Trusteeship," in "Comments and Suggestions on the Dumbarton Oaks Proposals," March 26, 1945, Box 55, File "UNCIO Charter: Comments and Proposals, United States Delegation," *Papers of Charles Taussig*, Franklin D. Roosevelt Presidential Library, Hyde Park, NY (hereafter *Taussig Papers*).

to dismantle the British, French, and Dutch empires and "place all dependent areas," as they were known then, "under complete international administration and control." He deemed equally unacceptable a "somewhat less drastic" trusteeship plan to put only the current mandates and colonies stripped from the Axis "under full international administration and control."[104]

Determined to maintain "good relations with our present associates" in France, Britain, and the Netherlands while offering some hope "to peoples seeking independence," the United States came up with a plan that was a blend of compromises. The State Department latched onto the idea that it would be prudent to create "a new and broadened version of the mandates system." The new terminology of "trusteeship" was to "avoid any suggestion that the new system is merely perpetuating an old regime which enjoyed only indifferent success."[105] The proposed new international organization, the United Nations, would, however, "handle only mandated and detached areas; the present colonial arrangements would not be disturbed." That was to mollify the Europeans. As a sop to those denied the right to self-determination, "the colonial powers would pledge ... to observe ... certain specified principles and would make public to the world essential information regarding their colonial administration" of the colonies.[106] The combination of international accountability and "higher standards" for education, health, and labor in the trust territories, the State Department hoped, would set the precedent for the rest of the Europeans' empires.[107]

Although that formula was supposed to quell discontent from both the colonized and colonizer, it did neither. Furthermore, the United States by now had some of its own "assets" to consider. The JCS, who had their eye on the mandated islands wrested from Japan, were, in the words of William Hastie, NAACP board member and former civilian aide to the secretary of war, "'fighting like hell' for the United States to declare that it will hold on to the bases we have established" in the Marshalls, Carolines,

---

[104] Draft of Report to the President and Congress: Dependent Territories and Arrangements for Trusteeship, June 6, 1945, Box 66, File "Trusteeship–Report to President," *Taussig Papers*.

[105] ibid.

[106] Memorandum for the President, November 17, 1943, Box 59, File "Trusteeship – Background Material before San Francisco," *Taussig*; Frey, "Visions of the Future," 365.

[107] Benjamin Gering to Isaiah Bowman, June 1, 1944, Box 1, File "Bowman, Isaiah, 1944," *Gerig Papers*.

Palaus, and northern Marianas Islands, "and to hell with trusteeship."[108] The JCS were emphatic that "the Japanese mandated islands … [were] essential to our security" and "there appear[ed] to be no valid reason why their future status should be the subject of discussion with any other nation." That, of course, included not only the virtually moribund League of Nations but also the proposed UN.[109] Two powerful senators, Tom Connally (D-TX), chair of the Foreign Relations Committee, and Arthur Vandenberg (R-MI), added their significant clout to the debate. They, too, "wanted assurances" that no trusteeship plan "would … in any way tie the hands of the United States" and "that in one way or another the United States would be in a position to have control of the Pacific Islands."[110] Connally drove home his point succinctly: "[T]ake them and hold them."[111]

Assistant Secretary of State James Dunn had to admit that nearly a year's worth of dickering, haggling, and compromising with the military over the Japanese mandated islands meant that the Americans "lost sight of the broad principles involved in the colonial issue."[112] That was readily apparent when one of the most respected advisers, Hamilton Fish Armstrong, editor of *Foreign Affairs*, recommended that in subsequent negotiations the United States needed to downplay or ignore altogether the Atlantic Charter.[113]

This was, in some ways, a dramatic shift. Initially, playing up its heritage as a former colony, the U.S. government had, in November 1942, conceived of "The Atlantic Charter in Relation to National Independence." Then, in March 1943, the State Department developed the "Draft Declaration by

108 Roy Wilkins to Walter White, memo, April 11, 1945, Box A639, File "United Nations: UNCIO, General, 1945, March–May 10," *Papers of the NAACP*.

109 Major Mathias F. Correa to Keith Kane, n.d., ca. April 1945, Box 77, File "U.N. Conference, 1945 Trusteeship (Photostats)," *Taussig Papers*; Japan: Mandated Islands, Status of Military Government, March 22, 1944, PWC-123, Reel 2, *State Post-War Committee*; Melvyn P. Leffler, "The American Conception of National Security and the Beginnings of the Cold War, 1945–48," *American Historical Review*, 89, no. 2 (April 1984), 349–350.

110 Meeting of the Advisers with the American Delegation, April 27, 1945, Box 77, File "U.N. Conference, 1945 Trusteeship (Photostats)," *Taussig Papers*.

111 "On April 16th when the Secretary of State opened the meeting, …" April 16, 1945, Box 59, File "Trusteeship–Background Material before San Francisco," *Taussig Papers*.

112 Memorandum for the Files: Conversation with Assistant Secretary of State Dunn at luncheon given by Secretary Stettinius to the Foreign Ministers, Union Pacific Club, May 1, 1945, Box 77, File "U.N. Conference, 1945 Trusteeship (Photostats)," *Taussig Papers*.

113 H. F. A. "Preamble," April 6, 1945, Box 84, Folder "5," *Papers of Hamilton Fish Armstrong*, Seeley Mudd Manuscript Library, Princeton University, Princeton, NJ (hereafter *Armstrong Papers*).

the United Nations on National Independence," which had as its "most significant provision ... that colonial peoples should be granted progressive measures of self-government and should be given full independence in accordance with a fixed time schedule."[114] Now, with questions about military bases and access to raw materials dominating deliberations, the indigenous peoples and their rights to self-determination were lost as collateral damage.[115]

The maneuvering by the European powers, South Africa, and the United States to entrench themselves in lands not their own set a daunting, seemingly impossible challenge for all those determined that the Second World War spelled the end, not the continuation, of colonial rule.[116] For the NAACP, in particular, there was another problem: a set of its own financial, structural, and personnel issues that called into serious question whether the Association had the ability to meet and sustain the challenge of a "people's revolution." Undercapitalized, with a fractured hierarchy that was embroiled in internecine squabbles, and facing opponents that were better resourced and less scrupulous, the NAACP had all of the hallmarks of many other organizations – such as Marcus Garvey's Universal Negro Improvement Association, the Student Non-Violent Coordinating Committee, and the Black Panthers – buried in the graveyard of social justice movements.[117]

[114] Ralph Bunche to Charles Taussig, Memorandum on the Issue of Trusteeship, n.d., Box 59, File "Trusteeship – Background Material before San Francisco," *Taussig Papers*.

[115] "Address by Mr. Henry S. Villard ... at the Chautauqua Institute," August 18, 1943, Box 33, File "20," *Phelps-Stokes Collection*; Summary: Dependent Areas, June 12, 1944, PWC-242, Reel 4, *State Post-War Committee*; Principles of Administration in Dependent Territories, March 8, 1945, Reel 1, *Confidential France Foreign Affairs*; Memorandum for the Files: Conversation with Assistant Secretary of State Dunn at luncheon given by Secretary Stettinius to the Foreign Ministers, Union Pacific Club, May 1, 1945, Box 77, File "U.N. Conference, 1945 Trusteeship (Photostats)," *Taussig Papers*; Henry Stimson and James V. Forrestal to Franklin Roosevelt, April 13, 1945, Box 66, File "Trusteeship–Report to President," *Taussig Papers*; "On April 16th when the Secretary of State opened the meeting, ..." April 16, 1945, Box 59, File "Trusteeship–Background Material before San Francisco," *Taussig Papers*; "At the afternoon meeting on April 17th, ..." April 17, 1945, Box 59, File "Trusteeship–Background Material before San Francisco," *Taussig Papers*; Memorandum for the President: State-War-Navy Agreement, April 18, 1945, Box 36, File "State Department Correspondence, 1945 [1 of 2]," *HST:WHCF:CF*; Ernst B. Haas, "The Attempt to Terminate Colonialism: Acceptance of the United Nations Trusteeship System," *International Organization*, 7, no. 1 (February 1953), 6.

[116] A Declaration of Negro Voters, November 20, 1943, Box A224, File "Declaration by Negro Voters: General, 1943," *Papers of the NAACP*.

[117] Joshua Bloom and Waldo E. Martin Jr., *Black against Empire: The History and Politics of the Black Panther Party* (Berkeley: University of California Press, 2013); Clayborne Carson, *In Struggle: SNCC and the Black Awakening of the 1960s* (Cambridge, MA:

The Association's founding in 1909 was in direct response to a bloody rampage in Springfield, Illinois, the year before, when whites, exercised by rumors of rape and murder, descended on the jailhouse bent on vengeance. When the sheriff thwarted their plans and spirited the two accused black men out of the city, a torrent of violence rained down. Over the span of three terrifying days, the mob lynched innocent black men, torched the African American neighborhood, and laid waste the black business district.[118] Troubled that gory racial violence happened not only north of the Mason-Dixon line but also in the birthplace of Abraham Lincoln, an interracial group, including rights activist Mary White Ovington, grandson of famed abolitionist William Lloyd Garrison, Oswald Garrison Villard, and W. E. B. Du Bois, convened a series of conferences that led to the creation of the NAACP.[119]

From the Association's very beginning, with rented furniture and intermittently paid salaries, its omnipresent problem was funding.[120] The Great Depression had only exacerbated the financial crisis. African Americans supplied nearly 75 percent of the NAACP's income.[121] But the global economic collapse had wreaked havoc on black Americans as they watched back-breaking "Negro jobs" suddenly transform into employment opportunities labeled "whites only." Pushed off of the land as sharecroppers, pushed out of jobs in hot, filthy locomotives, and pushed into horrific living conditions, more than half of all African Americans were simply unable to find work.[122] With its main source of revenue shut off,

Harvard University Press, 1981, 1995); Colin Grant, *Negro with a Hat: The Rise and Fall of Marcus Garvey* (New York: Oxford University Press, 2008).

[118] Roberta Senechal, "The Springfield Race Riot of 1908," http://www.lib.niu.edu/1996/iht329622.html. Accessed April 18, 2013.

[119] Patricia Sullivan, *Lift Every Voice: The NAACP and the Making of the Civil Rights Movement* (New York: New Press, 2009), 1–16. Other founding members include William English Walling, Henry Moscowitz, Joel and Arthur Spingarn, Josephine Ruffin, Mary Talbert, Inez Milholland, Jane Addams, Florence Kelley, Sophonisba Breckinridge, John Haynes Holmes, Mary McLeod Bethune, George Henry White, Charles Edward Russell, John Dewey, William Dean Howells, Lillian Wald, Charles Darrow, Lincoln Steffens, Ray Stannard Baker, Fanny Garrison Villard, and Walter Sachs. Ida B. Wells-Barnett and Mary Church Terrell signed the call for the convening conference.

[120] Sullivan, *Lift Every Voice*, 16–17.

[121] Walter White to [Caroline] Flexner, April 19, 1933, File "White, Walter, 1932–1942," *Papers of Herbert Lehman*, Rare Book and Manuscript Library, Columbia University, New York (hereafter *Lehman Papers*).

[122] David M. Kennedy, *Freedom from Fear: The American People in Depression and War, 1929–1945* (New York: Oxford University Press, 1999), 87, 164, 186, 193; Robert S. McElvaine, *The Great Depression: America, 1929–1941*, 2nd ed. (New York: Times Books, 1993), 187–195; Patricia Sullivan, *Days of Hope: Race and Democracy in the New Deal Era* (Chapel Hill: University of North Carolina Press, 1996).

by 1933 the Association had reduced its staff and cut its "already quite low" salaries by almost one-third. Nonetheless, despite the depleted staff and diminished revenues, the workload had nearly tripled because of the magnitude of the crises African Americans faced.[123]

The early years of the Second World War brought little relief. In January 1941, Secretary Walter White, who had already forgone his own salary that month, had to get board authorization to dip into the reserves to pay the rest of the staff in full – except Roy Wilkins, who was in Kansas City for a funeral. White could only "hope" that by the time the assistant secretary returned, "we will have enough to pay the balance of his salary."[124]

Even as the war progressed and African Americans, through vigorous mobilization, gained access to better paying defense industry jobs, financial worries continued to haunt the NAACP.[125] Despite a membership that had grown to nearly 500,000 and coffers that appeared to swell, White warned that "neither the Board nor the branches should be deluded by the present high income of the Association; ... there are inevitable years of very great hardship ahead for all Americans and in particular the Negro." The sudden prosperity, he emphasized, was illusory. "It is of the utmost importance that the national office and the branches abstain from any grandiose ideas that this prosperity is permanent." It was, White warned, "a matter almost of life and death for the Association to put aside every penny possible now for the hard years ahead."[126]

White's ominous forecast was prescient. The ensuing years saw the NAACP lurch from one financial crisis to the next. The never ending paradox for the Association was that its primary base of support – African Americans – had, because of centuries of slavery and discrimination, very little, if any, disposable income available to adequately fund the organization. The very conditions that had created the need for an NAACP meant that by definition the Association's workload outstripped its budget.

---

[123] Walter White to [Caroline] Flexner, April 19, 1933, File "White, Walter, 1932–1942," *Lehman Papers.*

[124] Walter White to Arthur B. Spingarn and Mary White Ovington, January 14, 1941, Box A146, File "Board of Directors: Arthur Spingarn, 1940–55," *Papers of the NAACP.*

[125] Cornelius L. Bynum, *A. Philip Randolph and the Struggle for Civil Rights* (Urbana: University of Illinois Press, 2010), 157–184; Carol Anderson, *Eyes Off the Prize: The United Nations and the African American Struggle for Human Rights. 1944–1955* (New York: Cambridge University Press, 2003), 24.

[126] Walter White to Thurgood Marshall, Roy Wilkins, and Ella Baker, December 4, 1944, Box 3, File "9," *Papers of Ella Baker*, Schomburg Center for Research in Black Culture, New York (hereafter *Baker Papers*).

In late 1946, Walter White confided to a colleague, "Frankly, the one problem we face is that of money. The virtual certainty of some recession during 1947 makes it imperative that we count our pennies even for the most valuable project."[127] As a result, when it tried to hire capable, seasoned staff to take on key aspects of the Association's work, such as managing public relations or solidifying the NAACP's relationship with black churches, the inability to offer competitive salaries hampered its efforts.[128] One editorial claimed that, by 1950, the once "powerful" and "militant" NAACP had been reduced to a "beggar" that had to go hat-in-hand to organized labor for a $28,000 bailout just to pay the staff and meet the Association's operating expenses.[129] And even that was not enough. Later that same year, famed contralto Marian Anderson issued a fundraising letter warning that "The N.A.A.C.P. [was] in dire straits. Its program [was] threatened drastically unless some emergency support [was] immediately forthcoming."[130] The problem was one of simple arithmetic. In 1950, the Association "took in $260,231.90 and spent $286,311.21, thus ending the year $26,079.31 in the red"[131] – or, in 2012 dollars, nearly a quarter of million in the hole.[132]

A way out might have been found in funding by charitable foundations. Indeed, in 1951, pleas directly from Walter White went out to Ford Foundation President Paul Hoffman. However, despite initial conversations in which Hoffman promised that the "Association had the inside track," subsequent tantalizing discussions about the foundation's keen interest in the "international aspect of the race question," and "considerable work" on the proposal and a virtual dream team of sponsors

---

[127] Walter White to Reverend James H. Robinson, December 27, 1946, Box A594, File "Staff: Walter Offutt, 1946–49," *Papers of the NAACP.*

[128] Henry [Moon] to Mollie [Moon], February 7, 1948, Box 2, File "Correspondence, 1947–1949," *Moon Papers*; Reverend James H. Robinson to Walter White, December 26, 1946, Box A594, File "Staff: Walter Offutt, 1946–49," *Papers of the NAACP*; Walter P. Offutt, Jr. to Roy Wilkins, memo, March 19, 1947, Box A594, File "Staff: Walter Offutt, 1946–49," *Papers of the NAACP*; Walter White to the Committee on Administration, March 22, 1947, Box A594, File "Staff: Walter Offutt, 1946–49," *Papers of the NAACP*; Roy Wilkins to Walter Offutt, July 10, 1947, Box A594, File "Staff: Walter Offutt, 1946–49," *Papers of the NAACP.*

[129] William O. Walker, "Down the Big Road," *Cleveland Call and Post*, March 25, 1950.

[130] Marian Anderson and Ruth Bryan Rohde to Wilhemina Adams, December 8, 1950, Box 4, File "NAACP – Correspondence, 1927–1959; Invitations, 1932–1959," *Papers of Wilhemina F. Adams*, Schomburg Center for Research in Black Culture, New York (hereafter *Adams Papers*).

[131] "Where Are the 'Race Patriots'?" *Pittsburgh Courier*, July 28, 1951.

[132] http://www.measuringworth.com/uscompare/relativevalue.php. In 2012, $26,079.31 is equivalent to $249,000.

including former First Lady Eleanor Roosevelt and Nobel Peace Prize winner Ralph Bunche, the NAACP's request for $2 million was flatly denied.[133]

As daunting as the perennial financial worries were, however, in some ways they paled in comparison to the rivalries and feuds that not only embroiled the Association in endless harangues but also siphoned valuable time away from the long, hard work of the organization's mission. Part of the problem was the NAACP's very structure. Director of Branches Ella Baker rightly observed that "there seems to be a tendency towards creating one-man departments and then expecting a first class job to be done."[134] Roy Wilkins even confided:

If anybody hereafter mentions the sending of the entire staff to do field work at the same time, they are going to have to meet me with a Winchester rifle. I am jumping sideways between conferences, luncheons, committee meetings, speaking engagements, youth work, branch work, substituting for Mr. White, covering up for Mr. Marshall, running to Washington, out to Detroit, up to Boston, answering the telephone and trying to answer a few letters, office conferences, staff conferences, etc., etc.[135]

Even worse was the propensity to provide "no objective yardstick" to evaluate the effectiveness of its administrators. This, Baker claimed, often led to the highly dysfunctional practice of "one's efficiency being rated in terms of whether one is or is not persona non grata." The end result, she concluded, was a toxic atmosphere that tended "to breed small, ingrown, or frustrated people."[136]

The executive staff, in particular Secretary Walter White and Assistant Secretary Roy Wilkins, seemed to come in for special scorn. White, with his chameleon-like contradictions, was an easy target. He was "jolly and engaging" to the outside world, "domineering, almost suffocating" at

---

[133] Minutes of the Board of Directors Meeting, February 13, 1951, *Papers of the NAACP*, History Vault, Accession #: 001410-001-0282, ProQuest History Vault: Papers of the NAACP, Part 01: Meetings of the Board of Directors, Records of Annual Conferences, Major Speeches, and Special Reports (hereafter History Vault); Minutes of the Meeting of the Board of Directors Meeting, March 12, 1951, *Papers of the NAACP*, History Vault, Accession # 001410-001-0282; Minutes of the Meeting of the Board of Directors, May 14, 1951, *Papers of the NAACP*, History Vault, Accession #: 001410-001-0282; Minutes of the Meeting of the Board of Directors," June 28, 1951, *Papers of the NAACP*, History Vault, Accession #: 001410-001-0282.

[134] Ella Baker to Walter White, May 15, 1946, Box 3, File "5," *Baker Papers*.

[135] Roy Wilkins to Ella Baker, March 27, 1942, Box 3, File "NAACP Correspondence (1936–1968)," *Baker Papers*.

[136] Ella Baker to Walter White, May 15, 1946, Box 3, File "5," *Baker Papers*.

work, and "silent and distant" at home. Not exactly religious, he made the NAACP his God. He was dedicated to revealing the truth about racism and injustice; he also published one invented personal history after the next to inflate his importance and prominence. Although fighting for democracy, he, like most autocrats, fused his identity with the organization and governed with an iron fist. The NAACP was his power base; it provided the narrative of his life, and it gave him access to politicians, world leaders, literary giants, and entertainment legends that far exceeded the low horizons of his previous career as an insurance salesman in Atlanta, Georgia. And, as far as he was concerned, he had earned every ounce of that new life. In his early work with the NAACP, he used his blond hair, blue eyes, and Georgia accent to "pass" as a white Southerner to investigate lynchings, publicize the mobs' shallow motives, and hammer on that evidence to demand change in the norms and laws that had made "decades of cruelty, greed, and savagery" prevalent in the land of democracy. He was tireless. Fearless. And smart. He was also reckless, ingratiating, and frankly, in the words of Du Bois, "unbearable."[137] (See Figure 1.2)

Many shared Du Bois's opinion of White. Baltimore *Afro-American* journalist L. F. Coles told Baker, "I have never been able to tolerate the Secy," Walter White.[138] African American attorney and army officer Colonel Campbell Carrington Johnson, in a withering conversation with Rayford Logan on the state of leadership in the black community, summed up White in one word – "egomaniac."[139] Baker herself "made no secret of her contempt for Walter White." As scholar Barbara Ransby noted, "[T]here seems to have been an almost universal consensus among the New York staff that Walter White was egotistical, vain, and shortsighted.... Baker recalled White as someone who went out of his way to remind everyone around him how important he was."[140]

Even supposed allies found the secretary of the NAACP distasteful. President Roosevelt's staff described White as "insulting" and "one of the

---

[137] Dyja, *Walter White*, 118–119. For White's fabrications and a scholar's meticulous attempt to unravel truth from fiction, particularly as deployed in White's autobiography, *A Man Called White*, see Kenneth Janken, *White: The Biography of Walter White, Mr. NAACP* (New York: New Press, 2003).

[138] L. C. Coles to Ella Baker, May 21, 1946, Box 3, File "5," *Baker Papers.*

[139] Rayford Logan, diary entry, August 2, 1942, Box 3, File "Diaries, 1942," *Logan Papers.*

[140] Barbara Ransby, *Ella Baker and the Black Freedom Movement: A Radical Democratic Vision* (Chapel Hill: University of North Carolina Press, 2003), 143.

FIGURE 1.2. Walter White, secretary of the NAACP, working the halls of power, testifying before Congress.
Source: Bettman/Corbis. Courtesy of Corbis, Stock Photo ID # U541553ACME.

worst and most continuous of trouble makers."[141] President Harry Truman was equally emphatic that he neither liked nor trusted the NAACP secretary. "I don't care for this white negro [sic]," Truman asserted, "and I am always doubtful of anything he says."[142]

Roy Wilkins brought another set of flaws and challenges to the table. Haunted by a childhood bathed in death and abandonment, disgusted by an itinerant jack-of-all-trades absentee father who used the clerical collar as a great hustle, the young boy Wilkins grew into a cynical, pugilistic,

[141] Stephen Early to Malvina Thompson, August 5, 1935, Box 173, File "White, Walter," *Papers of Franklin Delano Roosevelt, President's Secretary's File*, Franklin D. Roosevelt Presidential Library, Hyde Park, NY.
[142] Marginalia on Walter White to Harry Truman, November 23, 1945, attached to C[harles] G. R[oss] to David K. Niles, December 3, 1945, Box 1235, File "413 (1945–49)," *Papers of Harry S. Truman: Official File*, Harry S. Truman Presidential Library, Independence, MO. (Hereafter *HST:OF*).

FIGURE 1.3. Roy Wilkins, assistant secretary of the NAACP, showing the skepticism that was one of his hallmark traits.
Source: NAACP Collection. Courtesy of the Library of Congress, Prints and Photographs Division, LOT 13074, no. 595.

suspicious man, who was, above all else, a survivor[143] (see Figure 1.3). By his own admission, when sensing even the slightest threat, he would "fly off the handle," "make impulsive statements," and not be "as diplomatic as [he] could be."[144] After graduating with a degree in journalism from the University of Minnesota, Wilkins spent several years at the *Kansas City Call* as a reporter. But that was not enough. He had seen too much. Too much police brutality. Too many lynchings. Too many African Americans trying to survive by not fighting back. Merely writing about one racist incident after the next could no longer douse the fire to put an end to the degradation of black people once and for all. He remarked, "I wanted to shift from passively recording Jim Crow's hard knocks to fighting them."[145]

[143] Roy Wilkins, *Standing Fast: The Autobiography of Roy Wilkins*, introduction by Julian Bond (New York: De Capo, 1982), 19–21, 32–34, 37, 55, 75.
[144] Roy Wilkins to John Hammond, October 9, 1943, Box A613, File "Staff: Roy Wilkins-Hammond, John Controversy about Wilkins' Abilities, 1943," *Papers of the NAACP*.
[145] Wilkins, *Standing Fast*, 98–103.

Then came a letter from the Association's headquarters in New York City. "The Depression," Wilkins recalled, "had played hell with the finances of *The Crisis* and Dr. Du Bois wanted to hire me as the magazine's business manager to turn things around."[146] He came on board in 1931 as assistant secretary almost at the very moment that a palace coup led by Du Bois was in the works. Wilkins, the "opportunist," joined the rebellion only to realize that Walter White was not going anywhere. Du Bois, however, was on his way out.[147] Wilkins recanted, "confessing his deep regret for his role 'in that awful mess,'" and retrieved the situation and his job.[148] Although that storm had passed, he would continue to have a contentious working relationship with White in which Wilkins careened wildly between obedient Igor and treacherous Iago.

The assistant secretary displayed the traits that would haunt his long tenure at the NAACP when, in 1943, board member John Hammond, an heir to the Vanderbilt fortune, openly questioned Wilkins's ability to manage the Association if White took an extended leave of absence.[149] Hammond told the powerful Committee on Administration, which was the inner sanctum of the board of directors, that "Roy is jealous of Walter and his position and prestige." He then added that if White went away, the assistant secretary could "not be trusted" because Wilkins would "take advantage of the situation."[150]

Prickly, thin-skinned, short-tempered, and, as a trained journalist, with the ability to write multiple searing memos in a short space of time, Wilkins blasted White, whom he viewed as duplicitous for counseling him to "forget the whole thing," even though the secretary had been in

---

[146] Ibid., 93.
[147] Dyja, *Walter White*, 120.
[148] Sullivan, *Lift Every Voice*, 153.
[149] For some of the difficulties Wilkins experienced, see John Morsell to Lewis Steel, October 14, 1968, Box 31, File "Steel, Lewis: Dismissal Case, 1968," *Papers of Roy Wilkins*, Library of Congress, Washington, D C (hereafter *Wilkins Papers*); Robert Carter to Roy Wilkins, October 17, 1968, ibid.; Robert L. Carter to Roy Wilkins, ibid.; Roy Wilkins to Robert Carter, October 29, 1968, ibid.; Ingrid Celms to John A. Morsell, November 18, 1968, ibid.; "Kokomo NAACP Protests Wilkins Attorney Firing," *Anderson Herald*, October 16, 1968; for the revolt of the "Young Turks," see Gretchen Cassel Eick, "'Lift Every Voice': The Civil Rights Movement and America's Heartland, Wichita, Kansas, 1954–1972" (PhD diss., University of Kansas, 1997), 138–140; and Gilbert Jonas, *Freedom's Sword: The NAACP and the Struggle Against Racism in America, 1909–1969*, introduction by Julian Bond (New York: Routledge, 2005), 321–324.
[150] Roy Wilkins to John Hammond, September 25, 1943, Box A613, File "Staff: Roy Wilkins-Hammond, John Controversy about Wilkins' Abilities, 1943," *Papers of the NAACP*.

the room when Hammond "accused [Wilkins] of disloyalty, jealousy, and underhand work." How White could just "sit silent while such an attack was being made – well, I never would have believed it," Wilkins fumed. "I can scarcely believe it now." Conveniently forgetting his role in the abortive coup only a few years earlier, he insisted that he had never intrigued against White, he had never engaged in office politics, and he had backed the secretary without fail. "But," he fired at White, "you know all these things every one."[151]

Bruised and angry, Wilkins contemplated resigning. Then he demanded some sort of hearing because the charges were "too serious to be brushed off in the usual manner."[152] He poured out his soul to NAACP stalwart and board member Daisy Lampkin. Wilkins sensed that the "Association [was] on the verge of realizing its greatest possibilities *if* it can carry out the kind of program it should in these times."[153]

In that little word – *if* – the assistant secretary had subtly intimated, even while claiming to back White, that the secretary was a monumental hurdle to the NAACP's success. A board sub-committee had already decided to deal with the growth of the Association by restructuring and creating a new position that would take over many of the administrative tasks and responsibilities that absorbed the secretary. According to Wilkins, once White understood the full import of that recommendation, he was "reluctant to have anyone assume the power of what we have chosen to call an executive director." Moreover, when it became clear that Wilkins was slated for that new role, White allegedly sabotaged the effort. The assistant secretary complained that through tedious meetings, delaying tactics, and appointing clearly unqualified substitutes, Walter White was simultaneously blocking the necessary development of the NAACP and preventing Wilkins from having any real authority.[154]

Although he did not realize how closely his comments about his own ambitions and White's flawed leadership lived up to Hammond's accusations, Wilkins steadfastly maintained his trustworthiness and insisted that the only way he could "stay with self respect" was for Hammond to apologize.[155] Instead, Hammond played with, stalked, then

[151] Roy Wilkins to Walter White, September 27, 1943, ibid.; Roy Wilkins to Hubert Delany, September 28, 1943, ibid.
[152] Roy Wilkins to Arthur Spingarn, September 25, 1943, ibid.; Roy Wilkins to Hubert Delany, September 28, 1943, ibid.
[153] Roy Wilkins to Daisy Lampkin, September 28, 1943, ibid. Emphasis added.
[154] Roy Wilkins to Daisy Lampkin, September 28, 1943, ibid.
[155] Roy Wilkins to Daisy Lampkin, September 28, 1943, ibid.

devoured his prey. First, the board member owned up to virtually every word. He repeated exactly what he said in the meeting: the assistant secretary "cordially disliked Walter" and that Wilkins "thought [he] could do a better job as Secretary." With this Hammond baited the trap. "The basis for my remarks," he wrote Wilkins, "was a conversation you had with me a year-and-a-half ago in which you stated your beliefs about Walter in extremely emphatic and detailed terms." With the trap now set and ready to spring came the rapid uncoiling of the guillotine's rope. "If you wish to bring this whole matter up to the board for a decision, I will of course be prepared to report in detail our conversation."[156] A humbled Wilkins replied with a long, defanged letter, then dropped the matter.[157] But the grudge lingered. Nearly forty years later, his disdain for Hammond came through in a terse remembrance of the board member as a "young white firebrand ..., a rich kid from the Ivy League who was ... on good terms with left-wingers."[158]

Given the range of financial and administrative challenges, the board questioned whether fighting colonialism was an appropriate use of the NAACP's limited resources, especially given the scope of what needed to be done in the United States. NAACP President Arthur Spingarn, for example, "did not feel that the Association was in a financial position to undertake the job" of intervening on colonial issues.[159] He also questioned why White had to go "traipsing all over the world" when, in his opinion, "Negroes of the United States are not interested in what is happening in other parts of the world but only in jobs and security for themselves."[160] Similarly, board member Alfred Baker Lewis thought the whole idea of expanding the scope of the Association's work to Africa and anticolonialism was a "considerable undertaking" with ideological complications that had resource sinkhole all over it. The issue of African liberation, in Lewis's eyes, was too closely tied to "camouflaged Communist organizations" and the Soviet Union. "Of course the Communists today are on the ... right side of many ... issues," he warned Channing Tobias; "[T]his merely puts an additional burden upon those of us who are not Communist to work as actively as we can but completely separate from

[156] John Hammond to Roy Wilkins, October 8, 1943, ibid.
[157] Roy Wilkins to John Hammond, October 9, 1943, ibid.
[158] Wilkins, *Standing Fast*, 150.
[159] Minutes of the Meeting of the Board of Directors, December 9, 1946, Reel 3, NAACP.
[160] Walter White to Arthur Spingarn, n.d., Box 6, File "Spingarn, Arthur B.," *White Papers*.

Communists and Communist influenced organizations, for these socially valuable purposes."[161]

The response to these warnings diverged along two separate, distinct tracks. One group led by Channing Tobias and Walter White willingly entered into spirited debate to persuade hesitant board and staff to move in the direction of an anticolonial vision. For example, when Lewis raised the concern about aligning with so-called communist causes, Tobias volleyed that to "be quite frank ... it has been my policy ... to wear as few labels as possible so that I might be free to render helpful service to any group that might be rendering constructive help to humanity in general and to my people in particular."[162] Similarly, Tobias patiently but firmly explained to his fellow board members that "we cannot be ignorant of what is going on in Africa and be prepared to take care of our rights in the United States."[163]

White answered Spingarn in equally unequivocal terms. "From my quite extensive first hand contact with Negroes and other colored people here and abroad," the secretary sharply observed, "they are much more interested and concerned with the overall picture than would appear to be the case when seen only from the vantage point of New York City." He admonished Spingarn that "the NAACP will grow ... only as it recognizes that the problems of race and colonialism are world wide in their scope and, next to the question of U.S.–U.S.S.R. relations, the most important problem in the world today. We of the NAACP will be derelict in our duty if we do not recognize that fact and shape our program accordingly."[164]

The other response to the board's concerns was a more-or-less one-man campaign to redirect and radicalize the Association's anticolonial work. NAACP co-founder W. E. B. Du Bois had rejoined the Association in 1944 as director of Special Research expressly to provide the intellectual firepower needed for the organization to address the issues of colonialism and human rights. From the very beginning, however, he was on

---

[161] Minutes of the Meeting of the Board of Directors, December 9, 1946, Reel 3, *NAACP*; Alfred Baker Lewis to Channing Tobias, April 9, 1942, Biographical Record: Max Yergan, File "Council on African Affairs, Correspondence, 1937–1942," *Max Yergan Papers*, Kautz Family YMCA Archives, University of Minnesota, Minneapolis, MN. (Hereafter *Yergan-YMCA*).

[162] Channing Tobias to Alfred Baker Lewis, n.d., ca. April 1942, Biographical Record: Max Yergan, File "Council on African Affairs, Correspondence, 1937–1942," *Yergan-YMCA*.

[163] Minutes of the Meeting of the Board of Directors, December 9, 1946, Reel 3, *NAACP*.

[164] Walter White to Arthur Spingarn, n.d., Box 6, File "Spingarn, Arthur B.," *White Papers*.

a collision course with Walter White.[165] Their conflicting methods would eventually result in Du Bois's contemptuous dismissal of the Association's global efforts.

In many respects, it was not a fair fight. Du Bois was an intellectual behemoth; White a mimic, a pretender to the throne. Du Bois had a facile, conceptual grasp of the economic underpinning of white supremacy and exploitation; White knew it by what he read, saw, and was told. On the other hand, Walter White had a political ferocity and acumen that consistently eluded Du Bois. Whereas the scholar fought by Marquess of Queensbury rules, White's actions were more akin to a barroom brawl. In the end, what White won on the ground, Du Bois won in the history books.[166]

The heart and soul of their disagreement was that Du Bois was a lone avenger, whereas White was an organization man. That is to say, the scholar wanted the resources of the NAACP without its rules so that he could carry on his work of research, conferences, and publications to expose the horrors of colonialism. White, on the other hand, wanted to harness Du Bois's intellectual prowess in service of the NAACP's collective anticolonialism. Neither of these scenarios was possible nor even realistic. No more than genius can be confined in some jack-in-the-box structure can a maverick be allowed to run roughshod over an organization's budget, facilities, and staff.

Their initial skirmishes occurred over the mundane but all-important issues of offices and procedures. When, for example, Du Bois did not immediately receive the two rooms he was promised for his books, staff, and work, he flatly refused to wait a few months until the Association moved to larger headquarters. Instead, without authorization, he rented his own office in New York City and sent the bill to the NAACP.[167] Du Bois also believed that his stenographic support was inadequate, so he hired his own secretary again without discussing it with anyone – and sent the invoice to Roy Wilkins. Then there was the time when Du Bois

---

[165] Anderson, *Eyes Off the Prize*, 32–35.
[166] Ransby, *Ella Baker*, 109; Horne, *Black and Red*; Horne, *Mau Mau in Harlem?*; Horne, *Race Woman*; Horne, *Communist Front?*; Horne, *The End of Empires*; Roark, "American Black Leaders"; Harris Jr., "Ralph Bunche and Afro-American Participation in Decolonization"; Von Eschen, *Race Against Empire*; Von Eschen, *Satchmo Blows up the World: Jazz Ambassadors Play the Cold War* (Cambridge: Harvard University Press, 2004); Janken, *White*; Janken, "From Colonial Liberation to Cold War Liberalism"; Nesbitt, *Race for Sanctions*.
[167] Walter White to Lillian A. Alexander, November 29, 1945, Box A240, File "William E. B. Du Bois: General, 1945," *Papers of the NAACP*.

opted to take a trip to Haiti with his assistant, and, without inquiring how this fit into the organization's goals, workflow, or budget, expected the Association to cover all of the expenses for unauthorized travel. These episodes caused enormous friction and ill will.[168] Wilkins complained that Du Bois "seems to feel his Department is a detached entity having nothing to do with us except for us to pay the bills."[169] White asked the board, point blank, whether Du Bois was "to operate as an independent agent, merely financed by NAACP, or is he to conform to Assn administrative procedure."[170] As far as Du Bois was concerned, however, he had "strained every nerve to serve the Association" and it was "time for a careful reconsideration of [his] position in the organization."[171]

Those operational tensions careened into policy and, as one could expect, transformed discussions over strategy, programs, and tactics into personal mudslinging attacks and vendettas.[172] One of the most contentious and lingering issues concerned the Pan African Congress. Early on Du Bois pushed the NAACP to resurrect its 1920s sponsorship of this gathering. Within four months of his return to the Association, the board of directors "decided to sponsor a call for a Fifth Pan African Congress" in 1945 and was "prepared to assume a considerable proportion of the expense."[173] Part of Du Bois's urgency was "the threat of Jans [sic] Smut

[168] Walter White to W. E. B. Du Bois, September 22, 1944, Box A240, File "William E. B. Du Bois: General, 1943–44," *Papers of the NAACP*; Du Bois to White, memo, April 10, 1945, Reel 57, *Du Bois*; W. E. B. Du Bois to Vada Somerville, April 13, 1945, Reel 57, *Du Bois*; "Statement of Expenses for Secretarial Expenses at UNCIO, San Francisco, California," May 18, 1945, Box A240, File "William E. B. Du Bois: General, 1943–44," *Papers of the NAACP*; Roy Wilkins to Walter White, May 27, 1945, Box A639, File "United Nations – UNCIO – General, 1945 – May 11–June," *Papers of the NAACP*; Roy Wilkins to Walter White, memo, June 7, 1945, Reel 57, *Du Bois*; W. E. B. Du Bois to Walter White, January 3, 1946, Box A241, File "William E.B. Du Bois–General, 1946," *Papers of the NAACP*; W. E. B. Du Bois to Walter White, January 4, 1946, Reel 59, *Du Bois* ; Walter White to Arthur Spingarn, January 5, 1946, Box A241, File "William E.B. Du Bois – General, 1946," *Papers of the NAACP*; Re Dr. Du Bois, January 7, 1946, Box A241, File "William E. B. Du Bois–General, 1946," *Papers of the NAACP*.

[169] Roy Wilkins to Walter White, February 17, 1945, Box 8, File "Wilkins, Roy," *White Papers*.

[170] Re Dr. Du Bois, January 7, 1946, Box A241, File "William E. B. Du Bois–General, 1946," *Papers of the NAACP*.

[171] W. E. B. Du Bois to Walter White, January 3, 1946, ibid.

[172] Walter White to Lillian A. Alexander, November 29, 1945, Box A240, File "William E. B. Du Bois: General, 1945," *Papers of the NAACP*; Rayford Logan, diary entry, September 18, 1945, Box 4, File "Diaries, 1945–47," *Logan Papers*; W. E. B. Du Bois to Walter White, January 4, 1946, Reel 59, *Du Bois*; Anderson, *Eyes Off the Prize*, 139–151, 173.

[173] W. E. B. Du Bois to Harold A. Moody, February 15, 1945, Reel 57, *Du Bois*; W. E. B. Du Bois to Ladipo Solanke, April 11, 1945, Reel 58, *Du Bois*.

to call a Pan African Congress which virtually would be confined to the whites of South Africa, Tanganyika, and Kenya." Du Bois was clear: "I want to forestall any use of this name in a movement which would disfranchise the great mass of Africans and their descendants."[174]

George Padmore quickly stepped in to ease – and add to – Du Bois's worries by letting the scholar know that planning was already underway for this year's Pan-African Congress and, most important, that Africans would take the lead. The NAACP could, if it wanted to, "cooperate" and "organiz[e] the American delegation as well as the West Indian one," but "our task will be to contact all organisations in Africa, which I think," Padmore continued, "we should consider our sphere."[175]

Taken aback, Du Bois feared that "if we do not lead the way there is nothing to hinder them from forming a Pan-African movement of their own without the participation and guidance of American Negroes."[176] Therefore, without fully explaining the scope of Padmore's activities, the scholar put a budget request before the NAACP Board asking for $2,500 "including transportation for two delegates" but leaving unsaid what the total costs for the entire conference would be.[177] He soon followed up with a press conference announcing that the Pan-African Congress would be held in Paris in September 1945, "with the clear indication of NAACP sponsorship."[178] A barely contained Walter White could only characterize the news as "premature and unfortunate" given that none of the logistics – including place, date, lodging, transportation, and costs – had been finalized. In addition, he reprimanded Du Bois, "May I further suggest that future statements regarding the Congress be made through ... the regular Association channels as only by such cooperative clearance can confusion or misunderstanding be avoided."[179]

In a subsequent series of planning meetings and correspondence, the gulf between the two men became even more apparent as did their human frailties. Du Bois's vision was for a conference that would gather

---

[174] W. E. B. Du Bois to Ladipo Solanke, April 11, 1945, Reel 58, *Du Bois.*

[175] George Padmore to W. E. B. Du Bois, April 12, 1945, Reel 57, *Du Bois.*

[176] The Pan-African Movement, n.d., ca. July 1945, Reel 57, *Du Bois.*

[177] Irene Diggs to Roy Wilkins, May 12, 1945, Box A6, File "Africa: Pan-African Congress, 1945," *Papers of the NAACP.*

[178] Earl Conrad, "Pan-African Parley in Paris Set for September, Du Bois Announces," *Chicago Defender,* June 16, 1945; David Levering Lewis, *W.E.B. Du Bois: The Fight for Equality and the American Century, 1919–1963* (New York: Henry Holt and Company, 2000), 512.

[179] Walter White to W. E. B. Du Bois, June 14, 1945, Box A6, File "Africa: Pan-African Congress, 1945," *Papers of the NAACP.*

FIGURE 1.4. W. E. B. Du Bois, director of special research for the NAACP, was determined to apply the power of research and scholarship at the Pan-African Congress, 1945.
Source: Bettman. Courtesy of Corbis, Stock Photo ID # BE038887.

data on education, wages, housing, health, and ethnography throughout colonial Africa (see Figure 1.4). This was to be a fact-finding mission that secured information from the colonized, the colonizers, the diaspora in the United States and the Caribbean, and a range of organizations, such as labor, churches, and missionary bodies. He assumed, in turn, that the NAACP would "pay for an office in Paris ... and pay for a place of meeting." The Association would underwrite the costs of translators, secretaries, and printing, as well as travel and expenses. "All funds contributed by the NAACP," Du Bois proffered, would "be under the control of the delegates which it sends" – namely him. Similarly, the conference program and the determination of other sponsoring groups "would be entirely under the control of the Congress when organized." In this scenario, the Association would provide significant funding, roughly equivalent to more than $30,000 in 2011 dollars, and would have little to no say in what it financed.[180]

Board member William Hastie, who was on the Sub-Committee of the Committee on Pan-African Congress, pushed back. "Personally," he explained to White, "I am greatly concerned." Du Bois had not provided the level of specificity expected for someone planning an international conference that was to convene in only a few months, with delegates from several continents pouring into a war-torn city where the possibility of accommodations had not yet been determined and with the availability of trans-Atlantic transportation still unexamined.[181]

But logistics were not Du Bois's strength. Indeed, he went on a two-week vacation a little over a month before the proposed Pan-African Congress, when nothing, including budget, attendees, space, or transportation had been worked out.[182] While he was on vacation in Maine, it became clear that Padmore's group truly was taking the lead and planned to hold the conference not in Paris but in Manchester, England. Meanwhile, Du Bois had let his passport expire and did not even realize it until nearly two weeks before the conference.[183] By the time he returned from vacationing in Maine, his newly assigned role in Manchester would be that of an honored delegate at the Pan-African Congress but not the chief strategist. Moreover, the rapidly approaching date meant Du Bois would have to fly to England instead of taking a ship. As a result, the costs for his tickets nearly doubled from $1,200 to $2,000. Nonetheless, the board still authorized the increased expenditure so that Du Bois could arrive in time to have an impact.[184]

From Du Bois's perspective, however, he had not been saved by an organization that had just spent thousands of dollars to ensure his participation in a landmark anticolonial conference; rather, as he saw it, he had been undercut. Du Bois bitterly sniped at White that "while we

[180] W. E. B. Du Bois to Sub-Committee of Committee on Pan-African Congress, July 13, 1945, ibid.

[181] William H. Hastie to Walter White, July 17, 1945, ibid.; William H. Hastie to Walter White, telegram, July 11, 1949 ibid.

[182] W. E. B. Du Bois to Walter White, August 3, 1945, ibid.; Walter White to W.E.B. Du Bois, August 7, 1945, ibid.

[183] W.E.B. Du Bois to R.B. Shipley, telegram, September 27, 1945, Reel 58, *Du Bois*.

[184] J. B. Danquah to W. E. B. Du Bois, July 24, 1945, Reel 58, *Du Bois*; W. E. B. Du Bois to George Padmore, October 5, 1945, Reel 57, *Du Bois*; W. E. B. Du Bois to Walter White, memo, October 5, 1945, Reel 57, *Du Bois*; Ernest E. Johnson, "NAACP Holds Up Approval of Pan-African Meeting," *Atlanta Daily World*, July 22, 1945; Minutes of the Meeting of the Board of Directors, October 8, 1945, Reel 3, *NAACP*.

have been waiting, the convening committee of England ... have called a Pan-African Congress."[185] He complained to a colleague in Paris that "the National Association for the Advancement of Colored People has *finally* asked me to attend the Pan African Congress," adding that "it is pretty late for me to do anything but I am going to try."[186] He groused to Padmore about the conspiracy to keep him away from the conference but noted triumphantly that he, nonetheless, had prevailed – "against the desire of the secretary [Walter White] and several powerful members of the board."[187]

Although Du Bois was in part covering for his own failure to act effectively, there was some truth to his sense of a growing antipathy to him within the upper echelon of the NAACP.[188] White was convinced that Manchester was the dry run, perhaps even a planning session, for the major conference that would be held later in France. Rayford Logan, who was on the Association's Pan-African Congress Planning Sub-Committee, therefore, recalled that "Walter held me back after the meeting had disbanded to ask me whether I would be available for the 'real' Pan-African Congress in the spring in Paris because he did not want Du Bois to 'hog the whole show.'"[189] White's efforts to diminish the director of special research's influence were also reflected in the way the secretary chose to mount a case with the board against the scholar by patiently, carefully forwarding mail exchanges crafted to prove a point instead of resolve the issues.[190]

Nonetheless, it was not an anti-Du Bois conspiracy that caused William Hastie and others to raise concerns about the scholar's conceptualization of the Pan-African Congress. Hastie's experience as the civilian aide to the secretary of war had given him invaluable insight into the ways that powerful bureaucracies – such as the American and European

---

[185] W. E. B. Du Bois to the Secretary [Walter White] and Members of Pan-African Committee, August 15, 1945, Reel 57, *Du Bois.*

[186] W. E. B. Du Bois to Jean de la Roche, September 14, 1945, Reel 57, *Du Bois.* Emphasis added.

[187] W. E. B. Du Bois to George Padmore, December 30, 1946, Reel 59, *Du Bois.*

[188] Lewis, *W.E.B. Du Bois,* 511.

[189] Rayford Logan, diary entry, September 18, 1945, Box 4, File "Diaries, 1945–47," *Logan Papers.*

[190] Walter White to Arthur Spingarn, July 21, 1945, Box A6, File "Africa: Pan-African Congress, 1945," *Papers of the NAACP*; Walter White to Louis Wright, July 21, 1945, Box A6, File "Africa: Pan-African Congress, 1945," *Papers of the NAACP*; Re Dr. Du Bois, January 7, 1946, Box A241, File "William E. B. Du Bois–General, 1946," *Papers of the NAACP.*

governments – rationalized the irrational and blocked the inevitable.[191] As a result, he knew this high-stakes venture to demand independence had to be well planned, with a truly representative group of participants, not just some Africans who happened to be in Europe at the time, or the proceedings would "boomerang, both in the reaction of the colonial powers and in the reaction of the colonial peoples who have not been consulted."[192] Hastie, therefore, repeatedly voiced concerns that the logistical nightmare of the trans-Atlantic crossing had to be resolved. Before the Manchester conference was announced and the NAACP was still contemplating hosting one in Paris, he urged the committee to "not authorize [the] September conference without satisfactory detailed plans" concerning the budget, a list of participants, and guaranteed round trip transportation.[193] Given the number of ocean liners consigned to transport hundreds of thousands of troops, Hastie foresaw that delegates waiting for an open berth could get stranded in Europe for weeks or months on end and all the extra costs that would entail. Ralph Bunche, then one of the State Department's experts on colonialism, had, in fact, affirmed that "passage to Europe was going to be difficult but not impossible … but return passage [would be] even more difficult."[194]

In addition to logistics, the substance of the Pan-African Congress raised conflict. Du Bois wanted to amass the documentation about the human rights conditions in the colonies and, through publications and conferences, debunk the Europeans' narrative of "uplift" and "civilizing mission." White and Arthur Spingarn insisted that there had to be a "definite a program, not only of speeches but of action at the Congress." White contended that "there is not much value in merely meeting and letting it end there." There had to be an action plan to carry out the resolutions and seize on the political activism and ferment that was brewing and determine how to break the imperial powers' grip on lands and peoples that they had no business controlling.[195] Although it is easy to see now

---

[191] Phillip McGuire, "Judge Hastie, World War II, and Army Racism," *Journal of Negro History*, 62, no. 4 (October 1977), 351–362; Mark S. Cohen, review of *William Hastie: Grace under Pressure*, by Gilbert Ware, *Michigan Law Review*, 84, no. 4/5, (February–April 1986), 864; Simon Topping, "'Supporting Our Friends and Defeating Our Enemies': Militancy and Nonpartisanship in the NAACP, 1936–1948," *Journal of African American History*, 89, no. 1 (Winter 2004), 24.

[192] William Hastie to Walter White, July 17, 1945, Box A6, File "Africa: Pan-African Congress, 1945," *Papers of the NAACP*.

[193] William H. Hastie to Walter White, telegram, July 11, 1945, ibid.

[194] W. E. B. Du Bois to Walter White, July 20, 1945, ibid.

[195] Walter White to the Sub-Committee of the Committee on the Pan-African Congress, July 12, 1945, ibid.

that both Du Bois and White were right – conferences without activism would become mere academic exercises whereas political activism without a strong, verifiable knowledge base would lack the direction and the credibility to withstand the inevitable barrage of challenges from the colonizers – their mutual enmity blinded them to it at the time.

Disagreement reached even to the very demographic scope of the conference. In the summer of 1945, Wilkins, White, and Spingarn raised the specter that the name "Pan-African" was too limiting, especially given the tumult throughout the colonized world for independence. It was, after all, not just Africa demanding freedom from European rule. An incredulous Du Bois complained to a colleague in Paris, "[T]here has developed in the Association some opposition to a Pan-African movement. They want to expand it into a Congress of Dependent Peoples. I do not agree with this at all."[196] He *was* clear that the NAACP had to break out of its U.S.-based parochialism and decide whether it was "going to follow the wider vision of its founders and be interested in colored people everywhere." By "everywhere" he meant those in Africa and perhaps the Caribbean.[197] He firmly believed that "until Africa is free, the descendants of Africa the world over cannot escape chains."[198] His primary concern, therefore, did not extend to Malaysia, Indonesia, or India. As his biographer, David Levering Lewis, noted, the suggestion for a broad-based anti-imperial conference was simply unacceptable. "We have a 'pretty clear right to speak for Africa,' Du Bois snapped, but Asians would almost certainly 'repudiate such assumptions on our part.'"[199] "Asiatics do not need American Negroes to provide them leadership," the *Atlanta Daily World* reported one unnamed source, probably Du Bois, saying at the NAACP sub-committee meeting, but "Africans are desperately in need of aid in meeting problems peculiar to them."[200] At the end of the day, an exasperated Du Bois turned to Hastie and said, "I think we got exactly nowhere in our discussion and came so far as I can see to no conclusions."[201]

Actually, the stalemate over the scope of the NAACP's anticolonial work had been years in the making. In October 1941, the board

[196] W. E. B. Du Bois to Jean de la Roche, August 1, 1945, Reel 57, *Du Bois*.

[197] W. E. B. Du Bois to Gloster Current, December 3, 1946, Box A241, File "William E.B. DuBois–General, 1946," *Papers of the NAACP*.

[198] W. E. B. Du Bois to Walter White and Members of the Staff, October 10, 1946, ibid.

[199] Lewis, *W.E.B. Du Bois*, 512.

[200] Ernest E. Johnson, "NAACP Holds Up Approval of Pan-African Meeting," *Atlanta Daily World*, July 22, 1945.

[201] W. E. B. Du Bois to Walter White, July 20, 1945, Box A6, File "Africa: Pan-African Congress, 1945," *Papers of the NAACP*.

had approved the formation of a committee to "place before the Peace Conference the facts regarding the Negro and the colored peoples of the world." Then when the Phelps-Stokes Fund created its committee, the NAACP opted to wait until its members, who were crafting *The Atlantic Charter and Africa from an American Standpoint*, were free to devote significant time to the Association's initiative. From there, through faltering steps to form a committee, appoint personnel, and find the funds – because "this is one of the most important contributions the N.A.A.C.P. can make both now and in the post-war world" – the Association was on new terrain.[202] The more it thrashed about in unfamiliar waters dealing with international relations and colonialism, the more it became clear that, as Hastie advised, "[I]t certainly would be desirable to have a compensated Executive Officer devoting at least a substantial portion of his time to the work."[203] It was this setup that led the board to hire Du Bois despite concerns about his tense relationship with Walter White.[204]

On Du Bois's advice, the NAACP had convened in New York and generously financed a Colonial Conference on April 6, 1945, which included forty-nine delegates from ten colonies who provided insight into the global, not just European, demands and vision for a postwar world.[205]

[202] Franklin Reeves to Walter White, Roy Wilkins, et al., memo, August 24, 1942, Box A128, File "Board of Directors: Committee on Policy, Structure and Program, 1942–44," *Papers of the NAACP*; Proceedings of N.A.A.C.P. Program Analysis and Planning Conference Held in New York City, August 28–30, 1942, Box A128, File "Board of Directors: Committee on Policy Structure and Program, 1942–44," *Papers of the NAACP*; Walter White to the Board of Directors, February 8, 1943, Box A466, File "Peace Conference Committee, 1943," *Papers of the NAACP*; Walter White to William Hastie, February 15, 1943, Box A466, File "Peace Conference Committee to Present Views of Negroes at Upcoming Peace Conference," *Papers of the NAACP*; Walter White to William Hastie, September 23, 1943, Box A299, File "William H. Hastie–General, July 1943-August 1944," *Papers of the NAACP*; Walter White to William Hastie, November 12, 1943, Box A466, File "Peace Conference Committee, 1943," *Papers of the NAACP*; Walter White, memo for the files, December 16, 1943, Box A466, File "Peace Conference Committee, 1943," *Papers of the NAACP*.
[203] William Hastie to Walter White, May 6, 1943, Box A466, File "Peace Conference Committee to Present Views of Negroes at Upcoming Peace Conference, 1943–44," *Papers of the NAACP*.
[204] Minutes of the Meeting of the Board of Directors, July 14, 1944, Reel 3, *NAACP*; Anderson, *Eyes Off the Prize*, 32–34; Rayford Logan, diary entry, August 30, 1944, Box 4, File "Diaries, 1943–44," *Logan Papers*.
[205] Minutes of the Board for December 11, 1944, December 11, 1944, Box A240, File "William E.B. Du Bois: General, 1943–44," *Papers of the NAACP*; Roy Wilkins marginalia on W.E.B. Du Bois to Roy Wilkins, April 5, 1945, Box A197, File "Colonial Conference, 1945," *Papers of the NAACP*; "521,000,000 to be Represented at NAACP Colonial Conference," press release, March 29, 1945, Box A197, File "Colonial

The NAACP was determined, in Du Bois's own words, to fight "for the emancipation of the world."[206]

The recommendations from the Colonial Conference reaffirmed and buttressed the previous studies from the Phelps-Stokes Committee, as well as the African American ministers on the Federal Council Churches and the West African Press Delegation, and formed the broad objectives of the NAACP's anticolonialism.[207] The points were salient and nonnegotiable:

1. Colonialism must go for the reason that it has caused poverty, illiteracy and disease which affect not only the colonies but also the world and threaten world peace.

2. There should be an international body established to oversee the transition of peoples from colonial status to such autonomy as colonial peoples themselves may desire.

3. That on such an international body the colonial peoples themselves shall have effective representation.

4. That the primary object of this international body shall be to improve the economic and social condition of the colonial peoples.[208]

More specifically, the Colonial Conference attendees, including representatives from Ghana, Nigeria, and Burma, agreed that the "ownership of natural resources" and profits were to be used "primarily for the welfare of the natives of the colony," and that "no country like the Union of South Africa ... be recognized as capable of exercising a colonial mandate." The conference attendees also addressed the hard, cold reality of what settler colonialism had wrought. "We demand that in other parts of British Africa," such as Kenya, "no white minority be given privilege to rule over native majorities; that education for citizenship and work be undertaken for all native peoples and that the longstanding promise to admit native Africans to equal status with other citizens in the British Empire be

Conference, 1945," *Papers of the NAACP*; Annual Report of the Director of Special Research for the Year 1945 (October 4, 1944–July 1, 1945), Reel 57, *Du Bois*.

[206] Annual Report of the Director of Special Research for the Year 1945 (October 4, 1944–July 1, 1945), Reel 57, *Du Bois*.

[207] For the report from Benjamin Mays, Charles Wesley, and Channing Tobias, see Negro Churchmen and the Race Question: A Statement Prepared by Negro Members of the Commission on the Church and Minority Peoples of the Federal Council of the Churches of Christ in America, n.d., ca. 1944, File "Federal Council of Churches, 1944 [38]," *Tobias Papers*.

[208] Annual Report of the Director of Special Research for the Year 1945 (October 4, 1944–July 1, 1945), Reel 57, *Du Bois*.

implemented." And, "in the case of the French [and] Dutch ... colonies," any plans for eventual equality "cannot be carried out if these areas ... continue to be regarded as territory for trade, industry and investment to be carried on primarily for the benefit of non-resident Europeans without making the economic and social interests of the inhabitants of the colonies of first and continuous importance." Finally, for the colonies once controlled by Fascist Italy, the conference delegates "demand[ed] that ... the rights of natives in Libya, Eritrea, and Somaliland be safeguarded under an International Mandates Commission."[209]

On those points, the leadership of the NAACP was in full agreement; the tactics, however, were hotly contested. Du Bois envisioned a movement led by "American Negroes," hence, his emphasis on the liberation of African heritage peoples. White, surprisingly, was not so sure. On the domestic front, without question, the NAACP jealously guarded and fought for recognition as *the* leader in the civil rights struggle.[210] In fact, for many historians, the Association has a well-deserved and well-earned reputation for crushing, refusing to work with, absorbing, or co-opting perceived challengers.[211] However, White sensed that this anticolonial

[209] Specifically this Colonial Conference makes the following demands:, n.d., April 6, 1945, ibid.

[210] Alfred Baker Lewis for N.A.A.C.P. Program, n.d., ca. September 1943, Box 3, File "9," *Baker Papers*; Walter White to Roy Wilkins, December 12, 1944, Box A466, File "Peace Conference Committee, 1943," *Papers of the NAACP*; Walter White to Arthur Spingarn, November 21, 1946, Box A241, File "William E.B. Du Bois–General, 1946," *Papers of the NAACP*.

[211] John H. Bracey Jr. and August Meier, "'Allies or Adversaries?' The NAACP: A. Philip Randolph and the 1941 March on Washington," *Georgia Historical Quarterly*, 75, no. 1 (Spring 1991), 1–17; Hugh T. Murray Jr., "The NAACP versus the Communist Party: The Scottsboro Rape Cases, 1931–1932," *Phylon*, 28, no. 3 (3rd Quarter, 1967), 276–287; John Dittmer, *Local People: The Struggle for Civil Rights in Mississippi* (Champaign: University of Illinois Press, 1994), 78, 119, 274–275; Charles M. Payne, *I've Got the Light of Freedom: The Organizing Tradition and the Mississippi Freedom Struggle* (Berkeley and Los Angeles: University of California Press, 1995), 61; Manning Marable, *Race, Reform, and Rebellion: The Second Reconstruction in Black America, 1945–1990*, 2nd ed. (Jackson: University of Mississippi Press, 1991), 94–95; Adam Fairclough, *To Redeem the Soul of America: The Southern Christian Leadership Conference and Martin Luther King, Jr.* (Athens: University of Georgia Press, 1987), 39–40, 44–47, 64–65, 96, 104; Emilye Crosby, "'God's Appointed Savior': Charles Evers's Use of Local Movements for National Prestige," in *Groundwork: The Local Black Freedom Movement in America*, eds. Komozi Woodard and Jeanne Theoharis (New York: New York University Press, 2005), 165–192; Hasan Kwame Jeffries, *Bloody Lowndes: Civil Rights and Black Power in Alabama's Black Belt* (New York: New York University Press, 2009), 188–189; Taylor Branch, *Parting the Waters: America in the King Years, 1954–63* (New York: Simon and Schuster, 1988), 829–831; Sullivan, *Lift Every Voice*, 103, 161–162.

struggle was different. In the international realm, the NAACP was a relative neophyte, and, most important, it believed that the indigenous leadership and peoples were the ones to determine the trajectories of their own colonies – anything else would simply have been inappropriate. The Association, therefore, wisely opted not to even try to lead but to be more collaborative, more cooperative, more a team player – and to expand its vision to the liberation of all colonized peoples.

Du Bois saw this position as a failure of commitment: the "N.A.A.C.P. has taken no stand nor laid down any program with regard to Africa."[212] In fact, however, the Association was honoring the fundamental principle of self-determination. After fighting for decades for African Americans to have the right to vote and, therefore, the ability to choose the shape of the governments that made the laws and policies that directly affected their lives, the NAACP's anticolonial position reflected the same core belief.[213]

It is important to note, in light of the narrative of the radical Du Bois pressing up against a reactionary Association, that it was the scholar who paternalistically feared that Africans would have difficulty creating anything viable without black Americans' guidance. And, conversely, it was William Hastie who wanted to be sure that delegates at any NAACP-sponsored Pan-African Congress would be "representative of the genuine aspirations of their people" and not merely "expatriates or persons temporarily residing in England or France."[214] In the end, Hastie was right. George Padmore's leadership and insistence on being the "Elder Statesman behind the scene" was transformative.[215] In Manchester, England, while giving a nod to the previous Pan-African meetings that Du Bois organized, the delegates in 1945 acknowledged that "all these Congresses ... were not really representative. They were the pioneering work of one man, very great work, but definitely not of the same representative character as the Fifth Pan-African Congress."[216] Du Bois himself was awed by the breadth of representation and reported that the 1945 meeting had

[212] W. E. B. Du Bois to Walter White, November 14, 1946, Box A241, File "William E.B. Du Bois–General, 1946," *Papers of the NAACP*.

[213] For the extensive battle over the right to vote, see Manfred Berg, *"Ticket to Freedom": The NAACP and the Struggle for Black Political Integration* (Gainesville: University of Florida Press, 2005).

[214] William Hastie to Walter White, July 17, 1945, Box A6, File "Africa: Pan-African Congress, 1945," *Papers of the NAACP*.

[215] George [Padmore] to Cyril [Ollivierre], August 17, 1945, File "George Padmore," *Padmore*.

[216] Pan African Congress: Declarations and Resolutions, October 21, 1945, Reel 4, *Xuma*.

"nearly two hundred delegates from sixty different countries. In contrast with earlier congresses the majority of the delegates came directly from their countries with mandates from the countries."[217]

The success of the 1945 Congress did not end tension between Du Bois and the NAACP. An even more contentious area of disagreement was the question of communism, which had already been simmering. Du Bois believed that Marxist-Leninism, especially "what he understood as the ideal under experiment in Russia," could erase the inequalities that had bedeviled the existence of black people throughout the globe.[218] He consistently blasted the Association as being too timid "to take on any step which would lay it open to any sort of sympathy with Russia, Socialism, or Communism."[219] Du Bois intimated to the Association staff that its ideas were regressive, backward, and plodding because the "whole trend of the forward thinking world ... is toward economic planning to abolish poverty, curb monopoly and the rule of wealth, spread education, insure health and practice democracy. Here then," he exhorted, "the N.A.A.C.P. must take a stand ... we must not be diverted by witch-hunting for Communists." Simply put, he believed that only communism would provide for "the freedom of Africa in work and wage, education and health, the complete abolition of the colonial system."[220]

The Association leadership disagreed. However, the NAACP's anti-communism would prove to be more supple and less reactionary than Du Bois assumed.[221] Throughout the struggle for colonial independence, the Association would align with, run interference for, and provide invaluable support to activists whom the U.S. government labeled "communists" and "security risks" – putting its name and resources on the line for red-tinged freedom fighters.[222] That the NAACP flatly refused to follow without critique, question, or skepticism the Soviet Union – Walter White was, in fact, sure that communists "assail[ed]" him as an "Uncle Tom" because he did not "believe that the millenium [sic] of freedom and democracy has ... arrived in Soviet Russia" – was in no way a disavowal

[217] Report of the Department of Special Research, October to December 3, 1945, Reel 7, *NAACP.*

[218] Lewis, *W.E.B. Du Bois*, 517.

[219] W. E. B. Du Bois to George Padmore, September 22, 1947, Reel 60, *Du Bois.*

[220] W. E. B. Du Bois to Walter White and Members of the Staff, October 10, 1946, Box A241, File "William E.B. Du Bois–General, 1946," *Papers of the NAACP.*

[221] Manfred Berg, "Black Civil Rights and Liberal Anticommunism: The NAACP in the Early Cold War," *Journal of American History*, 94, no. 1 (June 2007), 75–96.

[222] See Chapters 2 and 3 on the NAACP's work with the Reverend Michael Scott of the Africa Bureau and Abdullahi Issa of the Somali Youth League.

of its anticolonialism.[223] The core of the fissure between Du Bois and the Association was whether communism was the ideological pathway that would put the NAACP at the "forefront."[224]

The outline of their dispute began to appear after the founding conference of the UN, which was held from May through June 1945 in San Francisco. Du Bois and White emerged from that ten-week baptism in diplomacy with very different perspectives about the possibilities for decolonization. It did not appear to start this way, however. As scholar David Levering Lewis noted, "It had been White's twenty-four hour pipeline into the White House and whirlwind lobbying on Capitol Hill that finally made possible the association's special UN status" as special consultants to the U.S. delegation.[225] Even before they came to San Francisco, the two men had called a truce because they knew they were going to need all of their energies to battle a powerful and recalcitrant foe.[226] Previously, at the Dumbarton Oaks Conference in October 1944, the United States had crafted with British and Soviet assent a draft charter for the UN that had, as Roy Wilkins remarked, "a total lack of consideration of colonial peoples and darker races."[227] The Association's representatives, therefore, went to San Francisco determined to right that wrong and ensure that the UN had the wherewithal to dismantle colonial empires, ensure indigenous control of natural resources, provide a full panoply of human rights, and establish a definite time line for independence.[228]

[223] Walter White, "My Critics," March 31, 1949, Box A81, File "Articles Walter White: Syndicated Columns, 1949," *Papers of the NAACP*.

[224] W. E. B. Du Bois to Walter White and Members of the Staff, October 10, 1946, Box A241, File "William E.B. Du Bois–General, 1946," *Papers of the NAACP*.

[225] Lewis, *W.E.B. Du Bois*, 505.

[226] Anderson, *Eyes Off the Prize*, 39–41; Roy Wilkins to Walter White, April 20, 1945, Box A639, File "United Nations: UNCIO, General, 1945, March-May 10," *Papers of the NAACP*; Lewis, *W.E.B. Du Bois*, 505.

[227] Roy Wilkins to Clark Eichelberger, telegram, February 19, 1945, Box A634, File "United Nations: Bretton Woods Conference, 1944–1946," *Papers of the NAACP*.

[228] Lewis, *W.E.B. Du Bois*, 503; Walter White to W. E. B. Du Bois and Mary McLeod Bethune, May 1, 1945, Box A639, File "United Nations: UNCIO, General, 1945, March-May 10," *Papers of the NAACP*; Walter White to Roy Wilkins, May 2, 1945, Box A639, File "United Nations: UNCIO, General, 1945, March-May 10," *Papers of the NAACP*; "Formal Demand Made for Race Equality at San Francisco Parley: American Delegation Asked by Consultants to Press Also for End of Colonial System and for International Bill of Rights," press release, May 3, 1945, Box A640, File "United Nations–UNCIO–Press Releases: Clippings, 1945," *Papers of the NAACP*; Walter White handwritten notes of Corps Committee meeting 9:30 a.m. May 4, 1945, Box A639, File "United Nations: UNCIO, General, 1945, July-1946," *Papers of the NAACP*.

However, it soon became clear that the Allies had other plans. As Trygve Lie, the first UN secretary general recalled, "At Dumbarton Oaks, ... the subject of trusteeship was not discussed at all. At San Francisco, it was one of the very last matters on which agreement could be reached during ten weeks of strenuous negotiations."[229] The Federal Council of Churches' analysts noted that the "Chapter on Trusteeships ... was written under an atmosphere of conflicting demands – the demand to promote the well-being of dependent peoples; and the demand, particularly by the United States, to enable the acquisition of strategic bases in the Pacific for security reasons."[230]

Similarly, all of the Atlantic Charter's human rights seemed to crumple beneath the "nationalistic, strategic, and economic imperatives unleashed by five years of warfare."[231] Powerful anti-discriminatory, antiracist language, which the NAACP had helped push into the founding document, was rendered virtually null and void by a joint backroom deal among the British, Americans, and Soviets to insert the "domestic jurisdiction" clause in the UN Charter. Article 2(7) laid out that "[n]othing contained in the present Charter shall authorize the United Nations to intervene in matters which are essentially within the domestic jurisdiction of any state or shall require the Members to submit such matters to settlement under the present Charter." In short, the clause blocked the UN from having any authority to investigate human rights violations without the prior and full approval of the alleged violator. The only exception was when international peace was threatened.[232]

By the time the San Francisco conference ended, a disgusted Rayford Logan dismissed the UN Charter as a "tragic joke."[233] A Nigerian paper, the *Daily Service*, saw the United Nations Conference on Independent

[229] "Opening Statement at First Meeting of the Trusteeship Council," March 26, 1947, in Andrew W. Cordier and Wilder Foote, eds., *Public Papers of the Secretaries-General of the United Nations*, Vol. 1, *Trygve Lie: 1946–1953* (New York: Columbia University Press, 1969), 75.

[230] Walter W. Van Kirk and O. Frederick Nolde, Memorandum No. 8: United Nations Conference on International Organization, July 3, 1945, File "Council of Churches, July–Dec. 1945, [40]," *Tobias Papers*; Stephen C. Schlesinger, *Act of Creation: The Founding of the United Nations, A Story of Superpowers, Secret Agents, Wartime Allies and Enemies, and Their Quest for a Peaceful World* (Boulder, CO: Westview Press, 2003), 232–235.

[231] Lewis, *W.E.B. Du Bois*, 507.

[232] Anderson, *Eyes Off the Prize*, 46–50; Charter of the United Nations, http://www.un.org/en/documents/charter/chapter1.shtml. Accessed December 19, 2013.

[233] Rayford Logan, diary entry, July 23, 1945, Box 4, File "Diaries, 1945–47," *Logan Papers*.

Organization (UNCIO) as a major defeat for the forces of liberation. "San Francisco and the world has once more returned to [a] terrific scramble for colonial territories and spheres of influence." The Nigerians looked at what appeared to be the wreckage of the UN Charter, human rights, and trusteeship and moaned that "[n]ew life has been infused into predatory imperialism."[234] A. B. Xuma tried to make sense of the incredible incongruity of Jan Christian Smuts, who oversaw one of the most racially oppressive nations on earth, helping to craft the human rights language in the UN Charter. Xuma wrote the prime minister that "Africans [were] still undergoing indiscriminate mass arrests, denial of freedom of speech and of assembly." It was time for "immediate relief in spirit of world security charter *you* signed."[235]

The left-wing Council on African Affairs (CAA), which was chaired by activist and entertainer Paul Robeson, denounced the UN Charter's trusteeship provisions as "inadequate and weak" and "filled with unctuous rhetoric" that "failed to establish the means for the United Nations … to insure the effective and rapid economic, social, and political advancement of colonial peoples throughout the world." In the CAA's estimation, what authority the proposed Trusteeship Council did have over the handful of colonies designated as "trusts" was "extremely limited." The only thing the provisions for trusteeship managed to do, the Council contended, was to make "it possible for the United States to arrange for a free hand in the administration of strategic islands taken from Japan." Article 73(e), which required the administering powers to provide information about the conditions in the colonies, was riven with "loopholes," which gave this clause "little if any value." The only saving grace, at least as far as the CAA could see, was that the Soviet Union would have a seat on the Trusteeship Council. This was doubly important because there had been no provision for indigenous people to be at the very table that would decide their future.[236]

Du Bois also was greatly troubled by what he saw in San Francisco. He told Metz Lochard of the *Chicago Defender*, "[W]e have conquered

---

[234] Marika Sherwood, "'There Is No New Deal for the Blackman in San Francisco': African Attempts to Influence the Founding Conference of the United Nations April–July 1945," *International Journal of African Historical Studies*, 29, no. 1 (1996), 93.

[235] A. B. Xuma to Jan Smuts, July 17, 1945, Reel 3, *Xuma*. Emphasis added.

[236] Council on African Affairs, "Text and Analysis of the Colonial Provisions of the United Nations Charter," n.d., ca. July 1945, Box 18, File "8," *Papers of Henry Callis*, Moorland-Spingarn Research Center, Howard University, Washington, DC (hereafter *Callis Papers*).

Germany but not their [sic] ideas. We still believe in white supremacy, keeping Negroes in their places and lying about democracy, when we mean imperial control of 750 million human beings in colonies."[237] He laid the lies, embrace of colonialism, and barely cloaked dominance of white supremacy at the feet of the West that was "bitterly opposed to the Russian economic program" and had tried to isolate the Soviets at the UNCIO.[238] "Everything that Russia did was given a sinister meaning," Du Bois complained.[239] Most frightening to the Americans and their European allies, the scholar asserted, was the "splendid frank straightforward statement" made by Foreign Minister Vyacheslav Molotov, who announced that the "Soviet delegation realizes that ... we must first of all see to it that dependent countries are enabled as soon as possible to take the path of national independence."[240] Instead of supporting this profound statement, Du Bois seethed, the United States was so intent on controlling the Japanese mandated islands that it turned its back on the prospect of aligning with the Soviet Union to ensure a world "which did not depend upon colonies" and whose "prosperity was not going to be built upon illiteracy, cheap labor, disease and crime."[241] Du Bois emphasized that the "San Francisco Conference ... did not go nearly far enough in facing realistically the greatest potential cause of war, the colonial system."[242] The domestic jurisdiction clause, for example, meant that "the broad generalization as to human rights 'without discrimination on account of race, creed or language' will not apply to colonial peoples unless England, Belgium, Holland and other colonial powers determine to apply it."[243] "Even the system of trusteeship for former mandates," he noted, was voluntary, "not compulsory, and applie[d] only to a few millions of the 750 millions of colonial peoples."[244] This analysis told only part of the story, however. Du Bois was so blinded by his faith in the USSR that he could not see Moscow's complicity in erecting the very

[237] W. E. B. Du Bois to Metz L. P. Lochard, telegram, May 4, 1945, Reel 56, *Du Bois.*

[238] W. E. B. Du Bois, "The Winds of Time," *Chicago Defender,* June 23, 1945.

[239] Earl Conrad, "Pan-African Parley in Paris Set for September, Du Bois Announces," *Chicago Defender,* June 16, 1945.

[240] W.E.B. Du Bois, "Lauds Molotov's Frankness in 'World Equality' Speech," *Chicago Defender,* May 26, 1945; "U.S. Failure to Back Freedom of Colonies Blasted," *Chicago Defender,* June 2, 1945.

[241] W. E. B. Du Bois, "The Winds of Time," *Chicago Defender,* June 23, 1945.

[242] W. E. B. Du Bois to Hamilton Fish Armstrong, July 9, 1945, Box 25, File "Du Bois, W.E.B., 1934–35, 1940, 1943–45, 1947, 1958," *Armstrong Papers.*

[243] Earl Conrad, "Pan-African Parley in Paris Set for September, Du Bois Announces," *Chicago Defender,* June 16, 1945.

[244] W. E. B. Du Bois to Editor *Harpers Magazine,* July 11, 1945, Reel 57, *Du Bois.*

barriers that made attaining decolonization and human rights that much more difficult.

Nonetheless, incensed by the domestic jurisdiction clause and the anemic trusteeship system, on July 11, 1945 (without Walter White's knowledge or consent), Du Bois testified during the treaty's ratification hearings before Tom Connally and the Senate Foreign Relations Committee.[245] The scholar, acting on his own but identified before Congress as the director of Special Research for the NAACP, noted that the "first duty of civilization is to see to it that no human being is deprived of" political, social, and economic rights "because of poverty, disease or ignorance." Yet, the UN Charter left virtually untouched the colonial system that is "undemocratic, socially dangerous and a main cause of war." It did so "because of the national interests, the economic rivalries, and the selfish demands of peoples represented at San Francisco," which left "the even more pressing cries of the 750,000,000 unrepresented ... not expressed and even forgotten." The provisions that were included in the Charter, Du Bois asserted, dealt with only a small number, roughly 25 million, who lived under colonial rule. Moreover, although there was some vague language for those in trust territories about "oral petition or of making any investigation into colonial conditions," this "widest grant of international power over colonies" was "evidently designed to reduce this power to a minimum and to give as little recognition as possible to the wishes of the colonial people themselves."[246]

That appeared to be the consensus.[247] However, the NAACP saw not only the many challenges, which, as Walter White observed, offered "scant hope for liberation," but also the possibilities.[248] Perhaps because the Association had to consistently and painstakingly work through broken legal systems, hostile bureaucracies, and inadequate political regimes to dismantle structural racism in the United States, the Association had the ability to see slivers of opportunities even in the most desolate spaces.

---

[245] W. E. B. Du Bois to Tom Connally, July 2, 1945, Reel 58, *Du Bois*; Robert V. Shirley to W. E. B. Du Bois, telegram, July 7, 1945, Reel 58, *Du Bois*; Walter White to Leslie Perry, July 18, 1945, Box A639, File "United Nations: United Nations Conference on International Organization–General, 1945–July, 1946," *Papers of the NAACP*; Minutes of the Meeting of the Committee on Administration, July 23, 1945, Box A127, File "Board of Directors: Committee on Administration, 1945," *Papers of the NAACP*.

[246] "Testimony of W.E.B. Du Bois," attached to W. E. B. Du Bois to Metz Lochard, July 11, 1945, Box 137-1, Folder "10," *Papers of Metz Lochard*, Moorland-Spingarn Research Center, Howard University, Washington, DC (hereafter *Lochard Papers*).

[247] Anderson, *Eyes Off the Prize*, 56.

[248] Ibid.

This was no Pollyanna moment. As far as White was concerned, the "Charter [was] woefully weak on colonial trusteeship."[249] And he knew why. "The pressures of the colonial powers and the cloakroom appeals to the preservation of white overlordship had been disastrously effective in preventing adoption of any really effective machinery to wipe out colonialism."[250] The Association believed, however, that there was still enough there, especially, Ralph Bunche surmised, in the provisions for oral petitions and Trusteeship Council visits to the colonies, to craft the means necessary to destroy colonialism. After all, Bunche, the senior African American in the State Department, noted "the administering authority could only do so much cleaning up even when it specifies the time for the periodic visits."[251] This meant that the sham of the "white man's burden" and the "civilizing mission" would be exposed. Over and over again.

The board of directors informed the U.S. Senate that, without question, the NAACP "would have been more enthusiastic" about the Charter "had the provision for establishment of international trusteeship been more forthright and far reaching in assuring to colored peoples participation in government, greater opportunities for self-development and ... independence. But," the board continued, "adoption of the Charter and entrance by the United States into full participation in a world organization will provide the beginning machinery to implement the ideals for which this war is being fought."[252]

That machinery was more powerful and effective than most assumed. Over the coming years, the deft use of the UN and the requirements for oral petitions, periodic visits, and annual reports transmitted to and reviewed by the Trusteeship Council and the Fourth Committee of the General Assembly transformed "inadequate and weak" provisions into chisels and sledgehammers that dismantled the imperial powers' legitimacy. UN Secretary General Trygve Lie observed that the "International Trusteeship System is no mere prolongation of the Mandate System under the League of Nations. It is a new system of international supervision. Its

---

[249] Walter White to John L. Childs, July 17, 1945, Box A639, File "United Nations: UNCIO, General, 1945, July–1946," *Papers of the NAACP*.

[250] Walter White, *A Man Called White: The Autobiography of Walter White* (New York: Viking Press, 1948), 298.

[251] Rayford Logan, diary entry, July 25, 1945, Box 4, File "Diaries, 1945–47," *Logan Papers*.

[252] Report of the Secretary for the July [1945] meeting of the Board, n.d., ca. July 1945, Reel 7, *NAACP*.

scope is wider, its powers broader, and its potentialities far greater than those of the Mandates System."[253]

Moreover, for the NAACP, the United Nations' hiring of both Bunche as the director of the Trusteeship Division and Channing Tobias's son-in-law, William Dean, as chief of the African Section, Economic Development and Stability, meant the Association had conduits of influence and information "strategically placed in the U.N."[254]

In the summer of 1945, however, none of this was a foregone conclusion. The NAACP was confident, however, that a new world order was within reach. To achieve a rights-based, decolonized world would require savvy, skill, and toughness, but the Association defined itself as "a David operating against a great many strongly supported, loud-talking Goliaths. We never forget, however, that the original David won."[255] The first rock in the slingshot, therefore, went straight at South Africa.

[253] Cordier and Foote, eds., "Opening Statement at First Meeting of the Trusteeship Council," March 26, 1947, *Trygve Lie, 1946–1953*, 74.
[254] William Dean to Walter White, October 28, 1946, Box A634, File "United Nations: General, 1945–46," *Papers of the NAACP*.
[255] Annual Report of the Washington Bureau, December 21, 1950, Box H163, File "Annual Reports, 1950–57," *Papers of the NAACP*.

2

"The White Man's Burden Has Not Been Very Heavy"

The NAACP's Anticolonial Struggle against South Africa, 1946–1951

> No country like the Union of South Africa can be recognized as capable of exercising a colonial mandate.
>
> – NAACP Colonial Conference, 1945

The NAACP's postwar agenda was firmly established at the April 1945 Colonial Conference. That meeting, in many ways, generated the Association's road map to colonial liberation: South Africa (South West Africa); Italy (Libya, Eritrea, Somalia); the Netherlands (Indonesia); France (Morocco and Tunisia); and Britain (Kenya). With a strategy similar to the methodical case-by-case approach it had used to expose the sham of separate but equal, the NAACP recognized that the way each colony was governed presented a prime opportunity to strategically undermine and delegitimize the rationales that had, for too long, transformed the brutality of white supremacy into the narrative of benevolent colonial rule.

South West Africa (current day Namibia), in particular, was a testament to how far the myth of the "white man's burden" had fallen short. The colony had been a mandate under the old League of Nations system and, as such, was a "sacred trust of civilization" administered, in this case, by South Africa. That jarring juxtaposition – a sacred trust held by a racially repressive regime – led the NAACP to emphasize two key principles that were essential for challenging the viability of colonialism in a world birthed by the Atlantic and UN Charters.

The first principle was that the administering power had to meet basic human rights standards. Certainly, the Association argued, a racially repressive state, especially one that, like South Africa, revered Nazi

Germany as a model of excellence, had no intention of implementing the improvements in education, housing, health care, and self-government that the UN Charter's Chapter XII required. A nation as determined as South Africa to dragoon more and more black bodies into the vortex of intolerable, exploitative working conditions was systemically incapable of honoring the human rights agenda that was essential for viable independence.[1]

The second principle was "international accountability." This concept was embedded in the reporting requirements for mandates and trust territories laid out by the League and, in an even more robust form, the UN. South West Africa was tailor-made for this challenge because Pretoria's rule was so brutal that the regime recognized that it could never, especially in a post-WWII world, convincingly defend its actions before an international forum. South Africa, therefore, patently refused to even acknowledge that it had to answer to the UN, which, in turn, generated the kind of backlash, indignation, and relentless pursuit of the truth that put not only colonialism but also apartheid on trial.[2]

[1] Chapter XII, Article 76, in part, notes that the goal of the trusteeship system is "b) to promote the political, economic, social, and educational advancement of the inhabitants of the trust territories, and their progressive development towards self-government or independence as may be appropriate to the particular circumstances of each territory and its peoples and the freely expressed wishes of the peoples concerned, and as may be provided by the terms of each trusteeship agreement; c) to encourage respect for human rights and for fundamental freedoms for all without distinction as to race, sex, language, or religion, and to encourage recognition of the interdependence of the peoples of the world." http://www.un.org/en/documents/charter/chapter12.shtml. Accessed May 3, 2013.

[2] "Named by U.N. to Study Segregation in South Africa: U.N. Names Bunche to Study Race Bias: Malan Regime in South Africa is Expected to Block Entry by 3-Man Commission," *New York Times*, December 23, 1952, Box A7, File "Africa: South Africa Petition to United Nations, 1953," *Papers of the NAACP*; Document 4: Letter dated 12 September 1952 addressed to the Secretary-General by the permanent representatives of Afghanistan, Burma, Egypt, India, Indonesia, Iran, Iraq, Lebanon, Pakistan, the Philippines, Saudi Arabia, Syria and Yemen, A/2138, *The United Nations and Apartheid, 1948–1994*, introduction by Boutros Boutros-Ghali, Blue Book Series, Vol. 1 (New York: United Nations Department of Public Information, 1994), 223–224; Document 5: Statement by Mrs. Vijaya Lakshmi Pandit, Chairperson of the delegation of India, introducing the item on apartheid in the Ad Hoc Political Committee of the General Assembly, A/AC.61/SR.13, 12 November 1952, ibid., 225–226; Document 7: General Assembly resolution: The question of race conflict in South Africa resulting from the policies of apartheid of the Government of the Union of South Africa, A/Res/616 A (VII), 5 December 1952, ibid., 227; Document 8: General Assembly resolution: The question of race conflict in South Africa resulting from the policies of apartheid of the Government of the Union of South Africa, A/Res/616 B (VII), 5 December 1952, ibid., 228; Document 9: Report of the United Nations Commission on the Racial Situation in the Union of South Africa, A/2505 and Add.1, 1953, ibid., 228–231; The Question of Race Conflict in South Africa Resulting from the Policies of *Apartheid* of the Government of the Union of South Africa: Report of the United

But it would be a "long night's journey into day."[3] South West Africa's initial descent into imperial bondage at the hands of Wilhelmine Germany had been horrific. Genocide, even before the international community knew exactly what to call it, stalked the land. The killing fields of the Kalahari exposed the lie of the "white man's burden" and served, instead, as a grim reminder of the reality of colonialism. Eighty percent of the Hereros and half of the Berg-Damaras and Namas lay dead at the hands of the Kaiser's imperial army.[4] For the West, and particularly for President Woodrow Wilson, South West Africa became the blood-drenched symbol of why, after the First World War, the colonial world also had to be made anew. Despite all of the secret clauses in all of the secret treaties finally revealed at Versailles, Wilson insisted that there would be no annexation of enemy territory nor would colonies be treated "as spoils of war." Instead, through the newly created League of Nations mandate system, there would be, for the first time in history, enforceable international accountability for the treatment of indigenous people.[5] In fact, those former German colonies were to be the hope of that new world, where the League's mandate system was "to ensure that never again would the

Nations Commission on the Racial Situation in the Union of South Africa, December 8, 1954, A/AC.76/L.22, Box A7, File "Africa: South Africa, press releases, 1950–55," *Papers of the NAACP*; U Thant to Robert McNamara, July 29, 1970, File "1740251: South Africa – General – United Nations/Bank Policy – Correspondence," *Papers of the World Bank*, World Bank Archives, Washington, DC (hereafter *Papers of the World Bank*); Ryan M. Irwin, "Apartheid on Trial: South West Africa and the International Court of Justice, 1960–1966," *International History Review*, 32, no. 4, (December 2010), 619–642; Irwin, *Gordian Knot: Apartheid and the Unmaking of the Liberal World Order* (New York: Oxford University Press, 2012), 17–99; Piero Gleijeses, "A Test of Wills: Jimmy Carter, South Africa, and the Independence of Namibia," *Diplomatic History*, 34, no. 5 (November 2010), 853–891; Ronald F. Dreyer, *Namibia and Southern Africa: Regional Dynamics of Decolonization, 1945–1990* (London; New York: Kegan Paul International, 1993); Carol Anderson, "International Conscience, the Cold War, and Apartheid: The NAACP's Alliance with the Reverend Michael Scott for South West Africa's Liberation, 1946-1952," *Journal of World History* 19, no. 3 (September 2008): 297–326.
3 *Long Night's Journey Into Day*, prod. and dir. by Deborah Hoffman and Frances Reid, California Newsreel, 2001. DVD, 94 min.
4 Jeremy Silvester and Jan-Bart Gewald, eds., *Words Cannot be Found: German Colonial Rule in Namibia, An Annotated Reprint of the 1918 Blue Book* (Boston: Brill, 2003), 62; Isabel V. Hull, "Military Culture and the Production of 'Final Solutions' in the Colonies: The Example of Wilhelminian Germany," in *The Specter of Genocide: Mass Murder in Historical Perspective*, eds. Robert Gellately and Ben Kiernan (New York: Cambridge University Press, 2003), 141–162.
5 Manela, *The Wilsonian Moment*; Gay J. McDougall, "International Law, Human Rights, and Namibian Independence," *Human Rights Quarterly*, 8, no. 3 (August 1986), 444–445; L. Adele Jinadu, "South West Africa: A Study in the 'Sacred Trust' Thesis," *African Studies Review*, 14, no. 3 (December 1971), 372–373.

African people be made to suffer from the misrule that they had had to endure under Germany."[6]

That steely "never again," however, had collapsed beneath the weight of the power politics that had engulfed the peace conference at Versailles in 1919. Tired and weary from the haggling, overly persuaded by South African troops already firmly ensconced in the region, and ignoring the patent disconnect between South Africa's racially oppressive domestic laws and the egalitarian "spirit of the mandate," which called for significant material improvement in the lives of the indigenous people, the Allies delivered the former German colony of South West Africa into the hands of South Africa.[7] This nation, as the Allies all well knew, was proud of both its overtly white supremacist foundation and its ruthless ability to "restrict the power and privileges of the African majority to such an extent that the preservation of white minority rule would be absolutely assured."[8]

Even while helping craft the guidelines of the new system, the leader of South Africa's delegation in Paris, Jan Christian Smuts, a man whom one British official described as "very determined and ruthless," made clear that the League's expectations for treating South West Africa and its people as "a sacred trust of civilization" were unrealistic and inapplicable.[9] Smuts declared that "the German colonies in … Africa are inhabited by barbarians who not only can not possibly govern themselves, but to whom it would be impracticable to apply any idea of political self-determination in the European sense."[10]

This ominous beginning for the mandate system evolved into decades of terror. Shortly after South West Africa fell into its hands, Pretoria unleashed an aerial bombing attack on the Namas for refusing to pay a dog tax, stripped nearly all arable land from the remaining Hereros, then transferred those property rights to thousands of German and Afrikaner immigrants, and, ultimately, pushed the Africans into Native reserves that

---

[6] Michael Scott, Phanuel Kozonguizi, and Samuel Nujoma, "The Commonwealth, the United Nations, and South West Africa," n.d., ca. 1961, Box 86, File "S.W. Africa, 1952–54, 1961," *Papers of Michael Scott*, Rhodes House, Bodleian Library, University of Oxford, UK (hereafter *Scott Papers*).

[7] Jinadu, "South West Africa," 374.

[8] George M. Frederickson, *White Supremacy: A Comparative Study in American and South African History* (New York: Oxford University Press, 1981), 240–241.

[9] Peter Henshaw, "South African Territorial Expansion and the International Reaction to South African Racial Policies, 1939 to 1948," *South African Historical Journal*, 50 (May 2004), 67.

[10] Jinadu, "South West Africa," 377.

had very little water and no means of sustaining any quality of life for inhabitants.[11]

A generation later, however, with the fight against Nazi Germany, South Africa's white supremacist defiance ran headlong into an equally powerful countervailing international force embodied in the *hopes* of the Atlantic and UN Charters.[12] Those charters of the early 1940s spoke of freedom; racial, religious, ethnic, and gender equality; human rights; and self-determination. They spoke of the promise of peace in a world ripped apart by Aryan supremacy. South West Africa, then "one of the most unrestrainedly exploited" colonies in the world, thus, became the battlefield for the ideas of international accountability, racial equality, and human rights against the unrelenting power of national sovereignty and white supremacy.[13]

South Africa, in the NAACP's estimation, was "notoriously one of the most vicious governments on earth."[14] This was, Du Bois noted, a government "where 2,000,000 white folk ... openly in their established government, hold 8,000,000 black natives in a subordination unequaled elsewhere in the world."[15] Clearly, Du Bois contended, South Africa was not part of the "civilized world."[16] It was a nation that had done everything in its power to retard the growth, development, and quality of life for Africans in "the sacred trust" of South West Africa. The NAACP had insisted at the founding conference that the United Nations have the power to sanction and remove colonies from the control of just such countries, which held the "sacred trust of civilization" in their grasp

---

[11] For South Africa's actions in South West Africa, see "Southwest Africans Appeal to the United Nations: Record of Interviews and Petitions with Certain Southwest African Tribesmen, Brought to the United Nations by the Reverend Michael G. Scott," July 20, 1947, FO 961/6; Jinadu, "South West Africa," 373–378; McDougall, "International Law," 445–446.

[12] "Dr. Anson Phelps Stokes on Africa and the Atlantic Charter," press release, January 29, 1944, Box 37, File "3," *Phelps-Stokes Collection*; The Committee on Africa, the War, and Peace Aims, *The Atlantic Charter and Africa from an American Standpoint* (New York: Federal Council of Churches in Christ, 1942), 54–58; Elizabeth Borgwardt, *A New Deal for the World: America's Vision for Human Rights* (Cambridge, MA: Harvard University Press, 2005), 14–86, 142–193; Anderson, *Eyes Off the Prize*, 8–57; A. W. Brian Simpson, *Human Rights and the End of Empire: Britain and the Genesis of the European Convention* (New York: Oxford University Press, 2001, reprint 2004), 157–220.

[13] Mandate Trust (by Michael Scott), n.d., ca. 1972, Box 4, File "Mandate Trust," *Scott Papers*.

[14] Attachment to W. A. Hunton from Rayford Logan, October 10, 1944, Box 4, File "Diaries: Personal, 1943–44," *Logan Papers*.

[15] Du Bois, *Color and Democracy*, 10.

[16] W. E. B. Du Bois to Editor of P.M., July 8, 1947, Reel 60, *Du Bois*.

but would "not keep their commitments in the colonies or ... make such commitments."[17]

The UN that emerged from San Francisco, however, did not quite have that power – at least not explicitly. As had been true under the League mandate system, the UN still had individual nations, such as Britain, France, Belgium, the United States, and South Africa, administer the colonies once controlled by Germany and the Ottoman Empire (from the First World War) and Japan and Italy (from the Second World War), and, as before, these colonies would remain international territories. Unlike the League, however, the UN, through the Trusteeship Council, would sponsor visits to the trust territories to ensure the inhabitants' progress toward self-governance.

For the NAACP, that was not enough. Self-governance was not independence. Rather, it appeared to be an attempt to pigeonhole the quest for freedom into some international purgatory of not-quite-a-colony-but-not-really-a-state-either. Equally troubling was that while the other colonial powers were, at least, placing their mandates in the UN's trusteeship system, South African Prime Minister Smuts announced before the end of the war in the Pacific that "at some future date the Union will ask and demand the annexation of the former German territories in Southwest Africa." Walter White heard those rumblings and exploded. This was a "sinister and dangerous ... device identical to the American pattern of calling Negroes in Mississippi citizens and then denying them all the privileges of citizenship."[18] Annexation would have removed hundreds of thousands of indigenous people from the protection of the international community, placed their lives behind the impregnable wall of South Africa's national sovereignty, and left them with absolutely no place to appeal for redress – not even the right to petition provided by the mandate system.

In fact, the South Africans made their proposal at the very first meeting of the UN General Assembly in 1946. Smuts and his team had few "illusions" about the difficulty of this task – of turning an international territory, where 90 percent of the population was African, into the fifth province of a racially oppressive state, and doing so with the sanction of

[17] Resolution Passed by the Board of Directors of the National Association for the Advancement of Colored People, March 12, 1945, Box A197, File "Colonial Conference, 1945," *Papers of the NAACP*.

[18] South African Delegation: South West Africa Mandate, June 22, 1945, DO 35/1937; Walter White to the Board, May 9, 1945, Box A639, File "United Nations: UNCIO, General, 1945, March-May 10," *Papers of the NAACP*.

an international body that was born out of the ashes of Germany's Aryan supremacy, Italy's mustard gas attacks on Ethiopia, and Japan's Rape of Nanjing.[19] But the South Africans believed that the time to strike was before the new international system gelled, and they hoped to smooth the way by relying on Smuts's inordinate prestige in the West as a dynamic leader, "who, by wisdom, craft, and sheer personality has guided his country through one internal and two world wars."[20] Smuts also played on his ability to "bully and blackmail" his Commonwealth ally, Great Britain, into supporting the effort.[21] Getting London on board was, initially, no easy feat. Indeed, the Colonial Office was violently opposed to the idea of annexation because of the trouble that would inevitably erupt in Britain's African colonies once it became known that the British, who had been working diligently on re-crafting their image as a human rights standard bearer in the colonial realm, had actually supported such a reactionary, regressive move. This was, after all, *the* South Africa whose embrace of white supremacy was infamous throughout the continent, and, in truth, throughout the world. To support South Africa's bid, the Colonial Office concluded, would be "unwise" beyond words.[22]

Yet, while the Colonial Office envisioned the eruption of uprisings throughout Africa and Asia, the Dominion Office worried mightily that South Africa would bolt right out of the Commonwealth if Britain did not openly support the quest for annexation. The Dominion Office was aided in this assessment by Smuts's threat that public opinion in South Africa (meaning, of course, white public opinion) would be so incensed at Britain's betrayal that his constituency would demand that South Africa leave the Commonwealth immediately. Smuts also coyly sang his own

---

[19] Ethiopian Ministry of Justice, *Documents on Italian War Crimes Submitted to the United Nations War Crimes Commission by the Imperial Ethiopian Government*, Vol. 1 (Addis Ababa: Ethiopian Ministry of Justice, 1949); Gavan McCormack, "Reflections on Modern Japanese History in the Context of the Concept of Genocide," in *The Specter of Genocide: Mass Murder in Historical Perspective*, 265–286.

[20] Dean Acheson to Harry Truman, memo, November 27, 1946, *Papers of Harry S. Truman: Personal Secretary's File*, Box 148, File "Subject File: Africa," Harry S. Truman Presidential Library, Independence, MO (hereafter *Truman:PSF*).

[21] Henshaw, "South African Territorial Expansion," 71.

[22] "Briton Outlines Human Rights Plan for U.N.," *New York Herald Tribune*, January 26, 1947, enclosed in Walter White to Ralph Bunche, February 3, 1947, Box A161, File "Bunche, Ralph, General, 1949," *Papers of the NAACP*; Simpson, *Human Rights and the End of Empire*; Memorandum by the Secretary of State for the Colonies to the Cabinet on Trusteeship, April 16, 1946, DO 35/1937; Minute of Sir J. Stephenson, February 2, 1946, DO 35/1933; Extract from the Conclusions of the 15th Meeting of the Cabinet on Monday, 13th May, 1946, at 11 a.m., May 17, 1946, DO 35/1937.

version of *après moi, le déluge*. The prime minister reported that he had
secessionist political foes back home, in the National Party, who were
Nazi-loving, English-hating, unrelenting Afrikaner white supremacists
who would not hesitate during the next election to use Britain's refusal
as a weapon to demolish him and seize the reins of power. Moreover,
Smuts continued, the British protectorates of Bechuanaland, Swaziland,
and Basutoland, which were surrounded by South Africa, would become
extremely vulnerable to that same enraged public opinion. Smuts would,
under the circumstances, have no choice but to absorb into the South
African state those enclaves of British colonialism.[23]

The bullying and blackmailing worked. Although the British Cabinet
and many ministers voiced concerns about the annexation of Africans into
a state whose "native policies" were absolutely odious, the government
was even more concerned about the ramifications on the Commonwealth
and the empire of the apocalyptic scenario that Smuts had so ruthlessly
outlined.[24]

While the British were handled, the UN was not. Part of the problem,
of course, was the South Africans themselves. Their overtly white supremacist ideology won them no converts. For example, during his testimony
before the Fourth Committee of the UN General Assembly, which handled
trusteeship issues, the South African delegate explained that the demand
to annex South West Africa was not about exploitation at all because
the territory was an "inhospitable," "sparsely populated region" whose
"natural resources are not very great."[25] There was simply no exploitation here, he suggested, because there was nothing to exploit.[26] Then, in
an attempt to assuage fears about the Union's "native policy," the South
African representative, seemingly unaware that his statement, in fact,
pointed to the absolute necessity for international accountability, "hoped

---

[23] Henshaw, "South African Territorial Expansion," 71–72; Extract from the Conclusions
of the 15th Meeting of the Cabinet on Monday, 13th May, 1946, at 11 a.m., May 17,
1946, DO 35/1937.
[24] Memorandum by the Secretary of State for Dominion Affairs to the Cabinet on
Trusteeship, April 15, 1946, DO 35/ 1937; To Field Marshal Smuts from Dominion
Office, May 14, 1946, DO 35/1937.
[25] Extract from U.N. Journal No. 8, January 18, 1946, DO 35/ 1933.
[26] Namibia actually is rich in natural resources. Its primary minerals are diamonds, copper,
uranium, gold, silver, lead, tin, lithium, cadmium, tungsten, and zinc. There are suspected
deposits of oil, coal, and iron ore. CIA, *World Fact Book*. https://www.cia.gov/library/
publications/the-world-factbook/fields/2111.html. Accessed May 3, 2013. Diamonds
were first discovered in what was then South West Africa in 1908. Also see Namibia,
Ministry of Mines and Ministry, "Geological Survey of Namibia." http://www.mme.gov.
na/gsn/diamond.htm. Accessed May 3, 2013.

that other countries would recognise that 'native' policies in South-West Africa had been different" than in the Union of South Africa, "and that black Africans had been treated more favourably" in the mandate than they had been in the nation itself.[27] Then, as if not understanding that the world's norms were headed in one direction, while South Africa was, at best, stuck in the seventeenth century, he waxed eloquently about the time when "South African pioneers" came to Africa, found the "whole continent ... steeped in primordial savagery," and "were engaged in a struggle against barbarism which had no parallel anywhere in the world." Finally he lamented that unlike the "other countries" where "the aborigines disappeared before the advance of civilization," in "Africa, they have multiplied exceedingly and maintained their identity."[28]

This testimony, laced with the unspoken racism of the "civilizing mission" and the barely disguised amazement that Africans, despite all that had been done to them, just refused to die and leave the continent to the white settler communities, greatly worsened the UN's concern about what South Africa's policies suggested for the Hereros, Namas, Berg-Damaras, and even the Ovambos, who had, up to this point, been pretty much left alone by the South African regime.[29] The Liberian delegate made it abundantly clear that he was neither persuaded nor duped by South Africa's story. It just "seemed strange," he remarked, "that while German South-West Africa was said to be barren, depopulated and unproductive, and thousands of pounds sterling had to be spent continuously therein, [that] the Union of South Africa still found this territory suitable and usable for incorporation into the Union."[30]

But it was the Indian government that really put South Africa's racial policies before the world, and in doing so, solidly linked the Union's domestic policies with what was happening and could happen in South West Africa. Outraged that Indians in South Africa had been subjected to racially discriminatory laws, including newly minted legislation denying those of Asian descent the right to own property or land, the Indian government took its case to the UN, charging that Pretoria had violated the

---

[27] Henshaw, "South African Territorial Expansion," 70.
[28] Extract from U.N. Journal, No. 8, January 18, 1946, DO 35/1933.
[29] The Ovambos were in the upper most northern region of South West Africa, on land not yet coveted by white settlers.
[30] Desirability of the Territorial Integration in, and the Annexation to, the Union of South Africa of the Mandated Territory of South West Africa, SD/A/C.4/2B, September 24, 1946, Box 29, File "SD/A/C.4/1–9," Lot File 82D211, Record Group 59: General Records of the Department of State, National Archives II, College Park, MD (hereafter RG 59).

human rights of Indians in South Africa. The Union's retort was damaging and revealing as the representatives explained that Indians were not singled out for mistreatment because "the basis of the governmental order in South Africa was racial discrimination" – that is, everyone "of color" was mistreated. As the British delegates watched this debacle unfold, they could only report back to the Foreign Office that any hope Smuts had of riding into South West Africa on the wave of his prestige as the Grand Old Statesman evaporated the moment the "Treatment of Indians in South Africa" came before the UN General Assembly. The "predominant factors operating against South Africa," the British remarked, "were … the antagonism generated by the Indian complaint and the 'rising tide of nationalism amongst the races of Asia' which rallied the 'coloured states' against a government 'avowing a policy of white supremacy.'"[31]

It was not, however, just the "coloured states" that refused to rally to the cause of annexation. This had become more than a referendum on the issue of the perpetuation and spread of white supremacy; it was also a challenge to UN authority, international law, and the question of the sanctity of international accountability. Thus, although South Africa was a valued ally, the United States flatly refused to back the Union's attempt to annex an international mandate. Although it "regretted" that Pretoria would not place the territory under the UN trusteeship system and believed that South Africa could not be forced to do so, under no circumstances would the United States support annexation. Still, that refusal was "couched in more conciliatory language than in the case of some of the other proposals" because, as John Foster Dulles, future secretary of state explained, the "United States, in view of its own record" of racial discrimination, was "not justified in adopting a holier-than-thou attitude toward the Union of South Africa."[32]

---

[31] Henshaw, "South African Territorial Expansion," 73; Implications of General Assembly Discussion Concerning Chapter XI of the Charter, December 18, 1946, Box 19, File "NSGT: Factors, etc. (Folder 2 of 2)," Lot File 60D257, *RG 59.*

[32] Mr. Thompson to Mr. Green, memo, November 13, 1946, Box 21, File "Trusteeship–Background Memos, etc.," Lot File 55D323, *RG 59*; Mr. Ross to Mr. Hiss, memo, October 25, 1946, Box 21, File "Trusteeship–Background Memos, etc.," Lot File 55D323, *RG 59*; Desirability of the Territorial Integration in, and the Annexation to, the Union of South Africa of the Mandated Territory of South West Africa, SD/A/C.4/2B, September 24, 1946, Box 29, File "SD/A/C.4/1–9," Lot File 82D211, *RG 59*; John Foster Dulles to Paul Robeson, December 7, 1946, Reel 1, *Papers of W. Alphaeus Hunton*, Schomburg Center for Research in Black Culture, microfilm (hereafter *Hunton Papers*). For U.S. relations with South Africa, see Thomas Borstelmann, *Apartheid's Reluctant Uncle: The United States and Southern Africa in the Early Cold War* (New York: Oxford University Press, 1993).

With Britain blackmailed into compliance and the Americans' "hands … completely tied" by their own Jim Crow democracy, it was Prime Minister Peter Fraser of New Zealand who decided to lead the charge of the Western nations against South Africa. After listening to that stunning testimony about "primordial savagery" and the need to continue on the path of the civilizing mission through annexation, Fraser declared that he was completely "at a loss regarding the position of the Union of South Africa." It just made no sense, particularly for a fellow member of the British Commonwealth, to come to the conclusions that Smuts and his government had so erroneously reached. "[N]o Power had the moral right to misappropriate territories placed under its control after the war of 1914–18," he asserted. That fundamental concept did not change because of the Second World War. If anything, at San Francisco, the "Committee on trusteeship, of which [Fraser] had been Chairman, had attempted to avoid all ambiguity … territories under mandate did not belong to the mandatory Powers, and [the] latter had no right to attach such territories to their sovereign territory." The New Zealander made a painful but pointed analogy: unless South Africa wanted to be thought of in the same vein as Nazi Germany, it would do well to remember that the "[m]embers of the United Nations should not violate the sanctity of international agreements as the enemy had done."[33]

The UN's stinging rebuke came as a shock to South Africa. The "dominant white minority," the State Department reported, "was poorly prepared for the blast of criticism from UN delegates." Their disbelief was deepened by the "overwhelming vote against annexation in the General Assembly – 37 to 0, with 9 abstaining," which "disturbed those who had expected that opposition would be limited mainly to colored and Communist delegates." Smuts now had to find some way to salvage his reputation, quell the negative reaction in the UN, and quiet the critics at home who believed that he had unnecessarily exposed South Africa to international censure. He worried aloud that "we are not out of the woods" yet, but he had devised a "subterfuge" whereby the Union would "submit reports to the UN … 'until the coast is clear.'"[34]

[33] Mr. Ross to Mr. Hiss, memo, October 25, 1946, Box 21, File "Trusteeship–Background Memos, etc.," Lot File 55D323, RG 59; Third Meeting of the UN General Assembly, Fourth Committee, A/C.4/4, January 22, 1946, *Papers of the United Nations*, Arthur Diamond Law Library, Columbia University, New York, NY (hereafter *UN*).
[34] "South African Attitudes and Policy Regarding South West Africa, November 1946–June 1947," July 17, 1947, OIR Report No. 4416, Reel 10, *OSS/Africa*.

At the next UN meeting, South Africa, appearing to be in compliance, actually provided an annual update on the conditions in South West Africa. Smuts's government also included a detailed analysis of a referendum held in the territory on the question of annexation. That referendum, the South Africans proudly claimed, showed that the "European community as a whole, which numbers about 31,000, is in favour of incorporation" and, even more significant, that "85 per cent of the natives have asked for incorporation."[35] Smuts then asserted that these results, which may have come as a surprise to some of the Union's critics, were to be expected because South Africa had "carried out the provisions of its mandate conscientiously." The Union had ensured that Africans had "the most fertile and richest arable soil in the country." The government had spent "millions of Pounds ... in purchasing additional land for the expanding needs of the Native population" and, equally important, had provided quality educational facilities from elementary schools to universities for Africans. Moreover, he beamed with pride, the cost had been borne by the "small European population, who are the main taxpayers" and who "carry willingly a very heavy financial burden in ... providing for the advance and uplift of the Native population."[36] In short, Africans were safe and prosperous under the benevolent, racialized sovereignty of South Africa. The UN could rest easy in approving the annexation.

An urgent appeal to NAACP board member Channing Tobias strongly suggested otherwise. Douglas Buchanan of the Anti-Slavery and Aborigines Protective Society, housed in Cape Town, called on Tobias "to do anything to help at this late hour."[37] Tobias's commitment to Africans was unquestioned and well known. He was a longtime official of the Colored YMCA (Young Men's Christian Association) and spent the bulk

[35] Meeting held in Sir Eric Machtig's Room with Mr. Forsyth, May 10, 1946, DO 35/1937.

[36] Submission by the Government of the Union of South Africa on the Territorial Integration in and the Annexation to the Union of South Africa of the Mandated Territory of South West Africa, SD/A/C.4/10, September 25, 1946, Box 29, File "SD/A/C.4/10–41," *RG 59*; Text of Speech by Field Marshal Smuts in Committee 4, United Nations press release PM/81, November 13, 1946, Box 44, File "2," *Bunche Papers*; Text of Speech by Sir Maharaj Singh Before Committee 4 (Trusteeship), United Nations press release PM/94, November 14, 1946, Box 44, File "Fourth Committee Working Papers, Speeches by Delegates, November 1946," *Bunche Papers*; Verbatim Record of the Seventh Meeting of Sub-Committee 1 of the Fourth Committee of the First Session of the General Assembly, November 23, 1946, Box 44, File "Sub-Committee One, 7th Meeting, November 1946," *Bunche Papers*.

[37] Douglas Buchanan to Channing Tobias, October 30, 1946, Box 54, File "13," *Phelps-Stokes Collection*.

of his career leading the Y's educational activities in Southern and West Africa. Tobias was also the director of the Phelps-Stokes Fund, which had not only built and run a university for Africans in South Africa but also provided thousands of dollars in tuition support for Africans to study in the United States. Buchanan knew he had an ally. In fact, a multinational network was coalescing to stop South Africa. Buchanan was the legal advisor for Bamangwato Regent Chief Tshekedi Khama, who was based in Bechuanaland. Tshekedi had originally tried to get the British to intervene but had been rebuffed. Then Tshekedi went to the American embassy in South Africa and explained why the United States had to stop the annexation – still, nothing. Buchanan, his lawyer, then reached out to Channing Tobias of the NAACP for help and explained that the Union was engaging in subterfuge, legerdemain, and outright lying to annex South West Africa. The referendum was rigged, Buchanan insisted. "The figures given by Field Marshall Smuts" to the UN "appear to include not only every male adult native but every woman, boy, girl, and babe in arms – if the issue were not so tragic it would be … an instance of political baby snatching and cradle robbing!" Moreover, Buchanan continued, it was highly improbable that the economic, educational, and land conditions for Africans were as pleasant as Smuts suggested. In fact, in all probability they were even worse than imagined because South Africa had flatly refused to allow any observers into South West Africa to see for themselves. The UN, Buchanan concluded, must be prodded to stop the annexation and live up to its own obligations toward this international mandate.[38]

His pleas resonated with an organization that was already primed for action on the issue. Earlier in the year, Du Bois had voiced his outrage at the "utterly indefensible position of the Union of South Africa in its treatment of Africans and Indians and its demand for absorption of Southwest Africa."[39] Pretoria's actions were all the more glaring because the UN was gearing up to craft, in some form or another, an international bill

---

[38] South Africa (B.B.S.) to D.O., telegram, May 6, 1946, DO 35/1937; Tshekedi Khama, Molefi S. Molefi, et al. to the High Commissioner for Basutoland, Bechuanaland Protectorate and Swaziland, April 29, 1946, Part Two, Enclosure Number 1 to Despatch Number 979, Reel 1, *Confidential British Africa*; Part Four, Enclosure Number 1 to Despatch Number 979 from the Legation at Pretoria, July 9, 1946, *Confidential British Africa*; T. Holcomb to the Secretary of State, 9 July 1946, *Confidential British Africa*; Douglas Buchanan to Channing Tobias, October 30, 1946, Box 54, File "13," *Phelps-Stokes Collection*.

[39] W. E. B. Du Bois to Rayford Logan, July 24, 1946, Box 181–3, Folder "14," *Logan-MSRC*.

of human rights. Walter White had, therefore, already called on Ralph Bunche, as well, for insight. The UN director of trusteeship's previous fieldwork in Cape Town led him to find "many parallels between the status and problems of these ['non-European'] South African groups and those of the American Negro." As a result, Bunche advised White not only to scrutinize the negotiations and drafting concerning the "special problems of human rights with relation to minority groups" but also to pay close attention to issues of enforcement and "the application of a bill of human rights" in "consideration of the special position of colonial peoples."[40] Thus, as White planned to breach the citadel of the UN lobbying for this combined program for human rights and anticolonialism, Du Bois instructed the secretary to "especially arraign South Africa for the way in which she has treated the mandates; ... for lack of education or of social uplift; and for [its] deliberate policy to ignore and degrade black people." Pulling from data that A. B. Xuma, a college classmate of Roy Wilkins, provided, Du Bois emphasized that in the Union 8 million Africans – that would be 83 percent of the population – were crammed into 17 percent of the land, that "there are no government schools for African children," that "95 percent of the African prison population is imprisoned for discriminatory regulations used against Africans only.... In short, Africans are underfed, underpaid, under-educated, underemployed, poorly housed and poorly and indirectly represented." The UN, Du Bois continued, "ought to recognize that no nation with the background of South Africa has any right to control black people."[41]

White could not have agreed more. To the powerful and influential – Eleanor Roosevelt, Sumner Welles, Senator Arthur Vandenberg – he openly praised the way that his friend and ally, Mme. Vijaya Pandit,

---

[40] Roger Baldwin et al. to Eleanor Roosevelt, May 2, 1946, Box A355, File "Leagues: American Association for the United Nations, Inc., 1945–46," *Papers of the NAACP*; Anne Winslow to Walter White, May 9, 1946, Box A355, File "Leagues: American Association for the United Nations, Inc., 1945–46," *Papers of the NAACP*; Final Report: Submitted by R. J. Bunche Fellow of the Social Science Research Council, 1936–1938, October 13, 1938, Box 23, File "South Africa Trips, 1937: Reports," *Bunche Papers*; Ralph Bunche to Walter White, May 13, 1946, Reel 59, *Du Bois*.

[41] Mr. White to Dr. Du Bois, memo, March 23, 1946, Box A634, File "United Nations: General, 1945–46," *Papers of the NAACP*; Roy Wilkins to Walter White, memo, November 4, 1946, Box A4, File "Africa: General, 1946," *Papers of the NAACP*; Roy Wilkins to A. B. Xuma, December 14, 1946, Box A4, File "Africa: General, 1946," *Papers of the NAACP*; W. E. B. Du Bois and L. D. Reddick, invitation to meet A. B. Xuma, November 21, 1946, Reel 4, *Xuma*; W. E. B. Du Bois to Editor of the *New York Times*, November 1, 1946, Reel 59, *Du Bois*; W. E. B. Du Bois to Mr. White, memo, March 26, 1946, Box A634, File "United Nations: General, 1945–46," *Papers of the NAACP*.

the Indian delegate to the Fourth Committee, had challenged the Union at every turn and refused to let South Africa sugarcoat its racially discriminatory policies.[42] White even boasted to Jawaharlal Nehru – India's prime minister, holder of an NAACP lifetime membership, and Mme. Pandit's brother – that "your sister has made so distinguished a record here in her fight against annexation of Southwest Africa ... as well as for racial equality" that the prime minister was going to have to work doubly hard to match her achievements.[43] With the full support of Tobias, White further led this effort to inform and shape public opinion with a widely syndicated column that went, at a minimum, to newspapers in New York, Chicago, and Detroit. He immediately addressed the sovereignty and resource issues:

If Southwest Africa with its vast mineral and agricultural resources were placed under a United Nations trusteeship arrangement, some likelihood of raising the standards of living and hope of the most cruelly exploited human beings on earth could be expected. But if the Union of South Africa is permitted to annex Southwest Africa, its natives would thereby become "citizens" of the Union and the United Nations could do precisely nothing about their fate.[44]

Then, White confronted the way South Africa, with its notorious domestic "native policy," had executed its international obligations as a mandatory power:

There are no government schools ... only ... mission schools for native and colored children.... Illiteracy, poverty and disease are rife throughout the colony among the native population. Over one hundred million dollars has been invested in the mines of Southwest Africa which are operated by what is virtually slave labor. Such has been the mandateship by the Union of South Africa which now demands the right to annex the colony which would mean that even the meager protection which the League of Nations attempted ... would be no longer required. This is what Smuts's demand on the United Nations means.[45]

---

[42] Walter White to Eleanor Roosevelt, January 31, 1947, Box A465, File "Madame Vijaya Lakshmi Pandit,1946–47," *Papers of the NAACP*; Arthur H. Vandenberg to Walter White, January 10, 1947, ibid.; Sumner Welles to Walter White, January 14, 1947, ibid.

[43] Walter White to Jawaharlal Nehru, December 9, 1946, ibid.

[44] From H. L. Oram, Inc. for Release to Subscribing Newspapers on Thursday November 21, November 21, 1946, Box A76, File "General Correspondence and Draft of Articles, 1946," *Papers of the NAACP*.

[45] From H. L. Oram, Inc. for Release to Subscribing Newspapers on Thursday November 21, November 21, 1946, Box A76, File "General Correspondence and Draft of Articles, 1946," *Papers of the NAACP*; Walter White, "Smuts' Threat Denounced: Peril to UN Seen," *Detroit Free Press*, November 24, 1946.

However, there was the nagging question of proof. South Africa's refusal to allow any independent organization to enter the territory, and its successful diplomatic efforts to quash an American recommendation for a UN-sponsored team to investigate, meant that the only real "facts" available were those that the Union had already presented: tall tales of high-quality educational facilities, abundant fertile land on which the African population lived, and the benevolence of Pretoria's intentions because of the supposed lack of exploitable natural resources. In the absence of hard data, South Africa confidently charged that all of its opponents were trading in speculation and rumors in a vile attempt to slander the Union's good name.[46]

The paramount chief of the Hereros, Frederick Mahareru, who was exiled in Bechuanaland, also demanded proof. He absolutely needed it. Mahareru had heard about the Union's plans, and he had to find a way to stop Smuts's regime, which he saw as just as ruthless, brutal, and genocidal as the Germans. It was then that he learned about a man – an Anglican priest; an Englishman who had lived in South Africa for years and whom the Union government disdained for stubbornly refusing to act like "he is a European."[47]

This Anglican minister had openly defied both South Africa's residential segregation laws and his Bishop by moving into Tobruk, an African shantytown just outside the city that gold built, Johannesburg. His movement into Tobruk was a protest against a "vast 'urban area'" with "between thirty and forty thousand people living as outlaws" and "hundreds of little streets and houses made of sackcloth and old tin cans. Without water or lighting, without any police or drains or latrines, with enormous mounds of accumulating rubbish comprising the entrails of oxen, human excreta and decaying garbage" and predatory, unchecked gang violence masquerading as the rule of law. All of this brought about, the priest asserted, because of a policy of exploitation of Africans "as raw materials ... to be discarded as useless refuse" in exchange for yet other black bodies that

---

[46] Alger Hiss to American Embassy, Pretoria, September 18, 1946, Box 21, File "Trusteeship–Background Memos, etc.," Lot File 55D323, *RG* 59; Implications of General Assembly Discussion Concerning Chapter XI of the Charter, December 18, 1946, Box 19, File "NSGT: Factors, etc, (Folder 2 of 2)," Lot File 60D257, *RG* 59; Text of Speech by Field Marshal Smuts in Committee 4, United Nations press release PM/81, November 13, 1946, Box 44, File "2," *Bunche Papers*.

[47] "Natives Championed is Warned," *News Chronicle*, March 4, 1949, Box 30, File "Quotations of South Africa/Statements on South Africa, 1947–49," *Scott Papers*.

FIGURE 2.1. The desolation in a shantytown on the outskirts of Johannesburg. This type of grinding poverty, in the midst of wealth, drove the Reverend Michael Scott and the NAACP to the UN to fight against apartheid South Africa.
Source: Hulton-Deutsch Collection/Corbis. Courtesy of Corbis, Stock Photo ID # HU038572.

would have nothing but squalor, disease, and destruction to show for the slave wages that a white man was willing to pay.[48] (See Figure 2.1)

---

[48] "I originally went to the squatters' camp known as Tobruk ..." n.d., Box 88, No File, *Scott Papers*.

That analysis and that decision to move into a place that the South African government had deemed absolutely unfit for European life had quickly landed the Anglican priest in prison. When he emerged from his prison cell, the man, the Reverend Guthrie Michael Scott, had earned among Africans a legendary reputation as a fearless freedom fighter who not only firmly believed in but also would actually stand up for racial equality. While his close friends and colleagues worried that he was drawn to "the lure of self-sacrifice which is the ill peculiar to saints" and that he had a "martyr complex" – they feared that he was "a quixotic figure battling against hopeless windmills" and "too much absorbed in suffering and the problems of the world, as if he took them on as a personal burden" – for those whom he was fighting to liberate, "Michael Scott was a household word in every African family." He was a man who "made no peace with oppression but rather committed himself totally to fight to end it!"[49]

Even two decades later, James Forman, a seasoned U.S. civil rights warrior who had abandoned nonviolence and passive resistance to embrace Black Power and armed liberation, found himself in awe of the Reverend Michael Scott. Initially, Forman thought of Scott as "an old time pacifist," "an old time preacher who still believes that religion is helpful." But then, as Scott began to speak about the destruction that colonialism and white supremacy had wreaked on this earth, including the "Myth of God as picker of chosen people," Forman leaned back and acknowledged that Martin Luther King Jr. "might have studied under him" because it was clear to even the most hardened that Scott "can preach! Halleluah [sic]!" And, even as Forman's cynicism pushed through with "Preach brother, preach in vain," the Black Power advocate nonetheless recognized that "the moralist is good, for he rekindles a spark of humanity."[50] That is what

[49] David Astor to Michael [Scott], n.d., ca. October 1950, Box 15, File "Correspondence: Astor, etc from GWS Papers at King Henry's Rd," *Scott Papers*; Father George Norton to Leon and Freda, February 12, 1949, Box 40, File "Letters from Fletcher, Troup, etc.," *Scott Papers*; Winifred Courtney to Ruth First, March 25, 1962, File "2/17/3," *Ruth First Papers*, Institute of Commonwealth Studies, University of London, London, England (hereafter *First Papers*); Mary Benson diary entry, n.d., Box 78, File "Mary Benson [A.Y. Only]," *Scott Papers*; Father George Norton to Leon and Freda [Troup], March 3, 1949, Box 40, File "Letters from Fletcher, Troup, etc.," *Scott Papers*; Michael Scott, *A Time to Speak* (London: Faber and Faber, 1958), 195; Episcopal Churchmen for South Africa to Mary Benson, telegram, November 15, 1983, Box 78, File "Mary Benson [A.Y. Only]," *Scott Papers*; In Memory of Michael Scott, September 29, 1983, Box 78, File "Mary Benson [A.Y. Only]," *Scott Papers*.

[50] Letter from James Forman, Second Letter, n.d., Box 7, File "9," *Baker Papers*.

Scott brought to the fight for South West Africa – humanity, fearlessness, and an unshakable faith in his God's commitment to equality.

After Scott met with Chief Frederick Mahareru and grasped the enormity and significance of the mission – go where the chief could not, discern the truth firsthand, and then tell the world – the Anglican priest "travelled a thousand miles by train and lorry [truck] and on foot, seeking out the Hereros and other peoples of South-West Africa."[51] Once he arrived, the stories he heard from Chief Hosea Kutako and the other Hereros, Namas, and Berg-Damaras, and the data he uncovered in the library at Windhoek, only confirmed the "serious misgivings" Scott already had about the annexation scheme.[52]

He learned, for example, how the so-called referendum was conducted. The South African representative, Major Hahn, explained to the people that this referendum was only to ensure that there would be no significant changes brought about by the Second World War. Then, when pressed, he assured the Africans that this meant that South West Africa would remain under the protection of the king of England, the very same England that had a favorable reputation among Africans because it had beaten the much-hated Germans, twice. Hahn failed to mention, of course, that this referendum actually signaled a seismic transformation that would obliterate an international mandate so that South West Africa could become the fifth province of South Africa. He also failed to mention that, although South Africa was a member of the Commonwealth, there had been serious rumblings about ending its status as a British Dominion and becoming an independent republic. If that happened, as it eventually did, there would be no formal tie to England or to the king. As Hahn spoke, Chief Hosea Kutako of the Hereros smelled treachery in the air and refused to sign off or endorse any referendum until the representatives of Great Britain, the United States, and France – the major powers that had crafted the mandate system in the first place – were there to witness and attest to the veracity of the referendum's language, meaning, and enforcement. Not surprisingly, the Hereros were immediately excluded from the process so that Major Hahn could find more pliable Africans to include in the tally of support.[53]

[51] John MacLaurin, *United Nations and Power Politics* (London: Allen & Unwin, 1951), 377.

[52] Scott, *A Time to Speak*, 219.

[53] Southwest Africans Appeal to the United Nations: Record of Interviews and Petitions with Certain Southwest African Tribesmen brought to the United Nations by the Reverend Michael G. Scott, July 20, 1947, FO 961/6; F. Tjerije to Honoured Chief F. S. Maherero,

Where he was going to find them was not quite clear because those who had come into contact with South African rule had learned, the hard way, the real meaning of white supremacy. One man, in fact, challenged Scott to ask "any of the Ovambos, in and out of Ovamboland, who have already worked amongst the [white] farmers in South-West Africa ... if they would like to join the Union and see what they will have to say." The treatment meted out to them was horrific. Like slaves, the "Ovambos are not allowed to leave on their own in search of employment. They are sold to the Public at from Eight to ten pounds each per year ... and many of them die in some way or another while they are here." The Africans' plea to Scott was wrenching. "We don't want to become the fifth-wheel of this donkey wagon of the Union of South Africa.... please do your utmost for South-West Africa to either become a British Protectorate or that we be handed over to America for Protection."[54] The Berg-Damaras were equally determined to be rid of South Africa and equally aware of what annexation really meant: "We do not want to be under the rule of the Boers. We do not want to join the Union Government." We "have suffered since the day the Union Government became the Trustee of South West Africa," and we are "still suffering."[55]

That suffering was tied directly to the issue of land. From his stint in Tobruk, Scott had fully grasped the destructive impact of the Union's policy of expropriating African land, allocating it to white settlers, and then pushing the indigenous people into areas where life could not be sustained. The effect was a soul-crushing "cheap migratory labour" system in which "thousands of Africans ... impelled, many of them, by land shortages, hunger and unemployment" and the subsequent "break-up of the social organisation of ... their whole tribal way of life" were forced to make the great "trek to the towns for the white man's work and wages."[56] The same pattern was emerging, on a smaller but equally vicious scale, in South West Africa. As South African forces drove the Hereros away from the land where their cattle could graze and funneled the people into dry,

February 20, 1946, Box 147, File "1," *Papers of the Africa Bureau*, Rhodes House, Bodleian Library, University of Oxford, UK (hereafter *Papers of the Africa Bureau*).

[54] J. A. Montgomery to Michael Scott, October 27, 1947, FO 961/6.

[55] Minutes of the Meeting between Mr. Allen (Additional Native Commissioner), Mr. Neser (Chief Native Commissioner), Major Hahn, and the Berg-Damaras – Native Inhabitants of South West Africa, August 1947, FO 961/6.

[56] "I originally went to the squatters' camp known as Tobruk ...," n.d., Box 88, No File, *Scott Papers*; the Rev. Michael Scott, "African View," *Observer*, August 20, 1950, KV2/2052/ Records of the Security Services on Suspected Communists: G. Michael Scott, January 1, 1942–December 31, 1950, National Archives, Kew Gardens, UK.

FIGURE 2.2. Herero Chief Hosea Kutako, leery of South Africa's plans to annex his homeland, aligned with Michael Scott to try to stop Pretoria's plans.
Source: Bettman/Corbis. Courtesy of Corbis, Stock Photo ID# 42–50589438.

hard, unforgiving terrain, the Hereros knew the fate Pretoria had planned for them. They exclaimed in agony, "[W]e know the best and worst parts of the whole country.... We are human beings. And we do not want to be changed into wild beasts. Only wild beasts can live without water."[57]

Therefore, during the final fact-finding meeting between Scott and the Africans, which took place at the hallowed ground in South West Africa where the Germans began the genocidal campaign that destroyed 80 percent of his people, Chief Hosea prayed, "O Lord, help us who roam about. Help us who have been placed in Africa and have no dwelling place of our own. Give us back a dwelling place" (see Figure 2.2). At that, Scott recalled, "my soul was sick with shame at the thought of the treatment which this proud people have received at the hands of the white

[57] Scott, *A Time to Speak*, 231–232.

race."[58] Now was the time to make it right, and he vowed to take their cause all the way to the UN.

The obstacles to fulfilling that promise were enormous. First, Scott was a poor, "ascetic," "shabbily dressed" man who, because of his dispute with the Anglican Church over the treatment of Africans, did not even have a parish to call his home.[59] Despite his constant pleas to the bishop to confront head on the desecration of Africans, the church demurred, saying that that was a political, not a religious, matter. The bishop "abhorred the idea of the Church as a reform society," and he "had little sympathy and perhaps a limited understanding of the kind of inspiration that burnt in ... Michael Scott." Thus, like the infamous scene in *Ben Hur*, the bishop warned that he did not want Scott "tying the Church or the Diocese" to the priest's "charriot [sic] wheels." Scott confided that he "felt betrayed by [his] own church." Similarly, most of Scott's liberal friends, who privately expressed distress at the racial conditions in South Africa, emphasized the importance of doing very little or, even better, nothing at all, so as not to antagonize the Union government.[60] That astonishing advice led Scott to rail the "trouble with moderates ... they are only moderately opposed to evil."[61] Scott recalled:

I felt that it was a very serious matter indeed, to go outside one's own nation in an appeal to the nations of the world. But the situation in South Africa was

[58] Ibid., 226.

[59] "A Stormy Petrel," March 5, 1949, DO 35/3811; Michael Scott to Lord Bishop of Johannesburg, October 12, 1946, Box 88, File "Correspondence with South African Clergy, 1947–1948," *Scott Papers*; Michael Scott to the Archdeacon, August 5, 1948, Box 88, File "Correspondence with South African Clergy, 1947–1948," *Scott Papers*.

[60] Michael Scott to Lord Bishop [Archbishop of Cape Town], October 17, 1943, Box 88, File "Correspondence with Clergy, Bishop," *Scott Papers*; Michael Scott to Lord Bishop [Archbishop of Cape Town], October 25, 1943, Box 88, File "Correspondence with Clergy, Bishop," *Scott Papers*; Michael Scott to Lord Bishop of Johannesburg, October 12, 1946, Box 88, File "Correspondence with South African Clergy, 1947–48," *Scott Papers*; Piers McGrandle, *Trevor Huddleston: Turbulent Priest*, foreword by Desmond Tutu; afterword by Rowan Williams (London: Continuum Press, 2004), 64; Anne Yates, review of *Apartheid and the Archbishop: The Life and Times of Geoffrey Clayton*, by Alan Paton, in *Journal of Southern African Studies*, 2, no. 2 (April 1976), 244; Father George Norton to Leon and Freda [Troup], March 3, 1949, Box 40, File "Letters from Fletcher, Troup, etc." *Scott Papers*; Jack [the Vicarage Hampton-in-Arden, Warwickshire, UK] to Ethel [Scott's aunt], April 24, 1947, Box 88, File "Correspondence with South African Clergy, 1947–48," *Scott Papers*; Mary Benson to Mr. Tomlinson, December 5, 1951, Box 15, File "David Astor Box, Correspondence with and Papers Connected with Rev. Michael Scott and S.W. Africa, 1950–1961," *Scott Papers*.

[61] Anthony Sampson, "Campaign of a Crusading Clergyman," review of *A Time to Speak* in *Saturday Review*, September 27, 1958, Box 15, File "Correspondence: David Astor, 1950s and 1960s," *Scott Papers*.

deteriorating.... In the past year alone there had been the repercussions from the Indian passive resistance movement in Natal, the Tobruk Shantytown and Bethal [a slave labor farm], and it seemed now as if the only hope for the African people was an appeal to the conscience of the world.[62]

Nonetheless, to travel to the UN meeting in New York and stay weeks and maybe months on end for the duration of that meeting would require resources well beyond his humble means.

Second, although they had asked him to be their voice to the UN, the Hereros were not a recognized state, and by design, only states could have direct access to that international body. Du Bois, in fact, had gleaned this glaring defect during the planning stages of the proposed United Nations. The NAACP co-founder was "'depressed' to realize how consistently the Allies had disfranchised the 750 million people who lived in the colonial world.... According to the proposals ... only states could join the UN, bring a complaint before the Security Council, or appeal to the International Court of Justice. Colonies had no rights." In fact, the UN could only "consider complaints filed by member states."[63] So, exactly where did a renegade cleric carrying a petition to the United Nations from Africans who lived in an area that was not a traditional colony, certainly not a nation, definitely not a UN trust territory, and, at best, a hotly contested and disputed international mandate created by an organization that had ceased to exist fit?

Third, U.S. immigration laws made it exceedingly hard for someone like Scott to ever set foot on American soil. During the 1930s, the Anglican priest spent many years working with the only organized force in South Africa that was as opposed to racial discrimination as he was, the Communist Party.[64] However, like so many who had been attracted early on to the party, Scott was quickly disillusioned by the Nazi-Soviet Non-Aggression Pact. In addition, he complained that the efforts to break the stranglehold of racism and inequality in South Africa, already a monumental battle, "were made even more ineffectual by the intriguing methods and cynicism of the Communists toward everything that was

---

[62] Scott, *A Time to Speak*, 232–233; "What the 'Searchlight' on South Africa's Native Policy Did Not See: Just an Aspect of Native Labour Conditions in South Africa," July 7, 1947, Box 54, File "13," *Phelps-Stokes Collection*; Alan Wieder, *Ruth First and Joe Slovo in the War Against Apartheid* (New York: Monthly Review Press, 2013), 14–15, 57.

[63] Anderson, *Eyes Off the Prize*, 38.

[64] Anthony Sampson, "Campaign of a Crusading Clergyman," review of *A Time to Speak*, in *Saturday Review*, September 27, 1958, Box 15, File "Correspondence: David Astor, 1950s and 1960s," *Scott Papers*.

not controlled by them or harnessed to their own cause."[65] Moreover, he "deplor[ed] their materialism and contempt for the [Christian] beliefs and values which [he] cherished."[66] After going through an agonizing period in which he weighed the implications of his deep, profound belief in equality against the painful reality that at this point in his life he could find no viable, organized structure to help him wage that struggle, Scott refused to accept the half a loaf that the communists offered and distanced himself. Nevertheless, although he was never a card-carrying member of the party, he was close enough. And in Cold War America, close enough was more than enough, particularly if the Departments of Justice or State ever found out.

Every turn – the lack of funding, the legal limbo of Scott's and the Hereros' status, and the inability to even enter the United States because of the minister's communist past – seemed to be a roadblock to stop him from telling the UN the truth about the conditions in South West Africa. But there had emerged on the international scene a confluence of forces that changed the rules of engagement.

First, the reality of Adolf Hitler's regime still resonated deeply in a war-stricken world. The Nuremberg trials were underway and the world had come to recognize that an ideology of unabashed white supremacy, particularly harnessed to an industrialized power, could only result in a staggering, unbearable loss of lives and resources. As a result, most of the colonial powers could no longer comfortably use the language of "the white man's burden" or the "civilizing mission" to justify their continuing presence in Asia, Africa, the Caribbean, and Central and South America and had to turn, instead, to the more neutral concepts of "modernization" and "development."[67] White supremacy was no longer the language of progress, as it had been during the rise of Jim Crow or the advent of

---

[65] McGrandle, *Trevor Huddleston*, 64.

[66] Michael Scott to Miss Levine, September 12, 1960, Box 43, File "GMS U. S. Visa," *Scott Papers*; Scott, *A Time to Speak*, 67.

[67] Frederick Cooper, *Africa since 1940: The Past of the Present (New Approaches to African History)*, ed. Martin Klein (New York: Cambridge University Press, 2002), 36–37; Nick Cullather, "Modernization Theory," in *Explaining the History of American Foreign Relations*, 2nd ed., eds. Michael J. Hogan and Thomas G. Paterson (New York: Cambridge University Press, 2004); David C. Engerman, Nils Gilman, Mark H. Haefele, and Michael E. Latham, eds., *Staging Growth: Modernization, Development and the Cold War* (Amherst: University of Massachusetts Press 2003); Michael E. Latham, *Modernization as Ideology: American Social Science and "Nation Building" in the Kennedy Era* (Chapel Hill : University of North Carolina Press, 2000); Nils Gilman, *Mandarins of the Future: Modernization Theory in Cold War America* (Baltimore, MD: Johns Hopkins University Press, 2003).

the "scramble for Africa"; it was now the murderous symbol of atavism, barbarism, and Auschwitz.

The second major change that created the political space for the challenge to South Africa was the unrelenting pressure coming from Africa and Asia for the dissolution of the European empires. As many historians have noted, the Second World War and Japan's initial stunning victories were crucial in destroying colonialism. Japan had proved that Europeans could be beaten decisively by a nation of color and, in doing so, exposed the lie of both European invincibility and "the doctrine of white supremacy," which was "[a]t the heart of the colonial system."[68] Further, a curtain had been lifted to reveal the obvious dependence of the Europeans on the colonies – and not the other way around. The ferocity of the Second World War made clear that without the support of millions of Africans and Asians in the empires and without their continents' resources, the European powers simply did not have the minerals or the manpower to defeat the Axis. At a certain level, the Europeans knew this brutal truth. And without question, colonial people knew it.[69] Therefore, as historian Frederick Cooper noted, after the Second World War "political debts fell due."[70]

One of the biggest debts to be paid was India's independence. As the former "Jewel in the Crown" of the vaunted British Empire, its freedom was a powerful symbol of the promise of a new world order. Moreover, Indian leaders were not content with their country's independence alone; they viewed themselves as the vanguard of colonial liberation movements throughout the world and had articulated a definition of colonial policy that carried the major themes voiced by the Hereros, Berg-Damaras, Namas, and the Reverend Michael Scott of oppression, exploitation, and the quest for freedom.[71]

---

[68] Mason Sears, *Years of High Purpose: From Trusteeship to Nationhood*, preface by Henry Cabot Lodge and introduction by Julius Nyerere (Washington, DC: University Press of America, 1980), 22.

[69] See, for example, F. N. Nkrumah et al. to Franklin Roosevelt, n.d., ca. 1943, Box A3, File "Africa: General, 1941–43," *Papers of the NAACP*; Clayton, *The Wars of French Decolonization*, 3–5.

[70] Cooper, *Africa since 1940*, 26.

[71] Richard M. Fontera, "Anti-Colonialism as a Basic Indian Foreign Policy," *Western Political Quarterly*, 13, no. 2 (June 1960), 423, 424; Manu Bhagavan, *The Peacemakers: India and the Quest for One World* (New Delhi: HarperCollins India, 2012); Swadesh Rana, "The Changing Indian Diplomacy at the United Nations," *International Organization*, 24, no. 1 (Winter 1970), 48–53; "Address of Her Excellency, the Ambassador of India, Mme. Vijaya Lakshmi Pandit, in presentation of the 34th Spingarn Medal to Dr. Ralph

India's desire to champion the worldwide anticolonial fight, and its place at the United Nations, became the third powerful force creating political room for the challenge to South Africa. One U.S. diplomat noted that the "impetus which the U.N. gave to African self-government can hardly be exaggerated.... It provided a worldwide forum from which the case against colonialism could be vigorously championed."[72] India's uncompromising leadership, about which the British fumed, the South Africans railed against, and the Americans resented for its lack of anti-communism, moderation, and gradualism, welded the Afro-Asian-Arab delegates in the General Assembly into a powerful voting bloc, attracted the support of the Soviets and Eastern Europeans, and consistently split the Latin Americans between the anticolonial and colonial powers. Thus, although the United States and the Western Europeans had spent an inordinate amount of time carefully managing the structure of the various committees – Human Rights, Trusteeship, and so forth – to maintain Western control, the challenge from India and its allies pushed the fight and the power out of those committees and directly into the General Assembly, where the anticolonial forces could marshal the votes to change the terms of the debate and international norms.[73]

The UN's central importance to the Hereros' cause, however, was not only because of Indian leadership but also because the organization itself refused to replicate the weakness of the League of Nations. South Africa's insistence on unilaterally absorbing international territory into its sovereign boundaries was an early and direct challenge to the UN's authority and went right to the core of the organization's determination to not be the League of Nations *part deux*. Although the UN Charter, as both Du Bois and White had pointed out, was rife with political compromises designed to keep the international organization from breaching the barrier of national sovereignty and particularly addressing the question of colonialism, legal maneuvering, and persistent, consistent, unrelenting debate with diplomatic, eloquent niceties veiling steely determination, allowed the United Nations to keep chipping away at the barrier of European "domestic jurisdiction" until colonialism, in toto – and not just

---

J. Bunche," July 17, 1949, Box A466, File "Pandit, Vijaya, Lakshmi, 1948–51," *Papers of the NAACP*.

[72] Sears, *Years of High Purpose*, 6–7.

[73] Mr. Sandifer to All Political Officers, memo, October 8, 1947, Box 15, File "Committee 4: Trusteeship," Entry 3039E, *RG 59*.

the former mandates – came within the purview of the organization.[74] Scott realized this when he admonished, "Most people are making the mistake of discounting the Trusteeship Council as a band of well-meaning talkers."[75] Indeed, he reproached his bishop for denigrating the UN as a "talk shop" by asking pointedly, "[W]hat other forum is there for those Africans to have appealed to and what other organised expression of the need for peace is there?"[76]

The final force that galvanized the assault of the voiceless against South African racial oppression was the mobilization of a phalanx of nongovernmental organizations (NGOs) eager and able to take on the fight for South West Africa. While historians have focused their attention on the left-wing and Communist contributions to this anticolonial movement, there was a larger, more powerful, better funded community of progressive, noncommunist organizations that vigorously waded into the struggle.[77] And although these progressive NGOs had their own separate emphases – religious, domestic, international – they had a shared core value system that created a natural synergy just waiting for the right opportunity and issue to emerge in the fight for a more just, humane, and democratic world. Therefore, the Reverend Michael Scott's affiliation with the International League for the Rights of Man (ILRM), American Friends Service Committee (the Quakers), Africa Bureau (which he would come to lead), India League, Anti-Slavery and Aboriginal Protection Society, American Committee on Africa (ACOA), and African National Congress seemed quite logical, as did the support of the NAACP.[78]

Indeed, Scott's intensity resonated in a particular way with Walter White. Although in many respects the two men could not have been more different – whereas Scott was shy and humble, White was vain and

---

74 Winifred Courtney to Ruth First, March 25, 1962, File "2/17/3," *First Papers*; Goronwy John Jones, *United Nations and the Domestic Jurisdiction of States* (Cardiff: University of Wales Press, 1979), 66–67, 71–77, 114–115; R. M. Douglas, Michael D. Callahan, and Elizabeth Bishop, eds., *Imperialism on Trial: International Oversight of Colonial Rule in Historical Perspective* (Lanham, MD: Lexington Books, 2006).

75 Michael Scott to Both [Leon and Freda Troup], February 6, 1948, Box A8, File "Southwest Africa, 1947–51," *Papers of the NAACP*.

76 Michael Scott to Archdeacon, August 5, 1948, Box 88, File "Correspondence with South African Clergy, 1947–1948," *Scott Papers*.

77 See, for example, Nesbitt, *Race for Sanctions*, which discounts the African American political center in the early years of this struggle.

78 See, for example, A. B. Xuma "A Mandate that Failed: South West Africa, Excerpts from the Twenty-nine Page Memorandum Forwarded to [UN] Secretary General Trygve Lie," n.d., Box 88, File "Union of South Africa," *Papers of Charles Fahy*, Franklin Roosevelt Presidential Library, Hyde Park, NY (hereafter *Fahy Papers*).

egotistical; whereas Scott lived a monastically simple life, White spent
lavishly as if it was his birthright; whereas Scott had suffered mightily
from childhood sexual abuse that made him unable to emotionally and
physically commit to his soul mate, White carried on a torrid, explosive
extramarital affair with a white, South African-born, thrice- and still-
married woman – when it came to the struggle for equality, both men
were resourceful, resilient, and virtually fearless.[79] White, during one of
his first assignments with the NAACP, left New York, donned his "pass-
ing" persona in rural Tennessee, and risked his very life to uncover how
a "relatively prosperous" black man, Jim McIlherron, could be burned at
the stake while being tortured with hot irons that, as witnesses described,
pulled off flesh with each thrust and sizzle. White exposed this well-
attended, advertised killing and then investigated the next lynching, and
the next, and the next, and the next.[80] Scott's determination to stand up
to the Union government, go to South West Africa, uncover the truth
about the actual conditions in the mandate, and publicize that spectacle
of oppression before the world spoke to White's and the NAACP's crusading spirit.

   That combination of forces – repulsion against white supremacy,
mounting pressure for decolonization, the emergence of India as an anticolonial champion, the UNs' determination to be stronger and more
effective than the League, and an array of well-organized, mobilized non-
governmental organizations – began to move the stumbling blocks out
of the Reverend Michael Scott's way. The Hereros themselves solved the
issue of funding by selling some of their cattle to finance Scott's journey
to New York.

   His visa problem remained, however. But help came from many directions. The NAACP, American Civil Liberties Union (ACLU), ILRM, and

---

[79] Mary Benson diary entry, December 5, 1953, Box 78, File "Mary Benson [A.Y. Only],"
   Scott Papers; Mary Benson diary entry, December 1953, Box 78, File "Mary Benson [A.Y.
   Only]," *Scott Papers*; fragment, December 1953, Box 78, File "Mary Benson [A.Y. Only],"
   Scott Papers; Mary Benson diary entry, January 1955, Box 78, File "Mary Benson [A.Y.
   Only]," *Scott Papers*; Mary Benson diary entry, January 30, 1955, Box 78, File "Mary
   Benson [A.Y. Only]," *Scott Papers*; Mary Benson diary entry, March 24, 1955, Box 78,
   File "Mary Benson [A.Y. Only]," *Scott Papers*; Michael Scott's handwritten notes, 1975,
   Box 78, File "Mary Benson [A.Y. Only]," *Scott Papers*; Anne Yates and Lewis Chester,
   The Troublemaker: A Biography of the Reverend Michael Scott (London: Aurum, 2006),
   173, 293; Poppy Cannon to Darling [Walter White], February 24, 1949, Box 8, File
   "White, Poppy Cannon (1949)," *White Papers*; Janken, *White*, 170, 171, 329–331, 335;
   Anderson, *Eyes Off the Prize*, 157–159.
[80] Walter F. White, "The Burning of Jim McIlherron: An N.A.A.C.P. Investigation," *Crisis*,
   16, no. 1 (May 1918), 16–20; Dyja, *Walter White*, 45–66.

other organizations, including the left-wing Council on African Affairs and the Communist-dominated Civil Rights Congress, now peppered the State Department with demands for an explanation as to why Scott's request for a visa had been denied. They insisted that he be allowed into the country. As Walter White explained, "[I]t is imperative that [the] opinion of natives on proposed annexation of Southwest Africa to Union of South Africa be heard and respected."[81] Scott applied additional pressure by writing directly to the secretary general of the UN, asking that office to inquire with the State Department about the status of his visa request.[82] As word began to spread that an Anglican minister had been ensnared in the tangle of U.S. anticommunist immigration laws, the press sensed a story and the State Department smelled a public relations nightmare.

Compounding the difficulties for officials at Foggy Bottom was that a government the United States was trying to woo, India, had now become involved. The Indian embassy had actually requested the State Department "to use its good offices to grant a visa to the Reverend Scott."[83] To continue to deny the man a visa, everyone recognized, would "put the United States in a bad light."[84] Yet although the initial analyses coming out of the American embassy in Johannesburg did not cast Scott as a Communist, the reports added that he was a "troublemaker" and that "through his support of the rise of the Heoroes [sic] in South West Africa, he had, not surprisingly, been associating with Communists. Therefore, under a strict interpretation of the Immigration Laws, he had been barred."[85] The State Department now scrambled to get him unbarred; however, that authority lay in the attorney general's hands, and because of Scott's "Communist" and "troublemaker" labels, the Department of Justice had placed the minister on the banned list.[86] "There will always be people like Scott," the

---

[81] Roger N. Baldwin to George J. Haering, telegram, October 3, 1947, Box 43, File "GMS U.S. Visa," *Scott Papers*; Max Yergen [sic] to Director, Visa Division Office of Controls, telegram, October 3, 1947, ibid.; Joseph J. Cadden to Secretary of State George C. Marshall, October 3, 1947, ibid.; Ira Latimer to George C. Marshall, October 6, 1947, ibid. ; Walter White to George C. Marshall, October 4, 1947, ibid.

[82] Fourth Committee: Communication Received by the Secretary-General Relating to South West Africa, A/C.4/97, September 26, 1947, Box 15, File "Committee 4–Future Status of South West Africa," Entry 3039E, *RG* 59.

[83] Thomas F. Power to Mr. Marcy, memo, September 27, 1947, Box 20, File "GA, 2d Session: Visa Cases of Courtade, Scott, et al.," Entry 3039E, *RG* 59.

[84] Mr. Sandifer to Mr. Bohlen, memo, n.d., ca., September 27, 1947, ibid.

[85] [Thomas F. Power], Memorandum on the Visa Application of Rev. Michael Scott, September 27, 1947, ibid.

[86] Mr. Green to Mr. Power, memo, September 30, 1947, ibid.

Justice Department derisively noted, "who feel they have business with the United Nations but in fact have no official connection."[87]

But as the India League, of which the NAACP was a member, searched to find a way around the State and Justice Departments and as Scott approached the Indian high commissioner in London for help, the need for an "official connection" proved to be the Achilles heel in the immigration laws. Because of Scott's "reputation as a fighter for Indian rights in South Africa," Sir Maharaj Singh, who led the Indian delegation at the UN, "appointed Scott as his personal adviser." This gave the heretical minister the "official connection" he needed to enter the United States and plead the Hereros' case before the Fourth Committee – almost.[88] When the visa was finally issued, "[I]t turned out to be the kind ... granted to communists attending the UN sessions. Scott was confined to Manhattan and Long Island, he was forbidden to make public appearances or even to preach by invitation."[89]

Despite this setback and although delayed by the visa wars, Scott was savvy enough to have previously sent to the secretary general's office a copy of the documentation he had amassed in South West Africa. The Indian delegation took over from there, ensuring that Scott's data about the *actual* status of land ownership, educational opportunities, available medical facilities, and employment opportunities circulated among the delegates on the UN's Fourth Committee. "This in itself gave the Herero case a head start."[90] By the time Scott arrived in New York, those data and the indigenous peoples' petitions had been accepted as official UN documents, which gave their statements of betrayal a level of power and cachet that cannot be overestimated. Having the petitions now marked as UN documents A/C.4/95 and A/C.4/96 "transform[ed] the contents of an ordinary piece of paper ... into something 'real,' something to be taken seriously."[91]

Here, at last, was the proof. Here were the data, not extrapolated or assumed from the misery that Africans suffered in the Union but directly from the inhabitants of South West Africa themselves. This is just what

[87] Yates and Lewis, *The Troublemaker*, 83.
[88] Ibid., 83–84.
[89] MacLaurin, *United Nations and Power Politics*, 381.
[90] Ibid., 84.
[91] Roger S. Clark, "The International League for Human Rights and South West Africa 1947–1957: The Human Rights NGO as Catalyst in the International Legal Process," *Human Rights Quarterly*, 3, no. 4 (November 1981), 109–110; Communication Received by the Secretary General Relating to South West Africa, A/C.4/95, September 26, 1947, Box 15, File "Committee 4–Future Status of South West Africa," Entry 3039E, *RG 59*.

the anticolonialist faction on the Fourth Committee had been trying
desperately to get its hands on.[92] Scott's petitions became the basis for the
UN's direct questioning of the annual report that South Africa had submitted previously – the very one in which Smuts glowed about the conditions in South West Africa and basked in the ringing endorsement of the
referendum. Scott, using his credentials as Singh's aide, began lobbying the
other delegates, explaining with insight and clarity the brutal discrepan-
cies between Smuts's report of a racial utopia and his findings of Dante's
Inferno. "Suddenly and mysteriously committee members from obscure
Latin American countries began asking cogent and penetrating questions
about a remote part of Africa wholly beyond their acquaintance."[93]

Armed with actual facts, the UN now confidently leveled fifty questions
at the South Africans. For example, Smuts spoke of the millions spent on
Africans annually, but could the government explain why 90 percent of
the population only received 10 percent of the budget? Or, for that matter, why 90 percent of the population was crammed into 42 percent of the
land, the least arable land? Again, in very pointed diplomatic language,
the UN sought clarification on the vaunted educational system Smuts
described, which now actually appeared to be for whites only. The only
schools available to Africans were those financed, run, and owned by
missionaries. Similarly the UN aimed questions at the lack of medical
facilities, the fact that there were no Africans whatsoever in governmental positions, and the fact that there appeared to be a skewed criminal
justice system that turned land-starved vagrancy into a criminal offense
punishable by debt slavery on white-owned farms. Just where, exactly,
was the Union government and its obligation for social, economic, and
political progress in all of this?[94]

The South African delegation, once confident and swaggering, was
now stumbling and on the defensive. And just when the Australian foreign
minister tried to intervene to salvage something of Smuts's reputation,
Mme. Vijaya Pandit rose, took Smuts's prestige, and threw it aside. "The
issues with which we are faced," she sternly reminded her colleagues,

---

[92] Fragment, n.d., ca., November 1946, Box 44, File "Fourth Committee Working Papers,
Statements by the Chairman, Nov. 1946," *Bunche Papers.*

[93] Yates and Lewis, *The Troublemaker,* 85.

[94] Report of the Government of the Union of South Africa on the Administration of South
West Africa for the Year 1946: T. C. Resolution of 12 December 1947, December 12,
1947, Box 30, File "SD/A/C.4/42–94," Lot File 82D211, *RG 59*; Report of the Trusteeship
Council Covering Its Second and Third Sessions: 29 April 1947–5 August 1948, Box
27, File "Background Book: Committee 4–Trusteeship (Folder 1 of 2)," Entry 3039E,
RG 59.

"far transcend personal considerations.... We should not forget the fate of hundreds of thousands of Africans in South West Africa who ... look to the Assembly for safeguarding their interests." To even think that one man's prestige weighed more on the scales of justice than the lives of more than 350,000 human beings was the ultimate in Western hubris.[95]

Clearly, India had the advantage and was not letting up. Prime Minister Nehru was unapologetic. India's goal was to "be recognised as the biggest moral power in the civilized world."[96] The prime minister thus explained, "This policy that we have so far pursued ... of standing up for the weak and the oppressed in various continents, is not a policy which is to the liking of the great powers who directly or indirectly share in their exploitation."[97] And that dislike suited the prime minister just fine. Later that year, Nehru told the UN General Assembly, "Let no one think that any nation, any community can misbehave. The United Nations is here to prevent any fear or hurt."[98] Particularly, it was understood, a UN that had India playing a starring role as the conscience of the globe.

But South Africa was not done yet, either. The Boer Republic regained its balance and fired back that the submission of the report was a courtesy, not an obligation, and the UN's intemperate response was an unacceptable and unwarranted treatment of a valued member of the international community. Clearly, the South Africans continued, the United Nations did not have the maturity, ability, or diplomacy to handle this matter appropriately. As a result, there would be no more reports. And, no, South Africa would not place the territory under the UN trusteeship system. At best, the Union would continue to administer it in the "spirit of the mandate."[99]

[95] Council on African Affairs, "U.N. Assembly Reverses Committee Decision on S.W. Africa and Colonies – Viewpoint of Colonial Powers Prevails," press release, November 4, 1947, Reel 2, *Hunton Papers.*

[96] Ramachandra Guha, *India after Gandhi: The History of the World's Largest Democracy* (New York: Ecco, 2007), 186–187.

[97] "We Lead Ourselves," speech before the Constituent Assembly (Legislative), March 8, 1948, in Jawaharlal Nehru, *India's Foreign Policy: Selected Speeches, September 1946-April 1961* (Delhi: Publications Division, Ministry of Information and Broadcasting, Government of India, 1961), 30–31.

[98] Rana, "The Changing Indian Diplomacy at the United Nations," 49.

[99] Fourth Committee, Question of South West Africa: Statement by the Delegation of the Union of South Africa, Regarding Documents A/C.4/95 and A/C.4/96, October 13, 1947, A/C.4/118, Box 15, File "Committee 4–Future Status of South West Africa," Entry 3039E, *RG 59*; Verbatim Record of the One Hundred and Forty-First Meeting of the General Assembly, A/PV 141, September 24, 1948, Box A635, File "United Nations: Geneva Conference, 1947–48," *Papers of the NAACP*; Deputy Permanent Secretary of the South African Delegation to the United Nations to the Secretary General of the United

The United States now tried to act as a buffer between South Africa and the UN. The U.S. delegation, walking a fine line between condoning and condemning, argued that "the question of South West Africa [was] one of great delicacy and difficulty," and, thus, it was important to recognize that South Africa, legally – maybe not morally, but legally – was well within its rights. The UN Charter did "not require a mandatory power against its will to place a mandated territory under trusteeship," and the fact that South Africa was the only nation to keep its mandate outside of the UN trusteeship system only and regrettably proved the point, in the State Department's opinion.[100]

The Fourth Committee, however, was in no mood for legalisms and temperate responses. It issued a stern resolution, watered down only by the full-throttle intervention of John Foster Dulles, that outlined South Africa's obligations as a mandatory power and the expectation that South West Africa would come under the trusteeship system without further delay. The State Department could only lament the yawning "gulf between world and South African opinion on the issues of trusteeship and domestic native policy." The department was equally concerned that the fireworks at the UN had "placed [Smuts's] government in an uncomfortable dilemma, particularly in view of the approaching general election" in South Africa.[101]

In fact, Smuts's difficulties at the UN became, just as predicted, a major part of the fodder that the National Party used to discredit him and his government.[102] Beating the drum of "protecting the white race," the Nationalists came to power like the four horsemen of the apocalypse. Future Minister of Finance Eric Louw said in words reminiscent of the party's hero, Adolf Hitler:

I wish to say tonight: White man, do not feel inferior. You come from the best blood in the world. Only when the nations of Europe allowed the Asiatic jews to

Nations, May 31, 1948, Box 27, File "Background Book: Committee 4–Trusteeship (Folder 2 of 2)," Entry 3039E, *RG 59*.

[100] Remarks by Francis B. Sayre, Alternate United States Delegate to the General Assembly, press release no. 291, October 30, 1947, Box 13, File "United Nations: Palestine and Southwest Africa," *Sayre Papers*; "United States Mission to the United Nations: South West Africa," October 27, 1947, US/A/712, Box 15, File "Committee 4, Future Status of South West Africa," *RG 59*.

[101] Future Status of South West Africa, SD/A/C.4/24, August 22, 1947, Box 29, File "SD/A/C.4/10–41," Lot File 82D211, *RG 59*; Mr. Green to Mr. Sandifer, memo, US/A/C.4/58, October 11, 1947, Box 15, File "Committee 4 Trusteeship," Entry 3039E, *RG 59*.

[102] Future Status of South West Africa, SD/A/C.4/24, August 22, 1947, Box 29, File "SD/A/C.4/10–41," Lot File 82D211, *RG 59*.

undermine their beliefs, ways of life, morals and culture, did the Europeans forfeit their leadership.... Let it never be said of the Grey Shirts, if the non-Europeans achieve a victory, that we have retreated as cowards. Let us rather die as heros of the European race and again lay the foundations for the future generations.[103]

Led by a minister of the Dutch Reformed Church, Daniel F. Malan, the Nationalists won the election in 1948 and brought to South Africa the policy of apartheid in which the "Afrikaner theorists ... applied the notion of a separate and God-given destiny for ... every nonwhite group to which it could assign a distinctive ethnic or tribal origin."[104] Apartheid, as public policy, translated into unvarnished, unapologetic, unrelenting white supremacy, without even the fig leaf that Smuts's regime had hung in front of it. One American diplomat's assessment was chilling. South Africa, he wrote, is not a

normal democratic community ... the Afrikaner (Boer) nationalists have ... already begun to create a police state. Furthermore, they are not a political party so much as the embodiment of resurgent anti-British Afrikanerdom. More than that, they are inspired by a religious belief in their racial superiority over the Africans. Put nationalism and religion together and add a universal fear of ultimately losing their racial identity in a sea of Africans and you have a party which is well nigh impossible to defeat by peaceful methods.[105]

Nonetheless, India circled back at the UN meeting in the fall of 1948 to expose what apartheid meant for the millions already trapped in its vise and for the 350,000 more that Pretoria was trying to annex. Ambassador Pandit launched a forceful argument that South Africa had no right to alter the status of an international territory and abrogate the rights of the inhabitants of that land. In addition, because this was international territory, the UN had the responsibility to send in a fact-finding team "to observe and report on the political, economic, social and educational conditions in the Territory."[106]

When the Fourth Committee voted against India's proposal and, instead, passed a watered-down version that expressed "regrets" that South Africa had refused to submit additional reports to the UN, Mme.

---

[103] Eric Louw as reported in the "Kruithoring," September 1947, Box 30, File "Quotations of South Africa/Statements on South Africa, 1947–49," *Scott Papers.*

[104] Frederickson, *White Supremacy,* 240.

[105] Mason Sears, first draft, n.d., Box 2, File "PMS Africa 1955 (Notes/Misc.)," *Papers of Mason Sears,* Massachusetts Historical Society, Boston, MA (hereafter *Sears Papers*).

[106] Trusteeship Questions, *Yearbook of the United Nations, 1948–1949,* 864–865, http://www.unmultimedia.org/searchers/yearbook/page.jsp?volume=1948-49&page=874&searchType=advanced. Accessed December 22, 2008.

Pandit described the resolution as a "complete surrender of principle." Even more infuriating, she was sure the U.S. delegation was behind it. The work that the Indians and Cubans in the UN had done to hold South Africa accountable had "lost by one vote due [to a] last minute bargain with Arab states and suppression of [the] Philippines."[107] But she planned to take this battle into the General Assembly and put up a "stiff fight." To do that she needed ammunition and called on the NAACP to give her "any material" that she could use in this slugfest.[108]

White responded to Ambassador Pandit's request immediately. In addition to sending his own analyses to her, he turned to Rayford Logan, who was the leading expert on mandates, for help. Logan promptly sent Ambassador Pandit a wealth of sordid data highlighting South Africa's "unconscionable" rule in South West Africa.[109]

During the debates in the General Assembly, Mme. Pandit went straight to the point. The resolution of "regrets" was "unsatisfactory," she insisted, because Malan's regime had taken steps to "bring the Territory to the verge of annexation" and had done so by trampling on the rights of the indigenous inhabitants of South West Africa. They had no voice. They had no opportunity for self-government. They had even been denied the "opportunity to present their views to the General Assembly or the Trusteeship Council." This was key "since a number of tribal leaders had protested the manner in which the referendum" that South Africa used to justify the annexation "had been held."[110] In her opinion, "the resolution almost seemed to condone an act which amounted to a violation of the Charter."[111] The South African delegate countered that his government would not "do anything in connexion with the Territory which might earn the ill-will of other nations." He urged the General Assembly to "keep the door open" – that is, trust the new South African regime to honor its international commitments instead of starting down a path that would create unnecessary animosity by putting undue pressure on the Nationalists. The UN, hoping that this was an indication of reasonableness, agreed to hold off on any visiting missions or demands for immediate reports because of

107 Vijaya Lakshmi Pandit to Walter White, telegram, November 21, 1948, Box A466, File "Pandit, Vijaya Lakshmi, 1948–51," *Papers of the NAACP.*
108 Ibid.
109 Walter White to Vijaya Lakshmi Pandit, November 23, 1948, ibid.; Rayford Logan to Walter White, November 26, 1948, ibid.; Rayford Logan to Vijaya Lakshmi Pandit, November 26, 1948, ibid.
110 *Yearbook of the United Nations,* 1948–49, 866.
111 Ibid.

the "assurance given by the representative of the Union of South Africa that the proposed new arrangement for closer association of South West Africa with the Union does not mean incorporation and will not mean absorption of the Territory by the Administering Authority."[112]

Despite all of those soothing "assurances," however, early in 1949, Malan's regime brazenly instituted the South West Africa Act, which, as the prime minister told the South African Parliament, would "knit South West Africa and the Union together in such a manner, knit them constitutionally in such a way that the countries will in the future be inseparably bound together."[113] This was, without question, an annexation in all but name. India would come to call it an "*Anschluss*, an invasion, a conquest."[114] It had to be done, Malan contended, because the UN was meddling in affairs in which it had absolutely no business. That meddling, he added, centered on the "improper motives" of "countries like India, Russia, and its satellites," which had actually used the Trusteeship Council to question why Africans "had no franchise, no eligibility for office and no representation on the Government." This interfering UN, Malan roared, "openly or by implication demanded full equality in all respects between all races and colours in South West Africa, including equal franchise, the removal of residential separation in urban areas, and the breaking up of Native reserves." Malan then scoffed, "Could anything more ridiculous ever be imagined?" Nonetheless, he concluded, this "was an indication to South Africa of what could be expected if South-West Africa was put under trusteeship ... South West Africa under such a council would be nothing but a festering sore in the body of South Africa."[115] (See Figure 2.3)

The virtual annexation of an international territory coupled with the advent of apartheid sent Scott racing to the British for help. In a meeting with the Secretary of State for Commonwealth Affairs, held under the auspices of the Anti-Slavery Society and several other organizations, the

[112] Ibid., 866, 867.
[113] "Speaking in the South African Parliament ...," February 16, 1949, Box 30, File "Quotations of South Africa/Statements on South Africa, 1947–49," *Scott Papers*.
[114] Provisional Verbatim Record, September 28, 1953, A/PV.448, CO 936/97.
[115] "Dr. Malan Resumes his Speech on SW Africa Amendment Bill, Juridical Grounds for Union's Refusal of U.N. Trusteeship," February 17, 1949, *Johannesburg Star*, Box 30, File "Quotations of South Africa/Statements on South Africa, 1947–49," *Scott Papers*; "South Africa and UNO: The Sort of Thing UNO Wants," Press Digest No. 50, December 13, 1951, *South African Press Digests, 1949–1972: South Africa, The Early Years of Apartheid* (Altair Publishing: Hebden Bridge, England, and New York, NY, 1994), Fiche 21 (hereafter *South African Press Digests*).

FIGURE 2.3. South African Prime Minister Daniel Malan was determined to annex South West Africa and bar the UN from having any access to or information about the troubling conditions in that international territory.
Source: New York World-Telegram & Sun Newspaper Photograph Collection. Courtesy of the Library of Congress, Prints and Photographs Division, LC-DIG-ds-04718.

Anglican minister pleaded with the British government to use whatever influence it had to compel the Union to place South West Africa, which was now in more jeopardy than ever, under a UN trusteeship. Scott's delegation warned that if "Britain continues to support the Union in her policy of annexation – which will result … in depriving the African inhabitants of land – she will be branded as having supported" a nation that violated "the paramountcy of international trusteeship." The British reply was cool, legalistic, and unresponsive: "[I]t would be quite wrong, and indeed … impossible, for the [Trusteeship] Council, of its own initiative, to attempt to concern itself with matters other than those arising directly from the affairs of territories already placed under Trusteeship." And, because South West Africa was not in that UN system, whatever legislation the Union passed, regardless of what anyone thought of it, was a matter of national sovereignty and, thus, well beyond the scope of the UN's authority. Meanwhile the internal consensus among British policy makers was that "no useful purpose would be served by our making any representations to the Union Government about South West Africa," and it would, "in fact, increase the influence of the hotheads among the Nationalists [sic] Party, make the Union more difficult to do business with and, in fact, drive the Union to further extremes of isolationism and defiance."[116]

A policy study by the U.S. State Department was also not sanguine about the possibilities of bringing South Africa in line. The virtual annexation of South West Africa and the "discontinuance of the annual report are means by which the Malan government hopes to insulate both the Union and South West Africa from external restrictions and interference." The reasoning behind such a move was to protect apartheid. South Africa, the policy analyst noted, "cannot carry out its promise to administer the territory 'in the spirit of the mandate' because its policies of racial repression and segregation are antithetical to that spirit. The refusal to submit either a trusteeship agreement or an annual report are [therefore] symptoms of the Union's inability to explain its racial policies to an international authority." The analysis warned that the United States could expect that Pretoria's actions would "be widely regarded as a provocative repudiation of the principle of international accountability." Moreover, "[a]dverse reaction will intensify when it is realized that the Union government intends to entrust the welfare of the third of a million colored inhabitants to the territory's small white population, which shares the views of the Union's own rural white population regarding white supremacy, ... the undesirability of Native progress financed from the general revenue," and the importance of applying "constant pressure ... to keep taxes down and the labor supply up."[117]

---

[116] Minute: The Anti-Slavery Society – for C. W. W. Greenridge, January 26, 1949, DO 35/3811; Anti-Slavery Society: Points Submitted to the Secretary of State for Commonwealth Affairs on South West Africa by a Joint Deputation from the Anti-Slavery Society, the Fabian Colonial Bureau, the League of Coloured Peoples, the Native Races Protections Committee of the Society of Friends and the United Nations Association, n.d., ca. March 1949, DO 35/3811; Deputation on South West Africa: received at the Commonwealth Relations Office, ... March 3, 1949, DO 35/3811; Letter sent to Sir A. Burns for signature, April 1949, DO 35/3811; Minute by J. T., May 31, 1949, DO 35/3811; Minute, Mr. Cumming Bruce, May 3, 1949, DO 35/3811.

[117] The Union and South West Africa, OIR Report No. 5021, August 11, 1949, Box 36, File "Background Book: Committee–4 Trusteeship (Folder 2 of 2)," Entry 3039E, RG 59.

The NAACP had been counting on international accountability. Rayford Logan, working as the Association's foreign policy consultant, had scoured the first Article 73(e) reports from the administering powers to the UN about the conditions in their colonial territories and concluded that it "is evident from this document that the 'White Man's Burden' ... has not been very heavy. But," he noted, "for the first time, it is possible for an international body to discuss the obvious ills in the colonies based on the reports of the colonial powers."[118] Not in South West Africa, however. Logan relayed to Walter White that "Malan, as you know, is even more vicious than Smuts."[119] And given that Logan considered the old field marshal to be a "goddamned vicious son-of-a-bitch," Malan's reign could only portend disaster.[120]

White knew. He knew directly from Scott. While in New York during the UN's previous meeting, the reverend worked "from an office loaned [him] by the National Association for the Advancement of Colored People," whose headquarters happened to be well within the visa boundaries the Justice Department had laid out for the priest.[121] And then, after his return to Southern Africa, Scott contacted White again, laying out the increasing stranglehold on the minister's movements, the attempts to "intimidate" the Africans whom he represented, and the censorship of UN information that the regime had imposed on the region. Scott needed White's help, again. "I informed the chiefs how very good you had been in helping me to get their opinions made known," but the fight was not yet won.[122]

By the time of the fall 1949 UN meeting, South Africa basically announced, in no uncertain terms, that it was ready to do battle. There would be no more groveling before the United Nations, asking permission for anything. In fact, when Eric Louw attended the meeting of the UN General Assembly, he boasted that he "did not go crawling like General Smuts." When the "Russians, Poles, Chinese, and others were slandering the good name of South Africa ... he hit back hard." For him that was the only option. The United Nations had far too many "coloured states ...

---

[118] Rayford Logan, "The Recently Published Reports of the United Nations on Non-Self Governing Territories," n.d., Box 29, File, "31," *Logan-MSRC.*

[119] Rayford Logan to Walter White, September 11, 1948, Box A635, File "United Nations: General Assembly, Oct. 1948," *Papers of the NAACP.*

[120] Logan, diary entry, June 26, 1945, Box 4, File "Diaries, 1945–47," *Logan Papers.*

[121] Michael Scott to Tshekedi Kama, January 14, 1948, Box A8, File "Southwest Africa, 1947–51," *Papers of the NAACP.*

[122] Michael Scott to Walter White, June 9, 1948, ibid.

trying to dictate how South Africa should treat its Indians, Coloureds, and Natives." Therefore, in its work at the UN, the mission was clear: the "Nationalist party intended to save white civilisation."[123]

And yet, although that swagger emboldened Malan's regime, the roil in the UN began to transform the Western perception of South Africa from valued military ally to political ball and chain. The CIA noted that "South African intransigence ... has made the country something of a propaganda liability to the US and the Western bloc."[124] Canadian officials recognized that "South Africa is, admittedly, a handicap to the western world in the struggle of moral supremacy over Communism." Malan's regime was "a liability to the white races" because "the behavior of the whites in South Africa ... increases the danger that the white world will not have the full support of the coloured peoples in Asia against the Soviet Union."[125]

For most members of the Fourth Committee the response to South Africa was disgust. Even the French, who were angling to weld their North African colonies into France, explained that South Africa did not have any legal grounds to annex South West Africa. "Obviously it had not been contemplated by the authors of the [League of Nations] Covenant that any Mandated Territory might be incorporated with the territory of the Mandatory Power," the French delegate explained. "Article 22 did not provide that the territory would be an integral part ... but that it should be

---

[123] "Mr. Eric Louw Attacks Gen. Smuts," March 2, 1949, *Johannesburg Star*, Box 30, File "Quotations of South Africa/Statements on South Africa, 1947–49," *Scott Papers*; "Mr. Strydom Discusses UNO and South Africa," November 30, 1950, *South African Press Digests*, Fiche 13; Memorandum of Conversation between the U.S. Ambassador to South Africa and the Minister of Agriculture, the Honorable S. P. LeRoux, November 26, 1951, 745a.13/11–2651, Reel 19, *Confidential U.S. State Department Central Files: South Africa, 1950–54* (Frederick, MD: University Publications of America, 1985) (hereafter *Confidential South Africa*).

[124] CIA, "The Political Situation in the Union of South Africa," July 31, 1949, ORE 1–49, Box 215, File "Central Intelligence Reports: O.R.E.: 1949: 1–16 [1–3, 6, 9, 11, 14, 16: January 31–August 2]," *Papers of Harry S. Truman: Personal Secretary File: Intelligence Reports*, Harry S. Truman Presidential Library, Independence, MO (hereafter *Truman:PSF:IR*).

[125] Memorandum from Commonwealth Division to Deputy Under-Secretary of State for External Affairs, March 23, 1949, No. 199, Canadian Department of Foreign Affairs and International Trade, http://www.international.gc.ca/history-histoire/documents-documents.aspx (hereafter *Canadian Foreign Affairs*); Memorandum by United Nations Division [K. B. Williamson], March 28, 1949, No. 201, *Canadian Foreign Affairs*; Memorandum from Deputy Under-Secretary of State for External Affairs [E. Scott Reid] to Commonwealth Division, March 26, 1949, No. 200, *Canadian Foreign Affairs*. Excerpt from Carol Anderson, "The Histories of African Americans' Anticolonialism during the Cold War," in *The Cold War and the Third World*, ed., Robert McMahon (New York: Oxford University Press, 2013), 178–191.

administered as an integral part. That was the core of the problem." The Cuban representative was even more blunt. The Fourth Committee was "dealing with a case of annexation hidden under the cloak of association, with a case of racial discrimination under the pretext of segregation." The Syrian delegate was equally clear about South Africa's annexation of international territory. There "was nothing in the mandate which could justify such intentions."[126]

The Fourth Committee's ire thus merged with Scott's and the NGOs' fears about what a regime of Nazi lovers would do to Africans. Unfortunately, before Scott could even get to the UN, the same old visa problems arose again. The label of "communist" dogged his every move. Scott's visa woes might have been intractable especially as the United States and the British were putting enormous pressure on the Indian government to keep the priest off the delegation, this time by warning that the precedent of allowing dissidents to become officially attached to legitimate delegations could wreak havoc. As an example they pointed to the chaos that would reign if Pakistan put a disaffected Indian on its delegation. At that point, however, the NGOs stepped in again. The International League for the Rights of Man, on whose board Walter White sat, and which had official class B consultative status with the UN, accredited Scott as its representative. Its official ties with the United Nations put the International League's designees under the protection of the Headquarters agreement. The chair of the ILRM, Roger Baldwin, confidently reminded the State Department's chief of visas that "persons coming from abroad as official representatives of recognized UN non-governmental organizations are admitted without question.... We trust that the Embassy in London will be promptly advised to grant him [Scott] a visa."[127] It did – although once again weighted down with "embarrassing" restrictions.[128]

[126] Fourth Committee, Provisional Summary Record of the Hundred and Thirtieth Meeting, 4th session, held on 21 November 1949, A/C.4/SR. 130, November 22, 1949, Box 81, File "Committee IV (Trusteeship Committee)," *Fahy Papers*.

[127] "[American Civil Liberties] Union Joins International League for the Rights of Man, Bulletin #79, October 1948, Box 1149, Folder "25," *Papers of the ACLU*, Seeley Mudd Manuscript Library, Princeton University, Princeton, NJ (hereafter *ACLU Papers*); Michael Scott to Both [Freda and Leon Troup], January 3, 1948, Box 40, File "Letters from Fletcher, Troup, etc.," *Scott Papers*; Roger Baldwin to H. J. L'Heureux, March 31, 1949, Box 43, File "GMS U.S. Visa," *Scott Papers*; Roger Baldwin to H. J. L'Heureux, April 26, 1949, Box 43, File "GMS U.S. Visa," *Scott Papers*.

[128] Michael Scott to the Bishop, January 8, 1947, Box 88, File "Correspondence with South African Clergy, 1947–1948," *Scott Papers*.

Once the International League got Scott into the United States, the organizations met other needs.[129] While a local seminary provided housing, the NAACP once again gave Scott invaluable office space. And although the organization was stretched to the limit in handling a myriad of civil rights issues in the United States, the Association also met the Anglican minister's insatiable need for secretarial support – a direct result of the way the United Nations operated.[130] Its delegates dealt with paper. Their debates circled around the reams and reams of data, memoranda, analyses, petitions, minutes, and reports that flowed through UN headquarters on a daily basis. The logistical support that the NAACP provided allowed Scott to participate in ways that would have been physically and practically impossible without it.

In addition to this tangible support, the Association also offered and delivered the intangibles of its good name, reputation, and clout to help the Hereros' emissary get access to key people, who, because of his visa restrictions, would have otherwise been well beyond the minister's reach. With public speaking engagements off-limits, articles written by him banned in the United States, and his travel severely restricted to several blocks in Midtown Manhattan, Scott was tethered and, for all intents and purposes, silenced beyond the walls of the UN. Walter White bristled at the disgraceful treatment of this "strong and beautiful disembodied spirit."[131] He decided that if the minister could not go out and spread the message about apartheid and South West Africa to those who really needed to hear it and who had the power and the influence to do something about it, then he [White] would solve that problem by bringing those people to the Reverend Scott. The secretary suggested to his board of directors that "it would be exceedingly useful for the Association to arrange for Rev. Scott to tell his story to influential Americans."[132] White, therefore, under the auspices of the NAACP, hosted a series of

[129] The ILRM had very few staff and virtually no resources. See Memorandum of a Meeting of Members of the Board and Invited Guests of the International League for the Rights of Man, February 26, 1948, Box 1149, File "25," *ACLU Papers*; Board of Directors Meeting: International League for the Rights of Man, March 5, 1948, Box 1149, File "25," *ACLU Papers*.

[130] Winifred Courtney to Ruth First, March 25, 1962, File "2/17/3," *First Papers*; Lovina Marlowe to Bobbie Branch, November 11, 1954, Box A6, File "Africa: Michael Scott, 1953–55," *Papers of the NAACP*.

[131] Walter White to Hubert T. Delany, November 20, 1952, Part 14, *Papers of the NAACP: Race Relations in the International Arena, 1940–1955*, Reel 4, (Bethesda, MD: University Publications of America, 1993), microfilm (hereafter *NAACP-Int'l*).

[132] Walter White to Mr. Wilkins and the Board of Directors, June 6, 1949, Box A8, File "Southwest Africa, 1947–51," *Papers of the NAACP*.

teas and cocktail parties at his Manhattan apartment with an A-list of invited guests – senators, mayors, clergy, media representatives, and labor leaders – and with Scott as the featured guest. Those teas and gatherings quickly evolved into fundraising activities, generating thousands of dollars to support Scott's work and, because he suffered from a "creeping intestinal disease" that turned out to be Crohn's, to cover his health care costs. Channing Tobias and Walter White even agreed that although the Association "[couldn't] afford" it, the NAACP would make a sizable contribution to offset Scott's living expenses because "Michael Scott has done so much to focus attention on the evil and dangerous situation in South Africa."[133]

The Association then joined with Scott and the International League's regular UN representative, Max Beer, in "an intensive lobbying effort among delegates aimed at disseminating information on the South West African issue and at allowing Scott to appear before the Fourth Committee"[134] (See Figure 2.4). In asking for the NAACP's help in this area, the priest had explained that it "is not only in the sphere of trusteeship but also in that of human rights that South Africa has seriously challenged the civilised standards which the peoples of the world

---

[133] "NAACP Joins Demonstration Against South African Annexation," press release, November 26, 1946, Reel 1, *NAACP-Int'l*; "Visa Granted S.W. African," October 10, 1947, press release, Reel 4, *NAACP-Int'l*; Minutes of the Board of Directors Meeting, "Picketing South African Delegation to the UN," October 13, 1952, Box A7, File "South Africa Petition to the United Nations, 1953," *Papers of the NAACP*; "Ban on Michael Scott," Secretary's Report, September 1952, Reel 4, *NAACP-Int'l*; "Reverend Scott Admitted to U.S." Secretary's Report, November 10, 1952, Reel 4, *NAACP-Int'l*; Sartell Prentice Jr. to Walter White, June 9, 1949, Reel 4, *NAACP-Int'l*; Walter White to Editor, October 30, 1950, Reel 4, *NAACP-Int'l*; Walter White to Board and Vice Presidents and Attached List, January 13, 1948, Reel 4, *NAACP-Int'l*; Henry Moon to Roy Wilkins, draft of letter to UN delegation (U.S.), November 8, 1949, Box A323, File "Italian Colonies, Disposition of, Correspondence Regarding, May 1949–50," *Papers of the NAACP*; Walter White to George C. Marshall, telegram, October 4, 1947, Reel 4, *NAACP-Int'l*; Walter White to Dean Acheson, September 21, 1950, Reel 4, *NAACP-Int'l*; Walter White to Robert C. Alexander, January 9, 1948, Reel 4, *NAACP-Int'l*; Margaret R.T. Carter to Walter White, October 4, 1950, Reel 4, *NAACP-Int'l*; Walter White to Roy Wilkins and the Board of Directors, memo, June 6, 1949, Reel 4, *NAACP-Int'l*; Michael Scott Meeting, Secretary's Report, November 10, 1952, Reel 5, *NAACP-Int'l*; Roy Wilkins to Warren Austin, November 9, 1949, Reel 5, *NAACP-Int'l*; Roy Wilkins to C.D.B. King, telegram, November 21, 1949, Reel 5, *NAACP-Int'l*; Roy Wilkins to Roger Baldwin, November 22, 1949, Reel 5, *NAACP-Int'l*; Joseph J. Chesson to Roy Wilkins, telegram, November 22, 1949, Reel 5, *NAACP-Int'l*; Walter White to Clarence Pickett, January 12, 1951, Reel 5, *NAACP-Int'l*; "Scott, according to a reliable source, is a dying fanatic ...," July 27, 1951, PA in PF 65, 777, KV2/2053.

[134] Clark, "The International League for Human Rights," 111–112; Roger Baldwin to Michael Scott, April 26, 1949, Box 43, File "GMS U.S. Visa," *Scott Papers*.

FIGURE 2.4. Michael Scott lobbying UN Philippine delegate Carlos Romulo for South West Africa's right to self-determination and international accountability. *Source*: Thomas D. McAvoy, Time & Life Pictures. Courtesy of Getty Images, #50523888.

through the United Nations are striving to establish. And it is therefore doubly important for ... the voices of the African people to be given a hearing."[135]

The anticolonialist delegates on the Fourth Committee, in fact, had begun to make noises that they just might allow the priest to provide *direct* testimony to compensate for the Union's dogmatic refusal even to submit annual reports on the conditions in South West Africa as the mandate required. This idea was beyond precedent setting, however; it carried major implications for decolonization. The colonial powers were greatly resistant to and decidedly concerned about allowing, essentially,

[135] Michael Scott to Walter White, April 10, 1949, Box A8, File "Southwest Africa, 1947–51," *Papers of the NAACP*.

a private citizen with complaints from the colonized to be heard before the UN.[136]

To help overcome this resistance and because he recognized that in Southern Africa he was dealing with a full-fledged human rights crisis, Scott sought an appointment with the revered Eleanor Roosevelt, former first lady, NAACP board member, and, most important, chair of the UN Commission on Human Rights. Initially, she wanted nothing to do with him. Roosevelt knew who he was; briefings from the State Department, via South Africa, had made that clear. Scott, according to the reports, was a criminal: an "eccentric," homeless, indigent "fanatic" who "belonged 'to all left-wing groups in the Union.'"[137] Roosevelt maligned him to her staff as a "troublemaker" and "a Commie," who had been "besieging" and "bothering everyone at the U.N." Roosevelt's secretary noticed, however, that Scott had called from the NAACP's office in New York and she decided to "check ... through them" to see what this man was all about.[138]

The Association was unequivocal. The charge of Scott "being a 'Communist'" was "ridiculous." Scott was "doing an extremely courageous and self-sacrificing job on about the worst sector on white interracial justice in the entire world." And it was because he had "the courage to fight for the rights of the native population" that this smear campaign began in the first place.[139] South Africa and its allies, the NAACP explained, were trying to "still Scott's small voice" and, in doing so,

[136] Clark, "The International League for Human Rights," 113; MacLaurin, *United Nations and Power Politics*, 382–383.

[137] Suresh Chandra Saxena, *Namibia and the World: The Story of the Birth of a Nation* (Delhi: Kalinga Publications, 1991), 66; Michael Scott, "South West African Referendum Misinterpreted by South African Government," n.d., Box 13, File "'S' (Folder 2)," *Papers of Harry S. Truman, Philleo Nash Files*, Harry S. Truman Presidential Library, Independence, MO (hereafter *Truman:Nash*); Walter White to Arthur Capper, January 21, 1948, Reel 4, *NAACP-Int'l*; Stanley Burch, "Scott 1," November 1949, Reel 4, *NAACP-Int'l*; Argyle R. Mackey to Roger Baldwin, December 23, 1952, Reel 4, *NAACP-Int'l*; Durward Sandifer to Charles Bohlen, memo, n.d., Box 33, File "United Nations Correspondence, 1947," *Papers of John Foster Dulles*, Seeley Mudd Manuscript Library, Princeton University, Princeton, NJ (hereafter *JFD-Princeton*); Freda Troup, *In Face of Fear: Michael Scott's Challenge to South Africa* (London: Faber and Faber Limited, 1950), 138.

[138] Handwritten and typed notes attached to Eleanor Roosevelt to Rev. Michael Scott, January 26, 1948, Box 3364, File "Scott, Rev. Michael, 1948–49," *Papers of Eleanor Roosevelt*, Franklin D. Roosevelt Presidential Library, Hyde Park, NY (hereafter *Roosevelt Papers*).

[139] White to Roy Wilkins and the Board of Directors, memo, June 6, 1949, Box A8, File "Southwest Africa, 1947–51," *Papers of the NAACP*; Alfred Baker Lewis to Walter White, January 15, 1948, Reel 4, *NAACP-Int'l*.

silence the cries of the oppressed in South West Africa. The Association leadership was, therefore, determined to give the Anglican priest "every assistance" in waging this battle against a regime that was "not fit to hold South West Africa as either a mandate or a trust area."[140] Barely persuaded, Roosevelt eventually agreed to meet with Scott.

She was already well aware of the human rights catastrophe emerging out of apartheid. In her negotiations for the UN Declaration of Human Rights, she came to realize that, under Malan's regime, there was "practically no hope for the native people of South Africa." This became most evident when the South African delegate to the UN Commission on Human Rights stated with no hesitation that "[t]here are certain people in South Africa who neither now nor ever can enjoy the guarantees of the Declaration of Human Rights." All of Mrs. Roosevelt's persuasive powers, and they were considerable, could not move him from that position.[141] Nonetheless, despite her understanding of the magnitude of the problem, and despite the NAACP's assurances, she still remained leery of the Reverend Michael Scott. After their meeting, her impression of the Anglican minister had not altered drastically. In Roosevelt's view, Scott was "too intense" to make an effective, "dispassionate presentation" before the UN's Fourth Committee. She was wrong.[142]

Increasingly resentful of South Africa's continuing defiance, the Fourth Committee did the unspeakable – at least in the minds of the colonial powers – and considered asking Scott to testify. This was unheard of; individuals simply had no standing before the UN. The Haitian delegate, however, was unwilling to "quibble" over legalities. Especially when it had become clear that South Africa had adopted "measures of racial discrimination in the manner of nazi [sic] Germany." The British, on the other hand, were aghast about the "very dangerous precedent" the Fourth Committee was setting. They argued that every country had a disgruntled minority group somewhere, and if Scott was allowed to testify, "representatives of all those minorities would take advantage of that precedent and the UN would be flooded with requests

[140] Secretary's Report, November 10, 1952, Reel 4, *NAACP-Int'l*; "Block African Merger, Wilkins Urges Acheson," press release, November 17, 1949, Reel 4, *NAACP-Int'l*; Roy Wilkins to Marguerite Cartwright, November 22, 1949, Box A8, File "Africa: Southwest Africa, 1947–51," *Papers of the NAACP*; Roy Wilkins to Roger Baldwin, November 22, 1949, Box A8, File "Africa: Southwest Africa, 1947–51," *Papers of the NAACP*.

[141] Rayford Logan, diary entry, n.d., Box 4, File "Diaries, Personal, 1948–49," *Logan Papers*.

[142] Eleanor Roosevelt to Mary A. Dingman, October 30, 1949, Box 3364, File "Scott, Rev. Michael, 1948–49," *Roosevelt Papers*.

for a hearing."[143] It was "illuminating," one scholar noted, "that [the British] seem to place the Africans," who live in Africa, "in the category of minorities."[144]

Whereas the British were resolute, the U.S. delegation was split. Some could only view the Reverend Michael Scott as a "problem," a "serious problem"; on the other hand, the U.S. representative on the Fourth Committee helped sanction Scott's credentials as the representative of the Hereros and almost cleared the pathway for his testimony.[145]

Another two hours of debates ensued largely over the following question: What authority did the Reverend Michael Scott have to represent Hereros, Namas, and Berg-Damaras? "Finally, Mr. Noriega, of Mexico grew impatient. 'Gentlemen,' he remarked, 'Jesus Christ was crucified because his credentials as King of the Jews were not in order; but that is no reason for us to play Pilate.'" At 10:30 at night, with the United States and the Soviet Union and many others voting against the British and South Africans, the Fourth Committee agreed to hear the Reverend Michael Scott's testimony.[146]

Scott's performance was riveting. In unwavering understated tones, he told "a story of endless treachery and tyranny imposed on the shattered tribes who have sent him" to the UN.[147] He laid out the Ministry of Justice's success in "manufacturing criminals" through a series of "Pass Laws and Masters and Servants Acts" that created a captive, cheap labor pool ready for exploitation. By criminalizing the sheer fact of being black, the Union government was able to "contract ... for three thousand labourers per year from South West Africa to work in the gold mines of Johannesburg." The South Africans also arrested "thousands of landless and homeless Africans ... every week" and forced them to work "in near slavery conditions" on the white-owned farms in the Transvaal.[148] In short, the "spirit of the mandate" had been violated. South Africa spent

[143] Fourth Committee, "Summary Record of the Hundred and Thirty-third meeting, 4th session held ... on Wednesday, 23 November 1949," November 24, 1949, A/C.4/SR.133, Box 81, File "Committee IV (Trusteeship Committee)," *Fahy Papers*.

[144] MacLaurin, *United Nations and Power Politics*, 384.

[145] Clark, "The International League for the Rights of Man," 113; Warren Austin to Roy Wilkins, November 17, 1949, Reel 5, *NAACP-Int'l*; Francis Russell to Roy Wilkins, December 14, 1949, Reel 5, *NAACP-Int'l*.

[146] MacLaurin, *United Nations and Power Politics*, 386.

[147] Stanley Burch, Scott 1a, November 1949, Reel 4, *NAACP-Int'l*.

[148] Barriers to Justice: An Open Letter to the Hon. Mr. H. G. Lawrence, M. P. Minister of Justice Union of South Africa, n.d., ibid.; Michael Scott to Members of the Trusteeship Council, December 6, 1947, ibid.; "Profile – Michael Scott," December 4, 1949, *The [London] Observer*, December 4, 1949, ibid.

100 times more on health care for the few whites in South West Africa than the Africans; it allocated barely 25 cents per capita on the education of Africans but nearly $20 per white child. It also reduced the maximum pay of $1.80 per month for African workers in rural areas "because of European complaints that the wage schedules were excessive and impractical!" There was also the "well substantiated reports of natives labouring under the crack of the sjambok," a fierce leather whip, as well as being "sometimes shot and buried."[149] Scott "pleaded for United Nations protection for Africans in the territory." He "detailed their degrading treatment at the hands of white farmers and the South African government, including the bombing and strafing of one tribe in order to remove it from land that whites wanted to seize."[150] One historian noted that when Scott finished, the "impact was overwhelming, even on the most hardened of the many hardened politicians in the room."[151]

Then the Haitian delegate, Stephen Alexis, who looked and spoke "like an Old Testament prophet with the added grace of a French orator," rose. Gripping his hand to his throat, Alexis exclaimed, "Now we know.... Now we know why everything was done to prevent this man from speaking. It – it chokes us." Alexis declared that Scott's testimony was

the most terrible indictment ever drawn up against men who called themselves civilized: ... machine-gunning and bombing natives like beasts; driving them from their land to die; giving the land back to their former cruel master the Germans; flogging them, rounding them up for forced labour, degrading them with the sense of inferiority, with the false idea that there are born masters and servants.

In a final burst of oratorical contempt, Alexis exclaimed " *Vous croyez qe ça ira sans châtiment*? [You think this will pass without punishment?]"[152]

Scott's testimony had compelled the General Assembly to finally do what it had been contemplating for years: it asked the International Court of Justice (ICJ) for an advisory opinion to establish, precisely, South West Africa's status and South Africa's responsibilities.

Scott's testimony also drove the South African government to an even higher pitch of fury against the Anglican priest. Eric Louw railed that Scott had committed "high treason" by "wag[ing] a sort of cold

---

[149] Reverend Michael Scott to the Members of the Trusteeship Council, December 6, 1947, Box A6, File "Africa: Michael Scott, 1947–49," *Papers of the NAACP*; Central African Council Memorandum No. 32/47, "Discussions with Union Government Regarding Migrant Labour," July 2, 1947, CO 525/201.

[150] Borstelmann, *Apartheid's Reluctant Uncle*, 121.

[151] MacLaurin, *United Nations and Power Politics*, 391.

[152] Ibid.

war against South Africa" and "act[ing] on the side of South Africa's enemies." Throughout the UN meeting Louw visibly resented "accusations ... that South Africa oppressed her non-European population and robbed them of their freedom." As far as he was concerned, there was no truth in any of it. The only truth was that those aspersions emanated from the most contemptible, lowest rungs of mankind. "This sort of story," he insisted, "comes in the first place from Indians in South Africa, from Communists in South Africa and from the so-called liberals among whom are the Michael Scotts."[153] Louw "declared that the time had come to 'take action' against the Rev. Michael Scott."[154] The Anglican priest's crime was simple and unforgivable. Scott "is a European and one would have expected him to stand by the Europeans." But, no. Instead, the priest used his passport as a weapon against the Union. He "went to the UN ... as a South African citizen and ... came to associate with the enemies of South Africa." "In time of war," Louw concluded, "if you associate with the enemy you are liable to be shot as a traitor."[155]

Louw's fury was aided and abetted by British intelligence, MI-5, which began to pass its highly classified dossier on the Anglican priest's activities and Communist links on to the South African government. Those reports were brutal in their assessment. They transformed Scott's faith into no more than a self-professed "racket" that would allow him to go "undercover" and use his clerical collar to move freely among Africans to "just say anything." Their depiction of Scott seemed to confirm everything that Malan's regime suspected about the priest and his so-called principled agitation for Africans' human rights.[156]

When the ICJ issued its ruling in 1950, it only heightened the rage of the South African government. Although the World Court ruled that the Union could not be forced to place South West Africa under the UN trusteeship system, the ICJ also insisted that Pretoria did not have the right or the power to change the international status of a mandate without the

---

[153] "More Threats to Civil Liberties: Eric Louw Suggests Measures Against 'Those Who Act on the Side of S. Africa's Enemies,'" *Forum*, January 15, 1949, Box 30, File "Quotations of South Africa/Statements on South Africa, 1947–49," *Scott Papers*.

[154] Extract from cutting from *Daily Worker* of January 10, 1949, headed "Meeting to Resist Malan" and mentioning Scott, January 25, 1949, KV2/2052.

[155] "Natives Champion Is Warned," *News Chronicle*, March 4, 1949, Box 30, File "Quotations of South Africa/Statements on South Africa, 1947–49," *Scott Papers*.

[156] Extract: Scott, Michael, PP.65777, January 13, 1943, KV2/2052; Percy Sillitoe to Barry, PF. 65,777/DG, February 9, 1950, ibid.; "The Reverend Michael Scott," April 13, 1950, ibid.; G. R. Mitchell for Sir Percy Sillitoe to General Palmer, P.F. 65777/B.1, April 13, 1950, ibid.

assent of the international community. As a result, the Court concluded, the mandate was still in existence and South Africa still had to adhere to the rules, including annual reports to the only recognized international body designed to handle this work, the United Nations. The Court's reasoning was simple. It "is not valid for South Africa to argue that, as the League of Nations is defunct, and the Mandate has lapsed, it can take over the Territory. In the Court's view, if the Mandate has lapsed, then the Union's authority has also lapsed. In effect, ... South Africa cannot assume rights derived from the Mandate and at the same time reject the obligations." [157]

Yet that is exactly what Malan's regime insisted it had the right to do. As he had made clear early in his reign, the prime minister had no intention of letting the UN, with its ideas of equality, anywhere near South West Africa. The World Court, Malan railed, has "put [the United Nations] in the vacant place of the League, perhaps even with somewhat increased power, and consequently, the unsavoury Michael Scott affair could easily be repeated in the future." This, for the prime minister, was a direct violation of national sovereignty because the United Nations "wants to thrust down our throats its ideology of equality between whites and blacks." "It must be clear to everyone that this could easily lead to the grossest interference in the internal affairs of both S.W.A. and the Union. We are not prepared to submit to such conditions." [158] South Africa's representative at the UN emphasized that the ICJ's advisory opinion was irrelevant, and as far his nation was concerned, the whole "question of South West Africa was almost academic." [159]

The United States had hoped for a more temperate response. "During the four years that the South West Africa question has been under consideration by the United Nations," a State Department analysis asserted, "the United States has exercised its influence in the direction of moderation. However," the report continued, "if the Union Government is

[157] International Status of South-West Africa, Advisory Opinion: I.C.J. Reports 1950, p. 128, Box 42, File "5th GA Background Book: Question of South West Africa," Entry 3039E, *RG* 59; "What the Decision Means," July 13, 1950, Press Digest No. 28, *South African Press Digests*, Fiche 11.

[158] "South-West Africa and the International Court's Decision," July 20, 1950, Press Digest No. 29, *South African Press Digests*, Fiche 11; "Union of South Africa: ... How Long?", n.d., *Together: The Reporter of the Chicago Urban League*, Box 10, Folder "214," *Papers of Edith Sampson*, Schlesinger Library, Radcliffe Institute, Harvard University, Cambridge, MA (hereafter *Sampson Papers*).

[159] "Report of the United Nations Debates on South-West Africa – 1950," attachment to Michael Scott to Walter White, January 19, 1951, Box A8, File "Southwest Africa, 1947–1951," *Papers of the NAACP*.

unwilling to even consider the opinion of the Court as a basis for its future policies regarding South West Africa, the United States would not be in a position to make further efforts on behalf of South Africa." In addition, the State Department stewed, it was "becoming increasingly difficult" to continue to "play a moderate role" in discussions involving South West Africa because "domestic public opinion ... is unsympathetic" to apartheid, South African intransigence, and the unilateral abrogation of an international mandate.[160]

Nevertheless, with the Korean War now raging and South Africa sending troops to fight on the Korean peninsula alongside American forces, the U.S. government was not about to do too much to antagonize an ally that had proven itself, particularly in the heat of war, to be steadfast and reliable. Moreover, the war had led to the implementation of NSC-68, the blueprint for waging the Cold War, which stressed enormous expenditures for defense and the stockpiling of strategic materials.[161] Mineral-rich South Africa was, therefore, crucial. "It is important," the British Dominions Affairs desk at the State Department wrote to the U.S. ambassador to South Africa, "that we maintain as friendly a political atmosphere as possible in our relations with South Africa because of our need for ... manganese exports and other strategic items. Unfortunately," the letter continued, "these United Nations disputes now serve to introduce sand into the gears of bilateral relations with South Africa."[162]

But the risk of losing South Africa as an ally was balanced by that of losing emerging nations to the Soviet camp in the Cold War. Not taking a firm stance against South Africa's policies exposed the West to charges of white supremacy and imperialism. One State Department analysis remarked that when it came to apartheid and South Africa, the Asian states were seized with the issue. And the colonial powers' overall legalistic protection of South Africa was creating resentment and an irreparable fissure. On the South West Africa issue, however, because of its special position as an international territory, there was a place for agreement. "Western as well as Asiatic opinion strongly holds that South Africa could

---

[160] Position Paper: Question of South West Africa: Advisory Opinion of International Court of Justice, SD/A/C.4/76, September 4, 1950, Box 42, File "5th GA Background Book: Question of South West Africa," Entry 3039E, *RG 59*; "United Nations Problem: Suggested Approach," n.d., Reel 19, *Confidential South Africa*.

[161] W. A. B. Illiff to S. R. Cope, November 21, 1952, File "1290930: Secret File – Union of South Africa," *Papers of the World Bank*; J. H. Collier to M. M. Rosen, July 17, 1953, "File 1290930: Secret File – Union of South Africa," *Papers of the World Bank*.

[162] J. Harold Shullaw to W. J. Gallman, December 17, 1951, Reel 18, *Confidential South Africa*.

take a more accommodating attitude, could agree for instance to the filing in the U.N. of annual reports. If South Africa," the report concluded wistfully, "could find a way to adopt a more accommodating attitude on this one case, it is our view that" there could be some moderation in the vituperative criticism coming out of the UN that is currently targeted at Pretoria and, possibly, driving the Asian states into the Soviet bloc.[163] U.S. policy toward South Africa, therefore, seemed to "tack back and forth" between protecting a Cold War anticommunist ally, on the one hand, and championing the principles of human rights, democracy, and equality against a white supremacist regime, on the other.[164]

For the Reverend Michael Scott, the International League, and the NAACP, there was no wavering. Given the prevailing McCarthyist winds howling through the American political landscape, the Association might have been, in its own way, in as much a quandary as U.S. officials. But it was not. That is to say, that even with the Korean War, the first "hot war" of the Cold War, tearing up and down the Korean peninsula; even with the Second Red Scare taking its toll on advocates for social justice by identifying their struggles with communism; even with W. E. B. Du Bois facing federal charges for aiding and abetting the Soviet Union for advocating a "Peace Movement"; even with "guilt by association" being used as *the* litmus test in an array of "loyalty" hearings to stamp the scarlet letter "C" on organizations and activists; even with all of that, the NAACP refused to back away from the clearly tainted Reverend Michael Scott.

Instead, gearing up for the next set of UN meetings, the "NAACP worked with the International League for the Rights of Man to secure a visa for the Anglican clergyman."[165] The Association also helped organize another round of fundraising for the priest, worked closely with the International League to distribute Scott's message to the black press and more than 643 targeted names on one of the NAACP's mailing lists, and arranged for a special screening of a documentary the Anglican priest had made, *Civilisation on Trial*, that provided visual proof of the horrific conditions under South African rule. Even more important, the NAACP's headquarters became the site for the formation of a broad-based coalition focused on South West Africa's freedom. This new Committee on South West Africa was to follow closely the developments at the UN in

[163] "United Nations Problem: Suggested Approach," n.d., Reel 19, *Confidential South Africa*.

[164] MacLaurin, *United Nations and Power Politics*, 384.

[165] "Rev. Scott Received Visa Following NAACP Appeal," press release, October 5, 1950, Box A6, File "Africa: Michael Scott, 1950–51," *Papers of the NAACP*.

terms of implementing the Court's decision and making sure that the Africans' voices remained an integral part of the discussion. The point, as Walter White summed it up, was "to make the issue so strong that neither the US, UK nor France could avoid it."[166]

South Africa had a different plan that included the United States, Britain, and France. Malan's government had, of course, rejected outright the ICJ's ruling on sending any report to the United Nations. Instead, as a "compromise," South Africa argued that it was not the League that actually awarded the mandate but, rather, the Associated and Allied Powers of the First World War. South Africa would, therefore, be willing to submit reports to those powers and only those powers – Britain, the United States, and France. In essence, South Africa was demanding that the major powers choose which side they were on. It was either the one that South Africa believed it represented, "Christianity and Western Civilisation," or the other side represented by "non-Christian" India, the Godless Soviet Union, and the "fanatical" Reverend Michael Scott.[167]

The United States refused to rise to the bait. Instead, it accepted membership on the UN's Ad Hoc Committee on South West Africa, which was to negotiate with the Union on the process for the submission of the annual reports. The U.S. representative, however, worked hard to put no new additional requirements on the reporting mechanism and even managed to hold a petition from Scott at bay, so as not to antagonize the Union.[168] Regardless of the conciliatory efforts, however, South Africa refused to negotiate except on the basis of its

---

[166] Walter White to Editor of the *Messenger*, October 27, 1950, Box A380, File "Leagues: International League for the Rights of Man, 1942–52," *Papers of the NAACP*; Madison S. Jones Jr. to John Pearmain, October 30, 1950, Box A380, File "Leagues: International League for the Rights of Man, 1942–52," *Papers of the NAACP*; John Pearmain to Madison Jones, November 28, 1950, Box A380, File "Leagues: International League for the Rights of Man, 1942–52," *Papers of the NAACP*; Madison S. Jones to John Pearmain, November 30, 1950, Box A380, File "Leagues: International League for the Rights of Man, 1942–52," *Papers of the NAACP*; Tentative Agenda: Meeting on South West Africa, December 1, 1950, Box 30, File "Correspondence with the International League for the Rights of Man and Other American Bodies, 1950–55," *Scott Papers*; Minutes of Meeting on 14 December 1950 to Discuss Formation of Ad Hoc Committee on South West Africa, December 14, 1950, Box A380, File "Leagues: International League for the Rights of Man, 1942–52," *Papers of the NAACP*; *Civilisation on Trial in South Africa*, prod. and dir. by Michael Scott and Clive Donner, Villon Films, 1948, 1994. Videocassette, 24 min.

[167] "South Africa and UNO: South Africa Withdraws from General Assembly of UNO," Press Digest No. 50, December 13, 1951, *South African Press Digests*, Fiche 21.

[168] Committee of the General Assembly on South West Africa, SD/AC.49/1, January 30, 1951, Box 18, File "SD/A/AC.49/1," Lot File 82D211, *RG 59*.

counterproposal, the one in which it would deal solely with the major, white, Western powers – no one else. Frankly, the Union contended, the United States needed to understand what a great compromise that was on the part of South Africa. After all, "some Western nations" have this "obsession with human rights" and "regard social colour distinction [as] devilish."[169] U.S. representatives tried to explain that the Ad Hoc Committee's proposals were "very reasonable." But South Africa scoffed. The one annual report that South Africa did submit, Minister of the Interior T. E. Donges retorted, had "led to some forty questions. The Union was not going to expose itself to this again." South Africa simply "refused to be the whipping boy" for the UN. If there was going to be an annual report, only the trusted, Western allies were going to receive it.[170] The United States and Britain, therefore, prepared for another difficult UN meeting, where South Africa's recalcitrance would cause the issue of South West Africa to, once again, "loom very large at the General Assembly."[171]

The American strategy of staying in a conciliatory mode was complicated at the fall 1951 UN meeting by the presence of two African Americans on the U.S. delegation to the United Nations. The scourge of Jim Crow, the steady incidences of lynching and Southern justice publicized throughout the world, the embarrassing episodes in which African, Indian, and Caribbean diplomats got caught in the wake of segregation laws and were harshly denied access to theaters, hotels, and restaurants led the State Department to search for "some outstanding Negroes" to place in international venues to counter the narrative of American

---

[169] "South Africa and UNO: Rev. Michael Scott to Appear before Trusteeship Committee," Press Digest No. 49, December 6, 1951, *South African Press Digests*, Fiche 21.

[170] Position Paper: The Question of South West Africa, SD/A/C.4/89, October 11, 1951, Box 44, File "6th GA (Committee 4: Trusteeship) Instructions to US Delegation," Entry 3039E, *RG 59*; Memorandum of conversation between the Ambassador and Mr. D. D. Forsyth, Secretary for External Affairs, October 30, 1951, 745a.13/10–3051, Reel 19, *Confidential South Africa*; Memorandum of conversation between the Ambassador and Minister of the Interior, Dr. The Honorable T. E. Donges, K. C., November 6, 1951, 745A.13/11–651, Reel 19, *Confidential South Africa*; Bernard C. Connelly to Department of State, November 2, 1951, 745a.13/10–2651, Reel 19, *Confidential South Africa*; Memorandum of Conversation with South African Ambassador, Dean Acheson, Mr. Shullaw, April 20, 1951, Reel 18, *Confidential South Africa*; W. J. Gallman to Secretary of State, October 26, 1951, Reel 19, *Confidential South Africa*.

[171] British Embassy in Washington to Foreign Office, September 5, 1951, DO 35/3842; Anglo-American Colonial Talks: Opening Meeting, October 10, 1951, DO 35/3842; Anglo-American Colonial Talks, October 10, 1951, CO 537/7137; Minute, Mr. Cockram, September 27, 1951, DO 35/3842.

racial oppression.[172] One such "outstanding Negro" was an attorney from Chicago, Edith Sampson, who had been brought in specifically to deal with another nagging problem dogging the State Department's heels: a petition from a black Communist organization, the Civil Rights Congress, charging the United States with committing genocide against African Americans.[173]

Sampson had a rose-colored vision of racism in the United States that could sometimes launch her straight into "Cloud Cuckoo Land" – she told a Swedish audience in 1951, for example, that there was no segregation in the United States, the Ku Klux Klan was a thing of the past, and black poverty was overstated because the African Americans she knew drove shiny Cadillacs – but even she was appalled that the U.S. delegation wanted to shield South Africa from international criticism. Pretoria, she insisted, simply could not treat the World Court's ruling like an a la carte menu from which the Union could pick and choose which pieces it wanted and ignore the rest. Her State Department handlers noted that although "she did not speak up often in delegation meetings, ... [s]he stood by her guns on the ... South West Africa item, insisting that the United States position should be clear-cut and in no sense protective of South Africa."[174]

Sampson laid out her case. South Africa's "virtual slave-system and color discrimination," she argued, "are exhibits of colonialism at its worst, and [are] so identified by the people of Asia, the Middle East and most of Latin America." Thus, if the United States backed South Africa and, by implication, its policies, America "would be 'damned' from the start" especially in "light of the Union's bad record and obvious steps to integrate SWA into the Union." She asked her colleagues to recognize that the United States could not stand before the UN and defend the

---

[172] Anderson, *Eyes Off the Prize*, 58–59, 72, 181, 186–187, 192.

[173] On the CRC's petition, *We Charge Genocide*, see Carol Anderson, "Bleached Souls and Red Negroes: The NAACP and Black Communists in the Early Cold War, 1948–1952" in *Window on Freedom: Race, Civil Rights, and Foreign Affairs, 1945–1988*, ed. Brenda Gayle Plummer (Chapel Hill: University of North Carolina Press, 2003), 93–114. On Edith Sampson's role in refuting the petition, see Anderson, *Eyes Off the Prize*, 203–206.

[174] Rea Stanton to Walter White, February 3, 1952, Box A638, File "United Nations: Sampson, Edith, 1949–52," *Papers of the NAACP*; Edith Sampson, "The Negro in a Maturing America," attached to Ernie Johnson, for Your Information, February 1952, Box A638, File "United Nations: Sampson, Edith, 1949–52," *Papers of the NAACP*; William Worthy, "In Cloud-Cuckoo Land," *Crisis*, April 1952, Box A638, File "United Nations: Sampson, Edith, 1949–52," *Papers of the NAACP*; "Record of Performance," n.d., ca. November 1951, Box 10, Folder "210," *Sampson Papers*.

indefensible. "America's survival is tied up with the amount of confidence we can engender in Asia and the Middle East," she asserted. "We can't buy it; we have to win it by standing for what they and we really believe in – human rights regardless of race or color."[175]

Then she came to the Reverend Michael Scott. Through Walter White, she had met with the Anglican priest several times throughout the previous year and was impressed. Scott, she asserted, was a "symbol of protest" – a voice for the otherwise "gagged natives of South West Africa." If the United States interfered with letting the world hear this man, it would "antagonize" the very members of the UN that the U.S. government was trying to attract to the West. Interestingly, Sampson was joined in this effort by Eleanor Roosevelt, who had also come to believe in the Reverend Michael Scott, even going so far as to anonymously donate funds, through the NAACP, to support his efforts. With this strong ally on her side, Sampson began to turn the tide in the delegation.[176]

It was now up to Channing Tobias, who was chair of the U.S. delegation on the Fourth Committee. *Ebony* magazine had described him as a "tall, scholarly, intensely-spiritual New Yorker … [who] operates in an air of secrecy, steering clear of spectacular high-pressure methods … but somewhere behind the scenes" getting the job done, nonetheless.[177] Benjamin Mays amplified that thought. Tobias, Mays observed, "would not say one thing to white people and another thing to Negroes." Instead, the NAACP board member was a man with "sane courage" who "never did allow the fear of losing position or prestige … interfere with his … stand on issues that he was convinced were right."[178] Thus, it was Tobias's years of work in Africa, particularly South Africa, of which the State Department was well aware, that spurred him on. He

---

[175] "Record of Performance," n.d., ca. November 1951, Box 10, Folder "210," *Sampson Papers*.

[176] Mary Benson, diary, December 1, 1950, Box 78, File "Mary Benson [A.Y. Only]," *Scott Papers*; Notes on UN meeting (Mrs. Edith Sampson: United States Mission to United Nations), n.d., Box 10, Folder "207," *Sampson Papers*; Edith S. Sampson to Mrs. Roosevelt et al., memo, November 28, 1951, Box 10, Folder "210," *Sampson Papers*; "Record of Performance," n.d., ca. November 1951, Box 10, Folder "210," *Sampson Papers*; Eleanor Roosevelt to Walter White, December 2, 1952, Box A6, File "Africa: Michael Scott, 1952," *Papers of the NAACP*. Anonymous financial support for Scott also came from W. Averell Harriman, see George M. Elsey to Walter White, December 9, 1952, Box A6, File "Africa: Michael Scott, 1952," *Papers of the NAACP*.

[177] "Mystery Man of Race Relations: Channing Tobias Meets and Influences More Top-level VIP's than Any Other Negro," *Ebony* (February 1951), File "Newspaper Clippings and Articles, 1937–1960 [4]," *Tobias Papers*.

[178] Benjamin E. Mays to Dalton F. McClelland, February 15, 1960, File "Biography Project, 1950–1960 [7]," *Tobias Papers*.

had informed his Foggy Bottom contacts from almost the moment the UN session began that, although he "was essentially a teamworker" and "could be relied upon to play the team game," there were some issues where he had "strong convictions" and would not tow the line. True to his word, for most of the session Tobias hewed very closely to U.S. policy. However, when the issue of the Hereros surfaced, he came into his own. "We must," he told Walter White, "do everything we can to see to it that [Scott's] ... 'small voice' is not drowned out by the noisy denunciations of him for which the representatives of the Union of South Africa are responsible."[179]

This was a bold stance for Tobias to take given that he had run into major difficulties in the Senate confirmation hearings concerning his appointment to the U.S. delegation. In typical Red Scare fashion, Tobias was assailed for his past membership in several organizations, such as the Council on African Affairs, which had now landed on the infamous Attorney General's list. Tobias was a fellow traveler, journalist Westbrook Pegler asserted. Tobias curried favor with Communists. Tobias was Red. The assault was so intense that it took intervention from the White House to push the confirmation through.[180] Yet here stood this black man, in 1951 Jim Crow America, proud of the stature and privilege associated with achieving the rank of U.S. delegate to the United Nations, risking it all so that the red-tainted Reverend Michael Scott could underline the crucial need for international accountability and give voice to the Hereros, Namas, and Berg-Damaras.

To be sure, Tobias's commitment had international support. Many had been alienated by South Africa's derisive treatment of the ICJ advisory opinion, its snub of the UN's Ad Hoc Committee on South West Africa, its refusal to submit an annual report even as required by the mandate, and its disdainful counterproposal that treated every other nation, particularly those in Asia, Africa, the Middle East, the Caribbean and Latin America, contemptuously. South Africa had only a few allies left and that small number would never be able to carry the day in the Fourth Committee of the UN General Assembly.

---

[179] Channing H. Tobias to John D. Hickerson, May 19, 1952, Box 2, File "6th General Assembly," Lot File 58D33, *RG 59*; Channing H. Tobias to Walter White, November 12, 1952, Reel 4, *NAACP-Int'l*.

[180] Walter White for release to subscribing newspapers, October 11, 1951, Box A81, File "Articles Walter White: Syndicated Column, 1951," *Papers of the NAACP*; Westbrook Pegler, "Dr. Tobias Leanings to Reds are Cited," October 16, 1951, File "United Nations, 1951–1952 [42]," *Tobias Papers*.

Thus, when the issue of South West Africa arose in November 1951, the Fourth Committee truly broke with precedent and considered inviting not just Scott, but the Hereros, Namas, and Berg-Damaras themselves to speak before the UN. The South Africans and British immediately protested. There was no right to petition for individuals who were not even in a trust territory. The UN Charter did not provide for this. The Fourth Committee's action, the South Africans charged, was a "violation of the Union's sovereignty." And, the Union warned, other nations, who were so smug now, would one day get "hanged on the gallows designed for South Africa."[181] The British, panicked, turned to the American delegation for support. But the cavalry was not coming. Tobias saw to that.

After the smoke had cleared and the Fourth Committee voted (37–7–7) to invite the Africans to the UN, the British complained bitterly that the United States did not use any of its considerable power and prestige to stop the Fourth Committee in its tracks. Rather, the "United States took no part in the debate" whatsoever. Even worse, the Cubans, who led the charge for the invitation, "were aware," even before the meeting began, that the Americans were going to sit stony faced throughout the whole ordeal. It was a setup; that was obvious. The British soon traced the Americans' deafening silence back to what they considered a most unlikely and inappropriate source, a black man. U.S. delegate Benjamin Gerig, the British learned, was "restrained from speaking in support of the United Kingdom by his coloured Adviser Dr. Channing Tobias." In fact, the report continued, although Gerig had carefully prepared an address to support the British position, at "the last moment, ... Tobias ... vetoed the American speech." "It is apparent," the report concluded, "that Anglo-American co-operation in the Fourth Committee will only operate, if at all, by grace and favour of Dr. Tobias."[182] (See Figure 2.5)

The British delegates not only told this tale of woe to the Foreign Office but also believed that the State Department had a right to know what was going on. They railed that "Channing Tobias ... the chief United States Delegate, prevent[ed] his Delegation from giving us the support we had been led to expect." They thought that any Anglo-American differences on colonial issues had been cleared up during a round of meetings held earlier in the year. At that time and others, they made their position perfectly clear. The "United Nations ha[d] no business dealing"

---

[181] "South Africa and U.N.O.: Dr. Donges Alleges 'Meddling' in Affairs of Members States," Press Digest No. 47, November 22, 1951, *South African Press Digests*, Fiche 20.
[182] From United Kingdom Delegation to the United Nations General Assembly Paris to Foreign Office, November 18, 1951, CO 537/7137.

FIGURE 2.5. NAACP board member, Channing Tobias, as the chair of the U.S. delegation in the Fourth Committee, blocked South Africa and Britain's initial attempt to stop the Herero, Nama, and Berg-Damara from providing direct testimony about the horrific conditions in South West Africa.
Source: NAACP Collection. Courtesy of the Library of Congress, Prints and Photographs Division, LOT 13074, no. 515.

with the "Southwest Africa question" because it was an "internal matter," and it was high time for the West to "speak up at the [General] Assembly and make it clear that colonialism ... was not necessarily a bad thing." The British had hoped that those meetings had handled any differences of opinion between the Anglo-Saxon powers, but obviously, as Tobias demonstrated, it had not. Thus, in a "frank exchange" with State Department representatives, the British asserted that Tobias had "gotten [the UN meeting] off to an extremely bad start." Instead of honoring the Anglo-American agreement and calming the "excitable atmosphere" in the Fourth Committee, Tobias had actually "paid tribute to the work" of the UN's anticolonial forces, "hoped that the time was past when non-self-governing territories were regarded as merely catering to the needs of peoples in other parts of the world," and "was glad to note from his own observations ... that the old colonialism was dead." The British warned their State Department colleagues that Foreign Secretary Anthony Eden was certainly going to take this up with the secretary of state and let him know about this "cypher" whose "lamentable" performance meant that "the precedent has now been set for the free-for-all discussion of political affairs of colonies."[183]

Channing Tobias's willingness to allow, in the words of the Foreign Office, that "unsavoury ... Michael Scott business" to occur also compelled the British to plot with the French and Belgians about how to rein in the bumptious Americans, whose maladroit leadership guaranteed "that the seeds of many and bitter controversies have been sown in the Fourth Committee." One British official fearfully spoke of the dragon's teeth planted by the U.S. delegation's fateful errors at that December 1951 meeting. At the next UN gathering, he warned, "[W]e shall be faced with applications for oral hearings from colonials ... and discussion of the political affairs of individual non-self-governing territories such as Cyprus, Malta, British Honduras, Morocco and Tunisia. All these horrors are at present just below the surface of the [Fourth] Committee."[184] This catastrophe, the British asserted, was the direct result of the State Department allowing "these casual American delegates" to subvert "the policy understood between our two Governments."[185] Kenneth Thompson, the attaché for colonial affairs, subsequently reported to the Foreign Office that in his "contacts with the State Department, I am conscious of a real sense of guilt on their part – an expectation that we are going to kick them pretty hard for letting us down."[186]

Meanwhile, the South African delegation was apoplectic about what had just transpired at the UN and went after Michael Scott with all of the top secret MI-5 ammunition it had stockpiled. Much to the horror of British Intelligence, the "South African delegation at the U.N.O.

---

[183] Mr. Jones to Mr. Hickerson, memo with attachment "Anglo-American Co-Operation in Fourth Committee of the General Assembly," November 30, 1951, Box 2, File "6th General Assembly," Lot File 58D33, *RG 59*; Anglo-American Colonial Talks, minutes, October 10, 1951, CO 537/7137; UK Delegation to the Foreign Office, November 23, 1951, CO 537/7137; UK Delegation to the Foreign Office, November 24, 1951, CO 537/7137; Statement by the Honourable Channing Tobias in Committee IV (Trusteeship on Non-Self-Governing Territories), November 21, 1951, File "United Nations, 1951–1952," *Tobias Papers*; "Tobias Urges Non-Self Governing Peoples Interests be Protected," November 29, 1951, File "United Nations, 1951–1952," *Tobias Papers*.

[184] B. O. B. Gidden to C. P. Hope, February 2, 1952, CO 936/94.

[185] Christopher Steel to Paul Mason, April 15, 1952, CO 936/94.

[186] J. K. Thompson to B. O. B. Gidden, February 25, 1952, CO 936/94.

session in Paris were making great play of Scott's past membership of the [Communist] Party and were apparently broadcasting this information among the other delegates." Even worse, from MI-5's perspective, was that the South Africans "claim to have obtained the information from two separate great powers," which was a horrific breach of protocol, and had ignored the revised intelligence analysis on Scott that noted that "he had been disassociated from the Party for the last six or seven years at least."[187]

While working to discredit Scott in Paris, the Union wrapped an iron fist around Southern Africa. Malan's government let Chief Hosea Kutako and his colleagues get as far as the city of Windhoek, where Scott had secured the funding, in part from the NAACP, to pay for their passage to the UN meeting in Paris. At Windhoek all progress stopped. Days passed before Malan's government finally announced that it had decided to refuse the African leadership passports to leave the country, ever.[188]

At this point, South Africa lost even more allies. The Canadians, who had been trying to play a moderating role, could not understand why South Africa was so intent on "burning bridges." The Union had set itself up as a "villain." It had continued to defy the UN and the World Court, it had refused to acknowledge the rock solid foundation in law of international accountability, and then it had tried to revert to legalisms by picking and choosing which sections of the ICJ's ruling best suited its case. At that, the Fourth Committee was so exasperated, the Canadians conceded, that "there seemed to be some substance in the contention that since South Africa had shown no inclination to accept that part of the International Court's opinion dealing with petitions and annual reports, the Assembly

---

[187] C. P. C. de Wesselow, note for P.F.65,777 (Scott), November 19, 1951, KV2/2053.
[188] Michael Scott to Chief Hosea Kutako, November 17, 1951, Box 15, File "David Astor Box, Correspondence with and Papers Connected with Rev. Michael Scott and S.W. Africa, 1950–1961," *Scott Papers*; "Scott Suggests Bechuanaland Hereros If S.W.A. Chiefs Are Refused Permission," *Sunday Times*, December 9, 1951, Box 5, File "South West Africa (Namibia): Press Comment on, 1950–51," *Papers of Joseph Sweeney*, Harry S. Truman Presidential Library, Independence, MO; Michael Scott to S. Garry Oniki, November 18, 1951, Box 30, File "Correspondence with Organisations in the US, 1949–55," *Scott Papers*; Mary Benson to Mr. Tomlinson, December 5, 1951, Box 15, File "David Astor Box, Correspondence with and Papers Connected with Rev. Michael Scott and S.W. Africa, 1950–1961," *Scott Papers*; "South Africa and U.N.O.: Union Withdraws from Trusteeship Committee," Press Digest No. 48, November 29, 1951, *South African Press Digests*, Fiche 21. In the mid-1960s, three Americans, working with Michael Scott, managed to record Chief Hosea's testimony and submit it to the UN. See Allard K. Lowenstein, *Brutal Mandate: A Journey to South West Africa*, foreword by Mrs. Franklin D. Roosevelt (New York: MacMillan Company, 1962), 166–167.

was morally justified in consulting representatives from that territory as a means of obtaining fuller information on local conditions."[189]

The denial of passports to Chief Hosea and his colleagues was part and parcel of the South African strategy to undermine international accountability and reinforce white supremacy. By this time, Scott had been banned from ever setting foot in South Africa again.[190] The Hereros could not get out. Tobias was certainly furious, particularly after he saw the smug, self-congratulatory air among the colonial powers when the Africans were denied direct access to the UN. Or, as he put it to Walter White, "I witnessed the brush-off." The others on the Fourth Committee saw it, too. Scott, however, was still on the scene, and Tobias, who received "counsel and advice throughout the sessions" from Ralph Bunche, signaled the other delegates that the United States would not be opposed to learning further about the plight of Chief Hosea and others stranded at Windhoek.[191] With that, the chair of the Fourth Committee, Max Henriquez Ureña of the Dominican Republic, "asked his reverence" to testify.[192] Scott said simply and powerfully that his was a poor substitute for the voices that the UN really needed to hear: those of the Africans themselves, who had endured the sufferings attendant with white supremacist rule.[193]

[189] Memorandum from Under-Secretary of State for External Affairs to Secretary of State for External Affairs, December 15, 1951, No. 228, *Canadian Foreign Affairs*; Chairman Delegation to United Nations General Assembly to Secretary of State for External Affairs, November 20, 1951, No. 217, *Canadian Foreign Affairs*; Secretary of State for External Affairs to Chairman, Delegation to the General Assembly of the United Nations, December 31, 1951, No. 213, *Canadian Foreign Affairs*; Chairman, Delegation to the General Assembly of the United Nations to Secretary of State for External Affairs, December 29, 1951, No. 212, *Canadian Foreign Affairs*.

[190] Mary Benson to Michael Scott, December 6, 1951, Box 78, File "Mary Benson [A.Y. Only]," *Scott Papers*; South African Secretary for the Interior to Michael Scott, December 19, 1951, Box 158, File "8," *Papers of the Africa Bureau*.

[191] Michael Scott, "South West African Referendum," n.d., Box 13, File "'S' (Folder 2)," *Truman:Nash*; Borstelmann, *Apartheid's Reluctant Uncle*, 162; Channing H. Tobias to John D. Hickerson, May 19, 1952, Box 2, File "6th General Assembly," Lot File 58D33, *RG* 59; Mr. Wainhouse to Mr. Hickerson, memo, April 24, 1951, Box 11, File "General Assembly Sixth Session, U.S. Delegation, Paris, 1951," Lot File 55D429, *RG* 59; Channing H. Tobias to Walter White, November 12, 1952, Reel 4, *NAACP-Int'l*; Phelps-Stokes Fund Board of Trustees Meeting Minutes, April 16, 1952, Box 6, File "Board of Trustees Minutes, 1952–1953," *Phelps-Stokes Collection*.

[192] Agatha Harrison to Friends House et al., December 10, 1951, Box 40, File "Letters from Fletcher, Troup, etc.," *Scott Papers*.

[193] "South Africa Strongly Criticised in U.N. Committee," *Manchester Guardian*, December 10, 1951, KV2/2053.

Although by 1951 the multinational coalition of which the NAACP was part was not able to fully achieve its goals in Southern Africa, the groundwork had been laid and the territory staked out. Du Bois had earlier written that "[t]he real radical ... is the man, who hits power in high places, white power, power backed by unlimited wealth; hits it and hits it openly and between the eyes."[194] That is what the battle for South West Africa revealed, as a marauding, maverick priest named Michael Scott and a "conservative, bureaucratic organization," the NAACP, risked the wrath of powerful governments, the destruction and ostracism that came with the "epithet" *Communist* and *Communist sympathizer*, and their respectable status in society to ensure that the atrocities of the apartheid regime would not go unnoticed.[195]

That fighting spirit is not surprising. As Scott's biographers noted, he had no use for a "gentle Jesus meek and mild." For him, the model "was Christ as a militant figure."[196] The Association similarly viewed itself as a "militant organization" and was, therefore, drawn to Scott, this warrior in a clerical collar.[197] As the emissary's emissary, the NAACP challenged the State and Justice Departments to help get Scott into the United States; provided him with office space and secretarial support; facilitated access, despite punitive restrictions on his visa, to power brokers and opinion makers; leveraged the combined and distinctive power of other organizations such as the ILRM and the India League at critical moments; and organized successful fundraising campaigns to pay his medical bills and living expenses. Despite the consistent attempts by the U.S. and British governments to pen Scott in the Soviet camp, the NAACP's unwavering support helped keep the issues of colonialism, international accountability, human rights, and the brutality of apartheid squarely on the UN's agenda. This work was further buttressed by Channing Tobias's key interventions, which, as the British complained mightily, brushed up against the imperial powers' claims of sovereignty in Africa and cracked open the door to the Fourth Committee's demand for information on the

---

[194] W. E. B. Du Bois, "Fisk," *Crisis*, 29, no. 6 (April 1925), 250. I want to thank Claudrena Harold for directing me to this source.

[195] August Meier and John H. Bracey Jr., "The NAACP As a Reform Movement, 1909–1965: 'To Reach the Conscience of America,'" *Journal of Southern History*, 59, no. 1 (February 1993), 27; G. R. Mitchell to G. N. Jackson, PF.65,777/B,1,g,.RT, December 7, 1950, KV2/2053.

[196] Yates and Chester, *The Troublemaker*, 294.

[197] Keynote Address by Dr. Channing H. Tobias, Chairman, Board of Directors, National Association for the Advancement of Colored People: An Address Prepared for Delivery at the 48th Annual NAACP Convention, June 25, 1957, *Tobias Papers*.

political progress of colonies toward independence. In a letter to Walter White, Scott conveyed the ways in which their collaboration had helped lead to a global recognition of South West Africa as "the symbol, on the one hand, of African people dispossessed of their lands and rights and, on the other, of the great efforts that have been made ... to establish the principle of international accountability."[198]

[198] The International League for the Rights of Man, January–February 1953 Bulletin, February 1953, Box 1154, File "9," *ACLU Papers*; Michael Scott to Walter White, January 12, 1951, Box A8, File "Southwest Africa, 1947–51," *Papers of the NAACP*.

3

"An Even Larger Issue Than 'Containing Communism'"

The NAACP and the Italian Colonies

> We demand that … the rights of natives in Libya, Eritrea, and Somaliland be safeguarded under an International Mandates Commission.
> – NAACP Colonial Conference, 1945

Southern Africa, unfortunately, was not the only place on the continent where an imperial power with a well-documented record of atrocities maneuvered to expand its control. In North Africa and the Horn, Italy sought to leverage its Cold War importance to the West, as well as its allies' influence in the UN, to regain dominion over people who were determined to break free of a colonial ruler who had bathed their lands in blood and mustard gas.

The visible agony of the Horn and North Africa coupled with Italy's astounding demand for return of all the African territory that its fascist incarnation had lost in the war was central to another key campaign the NAACP waged to undercut the legitimacy of colonialism. In this struggle over the Italian colonies of Libya, Somalia, and Eritrea, the Association used many of the same tools that it deployed against South Africa – the UN, media, progressive alliances, and sympathetic supporters within the halls of power – and focused on three key elements.

First, the Association elevated the principle of "the wishes of the inhabitants" and made that concept central to its sustained argument against the reimposition of Italian control. The NAACP was determined that the Atlantic Charter's pledges that there would be "no territorial changes that do not accord with the freely expressed wishes of the peoples concerned" and that the Allies would "respect the right of all peoples to choose the form of government under which they will live" would be more than just "eyewash" or a smoke screen for continued imperial rule.[1]

Second, the Association insisted on the principle, asserted initially during the battles with South Africa, that any administering power had to have the will and the ability to embed human rights into the political, economic, and social transformation of the colonies. Even after Rome agreed that it did not want the "old colonialism" but merely to hold a UN trusteeship over Libya, Eritrea, and Somalia, the Association was not assuaged. Italy's horrific legacy of mass slaughter, mass hangings, and mass poisonings, coupled with its destitute postwar status, proved that it did not and could not meet that standard.

Moreover, as the British, the Soviets, the Egyptians, the French, and the Ethiopians, in addition to the Italians, all vied for some additional sliver of territory in North Africa and the Horn, explaining their rationales in terms of military bases, strategic outposts, Red Sea access, or dumping grounds for "surplus population," the Association concluded that no nation was capable of honoring the wishes of the inhabitants and upholding the Charter's human rights commitments. This realization led to the third significant tenet in the Association's efforts: advocating for the UN itself to take on the extensive process of turning the Italians' genocidal wasteland of North Africa and the Horn into viable, democratic states.

Initially, U.S. foreign policy aligned, for the most part, with the NAACP's goals – keep Italy out and bring the United Nations in. The Association, therefore, spent the immediate postwar years focused on litigating and lobbying for equality at home; drafting its petition to the UN, *An Appeal to the World*, charging the American government with a range of human rights violations; and trying to stop Pretoria from annexing South West Africa. However, the onset of the Cold War was a game changer. The Defense and State Departments came to define U.S. national security in ways that put anticommunism – not human rights, not decolonization, not even democracy – at its center. The result was a haphazard, chaotic, and contradictory mosaic of U.S. foreign policy stances in North Africa and the Horn that treated the indigenous people and their wishes as absolutely irrelevant. It was at that point that the NAACP stepped in to defend the rights of Libyans, Eritreans, and Somalis. The Association directly challenged U.S. Cold War policy, reminded government officials

---

[1] The Avalon Project: Documents in Law, History, and Diplomacy, *Atlantic Charter*, August 14, 1941, http://avalon.law.yale.edu/wwii/atlantic.asp. Accessed May 13, 2013; George Padmore to Cyril Ollivierre, December 5, 1944, *Padmore*; Carol Anderson, "Rethinking Radicalism: African Americans and the Liberation Struggles in Somalia, Libya, and Eritrea, 1945–1949," *Journal of the Historical Society* 11, no. 4 (December 2011): 385–423.

and the public of Italy's brutal actions in Africa, and stepped in boldly where the black Left and the Soviets were unable to mount a coherent anticolonial campaign.

This important Cold War saga actually began decades earlier in Italy's hunger to attain Great Power status.[2] As a relative latecomer to nationhood and the imperial project, Italian colonialism dated back to only the 1890s. Although Italy tended to depict its rule in Libya, Eritrea, and Somalia as "benign," it was anything but. The Italians' tenure in Africa was marked by mass public hangings, slavery, poisoned water wells, and a genocidal pacification campaign that reduced the population in Libya by more than 40 percent.[3]

And, in the final analysis, none of the colonies proved to be the immigration magnets or economic assets that the Italian government had hoped for. Between 1890 and 1905, of the 3.5 million Italians who emigrated, fewer than 4,000 had moved to Eritrea. Indeed, during the entire fifty-year tenure of Italy's colonial rule, the Italian population in all three colonies barely approached 100,000; by contrast, the number who lived in New York City alone had surpassed that figure forty years earlier.[4] Moreover, the financial rewards of colonization also proved elusive. Even while adhering to a policy of "extremely limited economic development," the Italians had lost more than $1 billion financing their colonial empire, and there were no great mineral reserves to offset these staggering losses. (Oil had not been discovered in Libya until 1958, and Somalia's chief exports were frankincense and easily bruised bananas.)[5]

---

[2] Christopher Seton-Watson, "Italy's Imperial Hangover," *Journal of Contemporary History*, 15, no. 1, (January 1980), 169.

[3] Scott L. Bills, *The Libyan Arena: The United States, Britain, and the Council of Foreign Ministers, 1945–1948* (Kent, OH: Kent State University Press, 1995), 59; R. J. B. Bosworth, *Mussolini's Italy: Life under the Fascist Dictatorship, 1915–1945* (New York: Penguin Press, 2006), 381; I. M. Lewis, *A Modern History of the Somali: Nation and State in the Horn of Africa*, 4th ed. (Athens: Ohio University Press, 2002), 92–95; S. Pinkney Tuck to Secretary of State, April 8, 1946, Box 6968, 865C.00/4–846, RG 59.

[4] Haile M. Larebo, *The Building of an Empire: Italian Land Policy and Practice in Ethiopia, 1935–1941* (Oxford: Clarendon Press; New York: Oxford University Press, 1994), 25; E. A. Bayne, "Somalia on the Horn: A Counterpoint of Problems Confronting One of Africa's New Nations," *Publication of the American University Field Service Reports*, Vol. VII, no. 11 (New York: AUFS, 1960), 2–3; Lewis, *A Modern History of Somalia*, 101; Humbert Nelli, "Italian-Americans," in *Harvard Encyclopedia of American Ethnic Groups*, ed. Stephan Thernstrom (Cambridge, MA: Belknap Press of Harvard University Press, 1980), 545–560.

[5] Great Britain Ministry of Information, *The First to Be Freed* (London: His Majesty's Stationery Office, 1944), 6; Lewis, *A Modern History of Somalia*, 100–101; Bills, *The Libyan Arena*, 16, 18, 30; Larebo, *The Building of an Empire*, 15; MacGregor Knox,

Regardless of the financial toll and collapsed colonization schemes, however, Italy, ever desperate to maintain its tenuous hold on Great Power status, was on the prowl for additional colonies.[6] That hunt led straight to Ethiopia.[7] There the Italians not only failed to capture their prey in 1896 but also fell into their own trap. At Adowa, "ill-armed ... Ethiopians wiped out a seventeen thousand man Italian and auxiliary army" and handed Italy a stunning defeat on the battlefield.[8] From that moment on, "[r]evenge" became an insistent drumbeat for Italian politicians.[9] In 1935, fueled by the determination to "wipe out the shame of Adowa," Italy's fascist regime launched yet another invasion of one of the only independent nations on the continent of Africa.[10]

But as the twin pincer invasion from Eritrea and Somalia quickly stalled, Italian dictator Benito Mussolini saw his supposedly easy victory devolving into Adowa revisited. Panic and fear gripped him. Use "'any means' to assure victory" he ordered. Marshal Rodolpho Graziani responded accordingly. The field marshal wanted "maximum liberty" to saturate the "barbarous hordes" with "asphyxiating gas." The dictator approved Graziani's request and issued edict after edict calling for the execution, "extermination," and gassing of the Ethiopians. At first, Mussolini's air force dropped barrels of lethal yperite on the Ethiopians. However, after Il Duce's field marshals determined that the effect was "too localized" to change the tide of battle, the Italians decided to equip their planes with an "apparatus for spraying the liquid [mustard gas] in the manner that insecticides are sprayed over crops." This "deadly dew, destroying the eyes, burning through the clothing and the flesh to the very bones, ... had the most devastating effect." As if killing an

Mussolini Unleashed: 1939–1941, Politics and Strategy in Fascist Italy's Last War (New York: Cambridge University Press, 1982), 8–9; E. A. Bayne, "Somalia on the Horn: A Counterpoint of Problems Confronting One of Africa's New Nations," *Publication of the American University Field Service Reports*, Vol. VII, no. 8, (New York: AUFS, 1960), 3; Bayne, "Somalia on the Horn," Vol. VII, no. 11:3.

[6] Ruth Ben-Ghiat and Mia Fuller, eds., *Italian Colonialism* (New York: Palgrave Macmillan, 2005).

[7] Rene Albrecht-Carrie, "Italian Colonial Policy, 1914–1918," *Journal of Modern History*, 18, no. 2 (June 1946), 123–147.

[8] George Raudzens, "War-Winning Weapons: The Measurement of Technological Determinism in Military History," *Journal of Military History*, 54, no. 4 (October 1990), 416.

[9] Bills, *The Libyan Arena*, 11; George W. Baer, *The Coming of the Italian-Ethiopian War* (Cambridge, MA: Harvard University Press, 1967), 4.

[10] Seton-Watson, "Italy's Imperial Hangover," 170.

infestation of locusts, "clouds of deadly gas enveloped Ethiopian troops and peasants," and Haile Selassie's forces, "who lacked everything but valor," simply "didn't know how to fight this terrible rain that burned and killed."[11] The Ethiopian government could only futilely turn to the international community and denounce the "barefaced aggression by an armed great power against a practically unarmed and innocent black people."[12]

African Americans were in an uproar at this unprovoked attack – a clear attempt, in the words of anticolonial strategist George Padmore, "to destroy the last independent nation on the continent of Africa."[13] As Brenda Gayle Plummer noted, "[A] sacral belief in Ethiopia's importance was widespread in the black diaspora. Biblical allusions to ancient Ethiopian splendors ... and future glory ... stirred many. Modern Ethiopians had helped perpetuate the legend by remaining sovereign on a continent almost entirely subjugated to colonialism."[14] Anger, therefore, extended even to the "most rural and remote parts of Mississippi," columnist George Schuyler observed.[15] One black man called on God Almighty to have the "Red Sea repeat her Pharaoh act," part in two, and swallow Mussolini's troops whole.[16] As the war raged, the NAACP pleaded with another higher power, the president of the United States,

---

[11] Alberto Sbacchi, *Ethiopia Under Mussolini: Fascism and the Colonial Experience* (London: Zed Books, 1985), 25; Arthur H. Steiner, "The Government of Italian East Africa," *American Political Science Review* 30, no. 5 (October 1936), 884; Knox, *Mussolini Unleashed*, 3–5; Ethiopian Ministry of Justice, *Documents on Italian War Crimes*, iv, 5; Adam Clayton Powell Jr. to Warren R. Austin, April 13, 1949, attachment from *Congressional Record*, Box 43, File "Powell, Adam Clayton, Jr., 1949," *JFD-Princeton*; George W. Baer, review of "The Ethiopian War: 1935–1941," by Angelo Del Boca, *Journal of Modern History*, 42, no. 4 (December 1970), 708, 710.

[12] "Ethiopians Appeal for Moral Support," *New York Times*, October 5, 1935.

[13] Joseph E. Harris, *African-American Reactions to War in Ethiopia, 1936–1941* (Baton Rouge: Louisiana State University Press, 1994), 34–62, 97–98; George Padmore, "Ethiopia and World Politics," *Crisis*, 42, 5 (May 1935), 138. For the importance of the Italian invasion of Ethiopia to African American activism in international affairs, see Brenda Gayle Plummer, *Rising Wind: Black Americans and U.S. Foreign Affairs, 1935–1960* (Chapel Hill: University of North Carolina Press, 1996), 40–53. Also see, William R. Scott, *The Sons of Sheba's Race: African-Americans and the Italo-Ethiopian War, 1935–1941* (Bloomington: University of Indiana Press, 1993).

[14] Plummer, *Rising Wind*, 38.

[15] George Schuyler, "Views and Reviews," *Pittsburgh Courier*, November 23, 1935; S. K. B. Asante, "The Afro-American and the Italo-Ethiopian Crisis," *Race*, 15, no. 2 (1973), 176–177.

[16] F. Ernest Work, "Italo-Ethiopian Relations," *Journal of Negro History*, 20, no. 4 (October 1935), 447.

to do something, especially after it became clear that the "spineless," "moribund League of Nations was both unwilling and unable to intervene since the victim was dark skinned and the aggressor at least nominally white."[17]

The Association was especially contemptuous of the USSR, whose leadership at the League of Nations helped exacerbate that international organization's glaring timidity. Soviet Foreign Minister Maxim Litvinov, as president of the 86th Session of the League, had "pressed hard to settle the brewing conflict to Italy's benefit."[18] Just a year earlier, George Padmore complained bitterly that he had witnessed a series of actions by the Communist Party in Africa that could only be defined as "betrayal" and he knew why: "[T]oday Stalin has given up the idea of support to those who are still under the yoke, in order to win capitalist support."[19] For several years, especially with the rise of Nazi Germany, the Kremlin had been looking for some form of diplomatic entente with Fascist Italy to check Adolf Hitler on the European continent. The USSR was not going to let an unprovoked war against an African nation get in the way of its plans to woo Mussolini.[20] At the height of the invasion of Ethiopia, the Soviets, therefore, decided to "increase ... their oil shipments to Italy during January and February 1936."[21] In fact, as Plummer notes, "Soviet imports constituted 25 percent of the total Italian petroleum inventory."[22] For Moscow, the goal was not to defend a virtually unarmed nation from mustard gas attacks and aerial bombing, but rather to buy Italy's allegiance with Ethiopian blood.

As reports rolled in about the national "crucifixion" of Ethiopia, Walter White could only ask in anger, "Has Russia abandoned its alleged opposition [to] imperialism and its much publicized defense [of] weaker

---

[17] Walter White to Herbert Agar, December 4, 1941, Reel 1, *NAACP-Int'l*; Walter White, "Italy's Former Colonies and American Policy," August 26, 1948, Box A81, File "Articles: Walter White Syndicated Column, 1948, *Papers of the NAACP*.

[18] J. Calvitt Clarke III, "Soviet Russia and the Italo-Ethiopian War of 1935–36." http://users.ju.edu/jclarke/scss04.htm. Accessed June 24, 2008.

[19] George Padmore to Cyril Ollivierre, July 28, 1934, *Padmore*.

[20] J. Calvitt Clarke III, "Soviet Appeasement, Collective Security, and the Italo-Ethiopian War of 1935 and 1936," *Selected Annual Proceedings of the Florida Conference of Historians*, 4 (December 1996), 115–132. http://users.ju.edu/jclarke/wizzf.html. Accessed June 24, 2008.

[21] J. Calvitt Clarke III, "Italo-Soviet Military Cooperation in the 1930s," in *Girding for Battle: The Arms Trade in Global Perspective, 1815–1940*, ed. Donald J. Stoker Jr. and Jonathan A. Grant (Westport, CT: Praeger, 2003), 188–189.

[22] Plummer, *Rising Wind*, 49.

peoples?" Or, he challenged Litvinov, "Does your anti-imperialism stop at black nations?"[23] "Evidently" it did, one black scholar noted, because Ethiopia's independence was clearly being "sacrificed in an effort to maintain the peace of Europe."[24]

Indignation, however, was hardly universal, even in black activist circles. Paul Robeson, in particular, adopted a more aloof stance. "[N]aturally," he said, "my sympathy is all with the Ethiopians. It would seem that those people could get along without the kind of 'civilizing' that European nations do with bombs and machine guns."[25] But his analysis went no further. He ignored the USSR's role in this "civilizing mission," including the widespread reports that "the Soviets [were] raking in good capitalist profits selling wheat and coal tar to Italy for use in the war against Ethiopia."[26]

Robeson's long silence coincided with his full immersion in Marxist theory and growing affinity for what he (and so many other intellectuals) believed the Soviet Union had been able to achieve. Although, at that time, the USSR had just emerged from the Great Famine, where more than 5 million peasants had starved to death, all Robeson could see was a minority paradise, a thriving industrialized nation, and a virtual agricultural utopia. After a 1936 visit to the Soviet Union, he exclaimed with "boyish enthusiasm" that the "U.S.S.R. [was] The Land for Me." He dismissed outright the reports about the brutality of the regime. All "[t]his stuff about starvation is the bunk," he insisted to readers of the Communist Party's the *Worker* in 1936. "Wherever I went I found plenty of food," and the people were "very happy." Robeson continued, "I made it a point to visit some of the workers' homes.... They all live in healthful surroundings, with ... the most modern equipment ... plenty of light, fresh air, and space." Robeson, in fact, was so mesmerized by "the only nation in the world where racial discrimination is prohibited and where

[23] Walter White to Herbert Agar, December 4, 1941, Reel 1, *NAACP-Int'l.*; National Association [for the] Advancement [of] Colored People to Max Litvinov, telegram, May 22, 1935, Box 181–8, Folder "3," *Logan-MSRC.*

[24] Work, "Italo-Ethiopian Relations," 442.

[25] "Robeson Visions an Africa Free of Rule by Europeans," *New York Herald-Tribune*, January 12, 1936, in Paul Robeson, *Paul Robeson Speaks: Writings, Speeches, Interviews, 1918–1974*, ed. with introduction and notes by Philip S. Foner (New York: Brunner/ Mazel Publishers, 1978), 104.

[26] A. J. Barker, *The Civilizing Mission: A History of the Italo-Ethiopian War of 1935–1936* (New York: Dial Press, 1968), 10; "Editorials: Soviet Russia Aids Italy," *Crisis*, 42, no. 10 (October 1935), 305.

the people live freely" that he exhorted, "Say, do I like it! ... Why it's the only country in the world where I feel at home."[27]

Few other African Americans found anything to be so enamored of. The situation in Ethiopia was grim, and the Soviets (as well as the British and the French) had contributed to the bloodbath in the Horn of Africa. Scholars William R. Scott and S. K. B. Asante noted that "the racial implications of the Italo-Ethiopian conflict were paramount" as the black community "stated bluntly that the 'rape of Ethiopia is the rape of the Negro race.'"[28] The betrayal of Ethiopia would not be forgotten.

Meanwhile, as the Second World War erupted, Fascist Italy sensed that imperial glory was within reach. Mussolini calculated that a quick Axis victory, after Germany carved out its share, would allow the sizable crumbs of the French and British empires to fall in his lap. Thus, with France just weeks away from surrendering to the Nazis and the English fleeing across the Channel at Dunkirk, Italy attacked the French southern flank in May 1940.

That seemingly brilliant calculation was a miscalculation of monumental proportions. The declaration of war was an act of "national suicide" that branded the Italians as "jackals," exposed the fatal weaknesses in the Italian military, and destroyed Il Duce and his regime.[29] By 1943, the Italians were trying desperately to negotiate a separate peace with the Allies, withdraw their troops from the field of battle and redeploy them closer to home, and do all of this without raising the suspicions or the wrath of Nazi Germany. They failed. The *Wehrmacht* retaliated with blinding fury. What resistance the remnants of the "defeated," "disorganized," and "disintegrated" Italian armed forces could give was minimal and the resulting wholesale slaughter was exacerbated by the flight of the king, disarray in the government, and the evaporation of the supreme command of the armed forces. By the time the Germans were through,

[27] Robert Conquest, *The Harvest of Sorrow: Soviet Collectivization and the Terror-Famine* (New York: Oxford University Press, 1986); Timothy Snyder, *Bloodlands: Europe between Hitler and Stalin* (New York: Basic Books, 2010), 21–53, 67; David C. Engerman, *Modernization from the Other Shore: American Intellectuals and the Romance of Russian Development* (Cambridge, MA: Harvard University Press, 2003), 5, 194–243; "U.S.S.R. – The Land for Me," *Sunday Worker*, May 10, 1936, in Robeson, *Robeson Speaks*, 105–107; Martin Bauml Duberman, *Paul Robeson* (New York: Knopf, 1988), 349.

[28] William R. Scott, "Black Nationalism and the Italo-Ethiopian Conflict, 1934–1936," *Journal of Negro History*, 63, no. 2 (April 1978), 123; Asante, "The Afro American," 176.

[29] Rene Albrecht-Carrie, "Peace with Italy – An Appraisal," *Political Science Quarterly*, 62, no. 4 (December 1947), 482; Bills, *The Libyan Arena*, 11.

more than 700,000 Italian troops were captured and "only seven" out of the original sixty-one army divisions "were left" – and those were deep in Sardinia and southern Italy. Nonetheless, the next month, in a desperate bid to "avoid … the disgrace of being a defeated enemy," Italy, with virtually no remaining military capacity, committed another act of "national suicide" and declared war on Nazi Germany.[30] Italy, already vanquished, now fully exposed its defenseless people to the vengeance of Adolf Hitler.

As much as the Italians suffered at the hands of Nazi Germany, however – and they truly did – it was still difficult, if not impossible, for African Americans to erase the images of the cheering throngs who had once glorified Mussolini while Ethiopians collapsed under the rain of mustard gas.[31] Nor was it easy for the Allied Powers to forget Italy's cozy military alliance with the Nazis, its willingness to destroy the League of Nations to realize its imperialistic dreams in Ethiopia, or its self-serving eagerness to declare war on a prostrate France and badly wounded Britain.

Nonetheless, despite their full complicity in starting the war and then negligible contribution to the Allied victory, the Italians "indulged" in the ultimate fantasy that they, like the other late entrant into the war, the United States, would be treated as a full partner in the peace negotiations.[32] On Victory in Europe (VE) Day, Prime Minister Ivanoe Bonomi reminded President Truman of the great sacrifices the Italians had made to defeat the Nazis and asserted that the only thing his nation wanted, given that the tricolor flag of Italy flew alongside the stars and stripes of the United States, was a peace treaty that did not punish Italy for its brief fling with fascism and the return of all of the colonies, which were now,

---

[30] Elena Agarossi, *A Nation Collapses: The Italian Surrender of September 1943*, trans. Harvey Ferguson II (New York: Cambridge University Press, 2000), 1–2; Howard McGaw Smyth, "Some Recent Italian Publications Regarding World War II," *Military Affairs*, 11, no. 4 (Winter 1947), 245–253; Robert W. Komer, "The Establishment of Allied Control in Italy," *Military Affairs*, 13, no. 1 (Spring 1949), 21–25.

[31] Harcourt A. Tynes to Walter White, October 18, 1943, Box A466, File "Peace Conference Committee to Present Views of Negroes at Upcoming Peace Conference, 1943–44," *Papers of the NAACP*; "Open Ethiopian Legation: Minister Attends UNRRA," *New Africa*, 2, no. 5 (December 1943); Luisa Passerini, *Fascism in Popular Memory: The Cultural Experience of the Turin Working Class*, trans. Robert Lumley and Jude Bloomfield (London: Cambridge University Press, 1984, 1987), 5, 85.

[32] League of Nations, "Report of the League of Nations Council Committee," *American Journal of International Law*, 30, no. 1, Supplement: Official Documents (January 1936), 1–26; Albrecht-Carrie, "Peace with Italy – An Appraisal," 484.

as a result of the disastrous North African campaigns, occupied by the British military.[33]

The Allies were not in a generous, forgiving mood. They awarded Great Britain temporary control over all of the Italian colonies except an area in Libya known as the Fezzan, which the French would administer. This was a stopgap measure until the Council of Foreign Ministers (CFM), comprised of the United States, Britain, France, and the USSR, could decide the final fate of Eritrea, Libya, and Somalia.[34]

For African Americans, this political maneuvering could only mean that the war's victory was slipping away. The leery black press, concerned that the Allies' plans for the postwar gave nothing but "lip service" to anticolonialism, concluded that "the outlook [was] not only dark and confusing but discouraging" for people of color.[35] The *Pittsburgh Courier* warned that with the Council of Foreign Ministers meeting looming, "the ghosts of old world diplomacy" had revived to "concoct" a "witch's brew ... that bodes little good for either the native peoples or for the peace of the world."[36]

At least initially, however, the CFM's deliberations would prove to be more complex and more grounded in modern notions of self-determination and trusteeship than any previous international conference on Africa. Therefore, in addition to Italy's abominable record as a colonial power, the nation would have another hurdle to overcome to regain control of Libya, Eritrea, and Somalia. Rome was simply in no position to fulfill any of Chapter XII's basic requirements to construct a viable political, economic, and social infrastructure in North Africa and the Horn. As far as U.S. State Department officials were concerned, Italy was an impoverished nation, unable to feed its own people, struggling to buy enough coal to get through the coming winter, and wholly dependent on American largesse and relief funds just to survive. Secretary of State Byrnes, therefore, warned Italian Prime Minister Alcide De Gasperi to be "realistic" about what was going to occur at the upcoming Council of Foreign Ministers meeting because the United States had no intention of

[33] Bills, *The Libyan Arena*, 33, 59–60.

[34] Ibid., 38, 59–60. China was also a member of the Council of Foreign Ministers; however, it played no role in the decision on the Italian Colonies.

[35] A. M. Wendell Malliet, "Declares Postwar Outlook Dark for Colored Nations," *New York Amsterdam News*, April 7, 1945.

[36] Rayford Logan, "Colonial 'Spectres' Haunt London Peace Conference," *Pittsburgh Courier*, September 22, 1945.

watching its relief funds disappear down the "rathole" of Italian imperial ambitions in North Africa and the Horn.[37]

As promised, when the CFM did meet in September 1945, Byrnes entirely dismissed De Gasperi's pleas, made no distinction between Italian and Fascist rule, and noted that "oppression" and fiscal mismanagement defined the entire period of Italy's fifty-year colonial regime. Then the secretary of state, in a move designed to enhance the prestige of the newly created United Nations, keep the Soviets out of the Mediterranean and Red Seas, and lend credibility to America's image as an anticolonial power, proposed that Eritrea, Somalia, and Libya be held in "a genuine international trusteeship" with an administrator "appointed by, and responsible to, the Trusteeship Council of the U.N."[38]

This precedent-setting proposal to designate the UN and not any particular nation as the administering power was no spur-of-the-moment decision. Instead, the State Department had arrived at this conclusion "with some difficulty." As foreign policy consultant John Foster Dulles later noted, the United States "recognized that true international trusteeship ... was ... the sound solution"; however, the State Department was initially "frightened by the practical difficulties involved," such as how would order be maintained "among the rather turbulent tribes?" And, equally important, "Who would pay the budgetary deficits ... of such economically poor areas?" They first toyed with "a less ideal solution, namely, Italian trusteeship under the United Nations Organization." Dulles and Byrnes soon realized that an Italian trusteeship "would be difficult ... to defend" because "Italy had not established a good reputation as a colonial power" and "was both incompetent and an ex-enemy."[39] Byrnes, therefore, argued before the Council of Foreign Ministers that only an international trusteeship would "assist the inhabitants of the colonies to develop the capacity for self-government so that the people might

---

[37] Bills, *The Libyan Arena*, 38, 60.

[38] United States Department of State, "Memorandum Prepared in the Department of State: Chronological Summary of Correspondence and Exchanges of Views Leading up to the Discussions with the British on the Middle East, with Texts of More Important Documents Attached as Annexes," n.d., *Foreign Relations of the United States*, Vol. 5, *The Near East and Africa* (Washington, DC: Government Printing Office, 1971), 488, 543–544 (hereafter FRUS).

[39] "Extract from Notes Dictated in Advance of Meeting of Commission on a Just and Durable Peace and, in Substance, Used in J.F.D. Opening 'Off-the-Record' Statement to the Commission on November 8, 1945," November 8, 1945, Box 26, File "Byrnes, James F.," *JFD-Princeton*.

be granted independence." Moreover, he added, it would preclude any single power from militarily or economically exploiting these colonies.[40]

The other nations sitting around that table were not pleased. France, whose Great Power status had already been punctured by a panzer division through the Ardennes Forest, was beside itself at the proposal's implications. The stunning defeat by Nazi Germany and the weakened grip of Vichy France on the colonies had spurred nationalists throughout the French Empire to demand independence. Vietnam had already begun to break free, and the colonies in North Africa were not far behind. French Foreign Minister Georges Bidault was therefore greatly concerned that the very "concept" of Libyan independence "would be a fire brand in [France's] African possessions" of Algeria, Tunisia, and Morocco. As far as Bidault could see, neither a UN trusteeship nor the continued presence of the British, who, in his opinion, seemed to be getting soft on the issue of colonialism, could deliver what the French really needed – a return to the prewar colonial status quo. Only Italy, which was also struggling to reassert itself as a Great Power, could be counted on to keep an ironclad grip on Libya and refuse to entertain any dangerous notions of independence.[41]

Although France's traditional response was to be expected, the Soviets stunned everyone. Despite their vocal antipathy toward colonialism, they had, as early as 1944, begun to determine what colony along the Mediterranean they wanted for themselves. To lay the groundwork for this plan, Andrei Gromyko, while at the UN founding conference in San Francisco, probed then acting Secretary of State Edward Stettinius about the possibility of the Soviets becoming a trustee power under the UN. Of course, with the war still raging in Japan and the United States hoping to entice the Red Army to weigh in, the Americans "agreed in principle to support" the Soviets' bid for a trusteeship. By the time of the September CFM meeting, however, the Japanese had surrendered, and the United States now had little use for the Soviets and no desire to even ponder the possibility of the Kremlin gaining a toehold along the Mediterranean. Thus, when Byrnes dropped his little UN trusteeship bombshell, Molotov

---

[40] Emory Ross to Friend, September 28, 1945, Reel 1, *NAACP-Int'l*; James F. Byrnes, *Speaking Frankly* (New York: Harper, 1947), 93.

[41] Bills, *The Libyan Arena*, 39–40; "Extract from Notes Dictated in Advance of Meeting of Commission on a Just and Durable Peace and, in Substance, Used in J.F.D. Opening 'Off-the-Record' Statement to the Commission on November 8, 1945," November 8, 1945, Box 26, File "Byrnes, James F.," *JFD-Princeton*; Clayton, *The Wars of French Decolonization*, 3; Byrnes, *Speaking Frankly*, 95.

was "vehemently opposed" to the idea and reminded the secretary of state of Stettinius's promise. As a result of that understanding, Molotov asserted, the USSR had decided that Tripolitania would be an acceptable down payment on the yet-to-be-determined reparations that the Italians owed the Soviets.[42]

To try to ease the tension that now sizzled through the CFM meeting, Molotov offered that the USSR had no intention of imposing its political or economic system on the Libyans. Nor was this a move to put the Soviet Navy at the heart of the British maritime lifeline. Rather, he said, the USSR simply needed a "warm water port" for its "merchant fleet." Molotov also offered that, in his opinion, the ceding of Tripolitania to the USSR did not preclude the other victorious powers from taking possession of whatever colony they wanted. Byrnes was flabbergasted. He retorted that "these areas must ... not be regarded as spoils of war" and "colonial peoples ought not to be bartered about because of the misdeeds of their colonial masters." Molotov refused to back down. "So," the Russian asked, "you do not want to give us even a corner of the Mediterranean?"[43]

Notably, the CAA, which was founded nearly a decade earlier to secure the "political liberation of the colonized African nations," did not sound the alarm about North Africa and the Horn being carved up as if this was 1884 all over again.[44] Instead, the CAA fully endorsed the Kremlin's bid for a trusteeship over Tripolitania – even though it would have come at the steep price of expanded French and British control in the area. Robeson's Council argued that the USSR was "a state without any imperialist ambitions or designs." In fact, the CAA continued, "[B]ehind the Russian request at London lies a subtle plan (subtle does not necessarily mean insidious ...) to challenge the Western democracies to a race for the betterment of dependent peoples."[45] Robeson further explained that

[42] Byrnes, *Speaking Frankly*, 95–96; Bills, *The Libyan Arena*, 42–43; "Extract from Notes Dictated in Advance of Meeting of Commission on a Just and Durable Peace and, in Substance, Used in J.F.D. Opening 'Off-the-Record' Statement to the Commission on November 8, 1945," November 8, 1945, Box 26, File "Byrnes, James F.," *JFD-Princeton*.

[43] Vladimir O. Pechatnov, "The Allies Are Pressing on You to Break Your Will . .': Foreign Policy Correspondence Between Stalin and Molotov and Other Politburo Members, September 1945–December 1946," trans. Vladislav M. Zubok, Working Paper No. 26, Cold War International History Project (Washington, DC: Woodrow Wilson International Center for Scholars, September 1999), 2–3.

[44] Description of the Council's mission taken from Von Eschen, *Race Against Empire*, 20.

[45] "Interpreting the Foreign Ministers' Discussion on Italian Colonies," *New Africa*, 4, no. 9 (October 1945).

only the "Soviet Union has demonstrated how it is possible to wipe out colonialism and all that that word connotes within a single generation."[46] In casting the Kremlin in this way, Robeson and the CAA had to ignore the inconsistencies between the Soviets' rhetoric and their foreign policy. Granted, the Council may not have known that Soviet Ambassador to the UN Andrei Gromyko "went out of his way" to ensure that the Americans understood that the Kremlin had little interest in broader colonial matters and was particularly "not ... directly concerned with ... the African mandates."[47] Nonetheless, the CAA was fully aware, as reported in its own newsletter, *New Africa*, that the USSR had not shown up at any meetings of the UN Trusteeship Council for at least a year. Considering that after San Francisco, the CAA had put all of its anticolonial hopes on the Soviets' wielding their influence in that key UN body, the Kremlin's actions, or at least its inactions, should have provided some indication to Robeson about the low priority Moscow assigned to ending colonialism.[48] In addition, a *New York Times* article painstakingly and accurately detailed how the USSR was "not very interested in the trusteeship agreements for areas in Central Africa" or in "areas south of the Equator." The only colonial issues where "the Soviet Union was really concerned [were] in the Mediterranean and northern Pacific areas," especially regarding "the fate of the Italian colonies, Palestine and any islands north of the Equator in the Pacific."[49] In other words, the Soviets' interest in colonial issues was situation-specific and strategy-driven, not, as the CAA tried to convince itself, broad-based, philosophical, or ideological.

The *Pittsburgh Courier*, one of the leading black newspapers concerned with colonial liberation, had no illusions concerning the Soviets' bid for Tripolitania. "The hungry Russian Empire, 'defender of small nations' and 'champion of the world's workers,'" the *Courier* reported, "has already SWALLOWED half the Poles, many of the Finns, all of

---

[46] "Address by Paul Robeson," June 7, 1946, Reel 1, *The Paul Robeson Collection* (Washington, DC: University Publications of America. 1989), microfilm (hereafter *Robeson*).

[47] "Commentary on Principal Amendments to Trusteeship Agreements Proposed During the Second Part of the First Session of the General Assembly," February 4, 1947, SD/S/895, RG 59 Freedom of Information Act (FOIA) request; Durward Sandifer to George Kennan, memo, April 27, 1948, Box 11, File "USSR: Miscellaneous Memorandum," Lot 55D429, RG 59.

[48] "Soviet Absent, U.S. Gets Presidency as Trusteeship Council Convenes," *New Africa*, 6, no. 4 (April 1947).

[49] James Reston, "Soviet Interest in Colonies Held Specific, not General," *New York Times*, December 11, 1946, Reel 59, *Du Bois*.

the Baltic peoples, half the Koreans, millions of the Chinese and most of the Manchurians, and," the editorial continued, "is now asking for 'trusteeship' over Tripolitanians and Eritreans while calling for peace and 'an end to imperialism.'"[50] What the Soviets really wanted, the *Courier* explained, was not "an end to imperialism" but rather a "foothold on the Mediterranean and the Red Sea to checkmate the Anglo-Saxon Powers."[51]

The British certainly could feel the imperial ground dissolve from right under them. From England's perspective, the entire discussion at the CFM meeting had gone very badly. Indeed, Bevin remarked that "[i]f we are not careful, our victory in war may lead us to being plucked by our Allies."[52] "I must confess," the British foreign secretary warily said, "I was a little dubious about how this scheme" for a UN trustee-ship "would work out."[53] It looked like the Americans had concocted yet another mechanism to dismantle the British Empire. Then, of all things, Bevin observed, the Soviets were making an overt, determined bid to plunge the hammer and sickle "dangerously close to our throat."[54] Meanwhile, the French had proffered a plan that was all too embracing of the "jackal" Italians and, worse yet, carried the potential to unleash a bloodbath in North Africa. After years of slavery, torture, mass murder, and racial discrimination, there were bitter memories throughout Somalia, Libya, and Eritrea about the abject cruelty of Italian, not just Fascist, rule. Moreover, the Ethiopians were vehemently opposed to having to fend off yet another Italian encirclement. The British Military Administration (BMA) reported that the Arabs, and, to a lesser extent, the Africans, were armed and willing to go to war to prevent the Italians from ever stepping foot in Africa again. That kind of bloodshed would destroy everything the British had hoped to salvage in this new postwar world.[55]

The fact of the matter was that nationalism, no matter how much the French wanted to ignore it, just could not be denied. England's

---

[50] "The Cannibals," *Pittsburgh Courier*, January 11, 1947. Emphasis in original.

[51] "Italy's Former Colonies," *Pittsburgh Courier*, October 4, 1947.

[52] Quoted in Callum A. MacDonald, "Waiting for Uncle Sam: Britain, the United States, and the First Cold War," *Reviews in American History*, 17, no. 1 (March 1989), 128.

[53] "Mr. Bevin's Speech ... in the House of Commons, June 4th, 1946," press release, June 5, 1946, 741.0/6–546, Reel 1, *Confidential U.S. State Department Central Files: Great Britain Foreign Affairs, 1945–1949* (Frederick, MD: University Publications of America, 1987) (hereafter *Confidential Great Britain Foreign Affairs*).

[54] Kumar Goshal, "As an Indian Sees It: Hand of Great Britain Discerned Behind Dutch Offer to Indonesia," *Pittsburgh Courier*, February 23, 1946.

[55] Bills, *The Libyan Arena*, 22.

dire economic straits, therefore, dictated that accommodation with nationalism, not confrontation, was the only way to preserve the crumbling British Empire and "retain ... direct control ... of certain strategic sites." An essential element of this strategy, in addition to securing U.S. support, was the wartime promise of independence that the British had dangled before Senussi leader Sayyid Idris in Cyrenaica. The Libyan region of Cyrenaica had become "more important than ever for the successful implementation of British strategic policy" in the Middle East. Bevin therefore had no intention of reneging on the promise to Idris by allowing, of all things, the Italians to resume control of Libya.[56] Thus, although Bevin was as leery of the UN trusteeship idea as the other participants, he understood that the way to achieve his ultimate goal was not to attack Byrnes's idea outright but to appear to support elements of it while finding the common ground that would move the United States closer to the British position. Therefore, before the CFM meeting deadlocked over an unrelated, procedural question, Bevin gave a begrudging, lukewarm welcome to the notion of a UN trusteeship.[57]

Yet, as the outlines of the Cold War became clearer and clearer, British and U.S. foreign policy, especially in North Africa and the Horn, finally began to converge in earnest. By 1947, the JCS acknowledged that "Great Britain and her Empire" are "our most ... important allies," and for British, and hence, American, strategic policy to be effective "in the Middle East and Eastern Mediterranean," Britain would need military bases in North Africa. Cyrenaica had, because of the turmoil in Palestine, become the base of choice. The JCS, therefore, argued that it "would be contrary" to American interests to allow "the USSR[,] . . our ... enemy," to gain "control of any of the colonies" even under the "guise" of a UN trusteeship.[58] With that simple pronouncement, the Joint Chiefs, with the State Department's assent, buried Byrnes's proposal.

Still, the option of an Italian trusteeship was equally untenable. The JCS, Policy Planning Staff, and area specialists in the State Department all doubted the wisdom of encouraging or even allowing the Italians to

[56] "Memorandum from the State-War-Navy Coordinating Committee to the Department of State," July 8, 1947, *FRUS* (1947) 3:593.

[57] Interdepartmental Working Party Draft Report: Disposal of the Italian Colonies, February 25, 1946, FO 1015/34; Benjamin Rivlin, "The Italian Colonies and the General Assembly," *International Organization* 3, no. 3 (August 1949), 461; Byrnes, *Speaking Frankly*, 95; Bills, *The Libyan Arena*, 20, 39.

[58] Memorandum from the State-War-Navy Coordinating Committee to the Department of State, July 8, 1947, *FRUS* (1947) 3:592–593.

return to North Africa and the Horn. "A country in the pitiable state of Italy, impoverished and in need of restoring its economy ... is hardly suited to take on the onerous and expensive responsibilities of non-paying colonies," the State Department's John Utter wrote. "Holding territories purely for prestige," he continued, "is an obsolete conception and contrary to all of the declarations of the United Nations ... the Italians should be made to face the issue and turn their energies to more profitable occupations at home."[59] Moreover, there was the nagging issue that Italy's economic chaos made the election of a Communist-dominated government a distinct possibility, especially after the Italian Communist Party (PCI) received nearly 40 percent of the popular vote in 1946. As far as the JCS was concerned, a Communist regime in Italy was nothing but a means for the Soviets to slither into the Mediterranean, deny the United States and Britain key military bases, and put a stranglehold on the flow of oil and other critical raw materials to war-ravaged Europe. Similarly, the State Department's Policy Planning Staff asserted that "there can be no question of the ultimate aim of the Italian Communist Party; ... the complete subjugation of Italy to Soviet control." As long as there was a chance that a Communist regime would be installed in Rome, Italy had to be kept out of Africa.[60]

For all of its denunciations, the State Department had no viable alternative except to hope that the nearly bankrupt British, who also believed that a UN "collective trusteeship would be undesirable on military grounds," could hang on long enough for the United States to stumble on another solution. Not surprisingly, the stalemate dragged on for years.[61] By 1948, however, the combination of the stark, clear lines of the Cold War, the growing importance of Italy to European economic recovery and defense, and the heated electoral battles both in Italy and the United States compelled the State Department to grope for some way out.

---

[59] Quoted in Bills, *The Libyan Arena*, 33, 55.
[60] Ibid., 32–33; "Memorandum from the State-War-Navy Coordinating Committee to the Department of State," July 8, 1947, *FRUS* (1947) 3:592–593; "Memorandum of the Policy Planning Staff," September 24, 1947, *FRUS* (1947) 3:976–977; National Security Council, "Position of the United States with Respect to Italy in the Light of the Possibility of Communist Participation in the Government by Legal Means," Box 176, File "National Security Council Meetings: 7: March 11, 1948," *HST:PSF*; Murray Edelman, "Causes of Fluctuations in Popular Support for the Italian Communist Party Since 1946," *Journal of Politics*, 20, no. 3 (August 1958), 536; "The Acting Secretary of State to the Embassy in Italy," March 11, 1947, *FRUS* (1947) 3:574.
[61] "Memorandum from the State-War-Navy Coordinating Committee to the Department of State," July 8, 1947, *FRUS* (1947) 3:592–593; F. E. Stafford (War Office) to Foreign Office, Enclosure No. 7 to 033/4859 (CA2a), May 14, 1947, FO 1015/34.

In Italy, the issue of regaining the colonies had become a major touchstone in the 1948 election.[62] And, for "U.S. government leaders," historian Wendy Wall observed, "the 1948 Italian election ... [was] 'an apocalyptic test of strength between communism and democracy' – a test that might well determine the fate of democracy on the Continent."[63]

However, claims on Libya, Eritrea, and Somalia were actually more complex. At the deputies of the foreign ministers meeting held in London to gather testimony from "those nations directly concerned" with the Italian colonies, a tangled web of American allies all demanded their share of the same stretch of territory in North Africa and the Horn. Of course, the Italians waxed poetic about all of their "accomplishments" in North Africa; however, they stumbled badly when pressed by U.S. Ambassador Lewis Douglas "as to whether the colonies had been [an] economic and financial liability to Italy." With a dash of creative accounting, the Italians maintained that routine expenditures had been "met by revenues from [the] colonies." No amount of creative flair, however, could erase the fact that throughout the 1930s, in Somalia, "local revenue produced ... considerably less than half of the colony's budget." In fact, profits from frankincense and barely marketable bananas contributed only about one-third of the annual budget. Given their well-known budgetary shortfalls, the Italians tried, without much success, to explain that the deficits were either the result of one-time "military" or other "extraordinary expenses." But fifty years of "extraordinary expenses" was just too extraordinary to accept.[64]

As difficult as it may be to believe, the Ethiopians' performance was just as incredible. To be sure, they had been viciously attacked in 1935 and had to endure years of Italian savagery. Nonetheless, as poor as they were, and as fragmented as their nation was, the Ethiopians were insistent on becoming a colonial power themselves, and as a result, they "emphasized claim to all of Eritrea and all of Italian Somali." When asked to supply a legitimate reason for their claim to Somalia, the Ethiopians

[62] Arnaldo Cortesi, "Italy Is Hopeful in Colonies Issue: Sforza Reports to Cabinet – Announcement is Expected Before Elections April 18," *New York Times*, April 8, 1948.

[63] Wendy L. Wall, "America's 'Best Propagandists': Italian Americans and the 1948 'Letters to Italy' Campaign," in *Cold War Constructions: The Political Culture of United States Imperialism, 1945–1966*, ed. Christian G. Appy (Amherst: University of Massachusetts Press, 2000), 89; Lawrence S. Kaplan, *NATO 1948: The Birth of the Transatlantic Alliance* (New York: Rowman and Littlefield, 2007), 52–55.

[64] "The Ambassador in the United Kingdom (Douglas) to the Secretary of State," November 19, 1947, *FRUS* (1947) 3:618; Lewis, *A Modern History of Somalia*, 100; Bills, *The Libyan Arena*, 16.

stammered and said they would get back to the deputies with a position paper on that.[65]

Joining this three-ring circus were the Egyptians, who hoped to carve off some of Libya, Eritrea, and Somalia for themselves while also working behind the scenes to malign the Ethiopians at every turn. The Egyptian secretary general of the Arab League "even went so far as to say that the Eritreans would probably be better off under the Italians than subjected to the reactionary and benighted rule of Addis Ababa."[66] This morass of claims and counterclaims led Byrnes's successor, Secretary of State George Marshall, to postpone any further discussions on the Italian colonies.[67]

In addition to trying to avoid an international quagmire, Marshall was also responding to domestic concerns. In 1948, Harry S. Truman was running for president, and to win an election that most believed was already lost, he needed to garner both the large Italian-American voting bloc and the sizable African American one. In New York City, for example, with a population of 4.8 million people, more than 1 million were either Italian American or African American. Because these two groups were at opposite ends of the spectrum on the issue of the Italian colonies, a non-decision, it was hoped, just might keep either from going into open revolt against the president.[68]

The chairman of the American Italian Congress, Luigi Criscuolo, had already begun to complain bitterly that Truman, who had overrode

---

[65] "The Chargé in the United Kingdom (Gallman) to the Secretary of State," November 12, 1947, *FRUS* (1947) 3:615.

[66] "Memorandum of Conversation, by Mr. John E. Utter of the Division of African Affairs," May 3, 1947, *FRUS* (1947) 3:579, 582; Editorial Note, *FRUS* (1947) 3:607; "Proposals for the Disposition of the Italian Colonies," OIR Report No. 4326, April 17, 1947, Reel 3, *OSS/Africa*.

[67] "The Secretary of State to the Embassy in the United Kingdom," August 3, 1948, *FRUS* (1948) 3:931–932.

[68] Clark Clifford to Truman, November 19, 1947, Box 23, File "Confidential Memo to the President ... (1 of 2)," *Papers of Clark Clifford*, Harry S. Truman Presidential Library, Independence, MO; "Memorandum by Mr. Philip Bagby of the United States Mission to the United Nations: Minutes of Working Group on Italian Colonies," September 28, 1948, *FRUS* (1948) 3:953; Ira Rosenwaike, *Population History of New York City* (Syracuse, NY: Syracuse University Press, 1972), 204; Jason Parkhurst Guzman, ed., *Negro Yearbook: A Review of Events Affecting Negro Life, 1941–46,* (Tuskegee, AL: Department of Records and Research, Tuskegee Institute, 1947), 8; Walter White to Rayford Logan, October 19, 1948, Box A635, File "United Nations: General Assembly, Oct., 1948," *Papers of the NAACP*; J. Howard McGrath to Truman, memo, August 11, 1948, Box 62, File "Italian Correspondence D.N.C. Chairman," *Papers of J. Howard McGrath*, Harry S. Truman Presidential Library, Independence, MO (hereafter *McGrath Papers*).

the State Department and recognized Israel, "never let the Jews down," but when it came to the question of Eritrea, Somalia, and Libya, the president had consistently ignored the wishes of Italian Americans. It was time, Criscuolo asserted, for Truman to treat Americans of Italian descent with as much respect as the Jews received. Criscuolo demanded that the United States "not only insist on the colonies being given back to Italy, but grant Italy a large cash subsidy in order to enable her to administer those colonies without getting deeper into debt." Leonard H. Pasqualicchio, national deputy of the Sons of Italy, which was the "largest Italian society in the United States," met "several times" with J. Howard McGrath, chair of the Democratic National Committee, "to talk about it." Unsatisfied with McGrath's noncommittal responses, Pasqualicchio, waving the Italian vote under McGrath's nose, arranged for a delegation of Italian Americans to meet with Truman. Pasqualicchio acknowledged that the "problem was loaded with dynamite," but if the president could cut the Gordian knot of Palestine, then certainly he could see to it that Italy got its ex-colonies back. Like Israel, this, too, was a "moral issue" and a small price to pay to satisfy the Italian American vote, which, as everyone knew, "could not be minimized" especially in a "state such as New York."[69]

Republican presidential candidate and New York Governor Thomas Dewey certainly recognized the importance of that vote and openly campaigned for Italy to regain control of its colonies and again "contribute to the development" of Eritrea, Somalia, and Libya. In truth, however, Italy had never really done that. Instead, after fifty years of Italian "development," Somalia had what could only be described as an "economic skeleton." There were few paved roads, no railway system, and a totally imported economic "infrastructure" of administrators, financiers, and businessmen. Nonetheless, John Foster Dulles, laying the ground work for his own New York senatorial race in 1949 and ignoring his earlier misgivings about Italian competency, "worked with Governor Dewey" to once again "give the Italian people an opportunity to develop their former colonies" and an outlet for "their surplus population." Democratic New York City Mayor William O'Dwyer, afraid that Truman's silence

---

[69] Luigi Criscuolo to Luigi De Pasquale, August 19, 1948, ibid.; J. Howard McGrath to Truman, memo, August 11, 1948, ibid.; Luigi De Pasquale to Howard [McGrath], August 31, 1948, ibid.; Leonard H. Paqualicchio to J. Howard McGrath, August 24, 1948, ibid.; Luigi de Pasquale to Howard [McGrath], August 20, 1948, ibid.; marginalia on Clayton Knowles, "Democrats Roiled by Dewey Proposal on Italian Colonies," *New York Times*, August 19, 1948, ibid.

would prove to be a costly mistake, jumped into the fray and issued his own statement calling for the "just and honorable" return of Eritrea, Libya, and Somalia to Italy.[70]

Robeson knew "vote-bait" when he saw it. The CAA registered disgust at the way the Republican "Tweedledum" and Democratic "Tweedledee" were so eager to "sell ... Africa for votes." Sickened by the way the politicians and their supporters praised the Italians' heroic "struggle ... to develop the agriculture of these lands," the Council on African Affairs blasted both parties for selective amnesia. That so-called "struggle," the CAA reminded them, actually "consisted of outright siezure [sic] of most of the best land ... and converting the [African] farmers into miserable landless peons."[71]

The NAACP's characterization was equally unflattering. Dewey and company were no more than two-bit hustlers willing to "prostitute" the colonies "on the altar of domestic politics." Determined to stop this madness, the NAACP called together a group of twenty-two national black organizations to set out in clear, unambiguous language where African Americans stood on the issue of the Italian colonies. "Although Messrs. Dewey, Dulles, and O'Dwyer may have forgotten the facts," Walter White exploded, "the colored world most certainly has not." Italy started the war. Italy lost the war. Italy, therefore, should not be "rewarded" for either. "The shamelessness" of proposing to "'restore Italy's war-shattered economy' at the expense of Ethiopia, Eritrea, Somaliland and Libya [was] incomprehensible." The generational "scar" the Italians slashed across the Ethiopian intelligentsia and the "ruthless exploitation" and "unspeakable brutalities" imposed on the Eritreans and Somalis by "their Italian masters" meant that the Africans owed Italy nothing. It was the other way around.[72]

[70] Clayton Knowles, "Democrats Roiled by Dewey Proposal on Italian Colonies," *New York Times*, August 19, 1948, Box 62, File "Italian Correspondence D.N.C. Chairman," *McGrath Papers*; Bayne, "Somalia on the Horn," Vol. VII, no. 6 (1960), 4–6; John Foster Dulles, "What I Have Done for Italy," October 13, 1949, Box 44, File "Senate Campaign-Correspondence: Re: Italy, 1949," *JFD-Princeton*; Council on African Affairs, "Selling Africa for Votes," press release, August 27, 1948, Reel 2, *Hunton Papers*.

[71] Ibid.

[72] Rayford Logan, "Statement on Behalf of 22 National Negro Organizations Relative to the Disposal of the Former Italian Colonies in Africa," September 9, 1948, Box A322, File "Italian Colonies, Correspondence Regarding Disposition of, 1948–April 1949," *Papers of the NAACP*; Walter White to E. Albert Norris et al., telegram, September 3, 1948, Box A322, File "Italian Colonies, Disposition of, Correspondence Regarding, 1948–49," *Papers of the NAACP*; "Negroes Ask Plebiscite for Former Italian Colonies," September 9, 1948, Box 5, File "Diaries, Personal: 1948–49," *Logan Papers*; Logan, diary

The Association went even further and emphasized that it was not just Italy's past but also its present that should have made this entire discussion moot. First and foremost, in the peace treaty, which Italy signed in 1947, Rome had renounced "all right and title" to the colonies. As a consequence, the Italians had no legal claim to any stretch of land in North Africa and the Horn. That should have been the end of it. Because it was not, however, Rayford Logan, who helped organize this 1948 Conference on Colonial Policy, stressed that Italy could not even meet the basic criteria to serve as a UN trustee. Beyond the obvious condition that Italy was not a member of the UN, there was the simple issue of money. This was a nation whose admittance into the Bretton Woods economic system was highly questionable because Italy had neither the gold reserves nor the cash on hand to meet the minimum entry level requirements. Similarly, the Italians were so destitute that it was unclear how they could begin to fulfill the economic and political development obligations of a UN trustee. "How," the NAACP plainly asked, "can impoverished Italy, incapable of promoting her own welfare, undertake this responsibility for others?" It was equally impossible to fathom how Italy's return to North Africa and the Horn would meet the treaty's stipulation for promoting "peace and security" in the region. The reimposition of Italian rule was a direct "renewed threat" to Ethiopia, which, given all that it had gone through, had every reason to question "why the aggressor enemy should be rehabilitated at the expense of the victim ally." As Emperor Haile Selassie would later note, "[T]he Italian occupation had resulted [in] ... the entire liquidation ... [and] systematic destruction of the Ethiopian educated class." Italy's reign, in short, had left far too many corpses and memories. Thus, the Association argued, the treaty's requirement that any final resolution had to "be in conformity with the wishes of the inhabitants" demanded recognition of the fact that the last thing the Libyans, Eritreans, and Somalis wanted was Italy coming across the Mediterranean again.[73]

entry, September 5, 1948, Box 4, File "Diaries, Personal: 1948–49," *Logan Papers*; Walter White, "Italy's Former Colonies and American Policy," August 26, 1948, Box A81, File "Articles: Walter White Syndicated Column, 1949," *Papers of the NAACP*; Walter White, untitled article, September 10, 1948, Box A74, File "Articles – Walter White *Chicago Defender* Columns, 1948," *Papers of the NAACP*.

73 Logan, "Statement on Behalf of 22 National Negro Organizations Relative to the Disposal of the Former Italian Colonies in Africa," September 9, 1948, Box A322, File "Italian Colonies, Correspondence Regarding Disposition of, 1948-April 1949," *Papers of the NAACP*; "Secretary's Staff Committee: Summary of Action (Admission of New Members to Bretton Woods Institution)," March 2, 1946, SD/S/164, File "SD/S/160-70,"

The NAACP was disturbed that the policy contortions in the CFM had everything to do with the East and West jockeying for strategic advantage and absolutely nothing to do with improving the quality of life for the indigenous people. It was wary of Secretary of State Marshall's "ominous" silence on the issue and his refusal to discuss the Italian colonies because that subject was in the realm of "high politics."[74] It was equally suspicious of "Russia's role in this sorry business" because this supposedly avowed anticolonialist power had become one of the most passionate advocates for returning the Italians to North Africa and the Horn.[75]

The Soviet Union had jettisoned its direct bid for Tripolitania and, instead, came out full force in favor of an Italian trusteeship for all the colonies. It was a calculated bribe – pure and simple. In Rome, the government of Christian Democrat Alcide De Gasperi, which was coming up for reelection in 1948, was overwhelmed by the physical and moral destruction that had engulfed Italy. The industrial infrastructure lay in ruins, people were starving, and a powerful, well-organized, and popular Italian Communist Party challenged De Gasperi's regime.[76] The U.S.

RG 59 FOIA request; "Alternative to Recommendation (3) Proposed by Office of European Affairs," March 1, 1946, SD/S/163, File "SD/S/160–70," *RG 59 FOIA request;* Information telegram, April 22, 1946, Box 6968, 865C.00/4-2246, *RG 59;* William Henderson to Hamilton Armstrong, memo, June 17, 1954, Box 33, File "Haile Selassie Emperor, 1942, 1945, 1961," *Armstrong Papers;* John Utter, memo, June 13, 1946, Box 6968, 865C.00/6-1346, *RG 59;* S. Pinkney Tuck to Secretary of State (John Utter's Report on Tripolitania), April 8, 1946, Box 6968, 865C.00/4-846, *RG 59;* Orray Taft to Secretary of State, telegram, August 31, 1948, Box 6968, 865C.00/8-3148, *RG 59.*

[74] Logan, "Statement on Behalf of 22 National Negro Organizations Relative to the Disposal of the Former Italian Colonies in Africa," September 9, 1948, Box A322, File "Italian Colonies, Correspondence Regarding Disposition of, 1948-April 1949," *Papers of the NAACP.*

[75] Walter White, "People, Politics, and Places," *Chicago Defender,* September 25, 1948.

[76] "The Italian Ambassador (Tarchiani) to the Under Secretary of State for Economic Affairs (Clayton)," March 8, 1947, *FRUS* (1947) 3:874; "The Ambassador in Italy (Dunn) to the Secretary of State," April 12, 1947, *FRUS* (1947) 3:880; "The Acting Secretary of State to the Embassy in Italy," April 25, 1947, *FRUS* (1947) 3:886–887; "The Secretary of State to the Embassy in Italy," May 1, 1947, *FRUS* (1947) 3:889; "The Ambassador in Italy (Dunn) to the Secretary of State," May 3, 1947, *FRUS* (1947) 3:889–892; "The Ambassador in Italy (Dunn) to the Secretary of State," May 6, 1947, *FRUS* (1947) 3:893–894; "The Ambassador in Italy (Dunn) to the Secretary of State," May 7, 1947, *FRUS* (1947) 3:897–903; "The Ambassador in Italy (Dunn) to the Secretary of State," May 28, 1947, *FRUS* (1947), 3:911–913; "The Acting Secretary of State to the Embassy in Italy," August 27,1947, *FRUS* (1947) 3:957; "The Italian Ambassador (Tarchiani) to the Acting Secretary of State," August 28, 1947, *FRUS* (1947) 3:959–962; "Memorandum of Conversation, by the Assistant Secretary of State for Political Affairs (Armour)," September 11, 1947, *FRUS* (1947) 3:965–967; "The Ambassador in Italy (Dunn) to the Secretary of State," September 17, 1947, *FRUS* (1947) 3:973–975; "Memorandum

ambassador to Italy, James Clement Dunn, frantically pleaded with the State Department for additional grain shipments to stave off famine and bread riots and requested tons of additional coal, well beyond Italy's allotment, to keep thousands of Italians from freezing to death. As the United States tried to determine what else it could do to ameliorate the conditions that made Italy ripe for a Communist takeover, Dunn suggested a probable loan of $800 million. The dollar crisis, balance of payments problem, and ongoing food shortage showed no signs of abatement.[77]

With the economy in turmoil and the Communists and the Christian Democrats unable to offer sustenance to the Italian electorate, both parties chose, instead, to distract the body politic with the elixir of Great Power status. As one approving Italian editorial noted, "None would ... remember the Marshall Plan or count sacks of coal and flour. The poor are those who attach greatest importance to ... luxuries." In other words, although the hundreds of millions of dollars the United States had poured and would continue to pour into Italy to feed, house, and clothe the population was nice, the Italians wanted their colonies back and were willing, in traditional Italian diplomatic fashion, "to sell [them]selves" to the highest bidder to make that happen.[78]

of Conversation, by the Assistant Secretary of State for Political Affairs (Armour)," September 25, 1947, *FRUS* (1947) 3:981–983; "Memorandum of Conversation, by the Acting Secretary of State," October 20, 1947, *FRUS* (1947) 3:993–994.

[77] "The Italian Ambassador (Tarchiani) to the Undersecretary of State for Economic Affairs (Clayton)," *FRUS* (1947) 3:874; "The Ambassador in Italy (Dunn) to the Secretary of State," April 12, 1947, *FRUS* (1947) 3:880; "The Ambassador in Italy (Dunn) to the Secretary of State," May 6, 1947, *FRUS* (1947) 3:893–894; "The Secretary of State to the Embassy in Italy," May 7, 1947, *FRUS* (1947) 3:895–897; "Memorandum of Conversation by the Secretary of State," May 16, 1947, *FRUS* (1947) 3:904, 906–907; "The Ambassador in Italy (Dunn) to the Secretary of State," May 28, 1947, *FRUS* (1947) 3:911; "The Ambassador in Italy (Dunn) to the Secretary of State," July 26, 1947, *FRUS* (1947) 3:949–950; "The Acting Secretary of State (Lovett) to the Embassy in Italy," August 27, 1947, *FRUS* (1947) 3:957; "Memorandum of Conversation by the Assistant Secretary of State for Political Affairs (Armour)," September 11, 1947, *FRUS* (1947) 3:965–966; "The Italian Ambassador (Tarchiani) to the Acting Secretary of State," n.d., *FRUS* (1947) 3:959, 961; "The Ambassador in Italy (Dunn) to the Secretary of State," September 17, 1947, *FRUS* (1947) 3:973–974; "The Ambassador in Italy (Dunn) to the Secretary of State," October 10, 1947, *FRUS* (1947) 3:988–989; "The Ambassador in Italy (Dunn) to the Secretary of State," October 10,1947, *FRUS* (1947) 3:989–991.

[78] Dunn to Secretary of State, telegram, November 26, 1948, 865.9111 RR/11–2648, Box 6968, *RG 59*; Knox, *Mussolini Unleashed*, 35; Rivlin, "The Italian Colonies," 463. For U.S. intervention in the critical 1948 election, see Alan A. Platt and Robert Leonardi, "American Foreign Policy and the Postwar Italian Left," *Political Science Quarterly*, 93, no. 2 (Summer 1978), 198–202; Kevin A. O'Brien, "Interfering with Civil Society: CIA and KGB Covert Political Action during the Cold War," *International Journal of Intelligence and Counterintelligence*, 8, no. 4 (Winter 1995), 431–456.

This was an easy call for the Kremlin to make. According to historian Sergei Mazov, Soviet archival documents make clear that "Realpolitik imperatives ... dominated ideological considerations on this [the Italian colonies] issue."[79] The chances of securing Tripolitania in the CFM were nil. However, the Italian Communist Party's unexpected show of strength in the 1946 midterm elections convinced the Soviets that in 1948, with the appropriate bait, they could actually have a duly elected, Kremlin-controlled government in Western Europe.[80] Moscow was "keen that the colonial topic should become a prominent part of the election campaign, to give the Popular Democratic Front (communists and socialists) the opportunity of profiting from it as much as possible." Thus, just three days after the Italians inquired about the USSR's stance, Vice Foreign Minister V. A. Zorin "declared that the Soviet government confirmed its proposal to give Italy trusteeship of Somalia, Eritrea and Libya." In short, the Kremlin was more than willing to counter the United States' bid of the Marshall Plan and CIA dollars with the allure of renewed colonial rule. The Soviets believed they would bolster the PCI's chances in the upcoming election by demonstrating that the Communists and only the Communists had Great Power backing to make North Africa and the Horn Italian domains again.[81]

The Kremlin's new stance was reaffirmed as the Four-Power Commission of Investigation set out on its fact-finding tour of North Africa and the Horn in the spring of 1948. The French, whose "major concern [was] to have a firm buffer between" Morocco, Tunisia, and Algeria "and the Arab States," were now joined by the Soviets, who became even more

[79] Sergei Mazov, "The USSR and the Former Italian Colonies, 1945–50," *Cold War History*, 3, no. 3 (April 2003), 49.

[80] Central Intelligence Agency, "Consequences of Communist Accession to Power in Italy by Legal Means," ORE 6–48, March 5, 1948, Box 214, File "Central Intelligence Reports: O.R.E.: 1948: 6–15 [6, 7, 9–15 January 13–August 3]," *Truman:PSF:IR*; "The Secretary of State to the Embassy in Italy," May 1, 1947, *FRUS* (1947) 3:889; E. Timothy Smith, "United States Security and the Integration of Italy into the Western Bloc, 1947–1949," in *NATO: The Founding of the Atlantic Alliance and the Integration of Europe*, eds. Francis H. Heller and John R. Gillingham (New York: St. Martin's Press, 1992), 75–76, 81–84. For Soviet control of the Italian Communist Party, see Silvio Pons, "Stalin, Togliatti, and the Origins of the Cold War in Europe," *Journal of Cold War Studies*, 3, no. 2 (Spring 2001), 3–27; Richard Drake, "The Soviet Dimension of Italian Communism," *Journal of Cold War Studies*, 6, no. 3 (Summer 2004), 115–119.

[81] Mazov, "The USSR and the Former Italian Colonies, 1945–50," 70; C. L. Sulzberger, "U.S., Britain Seen Divided at Key Mediterranean Points: Soviet Union Encouraging Rifts in Palestine and over Former Italian Colonies," *New York Times*, June 11, 1948; Bills, *The Libyan Arena*, 133.

insistent on an Italian trusteeship, especially in Libya. The British warned
that reinserting Italy into North Africa, and possibly the Horn, "would be
little short of disastrous." There would be a massive uprising; of that they
were sure. They were also certain that Italy would have to "re-conquer
practically the whole of the territory" and, as the British remarked, the
last time Rome's forces tried that maneuver, "the Italian troops proved
themselves quite unequal to it." The push for an Italian trusteeship, the
Foreign Office kept reiterating, ignored the very simple reality that "opinion amongst the whole population has been hardening against the return
of Italian administration, of which they have such bitter memories."[82]
Nonetheless, "apparently disregarding what the [Africans and Arabs]
told them," the French and Soviet delegates clung to their "contention
that the colonies should be returned to Italy." The Soviets, in fact, "took
pains" to praise "the pre-war Italian regime" and, with their French ally,
searched "in vain" for genuine pro-Italian sentiment among the indigenous people. They tried every possible maneuver to "enhance Italy's colonial record, inflate pro-Italian sentiments in the colonies, and show that
the indigenous peoples were too unschooled to administer themselves."[83]
The French and the Soviets, of course, conveniently ignored the fact that
the lack of education in Somalia, Eritrea, and Libya was a direct result
of a colonial policy that deemed it a "fundamental political mistake" to
provide even elementary education "for natives," who, "solely because
they possess a veneer of education, will refuse to work in the fields."[84]

The Soviets' latest policy gyration, while causing immediate disgust
among the NAACP leadership, left Robeson and the Council on African
Affairs speechless. The man and the organization that had steadily monitored the situation in the Italian colonies and railed against the rampant
imperialism that appeared to guide virtually every policy option the Great
Powers uttered suddenly went mute. Even when the Kremlin's attempt to
hand over millions of Africans and Arabs to their most dreaded enemy,
the Italians, was widely reported in the *New York Times*, the New York-

[82] Former Italian Colonies: Brief for Sir Oliver Franks, n.d., ca. March 1948, J 3440/6/G,
FO 115/4378.
[83] Pechatnov, "The Allies Are Pressing on You,'" 16; Bills, *The Libyan Arena*, 37, 113;
Clifton Daniel, "Italian Colonies Cause Big 4 Split," *New York Times*, July 22, 1948,
11; "Memorandum by the Assistant Secretary of State for Occupied Areas (Hilldring)
to the State-War-Navy Coordinating Committee," May 29, 1947, *FRUS* (1947) 3:584;
"Memorandum from the State-War-Navy Coordinating Committee to the Department
of State," July 8, 1947, *FRUS* (1947) 3:592–593.
[84] Guglielmo Nasi to Commissars, memo, June 5, 1938, Ethiopian Ministry of Justice,
Documents on Italian War Crimes, 30.

based CAA issued no articles, no press releases, no "urgent action" pleas.[85] Nothing at all came from Robeson or the Council to give any indication about the Kremlin's harrowing plans for Libya, Eritrea, and Somalia.

What Robeson did say during this time was targeted at CAA executive director Max Yergan, who, cowed by the Second Red Scare, had tried in early 1948 to gain control of the organization and place its 100 members squarely within the right wing of U.S. Cold War foreign policy.[86] Robeson, who had warned Yergan in December 1947 that "you will find me getting tougher and rougher but I have to do what I am told to do," lashed out at both his heretical colleague and the U.S. government. He blasted the United States for "supporting 'an intensified drive to exploit the peoples of Africa'" and Max Yergan for being "unwilling to challenge the imperialist policy of the United States State Department."[87] Robeson strenuously argued that instead of capitulating, which was what Yergan advocated, the CAA "must oppose all policies, domestic or international which may threaten the success of the council's program ... to foster the independence and advancement of Africans."[88] In truth, however, the Council did not oppose "all policies" – only those of the United States and the West. Robeson voiced no public opposition when, as Mazov noted, the "architects of Soviet foreign policy were interested in the geostrategic position of Libya, Somalia and Eritrea, rather than in ... any revolutionary development there."[89] In other words, when confronted with the hard

[85] "Soviet Alters View on Italian Colonies," *New York Times*, February 14, 1948; Clifton Daniel, "Shift on Africa by Soviet Studied: British Link Moscow Stand for Italy as the Trustee to Coming Elections," *New York Times*, February 18, 1948; "Big 4 Deputies Differ on Italian Colonies," *New York Times*, February 24, 1948. A search of Robeson's microfilmed papers, the W. Alphaeus Hunton Papers at the Schomburg, all of the issues of CAA's publication *New Africa* during the time period, the W. E. B. Du Bois Papers, the FBI file on Paul Robeson, and the British Intelligence files on Paul Robeson indicated no public speeches, commentaries, etc. on the Soviets' plan to hand Eritrea, Somalia, and Libya back to Italy.

[86] Anderson, *Eyes Off the Prize*, 163; Glenda Elizabeth Gilmore, *Defying Dixie: The Radical Roots of Civil Rights, 1919–1950* (New York: W.W. Norton & Co., 2008), 432–439; "Africa: Next Goal of Communists – an Interview with Dr. Max Yergan, America's Foremost Authority on Africa," *U.S. News & World Report*, May 1, 1953; "Goldwater Joins [James O.] Eastland, and Yergan in Outcries Against Unity in Congo," January 26, 1963, Box 1, File "Personal Papers – Newspapers articles about Yergan, 1952–1958," *Papers of Max Yergan*, Moorland-Springarn Research Center, Howard University, Washington, DC.

[87] Gilmore, *Defying Dixie*, 436; "Robeson Accuses U.S. of Exploiting Africa," *New York Times*, April 7, 1948.

[88] "Robeson Says He'll Continue Work with Reds," *New York Herald Tribune*, April 7, 1948, Reel 7, *Robeson*.

[89] Mazov, "The USSR and the Former Italian Colonies, 1945–50," 49.

truth of the Kremlin's realpolitik masquerading as liberation ideology, Robeson "chose, as was his style with matters of deepest import, to say nearly nothing."[90]

The NAACP, however, refused to be silent. The Association voiced its "dismay that many 'enemies' of colonialism and imperialism who vigorously denounce oppression by the western states become absolutely mute and conscienceless when faced with the crimes of the rival imperialism of the Soviet Union."[91] The forced control of other peoples had to be resisted; that was the point. The Association's September 1948 Conference on Colonial Policy, whose participants were the "spokesmen for more than six million Negro Americans," therefore, asserted that if the Eritreans, Somalis, and Libyans were to have a fighting chance at political and economic independence, the CFM needed to acknowledge its inability to reach a decision, follow the dictates of the Italian peace treaty, and cede jurisdiction to the UN General Assembly. Only there – where the voices and votes from Ethiopia, Liberia, Haiti, and India could carry as much weight as those of the United States or the Soviet Union – would the Italian colonies stand a chance of having "the wishes of the inhabitants" respected. The NAACP then drew on the recommendations from its 1945 Colonial Conference, resurrected Byrnes's proposal, and urged the establishment of an "International Administration under a UN trusteeship" for the Italian colonies, to be followed by a plebiscite, and, then, within a limited, defined period of time, independence.[92]

When the CFM met later the same month, the U.S. ambassador began by remarking that, after years of negotiations and policy statements, it was

[90] Odd Arne Westad, *The Global Cold War: Third World Interventions and the Making of Our Times* (New York: Cambridge University Press, 2007), 39–72; Duberman, *Robeson*, 499. Duberman noted this tendency while discussing another matter but this is a pattern. Robeson similarly "clammed up" when he realized that the Soviet Union, after the Holocaust, was systematically executing Jews, ibid., 352–353.

[91] "NAACP Stand on Colonialism and U.S. Foreign Policy," *Crisis*, January 1955 Box 7, File "National Association for the Advancement of Colored People," *Papers of the International League for Human Rights*, New York Public Library, New York (hereafter *Papers of the ILHR*).

[92] Rayford Logan, "Statement on Behalf of 22 National Negro Organizations Relative to the Disposal of the Former Italian Colonies in Africa," September 9, 1948, Box A322, File "Italian Colonies, Correspondence Regarding Disposition of, 1948-April 1949," *Papers of the NAACP*; Council on African Affairs, "Selling Africa for Votes," press release, August 27, 1948, Reel 2, *Hunton Papers*; "Negroes Ask Plebiscite for Former Italian Colonies," September 9, 1948, Box 5, File "Diaries, Personal: 1948–49," *Logan Papers*; Logan, diary entry, September 5, 1948, Box 4, File "Diaries, Personal: 1948–49," *Logan Papers*; Walter White to Truman, telegram, September 9, 1948, Box 545, File "OF 93 Miscellaneous – 1945–March 1949 [2 of 2]," *HST:OF*.

clear that all of the foreign ministers had at least agreed on one point: that Italy should regain control of Somalia. But now the Soviets balked. In the spring of 1948, the PCI lost the Italian election; the Kremlin now had no intention of supporting any of Rome's demands. The Soviets declared it a "waste of time" to quibble about one colony or all for Italy and then recommended that Eritrea, Somalia, and Libya come under a UN trusteeship administered by the four powers sitting around the table. The British and Americans were stunned. The corpse of James Byrnes's 1945 proposal, which the NAACP had supported but the Joint Chiefs of Staff and State Department had long since buried, just awoke with a vengeance. And, yet if this proposal went through, it would legitimately put the Soviets – "enemy" – within stalking distance of the Anglo-Americans' vaunted Mediterranean defense system. Finally, at 11:30 p.m. on September 14, 1948, deadlocked and worn out, the Council of Foreign Ministers agreed to turn over the issue of the Italian colonies to the UN.[93]

The Kremlin's latest policy shift revealed the costly constraints of Robeson's ideological box. In 1945, he had fully endorsed the Soviets' land grab for Tripolitania. Then, in February 1948, Robeson acquiesced to the most dreaded of all possibilities – the return of the Italians to Africa – because the Soviets wanted to increase the PCI's chances in the upcoming election. Then, only three days after the CFM had deadlocked over the Kremlin's UN trusteeship proposal for the Italian colonies, Robeson chaired a Council on African Affairs meeting that crafted a petition urging the United States to support "a truly international administration directly responsible to the United Nations." In short, in the span of a few years, the Council had supported or left unchallenged three distinct plans for the Italian colonies, which just happened to align with the positions taken by the Soviet Union at that time. And, although the CAA's latest move, which broke its months-long silence on the issue, was cloaked in powerful liberation verbiage – "remember that Africa belongs to the Africans, and that the paramount considerations should be the needs and aspirations of the peoples of Libya, Eritrea, and Somaliland" – in truth,

---

[93] "The Proposal by Soviet Delegation on the Former Italian Colonies," September 14, 1948, C.F.M./48/IC/Paris 1, Box 261, File "Italian Colonies-Record of Decisions & Documents; Special CFM-Ministers Meeting, Paris, Sept. 1948," *Records of International Conferences, and Expositions*, Record Group 43, National Archives, Washington, DC (hereafter *RG 43*); "Record of Decisions," September 13–15, 1948, Box 261, File "Italian Colonies-Record of Decisions & Documents: Special CFM-Ministers Meeting, Paris, Sept. 1948," *RG 43*; Bills, *The Libyan Arena*, 133–154; Mazov, "The USSR and the Former Italian Colonies, 1945–50," 72–73.

FIGURE 3.1. Paul Robeson at a party at the Soviet embassy, 1950. His unshakable faith in the USSR prevented him from challenging or even responding to the Kremlin's attempt to hand over Somalia, Libya, and Eritrea to the Italians, despite vehement protests from the indigenous peoples.
Source: Bettman/Corbis. Courtesy of Corbis, Stock Photo ID# U1154712INP.

this widely swinging pendulum suggests that, in this case, the center of gravity for Robeson's anticolonialism was not necessarily the needs of the colonized but, in fact, Soviet foreign policy. Similarly, Robeson's situational anticolonialism led him, in 1948, to pillory the Republicans and Democrats for using the Italian colonies as "vote-bait" while overlooking the fact that the Soviets were the first to dangle Africa's freedom in shark-infested electoral waters.[94] (See Figure 3.1)

---

[94] "Interpreting the Foreign Ministers' Discussion on Italian Colonies," *New Africa*, 4, no. 9 (October 1945); "Action on Italian Colonies at Paris Conference is Test of Peace Aims," *New Africa*, 5, no. 7 (July–August 1946); "Petition to the United States Delegation to the United Nations Concerning the Disposition of Libya, Eritrea, and Italian Somaliland," *Spotlight on Africa: Action Appeal*, September 28, 1948, Reel 61, *Du Bois*; "Council Urges Just and Prompt Decision on Italian Colonies," press release, September 28, 1948,

While Robeson and the Council tacked with the Soviet wind, the NAACP would not be blown off course. White had already cabled the policy statement from the Conference on Colonial Policy to "Messrs. Stalin, Attlee, Auriol and Truman" and promised the Ethiopian legation that he would "continue this struggle" in Paris at the upcoming UN meeting. However, what the NAACP considered to be the "struggle" and what the Ethiopians were fighting for was quite different. To be sure, they were in complete agreement that Italy should never be allowed in Africa again. Beyond that, however, Ethiopia was intent on replacing Italy as the colonial power in Eritrea and Somalia and had set about massaging, guilting, and pressuring the Americans and British to make that happen. The NAACP, on the other hand, was just as insistent that the former Italian colonies should not be passed from one colonial master to the next and, instead, had to become independent. As a result, the Ethiopians were "quite dissatisfied" with the NAACP for not "pushing Ethiopian claims to Eritrea." The Association, however, was just as adamant that "black imperialism [was] no more to be condoned than white imperialism." It was just inconceivable that a commitment to Ethiopia's territorial integrity could or should automatically translate into Addis Ababa's right to control the economic and political destiny of the Eritreans and Somalis. In short, for the NAACP, colonialism, like slavery, was fundamentally, inherently wrong, regardless of the color of the master.[95]

Despite their reputations, neither the Council on African Affairs nor even W. E. B. Du Bois had as coherent an anticolonialist vision as the Association in this matter. Unlike the NAACP, the Council fully supported

KV/2/1829; Council on African Affairs, "Selling Africa for Votes," press release, August 27, 1948, Reel 2, *Hunton Papers.*

[95] Walter White to the First Secretary of the Imperial Ethiopian Legation, September 9, 1948, Box A322, File "Italian Colonies Disposition of, Correspondence Regarding, 1948–49," *Papers of the NAACP*; "Italo-Ethiopian Relations: Their Whys and Wherefores and Prospects," *Ethiopian Herald*, Box 1, File "Clipping," *Marion Clinch Calkins Papers*, Georgetown University, Washington, DC; Marshall to Secretary of State, telegram, October 3, 1947, Box 140, File "921–980, 10/2/47–10/9/47," *Records of the Foreign Service Posts*, Record Group 84, National Archives, Washington, DC (hereafter *RG 84*); E. Sylvia Pankhurst to Walter White, March 3, 1948, Box A404, File "Logan, Rayford, 1948–49," *Papers of the NAACP*; Logan, diary entry, September 5, 1948, Box 4, File "Diaries, Personal: 1948–49," *Logan Papers*; Logan, diary entry, October 1, 1948, Box 4, File "Diaries, Personal: 1948–49," *Logan Papers*; Logan, diary entry, May 28, 1949, Box 4, File "Diaries, Personal: 1948–49," *Logan Papers*; Madison S. Jones Jr. to Michael Roche, September 19, 1949, Box A323, File "Italian Colonies, Disposition of, Correspondence Regarding, May 1949–50," *Papers of the NAACP*; Roy Wilkins to Trygve Lie, September 29, 1949, Box A323, File "Italian Colonies, Disposition of, Correspondence Regarding, May 1949–50," *Papers of the NAACP.*

Ethiopia's "dubious" title to Eritrea and appeared quite comfortable with the negation of the Eritreans' rights and inevitable absorption into the Ethiopian metropole. Although the legitimacy of Ethiopia's historical claims on Eritrea were murky at best, and its profession of Pan-Ethiopian oneness undermined by the extensive linguistic, religious, and cultural diversity of Eritrea, the CAA regarded Ethiopia's demand for the "return of Eritrea [as] wholly justified." The Council contended that because the "economic and cultural interests of the Eritreans and Ethiopians [were] one," there "actually [was] no separate Eritrean nation." This supposed cultural, racial, and linguistic homogeneity, however, masked what Eritrea and Ethiopia really were – a colony with excellent ports on the Red Sea and a large, land-locked nation determined to get access to those maritime facilities. As a consequence, in the eyes of many, Eritrea's apparent sole raison d'etre was to enhance Ethiopia's economic and political advancement. The Council argued that the "progress of Ethiopia from semi-feudal backwardness into a developed modern state depend[ed] upon" the Ethiopians gaining control of Eritrea and its nearly 1,000-mile Red Sea coastline. That, in the Council's opinion, was "essential" for Ethiopia's "economic prosperity." Du Bois was even more direct. "Eritrea is a land which Ethiopia must control ...; it is a country which she should own if she is to have economic expansion and free access to the markets of the world." Not surprisingly, then, in one of his last acts as the NAACP's foreign affairs expert, Du Bois advised White, who was preparing for the UN meeting in Paris, to "demand that Eritrea and Somaliland be given to Ethiopia, ... with the distinct understanding" that they would "eventually ... become a part of the Ethiopian nation."[96] Of course, White did no such thing.

As clear-eyed as the Association was on this question, it is important to remember that the NAACP was as mired in turmoil, inconsistencies, and divided loyalties as the black Left.[97] One of the most tumultuous

[96] "Action on Italian Colonies at Paris Conference Is Test of Peace Aims," New Africa, 5, no. 7 (July–August, 1946); "Interpreting the Foreign Ministers' Discussion on Italian Colonies," New Africa, 4, no. 9 (October 1945); Ruth Iyob, The Eritrean Struggle for Independence: Domination, Resistance, Nationalism, 1941–1993 (New York: Cambridge University Press, 1995), 42; Martin Plaut and Patrick Gilkes, "Conflict in the Horn: Why Eritrea and Ethiopia Are at War," No. 1 (March 1999), The Royal Institute of International Affairs, 1; "A Six-Point Program for Africa and the Peace Settlement," New Africa, 4, no. 8 (August–September 1945); Du Bois to White, memo, August 23, 1948, Box A241, File "W.E.B. Du Bois – General (Jan-Sept 1948)," Papers of the NAACP; W. E. B. Du Bois, "Ethiopia and Eritrea," New Africa, 8, no. 3 (March 1949).

[97] For details on the power struggle between White and Du Bois, see Anderson, Eyes Off the Prize, 126–130;, 138–144; for the scuttling of the NAACP's human rights petition to the UN, see ibid., 149–152.

episodes occurred in early September 1948 when Du Bois, in a document leaked to the *New York Times*, charged that the secretary had "hand[ed] the NAACP over to Truman" and, in the process, abandoned Africa.[98] Journalist Louis Lautier followed with a searing portrayal of Walter White as an egomaniacal manipulator who refused to "subordinate ... his personal ambitions" and let Du Bois, the NAACP's international affairs expert, take the lead at the UN. Lautier was especially concerned in "view of ... the disposal of Italy's former African colonies which [was] to come before the General Assembly." The journalist noted that whereas Du Bois had already laid out a definitive anticolonial strategy, "if Mr. White has any program for changing the concept of colonies as a source of profit for Europe and the United States, he has never disclosed it."[99] White's silence, some members of the black press and community believed, was because the NAACP had tried to "carry the State Department on one shoulder and the cause of oppressed peoples on the other."[100] Those accusations of reckless ambition, amateurism, and collusion definitely grazed White, but it was Du Bois who got caught in the blowback. Within days, the Association Board of Directors fired its cofounder.[101]

Oddly enough, although scholars mark this moment as the end of the NAACP's anticolonialism, in truth, the Association's divorce from the "radical" Du Bois actually created an opening for a new, dynamic internationalist push. White explained to a *Chicago Defender* reporter: "At Paris I will face the toughest opposition in my 31 years with the Association. The issues will be human rights, the Italian colonies, and trusteeship. We've got to fight," he asserted, because even if "we don't win, we will have at least proved the hypocrisy of the liberal nations of the world."[102] Not surprisingly, then, when during the trans-Atlantic voyage, White and the other consultants heard a very complicated scheme unfold to dissect North Africa and the Horn, he girded for battle. Benjamin Gerig, the U.S. delegation's trusteeship expert, had given a "coldblooded" appraisal of the rationale behind the Americans' new plan to carve out a little piece for everyone – except, of course, the Soviets and

---

[98] Dyja, *Walter White*, 175.

[99] Louis Lautier, "In the Nation's Capital: Walter White Goes to UN Conference," *Norfolk New Journal and Guide*, September 25, 1948.

[100] Henry Arthur Callis to Du Bois, October 8, 1948, Reel 61, *Du Bois*; Anderson, *Eyes Off the Prize*, 144–147.

[101] Anderson, *Eyes Off the Prize*, 144.

[102] Lillian Scott, "Du Bois, White Clash over NAACP Policies: Blasts Trip to UN Confab," *Chicago Defender*, September 18, 1948.

the indigenous inhabitants. Somalia, the Americans hoped, would keep the Italians happy *and* non-Communist. Southeastern Eritrea would give Ethiopia a colonial possession, an outlet to the sea, and a territorial buffer against Italian encirclement. The British would maintain Cyrenaica and the priceless military rights there. The United States would simply postpone a decision on the Fezzan and Tripolitania and denounce Byrnes's international trusteeship plan as unworkable to "prevent Russia from getting a foothold" in Africa.[103]

For White, the "timidity of the American delegation on the question of colonies was startling." He declared that the U.S. proposal was so misguided by "fear, military necessity or opportunism" that it missed the much larger picture. When Gerig challenged him to come up with something better, White immediately met with the other consultants and began to develop a counterposition. As the finalized draft circulated, with its stinging critique of the U.S. plan and strong affirmation of an international trusteeship, the State Department's Chester Williams ripped into the consultants and especially Walter White for "breach" of trust and "violation ... of ... confidential information." Gerig's discussion, Williams declared, was "off-the-record," and he insisted that everyone who had a copy of White's report "burn it," "destroy" it. Duly intimidated, several consultants began to backtrack and even offered to amend the statement to make it more palatable to the United States.[104]

White would not back down. He informed Williams and Eleanor Roosevelt that although the others may cave in to State Department pressure, he had no intention of doing so. The "statement that I signed," White asserted, "must not be changed in any fashion." Moreover, he considered Williams's handling of the matter to be highly inappropriate and alarmist – and that was "putting it with unbelievable mildness."

[103] Walter White to Rayford Logan, October 22, 1948, Box A635, File "United Nations: General Assembly, Oct., 1948," *Papers of the NAACP*; Walter White to the United States Delegation to the United Nations, Box 166-21, File "21: Correspondence, United Nations," *Logan-MSRC*; "Report to the Office Not for Publication Until Later: Received from Walter White 10/19/48," October 8, 1948, Box A635, File "United Nations General Assembly, October 1948," *Papers of the NAACP*.

[104] White to the United States Delegation to the United Nations, October 17, 1948, Box 166-21, File "21: Correspondence, United Nations," *Logan-MSRC*; Chet (Chester Williams) to Walter White, October 22, 1948, Box A635, File "United Nations General Assembly, October 1948," *Papers of the NAACP*; Walter White to Chester Williams, October 25, 1948, Box 181-8, Folder 3, *Logan-MSRC*; Jay Krane to Mr. White, October 26, 1948, Box A322, File "Italian Colonies, Disposition of, Correspondence Regarding, 1948–49," *Papers of the NAACP*; Chet [Chester Williams] to Walter White, October 29, 1948, Box A635, File "United Nations: General Assembly, Oct., 1948," *Papers of the NAACP*.

White then made sure that Roosevelt understood that he was willing to "risk ... antagonizing or even ... alienating some members of the United States Delegation" by taking this issue directly "to the American public." The plan Gerig had outlined, White insisted, was based on keeping the Communists out, not on bringing democracy in. And that was the problem. This "negative" policy of "containing Russia," White explained, had to stop because it "play[ed] directly into the hands of the Communists."[105] It allowed the Soviets, like a "clever boxer," to maneuver the United States into a corner. A prime example was the way the United States abandoned its own principled UN trusteeship proposal and was afraid to even whisper the name simply because the Soviets had now paraded the plan around as if it was their own. Adrift, with nothing but nebulous "strategic concerns" to guide them, the Americans, White observed, had concocted an ill-considered scheme "to keep Russia out" and help Britain "hold on to her position or what [was] left of it in the middle East." As a result, the United States, "once again," appeared "to be protecting the status quo." There was no other word for this but "tragic."[106]

White then warned of impending doom. The European "struggle for raw materials, markets, and native labor" played a key role in launching two world wars within one generation. Millions were already dead. However, instead of having the "vision and courage to attempt new approaches," especially "where experience has demonstrated that the old ones lead only to disaster," the United States "surrender[ed]" to "opportunistic ... expediency," "carved" up Africa as "war booty," and set the stage for a revolt that would make the ongoing war in Indonesia look "mild in comparison." It was not too late to salvage the situation, he advised, but the United States had to act quickly. He urged the U.S. delegation to reconsider its position on a UN trusteeship for the Italian colonies. For White, there was no legitimate reason to have abandoned the idea in the first place. The fact that the Soviets now supported it seemed an odd reason to change course, especially when the USSR had articulated three different positions in as many years. Moreover, Gerig's statement that a UN trusteeship was "unworkable, untested, and unreliable,"

[105] Walter White to Chester Williams, October 25, 1948, Box 181-8, Folder 3, *Logan-MSRC*; Walter White to Eleanor Roosevelt, October 26, 1948, Box 4567 (no file), *Roosevelt Papers.*

[106] White to the United States Delegation to the United Nations, October 17, 1948, Box A635, File "United Nations General Assembly, November 1948–49," *Papers of the NAACP*; Walter White, "Russian Tactics in U.N. Criticized," October 28, 1948, Box A81, File "Articles: Walter White Syndicated Column, 1949," *Papers of the NAACP.*

was, in the end, unconvincing. "The fact that such precedent was lacking was as well known to the U.S. in 1945 when its original proposals were presented as it is today," White noted. "Neither was there any precedent of an international United Nations administrative staff or of U.N. agencies dealing with truce supervision, health, refugees, education, labor and other problems," but those were put in place and "have achieved commendable success." This was not pie-in-the-sky naiveté, White explained. He was completely sanguine about the need to have a "realistic foreign policy," and he conceded that given the "present tensions and threats of war which have been created by Russian intransigence," there would be "risks" involved in implementing a UN trusteeship. Nevertheless, he added, "we must take ... some calculated risks" because trying to prop up "dying colonialism," no matter how well "disguised," was going to "cost us in the long run."[107]

The *Chicago Defender* underscored White's point. The U.S. delegation was no more than a pack of "diplomatic jackasses" that had foolishly tried "to give the former Italian colonies in Africa back to Italy." But, the editorial warned, "fifteen million American Negroes are not going to countenance the sell-out of those colonies to a bunch of thugs." African Americans would "never forget" the "rape [of] Ethiopia" and the "imprint of the Italian boot [that] is still fresh on the bodies of African colonials whom Mussolini's mobsters machine-gunned at the opening of World War II." The *Defender*, therefore, "sound[ed] a warning" that if Italy regained control in Africa, there would be "hell to pay."[108]

The *Chicago Defender*'s editorial only summarized the concerns about American complicity in the reimposition of Italian rule that had been raised all along by the black press and civic organizations such as the Brotherhood of the Protective Order of the Elks and the National Council of Negro Women (NCNW). Knowing that Italy was teetering on

[107] Walter White to Chester Williams, October 25, 1948, Box 181-8, Folder 3, *Logan-MSRC*; Walter White to Eleanor Roosevelt, October 26, 1948, Box 4567 (no file), *Roosevelt Papers*; White to the United States Delegation to the United Nations, October 17, 1948, Box A635, File "United Nations General Assembly, November 1948–49," *Papers of the NAACP*; "Report to the Office Not for Publication Until Later: Received from Walter White 10/19/48," October 8, 1948, Box A635, File "United Nations General Assembly, October 1948," *Papers of the NAACP*; White to Friends, December 2, 1948, Box A322, File "Italian Colonies, Correspondence Regarding Disposition of, 1948-April 1949," *Papers of the NAACP*; White to John Foster Dulles, telegram, December 2, 1948, Box A322, File "Italian Colonies, Correspondence Regarding Disposition of, 1948-April 1949," *Papers of the NAACP*.

[108] "Our Opinions: Diplomatic Jackasses," *Chicago Defender*, October 30, 1948.

financial ruin and sullied by a horrific colonial history, the Elks declared that "[t]he Italian government has neither the capacity nor honor to merit a foothold in Africa." The NCNW, in a unanimous resolution, urged the United Nations "not to take any action which would result in the African Colonies and people being placed either under Italian trusteeship or being returned to Italian sovereignty." Even the conservative *Atlanta Daily World* reported that the "will of the African people is clear"; they were ready to go to war to stop Italy. Ethiopia, the paper conveyed, "was prepared to offer military aid to Africans on her borders resisting Italian penetration." Despite the obvious threat to the peace, the newspaper continued, the Americans still "claim to be undecided."[109]

As it turned out, several in the U.S. delegation were equally concerned. The current plan to dissect various regions of Africa and then dole them out so that Italy would get this slice but not this other strip because that would go to Britain, and another section would be carved in two so Ethiopia could get some but not all, and a couple of other pieces would be left dangling until the United States could figure out what to do with them was completely underwhelming, confusing, and unpalatable. Assistant Secretary of State Dean Rusk, after trying in vain to find some rational basis for this convoluted plan, could only "emphasize ... that literally the United States had no program." Or, to put it more accurately, what the United States did have was philosophically incoherent, politically indefensible, and violated the basic principles set down in the UN Charter.[110]

During the U.S. delegation's meetings, it soon became obvious why. "The main consideration," one State Department official explained, "was to keep Italy with the West." Unfortunately, he noted, that was not going to be easy. The "De Gasperi government was not too strong[,] ... was under continuing attack for collaborating too closely with the West," and, because the Italians wanted all of the colonies back, not just Somalia, "the Italian Communists could say that the West had let Italy down." Then,

---

[109] "Truman Declines to Comment on African Colonies: U.S. Policy on Disposition of Areas Concealed, Question of Italy's Former Colonies on Agenda of UN," *Norfolk New Journal and Guide*, September 18, 1948; "Elks Hit Return of Italian Colonies," *Atlanta Daily World*, September 1, 1948; "National Council of Women Makes 8 Recommendations," *Norfolk New Journal and Guide*, October 30, 1948; "Africans Protest Italian Rule: UN to Decide Fate of East Africa Lands, Most Africans Want Neither Britain nor Italy," *Atlanta Daily World*, August 15, 1948.

[110] "Minutes of the Twenty-Seventh Meeting of the United States Delegation to the Third Regular Session of the General Assembly," November 12, 1948, US(P)/A/M(Chr)/27, Box 60, File "US(P)/A/M/(CHR)/1–34," *RG 84*.

of course, there were the issues of military bases and national security. General Willis D. Crittenberger emphasized that "this was not simply a problem of the Italian colonies ... but involved the Middle East and the whole Mediterranean area." Admiral H. Kent Hewitt asserted that, from his standpoint, the "overriding" consideration was the "great strategic importance of Libya and Eritrea, not only to the British but also to the United States." The United States, Hewitt insisted, had to "insure that these territories [did] not fall into the hands of any potentially hostile power."[111]

In other words, in a discussion supposedly concerned with the political and economic future of millions of Africans and Arabs, the "main consideration" was whether U.S. policy would "strengthen the Italian government," "have a favorable effect upon Italian public opinion," and be "in line with the need to establish British bases in the area." Obviously, the "wishes of the inhabitants" had simply vanished beneath an avalanche of strategic concerns.[112]

Both the State Department's legal advisor, Earnest A. Gross, and the U.S. representative on the Trusteeship Council, Francis B. Sayre, were distressed. They described the current proposal as an "embarrassing" position that was "negative, negotiated, ... and ... no one's first choice." Sayre was openly "unhappy about the whole situation" because the "interests of the inhabitants of the area had been ignored." He noted that whereas the "original United States position had real strength because it kept the problem at a level above strictly political considerations," it had now "become a football of politics." Mrs. Roosevelt was equally candid. "She thought there was great merit in the original United States proposal" because it put the "United States in a logical position toward the problem of dependent peoples all over the world" and, she added, "satisfied domestic groups interested in colonial problems." Benjamin Cohen, the State Department's counselor, then added that "his own views started at the same place" as Mrs. Roosevelt's, and he "wanted to also express agreement with the things Mr. Sayre had said." Cohen, who had worked extensively on the Marshall Plan and, therefore, understood the dynamics of a "Europe first" policy, acknowledged that the "United States was in a difficult position, and [that] it was not easy to find a perfect solution." Nonetheless, "if it were not too late," he offered, "the idea of a collective trusteeship had great merit and possibilities."[113]

[111] Ibid.
[112] Ibid.
[113] Ibid.

Secretary of State Marshall, therefore, began to probe why a UN trusteeship, which seemed to be so philosophically in sync with the United States' image as an anticolonial power, had been dismissed so readily. Dulles, who had walked into the Paris meeting determined to "bring about a solution which would realize for Italians the goals ... set out in the Dewey statement," answered. He remarked that "in London in 1945 the solution of a United Nations" trusteeship "had appeared as the only alternative to an old-fashioned scramble for colonial rights in the area." At the time, however, Senator Vandenberg thought that a collective trusteeship was "impractical" because it would "require someone to put up the money ... [and] it was one thing to get Congress to put up money for U.S. aid and another thing for it to finance African colonial enterprises." As a consequence, Byrnes's proposal was rejected, and "the scramble had taken place." That was a fact, Dulles said, "and it was now necessary to attempt to divide the area on the basis of power politics." The "existing state of international relations," Dulles added, "made that inevitable." Thus, the task before the U.S. delegation, he asserted, was not to sit and bemoan this reality but to find a way to present American policy "more attractively," perhaps by appropriating the language of the Trusteeship Council and the UN Charter, so that the General Assembly would sign on and ignore the "power politics" behind this redistribution of Africa.[114]

The delegation was mystified about how it could possibly dress up the American plan to look like it was "meeting the wishes of the inhabitants." Moreover, it was impossible to reconcile Italy's well-known aversion to colonial independence with the goals of a UN trusteeship. Even if the intent was there, there was major doubt if Italy had the economic wherewithal to meet the wide-ranging demands and responsibilities of a UN trustee. John Utter explained to the secretary of state that the "administration of these areas would constitute a heavy financial burden for Italy particularly because it would be expected to carry on not only the usual colonial administration" but also would have to build, maintain, and operate "educational and social welfare facilities." Willard Thorp, the assistant secretary of state for economic affairs, then interjected that "there should be no suggestion" in whatever trusteeship agreement got drafted that "any financial assistance [from the United States] was contemplated" to subsidize Italy's colonial escapades.[115]

---

[114] Ibid.; John Foster Dulles, "What I Have Done for Italy," October 13, 1949, Box 44, File "Senate Campaign-Correspondence: Re: Italy, 1949," *JFD-Princeton.*

[115] "Minutes of the Twenty-Seventh Meeting of the United States Delegation to the Third Regular Session of the General Assembly," November 12, 1948, US(P)/A/M(Chr)/27,

This undercurrent of doubt was beginning to wear on Dulles. He was not going to sit idly by and let the United States back away from a policy that would guarantee that "the Italians [had] a favored position as regarded emigration and development in these areas," and, given Italy's "excess population" difficulties, he insisted that the United States "should go further in giving ... satisfaction to the Italians in this regard." Although one of his colleagues believed that only "birth control" and "badly needed land reforms" could solve Italy's overpopulation woes, Dulles was sure that the key was unrestricted migration to Africa. Early on in the UN session, he had even "suggested that something might be done for Italy ... in the African Colonies of other European powers." He therefore met with the British to ask them to let the Italians resettle in Cyrenaica. The British, of course, balked and told Dulles that war with the Arabs was imminent if Cyrenaica became a dumping ground for Italy's "excess population." Unconvinced, Dulles walked away from that meeting with the distinct "impression that the British had been playing up the hatred of the Senussi for the Italians out of all proportion to avoid an Italian trusteeship."[116]

John Utter strongly disagreed. Arab hatred of the Italians was no figment of the British imagination. When he was in Cyrenaica, Utter explained, "he had asked whether they would mind having the Italian settlers return, [and] they always expressed violent opposition." This, he continued, "was the opinion prevailing throughout the territory."[117]

The secretary of state, however, was as skeptical as Dulles and thought that the British had, in fact, "played up" the extent of Arab opposition "because it supported the British desires in Cyrenaica." Marshall, therefore, suggested that the United States aim toward a policy that encouraged the resettlement of Italians not only in Libya but also in Somalia and Eritrea. Pleased with this new direction, Dulles added that he wanted the

Box 60, File "US(P)/A/M/(CHR)/1–34," *RG 84*; "Minutes of the Twenty-Ninth Meeting of the United States Delegation to the Third Regular Session of the General Assembly," November 17, 1948, US(P)/A/M(Chr)/29, Box 60, File "US(P)/A/M(CHR)/1–34," *RG 84*.

[116] Phil Bagby to Samuel Reber, October 15, 1948, 865C.oo/10–1548, Box 6968, *RG 59*; "Minutes of the Twenty-Ninth Meeting of the United States Delegation to the Third Regular Session of the General Assembly," November 17, 1948, US(P)/A/M(Chr)/29, Box 60, File "US(P)/A/M(CHR)/1–34," *RG 84*; John Foster Dulles, "What I Have Done for Italy," October 13, 1949, Box 44, File "Senate Campaign-Correspondence: Re: Italy, 1949," *JFD-Princeton*.

[117] "Minutes of the Twenty-Ninth Meeting of the United States Delegation to the Third Regular Session of the General Assembly," November 17, 1948, US(P)/A/M(Chr)/29, Box 60, File "US(P)/A/M(CHR)/1–34," *RG 84*.

UN's immigration policies to "be as liberal as possible" and he believed that the "United Nations should set an example of not building up barriers against the natural movement of peoples." Of course, this was a little ironic coming from the man who had worked hard to design a domestic jurisdiction clause that would shield from UN scrutiny the immigration laws crafted to keep Italians and other "undesirables" out of the United States. Benjamin Cohen saw the contradictions and warned that although Dulles's proposal for barrier-free migration sounded good in theory, there might be an element of "danger in urging" the UN in this direction. Then, as if his meaning was not clear, he tossed out the term "Asiatic exclusion policies." The secretary of state understood the import of Cohen's warning and recommended that "this matter be considered again and brought back in a redrafted resolution for discussion."[118]

Compounding the State Department's difficulties were the backroom maneuvers of the Italians. Foreign Minister Count Carlo Sforza, relying on his nation's strong religious and emigre connections in South and Central America, had successfully lobbied the Latin American nations to protect Italy's interest in the General Assembly.[119] Because a two-thirds majority was required to ratify any proposal on the colonies, Sforza knew that no agreement could get through without the twenty votes from the Latin Americans, and they had agreed to demand Italian trusteeship for all of the colonies and to accept nothing less. In addition, Italy continued to play its traditional diplomatic game of "flirt[ing] first with east and then west," hoping that either the Soviets or the Americans would want "Miss Italy" bad enough to hand over Somalia, Eritrea, and Tripolitania. America's first offer of the Marshall Plan and "sacks of … flour" was haughtily dismissed as not enough. "Bread is not everything," one editorial warned, and if during this UN session, "America may show herself to be just as hostile" as the British, the Italians would remember that it was the "USSR … for [the] love of Italy [that] tore up her thesis of anticolonialism" and fought hard to give Italy what it wanted most. This was not about imperialism, the editorial asserted, because the Italians never "imitated [the] old examples of exploitation of natives." Instead, Italians had a "'profound spiritual tie' with the lands which they have turned their glance for 50 years" and which "their fathers and brothers bathed with blood and sweat before [the] advent of Fascism." Italy,

---

[118] Ibid.
[119] Dunn to Secretary of State, December 4, 1948, 865.9111 RR/12–448, Box 6968, RG 59.

the editorial insisted, did not want old-fashioned colonialism; its only desire was a "trusteeship, ... commercial possibilities and [an] outlet for [its] excess population" – who, actually, would prefer to go to America. Unfortunately, the editorial continued, America "does not want or need them." With immigration to the United States blocked because of the National Origins Act of 1924, another editorial declared, the colonies were now an "irreplaceable outlet for Italian labor."[120]

With intense dissension in the State Department's own diplomatic ranks and the Italians playing hardball, it was becoming increasingly apparent that it was futile to take on the Italian colonies issues right now. The UN was already inundated at this meeting by Palestine, which was in the process of exploding; the Berlin crisis, which had sent a death chill through the air; and the Declaration of Human Rights, which, because of the wave of postwar lynchings in the American South, the U.S. delegation needed to have ratified to demonstrate the nation's leadership of the "free world." As a result, the only viable option was to postpone discussion on the Italian colonies, which, after much wrangling, the UN did.

In the interim, the State Department hoped to win over the Latin American nations by stressing how important it was for them to not undermine the United States' "strategic concerns" in the Mediterranean. In addition, Acting Secretary of State Robert Lovett, in an effort to mollify the Italians, officially informed De Gasperi that the United States "fully and actively supported an Italian trusteeship for Somaliland," was considering an Italian trusteeship for Tripolitania, would argue forcefully for the "return of former Italian residents of Tripolitania and all of Eritrea," and would insist on a "guarantee [of] ... human rights" for those Italians in Eritrea. Lovett noted, almost apologetically, that "[a]lthough the proposed solution ... may be less favorable to Italy than that for which your Government has so earnestly appealed," the United States in reaching its decision "had to take into consideration ... the possibility that the burden of administration of some of the areas might seriously retard Italian recovery at home." Lovett added that he sincerely hoped that De Gasperi would "appreciate the reasons underlying this decision."[121]

---

[120] Dunn to Secretary of State, telegram, November 26, 1948, 865.9111 RR/11–2648, Box 6968, *RG 59*; Byington to Secretary of State, telegram, July 24, 1948, 865.9111 RR/7–2448, Box 6968, *RG 59*; Plain to Secretary of State, telegram, November 28, 1948, 865.9111 RR/11–2748, Box 6968, *RG 59*; Byington to Secretary of State, telegram, December 9, 1948, 865.9111 RR/12–948, Box 6968, *RG 59*.

[121] Robert A. Lovett to Alcide De Gasperi, December 4, 1948, SD/A/C.1/211, Box 21, File "SD/A/C.1/200–225," Lot File 82D211, *RG 59*.

Walter White most certainly did. It was obvious to him that the U.S.'s proposal, no matter how nicely "sugar-coated," was "dangerously imperialist." He warned that the United States could not "parcel" out Africans and Arabs as if they were no more than "chattel" and then not expect to have serious repercussions rain down on America's head. All one had to do, he observed, was follow what was happening in South Asia, where "Indonesian leaders who have fought Communism as well as imperialism" were being slaughtered by the Dutch. This kind of "insane course ... will play directly into the hands of Russia," because revolution was sure to follow and "will sweep throughout Asia, Africa and other parts of the world where" people were sick and tired of being "robbed for the benefit of absentee landlords in Europe." White was angry that the United States just did not seem to understand that there was "an even larger issue than 'containing Communism'. It [was] one of stopping greed based on racial arrogance."[122]

At the spring 1949 session of the UN, White's ire was raised even further when Sforza informed the Americans that without its colonies, Italy would have major difficulty signing the yet-to-be ratified North Atlantic Treaty (NATO), which was the defense cornerstone of European integration. The Italian press chimed in that "if western powers want[ed] Italy associated in western policy and Atlantic defense," then they needed to recognize that Italy had "Rights to Africa" and it was simply "mortify[ing]" and intolerable that the United States and Britain would "impoverish" Italy and "treat her as Cinderella in [this] new community" of the western alliance.[123]

Then, after dinner one evening at the Italian Embassy in Washington, Gastone Guidotti, director general of political affairs, continued to apply the pressure and "marshalled every argument" in Italy's arsenal to regain the colonies. In lobbying J. C. Satterthwaite, director of the State Department's Africa desk, Guidotti began with the "surplus population" argument, then the "it would be wrong to exclude Italy from

---

[122] Walter White to John Foster Dulles, telegram, December 2, 1948, Box A322, File "Italian Colonies, Correspondence Regarding, Disposition of, 1948-April 1949," *Papers of the NAACP*; Walter White to Muriel Blundell, December 2, 1948, Box A322, File "Italian Colonies, Disposition of, Correspondence Regarding, 1948-April 1949," *Papers of the NAACP*; Walter White, untitled article, December 24, 1948, Box A74, File "Articles: Walter White *Chicago Defender* Columns, 1948," *Papers of the NAACP*.

[123] "Memorandum of Conversation," April 13, 1949, US/A/C.1/802, Box 40, File "US/1/C.1/751–850," *RG 84*; Rayford Logan to Walter White, telegram, March 29, 1949, Box A404, File "Rayford Logan, 1948–49," *Papers of the NAACP*; Dunn to Secretary of State, May 9, 1949, Box 6968, 865.9111 RR/5-949, *RG 59*.

the economic development of backward" places argument, and, next, the "reward" for the "great work" Italy had already "accomplished" in developing North Africa and the Horn argument. Guidotti then zeroed in on what he really wanted. With Tripolitania and Somalia apparently in the bag, the Italians demanded Eritrea as well. To assuage any fears about Ethiopian encirclement, he offered that the Italians were more than willing to have a joint trusteeship with the Ethiopians, as long as it was clear that Italy would be "in effective control." When Satterthwaite raised the nettlesome questions about the "economic and military burdens which trusteeship ... would impose," Guidotti replied that it would cost only about $120 million the first year, and, because "they did not anticipate that there would really be much, if any, resistance," administrative costs "might be as little as $40,000,000" in the following years. Guidotti sidestepped, of course, how Italy, which was still on economic life support, could possibly afford to divert $120 million to colonial administration and then another $40 million annually thereafter. This was no minor issue; the idea that the Italians were prepared to spend roughly $6.78 billion (in 2011 dollars) for the first year of colonial administration and an additional $2.26 billion in the subsequent years was simply infeasible. Nor could Guidotti provide any credible plan for providing for security forces in *all* of the coveted areas "except to remark that this had been worked out in detail with the British." But, of course, that was only for Italian Somaliland, not for Tripolitania or Eritrea.[124]

Apparently uncomfortable with the direction the conversation had taken, Guidotti decided that the time had come to issue the threat that inevitably accompanied these interactions. It "would be unfortunate," he remarked, if Italy, which was "becoming a member of the North Atlantic group[,] ... should have to oppose the United States and make unpleasant speeches at [the UN meeting in] Lake Success." Of course, in addition to being "unfortunate," it would also be politically embarrassing, disruptive, and potentially harmful for prospective NATO members to be at each other's throats arguing over African colonies in front of the UN General Assembly. Satterthwaite understood, however, that the Italian delegation was prepared to make those "unpleasant speeches" "unless the United States agreed with the Italian position." Satterthwaite firmly replied that the United States had already made a commitment to Ethiopia for the

---

[124] "Memorandum of Conversation," April 1, 1949, US/A/C.1/773, Box 40, File "US/A/C.1/751–850," RG 84.

southeastern portion of Eritrea, which, to the Italians' horror, contained the "European" cities of Asmara and Massawa.[125]

Even more disconcerting from the Italian standpoint was that Tripolitania seemed to be slipping away as well. To be sure, Lovett had earlier indicated that the United States was considering throwing its support behind an Italian trusteeship in this region of Libya, but events since that time had called that decision into question. Reports began to pour out from Tripolitania about the rising agitation and disgust with the West for using Arab land to obtain Italy's allegiance. One searing Arab query asked, "Why buy Italy with our territory when historically Italy never stays bought?" Moreover, Arab leaders, who had recently returned from Rome, noted that the "officials they saw in the Ministry of Colonies [were] the same 'Fascist' officials as before the war." This was true. In Italy's version of denazification, only 587 out of 10,063 Fascists were removed from public office. Although the Italians in the colonial office gave assurances that all they wanted to do was assist in the economic development of Tripolitania, the Arabs seriously doubted it. After all, these were the same administrators who, before the war, "wholeheartedly subscribed to the theory that the ... Arab was by nature, ... a subservient person whose only use was as a servant of the dominant Italian." These "conflicting statements," American Consul Orray Taft Jr. warned, had only "strengthened [the] belief that Italy [would] promise anything to get in power" yet had no "intention of bringing Tripoli to independence." Arab leaders warned their community that "our Italian enemies ... want to enslave us again.... They want to exploit us." Why? Because "Italy is ... in a state of misery and extreme poverty and she desires to alleviate her worries at our expense." The Arab leadership then reminded their followers of the horrible toll that Italy had already exacted from them: "Every Arab in Tripolitania has had contact, usually disagreeable, with some Italian and in every family there [were] gaps left by Arabs killed by the Italians. We cannot forget this." Nor were they likely to forget how their land was confiscated and handed over to Italian settlers for development. The fact that "Italian politicians have clearly indicated that [the] settlement of Italians" was one of their chief "aims," the leadership asserted, could only mean that "our land [will be] taken from us again." Taft, therefore, wired the State Department that the "situation is tensest since my arrival here.... Country is politically and religiously united in face of threat or possibility of Italian return" and for the "first time [there is] religious

[125] Ibid.

opposition to Italian return. This is serious." Then Taft warned, "[i]t is generally accepted that disorders will follow upon the announcement of and entry of Italian control."[126]

The explosiveness of the situation had finally penetrated. John Foster Dulles began to understand that the British had not been exaggerating and manipulating the depths of anti-Italian sentiment. Throughout the ranks of the State Department, there was now raw skepticism about Italian Ambassador Alberto Tarchiani's claims concerning Italy's "great contributions to the advancement of Tripolitania" and the "excellent relations [the Italians had] with the native population." Department officials were equally wary of the ambassador's assertion that this harmonious relationship portended "an orderly transfer" of power with "no serious difficulties in taking over ... from the British." In clear, unadorned language, Dean Rusk told Ambassador Tarchiani that the United States "had serious doubts" that the Italians could return to Tripolitania "without the outbreak of open hostility on the part of the natives." As a result, Rusk asserted, the United States would not and could not support the reassertion of Italian rule in Libya because that could unleash bloodshed and destruction to rival that in Palestine.[127]

That decision only fed the sense of angst and desperation. In Rome, De Gasperi warned Ambassador Dunn that if the United States did not support the Italians' colonial aspirations, it "would make Italy's participation in the Atlantic Pact and Italy's rearmament futile." Then, raising the specter of the Red bogeyman, "De Gasperi ... said that his government [could] not continue to carry on effectively its battle against communism if it also ha[d] to face distrust on the part of democratic nations." Sforza had to admit, of course, that "on the basis of actual facts, and when viewed rationally," the prime minister's threats sounded "absurd." However, Sforza continued, it would be foolish to "underestimate" the "psychological and emotional factors" that govern the Italian electorate.

---

[126] "Memorandum of Conversation," April 13, 1949, US/A/C.1/802, Box 40, File "US/A/C.1/751–850," RG 84; Orray Taft Jr. to Secretary of State, memo, November 27, 1948, 865C.00/11–2748, Box 6968, RG 59; Orray Taft Jr. to Secretary of State, telegram, December 28, 1948, 865C.00/12–2848, Box 6968, RG 59; Kimber Quinney, "The United States, Great Britain, and Dismantling Italian Fascism, 1943–1948," (PhD diss., University of California, Santa Barbara, 2002), 284; Orray Taft Jr. to Secretary of State, telegram, March 9, 1949, 865C.00/3–949, RG 59; Orray Taft Jr. to Secretary of State, telegram, March 12, 1949, 865C.00/3–1249, Box 6968, RG 59; Orray Taft Jr. to Secretary of State, telegram, April 8, 1949, 865C.00/4–849, Box 6968, RG 59.

[127] "Memorandum of Conversation, by the Assistant Secretary of State for United Nations Affairs (Rusk)," March 25, 1949, FRUS (1949) 4:539–542.

Sforza expressed that he "had no desire or intent to suggest the use of blackmail in any form," but, he added ominously, if the Italian people believe that "their just rights are disregarded in the settlement of the Colonies question, ... support for continued close cooperation with the western powers, and support for the Atlantic Pact itself, would become dubious to say the least." Inevitably, he concluded, "the adverse reaction might be so grave as to seriously retard the growing integration of Western Europe."[128]

French Foreign Minister Robert Schuman, the chief architect of European integration, fearful that Great Power dissension over North Africa would jeopardize everything he had worked so hard to put in place, was ready to run the diplomatic gauntlet to "plug hard for the Italian effort to regain [the] colonies." His first stop was London. To Schuman's surprise, Foreign Secretary Bevin said that the British had no qualms about an Italian trusteeship over Tripolitania; the problem was not England. The problem was Italy's miserable colonial record. The U.S. consul had reported that at just the hint of the Italians returning to Libya, the Cyrenaicans published an old photo of an Italian-ordered mass execution and, even more ominous, made clear that they were prepared to "join [the] Tripolitanians in resistance." Faced with the possibility of a full-fledged colonial war, Bevin asserted that he had no intention of using British troops to prop up an Italian trusteeship and he seriously doubted "Italy's ability to maintain order in Africa, without wrecking her own finances." Of course, this was all mere speculation, Bevin observed, because there was no way that an Italian trusteeship for Tripolitania could ever muster a two-thirds majority vote in the General Assembly.[129]

To Schuman, the British were being totally unreasonable, and he therefore tried to persuade Dulles to work with the French Ministry of Foreign Affairs to develop a proposal that would satisfy Italy's "modest demands." Dulles, however, informed the foreign minister that the issue was much larger than the East/West conflict that everyone had focused

---

[128] "Memorandum of Conversation," April 13, 1949, US/A/C.1/802, Box 40, File, "US/A/C.1/751–850," *RG 84*.

[129] F[rank] K[enyon] Roberts to Ernest Bevin, December 29, 1948, FO 371/79336; F[rank] K[enyon] Roberts to Sir C. Sargent and Sir I. Kirkpatrick, December 30, 1948, FO 371/79336; James Clement Dunn to Secretary of State, telegram, January 14, 1949, 865.9111 RR/1-1349, Box 6968, *RG 59*; "The Chargé in the United Kingdom (Holmes) to the Acting Secretary of State," January 17, 1949, *FRUS* (1949) 4:526–528; "The Consul at Tripoli (Taft) to the Secretary of State," March 21, 1949, *FRUS* (1949) 4:535–536; "Memorandum of Conversation, by the Assistant Secretary of State for United Nations Affairs (Rusk)," March 25, 1949, *FRUS* (1949) 4:539–542.

on. The United States, Dulles asserted, now had "to think in terms of North-South." Africa's and the Middle East's vast resources were absolutely essential for Western European development, and, Dulles added, "if the Italian Colonies were dealt with in a manner which excited a Moslem holy war or a race war of black against white, then [those resources] would disappear." Moreover, Dulles noted, the flow of private capital and Marshall Plan funds would also dry up. "Already there was strong pressure in the United States to cut off aid to the Netherlands on account of Indonesia and a great deal would be risked if it seemed that American military and economic assistance to Western Europe was being employed to build up a colonial empire that would be resisted by the native population." More to the point, given Arab resistance and British refusal to "facilitate the reestablishment of Italian administration," there was a strong possibility that the Italians would have to "fight their way in" to administer Tripolitania, and he did not believe that Italy's fragile "prestige" was worth the costs. Schuman reminded Dulles that the "British had a quality ... of looking out for themselves," and he urged Dulles to rethink his position, especially because De Gasperi had made it very clear that if Italy did not regain control of Tripolitania, the Italians would have great difficulty in ratifying the North Atlantic Treaty. Dulles, however, was ready to call De Gasperi's bluff and told Schuman as much.[130]

Walter White also seethed at "the sheer impudence ... of the Italians," who, although their "economy [was] shored up almost entirely by the Marshall Plan," had the audacity to "tell ... the United States ... that they would not join the North Atlantic Pact unless they could have their imperialist way in ... Africa." This only reaffirmed White's conviction that "[n]o greater threat – including war with the Soviet Union – could be created than a North Atlantic Alliance which [was based] on the perpetuation

[130] "Schuman, Sforza Discuss Colonies: Italy's Part in Atlantic Pact Said to Depend on Allied Stand Toward Former Possessions," *New York Times*, December 21, 1948; Caffery to Secretary of State, December 25, 1948, 751.65/12–2448, Reel 2, *Confidential France Foreign Affairs*; James Clement Dunn to Secretary of State, telegram, January 14, 1949, 865.9111 RR/1-1349, Box 6968, *RG 59*; "The Ambassador in Italy (Dunn) to the Secretary of State," November 28, 1948, *FRUS* (1948) 3:966–967; "The Ambassador in Italy (Dunn) to the Secretary of State," December 28, 1948, *FRUS* (1948) 3:968–969. "Memorandum of Conversation, by Mr. John Foster Dulles of the United States Delegation to the U.N. General Assembly," April 12, 1949, *FRUS* (1949) 4:544–546; "Memorandum of Conversation, by Mr. John Foster Dulles of the United States Delegation to the U.N. General Assembly," April 13, 1949, *FRUS* (1949) 4:546–551; "Memorandum of Conversation," April 13, 1949, US/A/C.1/778, Box 40, File, "US/A/C.1/751–850," *RG 84*; "The Ambassador in Italy (Dunn) to the Secretary of State," June 29, 1949, *FRUS* (1949) 4:564–566.

of colonialism for the benefit of white, industrialized, war-shattered and intellectually and morally decadent Europe." He cabled the new secretary of state, Dean Acheson, that the "presumptuous and incredible" link between the North Atlantic Treaty and Italy's "imperialistic designs" was "regrettable" but "nonetheless dramatically revealed" by Count Sforza. Regardless of the Italian foreign minister's threat, White declared, the State Department needed to remember that Italy's behavior in Africa was "execrable," its "atrocities in Ethiopia" were "well-documented," and its record as a colonial administrator was the epitome of "inefficiency, arrogance and barbarity." From any angle, White insisted, Italy was unfit to become a UN trustee. The NAACP, therefore, quickly convened a "closed meeting" of nineteen national organizations to develop a detailed policy statement, which asserted that if the United States capitulated to the Italians' demands, it would "constitute … power politics at its worst" and make clear that North Africa was sold out as a "quid pro quo for Italy's adherence to the North Atlantic Treaty." One NAACP branch president, proud of the strident, defiant tone, sent his "congratulations on [the] stand against return of African colonies to Italy." He was "[g]lad National Office didn't miss the boat on this one."[131]

---

[131] Walter White, "White Fears Worst: New Deal on Colonies Brewing?" *Detroit Free Press*, April 17, 1949, Box A322, File "Italian Colonies, Disposition of, Correspondence Regarding, 1948–49, April," *Papers of the NAACP*; Walter White to Dean Acheson, telegram, n.d. [ca. March 29, 1949], Box A404, File "Rayford Logan, 1948–49," *Papers of the NAACP*; Walter White, handwritten note on "Sforza, Ital. Peace Treaty," n.d., Box A404, File "Logan, Rayford, 1948–49," *Papers of the NAACP*; Walter White, "The North Atlantic Alliance and Colonialism," February 24, 1949, Box A81, File "Articles: Walter White Syndicated Column, 1949," *Papers of the NAACP*; White to Warren R. Austin, April 13, 1949, Box A322, File "Italian Colonies, Disposition of, Correspondence Regarding, 1948–49, April," *Papers of the NAACP*; Warren Austin to Walter White, Box A323, File "Italian Colonies, Correspondence Regarding Disposition of, May 1949–50," *Papers of the NAACP*; James W. Swihart to White, April 27, 1949, Box A322, File "Italian Colonies, Correspondence Regarding Disposition of, 1948-April 1949," *Papers of the NAACP*; "Draft of a Statement to Be Presented for the Consideration of Organizations Invited to the Closed Conference at the Offices of the National Association for the Advancement of Colored People," April 8, 1949, Box 94–18, Folder 429, *Papers of Arthur B. Spingarn*, Moorland Springarn Research Center, Howard University, Washington, DC (hereafter *AB Spingarn Papers*); "Statement Adopted by a Conference Called by the National Association for the Advancement of Colored People in Support of an International Trusteeship for the Former Italian Colonies and Southwest Africa, and for the Independence of Indonesia," April 8, 1949, Box A404, File "Rayford Logan, 1948–49," *Papers of the NAACP*; White to Organizations Invited to Attend Conference on Colonial Policy, memo, April 8, 1949, Box A404, File "Rayford Logan, 1948–49," *Papers of the NAACP*; White to American Federation of Labor et al., telegram, March 31, 1949, Box A323, File "Italian Colonies, NAACP Meeting Regarding Disposition

The National Office was far from done. White pulled together a series of articles for Congress that explained that the current plan to divide up Africa as spoils of war was something "straight out of the Eighteen Eighties, with a kind of modern cellophane wrapping, tinted with trusteeship and international responsibility phrases." On the floor of the House of Representatives, Congressman Adam Clayton Powell Jr. (D-NY) carried the story forward noting that "World War II began when the world sat idly by and allowed Italy to rape Ethiopia. World War III will begin if this action is again allowed by the United Nations Organization. This is not a threat but a statement of logic." To even consider ceding any part of North Africa or the Horn to Italy, Powell contended, was "in direct contradiction to the treaty with Italy, to the stated purposes of the United Nations Organization and to every part of our conscience and religious concepts. It makes a complete mockery of World War II, and it definitely starts the world on the road to World War III." [132]

In his regular column in the *Los Angeles Sentinel*, Roy Wilkins voiced similar outrage. "The great and ominous crime sought to be committed here," the NAACP's assistant secretary wrote, "is the selling of the African people into further exploitation and slavery for the preservation of an American-European union apparently not strong enough to maintain itself without the blood and liberty of Africans." He railed that "America, which preaches so much about democracy and about self-determination," had "coldly ma[de] a deal to sell the African colonies back to Italy in order to strengthen a treaty designed to restore Western Europe and keep 'peace' with the Soviet Union." Well, he retorted, "there will be no peace on this basis. There will be no justice on this basis. Colonialism must go and not even the great strength of America will be sufficient to make Italy a satisfactory governor of the black men and women who want to be and demand to be free." [133]

of, 1948–49," *Papers of the NAACP*; Guy Brewer to Walter White, telegram, April 8, 1949, Box A322, File "Italian Colonies, Disposition of, Correspondence Regarding, 1948–49, April," *Papers of the NAACP*; Walter White to Congressman, April 29, 1949, Box A322, File "Italian Colonies, Disposition of, Correspondence Regarding, 1948–49, April," *Papers of the NAACP*.

[132] See, for example, Edward Martin to Walter White, May 2, 1949, Box A322, File "Italian Colonies, Disposition of, Correspondence Regarding, May, 1949–1950," *Papers of the NAACP*; Emory Ross, "Policy for Africa: Italian Trusteeship Opposed, U.N. Supervision Urged," *New York Times*, April 17, 1949, Box A322, File "Italian Colonies, Disposition of, Correspondence Regarding, 1948–49, April," *Papers of the NAACP*; Adam Clayton Powell Jr. to Warren R. Austin, April 13, 1949, attachment *Congressional Record*, Box 43, File " Powell, Adam Clayton, Jr., 1949," *JFD-Princeton*.

[133] Roy Wilkins, "The Watchtower," *Los Angeles Sentinel*, April 14, 1949.

An editorial in the *Chicago Defender* railed that with the proposed NATO-for-colonies swap, the Italians had connived "to restore their hated rule among Africans" and were behind the "dirtiest deal in big power politics of our time."[134] Columnist Joseph D. Bibb seethed in the *Pittsburgh Courier* at Sforza's "brass and unparalleled nerve to ask the [UN] convention to give back to Italy 'her' colonies," which were only initially seized "after a reign of murder and a cloud-burst of blood." Yet, Bibb continued, "nobody is asking the natives of Africa ... if they want the white people to rule over them.... There is no 'self-determination' for small nations." There is, instead, "a frantic snatch and grab by the grasping takers and greedy claws who whisper about the 'democratic way of life.'"[135] George Schuyler was equally clear. "It is a kind of black-mail these politicians [in Italy] are exacting, and the Allies do not mind because the real estate belongs to weak peoples." However, he continued, "a little picketing by Negroes" at the UN "will serve notice that at least some colored Americans know the score."[136]

Even the Council on African Affairs rejoined this fight, albeit with a Soviet twist. The CAA orchestrated a "delegation of twelve organizations, which paid a surprise visit to the United Nations and buttonholed UN delegates" to keep Italy out of Africa. The delegation "voiced their protests directly to John Foster Dulles" until he "was compelled to stop and listen."[137] The CAA labeled American support for Italian rule "a cynical repudiation of the war-time promise of self-determination for all peoples." "The primary aim of Britain and the United States," the Council complained, "was to safeguard the retention of the strategically placed colonies, particularly Libya, under their own control," while – and this appeared to be the most important point – "excluding the Soviet Union from having any voice whatsoever in the affairs of these areas."[138]

While the Council tried to bolster the Soviets' role in Africa – in vain given that the USSR's anticolonialist credentials were already tarnished – the NAACP remained focused on how to help free the colonies from the threat

---

[134] "The Big Swindle," *Chicago Defender*, April 30, 1949.

[135] Joseph D. Bibb, "Subject Dark People: Imperialism Holds Africa, Malaya, Indonesia, and Indo-China Under Heel," *Pittsburgh Courier*, April 23, 1949.

[136] George S. Schuyler, "Views and Reviews," *Pittsburgh Courier*, April 9, 1949.

[137] "UN Delegates Asked to Change Views on Disposition of Colonies," *Atlanta Daily World*, May 12, 1949; "Deal on Italian Colonies Stalled, Postponed; UN Assembly Rejects New Imperialist Sellout," *New Africa*, 8, no. 5 (May 1949).

[138] "Protest against Italian Colonial Program Urged," *Atlanta Daily World*, April 20, 1949; "Deal on Italian Colonies Stalled, Postponed; UN Assembly Rejects New Imperialist Sellout," *New Africa*, 8, no. 5 (May 1949).

of Italian rule.[139] The Association decided to launch a well-coordinated radio and print campaign to provide a forum for the Somali Youth League (SYL), which was *the* political organization in Somaliland, to present its perspective to the public and to the UN delegates. Henry Lee Moon, the NAACP's director of public relations, wrangled an exclusive interview for the Somali representatives with the *New York Times* and then used that to emphasize the importance of this story to other papers and radio stations in the New York area. Moon and White understood, however, that getting the media to grab onto the story and puncture the myth of Italian benevolence was only part of the solution. It was painfully obvious that few had taken the Somalis and their concerns seriously. In fact, a few years later Abdullahi Issa, who led the SYL and would become Somalia's first prime minister, explained to Dulles that although "the colonial powers controlling almost the entire Continent of Africa … [sought] the diplomatic support and the economic aid of the United States Government in order to continue their domination of Africa," it was "the National Association for the Advancement of Colored People, which generously offered its moral and material support to the legitimate efforts of the Somali people to secure their unity and independence."[140] Because the UN clearly had to hear the other side of the story, Issa noted, "Walter White, Roy Wilkins and other members of the NAACP staff" provided "invaluable assistance" in getting the Somalis' cause before the UN's First Committee (the political committee).[141] (See Figure 3.2)

---

[139] For the adverse effects on the Soviets' reputation because of the Italian colonies, see Lawrence S. Kaplan, *NATO and the UN: A Peculiar Relationship* (Columbia: University of Missouri Press, 2010), 16.

[140] Abdullahi Issa to John Foster Dulles, August 6, 1953, General Correspondence, Box 4, File "Somaliland (1953–57)," *Papers of the ILHR.*

[141] Bayne, "Somalia on the Horn," Vol. VII, no. 8 (March 8, 1960), 3; Henry Lee Moon to J. Raymond Walsh, April 7, 1949, Box A322, File "Italian Colonies, Disposition of, Correspondence Regarding, 1948–49, April," *Papers of the NAACP*; Henry Lee Moon to Don Irvin, April 5, 1949, Box A322, File "Italian Colonies, Disposition of, Correspondence Regarding, 1948–49, April," *Papers of the NAACP*; Henry Lee Moon to Ted Poston, April 5, 1949, Box A322, File "Italian Colonies, Disposition of, Correspondence Regarding, 1948–49, April," *Papers of the NAACP*; Henry Lee Moon to George Streator, April 22, 1949, Box A322, File "Italian Colonies, Disposition of, Correspondence Regarding, 1948–49, April," *Papers of the NAACP*; Henry Lee Moon to Edgar T. Rouzeau, April 22, 1949, Box A322, File "Italian Colonies, Disposition of, Correspondence Regarding, 1948–49, April," *Papers of the NAACP*; Henry Lee Moon to Robert Hallett, April 22, 1949, Box A322, File "Italian Colonies, Disposition of, Correspondence Regarding, 1948–49, April," *Papers of the NAACP*; Henry Lee Moon to Ted Poston, April 22, 1949, Box A322, File "Italian Colonies, Disposition of, Correspondence Regarding, 1948–49, April," *Papers of the NAACP*; "Memorandum to the United Nations from the Somali Delegation," April 5, 1949, Box A322, File "Italian

FIGURE 3.2. Roy Wilkins meets with representatives of the Somali Youth League, future prime minister of Somalia, Abdullahi Issa, and Ali Noor to map out their strategy before presenting petition to UN's Fourth Committee on April 21, 1949.
Source: NAACP Collection. Courtesy of the Library of Congress, Prints and Photographs Division, LC-DIG-ds-04715.

During its testimony and in its interviews, the Somali delegation appealed to the UN not to "sacrifice our people on the altar of political bargaining and expediency" and to understand that it was not a question of a trusteeship but rather a question of an *Italian* trusteeship that was completely unacceptable. The Somalis explained:

Under the 'colonia' system, men, women and children had been taken by force from remote places and condemned to an indefinite period of servitude on Italian farms.... Bachelors were forced to marry women who had been born and bred on the estate. Punishment ... for a first offence of disobedience [was] fifty lashes with a hippopotamus-hide whip ... and for a second offence the victim was strung up for several hours on a gallows, with his toes just clear of the ground.

Colonies, Disposition of, Correspondence Regarding, 1948–49, April," *Papers of the NAACP*; "Somali Leader Thanks NAACP for Aid at UN," press release, May 26, 1949, Box A323, File "Italian Colonies, Disposition of, Press Releases, Newspaper Clippings, and Statements Regarding, 1949, May-Dec.," *Papers of the NAACP*.

The Somalis asserted that they had "suffered enough of slavery, suppression and oppression under the Italian administration during and long before the Fascist regime." It was something that they "will never forget."[142]

Then the Somalis cut through the fiction of "surplus population," observing with angry bemusement that it was only when Italians moved to Africa that they insisted on "demanding the right to administer the ... countries to which they have migrated." The Somalis further noted that if the western nations were really concerned about solving Italy's "surplus population" woes, "they would do far better to let down the bars and permit a sufficient number of Italian immigrants into these prosperous lands rather than awarding to bankrupt Italy the infertile and desert lands of East Africa, where, because of former Italian oppression, emigrants from that land would not be welcome." If the UN tried to hand their country back to Italy, the Somalis asserted, it would "be regarded as an unforgivable betrayal," an "appeasement of an ex-enemy" that would be "resisted by our people with all the means at their disposal." In other words, the "Somalis will resist ... restoration of Italian administration of ANY kind even at the price of complete extermination": "True, we don't have modern weapons, but we can and will fight, and to the finish."[143]

The Italians, however, were just as determined to regain what they believed was rightfully theirs. Sforza, in his appeal before the UN, dismissed all of the concerns about colonial uprisings and the subsequent drain on the Italian treasury. Instead, he emphasized to UN members that it was unthinkable to put Eritrea, "containing a highly civilized 'European' town like 'Asmara,'" under the rule of the Ethiopians. And, although he had the

[142] "Address to the First Committee of the General Assembly by Abdullahi Issa, Representative of the Somali Delegation," UN press release, May 9, 1949, Box A323, File "Italian Colonies, Disposition of, Press Releases, Newspaper Clippings and Statements Regarding, 1949, May-Dec.," *Papers of the NAACP*; Abdullah Issa et al. to Trygve Lie, November 6, 1948, Reel 10, *NAACP-Int'l*; "Somalis Warn of Civil War If Italians Regain Colony," April 1949, Box A323, File "Italian Colonies, Disposition of, Press Releases, Newspaper Clippings and Statements Regarding, 1949, May-Dec.," *Papers of the NAACP*. Emphasis in original.

[143] "Address to the First Committee of the General Assembly by Abdullahi Issa, Representative of the Somali Delegation," UN press release, May 9, 1949, Box A323, File "Italian Colonies, Disposition of, Press Releases, Newspaper Clippings and Statements Regarding, 1949, May–Dec.," *Papers of the NAACP*; Abdullah Issa et al. to Trygve Lie, November 6, 1948, Reel 10, *NAACP-Int'l*; "Somalis Warn of Civil War If Italians Regain Colony," April 1949, Box A323, File "Italian Colonies, Disposition of, Press Releases, Newspaper Clippings and Statements Regarding, 1949, May-Dec.," *Papers of the NAACP*.

"deep[est] ... respect for Ethiopia," Sforza wanted the UN to know just how "illogical" it was "that a nation [like Ethiopia] ... so much in need of help and education should be given control over a country of many religions and races (some of them more advanced than the Ethiopians themselves)." After explaining with similar clarity why Somalia and Tripolitania should also be returned to Italy, Sforza stressed, with unintended irony, that the Italian emigres in Africa were just "like their fellow-farmers and industrialists of South Africa." And, he argued, it would be "unjust" and "an act of racial discrimination" to "chase them out of Africa after a toil of generations" simply because they were white.[144]

After miraculously transforming Italian overseers, plantation owners, and marauding armies into victims of racial discrimination, Sforza then launched into a barrage of "impetuous" off-the-cuff remarks that were too much even for the U.S. delegation. The foreign minister made repeated, albeit "somewhat extraneous ... references to the Atlantic Pact," intimating that if the Italians "did not measurably realize their present colonial aspirations, this might have a serious effect ... on Italy's ratification of the Atlantic Pact and entry into the European union." For the United States that was a horrendous gaffe. Even worse, however, was "the general tenor of [Sforza's] informal remarks," which implied "that Africa was essentially a European problem." One member of the U.S. delegation advised Guidotti that "[i]t might be well in the future to try to avoid any impression that Italy and the other Western European powers looked on ... Africa primarily from the point of view of the benefits which Europe would derive." In other words, the Italians needed to be a lot more subtle about their imperialism.[145] (See Figure 3.3)

For Italy, however, this was not the time for subtlety, this was the time for bold action. In the spring of 1949, Sforza met with British Foreign Secretary Ernest Bevin, with whom he had been at loggerheads, to work

---

[144] "Speech of Count Carlo Sforza Foreign Minister of Italy," April 11, 1949, Box A323, File "Italian Colonies, Disposition of, Press Releases, Newspaper Clippings, and Statements Regarding, 1948–49, April," *Papers of the NAACP.*

[145] Ibid.; "Memorandum of Conversation," April 5, 1949, US/A/C.1/718, Box 40, File "US/A/C.1/651–750," RG 84; "The Chargé in the United Kingdom (Holmes) to the Acting Secretary of State," January 17, 1949, *FRUS* (1949) 4:526–527; "Memorandum of Conversation," April 7, 1949, US/A/C.1/738, Box 40, File "US/A/C.1/651–750," RG 84; "Memorandum of Conversation," April 11, 1949, US/A/C.1/764, Box 40; File "US/A/C.1/651–750," RG 84; "Memorandum of Conversation, by Mr. John Foster Dulles of the United States Delegation to the U.N. General Assembly," April 12, 1949, *FRUS* (1949) 4:544–545; "Memorandum of Conversation," April 12, 1949, US/A/C.1/779, Box 40, File "US/A/C.1/751–850," RG 84.

FIGURE 3.3. Italian Foreign Minister Count Carlo Sforza played hardball and threatened to withhold Italian participation in NATO unless the United States ensured that Italy regained control of Somalia, Eritrea, and Libya.
Source: Photographer Haywood Magee/Hulton-Deutsch Collection/Corbis. Courtesy of Corbis, Stock Photo ID# HU056533.

out a compromise that they could submit to the UN General Assembly.[146] "On 23 February Sforza wrote privately to Bevin: 'Do not give me away: personally I would sooner prefer a gigantic reconstruction in our South and in Sicily than to spend a penny in Africa. But you know too well that certain traditions are a force one cannot ignore; we cannot go 'against the current.'"[147] Yes, Bevin knew. The continued limbo in North Africa and the Horn had put an enormous strain on the British treasury and he needed a way out.[148] As far as Bevin was concerned, all Britain had wanted since the end of the war was Cyrenaica and the communications

---

[146] P. M. Crosthwaite to Sir I. Kirkpatrick, December 31, 1948, FO 371/79336; Saul Kelly, *Cold War in the Desert: Britain, the United States, and the Italian Colonies, 1945–52* (New York: St. Martin's Press, 2000), 115–116.

[147] Seton-Watson, "Italy's Imperial Hangover," 172.

[148] Summary of Telegrams, December 2, 1948, Box 23, File "State Dept. Briefs File, September–December 1948," *Papers of Harry S Truman: Staff Member and Office Files: Naval Aide to the President Files, 1945–53*, Harry S. Truman Presidential Library, Independence, MO (hereafter *HST:SMOF:NA*).

facility in the Western Province of Eritrea.[149] Italy made clear, however, that it would demand that the Latin Americans vote against the British unless Bevin came out in favor of an Italian trusteeship in Tripolitania.[150] The resulting and controversial Bevin-Sforza agreement gave Cyrenaica to Britain, the Fezzan to France, Eritrea (except the Western Province) to Ethiopia, the Western Province to British-controlled Sudan, and Somalia to Italy, and, in 1951, the Italians would take over Tripolitania. The need for the two-year lag time in Tripolitania, the British explained, was "to allow passions to cool off and to give the inhabitants of that territory the opportunity to realize that they had nothing to fear from Italy."[151]

The Tripolitanians thought otherwise. They had already warned UN Secretary-General Trygve Lie that any plan that tried to dissect Libya or allowed Italy "to dominate them again" would be viewed "as aggressive and unjust" and would be dealt with accordingly. With news of the Bevin-Sforza agreement, Tripolitania erupted. Taft reported that "over 3,000 Arabs ... paraded through Tripoli streets rythmically [sic] chanting 'Russian' and 'Libya'" and "'long live Russia'... based on Russian advocacy of rapid independence without interim Italian trusteeship." The Council on African Affairs believed that this supposed support for the Soviet Union "indicated that they [the Arabs] were as conscious of their friends as of their enemies." A much more probable explanation, however, was that the Arabs could play the Red card as well as the Italians and believed that this was the opportune and critical moment to do so. Thus, in addition to reporting to Washington that the Bevin-Sforza agreement had unleashed the specter of Soviet influence in North Africa, Taft then had to report that a "general strike and two demonstrations" were also planned. Although all of the protests were, thus far, "orderly," Taft was extremely worried because the next day the number of demonstrators had doubled with "[t]empers rising." Soon "20,000 Arabs marched through the streets denouncing British, American and Italian governments, tearing and burning flags of these countries, and calling a general strike." It was immediately clear to Taft that the Bevin-Sforza agreement was "entirely unacceptable here ... because it installs Italy."[152]

---

[149] Former Italian Colonies: Brief for Sir Oliver Franks, n.d., ca. March 1948, J 3440/6/G, FO 115/4378.

[150] "Memorandum of Conversation," April 8, 1949, US/A/C.1/756, Box 40, File "US/A/C.1/751–850," *RG 84*.

[151] Rivlin, "The Italian Colonies and the General Assembly," 467, 469.

[152] Orray Taft Jr. to Secretary of State, telegram, April 7, 1949, Box 46, File "United Nations Correspondence, Includes Genocide, Declaration of Human Rights," *JFD-Princeton*;

In London, Ambassador Douglas reported that the press could only say that "Bevin ... must have been extremely badly advised" because "at least 75 percent of Tripolitanians would be prepared to accept any plan for their future except the return of Italy. It [was] not only that the Italians brutally killed tens of thousands – possibly hundreds of thousands – of Libyans, ... and appropriated a great deal of their land; [but] they did nothing whatsoever" during the thirty years they were in power "to fit the Libyans for eventual independence": there was "no Libyan doctor, lawyer, or administrator, and hardly a teacher" in the region. All it would take now was "one wrong move" by the UN "in favour of Italian trusteeship," and "widespread disorders and considerable bloodshed" would follow.[153]

As incredible as it may seem, given the mass demonstrations in Tripoli, it actually appeared that the UN was going to make that "one wrong move." State Department consultant Benjamin Rivlin observed that "[a]lthough the Bevin-Sforza agreement was bitterly attacked by the Arab-Asiatic bloc and the Soviet states, it received the support of Great Britain, the United States, France and the Latin-American states." With that kind of numerical backing, which remained impervious to the "prolonged and acrimonious debate that stretched far into the night," the Dulles-created subcommittee assigned to handle the Italian colonies issue manipulated and massaged the wording of the Bevin-Sforza agreement to secure "a vote of 34 to 16 with 7 abstentions." If that vote held in the General Assembly, the agreement would pass with the necessary majority, carve up Libya, and put Italy back in firm control of Tripolitania and Somalia.[154]

Walter White, therefore, decided that it was time to intensify the NAACP's efforts. Rayford Logan had already warned him, based on a March briefing at the State Department, that the United States had probably already gerrymandered the UN vote to get a "settlement acceptable to the US, the UK and France."[155] But the coalitions were fragile and barely stitched together – that was also clear. White immediately

---

Orray Taft Jr. to Secretary of State, memo, April 27, 1949, 865C.00/4-2749, Box 6968, RG 59; Orray Taft Jr. to Secretary of State, telegram, May 16, 1949, 865C.00/5-1649, Box 6968, RG 59; "Deal on Italian Colonies Stalled, Postponed: UN Assembly Reject New Imperialist Sellout," *New Africa*, 8, no. 5 (May 1949), Reel 63, *Du Bois*; Orray Taft Jr. to Secretary of State, telegram, May 17, 1949, 865C.00/5-1749, Box 6968, RG 59; Dean Acheson to Orray Taft Jr., telegram, May 14, 1949, 865C.00/5-1349, Box 6968, RG 59.

153   Lewis Douglas to Secretary of State, telegram, May 24, 1949, 865C.00/5-2449, Box 6968, RG 59.
154   Rivlin, "The Italian Colonies and the General Assembly," 467.
155   Rayford Logan to Walter White, March 21, 1949, Box A404, File "Logan, Rayford, 1948–49," *Papers of the NAACP*.

noticed that although the Bevin-Sforza agreement in its entirety captured a majority in the Dulles-engineered UN subcommittee, it was obvious in the paragraph-by-paragraph voting that the proviso that awarded Tripolitania to Italy could have difficulty getting through the General Assembly. Prior to the final vote in the UN, the Association's Roy Wilkins and Henry Lee Moon teamed up with the Somali and Libyan representatives to lobby, cajole, and persuade the wavering delegations to stand up against this "shameless compromise" to carve up Libya and Eritrea and hand over Somalia to the Italians.[156]

As the *Pittsburgh Courier* reported, "Heavy pressure had been brought to bear upon the UN General Assembly from all parts of the United States by Negro welfare organizations" and African student groups. That pressure, especially from the NAACP, bore fruit. The first sign that the Bevin-Sforza agreement was in serious trouble arose, as White predicted, over the issue of Tripolitania. India, which had already worked closely with the Association on UN issues, changed its abstention to a resounding "no," which put the necessary two-thirds majority in jeopardy. Then, in defiance of U.S. expectations, Haiti, to which the NAACP had a direct channel, cast the decisive "no" that rendered the Bevin-Sforza agreement dead on arrival.[157] To punctuate the point, the subsequent proposal on Somalia was "'doomed to failure' as a result of Indian, Ethiopian, Liberian and Haitian opposition" – that is to say, doomed by the very nations that the Association anticipated would use the General Assembly to stand up against the colonial powers. The CAA proudly observed that the United States and Britain had "suffered" a stinging "defeat when the final vote was taken at 2:32 A.M., May 18th." "The vote," *New Africa* noted, "reflected one of the first significant revolts of some of the smaller nations against the dominating influence of the U.S. in the UN."[158]

---

[156] Walter White, "A Short, But Significant Victory within Our Time," *Chicago Defender*, November 12, 1949.

[157] "Rebuffed on Ethiopian Colonies, 'White' Nations Lose Face at UN: Smashing Defeat for Western Bloc Backing Italy," *Pittsburgh Courier*, May 28, 1949; "Defeat of Colonial Plan Hailed by Walter White," press release, May 19, 1949, Box A323, File "Italian Colonies, Disposition of, Press Releases, Newspaper Clippings and Statements Regarding, 1949, May–Dec.," *Papers of the NAACP*. For the NAACP's relationship with Haiti, see Millery Polyné, *From Douglass to Duvalier: U.S. African Americans, Haiti, and Pan Americanism, 1870–1964*, New World Diasporas, ed. Kevin A. Yelvington (Gainesville: University Press of Florida, 2010), 132–133, 140–141.

[158] Kelly, *Cold War in the Desert*, 116–117; "Deal on Italian Colonies Stalled, Postponed; UN Assembly Rejects New Imperialist Sellout," *New Africa*, 8, no. 5 (May 1949).

Clearly, the West had blundered badly. The echoes of warnings that John Utter, Francis Sayre, and others raised in November now reverberated in the thunderous 14-37-7 vote in the General Assembly. Benjamin Rivlin delivered a sobering analysis of all that went wrong. He explained that in trying to reconcile the conflicts of "British and American security … Italian and French pride, and Ethiopian territorial claims," the Bevin-Sforza agreement just plain "failed to give adequate consideration to … the most basic interest involved: the people of the territories themselves." The plan only "paid lip-service" to the principles in the Atlantic and UN Charters. It "flew in the face of the findings of the Four Power Commission of Investigation," ignored the Arabs' and Africans' vehement opposition to an Italian trusteeship, and whitewashed Italy's "record of oppression," "economic difficulties," and "helplessness and stagnation."[159]

Joseph Palmer II, the assistant chief of the State Department's Division of African Affairs, convinced that "there [were] certain lessons to be learned" from this fiasco, performed an equally incisive *postmortem*. For Palmer, the United States was on very shaky ground. First of all, by aligning with the Bevin-Sforza agreement, the United States placed itself "in the position of supporting … a regime for Tripolitania which was not in accord with the wishes of the inhabitants." The emerging nations in the General Assembly were appalled at the ease with which the United States ignored the "immediate reaction of the inhabitants of Tripolitania." Not only was this a "source of great embarrassment to the U.S." but also it "dissipate[d]" any goodwill America may have earned in granting independence to the Philippines. Even the abstentions, Palmer noted, were no source of comfort. It was obvious that most would have voted against the Bevin-Sforza agreement and "abstained principally because of instructions from home not to oppose the U.S." And even with that pressure, Liberia and Ethiopia had broken ranks and voted against the American-backed plan for an Italian trusteeship for Somalia. "I think it is probable," Palmer predicted, "that in any future General Assembly they would find it even more difficult to maintain a neutral attitude on a question involving such important matters of principle for them and … would naturally gravitate toward the anti-Italian grouping." The United States made a bad situation worse, Palmer continued, when it supported a contradictory proposal that gave "lip service to the concept of Libyan unity" then "divided the region into three zones under [three] different regimes." No one was fooled. How could they be? Two of the regimes – France

---

[159] Rivlin, "The Italian Colonies and the General Assembly," 469–470.

and Italy – had horrendous imperial histories in North Africa and were known to be viscerally opposed to colonial independence.[160]

The only way the United States could recover from this debacle, Palmer asserted, was to identify a trustee with a "reputation" and a "willingness and capability" to prepare a *united* Libya for independence. The General Assembly would accept nothing less. And, if the United States wanted to hold onto its "reputation" as a "nation concerned with matters of principle," it had to realize that it could "not afford to support a proposal which [ran] counter to the obvious wishes of the inhabitants of a territory."[161]

The U.S. ambassador in London and a chastened Foreign Secretary Bevin agreed. It was now clear to them that Libyan "independence [was] inevitable" and it was time to take advantage of the situation, "climb on [the] band wagon," and thereby gain the goodwill of the Arabs. The most feasible solution appeared to be a British trusteeship for a united, soon-to-be independent Libya. Ambassador Douglas and Bevin recognized that this position would result in a "first-class row with the French." Nonetheless, the ambassador asserted, it was the only sensible direction to take. It was inane, he observed, to continue to bend U.S. and British policy "toward a further postponement of [the] evil day" when Libya would become independent simply because the French refused to come to grips with the "realities" of nationalism in North Africa. Douglas went on to explain that, despite America's best advice, the French insisted on sleepwalking through the minefield of Arab nationalism, refused to even contemplate the possibility of independence for Tunisia, Morocco, and Algeria, and, thus, were in the process of creating a "situation [in] French North Africa" that would be as deadly as the one in Vietnam. He therefore wanted Acheson to understand that France, and only France, could "cure" the problems in French North Africa and that it was not in "our best interests" to continue to squelch Libyan unification and independence just to satisfy France's suicidal vanity.[162]

The National Security Council (NSC) affirmed the State Department's analyses. The NSC noted that the "Arab, Asiatic, and Soviet opposition which defeated [the Bevin-Sforza] proposal was directed primarily against

---

[160] "Memorandum by the Assistant Chief of the Division of African Affairs (Palmer)," May 27, 1949, *FRUS* (1949) 4:558–561.
[161] Ibid.
[162] "The Ambassador in the United Kingdom (Douglas) to the Secretary of State," July 14, 1949, *FRUS* (1949) 4:566–567; "The Ambassador in the United Kingdom (Douglas) to the Secretary of State," July 22, 1949, *FRUS* (1949) 4:569–571.

the partition of Libya and Italian administration of Tripolitania." It was evident that this bloc was "so strong that it could probably defeat any proposal for the trusteeship of Libya in the future." Because Libya was indispensable for Anglo-American security, however, it was "essential for this Government to take a position which will not antagonize the Libyans in their efforts to achieve unity and independence. A contrary course," the NSC noted, "might jeopardize the continued use of our military facilities, particularly Wheelus Field, in Tripolitania and the continued use by the British of their facilities in Cyrenaica." The only way to ensure America's "strategic requirements in the area" was for the "U.K. and also the U.S. [to] have sufficiently strong influence with the government of an independent and united Libya ... in which Sayed Idriss would be Chief of State."[163]

The NSC's analysis effectively pulled Tripolitania off the auction block as a payoff to the Italians, and with the bulk of Eritrea promised to the Ethiopians, the only possible colonial option for Italy was Somaliland. It was here, the NSC decided, that the General Assembly might let an Italian trusteeship exist simply "because of the importance of saving as much face as possible for the Italian Government." The NSC, therefore, recommended that the United States support a plan for the upcoming fall 1949 UN meeting whereby Libya, under British guidance, would be united and, after a clearly stated, short-term period, independent. Eritrea, except for the Western Province, would go to Ethiopia. The Western Province would come under an Anglo-Egyptian-Sudanese trusteeship. And, Somaliland, of course, would go to Italy. This was a plan that the United States hoped would win the necessary support of the Arab-Asian bloc and, if Italy got behind it, the Latin American one.[164]

For France, the Anglo-American plan represented the worst of all possible worlds – a united Libya, with a guarantee of independence, under a short-term *British* trusteeship. The American embassy in Paris warned the State Department to be prepared for "strenuous French opposition to a united Libya," because they were convinced that Sayyid Idris was a "'British stooge'... that would probably complicate the situation in French North Africa by giving material support to the independence movements" in Morocco, Tunisia, and Algeria.[165]

---

[163] "Draft: Report by the National Security Council on U.S. Position on the Disposition of the Former Italian Colonies," August 4, 1949, *FRUS* (1949) 4:572–578.
[164] Ibid.
[165] Ridgway B. Knight to Douglas MacArthur II, November 29, 1949, 865C.00/1.2949, Box 6968, *RG 59*.

The Italians also chafed at the Americans' proposal but realized that their African options had effectively been whittled down to Somalia. Still scratching and clawing, however, the Italians insisted that their control of Somalia had to last "long enough to justify Ital[ian] expense," and they believed that "[t]wenty-five years of trusteeship" sounded about right. Of course, the Italians needed more than just time; they needed money. Sforza noted that if the United States would just provide millions in development funds, "Somaliland would be less of a burden on Italy."[166] Meanwhile, Dulles warned Acheson that Sforza and De Gasperi would "redouble their efforts to prevent Massawa and Asmara," the "two so-called 'Italian' cities," from "coming under Ethiopian sovereignty." He was right. Sforza easily convinced the Latin American bloc to make its vote for a united, independent Libya contingent on Arab support for an Italian trusteeship in Somaliland, and he also persuaded Italy's supporters to vote against an Ethiopian trusteeship in Eritrea.[167]

For the NAACP, it was irrelevant whether Italy, France, Britain, the Soviets, or even Ethiopia achieved full satisfaction. The point was that the Arabs and Africans who lived in those colonies had to have their wishes for political and economic independence respected *and* protected. Although Walter White was now on leave because of his abrupt divorce from a black woman and subsequent controversial nuptials to a thrice-married fashion editor, he continued to use his newspaper column to hammer on the issue of the Italian colonies. He blasted John Foster Dulles, who, while on the senatorial campaign trail in New York, "unashamedly made a bid for Italian votes at the price of independence for the natives of the African colonies." At a stop in Buffalo, Dulles insisted "that Italy ha[d] a 'right' to send emigrants to Africa and that the sending of them there [was] the only solution to Italy's economic plight." White railed, "Mr.

---

[166] "The Secretary of State to the Embassy in Italy," August 17, 1949, *FRUS* (1949) 4:579–580; "Memorandum of Conversation, by the Secretary of State," September 14, 1949, *FRUS* (1949) 4: 583–585; "Text of the Statement by the Italian Foreign Minister Carlo Sforza Before the Political Committee of the U.N. General Assembly, October 1, 1949, on the Question of the Disposition of the Former Italian Colonies," October 1, 1949, Reel 64, *Du Bois*; Iyob, *The Eritrean Struggle*, 74; "The Chargé in the United Kingdom (Holmes) to the Secretary of State," December 16, 1949, *FRUS* (1949) 4:610–611.

[167] John Foster Dulles to Dean Acheson, memo, June 9, 1949, Box 39, File "United Nations Correspondence: Includes Declaration of Human Rights and Genocide Convention," *JFD-Princeton*; "The United States Representative at the United Nations (Austin) to the Secretary of State," October 7, 1949, *FRUS* (1949) 4:586–588; "Memorandum by the Deputy Director of the Office of United Nations Political and Security Affairs (Wainhouse) to the Ambassador at Large (Jessup)," October 8, 1949, *FRUS* (1949) 4:589–591.

Dulles conveniently ignore[d] the grim fact that Italy's economic plight [was] in part due to the fact that she fought on the side of Germany in the last war." Nor had it "occurred to Mr. Dulles that if Italians want[ed] to migrate to Africa or anywhere else they [could] do so without being given political control over the countries" to which they had moved. Dulles, White remarked, "must surely ... know that additional bloodshed and turmoil will inevitably follow any steps to give Italy again any of the African colonies which she renounced totally and forever in the Treaty of Paris." Already, in Somaliland, seven had been killed and "twenty wounded by British troops during the past two weeks for protesting the proposed return of Italian political control over that unhappy colony." It should, therefore, be obvious even to John Foster Dulles, White asserted, "that any steps by the U.S. or the U.N. or anyone else to reestablish colonialism, however disguised, will set off a chain reaction of revolt all over Africa and Asia."[168]

White was amazed that the Italians and the United States, despite the overwhelming evidence, continued to ignore that the "colonies cost Italy money instead of being a source of revenue and that very few Italians ... migrated to Africa to escape overcrowding in Italy." White noted, for example, that "less than half as many Europeans lived in the Italian colonies in 1931 as there were Italians in the Borough of Manhattan." He then cited a study done by a New York Stock Exchange investment banker which concluded that "[m]odern colonialism [was] ... an increasingly expensive luxury" and, more than that, "an economic ... anachronism." The refusal to accept those basic facts, White asserted, was grounded in some misbegotten "sentimental" longing for the good old colonial days. It was time for the Italians to recognize that those old days were not so good and were now long gone.[169]

At the NAACP's National Office, Wilkins also continued the battle. He blasted the *New York Times* and the State Department for branding the Somali Youth League as Soviet-controlled, when, he insisted, Abdullahi Issa's organization was "a purely nationalistic anti-imperialist movement." The fact of the matter, Wilkins continued, was that the State

---

[168] Walter White, "Senator Dulles and Colonialism," October 20, 1949, Box A81, File "Articles: Walter White Syndicated Column, 1949," *Papers of the NAACP*; Walter White, "The Colonial Question," July 28, 1949, ibid.; Walter White, "Colonialism Does Not Pay," December 8, 1949, ibid.

[169] Walter White, "Senator Dulles and Colonialism," October 20, 1949, Box A81, File "Articles: Walter White Syndicated Column, 1949," *Papers of the NAACP*; Walter White, "The Colonial Question," July 28, 1949, ibid.; Walter White, "Colonialism Does Not Pay," December 8, 1949, ibid.

Department had "abandoned" the Somalis and aligned with the colonial powers to deny Somalia the right to self-determination. This "failure of the United States to support" the Somalis' "just claims," Wilkins declared, made it clear that "[t]his country ha[d] yielded … to the Russians the role of champion of oppressed peoples." So, just what did the United States expect? Of course this "surrender" would have a "tremendous and unfavorable impact upon the millions and millions of colonial and semi-colonial peoples throughout the world." However, instead of coming to terms with the effect of its political cowardice, Wilkins noted, "this country" continually expresses "great alarm" whenever "one of these emergent nations understandably leans toward Soviet power." All the while, Wilkins scolded, "we continue to ignore the simple and positive remedy – namely that we ourselves should champion the liberation of colonial peoples." Then, instead of trying to put distance between the Association and the now red-tainted SYL, Wilkins proudly announced that the "NAACP ha[d] worked closely with the Somali delegation" and "supported the Somalis in their uncompromising opposition to the restoration of the Italian rule in Somaliland." More important, the Association would continue to do so and would not be scared off by the Red hobgoblin. Similarly, the fact that the Soviets and the "subversive" CAA came to champion a UN trusteeship plan for the Italian colonies did not compel the Association leadership to back away.[170]

That resolve and more would be needed for the next round at the fall 1949 meeting of the UN. Wilkins was already "distressed" that "at the last session of the General Assembly, the United States delegation was lined up with the European powers in support of obsolete colonialism." Ralph Bunche now warned the acting secretary that a deal was "being cooked up behind the scenes," and it was imperative that the NAACP "have some one [sic] regularly on the job to do some lobbying." Bunche noted that the last vote was just a little too close for comfort and the NAACP might not be able, as it did in the spring, to "pull the rabbit out of the hat at the last minute" (see Figure 3.4). As soon as the Association realized that the behind-the-scenes deal involved letting the Italians save face by gaining control of Somalia, Wilkins blasted the whole idea as absolutely "unthinkable." He urged the Haitians to continue to protect the rights of the Somalis. He pleaded with the Liberians to "join forces"

---

[170] Roy Wilkins to Dean Acheson, September 15, 1949, Box A323, File "Italian Colonies, Disposition of, Correspondence Regarding, May 1949–50," *Papers of the NAACP*; Roy Wilkins to Editor *New York Times*, November 18, 1949, ibid.

FIGURE 3.4. UN official Ralph Bunche – seen here with Roy Wilkins and Henry Lee Moon, publicity director for the NAACP, in September 1949 – provided invaluable insider information regarding the latest political maneuvering at the UN concerning the fate of Libya, Eritrea, and Somalia.
Source: Corbis. Courtesy of Corbis, Stock Photo ID# IH179745.

with all other "liberty-loving delegations" to keep Italy out of Africa. And he lobbied the delegates from Britain, India, the Middle East, South America, Scandinavia, and Eastern Europe to "vote against the proposal to restore Italian administration" to Somalia. Wilkins stated that if "the United Nations [was] to maintain its prestige among colonial peoples and their friends in other lands, that organization [could] not afford to retreat to old imperialism." Instead, the UN had to protect "the interests of the welfare of the people of Somalia." With that as its paramount responsibility, he asserted, "[u]nder no circumstances should Italy be permitted to return ... in any administrative capacity."[171]

---

[171] Rayford Logan to Roy Wilkins, September 20, 1949, Box A404, File "Logan, Rayford, 1948–49," *Papers of the NAACP*; "Draft of Letter to Liberian Delegation to UN," October 3, 1949, Box A323, File "Italian Colonies, Disposition of, Correspondence Regarding, May 1949–50," *Papers of the NAACP*; Roy Wilkins to Joseph D. Charles, telegram, October 20, 1949, Box A323, File "Italian Colonies, Disposition of, Correspondence Regarding, May 1949–50," *Papers of the NAACP*; Logan, diary entry, September 12, 1949, Box 4, File "Diaries, Personal: 1948–49," *Logan Papers*; Roy Wilkins to B. N. Rau, October 7, 1949, Box A323, File "Italian Colonies, Disposition of, Correspondence

The NAACP's program was not simply about opposing an Italian trusteeship. It was about supporting a UN trusteeship, which in the Association's estimation held the only promise of providing the economic and political structure needed to create independent, viable states. The NAACP's plans seemed to receive a major boost when Secretary-General Trygve Lie also proposed that the Italian colonies come under "a direct United Nations trusteeship." Lie was certain that "this practical approach" would "diminish the political differences that blocked success last spring."[172]

Despite Lie's support and the NAACP's lobbying efforts, the United States countered with what Roy Wilkins called enormous "pressure upon countries in need of American economic assistance," and, in the end, the State Department's development dollars proved decisive. The General Assembly voted that Libya, under a British trusteeship, would become independent no later than January 1, 1952. However, Somalia, as the Association feared, would achieve its independence only after ten years of Italian trusteeship.[173]

Disappointed, Wilkins labeled the General Assembly's decision a "partial victory." Granted, Libya won its independence and freedom from Italian rule; however, Wilkins noted, "Believing in self-determination, as we do, we naturally regret the failure of the General Assembly to heed the clearly expressed and oft-repeated objections of the Somalis to the return of their former oppressors."[174]

Regarding, May 1949–50," *Papers of the NAACP*; Alexander Cadogan to Roy Wilkins, October 8, 1949, Box A323, File "Italian Colonies, Disposition of, Correspondence Regarding, May 1949–50," *Papers of the NAACP*; Roy Wilkins to Trygve Lie, September 29, 1949, Box A323, File "Italian Colonies, Disposition of, Correspondence Regarding, May 1949–50," *Papers of the NAACP*.

[172] Roy Wilkins to Trygve Lie, September 29, 1949, Box A323, File "Italian Colonies, Disposition of, Correspondence Regarding, May 1949–50," *Papers of the NAACP*; Clyde Eagleton, ed., *Annual Review of United Nations Affairs: 1949* (New York: New York University Press, 1950), 93.

[173] Roy Wilkins to Editor *New York Times*, November 18, 1949, Box A323, File "Italian Colonies, Disposition of, Correspondence Regarding, May 1949–50," *Papers of the NAACP*; U.N. General Assembly, 4th Session. Question of the disposal of the former Italian Colonies, Resolution 289 (IV), November 21, 1949, http://daccess-dds-ny.un.org/doc/RESOLUTION/GEN/NR0/051/08/IMG/NR005108.pdf?OpenElement. Accessed July 26, 2010; Eritrea's independence would take decades to achieve. See Iyob, *The Eritrean Struggle*.

[174] "Colony Settlement 'Partial Victory,' Roy Wilkins Holds," press release, November 23, 1949, Box A323, File "Italian Colonies, Disposition of Press Releases, Newspaper Clippings and Statements Regarding 1949, May–Dec.," *Papers of the NAACP*.

Even after the UN's decision, the NAACP would not let the issue of Somalia slip away and, instead, continued to help the Somalis "in every possible way ... to avert domination of their country by Italy."[175] The Association issued protest after protest about the excessive show of force and "heavy-handed manner in which the Italians tended ... to reassert their authority" in Somalia[176] (see Figure 3.5). Then, when the State Department and Immigration and Naturalization Service tried to deport Abdullahi Issa because of his supposed Communist ties, the NAACP sent in one of its strongest legal teams, Robert L. Carter and Constance Baker Motley, who had been focused on dismantling Jim Crow, to ensure the Somali Youth League leader had continued access to the UN.[177] The Association also "'emphatically' protested" the choice of General Guglielmo Nasi as Italian special commissioner for Somaliland. Earlier, the Ethiopians had singled him out as a particularly vicious war criminal, who had been responsible for a series of mass murders and mustard gas attacks. "Surely," Roy Wilkins declared, "the United Nations cannot conceive of General Nasi, a previously fascist conqueror of British Somaliland and governor of the Gondar section of Ethiopia, as a just

---

[175] "Introduction," fragment, n.d., Reel 4, *NAACP*.

[176] "NAACP Hits Italian Request for Somalia Military Bases," January 5, 1950, Box A323, File "Italian Colonies, Disposition of, Correspondence Regarding, May 1949–50," *Papers of the NAACP*; "Somaliland Police Sent from Italy: First Contingents Sail Right after Rome Senate Votes Expense Appropriation," *New York Times*, February 9, 1950, Box A323, File "Italian Colonies, Disposition of, Press Releases, Newspaper Clippings and Statements Regarding, 1949, May–Dec.," *Papers of the NAACP*; Lewis, *A Modern History of Somalia*, 139–140.

[177] Walter White to Clarence Mitchell, July 7, 1953, Box A5, File "Africa: Abdullahi Issa, 1953–54," *Papers of the NAACP*; Robert L. Carter to Walter White, memo, July 14, 1953, Box A5, File "Africa: Abdullahi Issa, 1953–54," *Papers of the NAACP*; Constance Baker Motley to Walter White and Clarence Mitchell, memo, July 16, 1953, Box A5, File "Africa: Abdullahi Issa, 1953–54," *Papers of the NAACP*; Clarence Mitchell to Walter White, July 17, 1953, Box A5, File "Africa: Abdullahi Issa, 1953–54," *Papers of the NAACP*; Abdullahi Issa to Walter White, July 18, 1953, Box A5, File "Africa: Abdullahi Issa, 1953–54," *Papers of the NAACP*; Abdullahi Issa to Walter Offutt, July 18, 1953, Box A5, File "Africa: Abdullahi Issa, 1953–54," *Papers of the NAACP*; Walter White to Abdullahi Issa, July 20, 1953, Reel 2, *NAACP-Int'l*; White to Herbert Brownell, July 20, 1953, Reel 2, *NAACP-Int'l*; Walter P. Offutt Jr. to Abdullahi Issa, August 3, 1953, Reel 2, *NAACP-Int'l*; Clarence Mitchell to Abdullahi Issa, September 10, 1953, Reel 2, *NAACP-Int'l*; Walter P. Offutt Jr. to Abdullahi Issa, October 13, 1953, Reel 2, *NAACP-Int'l*; Clarence Mitchell to Walter White, telegram, November 3, 1953, Reel 2, *NAACP-Int'l*; Abdullahi Issa to Walter Offutt, April 27, 1954, Box A5, File "Africa: Abdullahi Issa, 1953–54," *Papers of the NAACP*; Abdullahi Issa to Walter Offutt, May 11, 1954, Box A5, File "Africa: Abdullahi Issa, 1953–54," *Papers of the NAACP*.

FIGURE 3.5. The NAACP protested the Italian show of military force at Mogadishu in 1950 as Italy began its trusteeship over Somalia.
Source: Bettman/Corbis. Courtesy of Corbis, Stock Photo ID# U934413ACME.

and suitable administrator for a liberated colony preparing itself for democratic self-government."[178]

Although the initial show of force and Nasi's appointment were rankling, the United Nations had, in fact, put a tight leash on the Italians' trusteeship, with mandatory direct oversight by a UN Advisory Council housed at Mogadishu and periodic site visits by members reporting directly to the Trusteeship Council. Moreover, an administering power's financial responsibilities finally began to prick through the sentimental haze of Italian colonial euphoria. The initial appropriation alone to administer Somalia was a staggering $9.6 million – roughly $427 million in 2011 dollars. Thus, as E. A. Bayne noted, it soon became "clear to all Italians (as many had foreseen it earlier) that Italian colonialism would be too costly to be borne ... by a government confronted with ...

[178] Roy Wilkins to Carlos P. Romulo, telegram, January 5, 1950, Box A323, File "Italian Colonies, Disposition of, Correspondence Regarding, May 1949–50," *Papers of the NAACP*; Ethiopian Ministry of Justice, *Documents on Italian War Crimes*, 2.

reconstruction and development at home"; and this basic truth "involved a triumph for the realists in the Italian Government over the unrealistic nationalistic proponents of colonialism."[179]

Throughout this journey to liberation, a potent blend of realism and idealism shaped the NAACP's push to keep "the wishes of the inhabitants" and Italy's shortcomings front and center during the debates. The Association was appalled that the United States consistently put anticommunism above all else. Above principle. Above democracy. Above the Atlantic and UN Charters. Above the right to self-determination. The NAACP, therefore, overcame its own internal discord and mustered the stamina and strategic intelligence to help push the reality of the Somalis', Libyans', and Eritreans' objections back onto the U.S. and UN agendas, especially when NATO considerations had muffled the cries of the indigenous peoples. The Association dodged through the minefields of Cold War foreign policy, the hazards of electoral politics, and the sniping within its own constituency that defined working through the corridors of power as a sell out, a surrender. It was anything but. Although Eritrea became trapped in Ethiopia's clutches, the Association's intervention rendered some astonishing results. Libya, which had been on the butcher block ready to be cleaved in three, gained its independence within a year, and Somalia, looking down the long barrel of a generation of Italian rule, walked away with only a decade. These accomplishments were not easy, but years earlier when Wilkins first saw the NAACP in action, he had said, "Here at last was a fighting organization, not a tame band of status quo Negroes."[180]

As in any war, however, there were casualties. Tobias's son-in-law, William Dean, who led the UN mission to Somalia and organized the secretary-general's plan for the economic reconstruction of the Italian colonies, came back to the United States "physically exhausted." By the time he landed in New York, he was no more than "skin and bones." The Harvard-trained economist, who had proven invaluable in slipping trusteeship and human rights information to the NAACP, was visibly "overwork[ed]" and "depressed" by what he had encountered on the Red

---

[179] Lewis, *A Modern History of Somalia*, 139–140; Trusteeship Council Resolution 1255 (XVI): Financing of the Economic Development Plans of the Trust Territory of Somaliland under Italian Administration, July 21, 1955, Box 56, File "10th GA Committee 4 (Trusteeship) Position Papers," RG 59; Bayne, "Somalia on the Horn," Vol. VII, no. 10 (March 15, 1960), 9.

[180] Wilkins, *Standing Fast*, 93.

Sea. Distraught "since his return from Africa," Dean gave in to despair and committed suicide "in the gas-filled Harlem apartment of his father-in-law, Dr. Channing H. Tobias."[181]

[181] Bill Dean to Walter White, marginalia on, Resolution Related to the Reconstruction Problems of Devastated Areas not Included in the Reports of Temporary Subcommission on Economic Construction of Devastated Areas and to the Termination of Activities of That Subcommission (Approved March 28, 1947), April 2, 1947, Box A4, File "Africa: General, 1947–49," *Papers of the NAACP*; E(dna) M W(asem) to White, memo, January 29, 1948, Box A635, File "United Nations General Assembly, 1946-August 1948," *Papers of the NAACP*; "The Week's Census, Died: William Henry Dean, 41," *Jet*, January 24, 1952; "UN African Aide Suicide Victim," *Cleveland Call and Post*, January 12, 1952.

4

So Weak, So Seventeenth Century

Indonesia and the Domestic Jurisdiction of Dutch Colonialism

> "In the case of the ... Dutch ... colonies" any plans for eventual equality "cannot be carried out if these areas ... continue to be regarded as territory for trade, industry and investment to be carried on primarily for the benefit of non-resident Europeans without making the economic and social interests of the inhabitants of the colonies of first and continuous importance."
> – NAACP Colonial Conference, 1945

At the same time that the NAACP was helping with the battle against colonialism on the African continent – not to mention fighting Jim Crow at home – the Association's attention was drawn to the Indonesians' epic struggle for freedom, which was taking place more than 10,000 miles away in Southeast Asia. Because this battle played out primarily in the Security Council, which was less amenable to the suasion of appointed representatives and the lobbying of other delegations in the halls, the NAACP did not and could not play as direct a role.

Nonetheless, this did not signal impotency. On the contrary, the Association adopted a strategy that was an essential component in the campaign for Indonesian independence. Working closely with an interlocked network of NGOs, such as the Post-War World Council, the ILRM, and the India League, the NAACP identified the key weakness in Holland's colonial argument (domestic jurisdiction) and the necessary levers (the Marshall Plan and public opinion) to knock the imperial power off its stride. Of course, the confluence of interests – major pillars of U.S. foreign policy threatened, a seemingly viable nationalist alternative to indigenous Communists, and the Netherlands' uncanny ability to anger allies and enemies alike – was incredibly fortuitous and necessary.

But without the mobilization of an enraged public that vented its disbelief when U.S. funds intended for rebuilding Nazi-ravaged democracies were actually being used in the destruction of a viable Republic, the State Department would have had neither the leverage nor probably the will to take the tough stand that eventually broke the Dutch refusal to negotiate.

After the Second World War, Holland was determined to rebuild itself on the backs of people who not only refused to be exploited but also insisted that they were not going to taste colonial bondage again. The Indonesians called it "'100% merdeka' (100% freedom)."[1] The Hague insisted, however, that it and it alone controlled the life arc of the rebellious, independence-minded colony. The Dutch declared that the UN's domestic jurisdiction clause gave them the freedom to do whatever they deemed necessary, without outside interference, to control the insurgent nationalism that undermined their dominance and authority in a land far, far away.

At base, the challenge the NAACP and others faced was the reluctance of the United States to risk alienating a European Cold War ally. This was not going to be easy. The Soviet Union was *the* threat and Europe was ground zero. The Americans had funneled the bulk of their postwar resources, attention, and prioritization to their Atlantic partners. Even in the midst of the Korean War, President Truman assured Congressional leaders that "All [of] our program[s]" – the Marshall Plan, NATO, and more – were "to strengthen our Allies" in Europe.[2] Other areas languished or became collateral damage. Washington had, of course, given significant lip service to democracy, anticolonialism, self-determination, and human rights.[3] However, it had also defined national security in ways that undermined those very values. The State Department, Congress, and the White House, therefore, had to be convinced that U.S. national security was imperiled – not bolstered – by European colonial rule.

[1] Anne L. Foster, "Avoiding the 'Rank of Denmark': Dutch Fears about Loss of Empire in Southeast Asia," *Connecting Histories: Decolonization and the Cold War in Southeast Asia, 1945–1962*, eds. Christopher E Goscha and Christian F Ostermann, Cold War International History Project (Washington, DC: Woodrow Wilson Center Press; Stanford, CA: Stanford University Press, 2009), 76.

[2] Meeting of the President with Congressional Leaders, 11 a.m., Friday, December 1, 1950, Subject File Foreign Affairs, Box 148, File "Attlee Meeting – December 1950," *HST:PSF*.

[3] For European frustration with even the U.S.'s lip service to anticolonialism, see Paul Masar to Sir John Martin, June 11, 1952, CO 936/94; Letter for Signature in the Foreign Office to Monsieur G. Gaucher, n.d., ca. June 27, 1952, CO 936/94.

This unparalleled Cold War battle had begun, in fact, during the Second World War, which was a turning point for both Holland and Indonesia. By 1945, the Netherlands was in "turmoil" as that nation endured "a ruthless enemy who held it and bled it mercilessly during four long, dark years."[4] As the Dutch ambassador to the United States Eelco Van Kleffens recounted, the Netherlands was "a devastated country.... No country had been looted more thoroughly by the Germans, ... by the Hitler regime, than Holland had. We had to build our harbors from the ground up; we had to build our railways from the ground up; we had to start all our factories anew (they were empty shells)."[5] Meanwhile, from March 1942 to August 1945, the Japanese overran and occupied the jewel in Holland's own imperial crown, Indonesia, and subjected the people to the horrors of famine, torture, and rape.[6]

V-J Day only brought another set of challenges. Holland longed to step back in as if nothing had changed and resume the role of imperial power – running the colony, making its laws, extracting the resources, and shipping the wealth back to the Netherlands. In fact, prior to the war, "almost 14 percent of Dutch national income originated ... from Indonesia."[7] However, Japan's mad dash scramble in the aftermath of Hiroshima and Nagasaki, coupled with Holland's weakened and decimated armed forces, which could not get to the archipelago for months, created a chaotic "who's in charge?" atmosphere. As far as many Indonesians were concerned, the Dutch most certainly were not.

Walter White had gleaned from his travels and correspondence with the Indonesian leadership that the refusal to accept the reassertion of the Netherlands' rule was based, in large measure, on centuries of Dutch misrule. He learned that in 1938, the "average income of the Indonesian amounted to no more than the equivalent of one United States cent a day." "After 350 years of Dutch rule in Indonesia, 93% of Indonesian

---

[4] "The Netherlands Marines Are Coming ..." *Netherlands News Digest*, 3, no. 5 (May 15, 1944), 193.

[5] Eelco Van Kleffens Oral History, http://www.trumanlibrary.org/oralhist/vankleff.htm. Accessed June 9, 2013.

[6] "Japanese Methods of 'Winning Friends,'" *Netherlands News Digest*, 3, no. 17 (November 15, 1944), 694; Toshiyuki Tanaka, *Hidden Horrors: Japanese War Crimes in World War II*, foreword by John W. Dower (Boulder, CO: Westview Press, 1996), 11–78, 94.

[7] Foster, "Avoiding the 'Rank of Denmark,'" 68–71; David Jordan, "'A Particularly Exacting Operation': British Forces and the Battle of Surabaya, November 1945," *Small Wars and Insurgencies*, 11, no. 3 (Winter 2000), 90, 93; Pierre Van Der Eng, "Marshall Aid as a Catalyst in the Decolonization of Indonesia, 1947–49," *Journal of Southeast Asian Studies*, 19, no. 2 (September 1988), 336.

people were illiterate." In terms of access to health care, in 1940 there was, per capita, only "1 doctor for 60 thousand people."[8] Moreover, by "abandoning their colonial possession so rapidly and disgracefully in 1942," collapsing before Emperor Hirohito's military "'without any shadow of a proper attempt' to defend the Netherlands East Indies," and "their failure to provide adequate protection for the Indonesian people, [which] left them unarmed and helpless to face the invading Japanese forces," the Dutch lost any claims they may have had on the archipelago. By the same token, the millions of Indonesians who "'paid a very high price' in pain and bloodshed … 'to wrest power from the Japanese,'" had earned their freedom.[9] On August 17, 1945, the indigenous leadership, led by Mohammed Hatta and Achmed Sukarno, who had been engaged in "years of nationalist struggle," issued Indonesia's declaration of independence from the Netherlands.[10]

The Dutch were stunned. They "registered disdain for the … unilaterally proclaimed independent Republic."[11] They painted a lurid picture of the Republic of Indonesia as a tropical *Lord of the Flies* awash in "anarchy," "violence," "looting," and the "complete destruction of the social structure." They cajoled the British, who had military authority over Southeast Asia at the end of the war, to go in and restore order.[12] However, when General Sir Philip Christison, who headed the UK's forces in Indonesia, arrived to temporarily take control of the archipelago, he and his troops "were bewildered by the state of affairs they found in the East Indies." Expecting to see chaos, bedlam, and confusion, the British found, instead, "a functioning native government actively supported by the great majority of politically conscious Indonesians and operating at a high degree of efficiency."[13] The Foreign Office immediately advised The Hague to begin negotiations.[14]

[8] L. N. Palar to Walter White, May 4, 1949, Box A321, File "Indonesia, 1948–49," *Papers of the NAACP.*

[9] Frances Gouda, *American Visions of the Netherlands East Indies/Indonesia: US Foreign Policy and Indonesia Nationalism, 1920–1949*, with Thijs Brocades Zaalberg (Amsterdam: Amsterdam University Press, 2002), 124–125; L. N. Palar to Walter White, May 4, 1949, Box A321, File "Indonesia, 1948–49," *Papers of the NAACP.*

[10] McMahon, *Colonialism and Cold War,* 38.

[11] Gouda, *American Visions of the Netherlands East Indies/Indonesia,* 127.

[12] Document 164: "Annex A" in 301st Meeting of the Supreme Allied Command, December 6, 1945, *Officiële Bescheiden Betreffende de Nederlands-Indonesische Betrekkingen, 1945–1950* (The Hague: Martinius Nijhoff, 1972), 314.

[13] McMahon, *Colonialism and Cold War,* 86.

[14] Cees Wiebes and Bert Zeeman, "United States' 'Big Stick' Diplomacy: The Netherlands between Decolonization and Alignment, 1945–1949," *International History Review,* 14, no. 1 (February 1992), 47.

The Netherlands, however, stubbornly refused to believe that Indonesia could actually thrive without the Dutch. Refused to negotiate with the Republic about what role Holland would have, if any, in the new Indonesia. Refused to see Sukarno and Hatta as anything but Asian quislings, illegitimate representatives of an illegitimate government. In short, the Netherlands refused to believe that the relatively brief period of the Japanese occupation had destroyed what nearly 350 years of colonial rule had built. As historian Anne Foster noted, "many Dutch commentators ... have used the word 'trauma' to describe" the realization that the Netherlands East Indies was becoming Indonesia.[15]

To put the earth back on its axis, the Dutch desperately wanted the British to use the Indian Army to overthrow the Republic and hold Indonesia in European hands until the Netherlands had regained enough military strength to take control. Dutch Admiral Conrad Helfrich explained that "in his experience ... when dealing with native rabbles the most profitable way was to hit immediately and to hit hard."[16] The British, especially the Supreme Allied Commander for Southeast Asia, Lord Mountbatten, resisted. As the English saw it, their job was to "finish off the war against Japan" by disarming Tokyo's remaining forces on the archipelago and freeing the prisoners of war (POWs). "This was," the British made clear, "a very different thing to restoring by force the Dutch Government against the wishes of the population."[17] The Netherlands Foreign Minister Dirk Stikker bristled at England's unwillingness to step up to the plate for the imperial team. He recalled that Britain's reluctance "created an atmosphere of distrust. We didn't like Mountbatten's attitude at that time."[18]

Dutch Lieutenant Governor General Hubertus Van Mook tried to alleviate British concerns that a harsh regime would emerge from the level of violence necessary to destroy the Republic. He offered that "if a forcible restoration of order must precede the solution of the political problem, this will not mean that the solution itself will become less liberal." Van Mook then added, "[I]t should not be expected that the necessity of applying force [could] be avoided by political concessions."[19] In short, the

---

[15] Foster, "Avoiding the 'Rank of a Denmark,'" 69.
[16] Document 164: The 301st Meeting of the Supreme Allied Command, December 6, 1945, Vol. 2, *Officiële Bescheiden*, 303, 307–308, 309.
[17] Ibid., 307.
[18] Dirk U. Stikker Oral History, http://www.trumanlibrary.org/oralhist/stikker2.htm. Accessed June 8, 2013.
[19] McMahon, *Colonialism and Cold War*, 89–94; Document 164: The 301st Meeting of the Supreme Allied Command, December 6, 1945, Vol. 2, *Officiële Bescheiden*, 309, 311.

Netherlands had no intention of negotiating and, instead, expected the British to fight for Dutch colonialism, under the guise of liberalism, and use the Indian Army to do so.

Mabel Denning, chief political officer to Lord Mountbatten, was appropriately concerned that The Hague simply did not understand the full impact of the Second World War on Asia. "Nobody in Indonesia," he reported, "wanted 'the old gang back.'"[20] Republic Vice President Hatta made clear that "the Dutch [were] about as popular as the pox."[21] Hatta warned that "many years of bloodshed and bitter fighting [would] ensue if the Dutch attempted to take the colony by force of arms."[22] Mabel, therefore, relayed to his superiors that "if the Dutch cannot be persuaded of the truth that the East has changed and changed radically as a result of the war then a satisfactory solution is unlikely."[23]

However, the Dutch could not be persuaded. One U.S. State Department official, who had just returned from The Hague, laid bare the "resentment" coursing throughout the Netherlands government toward the British for their reluctance to use the Indian Army in what was essentially a war of colonial suppression. The Dutch, he chided, "have acquired [the] habit of looking to others for help without exerting maximum efforts themselves." He also warned of a disturbing, imperious air. The "Netherlands Government attitude [toward the] Indies situation," he asserted, could only be described as "stiff" and "slightly 'Colonel Blimpy.'"[24] That is to say, just like the satirical cartoon character, the Dutch were, he suggested, jingoistic and reactionary and, as illustrated in Van Mook's quizzical statement about liberalism through force, able to contradict themselves with no awareness of the incongruity. (See Figure 4.1)

Although the British and Americans agreed that Holland's policy was not based on reality, they also concurred, in the words of Lord Inverchapel (Sir Archibald Clark-Kerr), who would be sent in as a negotiator, that the Indonesian "demand for independence [was] foolish."[25] Britain, now under the helm of Prime Minister Clement Attlee, was, therefore, in "an awkward position. On the one hand, the Labour government wanted

---

[20] McMahon, *Colonialism and Cold War*, 90.

[21] Ibid., 96.

[22] "More Indians for Java to Occupy Surabaya," *Manchester Guardian*, October 19, 1945.

[23] McMahon, *Colonialism and Cold War*, 95.

[24] Winant to Secretary of State, telegram, November 3, 1945, Reel 4, *Confidential Great Britain Foreign Affairs*.

[25] Summary of Telegrams, March 8, 1946, Box 22, File "State Dept. Briefs File, January–May 1946," *HST:SMOF:NA*.

FIGURE 4.1. The State Department feared that the Dutch exhibited all of the worst traits of Colonel Blimp. The cartoon reads: Colonel Blimp: Gad, sir, Lord Reverbeer is right. We should explain to the natives in India that British troops are only there to protect them from massacre, and if they don't accept that, then shoot'em all down.
Source: British Cartoon Archive. Courtesy of the Atlantic Syndicate.

to pull out and avoid involvement in the colonial struggles of another European power; on the other, they [sic] refused to let down the Dutch government, which had just spent five years in exile in London and had contributed loyally to the allied war effort."[26] The British tried to split the difference. However, virtually the moment Christison landed in Java in late September 1945, it was clear that his limited and precise orders – free those who were still interned in POW camps and disarm the Japanese – ran headlong into the Indonesians' fear that the British were there "to crush the new republic for the Dutch."[27]

In Surabaya that fear exploded. The blast was triggered by a stupid mistake, a failure of the British right hand to communicate with the left. A carefully negotiated entente conducted by one set of officers that recognized the right of the Indonesian Army and police to keep their weapons was completely undone by another that showered Surabaya with fliers demanding immediate disarmament and capitulation to British authorities in all realms. The results were harrowing. Inflamed nationalistic mobs tortured, mutilated, and beheaded Allied internees, ambushed and

---

[26] Wiebes and Zeeman, "United States' 'Big Stick' Diplomacy," 47.
[27] Jordan, "'A Particularly Exacting Operation,'" 93.

killed Brigadier A. W. S. Mallaby, and deployed anti-aircraft weaponry, tanks, and artillery seized from the Japanese to try to push the British back into the sea.[28] Enraged, Christison warned that if the Indonesians did not cease and desist immediately and surrender Mallaby's killers, he would "[b]ring the whole weight of my land, sea and air forces to bear on Surabaya."[29] And he did. The Royal Air Force and Royal Navy, coordinating with ground troops, forcefully launched a series of assaults that pounded Indonesian strongholds.[30] "The streets of Surabaya and Bandung witnessed the spectacle of ranks of young Indonesian nationalists, the *pemuda*, 'advancing upon British tanks armed only with bamboo spears and knives' and being killed in their thousands."[31] The eventual bloody cowing of the uprising, however, brought a major surprise for the British. The Indonesian Army boldly entered the fray and "although outclassed in terms of equipment and tactics, ... were sufficiently motivated to continue fighting against great odds."[32] This sent the signal to the British that "the Indonesians were utterly determined to prevent the return of the Dutch as a colonising power and would fight to the death against it."[33] (See Figure 4.2)

Meanwhile, at the very moment when British forces were battling the Indonesian Army, England's financial team, led by Lord Halifax, ambassador to the United States, and John Maynard Keynes, economic adviser to the Chancellor of the Exchequer, were deep in meetings with American officials to secure a multibillion dollar loan.[34] The British were in serious financial trouble – indeed, at the very end of their tether. The Second World War had depleted the nation's assets. The "net gold and dollar reserves of the United Kingdom, estimated at $4.2 billion in August 1938, were drawn down to $12 million by April, 1941."[35] Four years later, by the time Japan surrendered, the "British had lost about 25 percent of

---

[28] Ibid., 96, 99.

[29] Ibid., 99.

[30] "British Troops Fighting for Surabaya: Warships and Planes Bombard Port, Nationalists Send Reinforcements," *Manchester Guardian*, November 11, 1945.

[31] John Newsinger, "A Forgotten War: British Intervention in Indonesia, 1945–46," *Race and Class*, 3, no. 4 (1989), 51.

[32] Jordan, "'A Particularly Exacting Operation,'" 106, 107.

[33] Ibid., 92.

[34] Philip A. Grant Jr., "President Harry S. Truman and the British Loan Act of 1946," *Presidential Studies Quarterly*, 25, no. 3, Civil Rights and Presidential Leadership (Summer 1995), 490–491.

[35] Judd Polk and Gardner Patterson, "The British Loan," *Foreign Affairs*, 24, no. 3 (April 1946), 431.

FIGURE 4.2. Sign of defiance painted on a building in the fall of 1945: Indonesia Never Again the Life Blood of ANY NATION.
Source: Perdjoeangan Indonesia. Courtesy of the Library of Congress, Prints and Photographs Division, LC-USZ62-43524.

their prewar wealth, had contracted about $14 billion in sterling debt, and had seen the volume of their exports decline by about two-thirds."[36] And now, having to pour precious pound sterling into quashing what was nearly a full-fledged revolt in Indonesia, which was not even a British colony, only exacerbated the problem.

The *Manchester Guardian* explained that, at this point, "Britain ha[d] one major interest in Java and that [was] to get our troops out." The newspaper made clear that "British opinion … will not tolerate either an indefinite occupation or the reconquering of the island."[37] Parliament, similarly, had "the gravest misgivings about our position in Indonesia." The manpower demands for rebuilding war-torn England were extensive, but with a sizable number of British troops now unable to get home because someone in "Surabaya kick[ed] up some trouble," the need to extricate the UK from another nation's fight seemed obvious enough.

[36] Melvyn P. Leffler, *A Preponderance of Power: National Security, the Truman Administration, and the Cold War*, Stanford Nuclear Age Series, ed. Martin Sherwin (Stanford, CA: Stanford University Press, 1992), 62–63.
[37] "Indonesia," *Manchester Guardian*, December 29, 1945.

Parliament declared that Prime Minister Attlee "must clear up ... the suspicion that we are identified with the Dutch Government's scheme of pacification and are being made the instrument of Dutch policy. The sooner we get out of Indonesia the better."[38]

The anger against the violence in Surabaya extended into the British Commonwealth as well. The *Chicago Defender* reported that "world-wide support of the Javanese nationalists was registered this week when dock workers in Singapore and Australia paralyzed all shipping by walking out in a sympathy strike against 'British and Dutch imperialism.'"[39] Similarly, the *New York Times* noted that labor's walkout was highly politicized because, whereas other unions were focused on higher wages, the "Australians [were] ... frankly backing the Indonesian revolt against the Dutch."[40]

The proposed U.S. loan to Britain for $3.75 billion, therefore, appeared to be a lifeline in a turbulent sea of debt, labor strife, and war. The NAACP, however, wanted self-determination tied firmly to that line. Shortly after the negotiations were announced, Walter White drafted a cable to Truman demanding that "no part of the ... loan from the United States ... be used for the perpetuation of imperialism and human bondage."[41] The final telegram insisted on firm "pledges that none of the money" from this loan or any other "shall be used to perpetuate imperialism or to deny any colonials of [the] British Empire full freedom and justice."[42]

The Americans, to be sure, had a problem with the empire, just not the one that troubled the Association. U.S. negotiators pressed hard, very hard, on Keynes and Lord Halifax to break open the imperial preference system that locked U.S. manufactures out of the British Empire. *That* was the colonial quid pro quo that the Americans demanded in exchange for a multibillion-dollar loan. The fracas in Indonesia, on the other hand, was not significant enough or understood in the way the NAACP had

---

[38] "Parliament Again," *Manchester Guardian*, January 22, 1946; "Demobilization," House of Lords Debate, November 15, 1945, Vol. 137, cc999–1010, http://hansard.millbank-systems.com/lords/1945/nov/15/demobilization#S5LV0137P0_19451115_HOL_157; "Demobilization," House of Lords Debate, November 20, 1945, Vol. 137, cc1014–58, http://hansard.millbanksystems.com/lords/1945/nov/20/demobilization#S5LV0137P0_19451120_HOL_58.

[39] "Allied Arms Being Used by Dutch in Java, Say Natives," *Chicago Defender*, October 27, 1945.

[40] "Three Dock Strikes," *New York Times*, October 15, 1945.

[41] Minutes of the Meeting of the Board of Directors, December 10, 1945, Reel 3, *NAACP*.

[42] Walter White telegram summary, December 13, 1945, Box 1235, File "413 (1945–1949)," HST:OF.

cast it to warrant pressuring the United States' closest ally.[43] Therefore, while White wanted a guarantee that U.S. aid would not prop up colonial empires or suppress liberation struggles, the Americans responded that "it would be most inappropriate to have the question of financial assistance to the United Kingdom linked to a wide range of political issues or to insist that the United Kingdom adopt the point of view of the United States on these issues as a condition of a loan."[44]

The NAACP understood, however, that most things in the political realm were conditional. The point was to make the costs of supporting wars of colonial conquest so steep, so untenable that the foreign policy bureaucracy could not withstand the barrage. The bloodbath in Indonesia was a powerful opportunity. Here was a nascent republic that had endured centuries of colonialism and then a brutal Japanese occupation only to now face the hail of mortar shells and bombings because its people had the audacity to want to rule themselves. Unlike the cases of South West Africa and the Italian Colonies, which the NAACP had already taken on, this was an actual war. Guns. Bullets. Bombs. Dead bodies.

It was necessary, therefore, to make visible how U.S. material and financial support propped up violent colonial rule and the brutal suppression of self-determination. In a stinging article in the *Chicago Defender*, the NAACP "characterized the reported use of American war materials by British troops" in Surabaya as "one of the greatest scandals and tragedies of recent history."[45] Similarly, the *Atlanta Daily World* railed against the way that "American Lend-Lease [was now] being used in the suppression of the liberties and freedom of the Indonesians."[46] The *Chicago Defender* intoned that "Allied war aims were taking a beating this week, as American and British arms were put at the disposal of Dutch imperialist authorities ... in suppressing Indonesian efforts at achieving independence."[47]

During Prime Minister Attlee's visit to the United States, the Association fired off a telegram protesting the "slaughter of Indonesian ... youths." The NAACP emphasized "that the victory over the Axis will have been

[43] Leffler, *A Preponderance of Power*, 61–63.

[44] M. R. T. Carter to Walter White, January 18, 1946, Box A616, File "State Department, 1945–1947," *Papers of the NAACP*.

[45] "NAACP Hits Loans Boosting Imperialism," *Chicago Defender*, December 22, 1945.

[46] Louis Lautier, "Capital Spotlight: Restless World," *Atlanta Daily World*, January 9, 1946.

[47] "Indonesians in Global Struggle," *Chicago Defender*, October 27, 1945.

lost 'if allied nations perpetuate upon dependent peoples the same slavery Germany and Japan would have imposed.'" Then, highlighting an unsettling irony for those who thought the end of Churchill's administration would usher in a new day for Great Britain, the Association concluded that "it [was] all the more inconceivable that a Labor government should be a party to the perpetuation of human slavery."[48] Walter White was particularly piqued at Attlee's regime for coming hat-in-hand for a multibillion dollar loan while Britain still "retain[ed] ... troops in Greece, Egypt, Indonesia, the Levant, Iraq and Palestine" and also had "military, administrative and economic domination ... in India, Nigeria, Ethiopia, Shanghai, South Africa, Kenya, the West Indies and other parts of the world which imperialism she [was] asking the United States to underwrite."[49]

The *Chicago Defender* bluntly asked "should we lend billions for this?" The "policies of Foreign Minister Bevin have reflected a greater callousness toward the colonial peoples, and a greater determination to hold them in bondage than did the policies of Churchill and the Tories." "British troops [were] still in Indonesia" and "a constant threat to the independence movement of 70 million people." No good would come from a loan to the British, the *Defender* concluded. "To lend their government money ... for the continued oppression of colonial peoples would worsen, rather than improve, [the indigenous people's] conditions."[50] In a heated debate in the U.S. House of Representatives, Congressman Adam Clayton Powell Jr. referenced "the record of Britain in Greece, in Indonesia, ... in Africa, in Palestine, in Ireland, ... and the Caribbean," then denounced the loan to the British as an American stamp of "approval on hypocrisy, imperialism, colonialism, and broken pledges."[51]

An editorial in the *Pittsburgh Courier* similarly noted that "although the British Government [was] now controlled by Socialists and the American Government [was] represented as liberal, they have lost no time in lending all possible support to the Dutch." It was clear, the editorial continued, that "unable herself to enter the vacuum created by the sudden collapse of Japan, Holland called upon its fellow white stockholder in Indonesian resources to prevent the 'catastrophe' of a new brown independent

---

[48] Report of Secretary, October 1945, Reel 7, NAACP.
[49] Walter White, "Russo-Iranian Dispute," *Chicago Defender*, April 20, 1946. Also see, "Walter White Pledges NAACP Drive Against S.C. White Primary," *Atlanta Daily World*, April 12, 1946.
[50] "Should We Lend Billions for This?" *Chicago Defender*, June 1, 1946.
[51] "Powell Dubs British Loan 'Approval on Hypocrisy,'" July 27, 1946, *Chicago Defender*.

nation." Let there be no mistake, however: the "sympathies of the entire colored world are with the Indonesians" because they are waging a battle against the same "curse afflicting all alike, whether they are enslaved by the British, the Americans, the French, or the Russians."[52]

In a speech before 4,000 people piled into an auditorium in South Carolina, Walter White "drew a dramatic picture of the plight of all minority groups, emphasizing British rule in Egypt, India, Indonesia and other countries and the U.S. tolerance of intolerable conditions in the South."[53] This sense of shared struggle meant that African Americans would "protest against the use of military equipment purchased with their taxes to suppress the ligitimate [sic] aspirations of the Indonesians … protest against the hypocritical 'hands off' policy of Secretary of State Byrnes which mouths neutrality while doing all possible to destroy the young Indonesian Republic." In short, the *Pittsburgh Courier* stated, "American Negroes [would] demand that this Government use its influence to get the British mercenaries out of Java."[54]

The State Department, however, seemed initially impervious to an outraged public and the carnage in Surabaya. Only when the question of Indonesia landed before the UN Security Council did it become clear that the war in the archipelago was as toxic and dangerous as the NAACP and the black press suggested.[55] At the Security Council's January 1946 meeting, the Ukrainian delegate charged that Britain's actions in Indonesia "created a threat to the maintenance of international peace and security," which was the tripwire for UN intervention.[56] Given that earlier in the meeting the Soviets had come under a barrage of accusations concerning the reality of Stalin's attempt to set up a puppet regime in northern Iran and the possibility of Kremlin-backed insurgents in the Greek Civil War, the Ukrainian's effort to put Indonesia on the Security Council's agenda looked suspiciously like a diversionary and retaliatory tactic.[57] And it

[52] "Indonesia – The Roots of War," November 17, 1945, *Pittsburgh Courier*.

[53] "Walter White Pledges NAACP Drive Against S.C. White Primary," April 12, 1946, *Atlanta Daily World*.

[54] "Indonesia – The Roots of War," November 17, 1945, *Pittsburgh Courier*.

[55] Lani Guinier and Gerald Torres, *The Miner's Canary: Enlisting Race, Resisting Power, Transforming Democracy* (Cambridge, MA: Harvard University Press, 2002).

[56] Report of the Secretary-General on the Work of the Organization, June 1946, A/63, Box 225, File "United Nations Documents," *Papers of John Winant*, Franklin D. Roosevelt Presidential Library, Hyde Park, NY.

[57] Report of the Security Council to the General Assembly Covering the Period from 17 January to 15 July 1946: Official Records of the Second Part of the First Session of the General Assembly, Supplement No. 1, October 3, 1946, A/93, 1–37.

was. However, as Walter White understood, it was more than that, as well.[58] The war against the Republic raised questions about the reassertion of colonialism, the right to self-determination, and how far national sovereignty and domestic jurisdiction would and could actually stretch. This initial skirmish in the Security Council merely staked out the terms of engagement.

The Ukrainian delegate began by lamenting that for "three and one-half years the Indonesian people suffered under the Japanese regime." Tokyo's defeat should have "encouraged the Indonesians ... that their national aspirations would at last be realized. However," he continued, "reality proved different." Instead of freedom, the British rolled in and "began to employ ... all kinds of modern armies against the poorly armed Indonesians." He acknowledged the importance of the UK's mission to disarm the Japanese and release the POWs; however, the Ukrainian said, it was inexcusable and "inadmissable that the British troops were used for the suppression of the national movement of the Indonesian people." He then called for the Security Council to create a task force to "investigate the situation on the spot and establish peace."[59]

The British immediately took umbrage. The representative from the UK retorted that the Supreme Allied Commander, General Douglas MacArthur, tasked the British with disarming the Japanese and freeing the POWs interned in Indonesia. That was the only reason British troops were there. Unfortunately, a horrific part of Tokyo's occupation was to "develop a fascist force" in which the Japanese "armed and trained many thousands and equipped them with rifles and light tanks." That, he explained, was what the British faced when they arrived in Indonesia – a fascist buzz saw. As for suppressing a nationalist movement, he concluded, the Soviet proxy needed to take that up with the actual sovereign, the Netherlands.[60]

The Dutch delegate then scoffed at the Ukrainian's assertion that there was any threat to international peace. There was nothing *international* about it. As far as Holland was concerned, Article 2(7) held hard and fast. Whatever was going on in Indonesia, he argued, was under the Netherlands' domestic jurisdiction, and, therefore, the UN had no authority or right to send in any kind of investigatory commission.[61]

---

[58] Walter White, "Russo-Iranian Dispute," *Chicago Defender*, April 20, 1946.
[59] Report of the Security Council, A/93, 37–38.
[60] Report of the Security Council, A/93, 38–39; Jones, *The United Nations and the Domestic Jurisdiction of States*, 78.
[61] Report of the Security Council, A/93, 39.

The Ukrainian delegate circled around again as he tried to convince the Security Council to authorize the task force. He disparaged the way that the British and Dutch had damned the Republic by implication and argued that the "Indonesian national movement should not be regarded as fascist but as a democratic movement." Moreover, he certainly did not trust the objectivity of the Dutch and British in describing the situation in Indonesia. He insisted that "the Security Council should secure its own information in order to arrive at the proper conclusion on the subject." Finally, he concluded, at a bare minimum, "the use of British troops against the Indonesian population was neither just nor right."[62]

The Dutch dug in. The Ukrainian delegate not only had "no justification for bringing the matter before the Council" but he also "did not have complete command of the facts." There were nearly 200,000 POWs still interned. Japanese troops, even at this late date, continued to roam throughout Indonesia, and they needed to be disarmed. But even more than that, the "representative of the Netherlands reminded the [Security] Council … that according to the Charter, the United Nations could not interfere with internal matters of any given State." Indonesia was Dutch territory. Make no mistake about it.[63] Holland's representative, therefore, "would refuse to support a commission which would busy itself with matters which came within the domestic jurisdiction of the Netherlands."[64]

However, the numerous press reports of "Moslem fanatics," "Indonesian nationalists," and British air, land, and sea forces battling in Surabaya suggested something that went much broader and deeper than a Dutch domestic issue.[65] The Egyptian representative on the Security Council, therefore, jumped into the fray seeking assurances that "British troops shall not be used in any circumstances against the National Indonesian

[62] Ibid., 40.

[63] Ibid., 41.

[64] Ibid., 45.

[65] "Moslem Fanatics Fight in Surabaya: Religious Leaders in Charges Against Tanks – New Peril is Feared in Batavia," *New York Times*, November 20, 1945; "Destroyers Assist Surabaya Advance: Soekarno Appeals to Stalin to Intervene – Three Japanese Generals Arrested," *New York Times*, November 13, 1945; "RAF Attacks Foes in Surabaya Again: Blasts Indonesian Army's Main Headquarters – Soekarno Reports Heavy Casualties," *New York Times*, November 12, 1945; "British Make Gain in Surabaya Fight: Justice and Government Buildings Seized against Stronger Nationalist Resistance," *New York Times*, November 16, 1945; "Surabaya Assault Pressed by British: Planes and Warships Blast Java Navy Base While Indians Move into the City," *New York Times*, November 11, 1945; "Surabaya Shelled in British Attack Indonesians State: Bombardment of Java Center after Ultimatum Deadline Said to be Intense," *New York Times*, November 10, 1945.

Movement, and they will be withdrawn as soon as" the remaining Japanese surrendered and the POWs were freed.[66]

The UK representative, tired of allegations about England's ulterior motives, turned the delegates' attention, instead, to the issue of peace. He said that Britain had already brokered a series of talks between Dutch and Republic leaders, and it was, therefore, important to let that process work itself out.[67] The U.S. delegate then offered that "no constructive purpose would be served by conducting an investigation." Instead, "the best hope for an amicable settlement lay in a successful conclusion of negotiations then in progress."[68] In the end, the promise of peace was intoxicating enough to forestall further discussion on the issue and powerful enough to short-circuit both the Egyptian and Ukrainian proposals.[69]

In a scathing article in the *Pittsburgh Courier*, Rayford Logan noted that "the greatest disappointment arising from the first session" of the UN was that "it settled no serious international controversy." Instead, a series of major issues were "shunted aside," including the "demand that a fact-finding commission be sent to Indonesia."[70] The *Chicago Defender*, in a decidedly unflattering editorial, complained that "as far as colonial countries [were] concerned the current sessions of the United Nations Security Council appear to be no more hopeful than was the San Francisco Conference."[71]

Indeed, just a few weeks after the Security Council "shunted aside" both the Ukrainian and Egyptian proposals, the Hoge Veluwe Conference between the Dutch and the Indonesians, which the British had worked so hard to arrange, "broke down nearly as soon as it began."[72] The Hague simply and openly held the Republic and the Indonesian leaders in such contempt that the Netherlands government did not understand why it should even have to negotiate with "collaborators" like Sukarno and Hatta.[73] "One Indonesian representative remembered that he knew within five minutes of the beginning of the talks that the conference would not succeed."[74] Similarly, the "American representative in Batavia

[66] Report of the Security Council, A/93, 46.
[67] Report of the Security Council, A/93, 41; McMahon, *Colonialism and Cold War*, 117.
[68] Report of the Security Council, A/93, 45; McMahon, *Colonialism and Cold War*, 117.
[69] Report of the Security Council, A/93, 46.
[70] Rayford W. Logan, "UNO Fails to Assure Peace," *Pittsburgh Courier*, March 2, 1946.
[71] "UNO Council Dodges Colonial Issue: Russia Incident A 'Smoke Screen,'" *Chicago Defender*, April 6, 1946.
[72] Foster, "Avoiding the 'Rank of Denmark,'" 75.
[73] Dirk U. Stikker Oral History.
[74] Foster, "Avoiding the 'Rank of Denmark,'" 75.

had little hope for the success of the talks." Van Mook was certainly "pessimistic."[75] Two major issues – in addition to Dutch disdain – dominated and signaled trouble. First, the Republic's leaders wanted "de facto recognition of their authority over most of Java and Sumatra." The Hague quashed that idea immediately and countered that the Republic only consisted of Java and Madura – never Sumatra, which was, as one American official noted, "actually the 'gold mine' of" the Netherlands East Indies (NEI), rich with "plantations and oil fields."[76] Second, the Dutch were unwilling to even consider immediate independence, despite the Republic's declaration in August 1945. Instead, Holland insisted that there had to be a probationary period when "Indonesia would be part of a Commonwealth of the Netherlands," administered, of course, by The Hague.[77] Still regarding itself as the party with the upper hand, in early June 1946 the Dutch issued an ultimatum to the Republic and said "that their present offer [was] final."[78] At that point the talks just stopped – for months.[79] The Dutch, increasingly annoyed by these "upstart extremists" who blocked Holland's access to wealth and greatness, finally threatened military action on the archipelago if the Indonesian leaders did not concede to the terms laid down by The Hague.[80]

The United States and the UK, however, had too much at stake to let that happen.[81] As historian Robert McMahon explained, "British and American representatives" interceded and "helped to break the logjam in Holland."[82] Lord Killearn mediated and "impressed upon them the significance of the imminent departure of British troops and the consequent urgency of resuming serious negotiations."[83] Within months at

---

[75] Summary of Telegrams, March 8, 1946, Box 22, File "State Dept. Briefs File, January–May 1946," *HST:SMOF:NA.*

[76] Southeast Asia Regional Conference, June 21–June 26, 1948, Bangkok, Siam, Section XII: Regional Repercussions of Success or Breakdown of Dutch-Indonesian Negotiations, n.d., ca. June 1948, Reel 3, *Confidential Southeast Asia.*

[77] Foster, "Avoiding the 'Rank of Denmark,'" 75.

[78] Summary of Telegrams, June 7, 1946, Box 22, File "State Dept. Briefs File, June–August 1946," *HST:SMOF:NA.*

[79] Summary of Telegrams, June 19, 1946, ibid.; Summary of Telegrams, September 10, 1946, ibid.

[80] Document 164: "Annex A" in 301st Meeting of the Supreme Allied Command, December 6, 1945, *Officiële Bescheiden,* 314; Foster, "Avoiding the 'Rank of Denmark,'" 69, 76.

[81] McParsons to Cumming, July 17, 1946, Reel 4, *Confidential Great Britain Foreign Affairs;* Summary of Telegrams, October 16, 1946, Box 22, File "State Dept. Briefs File, September–December 1946," *HST:SMOF:NA;* Gallman to Secretary of State [from London via War], September 19, 1946, Reel 1, *Confidential Great Britain Foreign Affairs.*

[82] McMahon, *Colonialism and Cold War,* 131.

[83] Ibid., 130.

Linggadjati "the Dutch and Indonesians ... reached an agreement which include[d] recognition by the Dutch of the Indonesian Republic in Java and Sumatra, the Republic to join a United States of Indonesia which would remain within the framework of the Netherlands Kingdom."[84]

The Linggadjati Agreement, brokered on November 12, 1946, and signed on March 25, 1947, appeared to have avoided the crisis.[85] In truth, however, the agreement was crippled before the ink was dry. The CIA noted that the chasm between the Netherlands' and Republic's interpretations was "so deep and fundamental that orderly progress toward final adjustment of Dutch and Indonesian aspirations in the islands [could] not be expected." The Agency predicted that the frustrations would run so high that Holland would "attempt to reach a decision by military force. This, in turn," the CIA continued, "will aggravate anti-Western sentiment throughout the Far East and might lead to a consideration of the dispute by the UN Security Council."[86]

For the Americans, that prediction was highly problematic. In March 1947, Secretary of State George Marshall had gleaned from his meeting with Stalin that the deprivation, hunger, and political turmoil in Europe suited the Soviet leader just fine. Marshall returned to the United States and, with his staff, began to craft the outlines of the European Recovery Program (the Marshall Plan or ECA), which was going to consume billions of dollars and be a very hard sell to a fiscally conscious Congress.[87] A colonial war in Southeast Asia would only complicate the already nearly impossible, especially when, as the CIA noted, the "Republic's struggle for independence ... engenders widespread sympathy throughout the world," and Holland's efforts to supply necessary armaments and troop levels would undermine the very rationale for the Marshall Plan and drain scarce resources from the Netherlands' ability to rebuild.[88]

---

[84] Summary of Telegrams, November 14, 1946, Box 22, File "State Dept. Briefs File, September–December 1946," *HST:SMOF:NA*.

[85] McMahon, *Colonialism and Cold War*, 135–136.

[86] Central Intelligence Group, "Basic Dutch-Indonesian Issues and the Linggadjati Agreement," June 9, 1947, ORE 20, Box 214, File "Central Intelligence Reports: O.R.E.: 1947: 15–39 [15–17, 19–21: February 28-August 5]," *Truman:PSF:IR*.

[87] Michael J. Hogan, *The Marshall Plan: America, Britain, and the Reconstruction of Western Europe, 1947–1952* (New York: Cambridge University Press, 1987), 26–53; Hogan, *A Cross of Iron: Harry S. Truman and the Origins of the National Security State, 1945–1954* (New York: Cambridge University Press, 1998), 89–95.

[88] Central Intelligence Group, "Basic Dutch-Indonesian Issues and the Linggadjati Agreement," June 9, 1947, ORE 20, Box 214, File "Central Intelligence Reports: O.R.E.: 1947: 15–39 [15–17, 19–21: February 28–August 5]," *Truman:PSF:IR*.

This worst-case scenario became reality when the Republic tested the Linggadjati Agreement's tensile strength and saw the truce snap like cheap glass. Interpreting the accord as the Netherlands' acknowledgment of their independence, the Indonesians "attempted to establish [their] own foreign relations with the United Kingdom, the United States, Australia, China, India, and several Arab states, all of which recognized the Republic *de facto*."[89] The Hague was furious. Its position was clear and nonnegotiable: the Netherlands had sovereignty, not the Republic. Immediately, "[r]eports from Batavia and Sumatra to the British Foreign Office suggest[ed] that the local situation [was] deteriorating with tension and provocation rising on both the Dutch and Indonesian sides."[90] Moreover, the "situation was likely to get out of hand soon" because "Dutch military and naval commanders" were spoiling for a fight and "have been recommending military action for some time now."[91] Thus, when the Republic refused to place the Indonesian police and army under Dutch command, the Netherlands moved in to demonstrate in no uncertain terms where sovereignty really lay.[92]

In July 1947, the "Dutch announced that they no longer considered themselves bound by the Linggadjati Agreement and resorted to what they called a 'police action.'"[93] In a series of punishing bombardments buttressed by a strangling blockade, Holland was determined to "gain control of … Java and Sumatra, … [and] the surplus rice-producing area of East Java" and break the will of the Indonesians.[94] The Republic, bloodied and frantic, radioed the international community for help. As India, Australia, and the Red Cross attempted to aid the wounded, the Netherlands retaliated. In late July 1947, "two Dutch fighter planes shot down an Indian Dakota plane on a mercy flight from Singapore to Jogjakarta with two tons of medical supplies for the Indonesian Red

[89] Philip C. Jessup, *The Birth of Nations* (New York: Columbia University Press, 1974), 44.

[90] Summary of Telegrams, June 16, 1947, Box 22, File "State Dept. Briefs File, June–August 1947," *HST:SMOF:NA*.

[91] Summary of Telegrams, May 26, 1947, Box 22, File "State Dept. Briefs File, January–May 1947," ibid.

[92] S.E.A. Conference, Bangkok, Siam, Capt. D. J. McCallum Naval Liaison Officer, Batavia, Java, NEI: Military Situation in N.E.I., n.d., Reel 3, *Confidential Southeast Asia*; Mr. Landon to Mr. Fisher, memo, July 8, 1947, Reel 3, *Confidential Southeast Asia*.

[93] Jessup, *The Birth of Nations*, 45.

[94] S.E.A. Conference, Bangkok, Siam, Capt. D. J. McCallum Naval Liaison Officer, Batavia, Java, NEI: Military Situation in N.E.I., n.d., Reel 3, *Confidential Southeast Asia*; "The Far East," *Atlantic Report on the World Today*, August 1947, Box A321, File "Indonesia, 1948–49, May," *Papers of the NAACP*.

Cross."[95] The Australian Red Cross then tried to step in to organize "the supply of drugs, surgical instruments, and dressings," but the Dutch initially refused to allow the humanitarian aid to reach the wounded and dying. The International Red Cross eventually sent a representative into Jakarta to investigate because, if the allegations against the Dutch were true, Holland had just violated the Geneva Convention.[96] In short, in its attempt to hold onto Indonesia at all costs, the Netherlands blew through a series of international tripwires that so outraged multiple publics that it put The Hague on the road to diplomatic isolation.

On July 23, 1947, American socialist and pacificist Norman Thomas, chairman of the Post-War World Council, in conjunction with the Indonesian League of America, which was chaired by the secretary-treasurer of the Congress of Industrial Organizations (CIO), Julian Ross, asked the NAACP to join in a démarche to Truman urging the president to do "all that lies in your power to stop [the] war in Indonesia." Thomas noted, and Walter White agreed, that by issuing unreasonable ultimatums, striking before its own deadline had passed, and ignoring the pleas and efforts of the British and the Americans to find a workable solution, "the Netherlands government [was] primarily responsible for this dangerous breach of peace." The Dutch had launched a war "'which [was] likely to endanger the maintenance of international peace and security' and hence [fell] directly within the scope of the Charter of the United Nations and international commitments undertaken by the United States." Walter White eagerly signed off on the statement that the Netherlands' so-called police action had "been prosecuted on the basis of all out colonial war." "It [was] the simple truth that the Dutch Empire cannot long be maintained by force, at least not without a direct or indirect American underwriting of that force, to which our people will never assent." The president had to understand – as bluntly, as powerfully, and as succinctly as possible – that "no Marshall Plan can save democracy and prosperity if the nations of Western Europe waste their substance in a continuance of an outworn imperialism."[97]

---

95 "Indian Dakota Plane Shot Down by Dutch," *Canberra Times*, July 31, 1947.
96 "Indonesia Will Receive Medical Aid," *Foreign Broadcast Information Service Daily Reports: Far Eastern Section Australia*, August 10, 1947; "Red Cross Relief to Indonesia," *Foreign Broadcast Information Service Daily Reports: Far Eastern Section Australia*, September 10, 1947.
97 Draft Letter to President Harry Truman from Norman Thomas, Attached to Norman Thomas to Dear Friend [Walter White], July 23, 1947, Box A393, File "Post-War World Council, 1946–49," *Papers of the NAACP*.

Meanwhile, in San Francisco, picketers "exhibited placards with slogans such as 'The Nazis Ravaged Holland (1940) The Dutch Ravaged Java (1947),' 'Imperialism is the Same in Every Language,'" and "Stop Use of US Material to Murder Indonesians." There was an additional demonstration at the Netherlands consulate in Los Angeles.[98] Both the CIO and the American Federation of Labor (AFL) issued resolutions, backed maritime union strikers, and exhorted U.S. officials to "exert outright pressure on the Dutch government rather than lobby in a desultory fashion while covertly supporting the Dutch side with copious American dollars."[99]

A few months later, the New York branch of the NAACP held a "mass meeting" highlighting the struggles of the "[d]arker races throughout the world." In addition to speakers from India and South Africa, John Andu, "president of the Indonesia League of America discussed the four-year old fight for independence now being carried on against the Dutch." This successful meeting was one of the major events in a membership campaign designed to attract 15,000 new recruits.[100]

Not only had the Netherlands' "police action" riled up influential sectors of American civil society, but also, as the Council on African Affairs noted, "Dutch aggression against the Indonesians" was "so shocking and flagrant" that the "United Nations was compelled to take action."[101] On July 30, 1947, the archipelago's largest and nearest neighbors, India and Australia, decided to "request that the Security Council find that the situation in Indonesia constitute[d] a breach of the peace under Article 39 of the Charter." Prior to the meeting Ralph Harry of the Australian delegation explained to the State Department that "every effort would be made to avoid pointing the finger of guilt at the Netherlands government" but, he insisted, The Hague would be "called upon ... to live up to its obligations and to accept the decision of the Security Council." He assured the Americans that he was not asking for an investigatory commission, which the United States opposed because it would have placed the Soviets

[98] Gouda, *American Visions of the Netherlands East Indies/Indonesia*, 154.
[99] Ibid., 156.
[100] "NAACP Branch to Hold Mass Meeting," *New York Amsterdam News*, November 15, 1947; "Indonesian Speaker at NAACP Meet," *New York Amsterdam News*, December 6, 1947.
[101] "U.N. Faces Crucial Test on Issue of Colonial Freedom," *New Africa*, 6, no. 7 (July–August 1947). This article, although mentioning Indonesia, focused primarily on Africa. The CAA did not expend much energy on Indonesia because it was outside of the organization's geographic purview and the Council was wracked with internal dissension until late fall 1948.

squarely in the archipelago. Harry noted quite bluntly that that kind of task force would be irrelevant anyway because "[h]ostilities had now been in progress for ten days and it was apparent to all the world that there was a breach of the peace."[102]

At the Security Council meeting, the Indian representative immediately drew the delegates' attention to the "large-scale military action, which Dutch forces had launched against the Indonesian people without warning."[103] The magnitude of the assault, more than 100,000 Dutch troops, led the Australian representative to insist that this was "no mere 'police action', but armed conflict between two States in international law, with far-reaching effects in Australia and other neighbouring countries."[104]

The Dutch strongly countered that there was a basic, fundamental flaw in the Australian argument – this was no clash "between two sovereign states." There was only one state involved: the Netherlands. The Republic was merely a component among several in a "federation" where the Dutch were sovereign. Consequently, he argued, the "'police action' being taken against the Indonesian nationalists was a matter essentially within the domestic jurisdiction of the Netherlands."[105] He repeated that mantra at every lull in the discussion, at every turn in the debate, and at every opportune and inopportune moment. "The Netherlands was sovereign in the region concerned ... this matter was solely within the domestic jurisdiction of the Netherlands."[106]

This time, however, American and British support of the Dutch was not nearly as hopeful or as steadfast as before. The UK was "very much disturbed about the situation in Indonesia and [its] probable repercussions." As Whitehall saw it, while "militarily the Dutch will gain an initial success; ... the resulting situation in South East Asia will make the position of the western powers very difficult indeed." The British further warned that the conflict in Indonesia "may be incalculably damaging to

---

[102] Mr. Ross to Mr. Rusk, July 30, 1947, Box 7, File "Indonesian Case," Lot File 55D323, RG 59.

[103] United Nations Security Council, *Report of the Security Council to the General Assembly Covering the period from 16 July 1947 to 15 July 1948, Official Records: Third Session,* Supplement No. 2, A/620 (Lake Success, NY: United Nations, 1948), 28.

[104] *Report of the Security Council,* A/620, 28. The CIA estimated that the Dutch had more than 100,000 troops in Indonesia. See Central Intelligence Group, "Basic Dutch-Indonesian Issues and the Linggadjati Agreement," June 9, 1947, ORE 20, Box 214, File "Central Intelligence Reports: O.R.E.: 1947: 15–39 [15–17, 19–21: February 28–August 5]," *Truman:PSF:IR.*

[105] *Report of the Security Council,* A/620, 29; Jones, *The United Nations and the Domestic Jurisdiction of States,* 79.

[106] *Report of the Security Council,* A/620, 28, 29, 32.

the peace and stability of Asia and to the revival of economic prosperity in that and other parts of the world." London and Washington believed they understood what was at stake for the West – even if the Dutch did not. The British, therefore, had met with U.S. representatives prior to the Security Council meeting to map out a strategy to "arrest ... the present tragic course of events." They considered Anglo-American arbitration but surmised that "the Dutch would 'dislike and perhaps resent'" it. As they floated one idea after the next, it seemed that there was no lever powerful enough to make The Hague listen to reason. The problem, the State Department believed, was that the Dutch felt like they had the upper hand; "that they [were] rolling along successfully," could gain what they wanted "militarily" and, therefore, "seem[ed] to view a Security Council case with relative equanimity." It just appeared that for the Netherlands, domestic jurisdiction was the talisman that rendered the UN powerless.[107]

What the Dutch did not grasp was that under the right circumstances, the Security Council could and would reinterpret Article 2(7) at will.[108] As the Canadian delegation observed, "Regardless of which articles of the charter have been quoted in connection with the Indonesian dispute, it [was] a fact that the majority of the members ... felt that this was a problem involving over 70,000,000 people and one with which the [Security] Council had a moral, if not strictly legal, right to be concerned."[109] Both the American and British delegates argued, as did the Soviets, that there was "fighting on such a scale and in such conditions as to endanger the peace of the region." That framing of the issue meant that regardless of what the Dutch asserted, domestic jurisdiction was inapplicable, and there was a role for the UN whether the Republic was sovereign or not.[110] Thus, scholar Goronwy Jones explains, the Indonesia case "established the precedent that the Security Council ... was competent to decide that a colonial conflict was a matter of international concern on which it could take some action." Jones adds that "since no guidance was given in the

[107] Memorandum of Conversation: The Under Secretary, Sir John Balfour, Mr. Graves, Mr. Penson, Mr. Matthews, July 24, 1947, Box 7, File "Indonesian Case," Lot File 55D323, RG 59.

[108] Warren R. Austin to Louis B. Wehle, May 4, 1949, Box 75, File "Indonesia – ECA – UN Bill," *Papers of Louis Wehle*, Franklin D. Roosevelt Presidential Library, Hyde Park, NY (hereafter *Wehle Papers*).

[109] Document 150: DEA/50054–40, Secretary of State for External Affairs to Permanent Delegate to United Nations, telegram, July 6, 1948, Documents onCanadian External Relations: General Policy: Sub-Section 4, Indonesia, *Canadian Foreign Affairs*.

[110] *Report of the Security Council*, A/620, 29.

Charter on how a matter essentially within the domestic jurisdiction of a state was to be determined, the Council was given the loophole to decide what was politically expedient without necessarily taking into account the criterion of international law or seeking the judicial opinion of the International Court of Justice."[111]

Within weeks, the UN had established a commission of consuls in Indonesia to supervise the cease-fire. The Security Council then formed a Committee of Good Offices (GOC) to moderate the negotiations that would eventually lead, in January 1948, to the next truce, the Renville Agreement.[112] But Frank Graham, who was the U.S. representative on the GOC at the time, soon warned that the Netherlands' demands under Renville gave "the Republican Government virtually no hope for recovering the status it held under the Linggadjati Agreement nor even assurance of its continued existence." Under those conditions, Graham "fear[ed] that the Republic will make little effort to implement the truce and the Indonesian moderates will be weakened at the expense of the militants with a consequent increase in violence."[113]

Thus, by the time Walter White sat down in January 1948 to testify before the Senate Foreign Relations Committee about the NAACP's stance on the proposed Marshall Plan, the British had pummeled Surabaya while asking for a sizable low-interest rate loan, and The Hague had already scrapped the Linggadjati Agreement, launched a "police action" in Indonesia using Lend Lease military equipment, begrudgingly signed the Renville Agreement, and was prepared to trash it in spectacular fashion. None of this was lost on the NAACP, and White's support for the European Recovery Program reflects the Association's powerful opposition to the ongoing wars in Indonesia.

The groundwork for White's stance was laid in 1944, when he toured several of the war zones, including what was then Dutch New Guinea. At first, he marveled at the outstanding medical facilities the Dutch had built, although "their funds were meagre." Their willingness, he believed, to construct hospitals for use by the indigenous people seemed to accord with "Queen Wilhelmina's pronouncement from exile in London that the Dutch were going to abandon their system of empire and give their colonials real freedom." Then reality set in. "Oh, it isn't our money we

[111] Jones, *The United Nations and the Domestic Jurisdiction of States*, 80.

[112] Ibid., 81. The Committee of Good Offices was comprised of three members: a Belgian, an American, and an Australian.

[113] Summary of Telegrams, January 7, 1948, Box 22, File "State Department Briefs Files: January–April 1948," *HST:SMOF:NA.*

spent," one colonial official explained to White. "It's your money – we built this with American lend-lease." Stunned, White continued to probe. He next asked about schools for the indigenous people. The response was equally frank and troubling: "We'll continue to leave that to the missionaries." White then inquired about training for self-government as promised by the Queen. That question was dismissed with an air of "smugness." There was no need. "We know better than the natives what is best for them." Unable and unwilling to let it go, White asked about economic development for the island. Rest assured, the Dutchman said, "We plan to develop mineral and natural gas resources which are enormous because the Netherlands will need every guilder it can lay its hands on to re-establish itself after the war is over." By that point, it was abundantly clear that Queen Wilhelmina's words "had no meaning whatever ... the natives were important only as producers of revenue for the Dutch." This was, White exclaimed, a "regime which offered nothing but endless slavery for the natives."[114] The indigenous people recognized it, too. White conveyed that although they were "isolated from the world" and "far less educated and in touch with the trends of world politics than the natives of other Dutch colonies like Java, Sumatra, and other units of Indonesia ... the war for human freedom had penetrated even into the most remote areas where neither newspapers, radio, or the omnipresent movies had reached before the war."[115] The head of the NAACP, therefore, left Asia in 1944 convinced that this "ferment" for freedom "will make trouble for the Dutch or anyone else" who tried to stop it.[116] (See Figure 4.3)

Three years later, as he looked at the rubble caused by the Netherlands' destruction of the Linggadjati Agreement, White sensed that the Dutch and the United States were about to get buried. Although the United States may have done some fancy footwork in the Security Council, it had escaped no one's attention that "American lend-lease and surplus Army equipment [were] now being used in a futile attempt to crush the demand for freedom in Indonesia." The people in Asia, he said, were particularly aware that the "United States [was] financing and supplying equipment to perpetuate the system exemplified by the Dutch officials ...

---

[114] Walter White, "The Indonesian Tragedy," September 4, 1947, Box A81, File "Articles Walter White: Syndicated Columns, 1947," *Papers of the NAACP*; Walter White, "Dutch Lying Has Been Incredible and Contemptible," *Chicago Defender*, January 8, 1949.

[115] White, *A Man Called White*, 290.

[116] Walter White, "The Indonesian Tragedy," September 4, 1947, Box A81, File "Articles Walter White: Syndicated Columns, 1947," *Papers of the NAACP*.

FIGURE 4.3. Walter White's visit during the Second World War to Dutch New Guinea gave him insight into Dutch colonialism and he walked away convinced that imperialism equals slavery.
Source: NAACP Collection. Courtesy of the Library of Congress, Prints and Photographs Division, LC-USZ-62-130668.

in Indonesia."[117] White recounted how "American airplanes, tanks, and guns bearing the familiar insignia of the United States Army were used

[117] Ibid.

by the Dutch ... to crush the independence movement in Indonesia."
However, he continued, "all the war weapons now in existence or which
may be devised will never be able to stifle the demands of non-white as
well as white men for a more decent and just way of life. We seem so
pathetically and abysmally unable to comprehend this simple fact."[118]

In November 1947, the Association's board of directors, therefore, had
an intense discussion about whether to endorse the proposed European
Recovery Program. Channing Tobias noted that there was nothing of this
"considerable magnitude proposed at the present time to relieve the situation in Europe," and, he added, "we could hardly withhold our support
from it while waiting for some other plan to be evolved." Philadelphia
attorney Sadie Alexander, however, countered that "our opinion was not
asked when the plan was being formulated and therefore she objected to
our being asked at this time." The primary question that confronted the
board, however, was, did the "Marshall Plan ... conflict ... with the principles of the Association[?] No member stated that it did." Nonetheless,
the board insisted, "we do not consider the Marshall Plan perfect," and it
was Walter White's job "to point out why we are supporting it and why
we feel it should be broadened."[119]

The issue, at its roots, was that the Marshall Plan could not be just about
Europe, nor should it be just about halting communism. It had to be about
democracy. What the Dutch were doing in Indonesia made that obvious.
The Netherlands had tried to portray its Lend-Lease fueled "police action"
as essentially an in-house squabble. But this was war. War with global
implications. Between North and South. Between the colonizer and the colonized. Between imperialism and freedom. The war had already attracted
the attention of Nehru, who called an All-Asia Conference to "discuss the
crisis" in the archipelago.[120] White conveyed to the Indian premier the
Association's hopes that the delegates at the meeting would have "success
in formulating ... effective plans to aid [the] Indonesian people in resisting Dutch imperialism."[121] On this side of the Atlantic, the NAACP drew
inspiration from its work with the India League, which issued a resolution

---

[118] White, *A Man Called White*, 290.
[119] Minutes of the Meeting of the Board of Directors, November 10, 1947, *Papers of
the NAACP*, History Vault, Accession #: 001412–003–0652; Madison Jones to Roy
Wilkins, memo, June 29, 1949, Box A417, "Marshall Plan Correspondence, 1949–50,"
Papers of the NAACP.
[120] Text of Proposed Resolution on Indonesia, January 4, 1948, Box A321, File "Indonesia,
1948–49, May," *Papers of the NAACP*.
[121] News Release, January 4, 1948, ibid.

blasting The Hague for launching a merciless war of colonial conquest – in the middle of the twentieth century. "Today, the most blatant example of ruthless imperialism in the world is to be found in Indonesia where the Netherlands have disregarded all precepts of humanity as well as the specific injunctions of the United Nations in an effort to suppress by naked force, the beginnings of independence among the Indonesian people." The India League, on whose board Walter White sat, "call[ed] upon the United States Government to take ... two steps immediately." The first demanded that the Americans cut off all "aid in any form to the Netherlands." The second was to "institute action in the Security Council to brand the Netherlands as an aggressor nation and to set in motion the maximum sanctions against the Netherlands provided for in the Charter."[122]

The secretary then assembled a team within the NAACP to iden- tify the most salient issues to convey to the Senate Foreign Relations Committee that "the Association ha[d] certain reservations with respect to the Marshall Plan which we would, of course, voice."[123] A suggestion from Clarence Mitchell, director of the NAACP's Washington Bureau, struck an important chord. Mitchell believed that "the Association testi- mony on the Marshall Plan should include a reference to those European powers holding colonies." "[W]e have," he insisted, "a moral obligation to require that these countries ... adopt ... programs under which people currently subject to their rule shall be given the right of self-determina- tion and a chance for freedom."[124]

White, however, took it one step further. He not only "reference[d]" colonialism, but "speaking on behalf of the 1,627 branches, youth coun- cils and college chapters of the Association and its bi-racial membership of more than one half million Americans," he transformed it into a major issue throughout his testimony.[125] Despite the NAACP's anticommunist stance, he did not dwell on the growing battle with the Soviet Union for control of Europe.[126] Although he alluded to communism occasionally,

---

[122] Text of Proposed Resolution on Indonesia, January 4, 1948, ibid.
[123] Walter White to Arthur Vandenberg, telegram, January 5, 1948, Box A417, File "Marshall Plan Correspondence, 1947–48," *Papers of the NAACP*; Walter White to Dean Acheson, telegram, January 5, 1948, ibid.; MARSHALL PLAN, n.d., ca. January 5, 1948, ibid.; Walter White to William H. Hastie, telegram, January 7, 1948, ibid.; Leslie Perry to Walter White, memo, January 12, 1948, ibid.
[124] Clarence Mitchell to Walter White, memo, January 13, 1948, ibid.
[125] "Testimony of Walter White .... before Senate Relations Committee on Foreign Relations," January 27, 1948, ibid.
[126] Melvyn P. Leffler, *For the Soul of Mankind: The United States, the Soviet Union, and the Cold War* (New York: Hill & Wang, 2007), 11–83.

what the Soviets did or did not do was not the point. As, White would later confide to Nehru, "those of us who are opposed to all forms of totalitarianism including communism are also aware ... that hunger, frustration, colonialism, and racism would have created unrest in Asia, Africa and Latin America even" if there had never been a "revolution in Russia."[127]

The real point, which White spent the majority of his time outlining, was the inevitable violence that loomed on the horizon if the colonized remain enslaved by imperialism. He fully realized that the "European nations which [were] to benefit from this relief plan ... receive much of their economic strength from colonies in Africa, the Caribbean, the Pacific, and Asia." However, he explained, "it would be utter folly for the United States to help white Europe" and still "permit it to continue to deny freedom and opportunity to colonial peoples." "Some of these European countries," he observed, "have made it clear" that the Second World War had altered nothing. Foolishly, "they contemplate no fundamental change [in] the status of their colonials." That, he emphasized, not only was political suicide but also undercut the "moral obligation" the United States had to ensure "the right to self-determination and the chance for freedom which these [European] nations ask for themselves." Alluding to the current war of liberation in Indonesia as a harbinger of things to come, he observed that any effort to prop up "the myth of white superiority ... will speed revolt among the hundreds of millions of brown, yellow, and black people who are determined to have freedom also." If the Marshall Plan was about creating the economic conditions for peace, then colonialism had to end. Otherwise, billions of dollars would be squandered in the service of a discredited ideology that the Second World War had "destroyed forever." "Nothing," he noted, "will speed World War III more than attempts to reestablish 'white supremacy,'" as the Dutch were frantically and brutally trying to do.[128]

[127] Walter White to Jawaharlal Nehru, May 4, 1953, Box A675, File "Yergan, Max, 1941–53," *Papers of the NAACP*. For the enduring effects of race and racism globally, see Alejandro De La Fuente, "The New Afro-Cuban Cultural Movement and the Debate on Race in Contemporary Cuba," *Journal of Latin American Studies*, 40, no. 4, (2008), 697–720; Lucila Bandeira Beato, "Inequality and Human Rights of African Descendants in Brazil," *Journal of Black Studies*, 34, no. 6 (July 2004), 766–786; Faye V. Harrison, "The Persistent Power of 'Race' in the Cultural and Political Economy of Racism," *Annual Review of Anthropology*, 24 (1995), 47–74.

[128] U.S. Congress Senate Committee on Foreign Relations, *Hearings Regarding European Recovery Program*, 2nd sess., 1948, 952–953; "Testimony of Walter White ... before Senate Relations Committee on Foreign Relations," January 27, 1948, Box A417, File

Moreover, the NAACP's larger vision for the Marshall Plan included a demand to level the playing field. To invest instead of extract. To recognize that "hunger is as painful to brown, yellow and black stomachs as it is to white ones."[129] The Association, therefore, urged that aid similar in scope and scale to the Marshall Plan "be extended as needed to peoples in Asia, the Middle East, the Near East, Africa, the Caribbean and Latin America." And, with the specter of the Netherlands hovering menacingly over 70 million Indonesians, "the Association further urge[d] that the State Department adopt and pursue the policy of discontinuing aid to countries receiving Marshall Plan aid when they engage in military action to suppress movements for colonial freedom."[130]

Meanwhile, oblivious to the mounting ground swell against Holland's actions in Indonesia and pie-eyed from imperial "auto-intoxication," the Dutch, in one of the first meetings of the Committee of Good Offices, blithely admitted that during the cease fire in late 1947, their "troops carried out ... 'mopping up operations.'" They "even confirmed that they [had] taken drastic measures ... against the increasingly ferocious actions of the roving bands in the Krawang area.... Those bands," the Dutch noted, had "now been partially rendered harmless" by the "killing of more than 300 civilians and the wounding of 200 other civilians."[131] The Canadian representative at the UN, General Andrew McNaughton, warned that "the Netherlands should appreciate that in these circumstances they [were] not likely to receive much sympathy and, in fact, with the hardening view against them which [was] evident, they [would] be laying themselves open to very drastic censure by the Security Council." There was, McNaughton noted, a "growing anxiety" in the UN about the "sincerity" of the Netherlands to establish "real conditions of democracy in Indonesia and ... terminat[e] colonialism.... Most unfortunately," he continued, "the Netherlands spokesmen have left the impression that

"Marshall Plan Correspondence, 1947–48," *Papers of the NAACP*; Anderson, "The Histories of African Americans' Anticolonialism in the Cold War," 178.

[129] Louis Lautier, "Aid Others Beside Europeans – White: Support for Marshall Plan is Expressed, NAACP Secretary Says War-Ravaged Peoples Need Help," *Atlanta Daily World*, February 1, 1948.

[130] Resolutions Adopted by the Fortieth Annual Convention NAACP, Los Angeles, California, July 16, 1949, *Papers of the NAACP*, History Vault, Accession #: 001412–012–0433.

[131] Gerlof D. Homan, "The Netherlands, the United States and the Indonesian Question, 1948," *Journal of Contemporary History* 25, no. 1 (January 1990), 127; Committee of Good Offices on the Indonesian question, Corrigendum to the First Interim Report of the Committee to the Security Council, February 12, 1948, S/649/Corr.1, Box 76, File "Security Council Records: UN Committee of Good Offices on the Indonesian Question," *Wehle Papers*.

the Netherlands authorities, both in Indonesia and at home, will in fact endeavour to give a unilateral interpretation of the agreed political principles [of the Renville Agreement] in order that they might operate to their advantage and to the disadvantage of the Indonesian Republic; and that while they may adhere to a strictly literal interpretation of the various clauses, they will nevertheless show little scruple in transgressing the spirit."[132]

Just as McNaughton feared, the Dutch navy continued to "maintain ... a sea blockade of Republican territory," which was so "effective" that only "a trickle of smuggled goods ... reach[ed] Sumatra from Malaya. This [has] cause[d] the Republican area now to be extremely lacking in essentials, and this situation [was] rapidly deteriorating."[133] Indonesians, in fact, would eventually "charge ... that Adolph Hitler's Storm Troopers behaved more decently and correctly in their day than the Dutch troops" who "had established a crippling blockade by air, land, and sea."[134]

The blockade was crippling in more than one direction: the Dutch had also stemmed the flow of Indonesia's resources onto the world's markets, and for the United States, that was a problem – a major problem. As one State Department official noted, "American economic and commercial interests in Indonesia [were] of considerable magnitude."[135] Because the archipelago was "the principal Far Eastern source of oil, ... produce[d] 15% of the world's tin and 34% of its natural rubber," the CIA warned that "instability in the area resulting from Dutch-Republic strife ha[d], since the war, made full exploitation of Indonesian raw materials impossible."[136] Impossible, just when Congress was getting ready to authorize billions to rebuild Europe, in part with resources that Holland had deliberately choked off. Dutch actions, in short, were now threatening key pillars of U.S. foreign policy.

Remaining oblivious to mounting opposition, The Hague also used the GOC to send another ultimatum to the Republic. Holland refused

[132] Document 145: DEA/50054-40, Permanent Delegate to United Nations to Secretary of State for External Affairs, telegram, March 3, 1948, Documents on Canadian External Relations: General Policy: Sub-Section 4, Indonesia, *Canadian Foreign Affairs*.

[133] S.E.A. Conference, Bangkok, Siam, Capt. D. J. McCallum Naval Liaison Officer, Batavia, Java, NEI: Military Situation in N.E.I., n.d., Reel 3, *Confidential Southeast Asia*.

[134] "Dutch Attacked at ECAFE Conference," March 31, 1949, Reel 3, *Confidential Southeast Asia*.

[135] Mr. Landon to Mr. Radin, memo, August 8, 1947, Reel 1, *Confidential Southeast Asia*.

[136] CIA, "The Prospects for a United States of Indonesia," ORE 26-48, June 4, 1948, Box 214, File "Central Intelligence Reports: O.R.E.: 1948: 21-29 [April 2-November 19]," *Truman:PSF:IR*.

to entertain any discussions of a "political nature" in its negotiations but insisted that the Netherlands' proposals for a United States of Indonesia (USI) be accepted in toto and, moreover, that the Indonesians had only four days to agree to every stipulation. This unreasonable demand was linked with a rejoinder that any questions or reservations or "qualified acceptance ... would be considered a rejection."[137]

The GOC spent months trying to intervene. Trying to find some middle ground. Some compromise. Some counterproposal. The GOC worried about the continued instability, the ongoing guerilla warfare as Indonesians searched for ways to neutralize the superior firepower of the Dutch, and the unrelenting blockade that was sending the economic conditions of the major islands of Indonesia into an apparent death spiral. The GOC members searched for anything that could break the impasse. They searched in vain. In July 1948, the *Pittsburgh Courier* reported that the "UN Good Offices Committee in Indonesia has called its mission of five months 'a failure.' Efforts to bring harmony between the Dutch and the 60,000,000 brown Indonesian natives, says the committee, have been 'largely a disappointment.'" The roadblock to peace appeared to be that "Holland want[ed] the copper, tea, silver, and other assorted wealth of Indonesia" and was willing to bulldoze the Republic, the UN's Good Offices Committee, the Security Council, and the United States to obtain those resources.[138]

Everyone else could see it, too. The CIA surmised that The Hague's proposed United States of Indonesia would effect "the preservation of Dutch influence in Indonesia to the degree necessary to maintain Dutch economic advantages based on the control of the material resources of the area."[139] The Indonesians explained that the USI was "part of a Dutch programme to progressively diminish the authority and influence of the Republic and to leave it as a weak, dependent unit in an eventual Federation under Dutch domination."[140] And John Davies, one of the

---

[137] Committee of Good Offices on the Indonesian Question: First Interim Report of the Committee to the Security Council, February 10, 1948, S/649, Box 76, File "Security Council Records: UN Committee of Good Offices on Indonesian Question," *Wehle Papers*.

[138] Trezzvant W. Anderson, "World News in a Nutshell," *Pittsburgh Courier*, July 3, 1948.

[139] CIA, "The Prospects for a United States of Indonesia," ORE 26–48, June 4, 1948, Box 214, File "Central Intelligence Reports: O.R.E.: 1948: 21–29 [April 2–November 19]," *Truman:PSF:IR*.

[140] Document 145: DEA/50054-40, Permanent Delegate to United Nations to Secretary of State for External Affairs, telegram, March 3, 1948, Documents on Canadian External Relations: General Policy: Sub-Section 4, Indonesia, *Canadian Foreign Affairs*.

State Department's premier Asia experts, noted that the USI plan was designed so the Dutch "could still 'milk' the colonies by ruling them through the non-Republican Indonesians."[141]

The State Department's initial response to this stalemate reflected divisions within the bureaucracy. The Europe desk dominated. As John Cady in the Southeast Asia Division (SEA) recounted:

The basic issue of disagreement was simple; Europe was important from their point of view and responsibility, while Southeast Asia was comparatively unimportant. They refused, as a rule, to say anything or do anything that might embarrass their relations with the local French, Dutch, or British Embassy. For example, anything that had to do with explaining the Indonesia situation had to be cleared with the Dutch desk in the Western European group. There was little possibility of our formulating any independent policy as far as the Southeast Asian Division was concerned.[142]

SEA did try, however. As early as September 1947, desk officer Charlton Ogburn argued that the Dutch had it all wrong. When "nationalist parties and the metropolitan power" clashed, domestic jurisdiction evaporated. "A generation ago," he wrote, "such conflicts might have been matters of local interest only. The world-wide repercussions of the outbreak of open Dutch-Indonesian hostilities have made it clear that this is no longer the case."[143] The Southeast Asian Division, however, did not have the internal clout to carry this argument.

Nonetheless, there were cracks in the armor of the Europe desk, which the Dutch themselves created. Jacob Beam, who went from staffing the Central European division to consul general in Indonesia, explained that part of the shift in American policy toward the Republic was because the "Dutch were so damn mean, my God they ... [were] cruel."[144] Holland's actions had also caused the European desk officers to question the reliability and objectivity of their own consular staff. Back in 1946, American Consul Walter Foote sent a series of missives from Batavia that accused Britain of fomenting chaos to undermine the Dutch and seize control of the resource-rich island. The "tone of Dr. Foote's three

---

[141] Southeast Asia Regional Conference, June 21–June 26, 1948, Bangkok, Siam, Section XII: Regional Repercussions of Success or Breakdown of Dutch-Indonesian Negotiations, n.d., ca. June 1948, Reel 3, *Confidential Southeast Asia*.

[142] John F. Cady Oral History, http://www.trumanlibrary.org/oralhist/cadyjf.htm. Accessed June 8, 2013.

[143] Mr. Ogburn to Mr. Hickerson, Mr. Satterthwaite, and Mr. Gerig, September 2, 1947, Reel 5, *Confidential Southeast Asia*.

[144] Jacob D. Beam Oral History, http://www.trumanlibrary.org/oralhist/beamjw.htm. Accessed June 8, 2013.

telegrams," officials on the European desk concluded, "suggests that he has been 'reached' by Dutch sources with axes to grind."[145] This creeping sense that Holland was somehow corroding the basic sinews of diplomatic etiquette extended beyond the consulate and the embassy straight into the negotiations themselves. The latest U.S. representative on the GOC, H. Merle Cochran, stressed that the Netherlands apparently had little to no intention of honoring Renville. Rather "the Dutch harassing tactics in Indonesia" were aimed at making it "impossible for Hatta to negotiate" and setting up "an excuse for police measures."[146] Cochran also suggested that it was time to begin to question seriously Holland's plunge into the imperial abyss. He foresaw only "long-range political and economic instability" if the Netherlands' plans for a vanquished Republic and Dutch-dominated USI went through. He further predicted that if the Americans could not resolve this problem, "US prestige in southeast Asia will sink to a new low and the usefulness of the UN Good Offices Committee will come to an end."[147]

The Dutch, however, were not worried about the UN's prestige and believed they were acting in ways that bolstered the West, especially the United States. The Hague stressed that the Dutch were all that stood between civilization and an archipelago overrun with communists. The Netherlands Combined Chiefs of Staff issued a "report [that] show[ed], step by step, the increasing importance, within the Republic, of the communist dominated left wing parties." This was a clarion call, a Paul Revere warning, that "trace[d], factually, the rise and development of

---

[145] Walter Foote to Secretary of State, telegram, July 10, 1946, No. 290, Reel 4, *Confidential Great Britain Foreign Affairs*; Walter Foote to Secretary of State, telegram, No. 294, July 12, 1946, ibid.; Walter Foote to Secretary of State, telegram, No. 295, July 12, 1946, ibid. ; McParsons to Cumming, July 17, 1946, ibid.

[146] Jessup, *The Birth of Nations*, 61.

[147] Summary of Telegrams, June 8, 1948, Box 22, File "State Dept. Briefs File, May–August 1948," *HST:SMOF:NA*. For additional U.S. concerns about its falling prestige in Southeast Asia, see Southeast Asia Regional Conference, June 21–26, 1948, Bangkok, Siam, Section V: Regional Implications of the Emergence of Burma and Other Neighboring Countries as Independent States, n.d., ca. June 1948, Reel 3, *Confidential Southeast Asia*; Southeast Asia Regional Conference, June 21–June 26, 1948, Bangkok, Siam, Section II: Communist Activity in Southeast Asia, June 22, 1948, Reel 3, *Confidential Southeast Asia*; Southeast Asia Regional Conference, June 21–June 26, 1948, Bangkok, Siam, Section XII: Regional Repercussions of Success or Breakdown of Dutch-Indonesian Negotiations, n.d., ca. June 1948, Reel 3, *Confidential Southeast Asia*; Southeast Asia Regional Conference, June 21–June 26, 1948, Bangkok, Siam, Section XIII: Regional Reaction to United States Polices and Information Programs, n.d., ca. June 1948, Reel 3, *Confidential Southeast Asia*.

communism in the Republic of Indonesia during the first ten months of 1948."[148]

Then came an incident that shifted the ground dramatically beneath the Netherlands, although The Hague clearly did not recognize it. As the Americans feared, Holland's blockade of and consistent pounding on the Republic had created conditions of deprivation, poverty, and starvation, which led to increasing disillusionment among the people and a "leftward drift" in Indonesia. In late September 1948, the Indonesian Communist Party (PKI), sensing an opportunity, "made its bid for power" and "boldly launched a revolt against the Hatta government" in Madiun.[149] The State Department "watch[ed] developments with concern." U.S. foreign policy makers, however, found it "encouraging ... that the nationalists who comprise the Republican Government, ... declared the Communists to be the enemies of the republic and appear to be making every effort to eliminate this menace. We hope that they succeed."[150] Within a month, Hatta's forces had crushed the revolt and, in the process, "impressed American officials ... who could no longer question the staunch anticommunism of the republic regime."[151]

In the end, Madiun added to the already brewing growing doubt brought about by Holland's course of action in Indonesia. When Foreign Minister Stikker tried to "stress ... the Communist menace and the Dutch willingness to help the United States fight communism," Philip Jessup, U.S. ambassador-at-large to the United Nations, groaned about the "usual ploy" to red bait the Indonesians.[152] When asked if there were Communist "influences with [the] Republicans," British Foreign Minister Bevin retorted, "I doubt it."[153] Senator George Malone (R-NV), who had never been a fan of the European Recovery Program, did not mince words when he asserted that it was the "Indonesian Republicans [that] recently gave the Communists a licking." However, he warned, "if we keep on financing the Netherlands" with Marshall Plan dollars, "there [was] no telling what movement the Republicans will join to get rid of

[148] Office of the Netherlands Representatives to the Combined Chiefs of Staff, "The Rise of Communism in Indonesia in 1948," Box 79, File "Rise of Communism in Indonesia," *Wehle Papers*.

[149] McMahon, *Colonialism and Cold War*, 242.

[150] Mr. Butterworth to the Under Secretary, September 21, 1948, Reel 3, *Confidential Southeast Asia*.

[151] McMahon, *Colonialism and Cold War*, 242–243.

[152] Jessup, *The Birth of Nations*, 61.

[153] Cabinet Meeting 82(48), December 22, 1948, CAB/195/6.

the Dutch."[154] In short, the picketers, editorials, telegrams, and questions from senators all led Jessup to conclude that "congressional attitudes and public opinion, generally, favored the Indonesians." Moreover, he continued, "Secretary of State George Marshall, with his experience in guerilla warfare in the Philippines, was convinced that the Dutch could not obtain a military victory and therefore supported plans favoring Indonesian independence."[155]

All of these streams – American disenchantment with the Netherlands' position on Indonesia, heightened respect in Washington for the Republic, State Department confidence that nationalism and communism were not synonymous in the archipelago, a stiffening position in the UN Security Council, and mobilization of public opinion from the NAACP, the black press, and organized labor insisting that the United States cut off all Marshall Plan dollars – funneled into the maelstrom of December 1948 and created, to borrow the words of scholar Derrick Bell, an "interest-convergence."[156] This time the alignment was among the U.S. foreign policy-making apparatus, British, Indonesians, United Nations, and NAACP, who from their own perspectives, wanted the Netherlands to stop its military destruction of the Republic. The Americans needed Indonesia to be a "show horse for the West in the Asiatic parade" to counter the inevitable "loss of China" to Mao Zedong and the Communists.[157] Both the United States and Britain wanted much greater access than the Dutch had allowed to the unbelievably rich minerals of the archipelago.[158] The Indonesians, for their part, wanted to control their own political and economic destiny and unify all of the islands under one government.[159]

[154] "Colonial Powers Said to Abuse ERP: Senator Malone, in New Delhi, Charges Aid Helps to Curb Freedom in Southeast Asia," *New York Times*, December 16, 1948. For Malone's opposition to the Marshall Plan, see Hogan, *A Cross of Iron*, 327.

[155] Jessup, *The Birth of Nations*, 51.

[156] Derrick A. Bell Jr., "Brown v. Board of Education and the Interest-Convergence Dilemma," *Harvard Law Review*, 93, no. 3 (January 1980), 518–533.

[157] Memorandum of Conversation with Dean Acheson, Ambassador Van Kleffens, Mr. Lacey, and Mr. Scott, March 21, 1950, Box 66, File "March, 1950," *Papers of Dean Acheson*, Harry S. Truman Presidential Library, Independence, MO (hereafter *Acheson Papers*).

[158] Probable Duration of Grant Programs in Southeast Asia and Formosa, June 25, 1951, Box 124, File "ECA Projects – Southeast Asia and Dependent Areas," *RG 220: Presidential Committees, Commissions and Boards: President's Materials Policy Commission, 1951–52*, Harry S. Truman Presidential Library, Independence, MO (hereafter *RG 220: PMPC*); Report of Meeting with Mr. Isadore Lubin, U.S. representative to ECOSOC, July 9, 1951 – 11:00 a.m., July 10, 1951, Box 124, File "United Nations," *RG 220: PMPC*; Cabinet Minutes 80(48), December 13, 1948, CAB/195/6.

[159] Mohammad Hatta, "Indonesia's Foreign Policy," *Foreign Affairs*, 31, no. 3 (April 1953), 441–452; "Indonesia's Fight Not Over Yet': Opposition to Retention of Sovereignty

Meanwhile, the UN was determined to demonstrate its peace-keeping resolve and ability.[160] And the NAACP simply wanted to see an enslaved people freed from imperialism. As varied as those groups' aims may have been, the Netherlands' brusque and violent actions led to a "vehement" response across the board, causing even State Department officials to say "flatly ... to one Dutch diplomat: 'If you want to be rough, we can be rough too.'"[161]

The eruption began in early December 1948 when, despite major concessions from Hatta, Dutch representatives announced that "further talks with the republic [were] useless," walked out of the negotiations, and announced their plan to form a United States of Indonesia without the nationalists.[162] The abrupt abrogation of talks, the *New York Times* reported, gave "rise to fears of an imminent explosion on the fabulous islands of the Dutch East Indies." "At stake," the newspaper noted, were "the gigantic economic interests of the Netherlands in this area" arrayed against the "desire of a large segment of the 76,000,000 inhabitants to assert their freedom from European imperialism." The Americans were not bystanders in this "grave and complicated colonial problem." "At stake, too," the *New York Times* continued, was "the urgent desire of the United States State Department to prevent a new outbreak of violence in Southeast Asia at a time when the Communists threaten to overrun all of China."[163] The U.S. representative on the Committee of Good Offices, Cochran, therefore, pleaded with Washington to send as strong a warning as possible – to threaten whatever was necessary – to bring the Dutch back to the negotiating table.[164]

Acting Secretary of State Robert Lovett obliged with an aide-mémoire that can only be described as a thunderous warning shot across the bow. On December 7 he sent the Netherlands a missive that bemoaned the "unconscionable delays" in the talks and indicated that the U.S.

by Dutch," enclosure to despatch no. 109 dated March 29, 1947, from George R. Merrell, Charge d'Affaires, American Embassy, New Delhi, Reel 7, *Confidential U.S. State Department Central Files: India, Internal Affairs, 1945–1949* (Frederick, MD: University Press of America, 1986).

[160] Memorandum of Conversation between the Secretary [Acheson], Trygve Lie, and Truman, attachment to Lincoln P. Bloomfield to Mr. Winslow, April 20, 1950, Box 53, File "United Nations: Lie, Trygve – Austin Communications, 1950–1952, n.d.," *Austin Papers*.

[161] Wiebes and Zeeman, "United States 'Big Stick' Diplomacy," 50.

[162] "Dutch Break Off Indonesia Talks," *Washington Post*, December 12, 1948.

[163] "Bitter Fight in Indonesia Nearing Explosive Phase," *New York Times*, December 12, 1948.

[164] McMahon, *Colonialism and Cold War*, 247.

government was "convinced that to postpone any longer resumption of bona fide negotiations [would] be more than ever dangerous." Against enormous odds, Lovett noted, Hatta had already pulled off a miracle; however, Dutch obstinacy had put the prime minister in a precarious position. The Indonesian leader, "while acting with skill and fortitude against the Communist revolt, ha[d] so far been able to offer his supporters neither amelioration of the Republic's economic plight," which Holland's blockade had exacerbated, "nor any degree of its nationalist satisfaction," which the Netherlands' actions had thwarted. If the Dutch proceeded with their proposal to create a United States of Indonesia "without participation of the Republic ... [it] would not only discredit ... the moderate and conciliatory policy which Hatta has sought to promote, but would in itself be unwarrantable in view of assurances given by the Netherlands Government that this step would not be taken so long as reasonable hope remained of achieving the Republic's participation in an interim government of all Indonesia." Frankly, it was time for the Dutch to stand up and honor their agreements, Lovett intoned. Too much was at stake. The economic viability of both the Netherlands and Indonesia stood on the precipice of disaster if The Hague continued down this path. The Dutch government needed to come to terms with "the preponderant desire of the Indonesian people to govern themselves [which] finds its chief expression in the Republic of Indonesia, which must be considered not as a geographical concept but as a political force."[165]

Then, in what must have been an infuriating inversion for The Hague, Lovett insisted that it was the *Republic* that had kept the extremists in check, whereas Dutch efforts to weaken or destroy the nationalist government had cracked open a Pandora's box of woes that the Netherlands would never be able to handle. Lovett named the evils that would pour out of Dutch-ravaged Indonesia as the Republic inevitably fought back with everything it had, including a "scorched earth strategy," "guerilla warfare," and "the destruction of factories, plantations and transportation facilities, by assassination of estate personnel and intimidation of workers." All of this "would transform Indonesia from an economic asset ... to an ever more costly liability." The subsequent financial drain of fighting a guerilla war, Lovett warned, would "seriously deplete the resources of the Netherlands and tend to nullify

---

[165] Document 31: Aide-mémoire [The Acting Secretary of State to the Consulate General at Batavia. December 6, 1948], Vol. 16, *Officiële Bescheiden*, 55–58.

the effect of [U.S.] appropriations to the Netherlands and Indonesia under [the Marshall Plan] or *jeopardize continuation thereof.*" In other words, if the Dutch planned to launch a military strike in hopes of a quick kill, they needed to think again. Not only would the reality of getting bogged down in a guerilla war turn into a physical and financial bloodbath with no end in sight, but also a "resort to military force would come as a profound shock to [the] American people." Thus came the even more explicit warning. If the Netherlands refused to return to the negotiating table, "the United States Government would regard itself as no longer bound by the restraints heretofore imposed by its membership on the Committee [of Good Offices] and would consider itself free to take such measures as the changed circumstances might require."[166]

The U.S. ambassador to the Hague reported that the "Dutch reaction after reading [the] *aide-memoire* was one of pained and angry surprise." A. H. J. Lovink, the Dutch high commissioner, "controlling himself with some difficulty, said this was very plain speaking and he understood fully what it meant."[167] However, although Lovett's note made clear that hundreds of millions of Marshall Plan dollars for the Netherlands and the NEI were in jeopardy, the Dutch went into full attack mode. They hurled a brush-back pitch at the Americans with their own stinging aide-mémoire; rebuffed an effort by Hatta, who was willing to make even more concessions if negotiations would just resume; and, as Cochran feared, planned a military assault to end once and for all the existence of the Republic of Indonesia.[168]

They tried to camouflage their intent by toying with the Republic's proposals, which were transmitted via the Americans. The Netherlands' representatives made vague, noncommittal statements and then, "to gain a little more time," indicated that a cabinet-level review was required. This, however, was a stalling tactic crafted to keep everything in limbo until the UN Security Council had adjourned for the holidays. Dutch officials asserted that it was important "that nothing leaves marks before any action begins." There was to be no trace that the Netherlands planned all

---

[166] Ibid. Emphasis added.

[167] The Chargé in the Netherlands (Steere) to the Secretary of State, December 7, 1948, *FRUS* (1948) 6:530.

[168] McMahon, *Colonialism and Cold War*, 248–249; Homan, "The Netherlands, the United States and the Indonesian Question, 1948," 134–135; Document 90: Ambassador to Washington to Minister of Foreign Affairs, December 14, 1948, Vol. 16, *Officiële Bescheiden*, 148–149.

along on attacking Indonesia while the rest of the world scurried around trying to forestall war.[169]

Scurried, perhaps, is not quite accurate. Scrambled furiously. On December 13, from Batavia, Cochran advised the State Department that with the Dutch refusing to negotiate through the GOC, "there [was] now 'no alternative'" but to put "the Indonesian question before the Security Council."[170] From Washington, on December 13, the Economic Cooperation Administration (ECA), which administered the Marshall Plan, "advised the Dutch that there was no commitment ... even when there was an allotment" to provide "further aid for" the NEI, which had its own allocation.[171] On December 15, in a show of unparalleled unity within State, Lovett and the chiefs of the Europe, Far East, and UN divisions crafted a memorandum – delivered by the chargé to The Hague, Loyd Steere – which "warned" that "we might be forced by public opinion in the United States to resort to punitive sanctions.... If the Dutch resorted to military action, the reaction in the United States might be so strong as to jeopardize Dutch participation in the military assistance plans [NATO] which the United States was offering to the governments of Western Europe."[172] That same day, after Senator George Malone charged that American "funds had been used by Holland to keep soldiers in Indonesia and maintain a blockade of Republican ports," the Netherlands had to "give ... assurances" to the ECA administrator in Holland "that no [Marshall Plan] aid had been used to supply military equipment to Dutch troops in Indonesia."[173] Despite clear warnings that the Netherlands' participation in the Marshall Plan and NATO was at risk, however, on December 17, the American embassy picked up "rumors of preparations of military action in Indonesia" at the same time that

---

[169] Document 73: Minutes of the Meeting of the Council of Ministers, December 13, 1948, Vol. 16, *Officiële Bescheiden*, 114–119; Summary of Telegrams, December 15, 1948, Box 23, File "State Dept. Briefs File, September–December 1948," *HST:SMOF:NA*; Summary of Telegrams, December 15, 1948, Box 23, File "State Dept. Briefs File, September–December 1948," *HST:SMOF:NA*.

[170] Summary of Telegrams, December 13, 1948, Box 23, File "State Dept. Briefs File, September–December 1948," *HST:SMOF:NA*; "Indonesia Good Office Committee Reports Failure to Security Council," *Palestine Post*, December 16, 1948.

[171] Jessup, *The Birth of Nations*, 66–67. For how the areas of Indonesia controlled by the Dutch gained their own line item allocation of Marshall Plan dollars, see Van Der Eng, "Marshall Aid as a Catalyst in the Decolonization of Indonesia, 1947–49," 337–339.

[172] Jessup, *The Birth of Nations*, 66–67.

[173] "No Aid for Dutch War," *Palestine Post*, December 15, 1948.

the Dutch demanded "immediate Republican participation in the interim government [of the USI]."[174]

As far as the State Department was concerned, the Dutch had issued nothing short of an "ultimatum"; Washington, therefore, tried to break through to The Hague that this so-called pretext for war was simply implausible. A "self generated emergency was not a bona fide emergency."[175] The excuse "lacked credibility."[176] The Americans warned the Dutch to revisit the aide-mémoire of December 7 to grasp fully "certain actions which might inevitably have to result" if the Netherlands launched a "police action" in Indonesia.[177] Philip Jessup acknowledged that the State Department had taken off the diplomatic gloves, but, he said, it was necessary because "we were saving an ally from catastrophe."[178]

The Netherlands, however, had determined that its salvation lay in Indonesia. The Dutch explained that "Holland's life blood was in the Indies, that without it Holland would sink into an economic backwater ... would sink back into the North Sea ... therefore she must fight if need be to secure survival."[179] On December 18, "prepared to face the consequences of their decision even if this meant United Nations sanctions," the Dutch used the pretense of "military and terrorist activities by the Republic" to launch their second "police action."[180] As the *Washington Post* reported, Holland's troops were "going through the Republican areas like a knife through butter."[181] Jakarta was quickly overrun, Sumatra seized, and the Indonesian leadership rounded up and arrested. All told it was a spectacular military victory. It was also a stunning diplomatic defeat whose intensity and breadth somehow, despite all

---

[174] Summary of Telegrams, December 17, 1948, Box 23, File "State Dept. Briefs File, September-December 1948," *HST:SMOF:NA*.

[175] Jessup, *The Birth of Nations*, 70; Memorandum of Telephone Conversation on December 18 by the Director of the Office of Far Eastern Affairs (Butterworth), December 18, 1948, *FRUS* (1948) 6:572–573.

[176] Document 147: Foreign Minister to Ambassadors to London, Washington, Brussels, Ottawa, Representative in the Security Council, and Chief Executive Far East to Batavia, December 18, 1948, Vol. 16, *Officiële Bescheiden*, 224. ·

[177] Ibid.

[178] Jessup, *The Birth of Nations*, 74.

[179] Charles A. Smith, "American and British Stock Fall in Holland as Result of Bad Relations," *Norfolk New Journal and Guide*, March 26, 1949.

[180] Document 155: DEA/5005 4–40, Ambassador in France to Secretary of State for External Affairs, telegram, December 20, 1948, Documents on Canadian External Relations: General Policy: Sub-Section 4, Indonesia, *Canadian Foreign Affairs*; Document 132: Notes from the Secretary-General to Dutch High Commissioner to Ministers of Foreign Affairs, December 17, 1948, Vol. 16, *Officiële Bescheiden*, 209.

[181] "Reminding the Dutch," *Washington Post*, December 23, 1948.

of the warnings, blindsided the Dutch, who "never really expected the storm of indignation that arose in late December."[182]

This "police action," Jessup declared, "unified the State Department in favor of the Indonesians."[183] It also outraged a wide swath of allies. British Foreign Secretary Ernest Bevin, who had been working furiously to forestall war, railed that the Dutch "double crossed" and "stabbed [him] in the back." The sheer "stupidity of [the] Dutch," another cabinet official smirked, was sure to raise the ire of the Americans, maybe even compel them to withdraw "M[arshall] Aid" from the Netherlands, especially when it was "used for this purpose."[184] In fact, "[r]epresentatives of both the Australian and British Foreign Offices ... indicated their strong displeasure at the Dutch action in resuming military operations, while [the US] Embassy in New Delhi ... received reliable information indicating that the Indian government [was] so exercised at these developments that it may break off relations with the Netherlands and deny the Dutch the use of Indian ports and airfields."[185] The fact that The Hague was "determin[ed] to continue [the] police action despite the threat of [UN] sanctions" represented a challenge that the State Department was not willing to ignore.[186] Dean Rusk outlined the multiple ways that the Netherlands' assault on the Republic jeopardized U.S. foreign policy – from the colonial world, to the Marshall Plan, to China – and was "lamentable from all points of view." "The United States," he insisted "did not want 'to condone or wink at Dutch action in Indonesia.'"[187]

Therefore, soon after Holland attacked the Republican stronghold of Yogyakarta, the United States cut off Marshall Plan aid to the NEI. In addition, the U.S. delegate on the Security Council, Philip Jessup – using words uttered previously by the Post-War World Council, the NAACP, the Australians, and the Indians – "told the United Nations the Dutch attack was unjustified" and "a possible threat to world peace."[188] Jessup,

---

[182] Document 184: Ambassador to Washington to Minister of Foreign Affairs, December 20, 1948, Vol. 16, *Officiële Bescheiden*, 258–259; Homan, "The Netherlands, the United States and the Indonesian Question, 1948," 136.

[183] Jessup, *The Birth of Nations*, 71.

[184] Cabinet Minutes 82(48), December 22, 1948, CAB/195/6; Cabinet Minutes 80(48), December 13, 1948, CAB/195/6.

[185] Summary of Telegrams, December 21, 1948, Box 23, File "State Dept. Briefs File, September–December 1948," *HST:SMOF:NA*.

[186] Ibid.

[187] Jessup, *The Birth of Nations*, 75–76.

[188] "Dutch Attack Cuts U.S. Aid to East Indies," *Los Angeles Times*, December 23, 1948; "Marshall Plan Aid to Dutch East Indies Suspended by ECA: Agency Withholds About $14 Million 'Pending Clarification' of Fighting in Indonesia," *Wall Street Journal*, December 23, 1948.

FIGURE 4.4. According to the British, U.S. Ambassador Philip Jessup, was the "angel with the flaming arrow, who drove the Dutch out of Indonesia."
Source: Bettman/Corbis. Courtesy of Corbis, Stock Photo ID# U973189ACME.

now the acting U.S. ambassador to the UN and struggling to shake off a severe bout of pneumonia, summoned the strength to virtually demand that the Soviets return from Moscow for an emergency meeting of the UN Security Council[189] (see Figure 4.4). As the diplomatic winds gathered strength to blow away Holland's house of cards, public opinion, just as the State Department warned, unleashed a hurricane on the U.S. government demanding justice for the Indonesians.

[189] Thomas J. Hamilton, "U.N. Council Meets on Indonesia Today: Emergency Session Asked by U.S. – Dutch to Challenge Jurisdiction of Body," *New York Times*, December 20, 1948; Jessup, *The Birth of Nations*, 69; Document 155: DEA/50054–40, Ambassador in France to Secretary of State for External Affairs, telegram, December 20, 1948, Documents on Canadian External Relations: General Policy: Sub-Section 4, Indonesia, *Canadian Foreign Affairs*.

The war against the Republic was so explosive that the director of branches for the NAACP, Gloster Current, whom no one would characterize as an internationalist, urged Walter White to take an explicit stand.[190] "The unilateral action of the Netherlands government in Indonesia," Current observed, "seems to me warrants a statement from you denouncing the resumption of hostilities there. The United States State Department should be asked not to give any aid and comfort to the Dutch and ERP [Marshall Plan] aid should be discontinued pending a solution of this problem by the United Nations." In addition to pressuring the State Department to do more, Current also believed that the NAACP needed to reach out across the Pacific to show the Association's solidarity with those fighting for their freedom. "I think," Current continued, that "the colored peoples all over the world, especially in Asia, would welcome a statement in behalf of the Indonesians by the representative of the largest colored group in the United States." Current emphasized that this was neither inappropriate nor outside the scope of the Association's agenda. Rather, "[t]his ties into our general attitude on colonies and independence for colonials."[191]

White agreed and soon followed with a telegram to Paul Hoffman, the director of the Economic Cooperation Administration, making clear that although the cessation of funds already allocated for the Netherlands East Indies was noteworthy, it certainly was not enough: the "National Association for the Advancement of Colored People urges immediate withdrawal of *all* Marshall Plan aid from the Government of The Netherlands." Returning to the theme of his Senate testimony, White explained that this "desperate attempt of The Netherlands government to re-establish pre-war imperialism in the East Indies cannot be sustained without American aid.... We urge," therefore, "the immediate cessation of all such aid."[192]

Hoffman's office, however, wanted only to focus on the suspension of funds to Indonesia (as Holland's colony). This aligned with the State Department's policy, which did "not intend to bring about a general

---

[190] For standard narratives about Current, see, for example, Fairclough, *To Redeem the Soul of America*, 46–47; Ransby, *Ella Baker*, 276, 343; Dittmer, *Local People*, 160–169; Emilye Crosby, *A Little Taste of Freedom: The Black Freedom Struggle in Claiborne County, Mississippi* (Chapel Hill: University of North Carolina Press, 2005), 199.

[191] Gloster B. Current to Walter White, memo, December 20, 1948, Box A321, File "Indonesia, 1948–49, May," *Papers of the NAACP*.

[192] Walter White to Paul G. Hoffman, telegram, December 28, 1948, ibid.; "Halt Aid to Dutch Walter White Urges," press release, December 23, 1948, ibid. Emphasis added.

break with the Dutch" and did "not intend to apply sanctions against the Netherlands in Europe." The sanctions were only to convey especially "to the Asiatic peoples the interest of the US in the development of self-government in Asia" and to be "certain" that it was understood "that the US [was] not supporting directly or indirectly the Dutch military action in Indonesia."[193]

White, however, argued to his leadership team that the NAACP should "press our point that ECA aid to the Netherlands ought also to be stopped" for two important reasons. First, domestic jurisdiction was irrelevant in a war of colonial conquest. The Security Council made that clear. Just as the Dutch made equally clear "their refusal to obey the [UN's] cease fire order." Second, Hoffman's argument missed the point. Hundreds of millions of Marshall Plan dollars gave Holland the liquidity it needed to divert The Hague's resources to the war.[194] In fact, Du Bois, who was completely estranged from and spending his last ten days at the NAACP, explained to the *New York Star* that the United States had "given impoverished Holland $16,000,000 for 'recovery' under the Marshall Plan" – roughly the equivalent of $896 million in 2011 – which would "go some distance toward financing her current war in Indonesia."[195] In fact, Du Bois had seriously underestimated American largesse. The ECA had actually "authorized some $296,085,000 in outright grants plus a loan of $95,000,000."[196] (The 2011 equivalents are a staggering $16.6 billion in Marshall Plan aid coupled with a $5.32 billion loan.[197]) Even without the exact figures, White recognized, as did his nemesis Du Bois, that the enormous "aid which we give to the Netherlands even if not used in Indonesia releases funds, materials and men for the crushing of the Indonesians."[198] Therefore, in a reply drafted by the president of the NAACP, Arthur

---

[193] Elizabeth A. Hanna to Walter White, December 23, 1948, Box A321, File "Indonesia, 1949, June-Dec," *Papers of the NAACP*; Office of the Administrator, Press Release: ECA No. 330, December 22, 1948, Box A321, File "Indonesia, 1949, June–Dec.," *Papers of the NAACP*; Summary of Telegrams, December 24, 1948, Box 23, File "State Dept. Briefs File, September-December 1948," *HST:SMOF:NA*.

[194] Walter White to Henry Moon and Roy Wilkins, memo, December 27, 1948, Box A321, File "Indonesia, 1948–49, May," *Papers of the NAACP*.

[195] W. E. B. Du Bois to the Editor of the [New York] Star, December 20, 1948, Reel 62, *Du Bois*; Sixteen million is the equivalent of $896 million, http://www.measuringworth.com/uscompare/relativevalue.php. Accessed July 1, 2013.

[196] "Aid to Indonesia Cut Off, More Funds Given Dutch," *Boston Globe*, December 23, 1948.

[197] http://www.measuringworth.com/uscompare/relativevalue.php. Accessed July 1, 2013.

[198] Walter White to Henry Moon and Roy Wilkins, memo, December 27, 1948, Box A321, File "Indonesia, 1948–49, May," *Papers of the NAACP*.

Spingarn, White sent another telegram to the ECA in which he "repeated his demand 'for cancellation of all aid to the Netherlands government in Europe as well as in the Far East.'"[199]

The *New York Amsterdam News*, the *Norfolk Journal and Guide*, the *Atlanta Daily World*, and the *New York Times* carried the story of the NAACP's efforts to shut down all Marshall Plan dollars flowing to the Dutch.[200] Walter White followed with a blistering column in the *Chicago Defender*, where he mocked the wartime "weepy promises of Queen Wilhelmina" to "abandon their old system of colonial exploitation and give their overseas subject real freedom and equal opportunity with the white people of the Netherlands." Instead of "real freedom," he wrote, Holland launched a war to crush the Indonesians' legitimate quest for independence. "To the credit of the United States whose record during the recent UN General Assembly with regard to the former Italian colonies in Africa was exceedingly evasive and dangerously imperialist," White noted, "the United States has taken a forthright stand against the cold-blooded attempt of the Dutch to use armed force, ECA aid from the United States, chicanery and downright lying to stop the Indonesian struggle for freedom."[201] However, he also noted, the Americans could do more, much more, to drop Holland to its bankrupt knees.

That was certainly the tenor of the flood of editorials and newspaper reports. The condemnation of the Netherlands was nearly universal. The confluence of Dutch imperialism, the millions siphoned from the Marshall Plan, the Indonesian Republic's valiant struggle for self-determination, and, frankly, the Christmas holiday season were powerful fodder for the media. Journalist Horace Cayton's article in the *Pittsburgh Courier* was a potent mix of anger and sadness as he detailed how the "mechanized might of the Dutch empire" poured down on the Indonesians' "poorly armed native army." This, regretted Cayton, was a "fine Christmas

---

[199] "White Repeats Demand: Stop Marshall Plan Aid to Dutch," press release, December 30, 1948, Box A321, File "Indonesia, 1949, June–Dec.," *Papers of the NAACP*; Walter White to Paul G. Hoffman, telegram, December 28, 1948, Box A321, File "Indonesia, 1948–49, May," *Papers of the NAACP*.

[200] "Halt Aid to Dutch, Walter White Urges," *Atlanta Daily World*, December 30, 1948; "America Urged Not to Help Dutch Attack," *Norfolk New Journal and Guide*, January 1, 1949; "Cease Aid to Dutch, NAACP Leader Urges," *New York Amsterdam News*, January 1, 1949; "Groups Here Voice Protest on Dutch," *New York Times*, December 24, 1948.

[201] Walter White, "Dutch Lying has Been Incredible and Contemptible," *Chicago Defender*, January 8, 1949.

present." This gift "of bitterness, death, and destruction which these native people fighting for their freedom [were] now enduring" was made possible only by the millions in Marshall Plan aid that we "the people of the United States financed.... Don't get me wrong," Clayton clarified, "I am for the European aid ... if it is used for ... bolstering the democratic force of the world." However, he noted, "when our money [was] used to subject colonial people by brute force and to prop up the sagging corners of the Dutch imperial empire, that's when I and the plan fall out." Therefore, Cayton exhorted, the "Indonese must win." Their battle was "symbolic of the unrest of all colored people in all countries against all forms of economic and social oppression."[202]

The *Chicago Defender* also blasted the "Bloody Dutch" who "opened fire on the defenseless Indonesian Republic in a determined bid to reduce the proud natives to slavery and to seize the natural resources of the islands for the robber barons of Holland.... Fortified with American dollars through the Marshall Plan," the editorial continued, "the crafty Dutch are eager to feather their nest at the expense of other people's money and blood." The United States, however, "cannot afford to give aid and comfort to an imperial power that defies all of the principles of the United Nations charter and resorts to warfare to subjugate peoples who have every right to freedom and independence.... The Netherlands government must be condemned," the *Chicago Defender* concluded, "and all aid be withdraw [sic] from it immediately."[203]

The *Chicago Tribune*, owned by isolationist and Truman nemesis Robert "Colonel" McCormick, gladly gave voice to one of the Republic's spokesmen who charged that "it [was] obvious 'that the Dutch government [was] putting Marshall plan dollars in one pocket and taking Dutch guilders out of another' to prosecute its war against the Indonesians." It was simple arithmetic. The costs of "'maintaining ... forces of 130,000 men in Indonesia [was] so enormous that this military effort *and* the rehabilitation of Holland both could not be financed without Marshall plan aid' said Charles Thamboe, the republic's observer to the United Nations." Of course, the specific charge could not be proven, said Thamboe, but what other source was available to finance the "million dollars a day for their military efforts against us"? Quoting Senator Malone, Thamboe reiterated that "the American people would

---

[202] Horace Cayton, "Dutch Are Using United States Money to Enslave People of Indonesia," *Pittsburgh Courier*, January 1, 1949.
[203] "Our Opinions: Bloody Dutch Go to War," *Chicago Defender*, January 1, 1949.

be terribly unhappy if they knew how their money was being spent thru the Marshall Plan."[204]

A few days later the *Chicago Tribune* published an editorial that alluded to a "conspiracy so immense" that it could only raise serious doubts about both aid to Europe and the Truman administration.[205] Not only were the Dutch seemingly unafraid "of what the U.N. may do to them," the *Tribune* observed, but also what "seems to us to be of a good deal more importance is that the Dutch haven't been deterred by official expressions of disapproval in this country." But how was that possible when the Netherlands was on "the Marshall plan dole"? "Now isn't it curious that Holland, thus dependent upon us for present welfare and future security, is still indifferent to sentiment in Washington? Could it be that the Dutch went ahead in Indonesia after having been told privately to disregard the formal protests?" Or, is it that "Mr. Truman and his state department boys really believe that this country is more dependent on Holland than Holland is on us?" Something was decidedly awry, the editorial concluded, because the Dutch were "evidently persuaded that nothing they do in Indonesia can cost them their Marshall plan money."[206]

For a short while the Netherlands did feel bulletproof, particularly as its "indignation ... was running high" at the Americans for daring to cut off aid to the NEI. "The United States will lose in the long run," commented one unnamed Dutch official. Another swaggered that it was "simply ridiculous for the United States to suppose that it can cajole and

[204] Joseph Hearst, "Charges Dutch Meet War Cost with U.S. Funds," *Chicago Daily Tribune*, December 23, 1948. Emphasis added.

[205] That phrase, of course, is about the Second Red Scare and the *Chicago Tribune*'s work with Senator Joseph McCarthy (R-WI) to impugn the loyalty of top-ranking officials in the Truman administration.

[206] "Hard Boiled Holland," *Chicago Daily Tribune*, December 28, 1948. For additional articles from the *Chicago Tribune* that questioned the Dutch, the State Department, and Truman's foreign policy, see Quentin Pope, "Java's 'States' Dutch Directed, Bulletins Show: Federalists Scorned by Republic Chiefs," *Chicago Tribune*, February 11, 1949, Box A321, File "Indonesia, 1948–49, May," *Papers of the NAACP*; Quentin Pope, "Refutes Dutch Claim Javanese Rule Indonesia: Most of Its Officials from Other Isles," February 22, 1949, *Chicago Tribune*, Box A321, File "Indonesia, 1948–49, May," *Papers of the NAACP*; Quentin Pope, "Threat to Cut Off Aid Hard Blow to Dutch: Revenues from Indies Still Lagging," February 24, 1949, *Chicago Tribune*, Box A321, File "Indonesia, 1948–49, May," *Papers of the NAACP*; Quentin Pope, "Java Republic Wars on Reds Dutch Create," February 25, 1949, *Chicago Tribune*, Box A321, File "Indonesia, 1948–49, May," *Papers of the NAACP*; Quentin Pope, "U.N. Delay Gives Dutch Chance to Gain in Indies: Plan to Trim Offer of Sovereignty," February 28, 1949, *Chicago Tribune*, Box A321, File "Indonesia, 1948–49, May," *Papers of the NAACP*.

threaten us."[207] Ambassador Van Kleffens, ensconced in Washington and aware of the mounting tide against the Dutch, however, pled with Stikker to rein in the "dismissive statements" from Holland's official spokespersons not only because it left a "bad impression" but also because it appeared that American public opinion was "completely and increasingly bitter" toward the Netherlands.[208]

Jessup recalled that "Dutch policies were helping the Soviets, creating a breach in the Western front, arousing opposition in American public opinion, and perhaps moving Congress to take punitive action by cutting aid to the Netherlands."[209] An editorial in the *Wall Street Journal* emphasized that the "Dutch military action in Indonesia" had presented American foreign policy with a daunting Hobson's Choice. On the one hand, Holland had "an important place in blueprints for European reconstruction. To take hostile action, even of an economic character, against the Netherlands [was] a distasteful prospect." It would also send a troubling, punitive signal to "the other countries with colonial empires with which we [were] politically associated.... On the other hand the tide of racialism and nationalism [was] running high in the Orient. The repercussions of the Dutch move [were] felt far beyond the frontiers of Indonesia." It had not only angered India but also allowed the communists to "argue that here [was] a new proof of the intention of the white man to hold the Asiatic masses in colonial bondage.... In short," the *Wall Street Journal* concluded, regardless of whether Washington tried to appease the Dutch or the Asians, "the United States [was] in the position of being 'damned if it does and damned if it doesn't.'"[210] Holland had, indeed, cracked open Pandora's box, or to use a more modern analogy, set off a cascading power failure across U.S. foreign policy.

First, the western alliance looked liked it could fracture and, in doing so, topple much of the architecture the Americans had built to contain the Soviet Union. Bevin had already informed his cabinet that "we cannot support action of [the] Dutch."[211] Australia wanted the Netherlands expelled from the UN, insisting that "the Dutch action [was] worse than

---

[207] David Anderson, "Dutch Are Indignant," *New York Times*, December 23, 1948.

[208] Document 257: Ambassador to Washington to Minister of Foreign Affairs, December 24, 1948, Vol. 16, *Officiële Bescheiden*, 330–331.

[209] Jessup, *The Birth of Nations*, 83–84.

[210] William Henry Chamberlin, "Indonesian Squabble: Dutch Action Presents U.S. Diplomacy with Distasteful Decision; Either Way We Lose Friends and Prestige," *Wall Street Journal*, January 4, 1949.

[211] Cabinet Minutes 82(48), December 22, 1948, CAB/195/6.

Hitler's against Holland eight years ago."[212] Even the Belgians, who had staunchly supported the Dutch, were incensed by Holland's "police action."[213] There were also concerns that the Brussels Pact, which was the precursor to NATO, "could be jeopardized by the present cleavage between the Netherlands Government and other western governments." Moreover, "the projected Atlantic defense pact could hardly survive a shattering of the Brussels alliance or a really serious breach between the Netherlands and other western powers."[214]

Second, Holland's actions called into question the credibility of the nascent international justice regime. The Dutch had attacked Indonesia just days before the execution of seven high-ranking Japanese officials convicted during the recent Tokyo War Crimes trial. Holland's surprise assault on the Republic had raised the specter of Pearl Harbor without, obviously, the same consequences for the perpetrators. "Many Japanese conclude[d] that western powers were sabotaging the principles on which Nipponese war criminals were convicted" because the "Dutch action paralleled what the Japanese had done."[215]

Third, Holland's assault made Cold War strategy in Asia more precarious than ever. The British were "'damned annoyed' over [the] Dutch 'police action' in Indonesia" because England "feared" that the assault on the Republic "may well shatter Britain's carefully prepared plan to create a general anti-Communist 'front' throughout Southeast Asia."[216] Bevin was certain that Holland's "police action" could transform Asia into a "ripe plum for Russia."[217] Most frustrating, however, was the irony that the Dutch had used the red bogeyman to justify their imperialist actions.[218] Walter White, after detailing the disjuncture between the Netherlands' anticommunist claims and its attempt to destroy the very government that put down the revolt at Madiun, railed that "Dutch lying

---

[212] "Australia Requests U.N. to Expel Netherlands," *Los Angeles Times*, December 24, 1948.

[213] Summary of Telegrams, December 15, 1948, Box 23, File "State Dept. Briefs File, September-December 1948," *HST:SMOF:NA*; Jessup, *The Birth of Nations*, 67.

[214] Volney D. Hurd, "Java Crisis Rocks UN – ERP and Atlantic Pact Periled," *Christian Science Monitor*, December 24, 1948.

[215] "Dutch Attack Backs Up What Japan Did, Is Comment in Tokyo," *Chicago Daily Tribune*, December 20, 1948.

[216] Benjamin Welles, "British Are 'Annoyed,'" *New York Times*, December 21, 1948.

[217] Cabinet Minutes 80(48), December 13, 1948, CAB/195/6.

[218] John H. Thompson, "Dutch Attempt to Prove Case for Midwest," *Chicago Daily Tribune*, December 24, 1948; Joan Thirlet, "Dutch Accused of By-Passing UN in Indonesia Development," *Christian Science Monitor*, December 20, 1948.

ha[d] been incredible and contemptible." More than that, however, White continued, Holland's "insane course" of destroying nationalists as if they were Soviet-blessed commandos could only lead to a real communist revolt that would engulf Asia, Africa, and the Caribbean.[219] An editorial in the *Boston Globe* also pointed out that "Dutch aggression" would be the wick that lit a communist explosion throughout Asia. "This aggressive action, clothed as usual in the specious claim that it is [a] 'police action against terrorists,'" the editorial continued, "reveals colonial imperialism [was] back in business at the old stand – as if nothing had happened in Asia since the early nineteen hundreds."[220]

Fourth, Holland's war to gain control of Indonesia had, as the *Boston Globe* intimated, all of the telltale signs of the bloody Ghost of Christmas Past. Colonialism had no place in a world teeming with twentieth-century nationalist fervor. The *Los Angeles Times* emphasized that the "repercussions" of Holland's war on Indonesia rippled far beyond the archipelago: "Indeed, all people of Asia and the Middle East see the Dutch action as a challenge to their awakened nationalism."[221] The *Washington Post* reported that "India and Pakistan slapped an embargo on all flights of KLM, the Royal Dutch Airlines. The Ceylon government already had barred all Dutch ships and aircraft carrying troops and materials to the East Indies."[222] The *London Times*, therefore, expressed "that the present situation [was] more than a crisis in the relations between the Netherlands and the Indonesian Republic; it also [held] ominous implications for the prospects of friendly cooperation between Asia and Europe–an important element in the structure of international security."[223]

Fifth, the credibility of the UN hung in the balance. Just thirteen years earlier the Italians had scoffed at the League of Nations, invaded Ethiopia, and fully exposed that international organization's debilitating weakness to the world. Now the Dutch had flouted the authority of the Security Council with such impunity that a columnist for the *Pittsburgh Courier* depicted UN resolutions as "about as effective as slapping the wrist of a gangster who threaten[ed] you with a tommy-gun."[224] The *Los Angeles*

---

[219] Walter White, "Dutch Lying Has Been Incredible and Contemptible," *Chicago Defender*, January 8, 1949.

[220] "Holland Goes to War," *Boston Globe*, December 20, 1948.

[221] Waldo Drake, "Concern in London over Dutch Attack," *Los Angeles Times*, December 26, 1948.

[222] "New Burdens Face Holland over Indonesia," *Washington Post*, December 24, 1948.

[223] "U.N. and Indonesia," *London Times*, December 24, 1948.

[224] J. A. Rogers, "The Rape of Indonesia, South Africa, Only Bodes Ill for the Oppressors," *Pittsburgh Courier*, January 22, 1949.

Times reported, it was "difficult to find any one in Paris tonight who believes the Dutch government will heed the United Nations Security Council's order to halt its latest attack on Indonesian Republicans and release President Soekarno and other Republican leaders seized at Jogjakarta a week ago."[225] The *New York Times* observed that the "prestige of the [UN Security] Council has already suffered, as has the prestige of the white man throughout Asia and the prestige of the democratic nations throughout the world.'"[226] The British press declared that it was "absurd" for the Dutch "now to assert that Indonesian problems [were] a domestic affair ... [when] they accepted the Security Council's intervention after their last 'police action.'"[227] It was, also, the *Cleveland Call and Post* insisted, rooted in imperialism. When, "the United Nations policy" of "trying to make the ... Indonesian Republic a reality ... ran counter to the Dutch's assumed rights" to "exploit the rich natural resources of the Pacific islands with the cheap labor of the natives, ... the soldiers of the Netherlands marched in and took over." However, the editorial asserted, what happens next in Asia will be the decisive "acid test of the United Nations as a force for world peace and freedom."[228]

Sixth, an inevitable long and protracted war lurked just around the bend from Holland's supposed quick military victory. Jessup predicted that "if the Dutch army tried to suppress the guerilla movement in Indonesia, they would be bled."[229] The Australians, therefore, "regard[ed] the Dutch actions as both futile and dangerous and assert[ed] that even if the Dutch overran all the Republican territory they would almost certainly find themselves in protracted guerilla warfare, which would unite the Indonesian moderates and extremists."[230]

Finally, as Jessup warned, the outbreak of war in Indonesia had indeed raised the hackles of Congress, which then put the European Recovery Program and more at risk.[231] Matthew M. Fox, president and chairman of the American Indonesian Corporation, who was livid that the war had cut off "many prospective business deals between the United States and Indonesia," told the *New York Times* that "sentiment in Congress was strongly against the Dutch for their military move against the Republic of

[225] Drake, "Concern in London over Dutch Attack," *Los Angeles Times*.
[226] "Indonesia and the U.N.," *New York Times*, December 26, 1948.
[227] Drake, "Concern in London Over Dutch Attack," *Los Angeles Times*.
[228] W. O. Walker, "Down the Big Road," *Cleveland Call and Post*, January 29, 1949.
[229] Jessup, *The Birth of Nations*, 75.
[230] "Australia Against Dutch," *New York Times*, December 22, 1948.
[231] For the amendment by Senator Owen Brewster (D-ME), see Jessup, *The Birth of Nations*, 89; McMahon, *Colonialism and Cold War*, 276–278, 285–286, 291–293.

Indonesia. He predicted that Congress would act to cut off Netherlands aid if the State Department did not."[232] Senator Malone railed that twice in his "lifetime we have left bloody tracks all over the Pacific in two world wars in order to get the colonial systems back for the colonial-minded nations." However, he continued, these imperial nations were obviously weak, could not protect their own territory, and were now relying on the United States to underwrite their empires. He "feared" that the Marshall Plan "tended to finance regimes that 'like the Dutch in Indonesia [were] already outmoded.'" He stated with assurance that "without the money we gave the Dutch under the Marshall Plan they could not do what they are doing in Indonesia."[233]

On December 30, Ambassador Van Kleffens sent his appraisal of public opinion in the United States to The Hague. He wearily explained that except for a few pockets of support, the news was not good. The police action had wrecked Holland's standing in the United States. First and foremost, Van Kleffens wrote, the "Man in the Street ... reactions [were] bad." The "typical American ... [has] an instinctive sympathy for the 'underdog'" and resents mightily when the weaker is "bullied." That was how the "average American" understood what the Dutch had done in Indonesia: bullied. But worse than that, he continued, it was bullying for "colonial oppression" against a people fighting for their freedom. The Netherlands compounded the problem when it defied the UN, which was "seen as a kind of panacea against all international evil." Holland's problems were further exacerbated by the "headlines ... that the Dutch rained bombs down on poor, defenseless women and children in Indonesia." That imagery was bad enough, but for a people, especially in the Midwest and Northwest, who were very religious, the fact that the Netherlands "unleashed" a war "at the beginning of Christmas week" was nothing short of "shocking, ...not 'Christian,' ... and an unadulterated 'sin.'" Van Kleffens relayed that "even more than in 1947," when Holland launched its first police action, "the current action of the Dutch Government has struck a deep wound." He noted that this highly unfavorable public opinion had eddied through into the labor unions, which were calling for global strikes and cessation of ECA funds to the Netherlands; Congress, which was more "important and difficult than expected" especially with

---

[232] "U.S. Urged to End Aid Plan for Dutch," *New York Times*, December 30, 1948.
[233] U.S. Congress, Senate, Senator Malone of Nevada speaking on the Extension of the European Recovery Program, S. 1239. 81st Cong., 1st sess. *Congressional Record 95*, pt. 3 (April 6, 1949), 3986; "Says We Finance Strife: Senator Malone Holds Dutch Regime in Indonesia Outmoded," *New York Times*, December 23, 1948.

the contingent that was already "against the Marshall Plan"; the State Department, which did "not appreciate" the way the Dutch made the Security Council look "impotent" and put the "discussions on the Atlantic Pact" in jeopardy; and the White House, where Truman owed his stunning November 1948 victory, in part, to the very unions that were lobbying hard and relentlessly against the Dutch. Now was the time, Van Kleffens advised, to find a way to repair this damage. And the only way appeared to be to work with "the nationalists in close cooperation with all moderate elements, who will be willing to help build an independent and free Indonesia."[234] (See Figure 4.5)

An independent Indonesia was precisely the point for the NAACP, as it began to strategize with the India League, the International League for the Rights of Man, and the newly formed Americans for the Indonesian Republic (AIR), which included theologian Reinhold Niebuhr, novelist Vincent Sheean, Roger Baldwin, the Republic's chief counsel Robert Delson, and Senator Hubert Humphrey (D-MN), to mount the next wave of campaigns.[235] Key to their mobilization was the steady stream of information flowing into the Association from U.S.-based representatives of the Republic.[236] The NAACP even worked briefly with the Emergency Committee for Indonesia, although the Association's partners in the India League, J. J. Singh, and the ILRM, Baldwin, warned that this group, which included prominent Communist and former head of the African Blood

[234] Document 352: Ambassador to Washington to Minister of Foreign Affairs, December 30, 1948, Vol. 16, *Officiële Bescheiden*, 432–440.
[235] J. J. Singh to Walter White, telegram, December 28, 1948, Box A321, File "Indonesia, 1948–49, May," *Papers of the NAACP*; Walter White to Roy Wilkins, Thurgood Marshall, and Henry Moon, memo, December 31, 1948, Box A321, File "Indonesia, 1948–49, May," *Papers of the NAACP*; Minutes of the Board of Directors for the International League for the Rights of Man, January 8, 1949, Box A380, File "Leagues: International League for the Rights of Man, 1953–55," *Papers of the NAACP*.
[236] Robert Delson to Walter White, January 3, 1949, Box A321, File "Indonesia, 1948–49, May," *Papers of the NAACP*; Soedarpo Sastroeatomo to Director, January 25, 1949, Box A321, File "Indonesia, 1948–49, May," *Papers of the NAACP*; Ali Sastroadmidjojo and Robert Delson, "The Status of the Republic of Indonesia in International Law," 49, *Columbia Law Review* (March 1949), Box A321, File "Indonesia, 1948–49, May," *Papers of the NAACP*; Republic of Indonesia to [NAACP], "On the Spot Reports of An American Correspondent in Indonesia," n.d., ca. April 1949, Box A321 File "Indonesia, 1948–49, May," *Papers of the NAACP*; Sudarpo Sastrosatomo to Gentlemen, July 7, 1949, Box A321, File "Indonesia, 1949, June-Dec," *Papers of the NAACP*; L. N. Palar to Walter White, May 4, 1949, Box A321, File "Indonesia, 1948–49, May," *Papers of the NAACP*; Madison Jones to Sudarpo Sastrosatomo, July 12, 1949, Box A321, File "Indonesia, 1949, June–Dec.," *Papers of the NAACP*.

FIGURE 4.5. The Netherlands Ambassador to the United States Eelco Van Kleffens relayed to The Hague how Holland's "police action" in Indonesia had turned the American public against the Dutch and threatened access to Marshall Plan funding.
Source: New York World-Telegram & Sun Newspaper Photograph Collection. Courtesy of the Library of Congress, Prints and Photographs Division, LC-DIG-ds-04719.

Brotherhood Richard B. Moore, was "not reliable" and that it would be "advisable to steer clear of it in the future."[237]

This array of organizations had a two-pronged strategy. The first was to continue to generate enough media-savvy events to keep the pressure

---

[237] Charles A. Jayne to Madison Jones, March 27, 1949, Box A321, File "Indonesia, 1948–49, May," *Papers of the NAACP*; Madison Jones to the Committee on Administration, memo, March 28, 1949, Box A321, File "Indonesia, 1948–49, May," *Papers of the NAACP*; Roger Baldwin to Donald Harrington, April 15, 1949, Box 6, File "Harrington, Donald (1948–1958)," *Papers of the ILHR*; Roy Wilkins marginalia on Walter White to Roy Wilkins, April 12, 1949, Box A321, File "Indonesia, 1948–49, May," *Papers of the NAACP*.

on the State Department and the Netherlands. The second was to lobby Congress to shut down the flow of Marshall Plan dollars into Holland as long as the Republic remained under siege and the UN ignored. As a result, there were press releases that swatted away all claims of domestic jurisdiction and, instead, urged the Security Council to "brand the Dutch government as an aggressor and to invoke the sanctions of Chapter VII of the charter," which provided for UN military intervention if necessary. The ILRM also pointed to its "grave concern that the attempt to subdue colonial people by force in the hands of the imperialist powers [could] only lead to the growth of totalitarian influences hostile to the principles of the rights of man."[238]

The India League called for a rally with "leading American public figures and representatives of Asian countries ... to protest the latest Dutch aggression against the Indonesia people."[239] Held in the Roosevelt Auditorium in New York, the January 10 event included Baldwin, who represented the American Civil Liberties Union; Clark Eichelberger, head of the American Association for the United Nations; Stephen Wise, president of the World Jewish Congress; L. N. Palar, the Republic of Indonesia's representative at the UN Security Council; and Madison Jones, administrator for the NAACP.[240]

The Emergency Committee for Indonesia monitored closely the Brewster Amendment in Congress, which sought to ban the use of Marshall Plan dollars to any nation that was in violation of a UN Security Council resolution. This was the very policy that "was called for by the CIO, the National Association for the Advancement of Colored People, United World Federalists, and many other organizations and leaders."[241]

The NAACP, meanwhile, sponsored another anticolonial conference, attended by representatives from fifteen organizations, where the imperialism that was crushing Indonesia took center stage along with the Italian Colonies and South West Africa. The conference's straightforward

---

[238] Minutes of the Board of Directors of the International League for the Rights of Man, January 8, 1949, Box A380, File "Leagues: International League for the Rights of Man, 1953–55," *Papers of the NAACP*; Charter of the United Nations, Chapter VII: Action with Respect to Threats to the Peace, Breaches of the Peace, and Acts of Aggression, http://www.un.org/en/documents/charter/chapter7.shtml. Accessed July 9, 2013.

[239] J. J. Singh to Walter White, telegram, December 28, 1948, Box A321, File "Indonesia, 1948–49, May," *Papers of the NAACP*.

[240] Protest Meeting against Dutch Aggression in Indonesia, January 10, 1949, Box A321, File "Indonesia, 1948–49, May," *Papers of the NAACP*; Madison Jones to Walter White, January 11, 1949, ibid.

[241] Charles A. Jayne Jr. to Roy Wilkins, April 4, 1949, ibid.

resolution rejected the very notion that Holland had any domestic jurisdiction over a land and a people who refused to be colonized. Instead, the Netherlands' so-called "'police action' threaten[ed] international peace and security." The group "therefore urge[d] the Security Council to take the necessary steps, including sanctions, to compel the Netherlands to begin negotiations based upon the recognition of the Indonesian people." Then, staying on script with what the phalanx of organizations had been advocating since the Post-War World Council initiative eighteen months earlier, "We further recommend that the United States cease to advance funds to the Netherlands under the ECA or any other form until this independence has been formally recognized."[242]

Similarly, Americans for the Indonesian Republic pounded on the way the Marshall Plan fueled Holland's ability to wage this war. AIR's press release asserted that "American taxpayer funds" were "being used to make up Dutch deficits brought about by Holland's one million dollar a day expenditure for war in Indonesia." This was an "insane" "waste [of] money, men and goods on colonial conquest." Without the necessary controls of the Brewster Amendment, AIR continued, the Marshall Plan had given "the Netherlands the strength to defy the truce ordered by the United Nations" and made the United States a "partner in crime" in the "brutal war against the Indonesian people."[243]

This agitation all came to a head in April 1949 when the Indian and Australian delegations, tired of the stalemate, pushed hard to move the issue of Dutch defiance in Indonesia out of the rarefied air of the Security Council and into the real court of world public opinion, the UN General Assembly. Australian Minister of External Affairs Herbert Evatt was "most anxious to place Indonesia on the agenda and plunge into discussion about it." He was adamant that "if the pressure were relaxed on the Dutch, there would be no action."[244] The British, who were dealing with an insurgency in Malaysia, and the French, who were in the middle of a full-blown revolution in Vietnam, strenuously

---

[242] Walter White to Rayford Logan, telegram, April 5, 1949, Box A404, File "Rayford Logan, 1948–49," *Papers of the NAACP*; Draft of a Statement to Be Presented for the Consideration of Organizations Invited to the Closed Conference at the Offices of the National Association for the Advancement of Colored People, April 8, 1949, Box A322, File "Italian Colonies, Correspondence Regarding Disposition of, 1948-April 1949," *Papers of the NAACP*.

[243] Emanuel Demby to [NAACP], n.d., ca. March 1949, Box A321, File "Indonesia, 1948–49, May," *Papers of the NAACP*.

[244] Dean Acheson to Dean Rusk, memo, April 12, 1949, Box 64, File "April, 1949," *Acheson Papers*.

argued against this move. Carlos Romulo, of the Philippines, however, countered with the obvious. To date, he noted, "it had to be admitted that the results achieved by the Security Council were not very encouraging." Yes, Britain and the United States, through a recent initiative, had finally managed to get the Dutch to agree to sit down with Republic leaders and negotiate at the Batavia Conference, but, Romulo continued, to have to wait until those talks yielded results, as the delegate from the UK advised, meant that "the Assembly might find itself condemned to inaction." Alluding to the years in which the Dutch trashed one peace conference after the next, one UN-brokered truce after the other, Romulo "again stressed the danger of dilatory tactics, which had already greatly harmed the prestige of the United Nations." L. N. Palar picked up the baton and explained that the Batavia conference, even before it had begun, had the Damocles' sword of Dutch imperialism hanging over it. The Netherlands had made clear, he noted, that sitting at a peace table did not prevent Holland's troops from continuing to wage full-scale war in Indonesia. Palar could only underscore that no stretch of the imagination could make this a truce. Therefore, clinging mightily to the power of public opinion, he asked that the question of Indonesia be placed on the General Assembly's agenda "so that Member States might have an opportunity to demonstrate their friendly feelings towards the Republic of Indonesia and to indicate clearly to the Netherlands what they thought of that country's conduct in Indonesia and of its disregard for the Security Council's decision."[245]

Then Romulo, exposing the way the Cold War had defined whose human rights were worthy of UN scrutiny and whose were not, noted the irony that the delegations which were now questioning the scope of the Assembly's authority were the same "members [who] had spoken with great eloquence about the protection of human rights in connexion with the trial of Cardinal Mindszenty," whom the Communist regime in Hungary had branded a traitor and imprisoned. Yet, Romulo insisted, those human rights, which had energized the West in the case of the Cardinal, were also at stake "with regard to seventy-five million Indonesians. There was no case in which the General Assembly had a greater obligation to make use of the great moral power at its disposal."[246]

---

[245] Summary Record of the Sixtieth Meeting of the General Committee, Third Session – Part II, April 9, 1949, A/BUR/SR.60, Box 76, File "Indonesia: UN General Assembly Records, 1949," *Wehle Papers.*

[246] Ibid.

Poland's representative seized on Romulo's argument and declared that "the same delegations which, at the previous meeting, had appeared to be very much concerned with the fate of a criminal [Mindszenty] by a court of justice of a sovereign country were now trying to prevent the General Assembly from discussing a question relating to the most basic human rights, the right to life and independence, to nationhood and national sovereignty." Meanwhile, he railed, "blood was being shed in Indonesia. The Republic had again fallen under foreign domination.... Yet some of those who claimed to be ardent champions of human rights and of the dignity of the United Nations were attempting to delay consideration." There could be only one reason for this, he surmised, and that was "to make it possible for the invaders to complete their conquest and thus to place before the United Nations a *fait accompli*."[247]

The Soviet delegate, Jacob Malik, also questioned the very validity of this "so-called conference which the representatives of the Netherlands and the Republic of Indonesia were to attend." He derisively observed that the Anglo-American brokered peace talks in Batavia were in "reality ... a conference between prisoners and their gaolers, because the Netherlands Government, in violation of a Security Council resolution ... was continuing to keep them in exile and forbidding them to return to Jogjakarta." How equal, Malik queried, could those negotiations really be? Inmates bargaining with their jailers![248]

The Dutch delegate had heard enough. He fired back "that before accusing certain delegations of changing their position from day to day, the representatives of Poland and the USSR should themselves demonstrate greater logic in their reasoning." Recapping the Soviet bloc's position concerning the General Assembly's authority to discuss the Mindszenty case, he asserted that it was clear that the Communist nations "eloquently expounded the argument that the United Nations had no competence to interfere in the internal affairs of any State." Well, he stated, "the Netherlands Government still exercised sovereignty over Indonesia," and as a result, "the Indonesian question was therefore within the domestic jurisdiction of the Netherlands."[249]

Although there were very few in the room who actually believed there was any merit whatsoever to Holland's stubborn claim to Article 2(7), it was Jacob Malik, the Soviet representative, who parried that assertion

247 Ibid.
248 Ibid.
249 Ibid.

with masterful aplomb. The "cases of Cardinal Mindszenty and the Bulgarian traitors were questions essentially within the domestic jurisdiction of the States concerned," he said. However, Indonesia, "on the other hand, had long since assumed an international character, as it affected the maintenance of international peace and security of the fate of millions of human beings in South-East Asia."[250] Malik's assertion built on Australia and India's July 1947 avowal of this very principle; the Americans' insistence that the Republic participate in the Security Council discussions and the de facto recognition of the Indonesians' independence by a number of states, including the United Kingdom, the United States, India, and others; and the fact that the Republic's representative, L. N. Palar, was in the very room during the current debate.[251] Malik, therefore, zeroed in on the deafening silences as The Hague continued to mouth its trenchant domestic jurisdiction defense. "The argument which the representative of the Netherlands had just advanced," Malik declared, "was based on criteria which had been valid in the seventeenth century." However, he continued, in 1949, in a war of colonial conquest, "it was so weak that even those delegations which supported the Netherlands did not dare to defend it." Domestic jurisdiction had nothing to do with Holland's destruction of the Republic of Indonesia, Malik asserted in the debate's last, definitive word.[252] In a subsequent 41-3-12 vote, only South Africa, Belgium, and the Netherlands voted against placing Holland's war in Indonesia on the General Assembly's agenda.[253]

The Americans, already singed by South Africa's and Italy's colonial problems before the UN, were not about to risk adding more fuel to the anti-West fire.[254] The State Department, which had been bearing down on the Netherlands since December 1948, exponentially increased U.S. pressure on the Dutch to come to terms with Indonesian

[250] Ibid.

[251] Jones, *The United Nations and the Domestic Jurisdiction of States*, 81; Jessup, *The Birth of Nations*, 86; Document 143: DEA/50054–40, Memorandum from Head, United Nations Division to Secretary of State for External Affairs, February 19, 1948, Documents on Canadian External Relations: General Policy: Sub-Section 4, Indonesia, *Canadian Foreign Affairs*.

[252] Summary Record of the Sixtieth Meeting of the General Committee, Third Session – Part II, April 9, 1949, A/BUR/SR.60, Box 76, File "Indonesia: UN General Assembly Records, 1949," *Wehle Papers*.

[253] General Assembly, Verbatim Record of the One Hundred and Ninetieth Plenary Meeting, Second Part of the Third Session, April 12, 1949, A/PV 190, Box 76, File "Indonesia: UN General Assembly Records, 1949," *Wehle Papers*.

[254] Dean Acheson to Dean Rusk, memo, April 12, 1949, Box 64, File "April, 1949," *Acheson Papers*.

independence.[255] By August 1949 Van Kleffens tried to push back. He thought Acheson should understand that the Netherlands "government and people were still smarting under the remarks of Dr. Jessup in the Security Council's session of last January." The Dutch ambassador "did not understand why the U.S. should go so far in castigating the Netherlands." More infuriating, however, Van Kleffens added, was "the continued suspension of ECA aid to Indonesia," which "had two effects – it added greatly to the feeling of the Dutch Government and people that they were being penalized by the US … and it added to the bargaining power of the Indonesians, who interpreted the continued suspension of ECA aid as an indication of US disapproval of the Dutch." Acheson's reply was simple: Marshall Plan support had "become a symbol of far greater importance than its dollar value," and the United States did not want to do anything with those funds that would "work against a prompt settlement of the Indonesian affair."[256]

Thus, through months of arduous negotiations at the Round Table Conference at The Hague; Foreign Minister Stikker threatening not to sign the North Atlantic Treaty; the "deadlock" in talks after the Republic was dumbfounded that the Dutch actually wanted the Indonesians to take on the $2.2 billion debt incurred by Holland for the Second World War and two "police actions," none of which benefitted the archipelago; and the Dutch losing "all their grace" by treating the Indonesians "like bad debtors" because the Republic would not use the oil and tin reserves as collateral to pay Holland's war costs – through it all, Indonesia finally won its independence.[257] The Netherlands and Republic of Indonesia

[255] Rusk to Acheson, March 13, 1949, Box 8, File "Indonesia," Lot File 55D429, *RG 59*; Memorandum of Conversation, Mr. Bancroft and Mr. Ross, March 17, 1949, Box 8, File "Indonesia," Lot File 55D429, *RG 59*; Rusk to Acheson, memo, March 28, 1949, Box 8, File "Indonesia," Lot File 55D429, *RG 59*; Mr. Hickerson to Acheson, March 31, 1949, Box 8, File "Indonesia," Lot File 55D429, *RG 59*; Position Paper: The Indonesian Case, May 2, 1949, SD/A/C.1/214, Box 30, File "Background Book: Indonesian Case in the General Assembly," Entry 3039E, *RG 59*.

[256] Memorandum of Conversation with Acheson and Van Kleffens, August 12, 1949, Box 65, *Acheson Papers*.

[257] For how arduous, see "Summary of the Indonesian Question," April 27, 1949, Box A321, File "Indonesia, 1948–49, May," *Papers of the NAACP*; for NATO threat, see Memorandum of Conversation with Mr. Stikker, Mr. Van Kleffens, the Secretary, Mr. Reed, Mr. Nolting, March 31, 1949, Box 64, File "March, 1949," *Acheson Papers*; Van der Eng, "Marshall Aid as Catalyst in the Decolonization of Indonesia, 1947–49," 349; Memorandum of Conversation between Secretary Acheson and Prime Minister Nehru, October 12, 1949, Box 65, File "October–November 1949," *Acheson Papers*; Summary of Telegrams, October 10, 1949, Box 23, File "State Dept. Briefs File, September-December

reached an "eminently satisfactory" agreement on November 2, 1949, and the Dutch officially recognized Indonesian independence on December 27, 1949.[258]

While there was a widespread sense of jubilation and relief, the Dutch, one State Department official reported, were "very bitter. They resent us and some are not even polite." The Dutch bristled that "they have lost a valuable prize; perhaps the most valuable in the world. They have invested millions ... and now it is all gone. It is a bitter pill to swallow." However, on the other hand, he added, "they have taken hundreds of millions out of the Islands." In this new era, he remarked, "they will have to learn to be contented *traders* instead of *rulers!*"[259]

The Indonesians were as overjoyed as the Dutch were dejected. A jubilant Palar praised the international community for its support. He noted that "[w]ithout the positive assistance which the United Nations rendered, Indonesia's fate would have been decided on the battlefield alone."[260] And, frankly, that was a fight that the Republic would have had major difficulty winning outright. Palar recognized that there were key nations that aided the Indonesians' efforts in the UN. One was the United States, especially when a pneumonia-hobbled Jessup demanded an emergency meeting of the Security Council and became, in the words of the British, "the Angel with the flaming sword who drove the Dutch out of Indonesia."[261] The pneumonia-ridden Angel, however, had enormous help. Palar expressed his nation's gratitude "to Australia and to India for having brought the Indonesian question before the Security Council and the General Assembly." He was particularly appreciative of the effort to get his nation's freedom struggle on the "agenda of the General Assembly." Palar understood that this seminal action

---

1949," *HST:SMOF:NA*; for the debt negotiations, see "Round Table Conference," September 9, 1949, *Report on Indonesia*, Box A321, File "Indonesia, 1949, June-Dec," *Papers of the NAACP*; "The Financial Question at The Hague," October 7, 1949, *Report on Indonesia*, Box A321, File "Indonesia, 1949, June–Dec.," *Papers of the NAACP*.

[258] William Henderson, "Pacific Settlement of Pacific Disputes: The Indonesian Question, 1946–1949," Box 76, File "Security Council Records: UN Committee of Good Offices on Indonesian Question," *Wehle Papers*.

[259] Extracts of Letters of A. C. Hawthorne written from Djakarta, Indonesia, Oct. 12, 1950, October 18, 1950, Reel 1, *Confidential Southeast Asia*. Emphasis in original. Also see Memorandum for the President, Re: Visit of Queen Juliana, April 1, 1952, Box 43, File "State Department Correspondence, 1952, [5 of 6]," *HST:WHCF:CF*.

[260] Statement of Mr. L. N. Palar – issued on the day of transfer at the UN, December 30, 1949, Box A321, File "Indonesia, 1949, June–Dec.," *Papers of the NAACP*.

[261] Jessup, *The Birth of Nations*, 92; Oliver Franks to William Strang, May 26, 1952, CO 936/94.

was the turning point that brought "about the quick conclusion of the dispute."[262]

The ambassador's announcement that independence was finally in sight led Roy Wilkins, now acting secretary of the NAACP, to cable Palar congratulating Indonesia and its people "on the fulfillment of their aspiration for freedom and self-determination." Wilkins noted that "the emergence of Indonesia as an independent state [was] a welcome and heartwarming sign to all those who cherish the hope that the era of colonialism and colonial exploitation [was] approaching its end."[263] Those congratulations, a capstone to years of support and advocacy, were soon followed by meetings as well as subsequent official state dinners and receptions that the NAACP leadership, which had a "continued keen interest ... in the new State of Indonesia," often attended.[264]

The important role of the NAACP, among other NGOs, in shaping the public's understanding and interpretation of what was happening in a land on the other side of the world cannot be overestimated. Their work was critical to creating the enormous pressure that forced the Dutch to realize that the Netherlands East Indies was, indeed, Indonesia.

This should not be surprising. The battle over Indonesia revealed further the complexity of the NAACP's postwar vision and provided an important opportunity for the Association to challenge – even dare – the United States of America to be the anticolonial, democratic nation that it claimed to be. Drawing on the liberatory ethos embodied in the Atlantic and UN Charters, and even, when necessary, the Cold War, the NAACP deployed the United States' stirring language of freedom, democracy, equality, and justice to take on colonialism, racism, and white supremacy.

---

[262] "Press Statement by Ambassador L. N. Palar, Chief of the Indonesian Delegation to the United Nations on the Occasion of the Termination of the RTC at The Hague, 11/2," November 4, 1949, *Report on Indonesia*, Box A321, File "Indonesia, 1949, June-Dec," *Papers of the NAACP*.

[263] Roy Wilkins to L. N. Palar, telegram, December 29, 1949, ibid.; L. N. Palar to Roy Wilkins, December 30, 1949, ibid.

[264] Hemendra K. Rakhit to Walter White, February 15, 1950, Box 3, File "India League of America," *White Papers*; Roy Wilkins to Sirdar J. J. Singh, March 31, 1950, Box A321, File "Indonesia, 1950–51, July," *Papers of the NAACP*; Walter White to Ambassador and Madame Sastroamidjojo, telegram, August 16, 1950, Box A321, File "Indonesia, 1950–51, July," *Papers of the NAACP*; "Walter White Attends Indonesia Reception," press release, August 17, 1950, Box A321, File "Indonesia, 1950–51, July," *Papers of the NAACP*; Soedjatmoko to Walter White, September 6, 1950, Box A321, File "Indonesia, 1950–51, July," *Papers of the NAACP*; Walter White to Soedjatmoko, September 13, 1950, Box A321, File "Indonesia, 1950–51, July," *Papers of the NAACP*; Walter White to Moekarto Notowidigdo, October 16, 1951, Box A321, File "Indonesia, Aug, 1951–52," *Papers of the NAACP*.

The Association juxtaposed America's creed of equal opportunity, and the promise of abundance that comes with it, against the stark reality of systemic discrimination to demonstrate – through stunted life expectancy rates, illiteracy, and poverty data – the unsustainable costs for societies built on the quicksand of racial oppression. The bloodshed in Indonesia was a powerful, cautionary tale about the path to war and strife. Whether the United States understood this and was finally ready to live up to its billing as the "leader of the free world" was, for the NAACP, the big question.

5

Regime Change

We demand that in other parts of British Africa [such as Kenya] no white
minority be given privilege to rule over native majorities; that education
for citizenship and work be undertaken for all native peoples and that the
longstanding promise to admit native Africans to equal status with other
citizens in the British Empire be implemented.
                              – NAACP Colonial Conference, 1945

The war for full colonial liberation was far from over. In fact, it was far
from won. The indigenous freedom fighters and their allies, including the
NAACP, had begun to shake the pillars that propped up the white man's
burden; but shaking and collapsing are two different things. The French,
for example, continued to claim that Tunisia and Morocco were integral
parts of France and, regardless of what happened in Indonesia, held fast
to the concept of domestic jurisdiction. The British response to an epic
insurgency in Kenya rose to a shocking level of brutality and seemed
to only further entrench settler colonialism. Economic devastation in
Africa, Asia, and the Caribbean demanded an investment at a magnitude
that no one was willing to make. Worse still, international agreement on
human rights, which the NAACP deemed essential for real freedom, was
ensnared in the Cold War, Jim Crow, and colonialism and, thus, stalled
at the UN.

In addition, over the course of the 1950s, the Association would face
a series of challenges that made its job of helping destroy colonialism
nearly impossible. Raging conflicts within the organization crescendoed
at the very moment when the NAACP had to maneuver against a new
regime in the White House that was openly hostile and blocked access

to policy makers; the UN was under siege from red-baiting American politicians; and U.S. national security paradigm diverted American economic aid into military hardware and strategic mineral extraction. As a result, the next wave of anticolonial work became a haphazard journey to a decolonized but certainly not independent Third World.[1]

Early on the possibilities still seemed hopeful. Truman, for his 1949 State of the Union address, wanted to deliver a game changer – some foreign policy initiative that would capture the imagination of the American public and, maybe, the world. For the president's speech, however, the State Department warmed up a tired rehash of what the United States was already doing. Truman aide George Elsey was "annoyed" and "disappointed." The department's "well written" and "eloquent" draft had nothing "new in it to excite the country or the world." But then, like "manna from Heaven," a State Department staffer, Ben Hardy, surreptitiously called the White House with an idea that had been repeatedly shot down by his Foggy Bottom bosses. He believed that with the Marshall Plan well underway, the United States could now direct its economic development efforts toward areas outside of Europe. The Americans, Hardy argued, "had the knowledge and the experts to help those countries greatly improve their farming practices, the health of their people, their public works, and their educational systems – indeed much of what was needed to bring them into the modern world."[2] Truman loved the idea, announced it as the fourth point in his 1949 Inaugural Address, and joked with his staff that the State Department and the Bureau of the Budget, which were caught flat-footed and unprepared, would just have to "catch up with me!"[3]

An "angry" State Department refused to budge. A group of staffers had already ripped to shreds an idea floated internally for an African Development Commission, and now, just a month later, out of the blue, Truman announced something similar *for the world*! "Bewildered" department officials argued that it was sheer folly for the United States to "cultivate" and falsely raise "great expectations" about "opportunities" when absolutely no one was contemplating creating individual

[1] Jason C. Parker, "Decolonization, the Cold War, and the Post-Columbian Era," in McMahon, *The Cold War in the Third World*, 124–138; Bradley R. Simpson, "Southeast Asia in the Cold War," in ibid., 48–66.

[2] George McKee Elsey, *An Unplanned Life: A Memoir* (Columbia: University of Missouri Press, 2005), 175; Thomas G. Paterson, "Foreign Aid under Wraps: The Point Four Program," *Wisconsin Magazine of History*, 56, no. 2 (Winter 1972–1973), 121.

[3] Elsey, *An Unplanned Life*, 176.

Marshall Plans for every region of the globe. Staff insisted that America simply "could not afford an amount of aid that would make a dent in the standard of living" in these areas and to try to do so would "open a vast Pandora's box with untold consequence to the United States Government." As a result, the department was determined to stall, hem, and haw to keep the innocuous sounding Point IV "under 'wraps'" for as long as possible.[4]

Oddly enough, Truman was himself part of the problem. Determined to balance the budget, he quickly sent the signal that, although he wanted the impact of the Marshall Plan, he had no intention of requesting the billions it would take to achieve Marshall Plan results. Instead, the majority of the costs were to be borne by private capital instead of the government. As the plan unfolded, the business community balked and refused to be lassoed in. Corporate leaders demanded that all loans made under the program had to be fully guaranteed by the federal government, "[o]therwise Point Four will be 'just another la-de-da plan of high hopes that will fall flat on its face.'"[5] On the other hand, concerns mounted just as quickly that a carte blanche government guarantee of capital investment in Africa, Asia, and the Caribbean would invite, if not incite, reckless lending.[6] The thought of billions squandered in one ill-advised project after the next led R. W. Gifford, the director of Borg-Warner, a Fortune 500 multinational company, to exclaim that "I think it would be almost criminal if we give the other countries the idea that we have ... [the] intention" of trying "to play 'God' to the rest of the world."[7]

---

[4] Paterson, "Foreign Aid under Wraps," 121–122; Kotschnig to Sanders, December 1, 1948, Box 16, File "Economic Commission for Africa," Lot File 55D429, *RG 59*; Memorandum of Conversation with PL Staff, May 11, 1950, Box 65, File "United Nations: Williams, Chester A. – Corres. and Misc., 1946–1952, 1956," *Austin Papers*; Samuel T. Parelman to Mr. Allison, memo, November 19, 1951, Reel 1, *Confidential Southeast Asia*.

[5] "Point IV: Has U.S. Private Capital Reason Enough to March Abroad and Fulfill the President's Rosy Promise?" *Fortune*, February 1950, Box A617, File "State Department: Point IV Program, 1949–54," *Papers of the NAACP*; "Public Discussion of the Point Four Program for Technical and Other Assistance to Underdeveloped Areas: April 13–May 4, 1949," *American Opinion*, Report No. 5, May 9, 1949, Box 62, File "Foreign Relations – Point IV (Public Opinion)," *Papers of George Elsey*, Harry S. Truman Presidential Library, Independence, MO (hereafter *Elsey Papers*).

[6] Staff Memorandum, Financial Aspects of Point IV, May 9, 1949, Box 40, File "State Department, Correspondence, 1948–49 [6 of 6]," *HST:WHCF:CF*.

[7] R. W. Griffin to Isadore [sic] Lubin, December 1, 1949, Box 164, File "Article, 'American Investment and Point IV,'" *Papers of Isador Lubin*, Franklin Delano Roosevelt Presidential Library, Hyde Park, NY (hereafter *Lubin Papers*).

In addition to balance sheet tremors, the "fuzzy" and "disembodied concept" of Point IV conjured up additional fears.[8] Tapping into the long-standing disdain in American society for supposed welfare programs, especially when the recipients were not white, the *Chicago Tribune* and other newspapers roundly denounced Point IV as an "unrealistic" and misguided attempt to "provide the Hottentots with a quart of milk a day."[9] Truman himself warned Elsey, "Just don't play into the hands of crackpots at home – no milk for Hottentots." The president insisted that this was no welfare giveaway program, rather the "'natives' would have to help themselves."[10]

It was not clear how that was possible, given, as even the State Department had to admit, the depth of the "grinding poverty and the lack of economic opportunity for millions in the economically under-developed parts of Africa, the Near and Far East, and certain regions of Central and South America." Isador Lubin, the U.S. representative to the UN Economic and Social Council, would later explain that in these areas there were "wide-spread, deplorable standards of living – so low as to be incomprehensible to the American mind, for few of us have ever experienced anything like it." Half of the world's population, he noted, "receive only 11% of the world income." Worse, yet, Lubin offered, "the tragic fact is that these disparities are widening rather than narrowing."[11] A bootstrap policy for those whom colonialism had stripped of boots, straps, and virtually everything else made a mockery of Truman's stated

---

[8] "Public Discussion of the Point Four Program for Technical and Other Assistance to Underdeveloped Areas: February 11–March 4, 1949," *American Opinion*, Report No. 2, March 7, 1949, Box 62, File "Foreign Relations – Point IV (Public Opinion)," *Elsey Papers*; Barry Hardy, "Measures to Implement President Truman's 'Point Four,'" September 12, 1949, Box 61, File "Foreign Relations – Point IV (correspondence)," *Elsey Papers*.

[9] Linda Gordon, *Pitied but Not Entitled: Single Mothers and the History of Welfare, 1890–1935* (New York: Free Press, 1994); Brent Ruswick, *Almost Worthy: The Poor, Paupers, and the Science of Charity in America, 1877–1917* (Bloomington: Indiana University Press, 2013); Ira Katznelson, *When Affirmative Action Was White: An Untold History of Racial Inequality in Twentieth-Century America* (New York: W.W. Norton, 2006), 25–52; "Public Discussion of the Point Four Program for Technical and Other Assistance to Underdeveloped Areas: August 1–October 5, 1949," *American Opinion*, Report No. 9, October 10, 1949, Box 62, File "Foreign Relations – Point IV (Public Opinion)," *Elsey Papers*.

[10] Paterson, "Foreign Aid under Wraps," 122.

[11] The Address by the Honorable Isador Lubin, United States Representative to the Economic and Social Council, before the National Conference of Catholic Charities, Cleveland, Ohio, Press Release No. 1533, September 12, 1952, Box 53, File "United Nations: Lubin, Isador Appointment and Corres., 1950," *Austin Papers*.

foreign policy plan that "prosperity nourished democracy."[12] Nonetheless, it was with this creaky, contradictory beginning that the vague outlines of a program "slowly but surely" took shape.[13]

The form that it was taking, not surprisingly, greatly worried the NAACP. When Secretary of State Acheson declared in an off-the-record briefing that "'Western Europe is the keystone to Point Four,'" Rayford Logan surmised that the "strategic interests of the Western Powers," not the indigenous people, were actually paramount. "Or, perhaps," the NAACP foreign policy consultant concluded, Truman's "bold new program" was "primarily for the purpose of making the underdeveloped area more profitable for private capital."[14] The NAACP was, in short, alarmed by the ongoing debates that centered solely on business interests and the protection of capital. Those worries were heightened by the constant invocation of the welfare bogeyman allegedly poised to siphon off hard-earned American taxpayer dollars to the "Hottentots" in Africa.

Therefore, in October 1949, Walter White, on leave from the NAACP but still using the media as his bully pulpit, denounced the anti-Point IV tirade spewing out of Congress. He pointedly asked how elected officials could malign a program that was "necessary to prove democracy works" by defining it as nothing more than "just another give-away plan," "charity," and a "welfare state." This was, White railed, "government by invective" and an attempt to "lynch ... as sane and sound a piece of legislation

---

[12] The President's Point Four Program: Recommendations to the Congress, Address by Assistant Secretary Allen, *Department of State Bulletin*, July 4, 1949, 862, Box A617, File "State Department: 1949," *Papers of the NAACP*; Paterson, "Foreign Aid under Wraps," 120.

[13] "Public Discussion of the Point Four Program for Technical and Other Assistance to Underdeveloped Areas" *American Opinion*, Report No. 7, June 9, 1949, Box 62, File "Foreign Relations – Point IV (Public Opinion)," *Elsey Papers*. There is a rich literature on foreign aid. See Michael E. Latham, *The Right Kind of Revolution: Modernization, Development, and U.S. Foreign Policy from the Cold War to the Present* (Ithaca, NY: Cornell University Press, 2011); Nick Cullather, *The Hungry World: America's Cold War Battle Against Poverty in Asia* (Cambridge, MA: Harvard University Press, 2010); David Ekbladh, *The Great American Mission: Modernization and the Construction of an American World Order* (Princeton, NJ: Princeton University Press, 2010); Amanda Kay McVety, *Enlightened Aid: U.S. Development as Foreign Policy in Ethiopia* (New York: Oxford University Press, 2012); Daniel Maul, *Human Rights, Development and Decolonization: The International Labour Organization, 1940–70*, ILO Century Series (New York: Palgrave Macmillan, 2012).

[14] Rayford W. Logan, "Bold New Program or Old Imperialism? Truman's 'Point Four' an Enigma," attached to James W. Ivy to Walter White, May 19, 1949, Box A617, File "State Department: Point IV Program, 1949–54," *Papers of the NAACP*; Rayford Logan to Walter White, March 21, 1949, Box A404, File "Logan, Rayford, 1948–49," *Papers of the NAACP*.

as has come before the Congress in many a session." He was visibly perplexed by the ease with which House Minority Leader Joseph Martin Jr. (R-MA), for example, could talk about the need to watch every nickel and dime when it came to the Caribbean or Asia and then "less than twenty-four hours" later vote "exactly 166 times as much money for military aid to Europe – a program whose success is far more dubious than that of helping nations like India and Haiti lick the problems of hunger, disease, poverty and illiteracy." Wary of the insistent drift toward militarization of foreign aid and U.S. policy, White averred that the "Point Four program is not perfect. But it charts a new course at a cost less than that of a single aircraft carrier or a few bombers." American foreign policy needed to refocus, he insisted. "We must prove something – that human beings all over the world will eat more and better food, live more secure and healthy lives, and be more content under democracy." That outcome can only be obtained, White concluded, with "Point Four, the abolition of colonialism, and the ending of race and religious prejudice."[15]

Rayford Logan, testifying before the House Foreign Affairs Committee as the NAACP's representative, therefore, pounced on one of the major imperfections in Point IV. "A great deal had been said before the Committee about the protection of capital, but he had not heard … 'one word about the protection of labor.'" And that was a problem. "If treaties can provide protection for capital, patents and copyrights, surely," he asserted, they "can also provide protection for labor." The NAACP had consistently noted that one of the foundational principles of colonialism was the systematic and brutal exploitation of labor. Logan cited statistic after statistic from the colonial powers' own reports to the UN, which showed "that in some areas wages are as low as $2.00 a month." If, he argued, the goal of the much ballyhooed Point IV was to raise "the standards of living" of people in "underdeveloped areas," that required protecting the very labor of those people.[16] (See Figure 5.1)

Not only did the Association take this message into the media and before Congress, but also it sought to sway the contingent of NGOs discussing this potential landmark economic development program. To

---

[15] Walter White, "Point Four Program Necessary to Prove Democracy Works," October 6, 1949, Box A81, File "Articles: Walter White Syndicated Column, 1949," *Papers of the NAACP.*

[16] Summary of Testimony of Rayford W. Logan: House Foreign Affairs Committee Hearings on Point IV, October 5, 1949, Reel 17, *NAACP-Int'l*; "Extend Aid to Africa, NAACP Urges Congress," press release, October 13, 1949, Box A4, File "Africa: General, 1947–49," *Papers of the NAACP.*

FIGURE 5.1. Kenyan mother and child's plight in Nairobi highlights the NAACP's twin concerns about colonialism and the grinding poverty that comes in its wake. It also demonstrated the need for a viable Point IV program, despite the disparaging comments about a welfare program for the Hottentots.
Source: Bettman/Corbis. Courtesy of Corbis, Stock Photo ID# 42-50589439.

be sure, groups such as Social Action recognized the need for Point IV because "hundreds of millions … live in underdeveloped areas" where their "average annual income is less than $100 per year per person."[17] Others were wary. As the Post-War World Council made clear, the "history to date of investment in the underdeveloped areas has given the people of those areas no reason to look forward with confidence to further development by means of Western capital." In fact, "the dismal indifference of previous investors to sociological factors [such as] as the land holding system and peasant credit has resulted *in an inverse relationship*

---

[17] "Christians and the Point IV Program," *Social Action*, October 15, 1949, Box 164, File "Article, 'American Investment and Point IV,'" *Lubin Papers*.

between development and living standards."[18] Indonesia was a case in point. Although the Dutch insisted that they had "invested millions," it was also evident that "like most white Colonists, they have neglected many fundamental, progressive things that might have made their position stronger." For example, there were "very few Indonesians who have even as much as a high-school education."[19] This conundrum was the impetus behind "an all-day" gathering of a number of organizations to discuss Point IV's "relationship ... to the containment of Communism, Point IV as a means of promoting world revolution among dependent peoples and the degree of control that should be exercised." Invited to the off-the-record meeting by the Post-War World Council, the Association leadership knew this would be "an excellent opportunity for the NAACP to present its views in the presence of a very influential panel."[20] The Association had a perspective and history that eluded the others who assembled. As Logan bluntly noted, "I was the only colored person in attendance."[21]

During the discussion, he first stressed "the need for the peoples of the underdeveloped areas to participate in the formulation and execution of policies." The NAACP wanted guarantees that indigenous peoples would be fully involved in the design and implementation of any economic development plan. Anything less would replicate the old, disastrous model in which Westerners ran rough shod over traditional cultures and practices and sent those societies spiraling into poverty and starvation. Logan's second point was that in the selection of personnel to be trained "there shall be no discrimination." That recommendation was born of hard-earned experience. Logan and many other black academics like him had dealt with the weight of Jim Crow and its uncanny ability to trample degrees, experience, intelligence, and ability with a mantra of "Negroes need not apply." Exporting Jim Crow and thereby eliminating people of color from

---

[18] Post War World Council Off the Record Conference, October 29, 1949, Box A617, File "State Department: Point IV Program, 1949–54," *Papers of the NAACP.* Emphasis in original.

[19] Extracts from Letters of A. C. Hawthorne, October 18, 1950, Reel 1, *Confidential Southeast Asia.*

[20] Mary W. Hillyer to Friend, September 30, 1949, Box A634, File "United Nations: General, 1948–49," *Papers of the NAACP;* Activities of Dr. Rayford W. Logan on Point Four, March 27, 1950, Box A404, File "Logan, Rayford, 1950–51," *Papers of the NAACP;* Rayford Logan to Roy Wilkins, October 22, 1949, Box A634, File "United Nations: General, 1948–49," *Papers of the NAACP.*

[21] Rayford Logan to Roy Wilkins, October 31, 1949, Box A404, File "Rayford Logan, 1948–49," *Papers of the NAACP.*

training and educational opportunities contradicted the very rationale for the program. Third, Logan stressed that to wipe out the condescending, paternalistic air of white supremacy that seemed to permeate and disrupt economic development programs, "personnel should be chosen for their skill in human relations as well as in technical matters." Finally, he concluded, Point IV would be incomplete and unsustainable unless there was "protection of labor in the underdeveloped areas." To Logan's "great surprise the representatives broke out in spontaneous applause."[22]

The NAACP's foreign policy consultant then took the vision into a meeting at the State Department. There he was confronted with the fundamental contradictions between principle and prejudice that consistently vexed American foreign and domestic policy. A few months earlier, in December 1948, the UN had completed the Declaration of Human Rights, which was the first full articulation of the array of rights that all people held. By design, however, it was just a declaration, not a legally binding treaty. That was next. And at State, Logan learned that the proposed Covenant on Human Rights, which was now being drafted in the UN, was going to be stripped of all of the "economic and social provisions of the International Declaration of Human Rights." Eleanor Roosevelt tried to explain that any attempt to place in the treaty the economic and social rights delineated in the Declaration, especially those protecting labor, ensuring a standard of living, and guaranteeing the right to education "would insure defeat by the UN and by the Senate."[23]

Realizing what was at stake, Logan pressed the issue. For him, the Senate's recalcitrance was easy enough to trace. The powerful Southern Democrats worried mightily that a human rights treaty, as the law of the land, would upend Jim Crow and break their stranglehold on electoral politics and federal policy. Channing Tobias later explained that contrary to the South's standard operating procedure, "human rights in a democracy are not privileges to be parcelled out condescendingly by the strong to the disadvantaged, but are inherent in citizenship in a democracy." The South was determined, however, to deny human rights and even the basics of life to maintain its inordinate and disproportionate power not only over African Americans but also over U.S. domestic and foreign policy. In short, the South had a pit bull-like grip on the Senate

---

[22] Ibid.

[23] Rayford Logan to Roy Wilkins, November 12, 1949, Box A634, File "United Nations: General, 1948–49," *Papers of the NAACP*; UN Declaration of Human Rights, Articles 23, 24, 25, and 26, http://www.un.org/en/documents/udhr/index.shtml#a19. Accessed September 21, 2013; Anderson, *Eyes Off the Prize*, 15, 135, 137.

and would keep human rights from escaping out of the Declaration and into a treaty. But the UN? Logan asked who, specifically, at the United Nations would balk at fundamental, basic economic and social rights. Roosevelt "flatly stated that all the colonial powers oppose the inclusion of these provisions."[24]

The NAACP consultant, who had once defined himself as "a bad Negro with a Ph.D.," connected the seemingly disparate policy dots. He pointedly asked, "How one can reconcile the omission of economic and social provisions in the Draft treaty with Point IV?"[25] That is to say, how, on one hand, can the United States talk about helping the indigenous people raise the standard of living, improve the quality of education, and enhance access to health care via Truman's "bold new program" and then simultaneously be willing to trash those very provisions in a landmark human rights treaty? The answer was simple – the American South and the Global North.

The combination of an entrenched Confederacy and bitter-end European colonizers was a powerful one-two punch. While the American South worked feverishly, as Mississippi Senator James O. Eastland revealed, "to maintain white supremacy," the State Department's Working Group on Colonial Problems explained that the European powers had a vested interest in slowing down independence and the ability of the colonized to govern:

[A]dministering powers, while accepting the need for advancing the welfare of the inhabitants of dependent areas, regard these areas as essential for national prestige and for economic and military reasons. Accordingly, their inclination is to move more slowly in the direction of self-government or independence than would clearly be possible if preparation of the peoples for these goals were the sole or even primary aim.[26]

The Association understood that to outmaneuver the European powers, the NAACP needed to work through other liberal organizations to

[24] Rayford Logan to Roy Wilkins, November 12, 1949, Box A634, File "United Nations: General, 1948–49," *Papers of the NAACP*; Anderson, *Eyes Off the Prize*, 135, 137; Channing Tobias, "Building Better Human Relations is Everybody's Business – the World View and America's Responsibility," September 2, 1952, attached to Channing Tobias to Mrs. Franklin D. Roosevelt, September 17, 1952, Box 3378, File "Tobias, Dr. Channing, 1946–52," *Roosevelt Papers*.

[25] Rayford Logan to Roy Wilkins, November 12, 1949, Box A634, File "United Nations: General, 1948–49," *Papers of the NAACP*; Anderson, *Eyes Off the Prize*, 15.

[26] Berg, *Ticket to Freedom*, 96; Working Group on Colonial Problems, August 1, 1952, CP D-5/2, Box 18, File "SP: Working Group on Colonial Problems," Lot File 60D257, RG 59.

shape the way the public and leadership understood Point IV. Logan conveyed that "even in this group it was apparent that it was necessary for some one to be present to emphasize Africa and the participation of Natives in the formulation and execution of plans under Point IV."[27] By February 1950, Logan was pleased to report that at the "meeting of the Non Governmental Organizations at the State Department ... two of the four points" that the NAACP had stressed at the initial gathering were "now generally accepted." The first was that those selected to provide training must have the expertise as well as the ability to work on a basis of equality with people of color. The second was that "there should be as much protection for labor as for capital."[28] Logan then followed up the next month at a meeting of the American Association for the United Nations. "It gave the NAACP an opportunity," he wrote, "to present its 'Four Point Program for Point Four' to representatives of other organizations who may not have heard it before." Logan was "gratified to see that other representatives," such as those from the ACLU and the AFL, "are now presenting some of our points and others are coming along to support them."[29]

All of this was groundwork for the full-scale Congressional debate held in the spring of 1950. Given the earlier rumblings about "welfare," and the rhetoric about providing blanket protection for business while leaving workers fully exposed, the NAACP was rightly worried that Point IV would be "emasculat[ed]" going through the legislative grinder.[30] Logan was eager to testify before the Senate and lay out the Association's agenda, but he had a previous, unbreakable commitment. The NAACP, therefore, sent in Howard University professor William Leo Hansberry, teacher and mentor to Nnamdi Azikiwe and Kwame Nkrumah, as its representative, not only to endorse "heartily the declared aims and objectives of" H.R. 7346 but also to identify "certain parts of its text ... which need to be amplified and clarified." Hansberry pointed out that the bill "will include operations in a number of colonial regions where, under present arrangements, the native inhabitants have very little, if any opportunity

[27] Rayford Logan to Roy Wilkins, January 2, 1950, Box A404, File "Logan, Rayford, 1950–51," *Papers of the NAACP*.
[28] Rayford Logan to Roy Wilkins, February 4, 1950, ibid.
[29] Rayford Logan to Roy Wilkins, March 8, 1950, ibid.
[30] M. D. Jackson to Roy Wilkins, March 27, 1950, Box A404, File "Logan, Rayford, 1950–51," *Papers of the NAACP*; Roy Wilkins to Rep. John Kee, Rep. John W. McCormack, and Rep. Joseph Martin, telegram, March 28, 1950, Box 1235, File "413 (1945–1949)," *HST:OF*.

to participate in the formulation of the larger policies which determine and regulate economic conditions in such regions." Because the indigenous voices have been silenced, Hansberry insisted, "most colonial peoples governed by these powers have derived little, if any, direct benefits" from previous development plans such as the ECA. This was no small matter because, as Hansberry noted, "under H.R. Bill 7346 ... there are no provisions which make it certain that native peoples ... in the colonies and protectorates will have the opportunity to make direct requests for assistance to the agencies which will administer the Point Four program." Without this provision, without the active participation of the indigenous inhabitants to devise and execute the proposals that will enhance the standard of living, "it is going to prove well nigh impossible to convince these peoples that the present 'Act for International Development' ... is not just another device, under a new guise, to strengthen the old-fashioned imperialism of the past." It was therefore essential that "specific legislative guarantees in the Act itself ... safeguard the rights of the colonial peoples." The European powers would, Hansberry predicted, sputter about their sovereignty, "but in view of the new emphasis which is now being placed upon human rights by democratic nations, I am confident that the safeguards that should be included in this legislation would provide no obstacles which the statesmen of our own and the other governments concerned could not surmount." Democracy, he concluded, depended on it.[31]

Yet the bill's movement through the House and Senate reflected, instead, a gnawing ambivalence about foreign aid, particularly in Asia, Africa, and the Caribbean. For a program that was ostensibly designed to "bring about conditions in the world in which democratic government and institutions can survive and flourish," especially in some of the most economically devastated areas throughout the globe, the administration had asked for only $45 million out of a proposed federal budget of $3.175 trillion. And, for some members in the House, especially future Secretary of State Christian Herter (R-MA), even that was too much. Logan reported that "Herter led the fight for the reduction of the appropriation from $45 million to $25 million." NAACP board member Senator Herbert Lehman (D-NY), in arguing for restoration of the full appropriation, countered that given the relatively small funding request,

[31] Testimony presented by William Leo Hansberry to the Senate Foreign Relations Committee on H.R. 7346, April 3, 1950, Box A404, File "Logan, Rayford, 1950–51," *Papers of the NAACP*.

which amounted to "less than 1 ½ percent of the total expenditure authorized in the bill," our "object in this program is not to get credit for playing Santa Claus, but rather to reap the greater benefits which would come from helping to dispel the atmosphere of economic hopelessness in which totalitarianism and tyranny thrive."[32]

The economic hopelessness was tied, of course, to the horrific exploitation of labor. Or, as Francis Sayre would later explain, "Peoples can be as effectively manacled by economic and social forms of servitude as by political oppression."[33] Although the Senate maneuvered to restore some of the funding cut by the House, key and powerful elements in the Upper Chamber worked feverishly to remove any mention of labor. The House of Representatives, for all of its parsimony, had included language in the Point IV legislation that placed "labor standards in relation to investment." The House noted that the success of this program was dependent upon "confidence on the part of the people of the underdeveloped areas that investors will conserve as well as develop local resources, will bear a fair share of local taxes and observe local laws, and will negotiate adequate wages and working conditions for local labor." Rayford Logan proudly observed that "this is one of the four points which I have presented from the beginning." However, the Senate Committee on Foreign Relations, chaired by arch-segregationist Tom Connally, "took out the clause for the protection of labor which the House had put in." Logan informed Wilkins that "Southern Senators saw in this clause a kind of international FEPC [Fair Employment Practices Committee]," and it was doomed. By the time the Senate and House versions of the bill emerged out of the conference committee, Point IV came into being at least $10 million short and with the protection of labor nowhere to be found.[34]

The implementation of the program was further compromised by the onset of the Korean War just a few months later. In 1945, with Tokyo's

---

[32] Report of Meetings of NGO's at the State Department, March 29 and 30, 1950, attached to Rayford Logan to Roy Wilkins, April 9, 1950, Box A404, File "Logan, Rayford, 1950–51," *Papers of the NAACP*; U.S. Congress, Senate, Senator Lehman of New York Speaking for the Foreign Assistance Bill, S. 3304, 81st Cong., 2nd sess. *Congressional Record* 96, pt. 5 (April 25, 1950), 5695, 5696.

[33] Francis B. Sayre, "The Problem of Underdeveloped Areas in Asia and Africa," *Proceedings of the American Academy of Arts and Sciences*, 81, no. 6 (April 9, 1952), Box 13, File "United Nations: Printed Matter," *Sayre Papers*.

[34] Report of Meetings of NGO's at the State Department, March 29 and 30, 1950, attached to Rayford Logan to Roy Wilkins, April 9, 1950, Box A404, File "Logan, Rayford, 1950–51," *Papers of the NAACP*; U.S. Congress, Senate, Technical Cooperation Program Bill, H.R. 7797, 81st Cong., 2nd sess., *Congressional Record* 96, pt. 6 (May 23, 1950), 7527.

defeat, the Allies divided the former Japanese colony at the 38th parallel until they had time to give some meaningful thought about what to do with Korea. In the interim, communists ruled the north and American allies the south. After a series of provocations from both sides of the dividing line, in April 1950 North Korean leader Kim Il Sung convinced Stalin that an attack on the South would be quick and easy and, most important, unify the peninsula under Marxist-Leninist rule. Eventually convinced, the Soviet leader gave the go-ahead with a caveat to have Mao Zedong approve the plan, as well.[35] On June 25, 1950, Kim Il Sung struck like a cobra and obliterated the dividing line. When Truman received word from Acheson, the president had "already concluded the worst." His daughter Margaret reported that "[m]y father ... made it clear, from the moment he heard the news, that he feared this was the opening of World War III."[36] As historian Steven Casey explained, for Truman "the invasion could denote only one thing: the Soviet Union had decided to escalate the Cold War, boldly switching its target from Europe to Asia and changing its expansionist methods from internal subversion to armed invasion and war."[37] The unprepared South Korean and American troops were quickly outgunned, outmanned, and overrun until they were clinging for dear life on the tip of Korea at the Pusan Perimeter.[38]

A defeat of this magnitude, coming on the heels of Mao Zedong's victory in China and the Soviets' unexpected and successful testing of an atomic device in 1949, would, many were sure, sound the death knell for the West. The United States, thus, hurled virtually everything it had into the inferno. While tens of thousands of troops were mobilized and dumped into the battle and the U.S. government poured billions into the

[35] Allan R. Millett, *The War for Korea, 1950–1951: They Came from the North* (Lawrence: University of Kansas Press, 2010), 47–52; William W. Stueck, *The Korean War: An International History* (Princeton, NJ: Princeton University Press, 1995); Bruce Cumings, *The Origins of the Korean War* (Princeton, NJ: Princeton University Press, 1981, 1990); Stalin to Kim Il Sung (Via Shtykov), telegram, March 18, 1950, document 110683, Cold War International History Project (hereafter CWIHP); Shtykov to Vyshinski Regarding Meeting with Kim Il Sung, telegram, March 21, 1950, document 112044, CWIHP; Roshchin to Stalin, telegram, May 13, 1950, document 112023, CWIHP; Cable from Roshchin to Stalin, Relaying Mao's Request for Clarification on North Korea Taking Action against South Korea, May 13, 1950, document 115977, CWIHP; Cable from Vyshinsky to Mao Zedong, Relaying Stalin's Stance on Permission for North Korea to Attack South Korea, May 14, 1950, document 115976, CWIHP.
[36] David McCullough, *Truman* (New York: Simon & Schuster, 1992), 774.
[37] Steven Casey, *Selling the Korean War: Propaganda, Politics, and Public Opinion, 1950–1953* (New York: Oxford University Press, 2008), 19.
[38] Millett, *The War for Korea*, 87–106; 128–143.

American South and West to build the defense industry infrastructure
to wage an unrelenting Cold War, foreign economic aid transformed,
virtually overnight, into military packages and schemes to extract and
stockpile strategic raw minerals.[39] Point IV was one of the first on the
chopping block as its $35 million appropriation got shredded by the
Korean War.[40]

It was clear to all that this was a new day.[41] Michael Scott, still working hard to free South West Africa, complained that "the atmosphere
at the UN has been very much clouded by the Korean War." And, he
continued, "uppermost in the minds of the great powers is the necessity to build up a system of military security against their opponents."
The result, Scott said, was an emphasis on "the more short term need
for bases" and collusion "with those ... in power" such as the apartheid
regime in Pretoria.[42]

But Scott also noticed "a great dearth of any strong pressure groups
behind those more long-term positive ideas" such as human rights.[43] The
NAACP, for its part, was becoming distracted by a scandal of soap opera
proportions. It all began years earlier on a rainy night, after White came
back from his father's funeral and fell into the arms and the bed of a
longtime and married friend, Poppy Cannon. More than a decade later,
the sometimes off and now passionately on lovers resolved to have the
"courage and the stamina" in Jim Crow America, where sexual relations
between a black man and a white woman were criminal in many states,
to grab at "a second chance at happiness." Both were in marriages that
had grown stale, cold, and routine while the passion – both physical
and mental – between the lovers was at a fevered pitch. Cannon anx-
iously wrote her "Beloved" that "[w]e can't keep living bored ... regret-
ting the past. We *mustn't* let ourselves become paralyzed by fears for the

---

[39] Paul G. Pierpaoli Jr., *Truman and Korea: The Political Culture of the Early Cold War*
(Columbia: University of Missouri Press, 1999), 16–47; James E. Webb to the President,
memo, December 18, 1950, Box 41, File "State Department Correspondence [5 of
5]," *HST:WHCF:CF*; William S. Paley to Henry G. Bennett, memo, May 10, 1951, Box
124, File "State Dept. of," *RG 220: PMPC*.

[40] Walter White to Herbert Lehman, Dennis Chavez, and Leverett Saltonstall, telegram, July
11, 1950, Box A617, File "State Department: Point IV Program, 1949–54," *Papers of the
NAACP*.

[41] Dorothy Norman to Walter White, March 28, 1952, Box A284, File "Foreign Affairs:
Asia, 1950–52," *Papers of the NAACP*.

[42] Michael Scott to David Astor, October 19, 1950, Box 15, File "Correspondence with
Papers Re: SWA, 1950–1961," *Scott Papers*.

[43] Ibid.

future."[44] After suffering a major heart attack and coming to grips with the reality of a life only half lived, by May 1949 White finally agreed and tried to resign in June from the NAACP citing his failing health. However, the board, which had no idea about Poppy Cannon, refused to accept his resignation and insisted on a medical leave of absence, instead, naming Wilkins as the acting secretary. When a few days later, White dropped the bombshell – he received a quickie divorce from his African American wife of twenty-seven years and immediately married Cannon – the uproar was intense. As Wilkins told it, "half of the NAACP's members with whom he spoke 'wanted to lynch Walter for leaving Gladys, and the other half wanted to string him up for marrying a white woman.'"[45]

The aftershock exposed underlying, simmering tensions in the NAACP. Board member Judge Jane Bolin had already clashed with the executive staff repeatedly. She particularly bristled at the sense that the board was mere window dressing for whatever the Association's administrators wanted to do. Her concerns came to a head in June 1949, when Bolin strenuously questioned the propriety of a press release that Wilkins authorized, which announced that the board had voted to appoint him as acting secretary during Walter White's leave of absence. The problem, as Bolin so clearly pointed out, was that the board had not even met, much less voted, before word of Wilkins's promotion was on the newsstands. Not only was it presumptuous and unacceptable, she asserted, but also that kind of stunt "made board members appear to be rubber stamps."[46]

Wilkins, resentful of Bolin's stinging (if legitimate) criticism, struck back. The Nominating Committee, led by his ally Daisy Lampkin, was not scheduled to convene for several months, yet within weeks Bolin's name mysteriously disappeared from the list of board members for the July meeting.[47] Then, in September her name could be found in neither the "Will Be Present" nor the "Regrets" columns for the board meetings. The fact that Bolin actually attended the meeting heightened the urgency of making her removal official.[48] In October 1949, the *Baltimore Afro-*

---

[44] Poppy Cannon to Walter White, February 24, 1949, Box 8, File "White, Poppy Cannon (1949)," *White Papers*; Janken, *White*, 329–330.
[45] Anderson, *Eyes Off the Prize*, 157–59.
[46] Minutes of the Meeting of the Board of Directors, June 13, 1949, Reel 3, *NAACP*.
[47] Minutes of the Meeting of the Board of Directors, July 14, 1949, Reel 3, *NAACP*. There is no meeting in August, following the annual convention.
[48] Minutes of the Meeting of the Board of Directors, September 12, 1949, Reel 3, *NAACP*.

American reported that a "staff meeting was called at the national office ... when it was stated that 'Bolin has to go'" because "we can't get along with her."[49] The director of the NAACP's legal department, Thurgood Marshall, swore that although there was a meeting, nothing like that was ever said.[50] Despite his insistence, it was clear that Bolin, who had been removed from the powerful board and demoted to the honorific role of vice president, had just been "liquidated."[51] Bolin, who was steel and brilliance personified, did not quietly accept her silencing; instead, she fired off a resignation "letter so hot the paper almost scorched."[52]

In truth, Jane Bolin came into the crosshairs not only because she questioned Roy Wilkins's judgment, but also because she demanded board autonomy, backed branches in their skirmishes with the National Office, and was openly unconvinced of a "communist threat" to the NAACP. Equally important, she was falling in love with and would soon marry a staff member, Reverend Walter Offutt Jr., who reported directly to Wilkins.[53]

Offutt, who was the Association's church secretary, had a well-known and well-earned reputation for having the "courage to speak up" when he saw a wrong.[54] The underhanded assassination of Bolin's character

[49] "Removal of Judge Bolin from NAACP Board Bared," *Afro American*, October 8, 1949.
[50] Thurgood Marshall to Carl Murphy, October 13, 1949, Box A124, File "Board of Directors: Bolin, Jane B., 1943–1950," *Papers of the NAACP*.
[51] Hubert Delany to Roy Wilkins, November 9, 1949, Box 3338, File "NAACP, 1949," *Roosevelt Papers*.
[52] Roy Wilkins to Judge Bolin, January 10, 1950, Box A124, File "Board of Directors: Bolin, Jane B., 1943–50," *Papers of the NAACP*; Minutes of the Meeting of the Board of Directors, February 14, 1950, Reel 3, *NAACP*; Lillian Scott, "Along Celebrity Row," *Chicago Defender*, March 25, 1950; William O. Walker, "Down the Big Road," *Cleveland Call and Post*, March 25, 1950; "Judge Jane Bolin Quits NAACP, Scores Board: Woman Justice Scores Roy Wilkins, Staff, Quits Vice Presidency," *Los Angeles Sentinel*, March 16, 1950; "N.A.A.C.P. Spokesmen Say Judge Bolin's Criticisms Unfair," *Cleveland Call and Post*, March 25, 1950.
[53] Roy Wilkins to Hubert Delany, November 1, 1949, Box 3338, File "NAACP, 1949," *Roosevelt Papers*; Hubert Delany to Roy Wilkins, November 9, 1949, Box 3338, File "NAACP, 1949," *Roosevelt Papers*; "N.Y. Branch Answers Charge," *Atlanta Daily World*, October 22, 1949; Minutes of the Meeting of the Board of Directors, November 14, 1949, Reel 3, *NAACP*; Minutes of the Meeting of the Board of Directors, December 12, 1949, Reel 3, *NAACP*; William Lloyd Imes, Hubert T. Delany, Earl B. Dickerson, James E. Allen, and Lindsay H. White to Branch President, November 16, 1949, Box A124, File "Board of Directors: Bolin, Jane B., 1943–50," *Papers of the NAACP*; Izzy Rowe's Notebook, *Pittsburgh Courier*, November 24, 1951; Ed R. Harris, "On the Town," *Philadelphia Tribune*, November 17, 1951; "Married," *Jet*, November 15, 1951.
[54] Madison Jones to Walter White, memo, January 17, 1947, Box A594, File "Staff: Walter Offutt, 1946–49," *Papers of the NAACP*.

infuriated him. He fearlessly told everyone in the room at the October meeting – board and executive staff alike – that "the Association [was] in a pitiful plight from within and from without.... The morale [was] as low as it can get short of violence." The leadership, he continued, had engaged in "indecent and unethical things." Decay and suspicion had permeated the National Office and were now seeping into the branches. Then Offutt concluded, in a barely deflected allusion to Wilkins, "like priest, like parish."[55]

Retribution was swift. Wilkins, who had once considered Offutt "a young, well trained, well educated minister, with a pleasing personality," now reversed course.[56] He demanded, in the most blistering, unyielding terms, immediate "proof" of Offutt's accusation of impending collapse, mismanagement, and ethical lapses in judgment.[57] The minister's matter-of-fact, terse response only further enraged Wilkins.[58] When, for example, Offutt questioned why his office had to go for more than a month without any secretarial support, Wilkins pointedly fired back, "You are not doing a full time job here at the NAACP."[59] The acting secretary then laid out more precisely what he considered to be Offutt's deficiencies. "You are not doing any original thinking about the Church department, initiating projects, or thinking up ways and means of making your work effective." In short, Wilkins asserted, "your work is not satisfactory, the Association is not getting out of your department what we have a right to expect, and unless you can show great improvement in ... six months ... we shall have to make other plans."[60]

---

[55] Minutes of the Meeting of the Board of Directors, October 10, 1949, Reel 3, *NAACP*.
[56] Roy Wilkins to Bishop John A. Gregg, March 24, 1948, Box A540, File "Speakers – Offutt, Walter, 1947–48," *Papers of the NAACP*.
[57] Minutes of the Meeting of the Board of Directors, October 10, 1949, Reel 3, *NAACP*; Wilkins to Offutt, memo, October 13, 1949, Box A594, File "Staff: Offutt, Walter, 1946–1949," *Papers of the NAACP*; Wilkins to Offutt, memo, October 21, 1949, Box A594, File "Staff: Offutt, Walter, 1946–49," *Papers of the NAACP*.
[58] Bobbie Branche to Roy Wilkins, March 22, 1950, Box A594, File "Staff – Offut, Rev. Walter, 1950–54," *Papers of the NAACP*; Walter Offutt to Walter White, draft letter, n.d., ca. June 9, 1950, ibid.; Roy Wilkins to Walter White, July 13, 1950, ibid.; Walter Offutt to Walter White, July 26, 1950, ibid.; Walter White to Roy Wilkins, October 13, 1950, ibid.; Roy Wilkins to Walter Offutt, March 17, 1952, ibid.; Walter White to Walter White, July 8, 1953, ibid.; Walter White to Mr. McClain, July 7, 1954, ibid.; Walter Offutt to Walter White, July 9, 1954, ibid.; Walter White to Walter Offutt, July 29, 1954, ibid.
[59] Roy Wilkins to Walter Offutt, March 30, 1950, ibid.; Walter Offutt to Bobbie Branche, March 17, 1950, ibid.
[60] Roy Wilkins to Walter Offutt, March 30, 1950, ibid.

Aside from its general effect on morale, this treacherous dispute had a direct impact on the NAACP's ability to be effective in its international efforts. As Logan became more and more absorbed in other work, Offutt was becoming, in addition to the liaison with the black churches, the Association's representative on key human rights organizations dealing with colonialism and the NAACP's eyes, ears, persuader, and anticolonial advocate at the United Nations.[61] And Wilkins's enmity ensured that minimal resources would trickle down to support his endeavors.

Further undercutting the Association's ability to respond effectively to the geopolitical roller coaster of Cold War America was the tug-of-war that occurred when White decided in early 1950 that he wanted to return to the NAACP. Given the furor that his divorce and subsequent marriage had caused, his less-than-honest posture with the board when submitting his resignation, that during the last few months of his leadership the Association had suffered a major political setback when the filibuster rule, which the Southern Democrats had used to block all civil rights legislation, was strengthened immeasurably, White's return was certainly not assured.[62] But he was wily and determined. Wilkins was just as determined. For years, the assistant secretary had thought he could do a much better job than White – he had made that clear to John Hammond years ago. And, now, as the acting secretary, he was ready to permanently assume the helm of the NAACP. In fact, several board members had intimated to him that once White's year-long medical leave was up, the position was Wilkins's.[63]

However, by early February 1950, according to the *New York Amsterdam News*, the board was supposedly "calling upon Mr. White to return to put the Association together because it [was] falling apart." Everyone, of course, denied it, but there it was, circulating in the black press, that under Wilkins's leadership, the NAACP was near ruins.[64]

---

[61] Roger Baldwin to James B. Orrick, October 28,1952, Box 8, File "United Nations Observers at U.N. Representing the League (1950–55)," *Papers of the ILHR*; Roger Baldwin to Walter Offutt, October 5, 1953, Box A5, File "Africa: Organizations, 1952–55," *Papers of the NAACP*; Minutes of the Board of Directors Meeting: International League for the Rights of Man, October 18, 1953, Box A5, File "Africa: Organizations, 1952–55," *Papers of the NAACP*; International League for the Rights of Man, March–April Bulletin 1954, Box A380, File "Leagues: International League for the Rights of Man, 1942–52," *Papers of the NAACP*.

[62] For the strengthening of the filibuster rule and how some board members blamed White, see Anderson, *Eyes Off the Prize*, 156–57, 158.

[63] Ibid., 159.

[64] Minutes of the Meeting of the Board of Directors, February 14, 1950, Box 3338, File "NAACP, 1950," *Roosevelt Papers*.

Meanwhile Eleanor Roosevelt was convinced that the acting secretary had written a vicious letter disparaging White's interracial marriage and she, therefore, threatened to resign from the board of directors. Wilkins swore that he never did anything of the sort, insisted, as diplomatically as he possibly could, that Mrs. Roosevelt produce the letter, and pleaded with the powerful and well-connected former first lady to remain on the board. But it was clear to all, as the dust settled, that only Walter White's presence could keep the highly valuable Roosevelt's name on the NAACP's letterhead.[65] A subcommittee of the board decided that the most workable solution to the problem was to off-load many administrative responsibilities, including, most important, control of the purse strings, onto Wilkins while allowing White to return to the helm with a seeming promotion to executive secretary.

This solved very little. Wilkins and White circled each other, each waiting for the other to make a false step. That moment came when White went to California, met with several branches, then asked to have travel expenses reimbursed ... for him and Poppy Cannon White, who had joined him on this trip. Wilkins flatly refused. "The NAACP," he asserted, "never has had a general rule which would permit the wives of staff members to accompany them on business trips and have such transportation charged to the Association."[66] White was indignant and began to strongly suggest to the NAACP leadership that Wilkins was backward, parochial, shortsighted, and in the end, divisive. As if chiding Eliza Doolittle for yelling obscenities at Ascot, White condescendingly laid out to Wilkins that every viable organization, business, and foundation grasps the critical role of wives in networking, making social contacts, fund raising, and increasing dues-paying memberships. Wilkins, White implied, was just a little too unpolished and a bit too unsophisticated to understand the nuances of real leadership.[67]

Enraged and insulted, Wilkins systematically demolished the executive secretary's arguments and then took the opportunity to unveil what he saw as the real motive behind White's insinuations. "I cannot escape the feeling," Wilkins shot back, "that a great deal of the tension which periodically has risen and fallen since the return of the Secretary June 1, 1950, has stemmed from the Secretary's inability or refusal, to recognize

[65] Anderson, *Eyes Off the Prize*, 170.
[66] Roy Wilkins to Arthur B. Spingarn, Louis T. Wright, and William H. Hastie, memo, April 29, 1952, Box 8, File "NAACP, 1948–74," *Moon Papers*.
[67] Walter White to Louis T. Wright, Arthur B. Spingarn, and William H. Hastie, memo, April 24, 1952, ibid.

that" since the redistribution of power authorized by the board, "the Secretary no longer has the sole and final word about the conduct of all the business of the Association."[68]

Wilkins remembered how resistant White was to change when the board had earlier recommended creating an executive director position and White cunningly undermined the effort. But years had passed since then. This was now a different, weakened Walter White. In this duel, the executive secretary was like an aging gunfighter, all too aware of his slowed reflexes, strapping on his six-shooter and taking that next step down the dusty Main Street, nonetheless. Just a few weeks earlier he had complained that he was laboring under the consequences of serving as one of the "honorary pall bearers" at William Dean's funeral, where "in a snowstorm" he was "lined up outside for photographs without overcoats or hats." The prolonged exposure to freezing cold sent him spiraling toward "what at first looked like ... pneumonia," spiked his blood pressure up to 230, and left him with "some heart damage."[69] Yet his sense of himself as "Mr. NAACP" compelled White to fight for what he saw as his rightful and proper place in the organization. He therefore expressed to the board how Wilkins's Machiavellian actions had driven away potential donors and squandered critical funding opportunities that could have pulled the Association from the financial abyss.[70]

Wilkins counterattacked. He particularly chafed at the implication that he was somehow the "prophet of 'dissension'" responsible for the Ford Foundation turning down a $2 million grant because of "rumors of 'friction' in the National Office of the NAACP." Those lies, Wilkins fired back, were "conjured up by the Secretary out of his complete belief that his decisions should not be questioned by anyone." Well, Wilkins continued, White simply needed to accept the new world order at the NAACP. "I remain convinced," Wilkins conveyed, "that much of what has taken place since June 1, 1950, has been part of an effort to nullify the action of the Board on May 8, 1950, and force me from the staff of the Association by building up the fiction that I, and I alone, have stirred up and am

---

[68] Roy Wilkins to Arthur B. Spingarn, Louis T. Wright, and William H. Hastie, memo, April 29, 1952, ibid.

[69] Walter White to Channing Tobias, February 11, 1952, Box A147, File "Board of Directors: Channing Tobias, 1950–53," *Papers of the NAACP*; Walter White to Dean Acheson, January 31, 1952, Box A617, File "State Department: General, 1952–54," *Papers of the NAACP*.

[70] Walter White to Louis T. Wright, Arthur B. Spingarn, and William H. Hastie, memo, April 24, 1952, Box 8, File "NAACP, 1948–74," *Moon Papers*.

continuing to stir up dissension and division within the NAACP, thereby doing such great damage to the Association that my services must be terminated."[71]

After that last salvo, it was obvious that White no longer had the power to take down his rival. He was outgunned, outmaneuvered, and outfoxed, and the board and staff easily sided with Wilkins.[72] The executive secretary would now have to figure out how to move, particularly on anticolonial and international issues, with diminished power and without the budget authority, which now lay in the hands of someone whom he had crossed and who never forgot or forgave.

Even more problems were on the horizon, however. In addition to reordering the U.S.'s budget priorities, the Korean War was having a big impact on the United Nations. Ralph Bunche told Walter Offutt the war had diverted the UN's attention from the turmoil in South Africa, Kenya, Tunisia, and throughout Africa.[73] And that was troublesome because the Association had "recognized the United Nations as a medium by which a protest against colonization, exploitation and the denials of the principles of self government as practiced against many colored peoples of the world" could be made.[74] Moreover, the Korean War had accelerated Republican and Southern Democrat vilification of the United Nations as a Soviet Trojan horse and intensified communist witch-hunts of UN personnel, which took down several staff members in the secretariat and specialized agencies and led to at least one suicide when UN Chief Counsel Abraham Feller leapt to his death from a New York high-rise. Ralph Bunche, for one, faced repeated investigations until 1960.[75]

[71] Roy Wilkins to Arthur B. Spingarn, Louis T. Wright, and William H. Hastie, memo, April 29, 1952, ibid.
[72] Thurgood Marshall to Walter White, memo, April 29, 1952, ibid.
[73] Walter White to Ralph Bunche, March 20, 1953, Box A161, File "Bunche, Ralph, General, 1950–55," *Papers of the NAACP.*
[74] Resolution #1, June 1952, Box A47, File "Annual Convention, Resolutions General, 1952," *Papers of the NAACP.*
[75] Edward Willard, "Hiss, Harvard, and F.D.R. Linked to U.N. Suicide: Education Leads Feller Down Leftist Path," *Chicago Tribune,* November 24, 1952; Holmes Alexander, "A Suicide Analyzed," *Los Angeles Times,* November 25, 1952; Anderson, *Eyes Off the Prize,* 261; Telephone Conversation with Allen Dulles, Amb. Lodge, and Wilbur Re: Ralph Bunche, June 29, 1953, Box 1, File "Telephone Memoranda (Excepting to or from White House) May–June 1953 (1)," *Dulles:TCS*; Charles P. Henry, "Civil Rights and National Security: The Case of Ralph Bunche," in *Ralph Bunche: The Man and His Times,* ed. Benjamin Rivlin, foreword by Donald F. McHenry (New York: Holmes & Meier, 1990), 55–56.

Nor was the White House immune to the Korean War's devastation. After June 25, 1950, President Truman's woes mounted like the bricks that sealed Fortunato in the "The Cask of Amontillado." Kim Il-Sung's surprise attack across the 38th parallel seemed to underscore concerns from the right wing that the president's "Europe first" policy had weakened U.S. national security. It also unleashed a torrent of congressional hearings and FBI investigations in search of the supposed traitors within the administration who had sold out the United States to the Communists. Although American anticommunism was always strong, the foreign policy setbacks transformed that sentiment into something virulent, reckless, and destructive. Then came the disastrous turn of events when an oh-so-near U.S. victory and brag that "the boys will be home by Christmas" quickly descended into a rout as 400,000 of Mao Zedong's forces crossed the Yalu River and sent American and UN troops fleeing south. Truman's political fate was sealed when he uttered the unheard-of concept of "limited war" to explain why there was no victory, only the mud of stalemate. It was so bad that the president dropped out of the primaries and endured what seemed like interminable broadsides on his foreign policy from Republican candidate and head of NATO General Dwight David Eisenhower, thus, ending the Democrats' twenty-year control of the executive branch.[76]

Eisenhower rode into the White House vowing to end the war. He also had a plan to end Jim Crow. Gradually. Very gradually. And under the control of the Southern governments. As his biographer Stephen Ambrose observed, it was obvious that "the sum total of Eisenhower's program for the 16 million Negro Americans who were outside of the federal establishment was to appeal to the southern governors for some sign of progress." However, "[s]ince every one of those governors had been elected by a virtually all-white electorate, and since every one of them was thoroughly committed to segregation, ... the President could not have anticipated rapid or dramatic progress."[77] Eisenhower's election, therefore, meant that, at a crucial moment on the international scene, the Association would have to concentrate its resources at home.

---

[76] McCullough, *Truman*, 847–856, 909; David M. Oshinsky, *A Conspiracy So Immense: The World of Joe McCarthy* (New York: Oxford University Press, 2005).

[77] Stephen Ambrose, *Eisenhower: The President* (New York: Simon & Schuster, 1984), 127. For a more favorable assessment of Eisenhower's commitment to civil rights, see David A. Nichols, *A Matter of Justice: Eisenhower and the Beginning of the Civil Rights Revolution* (New York: Simon & Schuster, 2007).

The NAACP looked at Eisenhower and saw a man who simply did not understand how Mississippi got to be Mississippi. Or, equally important, how Mississippi stayed Mississippi. For example, despite the stranglehold of the poll tax, literacy tests, and outright ballot box terrorism, which meant that by "1940, no more than 5 percent of the black voting-age population of the eleven former Confederate states ... were registered voters" or that "as late as 1960, fewer than two percent of Mississippi's Black adults were registered to vote," Eisenhower somehow thought that the way toward the "elimination of racial difficulties" in the South would be if African Americans ran for office, such as for the "school board" or as city and county commissioner. Of course, the president's remedy, which was designed to minimize federal responsibility and put the onus overwhelmingly on African Americans, ignored the stark, cold truth that blacks who were courageous enough to try to even register to vote, were often killed, beaten, or jailed. The president's solution would require African Americans to up the ante and cross the threshold from courageous to suicidal.[78] The disconnect between the actual conditions of terror under which black people lived and Eisenhower's so-called remedies was so profound that Walter White was beside himself at what the future held.[79]

The executive secretary was right to be concerned. One of Eisenhower's closest confidantes was South Carolina Governor James Byrnes, who, as a U.S. senator, had already driven a stake through federal anti-lynching legislation and was determined to do the same to the NAACP's legal challenge to Jim Crow, *Brown v. Topeka Board of Education*. Byrnes immediately conveyed that Eisenhower owed African Americans "nothing." The newly elected president came to the White House without the black vote, Byrnes declared, and could easily stay there without it.[80] On the other hand, the governor made clear, the so-called Eisencrats, the four states of the Old Confederacy that broke from the Democratic Party

---

[78] Berg, *The Ticket to Freedom*, 140; Charles M. Payne, *I've Got the Light of Freedom: The Organizing Tradition and the Mississippi Freedom Struggle* (Berkeley: University of California Press, 1995, 2007), 1; Dwight Eisenhower to Billy Graham, March 22, 1956, Box 16, File "Graham, Billy," Name Series, *Papers of Dwight D. Eisenhower: Ann Whitman File*, Dwight D. Eisenhower Presidential Library, Abilene, KS (hereafter *Eisenhower:AWF*). For example, in Mississippi, Robbie Brown, "First Black Mayor in City Known for Klan Killings," *New York Times*, May 21, 2009.

[79] Anderson, *Eyes Off the Prize*, 211–215.

[80] Ibid., 213.

and voted Republican, were essential for continued GOP success.[81] The price was small, Byrnes insisted. Eisenhower needed only to maintain "the position you have consistently taken, that the states should have the right to control matters that are purely local." This from the governor of a state that spent nearly five times more per capita on school buildings for whites than blacks, had no high school whatsoever for African Americans in nineteen counties, and assigned only eight school buses throughout the state to transport black children.[82]

Indeed, even in Eisenhower's own administration, progress on racial equality was glacial despite a presidency supposedly committed to equal opportunity, at least in the federal sphere, as E. Frederic Morrow, a loyal black campaign staffer, would soon discover. Sherman Adams, Eisenhower's right-hand man, had invited Morrow to work at the White House after the election. With a plum offer, Morrow quit his job at CBS in New York, made arrangements for the care of his semi-invalid mother, and moved to Washington. But then reality hit. Despite Adams's offer, there was no job. At first, there was some "hassle over the amount of salary" Morrow "could expect in any White House position" and then there was always "one more detail to be ironed out" before the administration could make an official offer. Days of endless negotiations dragged on into months of unemployed limbo. And then silence. "[D]ozens" of Morrow's calls to the White House were not returned, and his life savings, on which he now had to live, just evaporated. Finally, seventeen months later, the president's counsel, Bernard Shanley, informed Morrow that "it had been decided that there was nothing in the White House available ... period!" Morrow was devastated even after Val Washington, director of minorities, Republican National Committee, interceded and secured a position for him at the Department of Commerce. Morrow strongly suspected that "prejudice" was at the root of his employment problems. He knew his inability to secure a job at the White House had absolutely nothing to do with his qualifications, which were exemplary, his performance during the campaign, which was first-rate, or concerns about his loyalty because he easily sailed through the FBI security clearance.[83]

[81] J. F. B. to Eisenhower, August 26, 1953, Box 3, File "Byrnes, James F. (2)," Name Series, *Eisenhower:AWF*; James F. Byrnes to Eisenhower, August 27, 1953, ibid.

[82] James F. Byrnes to Dwight Eisenhower, November 20, 1953, Box 3, File "Byrnes, James F. (1)," Name Series, *Eisenhower:AWF*; Rebekah Dobrasko, "Equalization Schools in South Carolina, 1951–1959," 1–3, http://nationalregister.sc.gov/SurveyReports/EqualizationSchoolsHistoricContext.pdf. Accessed October 26, 2013.

[83] Governor Adams' Invitation to Me to Come to Washington, n.d., Box 1, File "Diary – E. Frederic Morrow (1)," *Papers of E. Frederic Morrow*, Dwight David Eisenhower Presidential Library, Abilene, KS (hereafter *Morrow Papers*).

His suspicions were later confirmed when he learned that Wilton B. Persons, an Alabaman and Eisenhower's liaison to Congress, was "adamant" that no white woman, secretary or not, should ever have to work for a black man, and thus, Morrow, by definition, was unemployable in any administrative capacity.[84] If, however, CBS executive Morrow wanted to come work at the White House as a butler, Persons was amenable to that and would not lead the secretarial pool "in a walkout."[85] Although Morrow, after dazzling the Commerce Department, would eventually secure his coveted White House position, it was more than obvious the sway that Southern sympathies had within the administration.

Morrow's difficulties were exacerbated by a seemingly "revolutionary" race-neutral policy that Eisenhower was determined to implement.[86] The president "firmly believed that appointments to particular positions should never be made ... merely to provide representation for a particular minority or a particular group." Instead, Eisenhower wanted to "insure that his administration was representative of all Americans." That is why, even as the landmark *Brown* decision was on the Supreme Court's doorstep and the Southern politicians had threatened a virtual Civil War if the ruling did not go their way, he "refused to have an Administrative Assistant for minority problems."[87]

In truth, however, no matter how seductive the terminology, supposedly race-neutral policies are not neutral at all. Instead, they are weighed down with the baggage of privilege and history and embed inequality into ongoing efforts while remaining draped in the conscience-soothing language of nondiscrimination.[88] Roy Wilkins saw it immediately. He informed black GOP stalwart Archibald Carey that Eisenhower "meant what nearly all Republican campaigners have meant ... that Negro

---

[84] Morrow, diary entry, December 19, 1956 (sic), ibid.

[85] Kenneth O'Reilly, "Racial Integration: The Battle General Eisenhower Chose Not to Fight," *Journal of Blacks in Higher Education*, no. 18 (Winter 1997–1998), 110.

[86] L. Arthur Minnich, note for file, February 10, 1953, Box 1, File "A(1) (January-May 1953)," L. Arthur Minnich Series, Miscellaneous Files Subseries, *White House Office, Office of the Staff Secretary Records of Paul T. Carroll, Andrew J. Goodpaster, L. Arthur Minnich, and Christopher H. Russell, 1951–1961*, Dwight D. Eisenhower Presidential Library, Abilene, KS (hereafter WHO:OSSR:LAM).

[87] L. Arthur Minnich, Appointments (Administrative) Minorities, February 26, 1953, ibid.

[88] For some of the seminal works on color-blind racism see, Eduardo Bonilla-Silva, *Racism without Racists: Color-Blind Racism and the Persistence of Racial Inequality in America*, 3rd ed. (New York: Rowman & Littlefield, 2009); Ian Haney Lopez, *White by Law 10th Anniversary Edition: The Legal Construction of Race* (New York: New York University Press, 2006); George Lipsitz, *The Possessive Investment in Whiteness: How White People Profit from Identity Politics* (Philadelphia, PA: Temple University Press, 2006).

Americans should not expect any special attention to their peculiar needs on the theory that they should not demand more than the general run of American citizens. This ignores," Wilkins continued, "the fact that Negro Americans are presently in a special position below the level of other Americans," because centuries of chattel slavery and now Jim Crow, which no one else had ever had to deal with, had wreaked havoc on black people's access to the polls, quality education, housing, and wealth creation opportunities. African Americans, Wilkins insisted, "therefore need[ed] corrective action to bring them up to the level where they can enjoy general benefits."[89] Who within Eisenhower's circle would have that vision? Wilkins could only hope that the "new Administration will be wise enough to heed the counsel of persons like [Archibald Carey] rather than the advice of the markedly conservative white Republicans and their Negro adherents."[90]

That was not going to happen. The staff tasked with identifying and vetting federal appointments fervently believed that their race-neutral, "merit-based" approach was more stringent and equitable than that used by the previous Democratic administrations. Therefore, although months into Eisenhower's term "only about 200 Presidential appointments have been made thus far," the staff was proud that "these have all been based strictly on merit, with none having been made to represent particular groups, ethnic or otherwise."[91]

Of course, on closer scrutiny, it was clear that only African Americans had to scale the jagged rocks of Mt. Merit. At a meeting in July 1953, Eisenhower, Byrnes, and others candidly talked about the need to find Catholics, Jews, and those from the Midwest to fill certain slots on the U.S. delegation to the UN. Then they began a derisive conversation "that went on for some time" about what do with the "Negro slot." Secretary of State John Foster Dulles argued that "qualified" was the most important attribute and that there really should not be a position designated for an African American. He stated firmly, "if we had an Asst Secy of State who was a negro [sic] we wouldn't always have to fill that same job with one."[92]

[89] Roy Wilkins to Archibald Carey, November 4, 1952, Box 13, File "91: November 1–10, 1952," *Papers of Archibald J. Carey, Jr.*, Chicago Historical Society, Chicago, IL (hereafter *Carey Papers*).

[90] Roy Wilkins to Archibald Carey, November 10, 1952, ibid.

[91] L. Arthur Minnich, Appointments (Administrative), May 15, 1953, Box 1, File "A(1) (January–May 1953)," *WHO:OSSR:LAM.*

[92] Telephone Conversation Re: UN Delegation (Gov. Byrnes, President, Gov. Adams) and Sen. Dirksen, July 20, 1953, Box 1, File "Telephone Memos (Except to and from White House) July–Oct. 31, 1953 (5)," *Dulles:TCS.*

Dulles's example actually underscored the inanity of the situation. There not only had never been an African American as an assistant secretary of state, but also in 1953, at "the GS-7 level and above in the department in Washington only fifteen of 6,700 total employees" were black.[93] The improbability of high-ranking African Americans in key posts at the State Department was driven home when several officials thought about scoring a Cold War public relations bonanza by appointing blacks to ambassadorships throughout the Soviet bloc. While the idea was tantalizing, the reality of racism's corrosive effect on the administration's commitment to merit quickly became apparent. Embassy staff stated that "the presence of a Negro ambassador, *no matter how highly qualified*, might well result in serious personnel problems," including indiscrete and inappropriate comments to the press about their overall disdain for the black ambassador. And with that, the idea – not the embassy staff – was dropped.[94]

Not surprisingly, the administration's team, which sought to recommend appointments to the Caribbean Commission, could not find "a single negro [sic] candidate who is both qualified and will also do us some positive political good."[95] And that was the other issue. For all of the self-congratulatory bromides about merit only, "qualified" was not enough. The trick was to identify an African American who could work some political magic, as well. That meant, in many ways, finding black people who could provide the illusion of racial equality while just being happy to serve.

They were few and far between. Many African Americans did not believe in Eisenhower's gradualism or in patiently waiting for the crumbs of civil rights that white Southern governments would grudgingly drop from the table.[96] For example, when Jessie Vann, co-owner of the *Pittsburgh Courier*, gleaned that her initial position as a regular delegate to the UN was downgraded to alternate, she refused to accept the appointment. If

---

[93] Michael L. Krenn, *Black Diplomacy: African Americans and the State Department, 1945–1969* (Armonk, NY: M.E. Sharpe, 1999), 64.

[94] David S. Smith to Mr. Hanes, memo, June 29, 1954, Box 3, File "Subject File (Strictly Confidential) Negro Problem," *Dulles:PS:CMS*. Emphasis added.

[95] Memorandum: Office of the Secretary, Department of State, April 2, 1953, Box 2, File "Name (Strictly Confidential) [T-V]," *Dulles:PS:CMS*.

[96] A Plan for Procedure and Organization, February 14, 1955, Box 731, File "OF 142-A Negro Matters-Colored Question (2)," *Papers of Dwight D. Eisenhower: White House Central File*, Dwight D. Eisenhower Presidential Library, Abilene, KS (hereafter *Eisenhower:WHCF*).

Vann could not be a regular delegate, "she [was] not in the mood."[97]
Even a GOP loyalist like Archibald Carey, who did not abandon the
party until Barry Goldwater's 1964 presidential campaign, could not tow
Eisenhower's line unblinkingly.[98] Carey had stepped in as the alternate
U.S. delegate to the UN, however, he refused to abide by Dulles's directive
to abstain on a critical vote on the Genocide Convention.[99]

The hunt, therefore, was on throughout Eisenhower's presidency for
blacks who would be more than content with a little prestige and virtually unmoved by the larger struggles for racial equality and justice. That
would be the real litmus test of "qualified." Dulles had noticed black
journalist Carl Rowan at a Chamber of Commerce function, made an
inquiry, and learned what should have been rather disquieting information – that there were "no indications ... that Rowan had ever done any
work for the Party." That, however, did not dissuade the secretary of state
or the president. Instead, the journalist's star seemed to rise immeasurably
because of the assessment of a trusted black Republican that "Rowan
is rather controversial, because many of the people around Minnesota,
especially Negroes, do not think his articles reflect the thinking of the
modern-day Negro. He is more or less liked by white people because he
is more to their way of thinking on the Negro question."[100] In essence,
Rowan's racial politics trumped his GOP agnosticism and led the White
House to believe that, "as a negro [sic] appointment ... he would be a fine
one to make."[101]

Rowan was no aberration. A few years later, Helen Edmonds, professor of history at North Carolina Central University, rose to the fore for
the State Department because "[s]he is very conservative and is against
any kind of forced integration."[102]

The other end of this spectrum was best exemplified by a black nomi-
nee who was an ably qualified Republican but active in the fight for civil
rights. Cincinnati Mayor Charles Taft, scion of a storied GOP family,

---

[97] Memorandum of Conversation with Mrs. Vann (Pittsburgh), July 13, 1953, Box 1,
File "Telephone Memos (Except to and from White House) July–Oct. 31, 1953 (5),"
Dulles:TCS.
[98] Letter for the record, July 14, 1964, Box 48, File "339: June–July 1964," *Carey
Papers.*
[99] Anderson, *Eyes Off the Prize*, 248–249.
[100] Val J. Washington to Elias McQuaid, June 29, 1953, Box 9, File "Roa-Rus (2),"
Dulles:PS:SLSS.
[101] Jean Jerolaman, Memorandum for the Record, July 1, 1953, ibid.
[102] Mary Stanley, Memorandum for the Record, July 22, 1957, Box 6, File "Edm-Ewi,"
Dulles:PS:SLSS.

recommended Theodore Berry for a position on a U.S. delegation. His endorsement should have been unimpeachable. Taft's stamp of approval was followed by the president of Procter and Gamble, Howard Morgens, writing to the State Department that he personally would "feel very good about having Ted Berry represent the United States at the UNESCO [United Nations Educational, Scientific and Cultural Organization] meeting." However, while Morgens described Berry as "a man of character ... and of obvious leadership qualities ... who [was] willing to work hard at his job," information soon slipped to the State Department that Berry was "very active in the National Association for the Advancement of Colored People."[103] Worse yet, he was a long-standing board member. And that was a problem. Berry may have been "well educated" and a man of integrity, but those qualities could not surmount the contention that his appointment, in the words of Val Washington, would be a "fatal blow."[104] Congressman William Hess (R-OH) emphatically explained that Berry's so-called attributes were really a threat. In Hess's assessment, the NAACP man "was quite intelligent and could probably cause some trouble" – in fact, "a lot of trouble for the party."[105] The State Department, therefore, determined that there was a "problem of appointing a person like Berry."[106] With that, the NAACP board member was unceremoniously dropped "from further consideration."[107]

The Eisenhower administration's fear of and contempt for the Association shut down the NAACP's access to many of the channels of political power. During the Truman years, the Association was regularly invited to attend a number of special, off-the-record briefings at the State Department on colonialism, economic development, U.S. foreign policy, and the United Nations.[108] Moreover, the NAACP's insight

---

[103] Charles P. Taft to John W. Hanes Jr., November 25, 1957, Box 4, File "Be-Bl," *Dulles:PS:SLSS*; Howard Morgens to John W. Hanes, Jr., November 29, 1957, ibid.; Robert E. Hampton, Note to File, January 13, 1958, ibid.

[104] Robert E. Hampton, Note to File, January 13, 1958, ibid.; Robert E. Hampton, Memorandum for the Record, January 10, 1958, ibid.

[105] Robert E. Hampton, Note to File, January 13, 1958, ibid.

[106] Robert E. Hampton, Memorandum for the Record, January 24, 1958, ibid.

[107] Robert E. Hampton, Note to File, January 13, 1958, ibid.

[108] Memorandum for the Files from Madison Jones, February 24, 1948, Box A634, File "United Nations: General, 1948–49," *Papers of the NAACP*; Francis Russell to Arthur Spingarn, May 7, 1949, Box 181–8, File "3," *Logan-MSRC*; Rayford Logan to Madison S. Jones Jr., July 30, 1949, Box A634, File "United Nations: General, 1948–49," *Papers of the NAACP*; Memorandum of Conversation with Walter White, Dean Acheson, Mr. Mathews, Mr. Mackay, February 9, 1950, Box 66, File "February, 1950," *Acheson Papers*; Francis Russell to Arthur Spingarn, January 4, 1950, Box A404, File "Logan,

during the Point IV discussions also led to an invitation to provide advice and insight to the International Development Advisory Board.[109] The advent of the Eisenhower presidency slammed the doors shut.[110] Wilkins lamented that he was "persona non grata at the White House" and that the "Eisenhower administration is scared stiff to be even thought of as consulting with an NAACP official."[111] Indeed, the president's staff considered Wilkins "to be the most militant" of the black leadership.[112] Not surprisingly, then, despite numerous pleas, especially as the South ruthlessly tortured and killed a 14-year-old boy, launched Massive Resistance and shut down public schools, bombed the homes of civil rights activists, and unleashed the National Guard on black children who were just trying to get a decent education, Eisenhower refused for years to meet with the NAACP and a delegation of African Americans. In fact, the president did not relent until 1958.[113] Even after the long-awaited conference at the

Rayford, 1950–51," *Papers of the NAACP*; George McGhee, *Envoy to the Middle World: Adventures in Diplomacy*, foreword by Dean Rusk (New York: Harper & Row, 1983), 115; Francis Russell to Walter White, April 3, 1952, Box A617, File "State Department: General, 1952–54," *Papers of the NAACP*; Francis Russell to Walter White, Box A284, File "Foreign Affairs: Asia, 1950–52," *Papers of the NAACP*; Francis Russell to Walter White, September 11, 1952, Box A617, File "State Department: General, 1952–54," *Papers of the NAACP*.

[109] Nelson Rockefeller to Arthur Spingarn, January 29, 1951, Box A617, File "State Department: Point IV Program, 1949–54," *Papers of the NAACP*.

[110] John Foster Dulles to Walter White, January 8, 1953, Box A6, File "Africa: Michael Scott, 1953–55," *Papers of the NAACP*; Walter White to John Foster Dulles, January 13, 1953, ibid.; John W. Hanes Jr. to Walter White, February 2, 1953, ibid.; Walter White to John W. Hanes Jr., February 10, 1953, ibid.

[111] Roy Wilkins to Pauli Murray, July 18, 1958, Box A231, File "Murray, Pauli, 1958–63," *Papers of the NAACP*, Part III, Series A, General Office File, 1956–1965, (hereafter *Papers of the NAACP-III*).

[112] Rocco C. Siciliano, Memorandum for the Files: Meeting of Negro Leaders with the President – June 23, 1958, June 24, 1958, Box 731, File "OF 141-A(3)," *Eisenhower:WHCF*.

[113] A. Philip Randolph to Dwight Eisenhower, July 9, 1953, Box 32, File "White House Conference: Eisenhower Correspondence, A-W, 1953–57," *Papers of A. Philip Randolph*, Library of Congress, Washington, DC (hereafter *Randolph Papers*); Rayford Logan to Dwight Eisenhower, n.d., telegram, Box 10, File "13," *Logan-MSRC*; A. Philip Randolph to Roy Wilkins, August 31, 1955, Box 32, File "White House Conference: Eisenhower Correspondence, A-W, 1953–57," *Randolph Papers*; A. Philip Randolph to Dwight Eisenhower, August 31, 1955, Box 32, File "White House Conference: Eisenhower Correspondence, A-W, 1953–57," *Randolph Papers*; A. Philip Randolph to Dwight Eisenhower, telegram, February 2, 1956, Box 32, File "White House Conference: Eisenhower Correspondence, A-W, 1953–57," *Randolph Papers*; Summary of Telegram from Adam C. Powell to Eisenhower, February 23, 1956, Box 733, File "142-A-6 Negro Bus Boycott in Montgomery, Alabama," *Eisenhower:WHCF*; A. Philip Randolph to Dwight Eisenhower, May 8, 1956, Box 32, File "White House

White House, the NAACP and black leadership walked away with "no assurances that Mr. Eisenhower or the Department of Justice will take vigorous action and throw the full weight of the Executive branch of the Federal Government behind ... our fight. Nor [could African Americans] expect immediate remedial action from Congress."[114]

Earlier, Walter White had noted that only two members of the cabinet "know and are sensitive to the grave problems faced by minorities" – Attorney General Herbert Brownell and Mutual Security Administrator Harold Stassen. The rest, White insisted, were obstacles to the fight for equality.[115] And that meant the United States had an administration that not only was frustratingly dense about the struggle for civil rights but also did not understand the anticolonial upheavals either.[116]

Conference: Eisenhower Correspondence, A-W, 1953–57," *Randolph Papers*; Martin Luther King Jr., E.D. Nixon, et al., August 27, 1956, Box 32, File "White House Conference: Eisenhower Correspondence, A-W, 1953–57," *Randolph Papers*; A. Philip Randolph to Lester Granger, January 4, 1957, Box 32, File "White House Conference: Eisenhower Correspondence, A-W, 1953–57," *Randolph Papers*; Statement by Roy Wilkins to Ted Poston of the New York Post, via Phone Re. President Eisenhower's Answer to Rev. Martin Luther King, February 1, 1957, Box A175, File "King, Martin Luther, Jr., General, 1956–61, n.d.," *Papers of the NAACP-III*; Roy Wilkins to Richard M. Nixon, telegram, May 2, 1957, Box A239, File "Nixon, Richard M., 1956–60," *Papers of the NAACP-III*; A. Philip Randolph to Dwight Eisenhower, June 10, 1957, Box 32, File "White House Conference: Eisenhower Correspondence, A-W, 1953–57," *Randolph Papers*; Roy Wilkins to E. Frederick [sic] Morrow, June 17, 1957, Box A231, File "Morrow, E. Frederick, 1957–60," *Papers of the NAACP-III*; E. Frederic Morrow to A. Philip Randolph, June 25, 1957, Box 32, File "White House Conference: Eisenhower Correspondence, A-W, 1953–57," *Randolph Papers*; Rocco C. Siciliano, Memorandum for the Files on Meeting of Negro Leaders with the President – June 23, 1958, June 24, 1958, Box 731, File "OF 142-A (3)," *Eisenhower:WHCF*.
[114] Pauli Murray to Channing Tobias, July 4, 1958, Box A231, File "Murray, Pauli, 1958–63," *Papers of the NAACP-III*.
[115] An Address Prepared for Delivery 44th NAACP Annual Convention by Walter White, June 28, 1953, File "391B: Walter White," *Lehman Papers*.
[116] George White Jr., *Holding the Line: Race, Racism, and American Foreign Policy toward Africa, 1953–1961* (New York: Rowman & Littlefield, 2005), 37–39; Mr. Key to Mr. Murphy, memo, April 20, 1955, Box 4, File "State Department Colonial Policy: Memoranda and Correspondence," *Gerig Papers*; James W. Barco to Samuel DePalma, October 15, 1956, Box 44, File "Trusteeship Council, 1956," Lot File 60D113, RG 59; National Security Council, "U.S. Policy Toward Africa South of the Sahara Prior to Calendar Year 1960," NSC 5719/1, August 23, 1957, Box 21, File "NSC 5719/1-US Policy toward Africa (1)," NSC Series, Policy Paper Subseries, *White House Office, Office of the Special Assistant for National Security Affairs: Records, 1952–61*, Dwight D. Eisenhower Presidential Library, Abilene, KS; Memorandum for the National Security Council re: new Independent Countries and U.S. Policy, April 13, 1959, Box 6, File "New Independent Countries [April 1959]," NSC Series, Subject Subseries, *White House Office, National Security Council Staff Papers, 1953–1961*, Dwight D. Eisenhower Presidential Library, Abilene, KS; P. J. Halla to Mr. Boggs, memo, September 17, 1959,

As late as 1959, U.S. Ambassador to the UN Henry Cabot Lodge Jr. was pleading with the State Department to assign him staff with expertise. "Here we are with Africa in turmoil, with the Cameroons, Nigeria, Togoland and Somaliland all about to come in," Lodge complained, "and the U.S. Mission has not one officer who specializes in these matters."[117] Beyond the lack of expertise was just plain ignorance. When, for example, in October 1953, the NAACP sent Eisenhower a telegram complaining about South Carolina trying to maintain *apartheid* in the public schools, the Western Union agent said that "the White House didn't know what that word meant and asked them to check with the sender to find out."[118] Nearly a year later, Dulles admitted that "we have not thought enough re Africa."[119] And when they did, it was through a Cold War lens that saw only the "hazards of freedom" if decolonization was not gradual and stage managed by the imperial powers.[120] The result, Lodge complained, was that because of the administration's "apparent sympathy with colonial powers and their interests," indigenous people, particularly the youth, "think that we are supporting outgoing regimes – the Colonel Blimps."[121]

The administration, quite frankly, had no plan for decolonization that did not rely on CIA coups, military might, and the European powers. Walter White railed that "the revolt against white domination and exploitation" was "not going to be stopped by bombs. It will not be stayed by treaties and pacts made in London, Paris, Washington, Brussels, or Moscow." Instead, he continued, "it will grow like a prairie fire in August

Box 5, File "National Security Council – General [July 1959–February 1960]," NSC Series, Administrative Subseries, *White House Office, Office of the Special Assistant for National Security Affairs: Records, 1952–61*, Dwight D. Eisenhower Presidential Library, Abilene, KS; Conference of Principal Diplomatic and Consular Officers of North and West Africa, Tangier, May 30 to June 2, 1960, Box 1, File "Africa, U.S. Policy toward," Lot File entry 3039A, *RG 59*.

[117] Henry Cabot Lodge Jr. to Francis Wilcox, March 13, 1959, Box 40, File "HCL-Francis Wilcox Correspondence, 1953–60," *Papers of Henry Cabot Lodge, Jr.*, Massachusetts Historical Society, Boston, MA (hereafter *Lodge Papers*).

[118] Henry Lee Moon to Walter White, memo, October 22, 1953, Box A7, File "Africa: South Africa, Petition to United Nations, 1953," *Papers of the NAACP*.

[119] Telephone Call from Congressman Judd, June 24, 1954, Box 2, File "Telephone Memos (Except to and from White House) May 1, 1954–June 30, 1954 (1)," *Dulles:TCS*.

[120] A. Campbell to T. W. Garvey, November 9, 1953, CO 936/96; "Communism in Colonies: Mr. Dulles on U.S. Policy, Hazards of Freedom," *London Times*, November 19, 1953, CO 936/96.

[121] Henry Cabot Lodge Jr. to Dwight Eisenhower, June 26, 1956, Box 2, File "Strictly Confidential – L (2)," General Correspondence and Memoranda Series, *Papers of John Foster Dulles*.

until the havenots of the world who have been hungry and ragged and sick and without hope for centuries win not only food and whatever measure of security which is possible in this war-torn world of ours but something which is equally important to them and all human beings – dignity and status."[122]

That quest for dignity, which is embedded in human rights, was looking more and more remote, however. Human rights had gained some traction during the Truman administration with the ratification of the Declaration, but almost the moment Eisenhower assumed the presidency he faced a full-blown revolt in the U.S. Senate. As the UN set out to transform the Declaration into a treaty, the Covenant on Human Rights, a coalition of isolationist Republicans and Southern Democrats falsely raised the alarm that treaties would exploit a glitch in the Constitution and topple the United States of America. The Founding Fathers, the right wing claimed, had supposedly erred by allowing treaties to become the law of the land by ratification of *only* two-thirds of the Senate. To correct this fatal flaw, Senator John Bricker (R-OH) proposed a Constitutional amendment that would add two increasingly difficult steps to the ratification process. The first was to throw treaties into the legislative grinder that turned bills into laws through the approval of both the U.S. Senate and the House. The second was to require that same Byzantine process in all forty-eight state legislatures before a treaty could become the law of the land. The proposed Bricker amendment, in essence, stripped the president of much of his latitude and power in foreign policy and transferred that authority back to individual states. This would ensure, of course, that no treaty that might upset a particular local interest – say agriculture in Kansas – could ever be ratified by the United States.[123]

Vice President Richard Nixon explained that it was the Genocide Convention, which was drafted in the shadow of the Holocaust, that had sent the senators into frenzy.[124] Behind closed doors, Senator Walter George (D-GA) denounced the Genocide Convention as "a backdoor method to a federal anti-lynching bill" although the State Department had offered assurances that "not enough blacks had been lynched to constitute genocide." In front of the cameras, however, the Senators told a tale of wide-ranging and deeply felt patriotism, of shoring up the Constitution

---

[122] An Address Prepared for Delivery 44th NAACP Annual Convention by Walter White, June 28, 1953, File "391B: Walter White," *Lehman Papers*.
[123] Anderson, *Eyes Off the Prize*, 218–224.
[124] Ibid., 228.

to protect all Americans from the crippling ideologies of socialism and communism that human rights and the UN supposedly embodied.[125]

Bricker's forces had gained enough traction, sown enough doubt, and created enough unease among the public that Eisenhower sent Dulles to bargain with them to preserve some sense of power in the executive branch. As the secretary of state tried to negotiate, he served up a peace offering of epic proportions. Dulles threw away treaties on genocide, antislavery, political and civil rights, economic and social rights, as well as the political rights of women, swearing that the administration would have nothing to do with these. And with that another important door slammed shut.[126]

It was, therefore, obvious that the NAACP's continued role in anticolonial struggles faced a number of challenges. Oddly enough, one of the most important barriers to the Association's deep, active engagement in Africa and Asia was the landmark *Brown* decision. Although Herbert Lehman gushed that this was an "hour of triumph," the truth was much more complicated.[127] As difficult as the situation had previously been, the NAACP was now "on the firing line."[128] Henry Moon explained to a colleague in South Africa that the Association was "exceedingly busy" trying to fend off "the new pressures being applied against our organization throughout the South."[129] Wilkins could not go to the opening ceremonies heralding Ghana's independence because, as he explained to Nkrumah, "certain developments in the United States with which the National Association for the Advancement of Colored people is deeply concerned will prevent my leaving the country at this period."[130] Walter White had to turn down an invitation from Eleanor Roosevelt to participate in an international meeting because "it would be unwise for me to be out of the United States at this time when so much must be done in implementation of the Supreme Court's decision on school

---

[125] Ibid., 180, 253.

[126] Ibid., 228–231. The Covenant on Human Rights had been broken into two separate treaties: one dealing with political and civil rights; the other with economic, social, and cultural rights.

[127] Herbert Lehman to Walter White, June 19, 1954, File "White, Walter, 1936–1975," *Lehman Papers*.

[128] Chester Bowles to Henry Lee Moon, Box A51, File "Bowles, Chester, 1955–59," *Papers of the NAACP-III*.

[129] Henry Lee Moon to Ronald Segal, January 30, 1957, Box A35, File "Africa: South Africa, 1956–65, Undated," *Papers of the NAACP-III*.

[130] Roy Wilkins to Kwame Nkrumah, February 18, 1957, Box A34, File "Africa: Ghana, 1957–63," *Papers of the NAACP-III*.

segregation."[131] Thurgood Marshall was even more explicit about the challenges ahead. The "question is ... how to best implement the decision. There are some who lean toward Teddy Roosevelt's theory of walking softly and carrying a big stick." However, Marshall continued, "there are others who want a knock-down-drag-out fight regardless of anything.... It is for those of us who have been in this fight for so long to work out a plan which will be non-compromising and will get results." Marshall then keenly observed, "When you put those two phrases together, you realize the difficulty immediately."[132]

A no-holds-barred fight is exactly what the Old Confederacy had in mind. The State of Georgia tried "to outlaw the NAACP as a 'subversive'" organization.[133] Eugene Cook, Georgia's attorney general, declared that "either knowingly or unwittingly, it [NAACP] has allowed itself to become part and parcel of the Communist conspiracy ... delivering this nation into the hands of international Communism."[134] Manning Johnson, one of Ralph Bunche's accusers, told a Louisiana legislative committee in 1956 "that the NAACP 'is nothing more than a vehicle of the Communist Party, in which the Communists are colonizing for the purpose of inciting racial rebellion in the South, with the ultimate object, in the insane confusion, to seize power and take over the reins of government in the United States.'"[135] Georgia fined the Association tens of thousands of dollars in supposed back taxes. White Citizens Councils, the middle-class Klan, declared that "when in the course of human events it becomes necessary to abolish the Negro" that "all whites are created equal with certain rights: among these are life, liberty and the pursuit of dead niggers."[136] One minister from Indiana wrote that on a trip to the

[131] Walter White to Eleanor Roosevelt, June 30, 1954, Box 3497, File "White, Walter, 1953–56," *Roosevelt Papers.*

[132] Thurgood Marshall to F. D. Patterson, June 21, 1954, Box 108, File "7," *Phelps-Stokes Collection.*

[133] Federal Bureau of Investigation, "Report 43723: Communist Infiltration of the National Association for the Advancement of Colored People," January 17, 1956, Reel 1, *FBI File on Eleanor Roosevelt*, Franklin D. Roosevelt Presidential Library, Hyde Park, NY.

[134] Joshua Sewell, "A Fateful Moment in the History of a Free Country": An Analysis of Supreme Court Rulings Governing the Right to Association for the Communist Party, USA and the NAACP" (Senior Honors Thesis, University of Missouri, 2004), 54.

[135] Ibid., 55.

[136] *NAACP v. Alabama ex. rel. Patterson*, 357 U.S. 449 (S. Ct. 1958); Numan V. Bartley, *The Rise of Massive Resistance: Race and Politics in the South during the 1950's* (Baton Rouge: Louisiana State University Press, 1969, 1997), 216–217; The White Citizen's Council: A Preview of the Declaration of Segregation, February 10, 1956, Box 1, File "Civil Rights," *Morrow Papers.*

South he saw "the awful iniquities and terrible atrocities of the Ku Klux Klan ... [and] the White Citizens Council." "While I was in Atlanta," he wrote, "the State Legislature met, passed a resolution to petition the Georgia representatives of the United States Congress to repeal the 13th, 14th, and 15th Amendments to the Constitution of the United States of America and to impeach the members of the Supreme Court." In Florida, "under the influence of the White Citizens Council," the governor and the general assembly launched an investigation of the Association, "preparatory to putting that great organization out of business in Florida."[137]

The NAACP tried to remain "defiant" as the Southern sharks circled.[138] Channing Tobias summed it up: "Court action was invoked to ban our activities in Louisiana, Alabama and Texas. Legislation was passed to cripple us in Virginia, South Carolina, Mississippi, Alabama, Tennessee and Arkansas." Association members were even banned from public employment in Georgia, Louisiana, Mississippi, South Carolina, and Arkansas. "The intent of all this," Tobias asserted, "has been to harass, cripple and run the NAACP out of business."[139] On the edge of its greatest triumph, the Association was suddenly driven to fight tooth and nail for its own existence.

Thus throughout the 1950s, through both administrations, the NAACP faced internal and external conditions that crippled its anticolonialism efforts by channeling its attention and resources in other directions. This was evident when confronted with the intransigence and exponential difficulties of settler colonialism in North and East Africa. In many ways, the Association was stymied and reduced to offering a few press releases and, in the case of Kenya, an awkward intervention with the State and Justice Departments to prevent a deportation.

Trouble was brewing in French North Africa shortly after the Second World War and Paris's desperation to hang onto its faltering empire at all costs exacerbated the problem.[140] Habib Bourguiba, leader of the

---

[137] L. K. Jackson to Richard Nixon, April 11, 1957, Box A239, File "Nixon, Richard M., 1956–60," *Papers of the NAACP-III.*

[138] Interview Mildred Roxborough with author, telephone, March 26, 2010.

[139] Keynote Address by Dr. Channing H. Tobias at the 48th Annual Convention, June 25, 1957, File "Speeches, 1932–1958," *Tobias Papers.*

[140] Department of State, "France: Policy and Information Statement," September 15, 1946, 711.51/9-1546, Reel 3, *Confidential France Foreign Affairs*; Summary of Telegrams, February 10, 1947, Box 22, File "State Dept. Briefs File, January-May 1947," *HST:SMOF:NA*; AmConsul, Calcutta, India to Department of State re: Tunisian Leader's Calcutta Visit, September 2, 1952, Box 80, File "United Nations – Tunisian Question," *McKay Papers.*

nationalist Neo-Destour Party in Tunisia, "hinted that bloody revolts will ensue if the Tunisian people do not receive their independence."[141] Bourguiba, "France's Public Enemy Number One in Tunisia," insisted that this was not about violence for violence's sake; rather, it was about survival.[142] It was about stopping the genocidal erasure of Arab culture and language by an imperialism that "seeks not only domination and the exploitation of the natural resources of a country, but the absolute domination of its people."[143]

Bourguiba, of course, was referring to France's imperial model, "a curious blend of federalism and centralization in the form of the 'French Union,'" which absorbed colonies into the metropole as associated states and transformed Arabs into French citizens.[144] Although President Truman lamented that the French "were way behind the times in colonial matters," one imperial official explained that "in many ways the French conception [of associated states] is more daring than the [UN] Charter" because it will "liquidate the old system and recognizes the equality of races, no matter how different they may be."[145] French ambassador to the United States Henri Bonnet offered that the policy of "'association' ... [was] not a colonial policy nor a policy of oppression or suppression."[146] In fact, the French explained, "within this framework" of the Union, "the inhabitants, without distinction of origin or status, enjoy political rights similar to those of citizens of metropolitan France."[147]

[141] "Latin Imperialism in North Seeks to Enslave the Soul of a Nation," press release, December 4, 1946, Box 20, File "Tunisia," *McKay Papers*.

[142] handwritten notes Habib Bourguiba at Institute of Arab-American Affairs, December 6 at 3:45, n.d., ca. December 6, 1946, Box 20, File "Tunisia," *McKay Papers*.

[143] "Latin Imperialism in North Seeks to Enslave the Soul of a Nation," press release, December 4, 1946, Box 20, File "Tunisia," *McKay Papers*.

[144] Central Intelligence Agency, "French North Africa," November 28, 1950, Box 218, File "Central Intelligence Reports: Situation Reports: 32, 26 [October 21, 1948; November 28, 1950]," *Truman:PSF:IR*.

[145] Henry S. Villard, "I Remember Harry Truman," Box 8, File "Memoir of Conversation by H.S. Villard with Pres. Truman, Jan. 1952, MHDC 247," *Miscellaneous Historical Documents Relating to Harry S. Truman*, Harry S. Truman Presidential Library, Independence, MO; Jean Chretien (pseud for Fr. Col. Admin), "The French Colonial Ideal," *Free World*, January 1946, pp. 23–26, Box 79, File "United Nations – Trusteeship Council," *McKay Papers*.

[146] Memorandum of Conversation between Dean Acheson, Ambassador Bonnet, Mr. Van Lacthem, Mr. Wainhouse, Mr. Knight, May 15, 1952, Box 70, File "May 1952," *Acheson Papers*.

[147] Information from Non-Self-Governing Territories: Summary and Analysis of Information Transmitted under Article 73 e of the Charter: Cessation of the Transmission of Information under Article 73 e of the Charter: Report of the Secretary, A/915, June 14, 1949, Box 80, File "Committee IV (Trusteeship Committee)," *Fahy Papers*.

While that sounded interesting in theory, the reality was very different. Without even consulting the Tunisians, the French crafted a new governing structure in which the white settlers, the colons, "enjoy[ed] privileges and protections in Tunisia over and above those granted the Tunisians themselves."[148] The so-called equality was also belied by the fact that the "native government [was] not allowed to make policies or pass laws, but [had to] administer the measures laid down by the French." The CIA noted, as well, that for the most part "Tunisians are disenfranchised." And "although the French authorities claim to be engaging in a campaign against illiteracy, school facilities are so inadequate that fewer than one-fifth of the children can be enrolled in school." In addition, the Tunisians were laboring under the weight of "extreme poverty."[149] As far as the Arab leadership could tell, therefore, "there had been no change, no progress, no amelioration in the situation of the Tunisians" since the end of the Second World War.[150]

The same held true for the Moroccans.[151] A State Department analysis asserted that "such economic development as has occurred has resulted in numerous benefits to the ever increasing number of French settlers (there are some 150,000 Frenchmen in Tunisia and 350,000 in Morocco) and a relatively small group of investors and absentee owners in France. The Tunisian and Moroccan people," on the other hand, "have derived relatively limited economic and social benefit from this development."[152] Thus, the State Department noted, the word "'association' is anathema to Tunisian [and Moroccan] nationalists ... [who] regard the associated state concept as only a sugar-coated form of assimilation designed to deprive Tunisia [and Morocco] of [their] sovereignty, ... international status as a state separate from France, and of all chances of

---

[148] Enoch Williams to R. Allen, June 14, 1952, FO 115/4290; Memorandum of Conversation, May 22, 1952, Box 2, File "Tunisia, 1952," Lot File 58D33, *RG 59*.

[149] Central Intelligence Agency, "French North Africa," November 28, 1950, Box 218, File "Central Intelligence Reports: Situation Reports: 32, 26 [October 21, 1948; November 28, 1950]," *Truman:PSF:IR.*

[150] McGhee, *Envoy to the Middle World*, 231.

[151] Mahdi Bennouna to George A. Marshall, July 12, 1947, Box 9, File "Morocco," Lot File 55D323, *RG 59*; "The United States and the French-Moroccan Problem – 'The Other Side,'" Seventy-second Annual Convention of the American Federation of Labor, September 25, 1953, Box 59, File "Policy Issues – Anti-Colonial Resolutions in the General Assembly," *McKay Papers.*

[152] Working Group on Colonial Problems, CP A-10, August 26, 1952, Box 18, File "SP: Working Group on Colonial Problems," Lot File 60D257, *RG 59*.

obtaining independence."[153] French attempts to cloak this maneuver in the "progressive" garb of "equality" led Bourguiba to conclude, "It is a dreadful imperialism."[154]

The Arab League fully agreed and branded France "Public Enemy No. 1 in North Africa."[155] Paris and the colons had insisted that the "two million Frenchmen in North Africa," including those in Algeria, "must be protected."[156] This concern for the Europeans translated into "reforms" that ensured the political dominance by the French settlers in every decision-making body, including the "municipal assemblies, ... the Tunisian Council of Ministers and in any national assembly."[157] This was no surprise. The State Department noted that the colons "exercise powerful political influence both in Paris and at the Residency in Tunis." The settlers asserted that "the country has been developed to its present state through the hard work of Frenchmen." As a result, their "absolute opposition to any concessions giving Tunisians greater political and economic rights at the expense of French dominance" was rooted in the sense that everything good about this Arab land came from the Europeans and would be jeopardized, if not lost, "under a Tunisian Government."[158]

The inherent racism that undergirded this policy of "association" was unwittingly confirmed by former Prime Minister Paul Reynaud, who "stressed that the French problem" in Tunisia, Algeria, and Morocco, "was more like that of South Africa," where there was a sizable, prosperous European community that was significantly outnumbered by the impoverished indigenous people.[159] The similarities between North and

---

[153] Department of State, Intelligence Report: Nationalist-French Difference in Tunisia, No. 5793, March 11, 1952, Box 52, File "7th GA: Background Book, Tunisia (Folder 2 of 2)," Entry 3039E, *RG* 59.

[154] Jean Chretien (pseud. for Fr. Col. Admin), "The French Colonial Ideal," *Free World*, January 1946, pp. 23–26, Box 79, File "United Nations – Trusteeship Council," *McKay Papers*; "Latin Imperialism in North Seeks to Enslave the Soul of a Nation," press release, December 4, 1946, Box 20, File "Tunisia," *McKay Papers*.

[155] S. Pinkney Tuck to the Secretary of State, February 20, 1947, Reel 2, *Confidential France Foreign Affairs*.

[156] Memorandum of Conversation between Dean Acheson, Ambassador Bonnet, Mr. Van Lacthem, Mr. Wainhouse, Mr. Knight, May 15, 1952, Box 70, File "May 1952," *Acheson Papers*.

[157] Department of State, Intelligence Report: Nationalist-French Difference in Tunisia, No. 5793, March 11, 1952, Box 52, File "7th GA: Background Book, Tunisia (Folder 2 of 2)," Entry 3039E, *RG* 59.

[158] Ibid.

[159] Memorandum of Conversation, Dean Acheson, M. Paul Reynaud, Ambassador Bonnet, Mr. McBride, May 6, 1952, Box 70, File "May, 1952," *Acheson Papers*.

South Africa extended into their treatment of the UN, as well. Just like Smuts' and Malan's governments, France insisted that it did not have to submit information to the Fourth Committee, because its so-called colonies were actually integral components of the French state and, hence, shielded from international scrutiny by Article 2(7), domestic jurisdiction.[160] Foreign Minister Schuman was emphatic that "no French Government would be willing to permit the UN becoming primarily a mechanism ('machinery') for getting the French out of North Africa."[161]

The State Department's legal division, however, conveyed that "with regard to Article 2(7), it is important to note that the significance of this article is being steadily diminished." The challenges concerning Indonesia, the treatment of Indians in South Africa, human rights in the Soviet bloc (a ploy used by the United States to embarrass the Kremlin), and more "have had the effects of steadily whittling away at the scope of Article 2(7)." It was likely, department officials predicted, that the French would "invoke 2(7) in case of an appeal from the Algerians, Moroccans or Tunisians against French rule in order to try to prevent the Assembly from discussing the issue," but, the State Department's attorneys argued, the domestic jurisdiction clause "does not bar the discussion … in the General Assembly."[162]

As France's hard line with the nationalist Moroccan Istiqal Party and then subsequent arrests of Neo-Destour leaders took North Africa to the brink of war, the Arab bloc in the UN pressed hard for a hearing before the General Assembly or Security Council.[163] The French, who

---

[160] Information from Non-Self-Governing Territories: Summary and Analysis of Information Transmitted under Article 73 e of the Charter: Cessation of the Transmission of Information under Article 73 e of the Charter: Report of the Secretary, A/915, June 14, 1949, Box 80, File "Committee IV (Trusteeship Committee)," *Fahy Papers*; Memorandum of Conversation, Acting Secretary, M. Plaisant, Ambassador Bonnet, Mr. O'Shaughnessy, Mr. Kopper, Mr. Scott, November 14, 1949, Box 18, File "Special Committee: 1949 and 1950," Lot File 60D257, *RG 59*.

[161] Memorandum of Conversation, Dean Acheson, Ambassador Bonnet, Mr. Van Lacthem, Mr. Wainhouse, Mr. Knight, May 15, 1952, Box 70, File "May 1952," *Acheson Papers*.

[162] Memorandum: How the French North African Question Might Come before the United Nations, September 15, 1950, Box 80, File "United Nations – Tunisian Question," *McKay Papers*.

[163] Memorandum: How the French North African Question Might Come before the United Nations, September 15, 1950, Box 80, File "United Nations – Tunisian Question," *McKay Papers*; Memorandum of Conversation, April 3, 1952, Box 70, File "April 1952," *Acheson Papers*; Porter McKeever to Warren Austin, March 1952, Carton VII, File "Correspondence: March 1952," *Austin Papers*; Letter Dated April 2, 1952, from the Representative of India to the President of the Security Council Concerning Tunisia, S/2580, Box 80, File "United Nations – Tunisian Question," *McKay Papers*; Letter Dated

were "determined to fight against … placing this question on the agenda even if they became convinced that they would lose the fight," deployed every argument they could – from defining Arab nationalists as Soviet-guided missiles, to apocalyptic visions of the loss of strategic military bases dotting North Africa, to the camaraderie of a NATO ally – to get the United States to stop the UN dead in its tracks.[164] It worked. Acheson ignored pleas from Eleanor Roosevelt and a policy opinion from State Department staff that the Americans have never opposed discussion of an item and to do so now would set an awful precedent.[165]

Le Monde, in fact, determined that the best "evidence for Atlantic Pact solidarity" and one which "bolstered the French position" immeasurably was the "American abstention from voting on the Assembly agenda." Although this may have seemed trivial, France's flagship newspaper noted that it was significant because "Washington has never been opposed to including grievances on the agenda."[166] Rayford Logan, who was at the fall 1951 UN meeting in Paris, surmised that the "French evidently believe that the United States will support them in placing security ahead of independence for colonies."[167] This was confirmed beyond all doubt when the U.S. delegate, in the subsequent April 1952 meeting, abstained on placing Tunisia on the Security Council's agenda.[168]

At that point, the NAACP launched a series of protests. Walter White cabled Truman that U.S. actions gave "the impression … that our country wishes to maintain European imperialism." "This is contrary," White

---

April 2, 1952, from the Representative of Yemen to the President of the Security Council Concerning Tunisia, S/2584, Box 80, File "United Nations – Tunisian Question," *McKay Papers*; Mr. Hickerson to Dean Acheson, memo, May 15, 1952, Box 2, File "Tunisia, 1952," Lot File 58D33, *RG 59*; McGhee, *Envoy to the Middle World*, 250–252.

[164] Memorandum of Conversation on Egyptian Complaint in UN on Moroccan Question, Dean Acheson, M. Bonnet, Mr. Hickerson, Mr. Bonbright, Mr. Van Lacthem, October 24, 1951, Box 69, File "October 1951," *Acheson Papers*; Memorandum of Conversation, Dean Acheson, George W. Perkins, et al., April 3, 1952, Box 70, File "April, 1952," *Acheson Papers*; Memorandum of Conversation, Dean Acheson, Ambassador Bonnet, Mr. Van Lacthem, Mr. Wainhouse, Mr. Knight, May 15, 1952, Box 70, File "May 1952," *Acheson Papers*; Memorandum of Conversation on the Moroccan Situation, October 9, 1951, Box 69, File "October 1951," *Acheson Papers*.

[165] Mr. Hickerson to the Secretary, memo, April 3, 1952, Box 2, File "Tunisia, 1952," Lot File 58D33, *RG 59*; Memorandum of Telephone Conversation, Mrs. Roosevelt and Mr. Acheson, April 3, 1952, Box 70, File "April 1952," *Acheson Papers*.

[166] "UN Faces Moroccan Question: America Will Abstain for Agenda Vote," *Le Monde*, October 29, 1951, Box A404, File "Rayford Logan, 1950–51," *Papers of the NAACP*.

[167] Rayford Logan to Walter White, October 29, 1951, ibid.

[168] Marginalia on Mr. Hickerson to the Secretary, memo, April 3, 1952, Box 2, File "Tunisia, 1952," Lot File 58D33, *RG 59*.

wrote, "to our tradition of supporting national independence for subject peoples." Therefore, he continued, the NAACP "urges you to instruct our delegation to vote to bring this issue before [the] United Nations."[169] The Association's Youth Division denounced the "recent debacle in the United Nations in which the United States delegations abstained from voting to place the French-Tunisian conflict on the agenda of the United Nations Security Council." It was just "difficult to reconcile the position of the United States government in this issue" with the long-standing "history of our country in championing the cause of all downtrodden peoples to a right to free and equal discussion of all issues."[170] Herbert Wright, youth secretary, and "ten members of the Association's New York Intercollegiate Coordinating Council" met with State Department official Ernest Gross "to protest the refusal of the U.S. delegation to vote to place the Tunisian issue on the agenda" and to emphasize how that action was a "repudiation of our belief in those fundamental concepts of human rights which the United Nations was established to preserve and protect."[171]

Ambassador-at-Large Philip Jessup was also "most uncomfortable about the position the United States had taken on the Tunisian affair." The geostrategic imperatives that drove the abstention decision, Jessup admitted, were "very much against the grain" of American public opinion.[172] Jessup had, therefore, asked the British to intercede with the French to help defuse the situation and allow the UN to just discuss the issue.[173] Churchill refused. "I think," he replied, "we should discourage the Americans from hampering the French in maintaining their position in North Africa where they have done so much splendid work and have many supporters among the people." Although the specter of apartheid hovered over this entire issue, as even Reynaud had intimated, the British prime minister insisted that "Malan's conduct in South Africa should not complicate our general policy in the Mediterranean."[174]

Dean Acheson explained to the U.S. ambassador to France that "it will be even more difficult for us this autumn than it was before to oppose inscription" of the Tunisian item on the UN agenda. There was,

[169] Walter White to Harry S. Truman, telegram, April 10, 1952, Box A634, File "United Nations: General, 1952," *Papers of the NAACP.*

[170] "?: A publication of the Youth Division of the NAACP," ca. April 1952, Box 3338, File "NAACP, 1952," *Roosevelt Papers.*

[171] "NAACP Youth Protest U.S. Stand on Tunisia," April 24, 1952, Box A634, File "United Nations: General, 1952," *Papers of the NAACP.*

[172] Oliver Franks to William Strang, May 26, 1952, CO 936/94.

[173] Sir O. Franks to Foreign Office, telegram no. 823, August 3, 1952, PREM 11/300.

[174] Winston Churchill, Prime Minister's Personal Minute, October 6, 1952, ibid.

as the French knew all too well, "practically unanimous public press criticism" in the United States "which followed our abstention last spring."[175]

In December 1952, as American officials continued to straddle the fence, the NAACP, working with the International League for the Rights of Man and several other organizations, issued a broadside linking French use of the domestic jurisdiction clause in Morocco and Tunisia with South Africa's racial policies and disdain for UN authority in colonial matters.[176] Walter White bristled at "M. Schuman's speech ... serving notice on the U.N. General Assembly that France will not permit any interference in the Tunisian and Moroccan situation." The stakes, White knew, were too high. "If France has her way," he exclaimed, "there are many of us who fear there will be no stopping Malan in defying the U.N. and world opinion."[177] However, at the end of the day, as Offutt reported back, the "U.S. Delegation supported the Brazilian resolution on Tunisia. It is one that carries the usual do-nothing attitude[:] '.... expresses confidence ... expresses the hope ....Appeals to the parties ...,'" but in the end, do-nothing.[178]

The advent of the Eisenhower administration and John Foster Dulles as Secretary of State raised the barrier significantly on the possibility of even a conversation about Tunisia. Although discussions in the General Assembly and Fourth Committee had begun to reshape international norms about colonialism and human rights, Dulles was adamant that the United Nations had very limited value. He did concede that for sparring with the Soviet bloc, "the UN was a good propaganda forum." However, "it was useless to submit things to it about which it could do nothing

---

[175] Acheson to Amembassy Paris, July 30, 1952, Box 52, File "7th GA: Background Book, Tunisia (Folder 1 of 2)," Entry 3039E, *RG 59*.

[176] Minutes of the Board Meeting of the ILRM, October 15, 1952, Box A380, File "Leagues: International League for the Rights of Man, 1953–55," *Papers of the NAACP*; Roger Baldwin to Member of the Board and Advisory Committee and all Affiliates, November 1952, Box A380, File "Leagues: International League for the Rights of Man, 1953–55," *Papers of the NAACP*; Walter P. Offutt Jr. to Walter White, memo, November 26, 1952, Box A7, File "Africa: South Africa, Petition to United Nations, 1951–52," *Papers of the NAACP*; Walter White to Dear Friend, December 1, 1952, Box A7, File "South Africa Petition to the United Nations, 1951–52," *Papers of the NAACP*.

[177] Walter White to K. E. Popleon, November 11, 1952, Box A634, File "United Nations: General, 1952," *Papers of the NAACP*.

[178] Memorandum from Rev. Offutt, December 8, 1952, Box A634, File "United Nations: General, 1952," *Papers of the NAACP*; Statement by Ambassador Jessup in Committee I on the Tunisian Question, press release no. 1604, December 6, 1952, Box 80, File "United Nations – Tunisian Question," *McKay Papers*.

[because] it only builds up the idea of futility."[179] Thus, he repeatedly shut down even the hope that the United States would return to its original position and vote for issues to be discussed in the General Assembly. Instead, Dulles instructed the U.S. delegates at the UN to "vote 'no' rather than abstain" on the Tunisian question.[180]

The unrelenting use of violence in the Mau Mau uprising in Kenya, which began in 1952, provided another challenge because now the NAACP had to decide how or even if to support an anticolonial struggle that had resorted to guerilla warfare. For decades moderate Kikuyu had worked through the courts and the government to get the entrenched white settlers and the handful of conservative, relatively wealthy African chiefs to address the squalor and poverty of the people.[181] In many ways, however, each petition, each court case, and each meeting with colonial officials were nothing more than exercises in futility. The white settlers had dug in and insisted on their right to the most arable, productive land. Period. As one British official would lament, " 500,000 Africans are easier to handle than one white settler."[182]

Some Kikuyu advocated stronger measures. Historian James Meriwether noted, "The backbone of the Mau Mau movement formed from dispossessed squatters from the White Highlands; poor peasants, tenants, and younger Kikuyu who had been transformed into a landless rural class.... Many of these people felt they had little to lose and much to gain by resorting to a campaign of violence."[183] Militant Kikuyu asserted that secret initiations and machetes would do what years of meetings, petitions, and court cases could not.

Although the British and the media billed the violence as a race war, black against white, the Mau Mau in fact primarily targeted Africans who "collaborated" with the settlers and the colonizer. Nonetheless,

[179] Telephone Conversation with Amb. Lodge 5:03 p.m., June 25, 1953, Box 1, File "Telephone Memoranda (Except to or from White House), May–June 1953 (1)," *Dulles:TCS.*

[180] Telephone Conversation with Amb. Lodge, April 9, 1953, Box 1, File "Telephone Memoranda (Except to or from White House), January 1953–April 1953 (1)," *Dulles:TCS*; USUN to SEC, August 24, 1953, Box 9, File "Morocco: Miscellaneous," Lot File 55D429, *RG 59.*

[181] Anderson, *Histories of the Hanged*, 12–13, 31.

[182] Chester Bowles to Family and Friends, January 5, 1955, Box 442, File "2," *Papers of Adlai Stevenson*, Seeley Mudd Manuscript Library, Princeton University NJ.

[183] James H. Meriwether, "African Americans and the Mau Mau Rebellion Militancy, Violence, and the Struggle for Freedom," *Journal of American Ethnic History*, 17, no. 4 (Summer 1998), 65.

although whites constituted barely 3 percent of the casualties, the settlers' punctured sense of invincibility demanded retribution.[184]

The British response was, therefore, "a blunt, brutal ... instrument of oppression." Concentration camps, scorched earth policies, mass public hangings on transportable gallows, and collective guilt punishments reminiscent of the Nazis at Lidice gave the lie to the language of civilization and human rights.[185] Kenya's British governor Sir Evelyn Baring convinced himself that Kenyan African Union (KAU) leader Jomo Kenyatta "was directly responsible [for Mau Mau]. Here," Baring concluded, "was the African leader to darkness and death."[186] At Jomo Kenyatta's show trial, where he would eventually be sentenced to seven years hard labor and then indefinite exile, the head of the KAU refused to shoulder the weight or blame for Mau Mau. He challenged the Crown. "Mau Mau would not be as it is now. You made it what it is, not Kenyatta."[187] (See Figure 5.2)

The *West African Pilot* in Nigeria mocked the British colonial officers "groping around for ... [Mau Mau's] brain" convinced that a "Frankenstein monster had no doubt been created in Africa!" For the Nigerians, the real "terrorists" were the "white men, now carrying pistols in their pants," who had subjected the "natives of Kenya" to "oppression, terrorism, unemployment, ... squalor misery and hunger."[188] The *Times of India* similarly "denounce[d]" British "measures ... as being unnecessarily repressive" and designed specifically to exaggerate the threat of the Mau Mau to "curb ... [the] political and economic aspirations of the African people." The "sheer desperation generated by failure to get their just grievances redressed has driven Kenya's Africans to violence," but, the newspaper insisted, "poverty and hunger cannot be put down by the sword."[189]

To be clear, most, including Nigerians, Indians, and African Americans, were not supportive of Mau Mau's violence. But they also understood that entrenched settler colonialism, the lack of redress, and the denial of

---

[184] Ibid., 64.
[185] Caroline Elkins, *Imperial Reckoning: The Untold Story of Britain's Gulag in Kenya* (New York: Henry Holt, 2005); Simpson, *Human Rights and the End of Empire*, 835.
[186] Andrew and Mitrokhin, *The World Was Going Our Way*, 425.
[187] Montagu Slater, *The Trial of Jomo Kenyatta* (London: Secker & Warburg, 1955), 174.
[188] Extract from the West African Press Survey – No. 176, November 18, 1952, CO 822/448.
[189] U.K. High Commissioner in India to Nairobi and U.K. High Commissioner in Pakistan, October 24, 1952, ibid.

FIGURE 5.2. Both moderate Kikuyu like Jomo Kenyatta and the more militant Mau Mau disdained what settler colonialism had done to Kenya. After his release from prison, Kenyatta meets "Field Marshal" Mwariama, a Mau Mau leader. *Source*: Bettman/Corbis. Courtesy of Corbis, Stock Photo ID# BE059989.

basic human rights had brought the situation in Kenya to the brink. The word out of Pakistan was that although the "activities of Mau Mau are generally deplored, ... they are ... an inevitable outcome of British misrule."[190] George Padmore compared the Mau Mau uprising to Spartacus's "slave revolt of Rome. A blind protest against intolerable conditions and for land."[191] Later, in an interview in *Crisis*, he further expounded that "the colonial governing system in Kenya is so repressive ... that 'unless the Africans resort to direct action, their rulers just refuse to recognize – much less redress – their grievances.'" But the solution to all of the bloodshed, Padmore asserted, was in British hands.

[190] Extract from Pakistan Fortnightly Summary Part II, No. 78, April, 16–27, 1953, ibid.
[191] George Padmore to Ivar Holm, July 7, 1953, Box 41, File "14: George Padmore Correspondence, 1952–1957," *Papers of Kwame Nkrumah*, Moorland-Spingarn Research Center, Howard University, Washington, DC (hereafter *Nkrumah Papers*).

To put an end to Mau Mau, ... the British government will have to give Africans 'an irrevocable guarantee' that it will 'open the Highlands to landless Kikuyus, abolish the color bar, reopen the Independent schools, expand educational facilities, pay Africans in the civil service equal pay for equal work,' and allow representation in local and central government councils.[192]

Herbert Wright, NAACP youth secretary, also charged that British repression would stop nothing because the "Colonial Office [was] tending to the symptoms rather than the real cause of the Kenyan conflict."[193] Indian Premier Nehru explained to one U.S. official that "unless [the] colonial powers adopt [a] more liberal policy he believed [the] whole [African] continent would be lost through violent revolution." Mau Mau, Nehru warned, was just a portent of things to come.[194]

Although there was an overall consensus that the Mau Mau's violence was provoked, nevertheless, the bottom line was that innocent bystanders could easily become collateral damage. One instance of this that caught the attention of the NAACP, was Reuel Mugo Gatheru, a Kenyan student at Lincoln University in Pennsylvania, whom the U.S. government was trying to deport for entering the United States on a fraud-tainted visa. Herbert Wright urged the National Office to take up the case. He explained that "Immigration and Naturalization has been under pressure from the British government to deport [Gatheru] and all other Kenyan students from this country." The youth secretary further explained that, although the United States claimed that the problem was a bogus visa, the questions immigration officials asked Gatheru dealt more with the Kenyan's "political beliefs and ideology, than with the matter of his alleged fraudulent action."[195] For Wright, it just reeked of "British aggression."[196] While the youth secretary asked the National Office to intervene, the president of the NAACP's Harvard chapter, Louis Sharpe, urged the State Department to act. Deportation would land Gatheru "in jail or subjected to bodily harm upon arrival in his 'native' land."[197]

---

[192] "Land Hunger Seen as Crux of Kenya Issue," press release, April 29, 1954, Box A5, File "Africa: Kenya, 1952–1955," *Papers of the NAACP*.

[193] NAACP Official Scores Needless Murders, press release, April 30, 1953, ibid.

[194] Hildreth to Secretary of State, telegram, May 22, 1953, Box 1, File "Dulles, John F. May, 1953," Dulles-Herter Series, *Eisenhower:AWF*.

[195] Herbert L. Wright to Mr. White, Mr. Wilkins, Mr. Marshall, Mr. Moon, memo, January 13, 1953, Box A5, File "Africa: Kenya, 1952–1955," *Papers of the NAACP*.

[196] Herbert L. Wright to Louis Sharpe, May 5, 1953, ibid.

[197] Louis Sharpe to African Desk, U.S. State Department, April 27, 1953, ibid.

More pronounced pressure had come from Edith Sampson in November 1952, who asked Ambassador Jessup to intervene.[198] Her friend, colleague, and fellow Chicagoan, sociologist St. Clair Drake, alerted her to Gatheru's plight and asked if she, as a U.S. delegate to the UN, could do anything to help. "Mugo is anti-Mau," Drake said. "If he goes home now, the Mau Mau crowd will probably kill him, if they get him." The "white settlers on the other hand will keep him in jail." Drake recalled "the attitude the North once took toward the Fugitive Slave Act. I think," he said "we should send no slaves back to Kenya slave-masters."[199]

Jessup did inquire and learned that State Department officials had heard from immigration authorities "that he [Gatheru] engaged in dubious political activities before he left Kenya. It [was] also felt apparently that he employed a certain amount of subterfuge to get into this country." However, with publicity about the case mounting in London, the UN, and now the United States, it was important, one official advised, to keep a low profile and let the slow, grinding wheels of bureaucracy do their work.[200]

Mugo Gatheru at this point contacted Ralph Bunche, who directed him to the NAACP.[201] Walter White, already alerted to the situation by Herbert Wright, had set up a meeting with Attorney General Brownell and laid out in a preliminary letter that there was no subterfuge or fraud. Gatheru "was never denied a visitors visa in Kenya because he never applied for one." White explained that as a critic of "British colonial policy in Kenya," Gatheru understood the futility of doing so. Instead, he used the laws of the Commonwealth, went legally to India then England, obtained his student visa through proper channels, came to the United States, and enrolled in college. There simply was no fraud. White then moved on to what was at stake for Gatheru and the United States. "There is a very real and present danger that if Mr. Gatheru is forced to return to Kenya at this time he will be in imminent danger of death at the hands of the Mau Maus whose terrorist tactics he has criticized" or that he will be "prosecuted by some of the terrified British officials in Kenya whom Mr. Gatheru has also criticized." White emphasized that this issue

[198] Edith Sampson to Philip Jessup, November 12, 1952, Box 3, File "UNGA 1952 – 4th Committee," Lot File 53D65, *RG* 59.

[199] St. Clair Drake to Edith Sampson, November 7, 1952, ibid.

[200] Mr. Strong to Ambassador Jessup, memo, November 13, 1952, ibid.

[201] Mugo Gatheru to Ralph Bunche, July 4, 1954, Box A5, File "Africa: Kenya, 1952–55," *Papers of the NAACP*; Ralph Bunche to Mugo Gatheru, July 14, 1954, ibid.; Ralph Bunche to Walter White, July 14, 1954, ibid.

was bigger than simply the fate of one person. It was counterproductive and foolhardy to send a college-educated man like Gatheru "to almost certain death in Kenya" when what the continent desperately needed was "trained native African leadership who through their first-hand contact with American democracy constitute about the only effective force against Communism or any other form of dictatorship." This was the Cold War, White reminded Brownell: Africa's people and raw materials would be essential in that struggle.[202]

Of course, on the surface this sounds much like the standard red-baiting and in-the-hip-pocket-of-U.S.-foreign-policy babble that has led both scholars and leftist contemporaries to criticize the NAACP's anticolonialism. However, it should also be clear that the Association's concerns about the colonial world extended far beyond mere Cold War considerations. The NAACP's efforts to render "the wishes of the inhabitants" sacrosanct, make international accountability the norm, pierce through domestic jurisdiction, ensure that a colonial power's work be based on human rights and not exploitation, and argue for indigenous control of natural resources and a key role in economic development was all to ensure that what emerged from the remains of ravaged colonies would be strong, viable nations. For the NAACP, *viable* meant democratic. Not, of course, the way the United States did democracy. The numerous protests, court cases, and media campaigns designed to highlight and rectify the horrific shortcomings in the United States were clear indications that the NAACP did not consider American democracy ideal. But for the Association that did not mean communism was the answer. What it would take to transform colonies that had labored under the weight of racism and imperialism was to develop a system in which, as White noted, the ability of a people "to achieve dignity and an opportunity to education, growth, economic opportunity, and social advance" was at the center of a governing ethos.[203]

However, as clear as was the Association's vision and its commitment that "one of the duties of the NAACP was to help end exploitation and

---

[202] Walter White to St. Clair Drake, June 23, 1954, ibid.; Walter White to Bureau of Immigration and Naturalization, June 23, 1954, ibid.; Main Developments in the R. Mugo Gatheru Case, June 1954, ibid. For the NAACP's continued interest in Kenyan independence, see Mary L. Dudziak, *Exporting American Dreams: Thurgood Marshall's African Journey* (New York: Oxford University Press, 2008).

[203] The National Association for the Advancement of Colored People, the International League for the Rights of Man, and associated groups to the United States Delegation to the United Nations, memo, December 5, 1952, Box A7, File "South Africa Petition to the United Nations, 1951–52," *Papers of the NAACP*.

colonialism throughout the world," the Association simply could not carry the load the way it had previously.[204] Although other organizations repeatedly looked to the Association to follow through on the "efforts the NAACP has been putting forth during the past few years," by the mid- to late 1950s it was clear that a changing of the guard was necessary.[205]

In March 1955, Walter White, while preparing to attend the Afro-Asian Conference in Bandung, died of a heart attack.[206] Although he had been ill, his death was unexpected. The National Council of Negro Women eulogized him as a "great and militant leader … known throughout the civilized world as the unequivocal champion of human rights."[207] Senator Lehman described how White's "leadership molded a small group of men and women, imbued with the ideals of justice and equality, into a great and influential organization, highly respected in many communities." Walter White, Lehman continued, "was a courageous and unflinching fighter not only for his own people but for the rights, freedoms and liberties of all people."[208]

It was now up to Roy Wilkins, who was immediately named executive secretary, to carry this legacy forward (see Figure 5.3). But he had to contend with an organization that was under siege. "The South was buckling up to run us out of existence," he charged.[209] "Many Americans," Wilkins observed, "simply cannot get it into their heads that this is not 1914. Of course," he added, "Southern whites talk and act as though it were 1858."[210] With Confederate flags everywhere and open, brutal attacks on black people, Wilkins sighed that it made one "wonder if there ever

[204] Handwritten edits in Walter White to Dear, draft letter, November 1952, Box A7, File "South Africa Petition to the United Nations, 1951–52," *Papers of the NAACP*.

[205] Wm. Bross Lloyd Jr. To Walter White, August 29, 1952, Box A634, File "United Nations: General, 1952," *Papers of the NAACP*; Wm. Bross Lloyd Jr. to Walter Offutt Jr., May 9, 1952, Box A380, File "Leagues: International League for the Rights of Man, 1942–52," *Papers of the NAACP*.

[206] For Bandung, see Jason Parker, "Cold War II: The Eisenhower Administration, the Bandung Conference, and the Reperiodization of the Postwar Era," *Diplomatic History*, 30, no. 5 (November 2006), 867–892; Mark Atwood Lawrence, "The Rise and Fall of Nonalignment," in *The Cold War in the Third World*, 139–155; Cary Fraser, "An American Dilemma: Race and Realpolitik in the American Response to the Bandung Conference, 1955," in *Window on Freedom*, 115–140.

[207] "Walter White," *Telefact*, XIV, no. 3 (March 1955), Box 5, File "NCNW – Printed Material, 1949–1960," *Adams Papers*.

[208] Herbert H. Lehman to Mrs. Walter White, March 22, 1955, File "White, Walter, 1936–1975," *Lehman Papers*.

[209] Wilkins, *Standing Fast*, 219.

[210] Roy Wilkins to Joel I. Judovich, August 25, 1958, Box A48, File "Black Nationalism, 1958, 1961," *Papers of the NAACP-III*.

FIGURE 5.3. Arthur B. Spingarn (left), president of the NAACP, congratulates Roy Wilkins, who was named to succeed Walter White as executive secretary of the organization. White died March 21 of a heart ailment.
Source: Photographer, Barney Coons/Bettman/Corbis. Courtesy of Corbis, Stock Photo ID# U1280202INP.

was a Civil War and ... if, indeed, slavery does not still exist."[211] African Americans just seemed to be on their own, while the Eisenhower administration had infinitely more concern about others. Referencing the Soviet takeover of Hungary in 1956, Wilkins remarked:

When Hungarians resist oppression they are called heroes; when American Negroes legally and peacefully resist oppression they are called agitators. Our government sends observers to Hungary, organizes airlifts, sets up refugee camps, and opens immigration doors; but it does not say a mumbling word to the Deep South states about persecution, nor does it offer to aid a single black refugee.[212]

[211] Address of Roy Wilkins at Closing Meeting of 48th Annual NAACP Convention, June 30, 1957, Box 94–13, File "333: Wilkins, Roy," *AB Spingarn Papers*.
[212] Ibid.

Thus, while fighting racism at home, the NAACP's work in the international realm, especially after the resignation of Walter Offutt in 1954,
changed dramatically. The Association virtually abandoned the groundwork of meetings, strategy sessions, and lobbying, which had been so
effective in the past. When asked to provide staffing for an anticolonial
meeting, Wilkins regretted that "at the present state of affairs in the deseg-
regation campaign, we have no one we can spare."[213] What was left was
star power. In the fall of 1958, with other groups, the NAACP sponsored
a major dinner in New York in honor of Ghana's Prime Minister Kwame
Nkrumah.[214] The Association had "hail[ed] the emergence of Ghana as
a new and independent nation" and saw this "historic event" as a bell-
wether for "the complete reclamation of the Continent of Africa by its
indigenous peoples."[215] Ralph Bunche assured the prime minister that
"no place in this world, beyond your native shores, will you feel so fully
at home, will you find so much of consanguinity, of mutual sympathy and
understanding as in Harlem"[216] (see Figure 5.4). As the first independent
nation on the African continent since the end of the Second World War,
Ghana, Wilkins observed, was the "embodiment of world-wide aspiration toward the ideals of human freedom to which we have so long been
dedicated."[217] In addition to hosting Nkrumah, the NAACP sponsored
visits by South Rhodesia's Joshua Nkomo, funded a dinner for Guinea's
Sekou Touré, and worked to have Nnamdi Azikiwe of Nigeria and the
ANC's Oliver Tambo speak at the Association's annual conventions.[218]

---

[213] Roy Wilkins to Donald Harrington, September 1955, Box A356, File "Leagues: American
Committee on Africa, 1953–54," *Papers of the NAACP.*

[214] George Houser to Seth Anthony, April 24, 1958, Box A34, File "Africa: Ghana, 1957–
63," *Papers of the NAACP-III*; Program for the Visit to the United States of America
of the Honorable Kwame Nkrumah, Prime Minister of Ghana, July 23 to August 2,
1958, July 15, 1958, Box 33, File "24," *Nkrumah Papers*; "NAACP Secretary Wilkins at
State Dinner for Nkrumah," press release, July 24, 1958, Box A34, File "Africa: Ghana,
1957–63," *Papers of the NAACP-III.*

[215] Roy Wilkins to Kwame Nkrumah, February 26, 1957, Box A34, File "Africa: Ghana,
1957–63," *Papers of the NAACP-III.*

[216] Introductory Remarks Made by Ralph J. Bunche at Reception in Honor of Dr. Kwame
Nkrumah, Prime Minister of Ghana, press release, July 27, 1958, Box 32, File "3,"
Nkrumah Papers.

[217] Roy Wilkins to Seth Anthony, April 30, 1958, Box A34, File "Africa: Ghana, 1957–63,"
Papers of the NAACP-III.

[218] Robert W. Saunders to James Farmer, telegram, October 5, 1959, Box 19, File "NSGT:
Committee on Non-Self Governing Territories – Interdepartmental (Folder 1 of 5),"
Lot File 60D257, *RG 59*; James Farmer to F. W. Jackson, October 19, 1959, Box A307,
File "Staff: Farmer, James, General, 1959, Oct.-Dec.," *Papers of the NAACP-III*; John
A. Morsell to Homer Jack, Box A34, File "Africa: General, 1956–59," *Papers of the*

FIGURE 5.4. Ghana President Kwame Nkrumah addresses crowd in front of the Hotel Theresa in Harlem. Nkrumah declared that the 20 million African Americans constituted the strongest link between the people of North America and Africa. Police estimated the crowd at 1,000 persons.
Source: Bettman/Corbis. Courtesy of Corbis, Stock Photo ID #U1250507.

Beyond those high-profile events, however, the NAACP's efforts lagged. After Offutt resigned, the Association's attendance at key meetings with the UN and the International League for the Rights of Man was spotty, at best.[219] Wilkins's right-hand man, John Morsell, admittedly had an "all-too-scanty knowledge of Africa" and could not step in.[220] It took nearly four years, with the hiring of Reverend Edward J. Odom as church secretary, before the NAACP could have "constant representation" both at the UN and on a number of human rights and anticolonial NGOs.[221]

NAACP-III; Roy Wilkins to Nnamdi Azikiwe, July 21, 1959, Box A34, File "Africa: Nigeria, 1957–61," *Papers of the NAACP-III*; Roy Wilkins to Oliver Tambo, May 13, 1960, Box A35: File "Africa: South Africa, 1956–65," *Papers of the NAACP-III*.

[219] Roger Baldwin to Roy Wilkins, December 17, 1954, Box A380, File "Leagues: International League for the Rights of Man, 1942–52," *Papers of the NAACP*.

[220] John Morsell to C. F. Clarke, July 24, 1956, Box A34, File "Africa: General, 1956–59," *Papers of the NAACP-III*.

[221] Roger Baldwin to Edward Dudley, June 2, 1955, Box 7, File "National Association for the Advancement of Colored People," *Papers of the ILHR*; Roger Baldwin to Edward Dudley, September 19, 1955, Box 7, File "National Association for the Advancement of Colored People," *Papers of the ILHR*; Edward R. Dudley to Roy Wilkins, memo, September 23, 1955, Box A271, File "Fighting Fund for Freedom, E. R. Dudley, 1953–55,"

As early as May 1952, therefore, the NAACP was prepared to pass the anticolonial baton. Roger Baldwin of the ILRM was convinced that the current SWAT team-like efforts to swoop into the United Nations and support the Herero, Michael Scott, the Somali Youth League, and more, although impressive, were too scattershot and haphazard to be effective, especially at this phase of the anticolonial struggle. He sent out a call to several organizations, including the Association, to systematize these efforts and help "set up a bureau here in New York to assist the colonial peoples in contact with the United Nations."[222] In the subsequent planning session Walter Offutt, who would not leave the Association for

---

Papers of the NAACP; Edward Dudley to Roger Baldwin, September 23, 1955, Box 7, File "National Association for the Advancement of Colored People," *Papers of the ILHR*; Roger Baldwin to Henry Lee Moon, January 10, 1956, Box A194, File "Leagues and Organizations: International League for the Rights of Man, 1956–65," *Papers of the NAACP-III*; Roger Baldwin to Roy Wilkins, September 26, 1955, Box 7, File "National Association for the Advancement of Colored People," *Papers of the ILHR*; John Morsell to George Houser, June 5, 1957, Box A193, File "Leagues and Organizations: American Committee on Africa, 1956–59," *Papers of the NAACP-III*; L. Sylvester Odom to Roy Wilkins, April 2, 1957, Box A312, File "Staff: Odom, Edward J., 1957–65," *Papers of the NAACP-III*; Roy Wilkins to Edward J. Odom Jr., Box A312, File "Staff: Odom, Edward J., 1957–65," *Papers of the NAACP-III*; John A. Morsell to Max McCullough, November 7, 1957, Box A194, File "Leagues and Organizations: International League for the Rights of Man, 1956–65," *Papers of the NAACP-III*; Mrs. F. Zimmerman to Roy Wilkins, January 8, 1958, Box A194, File "Leagues and Organizations: International League for the Rights of Man, 1956–65," *Papers of the NAACP-III*; Roy Wilkins to Mrs. F. Zimmerman, January 21, 1958, Box A194, File "Leagues and Organizations: International League for the Rights of Man, 1956–65," *Papers of the NAACP-III*; Edward J. Odom Jr. to John Morsell, memo, March 13, 1958, Box A194, File "Leagues and Organizations: International League for the Rights of Man, 1956–65," *Papers of the NAACP-III*; Edward J. Odom Jr. to A. M. Asraf, March 24, 1958, Box A194, File "Leagues and Organizations: International League for the Rights of Man, 1956–65," *Papers of the NAACP-III*; Edward J. Odom Jr. to Wallace Irwin, March 24, 1958, Box A194, File "Leagues and Organizations: International League for the Rights of Man, 1956–65," *Papers of the NAACP-III*; A. M. Ashraf to Edward Odom Jr., March 25, 1958, Box A194, File "Leagues and Organizations: International League for the Rights of Man, 1956–65," *Papers of the NAACP-III*; William Irwin to Edward Odom Jr., March 26, 1958, Box A326, File "United Nations, General, 1957–63," *Papers of the NAACP-III*; Edward J. Odom Jr. to Roy Wilkins, memo, March 26, 1958, Box A312, File "Staff: Odom, Edward J., 1957–65," *Papers of the NAACP-III*; Edward J. Odom Jr. to Roy Wilkins, memo, March 27, 1958, Box A326, File "United Nations, General, 1957–63," *Papers of the NAACP-III*; John A. Morsell to Wallace Irwin Jr., September 10, 1958, Box A326, File "United Nations, General, 1957–63," *Papers of the NAACP-III*; John A. Morsell to T. D. T. Banda, December 18, 1958, Box A34, File "Africa: General, 1956–59," *Papers of the NAACP-III*; Will Maslow to Robert C. Weaver, February 18, 1960, Box A326, File "United Nations, General, 1957–63," *Papers of the NAACP-III*.

[222] Roger Baldwin to Walter Offutt Jr., May 21, 1952, Box A380, File "Leagues: International League for the Rights of Man, 1942–52," *Papers of the NAACP*.

another two years, was asked, specifically, "to explore the question of how much of the proposed activities can be carried on by his organization, the N.A.A.C.P. – especially clerical work and documentation."[223]

Around the same time, an ad hoc group in the United States, which was formed to support the passive resistance campaign against apartheid, wanted to expand its scope beyond South Africa and develop a more permanent structure.[224] By 1953, these efforts merged as Baldwin of the ILRM, Offutt of the NAACP, and a core of the then ad hoc Americans for South African Resistance began planning in earnest to establish a new organization that would be able to work full-time on colonial issues with a singular focus on Africa, "the last continent where this system of economic exploitation [was] still prevalent."[225]

They met throughout the spring and summer, hashing out a number of details such as scope, mission, functions, funding, tax-exempt status, and relationship to other organizations and the UN. The goal was to have the American Committee on Africa up and running by the beginning of the fall 1953 United Nations session when petitioners from the colonies would pour into New York needing help with publicity, maneuvering through the UN's bureaucracy, and lobbying other delegations. Through it all, Walter Offutt, as a member of the steering committee, was central both to the planning and to keeping the NAACP leadership fully apprised of the progress in establishing an organization that could focus on African liberation in ways that the Association simply could not.[226]

---

[223] Minutes of the International League for the Rights of Man, re: Colonial Peoples, May 26, 1952, Box A5, File "Africa: Organizations, 1952–55," *Papers of the NAACP*; Secretary's Report, Church Department: The International League for the Rights of Man, July and August, 1952, Box A380, File "Leagues: International League for the Rights of Man, 1942–52," *Papers of the NAACP*.

[224] Peter Weiss, "American Committee on Africa: Rebels with a Cause," *Africa Today*, 10, no. 9 (Nov., 1963), 38.

[225] George Houser to Dear Friend, March 20, 1953, Box A356, File "Leagues: American Committee on Africa, 1955," *Papers of the NAACP*; George M. Houser to A. Philip Randolph, March 25, 1953, Box 4, File "Africa: 1949–68, Undated," *Randolph Papers*; fragment, NAACP Minutes: Creation of an Organization to Deal with African Problems, March 1953, Box A6, File "Africa: Publicity, 1951–55," *Papers of the NAACP*.

[226] Report of the Meeting of the American Committee on Africa, May 14, 1953, Box 2, File "8," *Papers of the American Committee on Africa*, Amistad Research Center, Tulane University, New Orleans, LA (hereafter *Papers of the ACOA*); George Houser to Walter White, May 22, 1953, Box A356, File "Leagues: American Committee on Africa, 1953–54," *Papers of the NAACP*; Roger Baldwin to George Houser, May 28, 1953, Box 5, File "American Committee on Africa (1953–59)," *Papers of the ILHR*; Agenda: NAACP Board of Directors, June 8, 1953, Box 3461, File "NAACP, 1953," *Roosevelt Papers*; George Houser to Steering Committee of the American Committee on Africa, memo,

George Houser, who would become the executive director of ACOA, noted, "Although many organizations in the United States have been closely following African events and reporting to their membership on certain aspects of the developments, it has become increasingly evident that no existing agency is set up satisfactorily ... to do an interpretive job and to take appropriate action when this was demanded."[227]

Throughout the next year, ACOA began with "virtually no budget, no paid staff, but with a few enthusiastic volunteers."[228] The organization defined its responsibility to Africa as "helping the emergence of democratic self-governing states from racialism, poverty, exploitation, and ignorance under which the people of Africa suffer today."[229] The strategy was to "work through the United Nations principally by influencing the United States delegations" and to "give all assistance to petitioners from Africa in cooperation with the International League for the Rights of Man, and the N.A.A.C.P."[230] Indeed, even after Channing Tobias joined

June 25, 1953, Box A356, File "Leagues: American Committee on Africa, 1953–54," *Papers of the NAACP*; Minutes of the Steering Committee Meeting – the American Committee on Africa, July 9, 1953, Box A356, File "Leagues: American Committee on Africa, 1955," *Papers of the NAACP*; Walter White to Homer Jack, July 27, 1953, Box A356, File "Leagues: American Committee on Africa, 1953–54," *Papers of the NAACP*; Minutes of the Steering Committee – the American Committee on Africa, July 29, 1953, Box A356, File "Leagues: American Committee on Africa, 1955," *Papers of the NAACP*; Agenda for August 6th Steering Committee Meeting, August 6, 1953, Box A356, File "Leagues: American Committee on Africa, 1955," *Papers of the NAACP*; Walter White to Ralph J. Bunche, William H. Hastie, Rayford W. Logan, Arthur B. Spingarn, Channing H. Tobias, Thurgood Marshall, Henry Lee Moon, and Roy Wilkins, memo, August 5, 1953, Box A356, File "Leagues: American Committee on Africa, 1953–54," *Papers of the NAACP*; Minutes of the Executive Committee Meeting – American Committee on Africa, August 13, 1953, Box 2, File "8," *Papers of the ACOA*; American Concern for Africa: A Midsummer 1953 Review by Homer A. Jack, August 14, 1953, Box 3, File "29," *Papers of the ACOA*; Minutes of Steering Committee Meeting – American Committee on Africa, August 27, 1953, Box A356, File "Leagues: American Committee on Africa, 1955," *Papers of the NAACP*; Minutes of the Meeting of the Provisional Executive Committee: American Committee on Africa, September 16, 1953, Box A356, File "Leagues: American Committee on Africa, 1955," *Papers of the NAACP*.

[227] George M. Houser to Dear, draft letter, June 26, 1953, Box A356, File "Leagues: American Committee on Africa, 1953–54," *Papers of the NAACP*. Also see Prospectus of the American Committee on Africa, November 1953, Box A7, File "Africa: South Africa, General, 1950–53," *Papers of the NAACP*.

[228] George M. Houser, "Human Rights and the Liberation Struggle ... The Importance of Creative Tension," *Africa Today*, 39, no. 4, Africa and Human Rights in the 1990's (4th Qtr., 1992), 6.

[229] George Shepherd, Executive Secretary, press release, April 28, 1954, Box 43, File "46," *Papers of the ACOA*.

[230] Minutes of the American Committee on Africa, June 1, 1954, Box 2, File "8," *Papers of the ACOA*.

its advisory board, the American Committee on Africa's leadership team still wanted someone from the Association to sit on the executive committee.[231] As ACOA's chairman Donald Harrington explained to Roy Wilkins, "we feel that it is *very important* to have as close as possible a working relations with the NAACP."[232]

Thus by the time the Association was forced to wind down its own anticolonial work, the American Committee on Africa was coming into its own. ACOA was sponsoring major conferences that included notable freedom fighters such as Julius Nyerere, the future prime minister of Tanzania; producing publications that outlined the anticolonial struggles in Africa; and coordinating with other organizations to provide representation "at the first Pan-African Conference ever held on African soil." In addition, it had tapped Rayford Logan to be its liaison with the State Department. ACOA, in turn, became a resource for the Association, which directed numerous inquiries to George Houser and his staff.[233]

This was particularly important because, as *Pittsburgh Courier* editor Percival Prattis exclaimed in 1959, "Africa [was] on fire."[234] The

[231] Donald Harrington to Channing Tobias, December 13, 1954, Box A356, File "Leagues: American Committee on Africa, 1953–54," *Papers of the NAACP*; Channing Tobias to Donald Harrington, December 20, 1954, ibid.

[232] Donald Harrington to Roy Wilkins, September 20, 1955, ibid. Emphasis in original.

[233] Minutes of Executive Meeting, ACOA, May 7, 1954, Box 2, File "8," *Papers of the ACOA*; George W. Shepherd to Walter White, May 18, 1954, Box A356, File "Leagues: American Committee on Africa, 1953–54," *Papers of the NAACP*; *Africa Today: Bulletin of the American Committee on Africa*, 1, no. 1 (May 1954), Box 45, File "28," *Papers of the ACOA*; "Theme of First ACOA Conference – 'Is Colonialism Dying in Africa?'" *Africa Today: Bulletin of the American Committee on Africa*, 1, no. 2 (June–July 1954), Box 3, File "Africa: American Committee, 1954–69 + Undated," *Randolph Papers*; Joint Statement: The U.N. and Non-Self Governing Peoples, attachment to George W. Shepherd Jr. to Dear Friend, November 8, 1954, Box 71, File "9," *Phelps-Stokes Collection*; Herbert Hill to American Committee on Africa, December 10, 1954, Box A356, File "Leagues: American Committee on Africa, 1955," *Papers of the NAACP*; Donald Harrington to Channing Tobias, March 18, 1955, Box A356, File "Leagues: American Committee on Africa, 1955," *Papers of the NAACP*; Minutes of the Executive Board of the American Committee on Africa, December 14, 1955, Box 2, File "Executive Committee Minutes – 1593, June, 1954, Dec., 1955," *Papers of the ACOA*; American Committee on Africa Press Release [on conference to compel United States to revise policies toward Africa], November 17, 1956, Box 43, File "46," *Papers of the ACOA*; John Morsell to Frank Schoell, February 5, 1957, Box A34, File "Africa: General, 1956–59," *Papers of the NAACP-III*; in George Houser to Roy Wilkins, Box A193, File "Leagues and Organizations: American Committee on Africa, 1956–59," *Papers of the NAACP-III*; Roy Wilkins to George M. Houser, August 22, 1958, Box A193, File "Leagues and Organizations: American Committee on Africa, 1956–59," *Papers of the NAACP-III*.

[234] P. L. Prattis to Padmore, March 10, 1959, Box 11, File "3: Correspondence-Padmore, George A.," *Papers of Percival Prattis*, Moorland Spingarn Research Center, Howard University, Washington, DC.

FIGURE 5.5. Ghana President Kwame Nkrumah meeting with President Dwight Eisenhower indicating the growing emergence and initial confidence of African states on the world scene.
Source: Bettman/Corbis. Courtesy of Corbis, Stock Photo ID# BE060440.

continent was "undergoing a wide-open political revolution."[235] At the First All-African People's Conference in Accra, the "300 delegates from 28 states and territories in Africa no longer asked if they should be free." That was a given. The "big question: When?"[236] Wilkins trumpeted the news that "colonialism [was] on the way out and freedom on the way in."[237] (See Figure 5.5)

However, that new freedom was still dogged by the difficulty of moving forward with human rights. The ILRM reported month after month that the UN General "Assembly did not produce any result on the covenants."[238] Another summary lamented that "no notable steps have

[235] Notes for Report, n.d. ca. September 1960, Box 430, File "Africa Visit, 1960," *Papers of W. Averell Harriman*, Library of Congress, Washington, DC.

[236] Independent Intelligence Service, "Africa X-Ray Report: Behind the Scenes Information about Significant Trends," January 1959, Box 82, File "Political Conferences – 1st All African Peoples Conference, Dec. 1958," *McKay Papers*.

[237] Roy Wilkins to All-African Peoples Conference, telegram, January 27, 1960, Box A34, File "Africa: General, 1960–65," *Papers of the NAACP-III*.

[238] Minutes of the Board of Directors Meeting: ILRM, February 21, 1957, Box A194, File "Leagues and Organizations: International League for the Rights of Man, 1956–65," *Papers of the NAACP-III*.

advanced human rights in the spring meeting."[239] Session after session, year after year, the only news was that the "human rights covenants [were] still stalled."[240]

A convergence of fear, disdain, and self-interest from the West, the East, and the nonaligned derailed this major engine of change. The Eisenhower administration, under threat of the Bricker Amendment and the revolt of the Southern Democrats, walked away from international human rights and disengaged the United States from the treaty-making process. In addition, the imperial powers, which had a vested interest in keeping the colonies as weak and dependent as possible, refused to include information in their reports to the Trusteeship Council or the Fourth Committee on the shaky to nonexistent status of human rights in these so-called non-self-governing territories.[241] Nor was the Kremlin any standard bearer for human rights. Moscow funneled millions of innocent people into its gulag system; censored the press and banned free speech; and crushed basic freedom movements throughout Eastern Europe.[242] Finally, there were indications that Kwame Nkrumah, despite all of the accolades about being the harbinger of freedom, did not place as high a priority on human rights as many believed.[243] In fact, Padmore wrote to him shortly before Ghana's independence that the opposition party was "pressing for safeguards to be written into the const[itution]" and had demanded some "statement on Human Rights." Padmore scoffed that these "fools" think "paper guarantees are like the laws of the Medes and Persians. After all," he concluded, "the Weimar German Const[itution] was the most liberal

[239] The Rights of Man: Bulletin of the International League for the Rights of Man (March and April 1957), May 1957, Box 1157, File "5," *Papers of the ACLU.*

[240] The Rights of Man: Bulletin of the International League for the Rights of Man (November and December 1956), January 1, 1957, ibid.

[241] Minutes of the Board of Directors Meeting: ILRM, April 18, 1957, Box A194, File "Leagues and Organizations: International League for the Rights of Man, 1956–65," *Papers of the NAACP-III*; Roger Baldwin to Rikhi Jaipal, April 30, 1958, Box 8, File "United Nations: Non-Self Governing Territories, Fourth Committee (1956–59)," *Papers of the ILHR*; R. Jaipal to Roger Baldwin, May 2, 1958, Box 8, File "United Nations: Non-Self Governing Territories, Fourth Committee (1956–59)," *Papers of the ILHR*; Mason Sears to Roger Baldwin, May 2, 1958, Box 8, File "United Nations: Non-Self Governing Territories, Fourth Committee (1956–59)," *Papers of the ILHR*; Roger Baldwin to M. Chalapathi Rau, October 9, 1958, Box 8, File "United Nations: Non-Self Governing Territories, Fourth Committee (1956–59)," *Papers of the ILHR.*

[242] Geoffrey Robertson, *Crimes against Humanity: The Struggle for Global Justice* (New York: New Press, 2006), 44–45; Anne Applebaum, *Iron Curtain: The Crushing of Eastern Europe 1944–56* (New York: Doubleday, 2012).

[243] Houser, "Human Rights and the Liberation Struggle," 10.

in the world yet Hitler just trampled it underfoot."[244] Thus, barely more than a decade after World War II, with all of the promises of the Atlantic Charter and the hopes placed in the UN in the rearview mirror, it became all too clear that human rights had very few, if any, powerful allies.

By the end of the 1950s, the two locomotives of real freedom, political independence and human rights, had openly diverged. In 1959 the ILRM reported that the UN General Assembly "was ... dominated by the ... rising nationalism of African trust and non-self governing territories which in 1960 will result in the independence of possibly half-a-dozen countries."[245] Indeed the nationalists blazed ahead so dramatically that, as the National Security Council observed, "the increase of the African group from 7.7 percent of U.N. members in 1945 to 24.6 percent in 1960 and an estimated 28.8 percent in 1962 will make this ... by far the largest single geographic group in the U.N."[246] Although political independence barreled ahead, human rights lost steam just a few blocks out of the station. Looking back, ACOA's George Houser confirmed that in "the euphoria of the upsurge of nationalism and the struggle for freedom in this period, not much attention was given to the concepts of human rights or democracy."[247] To be sure, the December 1960 United Nations Declaration on the Granting of Independence to Colonial Countries and Peoples was laced with elegant nods to human rights, but, in truth, it was just placebo language that cast this new era in the hopes of 1945 without grappling with or acknowledging the damage that had been done to those rights in the intervening years. Moreover, although the preamble evoked freedom for the people, the body of the text was all about the sovereignty of the nation.[248] In that sleight of hand, human rights were firmly decoupled from independence.[249]

[244] Postscript, October 9, 1956, Box 41, File "14: George Padmore Correspondence, 1952–1957," *Nkrumah Papers*.

[245] The Rights of Man: Bulletin of the International League for the Rights of Man, (November – December 1959), Box 1158, File "28," *Papers of the ACLU*; The Rights of Man: Bulletin of the International League for the Rights of Man (September – October 1960), November 1960, ibid.

[246] Briefing Note for PB meeting of 6/24/60: The Changing Character of the U.N., June 24, 1960, Box 8, File "U.N.," Special Staff File Series, *White House Office, National Security Council Staff*, Dwight D. Eisenhower Presidential Library, Abilene, KS.

[247] Houser, "Human Rights and the Liberation Struggle," 9.

[248] Declaration on the Granting of Independence to Colonial Countries and PeoplesAdopted by General Assembly Resolution 1514 (XV) of 14 December 1960, http://www.un.org/en/decolonization/declaration.shtml. Accessed November 4, 2013; Burke, *Decolonization and the Evolution of International Human Rights*, 55.

[249] Burke, *Decolonization and the Evolution of International Human Rights*, 56–58.

Just a few years earlier the NAACP had articulated a powerful human rights vision. The premise was that "[f]reedom of the individual from political, racial, and religious discrimination must go hand in hand with economic advancement in order to realize true self-respect and full dignity. In the last analysis," the Association asserted, "this is the real key to a permanent world peace."[250] After the events of 1960, this perspective not only looked quaint but also looked like the road not taken.

---

[250] Enclosure in Edward R. Dudley to Roger Baldwin, September 23, 1955, Box 7, File "National Association for the Advancement of Colored People," *Papers of ILHR.*

Conclusion

Beyond the Single Story

The NAACP is the nation's oldest, largest, baddest, boldest, most hated, most debated, most notorious, and most victorious civil rights organization.
– Benjamin Todd Jealous[1]

The NAACP was determined to fight for a freedom that was more robust, inclusive, and real than the U.S. government or the colonial powers were ever willing to support. When Churchill said that the Atlantic Charter did not apply to the British Empire, he meant it. When he insisted that "America and Europe ... will ... keep Negro Africa in its place," the prime minister more than meant it.[2]

When Southern Democrats blocked the UN's development of human rights in a self-serving effort to protect Jim Crow, they certainly meant it. When Truman and powerful members of the press defined economic development as welfare for the Hottentots, they surely meant it. When Daniel Malan roared that he would not have the "festering sore" of racial equality anywhere near his South Africa, he definitely meant it. When Carlo Sforza and Paul Reynaud compared the entrenched Italian and French settlers in their respective colonies to whites in South Africa, they so meant it. And, when the Dutch made clear that they were willing to fight to the last man in the Indian Army and the last red cent of the Marshall Plan to control Indonesia, they meant every word.

The NAACP meant it, too. The Second World War had raised the militancy quotient exponentially. The "aggressive spirit of the NAACP" was

[1] *Columbia Magazine*, Spring 2013, cover. Thank you Henry Krisch for sending this to me.
[2] W[inston] S. C[hurchill] to Foreign Secretary, August 4, 1952, PREM 11/300.

on display for all to see.[3] The black press certainly noticed. The *Atlanta Daily World* trumpeted in 1942 "Democracies Face the 'New Negro.'"[4] According to the *Baltimore Afro-American,* that New Negro did not seek or ask, nor did it come "hat-in-hand."[5] Rather, it demanded. "Revolutionary," in fact, was the *Pittsburgh Courier*'s description of the transformation. The NAACP in South Carolina "brought a new type of leadership to the Negro's fight for his rights. Bold, daring, unmindful of threats and intimidation they have realized that politics at best is a rough and tumble affair and have fashioned Uncle Tom's walking cane into a rapier to impale white supremacy.... They have called the white man's bluff."[6]

This militancy survived the Second World War. It even braved the Cold War, and, most important, it did not stop at the water's edge. In early 1949, Walter White insisted that given the global scope of racism "the program of the association had [to] grow ... both by choice and necessity." It was the NAACP's job, he said, to undercut "the attempts, subtle or brazen, to perpetuate colonialism in Eritrea, Libya, Somaliland, Southwest Africa, [and] Indonesia," as well as additional areas in Asia, the Caribbean, and Africa. "All of these and other efforts," he lamented, "had to be carried out on a shoestring, because the increasing complexity and expensiveness of the problem at home left little money for the task in other parts of the world." However, White added, "increasingly it became clear that it was as short-sighted and futile to think of the race question in an exclusively American framework as it would be to believe that what happened to Negroes in Mississippi had no bearing on what happened to Negroes in Massachusetts and vice versa."[7]

The NAACP therefore brought to the freedom table vision, access to power, a well-oiled public relations/media capacity, and keen strategic thinking on how to change the terms of debate and redefine a narrative. The point was to put white supremacy, which was the engine driving colonialism and Jim Crow, on a collision course with a rights-based society. One staff member remarked that "the struggle of the Africans for

[3] "Healy Raps 'Uncle Toms'; 6,000 Join Ranks of NAACP," *Afro-American,* October 24, 1942.
[4] Wittie Anna Higgins, "The Democracies Face the 'New Negro,'" *Atlanta Daily World,* June 20, 1942.
[5] "Healy Raps 'Uncle Toms'," *Afro-American.*
[6] John H. Young, III, "South Carolina Debauches Voting, But Revolutionary Spirit Spurs Negro Leaders," *Pittsburgh Courier,* January 20, 1945.
[7] Walter White, "A Suggestion for Change in the Name of the NAACP," *Chicago Defender,* September 3, 1949.

political equality helps our fight for civil rights in America, just as our fight helps theirs."[8]

This sense of shared struggle brought out a tried-and-true strategy. Just as the NAACP eyed Jim Crow like a Jenga tower, then carefully selected specific legal cases to compromise the structural integrity of de jure segregation, the Association also strategically attacked the pillars that propped up "the white man's burden."

The work for South West Africa, Somalia, Libya, Eritrea, and Indonesia was specifically designed to put the legitimacy of colonialism under intense scrutiny – scrutiny that it could never withstand. For example, South Africa's white minority rule was tailor-made for demanding both international accountability and an administering power's demonstrated commitment to human rights. As State Department officials made clear, Pretoria could not realistically defend its racist policies to the UN or, for that matter, to any credible international audience. And that inability undercut not only South Africa's claims but also the legitimacy of the regime itself. Similarly, the combination of Italy's genocidal campaigns, economic devastation after the war, and geostrategic avarice allowed the NAACP to make the wishes of the inhabitants paramount, highlight the inability of impoverished Rome to fulfill the human rights standards expected in trusteeships, and explore the possibility of the UN as a trust power. Meanwhile, the Netherlands' stubborn refusal to acknowledge Indonesian independence put into play the full force of public opinion in pressuring governments to honor the right to self-determination, and, equally important, to set the precedent that domestic jurisdiction cannot be stretched to mask a much-hated and hotly contested alien rule. These were some of the most important battles that began to transform colonial empires from status symbols to badges of shame.

But this work is missed unless the scholarly lens pulls back from the black Left to the NAACP. That refocusing on African American liberals, as I noted in another venue,

lays open the circuits of informal power that transcended national, racial, ideological, and historical boundaries to take on a system of oppression that had reigned for hundreds of years. It reveals the ways that the seemingly powerless conceptualized their individual and collective strengths to challenge the dominant economic and political regimes. In fact, this battle to dismantle empires of racism in the midst of the Cold War reveals something about the possible. This struggle,

---

[8] James Farmer to H. I. Bearden, September 25, 1959, Box A307, File "Staff: Farmer, James General, 1957, 1959, Jan–Sept.," *Papers of the NAACP-III.*

frankly, should have been stillborn given the disproportionate financial, political, and technological power arrayed by the Europeans and Americans. It should have been an exercise in futility because of the ideological straitjacket of East and West that construed challenges to that discourse as traitorous. And, it should have been impossible given the geographic dispersion of racial allies spread across [four] continents with limited access to the technologies that revolutionized communications. Yet, in the end, African Americans found ways to circumnavigate around those challenges and work with and for those whom they saw as waging a similar struggle.[9]

By 1960, as colony after colony emerged onto the international scene as the nations of Somalia, Republic of Congo, Madagascar, and more, the *New York Times* stood in awe of this "breath-taking transformation of Africa."[10] Roy Wilkins was also impressed. The hopes of the 1940s were now bearing fruit and he knew that the NAACP played a role. He congratulated Abdullahi Issa on Somalia's independence then added that the Association was "proud to have been of small assistance in your appearances before the United Nations when you were struggling for the freedom you have now attained."[11]

The tragedy, however, for Somalia – and many other newly emerged nations – was that real freedom was never truly attained. Political independence, yes. Freedom, no. Somalia (and many other Third World nations) got caught in the vise of the Cold War, as well as the chaos that descended from colonial boundaries that disrupted lives, identities, and alliances.[12] More than that, however, Somalia is representative of the chaos, bloodshed, violence, and instability that comes when political independence is severed from human rights.

Scholars, such as economist Paul Collier, identified the "traps" that have ensnared a billion people in abject poverty; and political scientist Robert Bates charted the endemic violence brought on by a convergence of coercive authoritarian regimes and untold wealth in the hands of elites.[13] However, the core of the problem through a historian's lens

---

[9] Anderson, "The Histories of African Americans' Anticolonialism during the Cold War," 179.

[10] "African 'Independence Week,'" *New York Times*, June 30, 1960.

[11] "NAACP Hails New African Nations," press release, July 1, 1960, Box A34, File "Africa: General, 1960–65," *Papers of the NAACP-III*.

[12] Westad, *The Global Cold War*; William T. Mountz, "Americanizing Africanization: The Congo Crisis, 1960–1967" (PhD diss., University of Missouri, 2014).

[13] Paul Collier, *The Bottom Billion: Why the Poorest Countries Are Failing and What Can Be Done about It* (New York: Oxford University Press, 2007), 5–8; Robert H. Bates, *When Things Fell Apart: State Failure in Late-Century Africa* (New York: Cambridge University Press, 2008), 3–14.

is that independence was seriously compromised before it even began because the human rights essential for viability and freedom – strong, functional educational systems, respect for and adherence to labor standards, quality accessible health care, adequate housing, the right and ability to choose one's own government, and so much more – were never instituted.[14]

To be clear, the story of the Third World is not confined to "a genocide inside a failed state inside a dictatorship."[15] The point is that the inability of human rights to take hold in the UN with the same intensity and ferocity as decolonization portended a world of trouble. The rigid stances of the major stakeholders made clear that human rights were much more threatening to the status quo than even decolonization. As Wm. Roger Louis and Ronald Robinson demonstrated, once the West conceded that colonial liberation was a given, the goal was to make sure that independence was as hollow as possible to maintain Anglo-American control.[16] Unfortunately, shortsighted and self-serving actions were not confined to the colonial powers. After many of the freedom fighters became prime ministers, alleviating the continued suffering of their people took a backseat. The lesson learned once independence had been achieved, historian Roland Burke noted, was that "[i]ndividual rights had to be violated to secure national sovereignty, the opposite of the ideology that had animated the self-determination campaigns of the 1950s."[17] The NAACP feared as much and consistently stressed the importance of applying to the colonies "Articles 22 to 27 … of the Universal Declaration of Human Rights," which include "the rights … to equal pay for equal work, … to a standard of living adequate for the health and well-being of one's family, [and] education" to ensure a smooth transition to viable nationhood.[18]

The Italian trusteeship for Somalia, for example, was supposed to "foster the development of free political institutions … promote the economic

---

[14] Amartya Sen, *Development as Freedom* (New York: Anchor Books, 1999), 5–10; 148–151. For histories after independence see, for example, Bradley R. Simpson, *Economists with Guns: Authoritarian Development and U.S.-Indonesian Relations, 1960–1968* (Stanford: Stanford University Press, 2008); James Fergusson, *The World's Most Dangerous Place: Inside the Outlaw State of Somalia* (Boston, MA: De Capo, 2013).

[15] Nicholas D. Kristof, "Bright Continent: Why Africa's Success Stories Are Too Often Overlooked," *New York Times Upfront*, April 19, 2010.

[16] Wm. Roger Louis and Ronald Robinson, "The Imperialism of Decolonization," *Journal of Imperial and Commonwealth History*, 22, no. 3 (1994), 487.

[17] Burke, *Decolonization and the Evolution of International Human Rights*, 58.

[18] International and Colonial Problems, June 1951, Box A44, File "Annual Convention: Proposed Resolutions, 1951," *Papers of the NAACP*.

advancement and self-sufficiency of the inhabitants ... protect the rights and fundamental freedoms of all elements of the population" and to do so by "recognizing the fact that education in its broadest sense is the only sure foundation" to "national independence with due respect for freedom and democracy."[19] Yet at the onset of Somalia's independence, 90 percent of the population was illiterate and there were fewer than 250 college graduates to run a nation of 1.8 million people spread out over 246,000 square miles.[20]

How the human rights hopes of the Somalis and many more like them intersected with the anticolonial struggle waged by African Americans are critical for understanding the arc of the post-Second World War world. That analysis provides a much clearer understanding of what was done, undone, and why. The role of African Americans, particularly those in the NAACP, in helping "strip the global system of its urbane veneer to reveal the structures of racist power deepens the story about the strategies and tactics used by Third World freedom fighters."[21] It also reveals further how local and domestic concerns over power and status undermined the development and application of human rights globally.

However, this complex narrative remains hidden if scholars only see the black Left and posit what the turn toward or away from communism entailed.[22] Indeed, tracking the NAACP's anticolonial activism explodes the "danger of the single story" that has focused solely on a type of radicalism reserved for die-hard Communists.[23]

My glance at Jupiter's moons, therefore, began with the finding aid for the NAACP papers at the Library of Congress. Given the Ptolemaic

[19] Committee for Italian Somaliland Draft Report of the Committee to the Trusteeship Council, T/AC.18/L.9, January 18, 1950, UN.

[20] E. A. Bayne, *Four Ways of Politics: State and Nation in Italy, Somalia, Israel, Iran* (New York: American Universities Field Staff, 1965), 102, 112.

[21] Anderson, "The Histories of African Americans' Anticolonialism during the Cold War," 180.

[22] It is important to note that African and Asian nations that had communist governments could be as brutal as right-wing dictatorships. See Michela Wrong, *In the Footsteps of Mr. Kurtz: Living on the Brink of Disaster in the Congo* (London: Fourth Estate, 2000); Benedict R. O'Gorman Anderson, ed., *Violence and the State in Suharto's Indonesia* (Ithaca, NY: Cornell University Press, 2001); Philip Short, *Pol Pot: The History of a Nightmare* (London: John Murray, 2004); Steve Bloomfield, "Mengistu Found Guilty of Ethiopian genocide," *Independent*, December 13, 2006, http://www.independent.co.uk/news/world/africa/mengistu-found-guilty-of-ethiopian-genocide-428233.html. Accessed December 5, 2013.

[23] Chimamanda Ngozi Adichie, "The Danger of a Single Story," TED Talk, http://www.ted.com/talks/chimamanda_adichie_the_danger_of_a_single_story.htm. Accessed December 5, 2013.

logic, there were just far too many boxes marked "Africa" and "Asia" in the collection. Like the lunar objects orbiting the largest planet, they should not have existed. Yet there they were opening up galaxies of inquiry.

Bibliography

Primary Sources

Archival Materials

AMISTAD RESEARCH CENTER, TULANE UNIVERSITY,
NEW ORLEANS, LA

American Committee on Africa
Marguerite Cartwright
Edward Dudley

BEINECKE MANUSCRIPT LIBRARY, YALE UNIVERSITY,
NEW HAVEN, CT

Walter Francis White and Poppy Cannon White Correspondence

BODLEIAN LIBRARY, RHODES HOUSE, UNIVERSITY OF
OXFORD, OXFORD, UK

Africa Bureau
Guthrie Michael Scott

CHICAGO HISTORICAL SOCIETY, CHICAGO, IL

Archibald J. Carey Jr.

COLUMBIA UNIVERSITY, NEW YORK, NY

Herbert Lehman
Papers of the United Nations

DWIGHT D. EISENHOWER PRESIDENTIAL LIBRARY, ABILENE, KS

Dwight Eisenhower Papers as President
John Foster Dulles
Dennis Fitzgerald
National Security Council Staff Papers
Office of the Special Assistant for National Security Affairs

FRANKLIN DELANO ROOSEVELT PRESIDENTIAL LIBRARY,
HYDE PARK, NY

Louis Bean
Adolph Berle
Francis P. Corrigan
Oscar Cox
Ernest Cuneo
Charles Fahy
Leon Henderson
Gardner Jackson
Isador Lubin
Henry Morgenthau, Jr.
Henry Morgenthau, III
Eleanor Roosevelt
Franklin Delano Roosevelt: Personal Secretary's File
Whitney Hart Shepardson
Charles W. Taussig
Rexford G. Tugwell
Henry Wallace
Louis B. Wehle
Sumner Welles
John G. Winant
Vertical File

GEORGETOWN UNIVERSITY, SPECIAL COLLECTIONS DIVISION,
WASHINGTON, DC

Cecil Lyons
George McGhee
Marion (Clinch Calkins) Merrell Family Papers
Cornelius Von Engert

HARRY S. TRUMAN PRESIDENTIAL LIBRARY, INDEPENDENCE, MO

Dean Acheson
Stanley Andrews
Henry Bennett
John F. Cady Oral History
George Elsey

W. J. Gallman Manuscript
Stanton Griffis
William H. Hastie Oral History
Harry N. Howard
Philip M. Kaiser
Isador Lubin Oral History
Jesse MacKnight
George McGhee
Miscellaneous Historical Documents Relating to Harry S. Truman
Record Group 220: President's Materials Policy Commission
John M. Redding Oral History
William Sanders Oral History
Durward Sandifer Oral History
Dirk U. Stikker Oral History
Joseph Sweeney
Harry S. Truman: Official File
Harry S. Truman: President's Personal File
Harry S. Truman: President's Secretary's File
Harry S. Truman: Staff Member and Office Files: Naval Aide to the President
    Files, 1945–53
Harry S. Truman: White House Central File
Eelco Van Kleffens Oral History

HARVARD UNIVERSITY, CAMBRIDGE, MA

William H. Hastie

INSTITUTE OF COMMONWEALTH STUDIES, UNIVERSITY OF LONDON,
LONDON, UK

Ruth First

KAUTZ FAMILY ARCHIVES, UNIVERSITY OF MINNESOTA,
MINNEAPOLIS, MN

Channing Tobias
Max Yergan
YMCA Files on South Africa

LIBRARY OF CONGRESS, WASHINGTON, DC

O. Benjamin Gerig
W. Averell Harriman
Loy Henderson
Rayford Whittingham Logan
National Association for the Advancement of Colored People, Part II
    (1940–1955)
    Series A (Office Files)

Series B (Legal)
Series C (Branch)
Series H (Washington Bureau)
National Association for the Advancement of Colored People, Part III
(1956–1965)
Series A (Office Files)
Series B (Legal)
Series C (Branch)
Series H (Washington Bureau)
Leo Pasvolsky
A. Philip Randolph
Francis B. Sayre
Roy Wilkins

MASSACHUSETTS HISTORICAL SOCIETY, BOSTON, MA

Henry Cabot Lodge, II
Mason Sears

MELVILLE J. HERSKOVITS LIBRARY OF AFRICAN STUDIES, NORTHWESTERN
UNIVERSITY, EVANSTON, IL

D. Vernon McKay

MOORLAND-SPINGARN RESEARCH CENTER, HOWARD UNIVERSITY,
WASHINGTON, DC

Henry Arthur Callis
Abram Harris
Rayford Logan
Kwame Nkrumah
William Patterson
Percival Prattis
Paul Robeson
Arthur B. Spingarn
Louis T. Wright
Max Yergan

NATIONAL ARCHIVES, KEW, UK

CAB/195: Cabinet Secretaries' Notebooks
CO 525: Colonial Office: Nyasaland Original Correspondence, 1904–1951
CO 537: Colonial Office and Predecessors: Confidential General and
Confidential Original Correspondence, 1759–1955
CO 554: Colonial Office: West Africa Original Correspondence
CO 822: Colonial Office: East Africa: Original Correspondence, 1927–1964

CO 936: Colonial Office: International Relations Departments

CO 1015: Colonial Office: Central Africa and Aden: Original Correspondence, 1950–1962

DO 35: Dominions Office and Commonwealth Relations Office: Original Correspondence, 1915–1971

FO 115: Foreign Office: Embassy and Consulates, United States of America: General Correspondence, 1791–1967

FO 371: Foreign Office, Political Departments – General Correspondence

FO 954: Foreign Office: Private Office Papers of Sir Anthony Eden, Earl of Avon, Secretary of State for Foreign Affairs, 1935–1946

FO 961: United Kingdom Delegation to the United Nations: Correspondence and Papers, 1946–1967

FO 1015: War Office and Foreign Office, Administration of African Territories: Registered Files, 1915–1952

KV 2: Records of the Security Service: Personal Files, Communists and Suspected Communists, including Russians and Communist Sympathisers

PREM 11: Prime Minister's Office: Correspondence and Papers, 1951–1964, 1944–1964

NATIONAL ARCHIVES II, COLLEGE PARK, MD

Record Group 43: International Organization
Record Group 59: Records of the State Department
Record Group 84: Foreign Service Posts including U.S. Mission to the United Nations

NEW YORK PUBLIC LIBRARY, NEW YORK, NY

International League for Human Rights, 1948–1990

PEACE COLLECTION, SWARTHMORE COLLEGE, SWARTHMORE, PA

John Nevin Sayre

SCHLESINGER LIBRARY, RADCLIFFE COLLEGE, CAMBRIDGE, MA

Edith Sampson

SCHOMBURG CENTER FOR THE STUDY OF BLACK CULTURE, NEW YORK, NY

Ralph Bunche
W. Alphaeus Hunton
George Padmore
Phelps-Stokes Collection
Hugh Smythe
Channing Tobias

SEELEY G. MUDD LIBRARY, PRINCETON UNIVERSITY, PRINCETON, NJ

American Civil Liberties Union (ACLU)
Hamilton Fish Armstrong
John Foster Dulles
Adlai Stevenson

UNIVERSITY OF VERMONT, BURLINGTON, VT

Warren Austin

WORLD BANK ARCHIVES, WASHINGTON, DC

Papers of the World Bank

Microfilm

EMORY UNIVERSITY, ATLANTA, GA

The Paul Robeson Collection

OHIO STATE UNIVERSITY, COLUMBUS, OH

Confidential U.S. State Department Central Files: South Africa, 1950–1954
OSS/State Department Intelligence and Research Reports, Part XIII – Africa:
1941–1961.
*South African Press Digests, 1949–1972/South Africa: The Early Years of
Apartheid*

THOMAS J. DODD RESEARCH LIBRARY, UNIVERSITY OF CONNECTICUT,
STORRS, CT

A. B. Xuma

UNIVERSITY OF MISSOURI-COLUMBIA, COLUMBIA, MO

Bayard Rustin
Confidential U.S. State Department Central Files: British Africa, 1945–1949
Confidential U.S. State Department Central Files: British Africa, 1950–1954
*Confidential U.S. State Department Central Files: France, Foreign Affairs,
1945–1949*
*Confidential U.S. State Department Central Files: Great Britain, Foreign
Affairs, 1945–1949*
*Confidential U.S. State Department Central Files: India, Internal Affairs, 1945–
1949, Part 1.*
*Confidential U.S. State Department Central Files: India, Foreign Affairs,
1950–1954*
*Confidential U.S. State Department Central Files: Italy, Internal Affairs,
1940–1944*

Confidential U.S. State Department Central Files: Southeast Asia, 1944–1958
W. E. B. Du Bois
Marshall/Lovett Memorandums to President Truman, 1947–1948
NAACP, Part 14. Race Relations in the International arena, 1940–1955
Papers of the NAACP
State Department Documents of the Post-War Programs Committee, 1944

Published Government Documents

Canadian Department of Foreign Affairs and International Trade. http://www.international.gc.ca/history-histoire/documents-documents.aspx.

CIA. *World Fact Book.* https://www.cia.gov/library/publications/the–world–fact-book/fields/2111.html.

Ethiopian Ministry of Justice. *Documents on Italian War Crimes Submitted to the United Nations War Crimes Commission by the Imperial Ethiopian Government,* Vol. 1. Addis Ababa: Ethiopian Ministry of Justice, 1949.

FBI. *File on Eleanor Roosevelt.* Wilmington, DE: Scholarly Resources, 1996.

Great Britain Ministry of Information. *The First to Be Freed.* London: His Majesty's Stationery Office, 1944.

League of Nations. "Report of the League of Nations Council Committee," *American Journal of International Law,* 30, no. 1, Supplement: *Official Documents* (January 1936): 1–26.

Namibia, Ministry of Mines and Ministry. "Geological Survey of Namibia." http://www.mme.gov.na/gsn/diamond.htm. Accessed May 3, 2013.

Nehru, Jawaharlal. *India's Foreign Policy: Selected Speeches, September 1946–April 1961.* Delhi: Publications Division, Ministry of Information and Broadcasting, Government of India, 1961.

Officiële Bescheiden Betreffende de Nederlands-Indonesische Betrekkingen, 1945–1950. The Hague: Martinius Nijhoff, 1972.

The Avalon Project: Documents in Law, History, and Diplomacy. *Atlantic Charter,* August 14, 1941. http://avalon.law.yale.edu/wwii/atlantic.asp.

U.S. Congress. Senate. Committee on Foreign Relations. *Hearings Regarding European Recovery Program.* 80th Congress, 2nd sess., January 16, 19–24, 26–28, 1948.

Congressional Record (April 6, 1949), vol. 95, pt. 3.

Congressional Record (April 25, 1950), vol. 96, pt. 5.

Congressional Record (May 23, 1950), vol. 96, pt. 6.

U.S. Department of State. *Foreign Relations of the United States,* 1947. Vol. 3, *The British Commonwealth; Europe.* Washington, DC: Government Printing Office, 1972.

Foreign Relations of the United States, 1947. Vol. 5, *The Near East and Africa.* Washington, DC: Government Printing Office, 1971.

Foreign Relations of the United States, 1948. Vol. 3, *Western Europe.* Washington, DC: Government Printing Office, 1974.

Foreign Relations of the United States, 1948. Vol. 6, *The Far East and Australasia.* Washington, DC: Government Printing Office, 1974.

Foreign Relations of the United States, 1949. Vol. 4, *Western Europe.* Washington, DC: Government Printing Office, 1975.

Foreign Relations of the United States, 1950. Vol. 2, *United Nations; Western Hemisphere.* Washington, DC: Government Printing Office, 1976.

U.S. National Archives and Records Administration. *Power of Persuasion: Four Freedoms.* http://www.archives.gov/exhibits/powers_of_persuasion/four_freedoms/four_freedoms.html. Accessed June 19, 2012.

United Nations. Charter of the United Nations, Chapter VII: Action with Respect to Threats to the Peace, Breaches of the Peace, and Acts of Aggression. http://www.un.org/en/documents/charter/chapter7.shtml.

Charter of the United Nations, Chapter XII, Article 76. http://www.un.org/en/documents/charter/chapter12.shtml.

Declaration of Human Rights. http://www.un.org/en/documents/udhr/index.shtml#a19.

Declaration on the Granting of Independence to Colonial Countries and Peoples Adopted by General Assembly resolution 1514 (XV) of 14 December 1960. http://www.un.org/en/decolonization/declaration.shtml.

Question of the disposal of the former Italian colonies, Resolution 289 (IV), November 21, 1949. http://daccess-dds-ny.un.org/doc/RESOLUTION/GEN/NR0/051/08/IMG/NR005108.pdf?OpenElement.

Yearbook of the United Nations, 1948–1949. http://www.unmultimedia.org/searchers/yearbook/page.jsp?volume=1948-49&page=874&searchType=advanced.

Andrew W. Cordier and Wilder Foote, eds. *Public Papers of the Secretaries-General of the United Nations*, Vol. 1, *Trygve Lie: 1946–1953.* New York: Columbia University Press, 1969.

Report of the Secretary-General on the Work of the Organization. June 1946, A /63.

The United Nations and Apartheid, 1948–1994. Introduction by Boutros Boutros-Ghali, Blue Book Series, Vol. 1. New York: United Nations Department of Public Information, 1994.

United Nations Security Council. *Report of the Security Council to the General Assembly Covering the Period from 17 January to 15 July 1946: Official Records of the Second Part of the First Session of the General Assembly,* Supplement No. 1, October 3, 1946, A/93.

Report of the Security Council to the General Assembly Covering the Period from 16 July 1947 to 15 July 1948, Official Records: Third Session. Supplement No. 2, A/620. Lake Success, NY: United Nations, 1948.

Court Cases

Brown v. Board of Education, 347 U.S. 483 (S. Ct. 1954).

NAACP v. Alabama ex. rel. Patterson, 357 U.S. 449 (S. Ct. 1958).

Memoirs

Byrnes, James F. *Speaking Frankly.* New York and London: Harper & Brothers Publishers, 1947.

Elsey, George McKee. *An Unplanned Life: A Memoir.* Columbia: University of Missouri Press, 2005.

Jessup, Philip C. *The Birth of Nations.* New York and London: Columbia University Press, 1974.

McGhee, George. *Envoy to the Middle World: Adventures in Diplomacy.* Foreword by Dean Rusk. New York: Harper & Row, 1983.

Robeson, Paul. *Paul Robeson Speaks: Writings, Speeches, Interviews, 1918–1974.* Edited with introduction and notes by Philip S. Foner. New York: Brunner/Mazel Publishers, 1978.

Scott, Michael. *A Time to Speak.* London: Faber and Faber, 1958.

Sears, Mason. *Years of High Purpose: From Trusteeship to Nationhood.* Preface by Henry Cabot Lodge and introduction by Julius Nyerere. Washington, DC: University Press of America, 1980.

White, Walter. *A Man Called White: The Autobiography of Walter White.* New York: Viking Press, 1948.

Wilkins, Roy. *Standing Fast: The Autobiography of Roy Wilkins.* Introduction by Julian Bond. New York: Viking Press, 1982.

Interview

Mildred Roxborough

Databases

Foreign Broadcast Information Services
Hansard Millbanks House of Lords and Commons Debates
ProQuest Black Freedom Struggle History Vault: Papers of the NAACP
ProQuest Historical Black Newspapers

Web sites

Cold War International History Project: The Korean War. http://digitalarchive.wilsoncenter.org/collection/134/korean-war-origins-1945-1950

Measuring Worth: Relative Calculators and Data Sets http://www.measuring-worth.com/uscompare/

Contemporary Periodicals

Atlanta Daily World
Boston Globe
Canberra Times
Chicago Defender
Chicago Tribune
Christian Science Monitor
Cleveland Call and Post

Columbia Magazine
Jet
London Times
Los Angeles Sentinel
Los Angeles Times
Manchester Guardian
Netherlands News Digest
New Africa
New York Amsterdam News
New York Times
Norfolk New Journal and Guide
Palestine Post
Pittsburgh Courier
The Times of India
Wall Street Journal
Washington Post

Videos and Recordings

Adichie, Chimamanda Ngozi. "The Danger of a Single Story," *TED Talk.* http://www.ted.com/talks/chimamanda_adichie_the_danger_of_a_single_story. html. Accessed December 5, 2013.
Civilisation on Trial in South Africa, prod. and dir. by Michael Scott and Clive Donner, Villon Films, 1948, 1994. Videocassette, 24 min.
Long Night's Journey Into Day, prod. and dir. by Deborah Hoffman, and Frances Reid, California Newsreel, 2001. DVD, 94 min.

Secondary Sources

Achebe, Chinua. *Things Fall Apart.* New York: Fawcett Crest, 1959.
Agarossi, Elena. *A Nation Collapses: The Italian Surrender of September 1943*, trans. Harvey Ferguson. New York: Cambridge University Press, 1999.
Albrecht-Carrie, Rene. "Italian Colonial Policy, 1914–1918," *Journal of Modern History*, 18, no. 2 (June 1946): 123–147.
   "Peace with Italy – An Appraisal," *Political Science Quarterly*, 62, no. 4 (December 1947): 481–503.
Ambrose, Stephen. *Eisenhower: The President.* New York: Simon & Schuster, 1984.
Anderson, Benedict R. O'Gorman, ed. *Violence and the State in Suharto's Indonesia.* Ithaca, NY: Cornell University Press, 2001.
Anderson, Carol. *Eyes Off the Prize: The United Nations and the African American Struggle for Human Rights, 1944–1955.* New York: Cambridge University Press, 2003.
   "Bleached Souls and Red Negroes: The NAACP and Black Communists in the Early Cold War, 1948–1952" in *Window on Freedom: Race, Civil Rights, and Foreign Affairs, 1945–1988*, ed. Brenda Gayle Plummer. Chapel Hill: University of North Carolina Press, 2003.

"The Cold War and the Atlantic World," in *The Atlantic World: 1450–2000*, ed. Toyin Falola and Kevin D. Roberts. Bloomington: Indiana University Press, 2008.

"The Histories of African Americans' Anticolonialism during the Cold War," in *The Cold War in the Third World*, ed. Robert McMahon. New York: Oxford University Press, 2013.

"International Conscience, the Cold War, and Apartheid: The NAACP's Alliance with the Reverend Michael Scott for South West Africa's Liberation, 1946–1952," *Journal of World History* 19, no. 3 (September 2008): 297–326.

"Rethinking Radicalism: African Americans and the Liberation Struggles in Somalia, Libya, and Eritrea, 1945–1949," *Journal of the Historical Society* 11, no. 4 (December 2011): 385–423.

Anderson, David. *The Histories of the Hanged: The Dirty War in Kenya and the End of Empire*. New York: W. W. Norton, 2005.

Andrew, Christopher and Vasili Mitrokhin. *The World Was Going Our Way: The KGB and the Battle for the Third World*. New York: Basic Books, 2005.

Applebaum, Anne. *Iron Curtain: The Crushing of Eastern Europe 1944–1956*. New York: Doubleday, 2012.

Apraku, Kofi. *Outside Looking In: An African Perspective on American Pluralistic Society*. Westport, CT: Praeger, 1996.

Asante, S. K. B. "The Afro-American and the Italo-Ethiopian Crisis," *Race*, 15, no. 2 (1973): 167–184.

Atkinson, Rick. *An Army at Dawn: The War in North Africa, 1942–1943*. New York: Henry Holt and Company, 2002.

Baer, George W. *The Coming of the Italian-Ethiopian War*. Cambridge, MA: Harvard University Press, 1967.

Review of "The Ethiopian War: 1935–1941" by Angelo Del Boca. *Journal of Modern History*, 42, no. 4 (December 1970): 708–710.

Balaji, Murali. *The Professor and the Pupil: The Politics and Friendship of W.E.B. Du Bois and Paul Robeson*. New York: Nation Books, 2007.

Baldwin, Kate. *Beyond the Color Line and the Iron Curtain: Reading Encounters between Black and Red, 1922–1963*. Durham, NC: Duke University Press, 2002.

Barker, A. J. *The Civilizing Mission: A History of the Italo-Ethiopian War of 1935–1936*. New York: Dial Press, 1968.

Bartley, Numan V. *The Rise of Massive Resistance: Race and Politics in the South During the 1950's*. Baton Rouge: Louisiana State University Press, 1969, 1997.

Bates, Robert H. *When Things Fell Apart: State Failure in Late-Century Africa*. New York: Cambridge University Press, 2008.

Bayly, Christopher and Tim Harper. *Forgotten Armies: The Fall of British Asia, 1941–1945* London: Allen Lane, 2004.

Bayne, E. A. *Four Ways of Politics: State and Nation in Italy, Somalia, Israel, Iran*. New York: American Universities Field Staff, 1965.

"Somalia on the Horn: A Counterpoint of Problems Confronting One of Africa's New Nations," *Publication of the American University Field Service Reports*, Vol. VII, no. 8. New York: AUFS, 1960.

"Somalia on the Horn: A Counterpoint of Problems Confronting One of Africa's New Nations," *Publication of the American University Field Service Reports*, Vol. VII, no. 11. New York: AUFS, 1960.

Beato, Lucila Bandeira. "Inequality and Human Rights of African Descendants in Brazil," *Journal of Black Studies*, 34, no. 6 (July 2004): 766–786.

Bell, Jr., Derrick A. "Brown v. Board of Education and the Interest-Convergence Dilemma," *Harvard Law Review*, 93, no. 3 (January 1980): 518–533.

Ben-Ghiat, Ruth and Mia Fuller, eds. *Italian Colonialism*. New York: Palgrave Macmillan, 2005.

Berg, Manfred. *"Ticket to Freedom": The NAACP and the Struggle for Black Political Integration*. Gainesville: University of Florida Press, 2005.

"Black Civil Rights and Liberal Anticommunism: The NAACP in the Early Cold War," *Journal of American History*, 94, no. 1 (June 2007): 75–96.

Bhagavan, Manu. *The Peacemakers: India and the Quest for One World*. New Delhi: HarperCollins India, 2012.

Bills, Scott L. *The Libyan Arena: The United States, Britain, and the Council of Foreign Ministers, 1945–1948*. Kent, OH: Kent State University Press, 1995.

Bimberg, Edward L. *Tricolor over the Sahara: The Desert Battles of the Free French, 1940–1942*. Westport, CT: Greenwood Press, 2002.

Bloom, Joshua and Waldo E. Martin Jr. *Black against Empire: The History and Politics of the Black Panther Party*. Berkeley: University of California Press, 2013.

Bloomfield, Steve. "Mengistu Found Guilty of Ethiopian Genocide," *Independent*, December 13, 2006. http://www.independent.co.uk/news/world/africa/ mengistu–found–guilty–of–ethiopian–genocide–428233.html. Accessed December 5, 2013.

Bonilla-Silva, Eduardo. *Racism without Racists: Color–Blind Racism and the Persistence of Racial Inequality in America*. 3rd ed. New York: Rowman & Littlefield, 2009.

Borgwardt, Elizabeth. *A New Deal for the World: America's Vision for Human Rights*. Cambridge, MA: Harvard University Press, 2005.

Borstelmann, Thomas. *Apartheid's Reluctant Uncle: The United States and Southern Africa in the Early Cold War*. New York: Oxford University Press, 1993.

Bosworth, R. J. B. *Mussolini's Italy: Life under the Fascist Dictatorship, 1915–1945*. New York: Penguin Press, 2006.

Boyle, Kevin and Juliet Sheen, eds. *Freedom of Religion and Belief: A World Report*. London and New York: Routledge, 1997.

Bracey, John H., Jr. and August Meier. "'Allies or Adversaries?' The NAACP: A. Philip Randolph and the 1941 March on Washington," *Georgia Historical Quarterly*, 75, no. 1 (Spring 1991): 1–17.

Branch, Taylor. *Parting the Waters: America in the King Years, 1954–63*. New York: Simon and Schuster, 1988.

Buhle, Paul. *Tim Hector: A Caribbean Radical's Story*. Jackson: University Press of Mississippi, 2006.

Bullock, Alan. *Hitler, A Study in Tyranny*, rev. ed. New York: Harper & Row, 1964.

Burke, Roland. *Decolonization and the Evolution of International Human Rights.* Philadelphia: University of Pennsylvania Press, 2010.

Burrin, Philippe. *Living with Defeat: France under the German Occupation, 1940–1944,* trans. Janet Lloyd. London: Arnold, 1996.

Bynum, Cornelius L. *A. Philip Randolph and the Struggle for Civil Rights.* Urbana: University of Illinois Press, 2010.

C. M. C. "French North Africa since June 1940: Main Political Developments," *Bulletin of International News,* 19, no. 25 (December 12, 1942): 1125–1131.

Carson, Clayborne. *In Struggle: SNCC and the Black Awakening of the 1960s.* Cambridge, MA: Harvard University Press, 1981, 1995.

Casey, Steven. *Selling the Korean War: Propaganda, Politics, and Public Opinion, 1950–1953.* New York: Oxford University Press, 2008.

Clark, Roger S. "The International League for Human Rights and South West Africa 1947–1957: The Human Rights NGO as Catalyst in the International Legal Process," *Human Rights Quarterly,* 3, no. 4 (November 1981): 101–136.

Clarke, J. Calvitt. "Italo-Soviet Military Cooperation in the 1930s," in *Girding for Battle: The Arms Trade in Global Perspective, 1815–1940,* eds. Donald J. Stoker Jr. and Jonathan A. Grant. Westport, CT: Praeger, 2003.

"Soviet Appeasement, Collective Security, and the Italo-Ethiopian War of 1935 and 1936," *The Selected Annual Proceedings of the Florida Conference of Historians,* 4 (December 1996): 115–132. http://users.ju.edu/jclarke/wizzf.html. Accessed June 24, 2008.

"Soviet Russia and the Italo-Ethiopian War of 1935–36." http://users.ju.edu/jclarke/scss04.htm. Accessed June 24, 2008.

Clayton, Anthony. *The Wars of French Decolonization, Modern Wars in Perspective,* eds. B. W. Collins and H. M. Scott. London and New York: Longman, 1994.

Cohen, Mark S. Review of *William Hastie: Grace under Pressure* by Gilbert Ware. *Michigan Law Review,* 84, no. 4/5 (February – April 1986) 861–866.

Collier, Paul. *The Bottom Billion: Why the Poorest Countries Are Failing and What Can Be Done About It.* New York: Oxford University Press, 2007.

Comaroff, Jean and John Comaroff. *Of Revelation and Revolution: Christianity, Colonialism, and Consciousness in South Africa,* 2 vols. Chicago: University of Chicago Press, 1991, 1997.

Committee on Africa, the War, and Peace Aims. *The Atlantic Charter and Africa from an American Standpoint.* New York: Federal Council of Churches in Christ, 1942.

Conquest, Robert. *The Harvest of Sorrow: Soviet Collectivization and the Terror-Famine.* New York: Oxford University Press, 1986.

Cooper, Frederick. *Africa since 1940: The Past of the Present (New Approaches to African History),* ed. Martin Klein. New York: Cambridge University Press, 2002.

Crosby, Emilye. *A Little Taste of Freedom: The Black Freedom Struggle in Claiborne County, Mississippi.* Chapel Hill: University of North Carolina Press, 2005.

"'God's Appointed Savior': Charles Evers's Use of Local Movements for National Prestige," in *Groundwork: The Local Black Freedom Movement in America*, eds. Komozi Woodard and Jeanne Theoharis. New York: New York University Press, 2005.

Cullather, Nick. *The Hungry World: America's Cold War Battle against Poverty in Asia*. Cambridge, MA: Harvard University Press, 2010.

"Modernization Theory," in *Explaining the History of American Foreign Relations*, eds. Michael J. Hogan and Thomas G. Paterson, 2nd ed. New York: Cambridge University Press, 2004.

Cumings, Bruce. *The Origins of the Korean War*. Princeton, NJ: Princeton University Press, 1981, 1990.

Davis, Mary. "Labour, Race, and Empire: The Trades Union Congress and Colonial Policy, 1945–51," in *The British Labour Movement and Imperialism*, eds. Billy Frank, Craig Horner and David Stewart. New Castle upon Tyne: Cambridge Scholars Publishing, 2010.

de Jong, Louis. *The Netherlands and Nazi Germany*. Foreword by Simon Schama. Cambridge, MA: Harvard University Press, 1990.

De La Fuente, Alejandro. "The New Afro-Cuban Cultural Movement and the Debate on Race in Contemporary Cuba," *Journal of Latin American Studies*, 40, no. 4 (2008): 697–720.

Dittmer, John. *Local People: The Struggle for Civil Rights in Mississippi*. Champaign: University of Illinois Press, 1994.

Dixie, Quinton and Peter Eisenstadt. *Visions of a Better World: Howard Thurman's Pilgrimage to India and the Origins of African American Nonviolence*. Foreword by Walter Earl Fluker. Boston: Beacon Press, 2011.

Dobrasko, Rebekah. "Equalization Schools in South Carolina, 1951–1959." http://nationalregister.sc.gov/SurveyReports/EqualizationSchoolsHistoricContext.pdf. Accessed October 26, 2013.

Dorsey, Allison. *To Build Our Lives Together: Community Formation in Black Atlanta, 1875–1906*. Athens: University of Georgia Press, 2004.

Douglas, R. M. Michael D. Callahan, and Elizabeth Bishop, eds. *Imperialism on Trial: International Oversight of Colonial Rule in Historical Perspective*. Lanham, MD: Lexington Books, 2006.

Drake, Richard. "The Soviet Dimension of Italian Communism," *Journal of Cold War Studies*, 6, no. 3 (Summer 2004): 115–119.

Dreifort, John E. "Japan's Advance into Indochina, 1940: The French Response," *Journal of Southeast Asian Studies*, 13, no. 2 (September 1982): 279–295.

Dreyer, Ronald F. *Namibia and Southern Africa: Regional Dynamics of Decolonization, 1945–1990*. London; New York: Kegan Paul International, 1993.

Du Bois, W. E. B. "Fisk," *Crisis*, 29, no. 6 (April 1925): 250.

  The World and Africa: An Inquiry into the Part Which Africa Has Played in World History. New York: International Publishers, 1946.

  Color and Democracy: Colonies and Peace. Introduction by Herbert Aptheker. New York: Harcourt Brace, 1945; reprint, Millwood, NY: Kraus-Thomson Organization Limited, 1975.

Duany, Jorge. "Reconstructing Racial Identity: Ethnicity, Color, and Class among Dominicans in the United States and Puerto Rico," *Latin American Perspectives*, 25, no. 3 (May 1998): 147–172.

Duberman, Martin Bauml. *Paul Robeson.* New York: Knopf, 1988.

Dudziak, Mary L. *Exporting American Dreams: Thurgood Marshall's African Journey.* New York: Oxford University Press, 2008.

Dyja, Thomas. *Walter White: The Dilemma of Black Identity in America.* Chicago: Ivan R. Dee, 2008.

Eagleton, Clyde, ed. *Annual Review of United Nations Affairs: 1949.* New York: New York University Press, 1950.

Edelman, Murray. "Causes of Fluctuations in Popular Support for the Italian Communist Party Since 1946," *Journal of Politics*, 20, no. 3 (August 1958): 535–552.

"Editorials: Soviet Russia Aids Italy," *Crisis*, 42, no. 10 (October 1935), 305.

Eick, Gretchen Cassel. "'Lift Every Voice': The Civil Rights Movement and America's Heartland, Wichita, Kansas, 1954–1972." PhD diss., University of Kansas, 1997.

Ekbladh, David. *The Great American Mission: Modernization and the Construction of an American World Order.* Princeton, NJ: Princeton University Press, 2010.

Elkins, Caroline. *Imperial Reckoning: The Untold Story of Britain's Gulag in Kenya.* New York: Henry Holt, 2005.

Engerman, David C. *Modernization from the Other Shore: American Intellectuals and the Romance of Russian Development.* Cambridge, MA: Harvard University Press, 2003.

Engerman, David C., Nils Gilman, Mark H. Haefele, and Michael E. Latham, eds. *Staging Growth: Modernization, Development and the Cold War.* Amherst: University of Massachusetts Press, 2003.

Fairclough, Adam. *To Redeem the Soul of America: The Southern Christian Leadership Conference and Martin Luther King, Jr.* Athens: University of Georgia Press, 1987.

Fergusson, James. *The World's Most Dangerous Place: Inside the Outlaw State of Somalia.* Boston: De Capo, 2013.

Fontera, Richard M. "Anti-Colonialism as a Basic Indian Foreign Policy," *Western Political Quarterly*, 13, no. 2 (June 1960): 421–432.

Foster, Anne L. "Avoiding the 'Rank of Denmark': Dutch Fears about Loss of Empire in Southeast Asia," in *Connecting Histories: Decolonization and the Cold War in Southeast Asia, 1945–1962*, Cold War International History Project, eds. Christopher E Goscha and Christian F Ostermann. Washington, DC: Woodrow Wilson Center Press; Stanford, CA: Stanford University Press, 2009.

Frank, Billy. "Labour's 'New Imperialist Attitude': State-Sponsored Colonial Development in Africa, 1940–51," in *The British Labour Movement and Imperialism*, eds. Billy Frank, Craig Horner and David Stewart. New Castle upon Tyne: Cambridge Scholars Publishing, 2010.

Fraser, Cary. "An American Dilemma: Race and Realpolitik in the American Response to the Bandung Conference, 1955," in *Window on Freedom: Race,*

Civil Rights, and Foreign Affairs, 1945–1988, ed. Brenda Gayle Plummer. Chapel Hill: University of North Carolina Press, 2003.

Frederickson, George M. *White Supremacy: A Comparative Study in American and South African History.* New York: Oxford University Press, 1981.

Frey, Marc. "Visions of the Future: The United States and Colonialism in Southeast Asia, 1940–1945," *American Studies*, 48, no. 3 (2003): 365–388.

Gilman, Nils. *Mandarins of the Future: Modernization Theory in Cold War America.* Baltimore, MD: Johns Hopkins University Press, 2003.

Gilmore, Glenda Elizabeth. *Defying Dixie: The Radical Roots of Civil Rights, 1919–1950.* New York: W.W. Norton & Co., 2008.

Gleijeses, Piero. "A Test of Wills: Jimmy Carter, South Africa, and the Independence of Namibia," *Diplomatic History*, 34, no. 5 (November 2010): 853–891.

Godshalk, David Fort. *Veiled Visions: The 1906 Atlanta Race Riot and the Reshaping of American Race Relations.* Chapel Hill: University of North Carolina Press, 2005.

Gordon, Linda. *Pitied but Not Entitled: Single Mothers and the History of Welfare, 1890–1935.* New York: Free Press, 1994.

Gouda, Frances. *American Visions of the Netherlands East Indies/Indonesia: US Foreign Policy and Indonesia Nationalism, 1920–1949* with Thijs Brocades Zaalberg. Amsterdam: Amsterdam University Press, 2002.

Grant, Colin. *Negro with a Hat: The Rise and Fall of Marcus Garvey.* New York: Oxford University Press, 2008.

Grant, Jr., Philip A. "President Harry S. Truman and the British Loan Act of 1946," *Presidential Studies Quarterly*, 25, no. 3 (Summer 1995): 489–496.

Guha, Ramachandra. *India after Gandhi: The History of the World's Largest Democracy.* New York: Ecco, 2007.

Guinier, Lani and Gerald Torres. *The Miner's Canary: Enlisting Race, Resisting Power, Transforming Democracy.* Cambridge, MA: Harvard University Press, 2002.

Guzman, Jason Parkhurst, ed. *Negro Yearbook: A Review of Events Affecting Negro Life, 1941–46.* Tuskegee, AL: Department of Records and Research, Tuskegee Institute, 1947.

Haas, Ernst B. "The Attempt to Terminate Colonialism: Acceptance of the United Nations Trusteeship System," *International Organization*, 7, no. 1 (February 1953): 1–21.

Harris, Joseph E. *African-American Reactions to War in Ethiopia, 1936–1941.* Baton Rouge: Louisiana State University Press, 1994.

Harris, Robert L., Jr. "Ralph Bunche and Afro-American Participation in Decolonization," in *The African American Voice in U.S. Foreign Policy since World War II*, ed. Michael L. Krenn. New York: Garland, 1999.

Harrison, Faye V. "The Persistent Power of 'Race' in the Cultural and Political Economy of Racism," *Annual Review of Anthropology*, 24 (1995): 47–74.

Hatta, Mohammad. "Indonesia's Foreign Policy," *Foreign Affairs*, 31, no. 3 (April 1953): 441–452.

Headrick, Rita. "African Soldiers in World War II," *Armed Forces and Society*, 4, no. 3 (Spring 1978): 501–526.

Henry, Charles P. "Civil Rights and National Security: The Case of Ralph Bunche," in *Ralph Bunche: The Man and His Times*, ed. Benjamin Rivlin. Foreword by Donald F. McHenry. New York: Holmes & Meier, 1990.

Henshaw, Peter. "South African Territorial Expansion and the International Reaction to South African Racial Policies, 1939 to 1948," *South African Historical Journal*, 50 (May 2004): 65–76.

Hirschfeld, Gerhard. *Nazi Rule and Dutch Collaboration: The Netherlands under German Occupation, 1940–1945*. Oxford, New York and Hamburg: Berg, 1988.

Hogan, Michael J. *The Marshall Plan: America, Britain, and the Reconstruction of Western Europe, 1947–1952*. New York: Cambridge University Press, 1987.

A Cross of Iron: Harry S. Truman and the Origins of the National Security State, 1945–1954. New York: Cambridge University Press, 1998.

Homan, Gerlof D. "The Netherlands, the United States and the Indonesian Question, 1948," *Journal of Contemporary History*, 25, no. 1 (January 1990): 123–141.

Horne, Gerald. *Black and Red: W.E.B. Du Bois and the Afro-American Response to the Cold War, 1944–1963*. Albany: SUNY Press, 1986.

Communist Front? The Civil Rights Congress, 1946–1956. London: Associated University Presses, 1988.

Race Woman: The Lives of Shirley Graham Du Bois. New York: New York University Press, 2000.

The End of Empires: African Americans and India. Philadelphia: Temple University Press, 2008.

Mau Mau in Harlem? The U.S. and the Liberation of Kenya. New York: Palgrave MacMillan, 2009.

Houser, George M. "Human Rights and the Liberation Struggle... The Importance of Creative Tension," *Africa Today*, 39, no. 4 (4th Qtr., 1992): 5–17.

Huff, W. G. "Entitlements, Destitution, and Emigration in the 1930s Singapore Great Depression," *Economic History Review*, 54, no. 2 (May 2001): 290–323.

Hull, Isabel V. "Military Culture and the Production of 'Final Solutions' in the Colonies: The Example of Wilhelminian Germany," in *The Specter of Genocide: Mass Murder in Historical Perspective*, eds. Robert Gellately and Ben Kiernan. New York: Cambridge University Press, 2003.

Irwin, Ryan M. "Apartheid on Trial: South West Africa and the International Court of Justice, 1960–1966," *International History Review*, 32, no. 4 (December 2010): 619–642.

Gordian Knot: Apartheid and the Unmaking of the Liberal World Order. New York: Oxford University Press, 2012.

Iyob, Ruth. *The Eritrean Struggle for Independence: Domination, Resistance, Nationalism, 1941–1993*. New York: Cambridge University Press, 1995.

Jackson, Julian. *France: The Dark Years, 1940–1944*. New York: Oxford University Press 2001.

James, C. L. R. *Fighting Racism in World War II*. London: Pathfinder, 1980.

Janken, Kenneth. "From Colonial Liberation to Cold War Liberalism: Walter White, the NAACP, and Foreign Affairs, 1941–1955," *Ethnic and Racial Studies*, 21, no. 6 (November 1998): 1074–1095.

White: The Biography of Walter White, Mr. NAACP. New York: New Press, 2003.

Jeffries, Hasan Kwame. *Bloody Lowndes: Civil Rights and Black Power in Alabama's Black Belt*. New York: New York University Press, 2009.

Jennings, Eric T. *Vichy in the Tropics: Pétain's National Revolution in Madagascar, Guadeloupe, and Indochina, 1940–1944*. Stanford, CA: Stanford University Press 2001.

Jinadu, L. Adele. "South West Africa: A Study in the 'Sacred Trust' Thesis," *African Studies Review*, 14, no. 3 (December 1971): 369–388.

Jonas, Gilbert. *Freedom's Sword: The NAACP and the Struggle Against Racism in America, 1909–1969*. Introduction by Julian Bond. New York: Routledge, 2005.

Jones, Goronwy John. *United Nations and the Domestic Jurisdiction of States*. Cardiff: University of Wales Press, 1979.

Jordan, David. "'A Particularly Exacting Operation': British Forces and the Battle of Surabaya, November 1945," *Small Wars and Insurgencies*, 11, no. 3 (Winter 2000): 89–114.

Kaplan, Lawrence S. *NATO 1948: The Birth of the Transatlantic Alliance*. New York: Rowman and Littlefield, 2007.

NATO and the UN: A Peculiar Relationship. Columbia: University of Missouri Press, 2010.

Katznelson, Ira. *When Affirmative Action Was White: An Untold History of Racial Inequality in Twentieth-Century America*. New York: W.W. Norton, 2006.

Kelemen, Paul. "The British Labor Party and the Economics of Decolonization: The Debate over Kenya," *Journal of Colonialism and Colonial History*, 8, no. 3 (Winter 2007): 1–33.

Kelly, Saul. *Cold War in the Desert: Britain, the United States, and the Italian Colonies, 1945–52*. New York: St. Martin's Press, 2000.

Kennedy, David M. *Freedom from Fear: The American People in Depression and War, 1929–1945*. New York: Oxford University Press, 1999.

Knox, MacGregor. *Mussolini Unleashed: 1939–1941, Politics and Strategy in Fascist Italy's Last War*. New York: Cambridge University Press, 1982.

Komer, Robert W. "The Establishment of Allied Control in Italy," *Military Affairs*, 13, no. 1 (Spring 1949): 20–28.

Krenn, Michael L. *Black Diplomacy: African Americans and the State Department, 1945–1969*. Armonk, NY: M.E. Sharpe, 1999.

Kristof, Nicholas D. "Bright Continent: Why Africa's Success Stories Are too Often Overlooked," *New York Times Upfront*, April 19, 2010.

Larebo, Haile M. *The Building of an Empire: Italian Land Policy and Practice in Ethiopia, 1935–1941*. Oxford: Clarendon Press; New York: Oxford University Press, 1994.

Latham, Michael E. *Modernization as Ideology: American Social Science and "Nation Building" in the Kennedy Era*. Chapel Hill: University of North Carolina Press, 2000.

The Right Kind of Revolution: Modernization, Development, and U.S. Foreign Policy from the Cold War to the Present. Ithaca, NY: Cornell University Press, 2011.

Lattis, James M. *Between Copernicus and Galileo: Christoph Clavius and the Collapse of Ptolemaic Cosmology*. Chicago: University of Chicago Press, 1994.

Lauren, Paul Gordon. *The Evolution of International Human Rights: Visions Seen*, 2nd ed. Philadelphia: University of Pennsylvania Press, 2003.

Lawrence, Mark Atwood. "The Rise and Fall of Nonalignment," in *The Cold War in the Third World*, ed. Robert McMahon. New York: Oxford University Press, 2013.

Leffler, Melvyn P. "The American Conception of National Security and the Beginnings of the Cold War, 1945–48," *American Historical Review*, 89, no. 2 (April 1984): 346–381.

A Preponderance of Power: National Security, the Truman Administration, and the Cold War. Stanford, CA: Stanford University Press, 1992.

For the Soul of Mankind: The United States, the Soviet Union, and the Cold War. New York: Hill & Wang, 2007.

Lellouche, Pierre and Dominique Moisi, "French Policy in Africa: A Lonely Battle against Destabilization," *International Security*, 1.3, no. 4 (Spring 1979): 108–133.

Lewin, Ronald. *Rommel as Military Commander*. New York: Ballantine Books, 1968.

Lewis, David Levering. *W.E.B. Du Bois: The Fight for Equality and the American Century, 1919–1963*. New York: Henry Holt and Company, 2000.

Lewis, I. M. *A Modern History of the Somali: Nation and State in the Horn of Africa*, 4th ed. Athens: Ohio University Press, 2002.

Lipsitz, George. *The Possessive Investment in Whiteness: How White People Profit from Identity. Politics*. Philadelphia: Temple University Press, 2006.

Lopez, Ian Haney. *White by Law 10th Anniversary Edition: The Legal Construction of Race*. New York: New York University Press, 2006.

Louis, Wm. Roger. *Imperialism at Bay: The United States and the Decolonization of the British Empire, 1941–1945*. New York: Oxford University Press, 1978.

Louis, Wm. Roger and Ronald Robinson. "The Imperialism of Decolonization," *Journal of Imperial and Commonwealth History*, 22, no. 3 (1994): 462–511.

Lowenstein, Allard K. *Brutal Mandate: A Journey to South West Africa*. Foreword by Mrs. Franklin D. Roosevelt. New York: Macmillan Company, 1962.

MacDonald, Callum A. "Waiting for Uncle Sam: Britain, the United States, and the First Cold War," *Reviews in American History*, 17, no. 1 (March 1989): 125–130.

MacLaurin, John. *United Nations and Power Politics*. London: Allen & Unwin, 1951.

Malcolm X and Alex Haley. *The Autobiography of Malcolm X*. New York: Ballantine Books, 1964.

Manela, Erez. *The Wilsonian Moment: Self-Determination and the International Origins of Anticolonial Nationalism*. New York: Oxford University Press, 2009.

Marable, Manning. *Race, Reform, and Rebellion: The Second Reconstruction in Black America, 1945–1990*, 2nd ed. Jackson: University of Mississippi Press, 1991.

Maul, Daniel. *Human Rights, Development and Decolonization: The International Labour Organization, 1940–70*. ILO Century Series. New York: Palgrave Macmillan, 2012.

Mazov, Sergei. "The USSR and the Former Italian Colonies, 1945–50," *Cold War History*, 3, no. 3 (April 2003): 49–78.

McCormack, Gavan. "Reflections on Modern Japanese History in the Context of the Concept of Genocide," in *The Specter of Genocide: Mass Murder in Historical Perspective*, eds. Robert Gellately and Ben Kiernan. New York: Cambridge University Press, 2003.

McCullough, David. *Truman*. New York: Simon & Schuster, 1992.

McDougall, Gay J. "International Law, Human Rights, and Namibian Independence," *Human Rights Quarterly*, 8, no. 3 (August 1986): 443–470.

McDuffie, Erik. "Black and Red: Black Liberation, the Cold War, and the Horne Thesis," *Journal of African American History*, 96, no. 2 (Spring 2011): 236–247.

McElvaine, Robert S. *The Great Depression: America, 1929–1941*, 2nd ed. New York: Times Books, 1993.

McGrandle, Piers. *Trevor Huddleston: Turbulent Priest*. Foreword by Desmond Tutu, afterword by Rowan Williams. London: Continuum Press, 2004.

McGuire Phillip. "Judge Hastie, World War II, and Army Racism," *Journal of Negro History*, 62, no. 4 (October 1977): 351–362.

McMahon, Robert. *Colonialism and Cold War: The United States and the Struggle for Indonesian Independence, 1945–49*. Ithaca, NY: Cornell University Press, 1981.

McVety, Amanda Kay. *Enlightened Aid: U.S. Development as Foreign Policy in Ethiopia*. New York: Oxford University Press, 2012.

Meier, August and John H. Bracey Jr. "The NAACP as a Reform Movement, 1909–1965: 'To Reach the Conscience of America,'" *Journal of Southern History*, 59, no. 1 (February 1993): 3–30.

Meriwether, James H. "African Americans and the Mau Mau Rebellion Militancy, Violence, and the Struggle for Freedom," *Journal of American Ethnic History*, 17, no. 4 (Summer 1998): 63–86.

"'Worth a Lot of Negro Votes': Black Voters, Africa, and the 1960 Presidential Campaign," *Journal of American History*, 95, no. 3 (December 2008): 737–763.

Millett, Allan R. *The War for Korea, 1950–1951: They Came from the North*. Lawrence: University of Kansas Press, 2010.

Moore, Bob. "Unruly Allies: British Problems with the French Treatment of Axis Prisoners of War, 1943–1945," *War in History*, 7, no. 2 (2000): 180–198.

Mountz, William T. "Americanizing Africanization: The Congo Crisis, 1960–1967." PhD diss., University of Missouri, 2014.

Moyn, Samuel. "Imperialism, Self-Determination, and the Rise of Human Rights," in *The Human Rights Revolution: An International History, eds.* Akira Iriye, Pedtra Goedde and William I Hitchcock. Reinterpreting American History, ed. Wm. Roger Louis. New York: Oxford University Press, 2012.

Munholland, Kim. "The Trials of the Free French in New Caldeonia, 1940–1942," *French Historical Studies*, 14, no. 4 (Autumn 1986): 547–579.

Murray, Hugh T., Jr. "The NAACP versus the Communist Party: The Scottsboro Rape Cases, 1931–1932," *Phylon*, 28, no. 3 (3rd Qtr., 1967): 276–287.

My–Van, Tran. "Japan through Vietnamese Eyes, 1905–1945," *Journal of Southeast Asian Studies*, 30, no. 1 (March 1999): 126–146.

Nelli, Humbert. "Italian-Americans," in *Harvard Encyclopedia of American Ethnic Groups,* ed. Stephan Thernstrom. Cambridge, MA: Belknap Press of Harvard University Press, 1980.

Nesbitt, Frances Njubi. *Race for Sanctions: African Americans against Apartheid, 1946–1994.* Bloomington: Indiana University Press, 2004.

Newsinger, John. "A Forgotten War: British Intervention in Indonesia, 1945–46," *Race and Class*, 3, no. 4 (1989): 51–66.

Nichols, David A. *A Matter of Justice: Eisenhower and the Beginning of the Civil Rights Revolution.* New York: Simon & Schuster, 2007.

O'Brien, Kevin A. "Interfering with Civil Society: CIA and KGB Covert Political Action during the Cold War," *International Journal of Intelligence and Counterintelligence*, 8, no. 4 (Winter 1995): 431–456.

The Oilfields Workers' Trade Union, "OWTU History: 1937–1947." http://www.owtu.org/content/owtu–history. Accessed October 29, 2012.

O'Reilly, Kenneth. "Racial Integration: The Battle General Eisenhower Chose Not to Fight," *Journal of Blacks in Higher Education*, no. 18 (Winter 1997–1998): 110–119.

Oshinsky, David M. *A Conspiracy So Immense: The World of Joe McCarthy.* New York: Oxford University Press, 2005.

Ovendale, Ritchie. "The South African Policy of the British Labour Government, 1947–51," *International Affairs*, 59, no. 1 (Winter 1982–1983): 41–58.

Padmore, George. "Ethiopia and World Politics," *Crisis*, 42, no. 5 (May 1935): 138.

How Britain Rules Africa. London: Wishart Books, 1936; New York: Negro Universities Press, 1969.

Parker, Jason C. "Cold War II: The Eisenhower Administration, the Bandung Conference, and the Reperiodization of the Postwar Era," *Diplomatic History*, 30, no. 5 (November 2006): 867–892.

Brother's Keeper: The United States, Race, and Empire in the British Caribbean, 1937–1962. New York: Oxford University Press, 2008.

"'Made-in-America Revolutions'?: The 'Black University' and the American Role in the Decolonization of the Black Atlantic," *Journal of American History*, 96, no. 3 (December 2009): 727–750.

"Decolonization, the Cold War, and the Post-Columbian Era," in *The Cold War in the Third World*, ed. Robert McMahon. New York: Oxford University Press, 2013.

Passerini, Luisa. *Fascism in Popular Memory: The Cultural Experience of the Turin Working Class*, trans. Robert Lumley and Jude Bloomfield. London: Cambridge University Press, 1984, 1987.

Paterson, Thomas G. "Foreign Aid under Wraps: The Point Four Program," *Wisconsin Magazine of History*, 56, no. 2 (Winter 1972–1973): 119–126.

Payne, Charles M. *I've Got the Light of Freedom: The Organizing Tradition and the Mississippi Freedom Struggle.* Berkeley: University of California Press, 1995, 2007.

Pechatnov, Vladimir O. "'The Allies Are Pressing on You to Break Your Will ...':
Foreign Policy Correspondence Between Stalin and Molotov and Other
Politburo Members, September 1945-December 1946," trans. Vladislav M.
Zubok. Working Paper No. 26 of the Cold War International History Project.
Washington, DC: Woodrow Wilson International Center for Scholars,
September 1999.

Pierpaoli, Jr., Paul G. *Truman and Korea: The Political Culture of the Early Cold
War*. Columbia: University of Missouri Press, 1999.

Platt, Alan A. and Robert Leonardi, "American Foreign Policy and the Postwar
Italian Left," *Political Science Quarterly*, 93, no. 2 (Summer 1978):
198–202.

Plaut, Martin. "The Africans Who Fought in WWII," BBC, November 9, 2009.
http://news.bbc.co.uk/2/hi/africa/8344170.stm. Accessed November
23, 2012.

Plaut, Martin and Patrick Gilkes. "Conflict in the Horn: Why Eritrea and
Ethiopia Are at War," No. 1. The Royal Institute of International Affairs
(March 1999).

Plummer, Brenda Gayle. *Rising Wind: Black Americans and U.S. Foreign Affairs,
1935–1960*. Chapel Hill: University of North Carolina Press, 1996.

  In Search of Power: African Americans in the Era of Decolonization, 1956–1974.
New York: Cambridge University Press, 2012.

Polk, Judd and Gardner Patterson. "The British Loan," *Foreign Affairs*, 24, no. 3
(April 1946): 429–440.

Polyné, Millery. *From Douglass to Duvalier: U.S. African Americans, Haiti,
and Pan Americanism, 1870–1964*. New World Diasporas, ed. Kevin A.
Yelvington. Gainesville: University Press of Florida, 2010.

Pons, Silvio. "Stalin, Togliatti, and the Origins of the Cold War in Europe," *Journal
of Cold War Studies*, 3, no. 2 (Spring 2001): 3–27.

Quinney, Kimber. "The United States, Great Britain, and Dismantling
Italian Fascism, 1943–1948." PhD diss., University of California, Santa
Barbara, 2002.

Rana, Swadesh. "The Changing Indian Diplomacy at the United Nations,"
International Organization, 24, no. 1 (Winter 1970): 48–73.

Ransby, Barbara. *Ella Baker and the Black Freedom Movement: A Radical
Democratic Vision*. Chapel Hill: University of North Carolina
Press, 2003.

Raudzens, George. "War-Winning Weapons: The Measurement of Technological
Determinism in Military History," *Journal of Military History*, 54, no. 4
(October 1990): 403–434.

Rivlin, Benjamin. "The Italian Colonies and the General Assembly," *International
Organization*, 3, no. 3 (August 1949): 459–470.

Roark, James. "American Black Leaders: The Response to Colonialism and the
Cold War, 1945–1953," *African Historical Studies*, 4 (1971): 253–270.

Robertson, Geoffrey. *Crimes against Humanity: The Struggle for Global Justice*.
New York: New Press, 2006.

Robinson, Nehemiah. "Problems of European Reconstruction," *Quarterly Journal
of Economics*, 60, no. 1 (November 1945): 1–55.

Rogers, Ruel. "Black Like Who?: Afro–Caribbean Immigrants, African Americans, and the Politics of Group Identity," in *Islands in the City: West Indian Migration to New York*, ed. Nancy Foner. Berkeley: University of California Press, 2001.

Rosenwaike, Ira. *Population History of New York City*. Syracuse, NY: Syracuse University Press, 1972.

Ruswick, Brent. *Almost Worthy: The Poor, Paupers, and the Science of Charity in America, 1877–1917*. Bloomington: Indiana University Press, 2013.

Saxena, Suresh Chandra. *Namibia and the World: The Story of the Birth of a Nation*. Delhi: Kalinga Publications, 1991.

Sbacchi, Alberto. *Ethiopia under Mussolini: Fascism and the Colonial Experience*. London: Zed Books, 1985.

Schlesinger, Stephen C. *Act of Creation: The Founding of the United Nations, A Story of Superpowers, Secret Agents, Wartime Allies and Enemies, and Their Quest for a Peaceful World*. Boulder, CO: Westview Press, 2003.

Scott, William R. "Black Nationalism and the Italo-Ethiopian Conflict, 1934–1936," *Journal of Negro History*, 63, no. 2 (April 1978): 118–134.

   The Sons of Sheba's Race: African-Americans and the Italo-Ethiopian War, 1935–1941. Bloomington: University of Indiana Press, 1993.

Sen, Amartya. *Development as Freedom*. New York: Anchor Books, 1999.

Senechal, Roberta. "The Springfield Race Riot of 1908." http://www.lib.niu.edu/1996/iht329622.html.

Senghor, Lamine. "The Negro's Fight for Freedom," in *Ideologies of Liberation in Black Africa 1856–1970: Documents on Modern African Political Thought from Colonial Times to the Present*, ed. J. Ayo Langley. London: Rex Collings, 1979.

Seton-Watson, Christopher. "Italy's Imperial Hangover," *Journal of Contemporary History*, 15, no. 1 (January 1980): 169–179.

Sewell, Joshua. "'A Fateful Moment in the History of a Free Country': An Analysis of Supreme Court Rulings Governing the Right to Association for the Communist Party, USA and the NAACP." Senior Honors Thesis, University of Missouri, 2004.

Shaw, Rosiland. "The Invention of 'African Traditional Religion,'" *Religion*, 20 (1990): 339–353.

Sherwood, Marika. "'There Is No New Deal for the Blackman in San Francisco': African Attempts to Influence the Founding Conference of the United Nations, April–July, 1945," *International Journal of African Historical Studies*, 29, no. 1 (1996): 71–94.

Short, Philip. *Pol Pot: The History of a Nightmare*. London: John Murray, 2004.

Silvester, Jeremy and Jan-Bart Gewald, eds. *Words Cannot Be Found: German Colonial Rule in Namibia, An Annotated Reprint of the 1918 Blue Book*. Boston: Brill, 2003.

Simpson, A. W. Brian. *Human Rights and the End of Empire: Britain and the Genesis of the European Convention*. New York: Oxford University Press, 2001; reprint 2004.

Simpson, Bradley R. *Economists with Guns: Authoritarian Development and U.S.-Indonesian Relations, 1960–1968*. Stanford: Stanford University Press, 2008.

"Southeast Asia in the Cold War," in *The Cold War in the Third World,* ed. Robert McMahon. New York: Oxford University Press, 2013.

Slate, Nico. *Colored Cosmopolitanism: The Shared Struggle for Freedom in the United States and India.* Cambridge, MA: Harvard University Press, 2012.

Slater, Montagu. *The Trial of Jomo Kenyatta.* London: Secker & Warburg, 1955.

Sluimers, László. "The Japanese Military and Indonesian Independence," *Journal of Southeast Asian Studies,* 27, no. 1 (March 1996): 19–36.

Smith, E. Timothy. "United States Security and the Integration of Italy into the Western Bloc, 1947–1949," in *NATO: The Founding of the Atlantic Alliance and the Integration of Europe,* eds. Francis H. Heller and John R. Gillingham. New York: St. Martin's Press, 1992.

Smyth, Howard McGaw. "Some Recent Italian Publications Regarding World War II," *Military Affairs,* 11, no. 4 (Winter 1947): 245–253.

Snyder, Timothy. *Bloodlands: Europe between Hitler and Stalin.* New York: Basic Books, 2010.

Steiner, H. Arthur. "The Government of Italian East Africa," *American Political Science Review,* 30, no. 5 (October 1936): 884–902.

Stueck, William W. *The Korean War: An International History.* Princeton, NJ: Princeton University Press, 1995.

Sullivan, Patricia. *Days of Hope: Race and Democracy in the New Deal Era.* Chapel Hill: University of North Carolina Press, 1996.

  Lift Every Voice: The NAACP and the Making of the Civil Rights Movement. New York: New Press, 2009.

Tanaka, Toshiyuki. *Hidden Horrors: Japanese War Crimes in World War II.* Foreword by John W. Dower. Boulder, CO: Westview Press, 1996.

Thomas, Martin. "Deferring to Vichy in the Western Hemisphere: The St. Pierre and Miquelon Affair of 1941," *International History Review,* 19, no. 4 (November 1997): 809–835.

Thorne, Christopher. *Allies of a Kind: The United States, Britain, and the War against Japan, 1941–1945.* New York: Oxford University Press, 1978.

Tillery, Alvin B., Jr. *Between Homeland and Motherland: Africa, U.S. Foreign Policy, and Black Leadership in America.* Ithaca, NY: Cornell University Press, 2011.

Topping, Simon. "'Supporting Our Friends and Defeating Our Enemies': Militancy and Nonpartisanship in the NAACP, 1936–1948," *Journal of African American History,* 89, no. 1 (Winter 2004): 17–35.

Touwen-Bouwsma, Elly. "The Indonesian Nationalists and the Japanese 'Liberation' of Indonesia: Visions and Reactions," *Journal of Southeast Asian Studies,* 27, no. 1 (March 1996): 1–18.

Troup, Freda. *In Face of Fear: Michael Scott's Challenge to South Africa.* London: Faber and Faber Limited, 1950.

Tully, John A. *The Devil's Milk: A Social History of Rubber.* New York: Monthly Review Press, 2011.

Van Der Eng, Pierre. "Marshall Aid as a Catalyst in the Decolonization of Indonesia, 1947–49," *Journal of Southeast Asian Studies,* 19, no. 2 (September 1988): 335–352.

Von Eschen, Penny. *Race Against Empire: Black Americans and Anticolonialism, 1937–1957.* Ithaca, NY: Cornell University Press, 1997.
  Satchmo Blows up the World: Jazz Ambassadors Play the Cold War. Cambridge, MA: Harvard University Press, 2004.
W. G. E. "France, Syria, and the Lebanon," *World Today*, 2, no. 3 (March 1946): 112–122.
Wall, Wendy L. "America's 'Best Propagandists': Italian Americans and the 1948 'Letters to Italy' Campaign," in *Cold War Constructions: The Political Culture of United States Imperialism, 1945–1966*, ed. Christian G. Appy. Amherst: University of Massachusetts Press, 2000.
Walter, Barbara F. "Does Conflict Beget Conflict? Explaining Recurring Civil War," *Journal of Peace Research*, 41, no. 3 (2004): 371–388.
Washington, Robert E. "Brown Racism and the Formation of a World System of Racial Stratification," *International Journal of Politics, Culture, and Society*, 4, no. 2 (Winter 1990): 209–227.
Waters, Mary C. "Ethnic and Racial Identities of Second–generation Black Immigrants in New York City," *International Migration Review* 28, no. 4 (Winter 1994): 795–820.
  Black Identities: West Indian Immigrant Dreams and American Realities Cambridge, MA: Harvard University Press, 1999.
Weiss, Peter. "American Committee on Africa: Rebels with a Cause," *Africa Today*, 10, no. 9 (November 1963): 38–39.
Westad, Odd Arne. *The Global Cold War: Third World Interventions and the Making of Our Times.* New York: Cambridge University Press, 2007.
White, Jr., George. *Holding the Line: Race, Racism, and American Foreign Policy toward Africa, 1953–1961.* New York: Rowman & Littlefield, 2005.
White, Walter F. "The Burning of Jim McIlherron: An N.A.A.C.P. Investigation," *Crisis*, 16, no. 1 (May 1918): 16–20.
  A Rising Wind. Garden City, NY: Doubleday, 1945.
Wiebes, Cees and Bert Zeeman, "United States' 'Big Stick' Diplomacy: The Netherlands between Decolonization and Alignment, 1945–1949," *International History Review*, 14, no. 1 (February 1992): 45–70.
Wieder, Alan. *Ruth First and Joe Slovo in the War Against Apartheid.* New York: Monthly Review Press, 2013.
Work, F. Ernest. "Italo-Ethiopian Relations," *Journal of Negro History*, 20, no. 4 (October 1935): 438–447.
Wrong, Michela. *In the Footsteps of Mr. Kurtz: Living on the Brink of Disaster in the Congo.* London: Fourth Estate, 2000.
Yates, Anne and Lewis Chester. *The Troublemaker: A Biography of the Reverend Michael Scott.* London: Aurum, 2006.
Yates, Anne. Review of *Apartheid and the Archbishop: The Life and Times of Geoffrey Clayton* by Alan Paton. *Journal of Southern African Studies*, 2, no. 2 (April 1976): 243–244.
Yelvington, Kevin A. "A Life In and Out of Anthropology: An Interview with Jack Sargent Harris," *Critique of Anthropology*, 28, no. 4 (2008): 446–476.

Index

Acheson, Dean, 181, 264, 309, 310
ACLU. *See* American Civil Liberties Union
ACOA. *See* American Committee on Africa
Africa Bureau, 95
African Americans
  and Eisenhower administration,
    291, 295
  Indonesia, position on, 216
  Italian colonies, position on, 153, 168
  and Italy's invasion of Ethiopia,
    137, 140
  living conditions of, 38
  social status of, 24
African Charter, 19
African National Congress (ANC), 7,
  19, 95
Africans' Claims in South Africa, 20
Alexander, Sadie, 230
Alexis, Stephen, 116
Algeria, 144, 193, 194, 307
Ambrose, Stephen, 290
American Association for the United
  Nations, 278
American Civil Liberties Union (ACLU), 96
American Committee on Africa (ACOA),
  8, 95, 323
  NAACP, role of in founding, 323
American Federation of Labor, 224
American Friends Service (Quakers), 95
Americans for South African
  Resistance, 323
Americans for the Indonesian Republic,
  257, 260
ANC. *See* African National Congress
Anderson, Marian, 40
Andu, John, 224
anticommunism, 2, 3, 4, 5, 134, 202, 290

Anti-Slavery & Aborigines Protective
  Society, 80
Anti-Slavery and Aboriginal Protection
  Society, 95
apartheid, 70, 102, 104, 106, 119, 310
Arab League, 307
Arab-Asian bloc in UN, 190, 193
Armstrong, Hamilton Fish, 36
Asante, S.K.B., 140
Atlanta Daily World, 23, 56, 169, 214,
  249, 331
Atlantic Charter, 14, 16, 33, 63, 328
  as basis for Africans' decolonization
    plans, 17, 19, 133
  as basis for US's decolonization plans, 36
Attlee, Clement, 213, 215
Australia
  Indonesian independence, position
    on, 213, 222, 224, 245, 252, 255,
    260, 265
  South West Africa, position on, 99
Azikiwe, Nnamdi "Zik", 7, 18, 19

Baker, Ella, 41, 42
Balaji, Murali, 3
Baldwin, Roger, 109, 257, 322
Baltimore Afro-American, 284, 331
Baring, Evelyn, 313
Bates, Robert, 333
Bayne, E. A., 201
Beam, Jacob, 236
Beer, Max, 111
Bell, Derrick, 239
Berg-Damaras, 71, 77, 87, 88, 115
Berry, Theodore, 297
Bevin, Ernest, 147, 148, 179, 187, 193,
  215, 245, 252, 253

Bevin-Sforza agreement, 189, 190
  failure of, 192
Bibb, Joseph D., 183
Bidault, Georges, 144
black Left, 164, 332, 335
black press, 142, 168, 216, 286, 331,
  See also individual newspapers
Bolin, Jane, 283, 284
Bonnet, Henri, 305
Bonomi, Ivanoe, 141
Boston Globe, 254
Bourguiba, Habib, 304, 307
Brewster Amendment, 259
Bricker Amendment, 301, 327
Britain
  anticolonialism in the Empire, 11, 268
  Commonwealth, 75
  economic condition of, 27, 211
  Empire, importance to, 28
  India, position on, 20
  Indonesian independence, position on,
    209, 212, 217, 225, 253
  Italian colonies, position on, 142, 147,
    158, 172, 188, 193
  Kenya, colonialism in, 312
  Labour Party, policy on colonialism, 215
  the Netherlands, relationship with, 207,
    208, 209, 213, 220, 225, 245
  South Africa, relationship with, 75, 78,
    105, 117, 119, 126
  United States, dispute with over
    colonialism, 28, 33, 126
  US loan to, 211, 213, 215
British. *See* Britain
British Commonwealth. *See* Britain
British West Africa, 11, 18
Brotherhood of the Protective Order of the
  Elks, 168
Brown v. Topeka Board of Education,
  291, 302
Buchanan, Douglas, 80, 81
Bunche, Ralph, 41, 55, 67, 68, 130,
  289, 320
  NAACP, working with, 82, 197
Burke, Roland, 334
Butler, Tubal Uriah "Buzz", 16
Byrnes, James F., 142, 143, 144, 161, 291

Cady, John, 236
Canadian Foreign Office
  Indonesia, views on, 233
  South Africa, views on, 108, 129
capitalism, 7
Carey, Archibald, 293, 296
Carter, Robert L., 200
Casey, Steven, 281
Cayton, Horace, 249

Central Intelligence Agency (CIA), 11, 108,
  221, 234, 306
Chandrasekhar, S., 24
Chicago Defender, 31, 165, 168, 183, 213,
  214, 219, 249, 250
Chicago Tribune, 250, 271
Christison, Philip, 207, 210
Churchill, Winston, 21, 310
  and Atlantic Charter, 14, 20, 330
  and British colonies, 28
CIA. *See* Central Intelligence Agency
CIO. *See* Congress of Industrial
  Organizations
Civil Rights Congress, 97, 123
Clayton, Anthony, 31
Cleveland Call and Post, 255
Cochran, H. Merle, 237, 240, 243
Cohen, Benjamin, 170, 173
Cold War, 2, 5, 119, 134, 148, 205, 281,
  331, 333
Coles, L. F., 42
Collier, Paul, 333
colonial independence, 7, 28
  severed from human rights, 328, 333
  timetable for, 18, 28, 37
colonialism
  "civilizing" mission, to justify, 17, 26,
    55, 77
  domestic jurisdiction, to justify, 204
  education, poor state of because of,
    158, 306
  geostrategic and military bases, to justify,
    27, 37, 63, 134
  great power status dependent upon, 27
  Jim Crow compared to, 5, 332
  legitimacy weakened, 133
  Nazi ideology, compared to, 22
  raw materials, need for to justify, 27, 37
  surplus population in metropole, to
    justify, 134, 196
  US Cold War foreign policy, impact on,
    134, 205
  violence used to end, 31, 196, 210, 232,
    305, 312
  violence used to maintain, 15, 208
  white supremacy, to justify, 93
Committee on Africa and Peace
  Aims, 16–18
communism, 61, 91, 120, 231, 238, 254,
  303, 335
  and anticolonialism, 5
Congress of Industrial Organizations, 223
Connally, Tom, 36, 66, 280
Cook, Eugene, 303
Cooper, Frederick, 93
Council of Foreign Ministers, 142,
  147, 160

Council on African Affairs, 64, 97, 125, 164, 224
  Italian colonies, position on, 145, 153, 158, 163, 183, 191
  Soviet Union, belief in, 161, 183, 189
Creech-Jones, Arthur, 29
Criscuolo, Luigi, 151
Crisis, 12, 45
Crittenberger, Willis D., 170
Current, Gloster, 247
Cyrenaica, 148, 166, 172
  British military facilities in, 194

Daily Service, 63
Davies, John, 235
De Gasperi, Alcide, 142, 155, 174, 178
De Gaulle, Charles, 30
Dean, William, 68, 202
democracy
  and end of imperialism, 14, 21
Denning, Mabel, 209
Dewey, Thomas, 152
domestic jurisdiction, 6, 63, 65, 94, 173
  and Dutch colonialism, 204, 217, 218, 225, 248, 262, 332
  and French colonialism, 308
  NAACP's position on, 260
Donges, T. E., 122
Douglas, Lewis, 150, 190, 193
Drake, St. Clair, 316
Du Bois, W.E.B.
  anticolonial vision, 1, 4, 5, 59, 64, 131
  communism, belief in, 5, 61
  and Ethiopia, 164
  and founding of NAACP, 38
  and Indonesia, 248
  NAACP anticolonial program, attempt to radicalize, 3, 48
  NAACP, criticism of, 3, 60, 61
  Pan-African Congress, planning and vision for, 50–56
  primacy in NAACP historiography, 1
  South Africa, criticism of, 73, 81, 82
  Soviet Union, importance of to, 65
  UN Charter, criticism of, 66
  White, Walter, dispute with, 42, 45, 48–50, 54, 56, 165
Dulles, John Foster, 33, 78, 101, 143, 152, 171, 172, 178, 179, 195, 294, 296, 302, 311
Dunn, James Clement, 36, 156
Dutch. *See* Netherlands, the

Ebony, 124
Eden, Anthony, 28, 128
Edmonds, Helen, 296
Egypt, 151

Eisenhower, Dwight D., 8, 290
  colonialism, policies on, 300
  and NAACP, 297
  race-neutral appointment policy, 293, 294
Elsey, George, 269
Emergency Committee for Indonesia, 257, 259
Eritrea, 7, 8, 133, 135, 143, 150, 163, 174, 186, 194, 202
Ethiopia
  African Americans' response to Italy's invasion of, 137, 140, 153
  Eritrea, claims on, 7, 150, 163, 164, 176
  Italian colonies, position on, 147, 150, 154, 163, 192
  Italy's attack on, 75, 136
  Somalia, claims on, 150
  Soviet Union's support to Italy during invasion of, 138
European Recovery Program. *See* Marshall Plan
Evatt, Herbert, 260

Fezzan, 142, 166
Foote, Walter, 236
Ford Foundation, 40
Forman, James, 86
Foster, Anne, 208
Four Freedoms. *See* Atlantic Charter
Four-Power Commission of Investigation, 157
Fox, Matthew M., 255
France. *See also* Algeria; Morocco; Tunisia
  African colonies, 144, 193, 194, 268, 304
  colonialism, 32, 305
  colons, 306, 307
  domestic jurisdiction, use of, 308
  economic conditions of colonies, 306
  great power status, need to regain, 30, 31
  Italian colonies, position on, 144, 147, 157, 193, 194
  South Africa, compared to, 307, 311
  South Africa, views on, 108
  United States, dispute with over colonialism, 29
  and Vietnam, 144
  World War II, effects of on, 29
Fraser, Peter, 79
Free French, 30

Gambia, 18
Gandhi, Mahatma, 21, 23
Gatheru, Reuel Mugo, 315
Genocide Convention, 301

George, Walter, 301
Gerig, Benjamin, 126, 165
Germany
  and Aryan supremacy, 75
  and Italy in World War II, 140
  South West Africa, imperial army in, 71
Ghana, 12, 17, 18, 302, 320, 327
Gifford, R. W., 270
Graham, Frank, 227
Graziani, Rodolpho, 136
Gromyko, Andrei, 144, 146
Gross, Earnest A., 170
Guidotti, Gastone, 175

Haiti's UN delegation, 114, 116, 191
Hammond, John, 45, 46
Hansberry, William Leo, 278
Hardy, Ben, 269
Harriman, W. Averell, 124n. 176
Harrington, Donald, 325
Harris, Robert L., Jr., 3
Harry, Ralph, 224
Hastie, William, 35, 53, 54, 57, 60
Hatta, Mohammed, 207, 209, 238, 241
Helfrich, Conrad, 208
Hereros, 71, 72, 77, 87, 88, 91, 96,
    115, 130
Herter, Christian, 279
Hess, William, 297
Hewitt, H. Kent, 170
Hitler, Adolf, 21, 141, 328
Hoffman, Paul, 40, 247
Holland. *See* Netherlands, the
Horne, Gerald, 1, 3, 5
Houser, George, 324, 328
Hull, Cordell, 24, 33
human rights
  adminstering power must adhere to, 69
  and colonial independence, 7
  devaluing of, 327
  importance in NAACP anticolonial
    plans, 7, 134
  severed from colonial independence,
    328, 333
  stalled at the UN, 268, 327
  in the US South, 276
Hungary, 319

imperialism, 5, 14, 255
  Soviet Union's opposition to, 138
  US opposition to, 33
India
  and African Americans, 22, 23
  anticolonial leadership in the UN,
    94, 100
  and Atlantic Charter, 20
  independence of, 93

Indonesian independence, position on,
    222, 224, 245, 265
  NAACP, relationship with, 191
  South Africa, criticism of, 77, 100, 103
India League, 95
  Indonesia, work toward independence
    of, 204, 231, 259
  NAACP, relationship with, 98,
    230, 257
  South West Africa, work towards
    independence of, 98
Indonesia, 180
  Batavia Conference, 261, 262
  Committee of Good Offices, 227,
    233, 234
  Dutch need for, 27, 206, 220, 244
  economic conditions of, 206, 228
  Hoge Veluwe Conference, 219
  independence, struggle to achieve and
    maintain, 13, 205, 207, 211, 222, 231,
    241, 264
  Indonesia Communist Party, 238
  and Japanese occupation during WWII,
    13, 206, 207
  Linggadjati Agreement, 221, 222, 227
  Madiun, 238
  NAACP support of independence
    for, 204
  Renville Agreement, 227
  Round Table Conference at The
    Hague, 264
  Surabaya, 210, 213, 216
Indonesian League of America, 223
international accountability, 29, 70, 71, 73,
    76, 107, 129, 132
International Court of Justice, 116, 117
International League for the Rights of
    Man, 95, 96, 109, 120, 204, 257, 311,
    326, 328
International Red Cross, 223
Issa, Abdullahi, 184, 196, 200, 333
Italian Americans
  advocacy of Italy, 152
Italian colonies
  Britain's position on, 147, 158, 172, 188
  and Council of Foreign Ministers, 142
  economic conditions of, 135, 150
  Egypt's position on, 151
  Ethiopia's position on, 147, 150, 163
  France's position on, 144, 147, 157
  geostrategic issues concerning, 148, 159,
    170, 180, 194
  human rights violated by Italy in, 134,
    135, 185
  Italy's position on, 150, 175, 195
  Latin American nations' position on,
    173, 189

Soviet Union's position on, 145, 146, 155, 157, 161, 183
surplus population, as outlet for Italy's, 135, 172, 174, 186, 196
Tripolitanians' position on, 189
violence, Arabs and Africans willing to use to end, 147
Italy
1948 election, 150
colonial power, record as, 133, 173, 179
Communist Party of Italy, 149, 157
economic difficulties, 135, 142, 154, 155
Ethiopia invaded by, 136
great power status, importance of to, 135, 156
Italian colonies, attempt to regain, 133, 150, 175, 176, 186
mustard gas, use of, 75, 133, 136
NAACP's critique of colonialism, 153, 332
NATO, use of as leverage to regain colonies, 175, 176, 179, 182
in World War II, 140

Japan, 13, 75, 206
Japanese mandated islands, 35, 64
Java. *See* Indonesia
Javabu, Davidson Don Tengo, 19
JCS. *See* Joint Chiefs of Staff
Jessup, Philip, 238, 244, 245, 252, 255, 265, 310, 316
Jim Crow compared to colonialism. *See* colonialism
Johnson, Campbell Carrington, 42
Johnson, Manning, 303
Joint Chiefs of Staff, 33, 35, 148, 149
Jones, Goronwy, 226
Justice Department, 98

Kenya, 58, 268, 304, 312, 316
British response to uprising in, 313
Mau Mau, 312, 313
white settlers, 15, 312
Kenyatta, Jomo, 313
Khama, Tshekedi, 81
Kikuyu, 312
Kim Il-Sung, 281, 290
Korean War, 119, 120, 280, 289
Kutako, Hosea, 87, 129

Lagos, 26
Lampkin, Daisy, 46, 283
Lautier, Louis, 165
Le Monde, 309
League Against Imperialism, 10
League of Nations, 36, 94, 141
and Italy's invasion of Ethiopia, 138

Mandate system, 29, 33, 71
South West Africa, as mandate, 69
Lebanon, 30
Lehman, Herbert, 279, 318
Lewis, Alfred Baker, 47
Lewis, David Levering, 56, 62
Liberia's UN delegation, 192
Libya, 8, 133, 143, 144, 148, 150, 177
independence of, 193, 194, 199, 202
Italian colonialism, effects on, 190
Italy's genocidal campaign in, 135
Lie, Trygve, 63, 67, 189, 199
Litvinov, Maxim, 138
Lochard, Metz, 64
Lodge, Henry Cabot, Jr., 300
Logan, Rayford, 23, 42, 54, 63, 103, 154, 190, 219, 272, 275, 278, 309
as liaison for ACOA, 325
as NAACP's foreign policy consultant, 107, 273, 277
London Times, 254
Lord Mountbatten, 208, 209
Los Angeles Sentinel, 182
Los Angeles Times, 254, 255
Louis, Wm. Roger, 334
Louw, Eric, 101, 107, 116
Lovett, Robert, 174, 177, 240
Lovink, A. H. J., 242
Lubin, Isador, 271

MacArthur, Douglas, 217
Mahareru, Frederick, 84, 87
Malan, Daniel F., 102, 104, 107, 118, 311, 330
Malaysia, 15
Malik, Jacob, 262
Malone, George, 238, 243, 250, 256
Manchester Guardian, 212
Mao Zedong, 281, 290
Marshall Plan, 156, 170, 173, 204, 221, 230, 232, 238, 242, 245, 256, 260, 264
Marshall, George C., 151, 155, 171, 172, 221
Marshall, Thurgood, 284, 303
Mays, Benjamin, 124
Mazov, Sergei, 157, 159
McGrath, J. Howard, 152
McIlherron, Jim, 96
McMahon, Robert, 27, 220
McNaughton, Andrew, 233
Meriwether, James, 6, 312
Mitchell, Clarence, 231
Molotov, Vyacheslav, 65, 144
Monnerville, Gaston, 31
Moon, Henry Lee, 184, 191, 302
Morgens, Howard, 297

Morocco, 144, 193, 194, 268, 306
Morrow, E. Frederic, 292
Morsell, John, 321
Motley, Constance Baker, 200
Mussolini, Benito, 136, 140

NAACP
American Committee on Africa, role in
  founding, 323
American South's pressure on, 302, 304
anticolonial activism, questions about
  pursuing, 22, 47
anticolonial vision, 1, 3, 6, 7, 48, 58, 60,
  160, 163, 317, 331
anticolonialism and domestic
  jurisdiction, 248
anticolonialism and human rights, 134,
  329, 334
anticolonialism and international
  accountability, 107
anticolonialism and public opinion, 258
anticolonialism and wishes of the
  inhabitants, 7, 60, 133, 154
and anticommunism, 3, 5, 61, 231
Colonial Conference, 57
and communism, 303
Du Bois, W.E.B., criticism of by, 3, 60, 61
Eisenhower administration, relationship
  with, 8, 297
Eritrea, response to Ethiopia's attempt to
  annex, 164
Ethiopia, response to Italy's invasion
  of, 137
financial woes of, 38–41, 288
founding of, 38
French colonies, working for
  independence of, 309, 311
India, work with government
  officials, 103
Indonesia, working for independence
  of, 204, 213, 214, 223, 247, 257,
  259, 266
Italian colonies, advocating UN
  trusteeship over, 134, 160, 167, 199
Italian colonies, working for
  independence of, 133, 134, 153,
  160, 163, 181, 183, 190, 195, 197,
  202, 332
Kenya, response to uprising in, 315
leadership issues, 37, 46, 286
Marshall Plan, position on, 227, 230,
  231, 233, 247
militancy of, 131, 330
organizational structure, problems, 37,
  41, 268
Pan-African Congress, sponsorship and
  plan for, 50, 52

Point IV, position on, 272, 275, 277
Scott, Michael, working with, 95, 96,
  107, 110, 113, 120, 131
Somali Youth League, working with, 197
South Africa, criticism of by, 81, 82–83
South West Africa, working for
  independence of, 107, 111, 120, 131
Third World War, convinced colonialism
  will lead to, 21, 232
transnational alliances, 25
Truman administration, relationship
  with, 3, 4, 8
United Nations, working through, 62,
  67, 68, 191, 197
and US Cold War foreign policy, 4
White-Du Bois feud, 45, 48–50
White-Wilkins feud, 45, 287
Namas, 71, 72, 77, 87, 115
Nasi, Guglielmo, 200
National Association for the Advancement
  of Colored People. *See* NAACP
National Council of Negro Women,
  168, 318
National Party (South Africa), 76, 101
national sovereignty, 6, 73, 94, 106, 334
nationalism, 11, 78, 147, 328
  in Indonesia, 205, 239
  in North Africa, 193
Nationalist Party (South Africa), 108
Nehru, Jawaharlal, 83, 100, 230
Nesbitt, Francis Njubi, 3, 6
Netherlands, the, 204
  Britain, relationship with, 207, 208,
    210, 225
  domestic jurisdiction clause, use of, 217,
    218, 225, 262
  Indonesia, need for to rebuild, 27,
    205, 244
  Indonesian independence, policies and
    views toward, 207, 208, 220, 222,
    235, 242, 332
  international isolation, growing, 223
  and Marshall Plan, 221, 233, 242, 243,
    245, 248, 260
  NAACP's critique of colonialism,
    223, 224
  Nazi occupation of, 27
  red-baiting Indonesian nationalists,
    237, 238
  United States, relationship with, 180
  World War II, effects of on, 206
New Africa, 191
New York Amsterdam News, 249, 286
New York Star, 248
New York Times, 146, 165, 184, 213, 240,
  249, 255, 333
New Zealand, 79

Nigeria, 17, 18, 26
Nixon, Richard, 301
Nkrumah, Kwame, 12, 320, 327
Norfolk Journal and Guide, 249
North Atlantic Treaty Organization
(NATO), 175, 176, 182, 243, 253

O'Dwyer, William, 152
Odom, Edward J., 321
Office of Strategic Services (OSS), 11,
26, 32
Offutt, Walter, Jr., 284, 311, 322
Ogburn, Charlton, 236
OSS. *See* Office of Strategic Services
Ovambos, 77, 88
Ovington, Mary White, 38

Padmore, George, 12, 15, 51, 60, 137, 138,
314, 327
Palar, L. N., 261, 263, 265
Palestine, 146, 148, 174
Palmer, Joseph, II, 192
Pan-African Conference, 32
Pan-African Congress, 50–56, 60
Pandit, Vijaya, 82, 99, 102
Parker, Jason, 6
Pasqualicchio, Leonard H., 152
Pegler, Westbrook, 125
Phelps-Stokes Fund, 16, 19, 57, 81
Philippines, 26
Pittsburgh Courier, 22, 142, 146, 183, 191,
215, 219, 235, 249, 254, 325, 331
Plummer, Brenda Gayle, 6, 137, 138
Point IV, 270
and Korean War, 282
protection of capital, concerns about,
270, 272
protection of labor, concerns about, 273,
275, 280
welfare giveaway program, dismissed
as, 271
Poland's UN delegation, 262
Post-War World Council, 204, 274, 275
Powell, Adam Clayton, Jr., 182, 215
Prattis, Percival, 325

Ransby, Barbara, 42
Reynaud, Paul, 307, 330
Rivlin, Benjamin, 190, 192
Roark, James, 3, 4, 5
Robeson, Paul, 64
anticolonialism, 5, 162
Ethiopia, response to Italy's invasion
of, 139
Italian colonies, policy on, 153, 158, 161
Soviet Union, belief in, 139, 145,
159, 161

Robinson, Ronald, 334
Romulo, Carlos, 261
Roosevelt, Eleanor, 41, 82, 113, 114, 124,
166, 170, 276, 287, 302, 309
Roosevelt, Franklin D., 14, 24
colonies, plans for, 34
Ross, Julian, 223
Rowan, Carl, 296
Rusk, Dean, 169, 178, 245

Sampson, Edith, 123, 316
Satterthwaite, J. C., 175, 176
Sayre, Francis B., 26, 170, 192, 280
Schuman, Robert, 179, 180
Schuyler, George, 137, 183
Scott, Rev. G. Michael
Africans' view of, 86
character of, 86, 95
Church of England, relationship
with, 90
and communism, 91, 128
medical problems of, 111
NAACP supportive of, 95, 107, 110,
113, 120
Roosevelt, Eleanor, view of, 113, 124
Sampson, Edith, meetings with, 124
South Africa, relationship with
government of, 84, 116, 128
South West Africa, working to stop
annexation of, 89, 98, 104, 111,
132, 282
testimony at UN, 115
Tobruk shantytown, life in, 84
United Nations, importance
of to, 95
visa difficulties with US government, 91,
97, 109
Scott, William R., 140
Second Red Scare, 5, 120
Selassie, Haile, 137, 154
self-determination, 10, 11, 37, 60, 183,
199, 213, 266, 332
Senghor, Lamine, 10
Sforza, Carlo, 173, 175, 178, 186, 187,
195, 330
Sharpe, Louis, 315
Sierra Leone, 17, 18
Singh, J. J., 257
Singh, R. Lal, 22
Slate, Nico, 24
Smuts, Jan Christian, 32, 64, 72, 74, 75, 79
discredited by National Party, 101
prestige as leader, 75, 99
UN report on conditions in South West
Africa, 80, 99
Social Action, 274
Somali Youth League, 184, 196

Somalia, 8, 133, 143, 150, 161, 166, 174,
     194, 195, 202, 334
   colony's revenue, 150
   economy of, 152
   independence of, 199, 333
   NAACP's support for, 197, 200
   testimony to UN, 184, 185
South Africa
   African critics, attempt to silence, 87,
     113, 129
   African population, government fearful
     of, 32
   apartheid, 102, 106, 119
   and Atlantic Charter, 19
   Britain, relationship with, 75
   conditions for Africans in, 20, 32, 82,
     83, 84
   criticism of, 77, 79, 123
   India, relationship with, 77
   international accountability, refusal to
     accept, 70, 106, 129
   International Court of Justice, reaction
     to ruling of, 117, 121
   international pariah, becoming, 108, 125
   NAACP criticism of, 73
   South West Africa, attempt to annex, 32,
     33, 74, 76, 78, 80, 81, 103, 104
   South West Africa, conditions for
     Africans in, 70, 72, 80, 81, 115
   South West Africa, mandate of, 69
   United Nations, relationship with, 70,
     99, 100, 107, 118
   United States, relationship with, 78,
     101, 120
   white minority rule in, 72, 332
   white supremacy in, 73, 75, 78
South West Africa
   conditions for Africans in, 70, 72, 80,
     81, 115
   genocide committed by Germany in, 71
   mandate, 69
   South Africa's attempt to annex, 32, 33,
     74, 76, 78, 80, 81, 103, 104
Soviet Union, 4, 65
   in Cold War, 205, 281
   colonialism, position on, 144, 146
   Ethiopia, response to Italy's invasion of,
     138, 139
   Italian colonies, position on, 145, 146,
     155, 157, 158, 161, 183
   NAACP's critique of, 61, 138, 155, 160
   UN Trusteeship Council, 64, 146
Spingarn, Arthur, 47, 48, 55, 249
Stalin, Josef, 281
State Department
   anticolonialism, assessment of, 14, 25
   colonialism policy, 34, 35

decolonization, assessment of need
     for, 28
   Division of Dependent Areas Affairs, 29
   and domestic jurisdiction, 308
   and Dutch colonialism in Indonesia,
     205, 209, 226, 236, 238, 244,
     247, 263
   and French colonialism in Africa, 306
   Italian colonies, position on, 142, 149,
     173, 174, 178, 193, 197
   Point IV, position on, 269, 277
   Scott, Michael, attempt to deny visa
     for, 97
   South Africa's attempt to annex South
     West Africa, response to, 101,
     106, 118
Stettinius, Edward, 144
Stikker, Dirk, 208
Stokes, Anson Phelps, 17, 21
Sukarno, Achmed, 207

Taft, Charles, 296
Taft, Orray, Jr., 177, 189
Tarchiani, Alberto, 178
Thamboe, Charles, 250
Thomas, Norman, 223
Thomspon, Kenneth, 128
Thorp, Willard, 171
Tillery, Alvin B., Jr., 6
Times of India, 313
Tobias, Channing, 16, 21, 47, 48, 80, 230,
     276, 304, 324
   as US delegate to the UN, 124, 126, 127,
     130, 131
Trinidad, 16
Tripolitania, 145, 146, 155, 157, 161,
     166, 174
   Arabs' response to Italy's colonialism in,
     177, 189
   US miliary facilities in, 194
Truman, Harry S., 3, 4, 43, 205, 257, 281,
     290, 330
   1948 election, 151
   1949 State of the Union address, 269
   Point IV, 270
Tunisia, 144, 193, 194, 268, 305, 306,
     309, 311

Ukrainian UN delegate, 216, 218
United Nations, 6
   African group, increase of, 328
   Article 2(7), domestic jurisdiction clause,
     63, 217, 226, 308
   Article 73(e), transmission of reports
     from colonizers, 64, 107
   Chapter VII, threat to international
     peace, 259

Chapter XII, Article 76, trusteeship
human rights standards, 70, 142
Charter, criticism of, 63
Charter, foundation of rights-based
world, 73
Covenant on Human Rights, 276, 301
Declaration of Human Rights, 114, 174,
276, 334
Declaration on the Granting of
Independence to Colonial Countries
and Peoples, 328
decolonization, important role in, 289
Fourth Committee, 67, 76, 98, 101, 108,
114, 126, 128, 308
French colonialism, debate over, 308
General Assembly, 74, 78, 103, 192, 260,
261, 265, 311
and human rights, 7, 64, 114, 327,
328, 334
India's anticolonial leadership role in, 94
Italian colonies, debate over, 134, 143,
148, 161, 167, 169, 174, 182, 190,
192, 198, 201
prestige of, 254, 261
red-baited, 269, 289
San Francisco Conference (UNCIO),
62, 63
Security Council, debate over Indonesia,
216, 217, 218, 219, 226, 233
Security Council, debates over
Indonesia, 224
South Africa, relationship with, 70, 76,
77, 79, 99, 100, 103, 107, 118, 121
and testimony from individuals,
114, 126
and trusteeship, 35, 63, 64, 67, 74, 79,
101, 105, 201
United States. *See also* State Department
1948 election, 151
anticolonial reputation of, 33, 143,
192, 193
and anticommunism, 4, 5
Britain, as ally, 14, 148, 214
Britain, dispute with over colonialism,
28, 33
colonial independence, plans for, 28
colonial trusteeship, plans for, 28
Constitution and treaties, 301
France, relationship with, 29, 309
French colonialism, position on,
309, 312
Indonesian independence, position on,
213, 239, 263, 265
Italian colonies, position on, 134, 143,
165, 169, 170, 174, 178, 193, 199
Italy, relationship with, 141, 152, 187
and Marshall Plan, 221

national security, 134, 193, 205
South Africa, relationship with, 78, 101,
118, 120, 121, 123
the Netherlands, relationship with, 205,
221, 225, 229, 242, 243, 251, 256
trusteeship, debates within the
government over, 36
US Congress, 221, 234, 252, 255, 259, 272
H.R. 7346, 278
House of Representatives, 182, 215, 280
Senate, 66, 67, 227, 231, 276, 278
USSR. *See* Soviet Union
Utter, John, 149, 171, 172, 192

Van Kleffens, Eelco, 206, 252, 256, 264
Van Mook, Hubertus, 208, 220
Vandenberg, Arthur, 36, 82, 171
Vann, Jessie, 295
Versailles Peace Conference, 10, 11, 20, 72
Vietnam, 144
Villard, Henry, 26
Villard, Oswald Garrison, 38
Von Eschen, Penny, 3, 5

Wall Street Journal, 252
Wall, Wendy, 150
Washington Post, 244, 254
Washington, Val, 292, 297
Welles, Sumner, 82
West African Pilot, 313
White Citizens Council, 303
white man's burden, 6, 34, 69, 92, 107
white supremacy, 6, 25, 49, 65, 73, 75,
78, 331
recognized as faulty ideology, 92
in US South, 277
White, Walter, 24, 55, 61, 286
anticolonial statements, 11, 21, 25, 48,
74, 232, 331
Cannon, Poppy, relationship with,
195, 282
character issues, 41–43, 95
death of, 318
Du Bois, W.E.B., feud with, 48–50, 51,
54, 56, 165
and Eisenhower administration, 299,
300, 302
and Ethiopia, 138
and French colonies, 309, 311
Gatheru, Mugo, support for, 316
and Indonesia, 206, 213, 216, 223, 227,
228, 231, 247, 249, 253
and Italian colonies, 153, 165, 166, 167,
175, 180, 195
and NAACP finances, 39
and Point IV, 272
and South Africa, 82–83, 110, 121

White, Walter (*cont.*)
  UN Charter, criticism of, 66
  Wilkins, Roy, relationship with, 45,
    46, 287
Wilkins, Roy, 25, 39, 41, 62, 286, 318, 333
  Bolin, Jane, clash with, 283
  and Eisenhower administration, 293,
    298, 302
  and Indonesia, 266
  and Italian colonies, 182, 191, 196,
    197, 199
  Offutt, Walter, clash with, 285
  personal characteristics, 43
  White, Walter, dispute with, 45, 46, 287
Williams, Chester, 166
Wilson, Woodrow, 71
Wilsonian principles, 10

wishes of the inhabitants, 133, 154, 170,
    192, 193
World War II
  Britain, economic effects on, 27, 211
  colonialism, effects on, 22, 93, 232
  Dutch colonialism, effects on, 13, 207
  Free French involvement in, 30
  Italian colonialism, effects on, 141
  the Netherlands, economic effects on,
    27, 206
Wright, Herbert, 310, 315

Xuma, A. B., 7, 19, 20, 64, 82

Yergan, Max, 159

Zorin, V. A., 157

Printed in the United States
By Bookmasters